We wait for the sun to turn back for us,
that we may return to our place,
that we may hunt and dance again,
that we may eat flesh that is good,
that we may go where we like.

(From: Capture and Captivity. Markowitz, Arthur 1956)

Legal Anthropology

Volume 1

IWGIA

LIT

Manuela Zips-Mairitsch

LOST LANDS?

(Land) Rights of the San in Botswana
and the Legal Concept of Indigeneity
in Africa

LIT

Cover Images: G|wi, !Xõó and Ju|'hoansi (-San) on a so-called
"authentic Bushman Walk" near Ghanzi in Botswana,
© by Manuela Zips-Mairitsch
All pictures inside the book: © by Manuela Zips-Mairitsch

Published with the support of the Austrian Science Fund (FWF)

Der Wissenschaftsfonds.

Translated into English by: Daniel Stevens
Typesetting: Patric Kment
German Edition:
"Verlorenes Land. Indigene (Land)Rechte der San in Botswana.",
© Dietrich Reimer Verlag GmbH, Berlin 2009, www.reimer-verlag.de

Bibliographic information published by the Deutsche Nationalbibliothek
The Deutsche Nationalbibliothek lists this publication in the Deutsche
Nationalbibliografie; detailed bibliographic data are available in the Internet at
http://dnb.d-nb.de.

ISBN 978-3-643-90244-3 (LIT)
ISBN 978-87-92786-35-7 (IWGIA)

A catalogue record for this book is available from the British Library

©LIT VERLAG GmbH & Co. KG Wien,   LIT VERLAG Dr. W. Hopf
Zweigniederlassung Zürich 2013   Berlin 2013
Klosbachstr. 107   Fresnostr. 2
CH-8032 Zürich   D-48159 Münster
Tel. +41 (0) 44-251 75 05   Tel. +49 (0) 2 51-62 03 20
Fax +41 (0) 44-251 75 06   Fax +49 (0) 2 51-23 19 72
E-Mail: zuerich@lit-verlag.ch   E-Mail: lit@lit-verlag.de
http://www.lit-verlag.ch   http://www.lit-verlag.de

©International Work Group for Indigenous Affairs
Classensgade 11 E
DK-2100 Copenhagen, Denmark
Distribution:
In Germany: LIT Verlag Fresnostr. 2, D-48159 Münster
Tel. +49 (0) 2 51-620 32 22, Fax +49 (0) 2 51-922 60 99, E-mail: vertrieb@lit-verlag.de

In Austria: Medienlogistik Pichler-ÖBZ, e-mail: mlo@medien-logistik.at
In Switzerland: B + M Buch- und Medienvertrieb, e-mail: order@buch-medien.ch
In the UK: Global Book Marketing, e-mail: mo@centralbooks.com
In North America: International Specialized Book Services, e-mail: orders@isbs.com
e-books are available at www.litwebshop.de

Contents

Acknowledgements 9
Preface by René Kuppe 13
Introduction 21

Part 1: Indigenous Peoples in International Law

I. Historical Overview 29
II. "Indigenous Peoples": Term, Concepts, and Definitions 34
    Differentiation from the Term "Minority" 40
III. Special Indigenous Rights or Special Circumstances? Indigenous
    Protection Standards, Rights of Freedom, and Self-Determination 42
    1.   Sources of Law 42
    1.1   Binding Norms 43
    1.1.1 ILO Convention 169 43
    1.1.2 UN Convention on Biological Diversity 45
    1.2   "Soft law" Instruments 46
    1.2.1 Agenda 21, Chapter 26 (1992) 47
    1.2.2 UN Declaration on the Rights of Indigenous Peoples 47
    1.2.3 Declarations and Policies of various International Bodies 52
    1.3   Indigenous Rights as Part of Customary International Law 56
    2.   "Sources of Life": Lands and Natural Resources 57
    2.1   Material Standards of Protection 57
    2.1.1 Cause of Action 58
    2.1.2 The Relationship between Indigenous Peoples
           and their Territories 59
    2.1.3 Collective Land Rights 61
    2.1.4 Scope of Indigenous Territories 63
    2.1.5 Restriction of Alienation and Disposal 64
    2.2   Universal Human Rights Treaties 64
    2.2.1 Right of Ownership 65
    2.2.2 Right to Culture 66
    2.2.3 Right to Private and Family Life 66

2.3	Jurisdiction of International Monitoring Bodies	67
2.3.1	Human Rights Committee	67
2.3.2	Committee on the Elimination of Racial Discrimination	68
3.	Sources of Freedom and Equality: Self-Determination	70

Part 2: "Being Indigenous in Africa": Legal Developments of Indigenous Peoples Law in Africa

I.	Historical Overview	79
	1. Nature Conservation v. Human Rights Protection	81
	2. African Initiatives for the Protection of Indigenous Rights	83
II.	"Indigenous Peoples in Africa": Applying the Concept	88
III.	Indigenous Rights in the African Context	93
	1. Regional Indigenous Rights	94
	1.1 The African Charter on Human and Peoples' Rights	94
	1.2 The African Commission on Human and Peoples' Rights	101
	1.3 The African Court on Human and Peoples' Rights	104
	2. National Indigenous Rights	110
	2.1 Selected Constitutional Guarantees	110
	2.2 Jurisdiction using the example of South Africa	116
	2.2.1 The Case of the ǂKhomani San	117
	2.2.2 Richtersveld Case	120
	Excursus: "Aboriginal Title"	122
	2.2.2.1 "Aboriginal Title" before the South African Constitutional Court	128
	2.2.3 "Hoodia Gordonii" Case	132

Part 3: Legal Perspectives of San Communities

I.	Terminology: San, "Bushmen", Basarwa, Khoesan, N/oakwe or Kwe?	155
II.	Historical Overview until the End of Colonial Times	161
	1. Regional Historical Differences	169
	1.1 Botswana	169
	1.2 Namibia	172
	1.3 South Africa	173
	1.4 The "Northern San"	174
III.	Reflections on Indigenous Legal Perspectives and World Views	177

Part 4: Botswana: State and Society

I. Sociopolitical History 187
    1. Pre-colonial Phase 187
    2. Protectorate Bechuanaland 189
    3. Republic of Botswana 199

II. Sources of Law and Legal Pluralism 216
    1. Constitutional Law 216
    2. Customary Law 219
    3. Common and Statutory Law 222
    4. International Law 223
    5. Fundamental and Human Rights 225

Part 5: San in Botswana

I. San as Citizens: Basarwa and/or Batswana? 237
II. Dominant Views of the San in Botswana 241
III. Development Policies 246
    1. Remote Area Development Programme 246
    2. Community Based Natural Resource Management 253
IV. Development – Nature Conservation: A Contradiction? 260
V. NGO Initiatives 265
    1. National San NGOs 265
    2. Regional San NGOs 268

Part 6: "The Lost Lands": Relocation from the *Central Kalahari Game Reserve*

I. History of the *Central Kalahari Game Reserve* 291
II. The Relocation of the G|wi and ||Gana (San) 305
III. The Legal Dispute over the (temporarily?) "Lost Lands" 322
    1. Roy Sesana v. Government of Botswana 322
    1.1 Termination of Basic and Essential Services 326
    1.2 Restoration of Basic and Essential Services 328
    1.3 Lawful Occupation 329
    1.4 Deprivation of Land Possession 332

	1.5	Special Game Licences	337
	1.6	Access to the *Central Kalahari Game Reserve* (CKGR)	339
	1.7	Conclusions	343
	2.	Consequences of the High Court's Decision: Summary	345
IV.	The Legal Dispute over Access to Water		359
	1.	Matsipane Mosetlhanyane, Gakenyatsiwe Matsipane & further applicants v. Attorney General of Botswana	360
	2.	Matsipane Mosetlhanyane & Gakenyatsiwe Matsipane v. Attorney General of Botswana, Court of Appeal	365
	3.	Consequences of the Courts' Decisions: Summary......................	369

Part 7: Conclusion.. 379

The Return of the Outlaws: An Epilogue by Werner Zips............................ 385

Appendix

Examples of Indigenous Peoples in Africa (not exhaustive!) 392

Abbreviations.. 394

Bibliography 395

(Selected) Legal Texts 419
    1.   International Instruments 419
    2.   National Laws, Regulations and Policies 421
    3.   Court Cases 423
    4.   Interviews 424

Index of Figures.. 425

Index 427

About the Authors.. 431

Acknowledgements

I would like to begin my acknowledgements with a few personal remarks that have become, as jurists like to call the indispensable and essential condition of existence of facts, a "conditio sine qua non" for this book. Just before finishing my studies in law at the University of Vienna, I planned to reward myself for passing the last exam with my second journey to Botswana. If you are interested in nature and wildlife, this rather large country in the Kalahari semi-desert is probably second to none. My partner Werner Zips, professor at the Department of Social and Cultural Anthropology, was already there to prepare a field trip with students. So after I had passed the mentioned exam, I met him in Maun. He could not wait until we had left the airport and welcomed me with what at that time was a rather threatening sentence, "I have found the topic for your dissertation."

As my reaction was not all too enthusiastic, he started telling me about what he had seen during a trip with a friend of ours to the *Central Kalahari Game Reserve*. The reserve's administration had only allowed them to stay north of Piper's Pan. Of course they had asked why they could not go any further south and were finally told that there were too many trucks driving around "down there": Trucks in the Central Kalahari which at that time was hardly frequented at all and showed next to none touristic infrastructure? Ultimately a *Wildlife Department* officer came out with the truth that at that time (mid-February 2002) the last remaining San in the Kalahari were resettled. While we were travelling to various regions of the Kalahari for the next three weeks, my initial scepticism of writing a dissertation virtually blew away in the sandy Kalahari winds. I increasingly realized that I just felt concerned about developmental policies that appeared to leave no space for alternative lifestyles and their related world views. How could there be no place left for a few hundred individuals in an area of over 52,000 km² who wanted to lead their lives in a different way from what "modern" times dictated and "modern" governments allowed? Therefore, this direct confrontation with the plight of the Kalahari suggested a rights-based approach that I decided to apply to my further studies.

My central focus evolved around the question how a more or less forced relocation from the reserve related to national and international legal standards. So-called internal displacements and relocations are nothing new or rare in the international context. Although there was an abundance of especially anthropological literature, hardly any book or study addressed any legal questions the San were facing, not least their own understanding of law or indigenous rights that were concerning their entire existence. These were and still are highly contested in the African context. After several research periods in southern Africa, I published my revised dissertation "Verlorenes Land? Indigene (Land)Rechte der San in Botswana" (Lost Lands? Indigenous (Land) Rights of the San in Botswana) in the publishing house Reimer in 2009. The present publication is an updated and revised translation of the German book.

This would have hardly been possible without the financial support of the Austrian Science Fund (FWF). I would like to cordially thank Doris Haslinger in particular for her great advice and support. Furthermore, I am much obliged to the two publishers *International Work Group for Indigenous Affairs* (IWGIA) and LIT Verlag for their trust and willingness alike to publish this book. Cæcilie Mikkelsen (IWGIA) has been an extremely sensitive, amicable and simply the best publication coordinator anyone could wish for. In addition, I would like to thank Diane Vinding for editing my book in such a detailed and considerate way, also paying attention to questions of content. Aside from his creative cover design, Richard Kiesling (LIT Verlag) has always engaged me in constructive conversations and offered valuable advice during countless "coffee sessions". My thanks go to Patric Kment for his meticulous setting and layouting as well as to Maggie Kolb for her inputs to the cover design. At a time when hardly anybody was talking about indigenous rights in the African context, René Kuppe was not only one of the first to regard them as legally justified but he supported my dissertation, offered indispensable advice and even wrote the preface to my book. For all that, I owe him my sincere thanks! Notwithstanding all his other obligations, my translator Daniel Stevens performed outstandingly, edited the German text and provided numerous content-wise suggestions. This book is also yours!

Above all, I am certainly most indebted to my "partner in crime" Werner Zips: of course for his emotional support but especially for his suggestions and critical remarks in countless discussions, for his commitment during proofreading, for his inputs concerning cover design and the selection of photographs, for our many adventures and so much more …

Numerous NGOs of civil society, interest groups, colleagues, indigenous representatives and San communities have supported my scientific research. Therefore, I would like to collectively thank them (also because I do not want to for-

Acknowledgements 11

get anyone) and just point out the extraordinary help of a few through long interviews, professional advice and likewise support: Roger Chennells, Alice Mogwe (DITSHWANELO), Mathambo Ngakaeaja (WIMSA), and Gordon Woodman. I refrain from mentioning any specific San communities or individual San who have helped me in various ways due to the highly charged situation and precarious political conditions and ongoing legal conflicts. Nevertheless, I would like to express my utmost solidarity and attachment to them. This is not the only reason why I dedicate this book to them, hoping that they can finally find some peace and lead a self-determined life in what they "thought to be their lost lands".

March 2013
Manuela Zips-Mairitsch

Preface

René Kuppe

"When a culture is destroyed in the name of progress, it is not progress, it is a loss for our world".
Archbishop Desmond Tutu, Honorary Doctor of the University of Vienna (Nov. 2006, on Botswana's government policies concerning members of the San living in the Central Kalahari).

This book is far more relevant than the issues – a legal dispute over land rights in southern Africa – it directly addresses: the author shows how a small and marginalized group fights for their "lost lands" and how ethnic groups mobilize and take up the discourse of indigenous rights. The African context in particular makes it possible to emphasize the essence of this legal discourse – a discourse that has become crucial in many countries of the world and is globally based on one of the most dynamic new social movements of our time. At first sight, however, Africa does not seem to be ready to address such rights in a reasonable way. With its etymological origins in Latin, the term indigenous literally refers to *those rooted in land*. This classic connotation was developed in the Americas and Australia where originally European colonist populations had formed postcolonial states and continued to impose foreign political structures on the descendants of the original population. Although "their country" was politically decolonized, these "original populations" were deprived of their right of self-determination and lived under conditions of neocolonialism.

Now in Africa, not the originally European settler communities but the descendants of colonized Africans were able to achieve decolonisation (with the by now historically overcome exceptions of South Africa and Southern Rhodesia); keeping all this in mind, *all* – at least African – inhabitants of the continent's new states could be considered indigenous population. This situation levels out the term due to excessive use and strips it of the specific and legally-based function it assumes in Australia and the Americas.

Remarkably enough, a network attending to the interests of the most discriminated and marginalized ethnic group – the San – in southern Africa was formed in 1996. In German and various other European languages, they were known as "Buschmänner" or "Bushmen" for a long time. The international San organization called itself "Working Group of Indigenous Minorities in Southern Africa" (WIMSA) and saw its mission in supporting the San, amongst other things, to be politically recognized, to protect their access to natural, human and financial resources, to regain a distinct identity, and to determine their development themselves. In many ways these objectives can be compared to the issues of indigenous peoples in Australia and the Americas. They all live in states that suppress their political rights, deny them access to needed resources, and impose a new identity based on the nation state on them. Also within the postcolonial political context, the states of today's southern Africa face an interethnic imbalance in power. Therefore, it is obviously reasonable for the San to insist on their "indigeneity". The present situation of the San is not only the consequence of a historical development that started with the beginning of European colonialism or modern, independent states though.[1]

Long before the first Europeans entered southern Africa, Bantu-speaking groups little by little migrated from northern regions into the territory of the ancestors of today's San. While these immigrants formed the subgroups ("tribes") of today's Tswana people, they deprived the San of their control over land and pushed them to the margins of society as well. Of course the internal organization of Tswana society has often been characterized as a form of *African democracy*: legal and political decisions were made by the *kgotla*, the so-called community council. Individuals were only allowed to participate in this council, if they were full members of Tswana society. This was the only way to influence public decisions and to possibly benefit from the cyclic assignments of farming land. Although nobody was permanently entitled to such land, the right was exclusive for the assigned period. Access to land intended for cattle breeding was originally free but soon changed to be reserved for social organization units of Tswana society only.

---

1 For more details to the historical background of the legal discrimination against the San, see also the following literature I have used: Nicolas Olmsted (2004): Indigenous Rights in Botswana: Development, Democracy and Dispossession. In: *Washington University Global Studies Law Review* Vol. 4: 799–866; Clement Ng'ong'ola (1997): Land Rights for Marginalized Ethnic Groups in Botswana, with Special Reference to the Basarwa. *Journal of African Law* Vol. 41: 1–26; Hitchcock, Robert (2001): "Hunting is our Heritage": The Struggle for Hunting and Gathering Rights among the San of Southern Africa. In: Anderson, David/Ikeya, Kazunobu (Hg.): *Parks, Property and Power: Managing Hunting Practice and Identity within State Policy Regimes*. Senri Ethnological Studies no. 59. National Museum of Ethnology, Osaka, 139–156.

After Bechuanaland was established as a British protectorate (at least formally in 1885), three types of land slowly developed under European influence: firstly, Tswana "tribes" kept the land they had previously controlled in so-called "tribal reserves" but "tribal councils" administrating the land according to their own customs and traditions were integrated into the looming system of colonial administration. A second type of land was created, when "tribal" representatives surrendered huge areas of farmland to white settlers. British authorities increasingly supported these settlers to "defend" their territory against German colonial expansion from adjacent German South-West Africa. At the estates of these settlers, titles to private property were also recognized. The third and remaining type of land was neither considered autonomous collective land of Tswana "tribes" nor private property of European settlers but was classified as public crown land (legally meaning state land).

In the context of these three types of land, there was no more room for a separate legal status of land used by the San. They either lived on Tswana "tribal reserves" where they were not entitled to use land under Bantu customary law or they were de-facto tolerated on crown land or the private farms of white settlers. Although the formal classification of San territories as crown land did not directly change the system of land use, big-game hunting became more and more important and trophy hunters doubled the pressure by limiting the remaining freedoms of the San. The reduction of wildlife could of course not be balanced by low-paid work on white farms. Quite in contrast, wages rather hit rock bottom because the San had to compete with better-qualified Tswana workers.

This book offers a complex picture of the "Bushmen" of southern Africa in the 20th and 21st century. While the public still sees them as isolated and hunting "Stone Age people", they are really suffering from a situation that has its roots in historical interactions with Bantu people and the British colonialism of later times. Just before the British protectorate of Bechuanaland ended, the government recognized their situation due to an officially-commissioned report by "Bushman Survey Officer" George Silberbauer. The situation of many San living in the Kalahari was already comparable to conditions under slavery and quite similar to situations of marginalized "hunters and gatherers" in other countries, e.g., right now the Ayoreo in eastern Bolivia. Today governments can learn from the experiences with policies of protection of the San: it seems paradoxical to imagine that the foundation of today's conflict was laid when the government tried to establish an "area of retreat" for "hunters and gatherers" as well as endangered natural resources. Later on, the San became involved in this conflict – the present book's central issue – as well. The truth of the matter is that the establishment of the *Central Kalahari Game Reserve* was the only specific and political measure to protect the San way of life ever undertaken by a government for the territory of today's Botswana. Even when non-inhabitants were soon strictly forbidden to enter the reserve, this protection policy did not recognize the rights of the San; the land of the reserve – one of Africa's largest protected areas – formally remained crown land. As it was a general rule for the entire crown land, only governments were entitled to monitor hunting activities – quite in contrast to Tswana "tribal reserves" for which the protectorate government had granted them extensive autonomy in terms of hunting.

The San who had been marginalized by Tswana society in pre-colonial times were ultimately deprived of their right of self-determination under formal law as well and became subjects of paternalistic protection policies.

The precarious situation of the San even intensified in various ways when Botswana became independent in 1966. Similar to other parts of Africa, the policy of nation-building manifested itself in both state and law being allegedly blind to ethnicity and cultural diversity. All state citizens were supposed to be equals before the law. At the same time, the legal system of independent Botswana took up some aspects of the former protectorate: while the first – and later often amended – Land Act of the independent state recognized the "tribes'" customary patterns of land use, the term "tribe" did not comprise the sociopolitical organization of the San (and other minorities such as the Kgalagadi). Without specifically applying categories concerned with "ethnicity", the state nevertheless granted Tswana forms of land use but denied the same to the San. The administration of land was transferred from the former "tribal" authorities to state councils, the so-called land boards. This is how the power of traditional chiefs could be limited, while the access to authorities administrating the land could still be offered to members of Tswana society.

The crown land outside the "tribal reserves", which for the most part represented the remaining hunting areas for the San, was now owned by the state of Botswana. While Tswana authorities were generally consulted to control hunting on "tribal reserves", the state increasingly tried to exclusively control hunting on state land. Starting in the 1990s, it became more and more difficult for members of the San to obtain the hunting licenses they legally needed. At the same time, government authorities made most San subjects to an integral rural development programme which was supposed to turn San into full citizens of the state.

The present book demonstrates the virtually classic problem of an integrationist development approach focusing on poverty, poor economic opportunities, a lack of access to education and other social achievements, a policy that does not – specifically – address the reasons and special conditions of marginalization of certain sociocultural groups. Accordingly, Botswana's social programmes do not call their beneficiaries "Bushmen" or "San" but rather speak of "inhabitants of remote areas". Thus they fictitiously keep up the official version of the social backwardness of desert people without recognizing their cultural needs or their specific sociocultural marginalization.

It is a truism, however, that social and economic opportunities of individuals often spread along ethnic "dividing lines" to a significantly different extent. Ethnicity may cause structural inequalities and an effective solution to this problem must keep in mind how ethnicity affects the access to rights and opportunities. The mobilization of the San in Botswana and other countries seeks to articulate the cultural reasons of discrimination and to establish specific claims against present states by expressing their own indigeneity. In this sense, indigeneity is a concept of several dimensions; it connects compensation claims of ethnic groups based on historically experienced injustices to demands to overcome present discrimination as well as respect for a self-determined cultural otherness.[2]

The present book impressively describes how Botswana's San were dominated by other (Bantu-speaking) groups who had not immigrated from another continent or "across the sea" but from other parts of Africa into present-day Botswana in the course of a long historical process. This African "internal colonisation" has not only forced the San into the characteristically marginal position they assume today, it has also established rules of statehood in cooperation with colonial law, which block out the cultural logics and social patterns of the San. This can be most clearly seen in cases where the state of Botswana neither recognizes the San's characteristic forms of resource use nor their forms of social coexistence – in contrast to Tswana land ownership and "tribal organizations", which today even form a constitutive element of modern Botswana society.

Keeping all this in mind, the concept of "indigeneity" makes sense even in the African context unless it is trivially reduced to the mere historical priority of a group. It should rather comprehend recent complex interactions between groups and the dominant state and focus on establishing indigenous rights. Zips-Mairitsch shows exceptional skills and empathy in explaining the specific conflict situation of her research area. She enables an audience to understand why the African San legitimately use the concept of indigeneity which, as she puts it, makes it possible to recognize "differentiation within a democratically negotiable relationship". Therefore, this concept refers to neither essentialist nor historical characteristics of certain ethnic groups but to an imbalance of power in the sense of a correcting mechanism in the reciprocal relationship between the state and the local, thus indigenous, population.

The discussion about the San's indigeneity presents the crucial context of this book's main issue: presenting and analyzing the *High Court of Botswana's* decision of the case *Sesana v. the Attorney General* in late 2006. In this case, 215 individual San claimants took legal steps against their relocation from the *Central Kalahari Game Reserve* as well as the denial of hunting licenses. Furthermore, they criticized the discontinuation of state infrastructure and welfare benefits. After 130 days of trial and almost 19,000 pages of minutes, this was the most comprehensive case any court in Botswana had ever had. At the same time, it shows the lim-

---

2   Cf. René Kuppe (2009): The Three Dimensions of the Rights of Indigenous Peoples. In: *International Community Law Review* 11(1): 103–118.

its of the claimants' legal strategy: although significant progress has been made in recognizing the land rights of indigenous peoples in the last few years – for further details see Zips-Mairitsch – it becomes clear how difficult it is to implement this progress for the benefit of a community's way of life like the San.

The most important and legally binding instrument for the protection of the rights of indigenous peoples is Convention 169 of the International Labour Organization. Art. 14 explicitly guarantees the full recognition of the right of ownership and possession over land that indigenous peoples traditionally occupy (first sentence, Art. 14, ILO 169). Although Botswana has not ratified this convention, it is nonetheless a crucial point of reference for the assessment of indigenous claims. It certainly remains doubtful, however, whether the characteristic San way of life meets the requirements of the convention in respect to the legal recognition of traditional occupation. In this context, "traditionally occupy" generally refers to a close relationship to land, which excludes third parties from using it as well. Thus, land must be occupied exclusively.[3]

Today it is without doubt scientifically confirmed that the San's so-called "nomadism" cannot be interpreted as unstructured "wandering around" in the relevant regions of southern Africa. Moreover, the relationship between the San (other nomadic peoples too) and land is shaped by normative logics and practices. This foundation often establishes an extremely close connection between these peoples and their territories and resources. When it comes to the legal logics of state law, we have to ask what the nature of this connection would have to be as well as how "close" it would have to be to provide a basis for land rights. In his classic work about indigenous land rights, McNeil already explained that the ownership and possession of indigenous peoples over a territory also includes "not just land in actual use by them at any given moment, but all land within their habitual range, for occupation, once acquired, is not necessarily lost by temporary absence (particularly if seasonal)".[4] Their intent and ability to control exclusively these lands must be given though.

It is generally recognized in legal doctrine as well as national and international case law that the relationship to land under the "aboriginal title" may vary in intensity. Recent Canadian court rulings, for example, nevertheless stipulated that a nomadic way of life may be sufficient to establish limited rights to a certain location but it would not be enough for a – legally relevant – relationship to land unless evidence of the permanent and intense use of the land is provided.[5] This is why the nomadic and semi-nomadic use of land may disqualify indigenous peoples from a legal title over land.

---

3 See Jérémie Gilbert (2007): Nomadic Territories: A Human Rights Approach to Nomadic Peoples' Land Rights. In: *Human Rights Law Review* 7(4), 681–716: 701–702.
4 McNeil, Kent (1989): *Common Law Aboriginal Title*. Oxford: Clarendon Press: 204.
5 See R. v. Marshall; R. v. Bernard, [2005] 2 S.C.R. 220, 2005 SCC 43, para. 126.

Such a restrictive interpretation of the claim over a direct right to land is in a certain way also supported by the second and third sentence of Art. 14 ILO Convention 169, "... measures shall be taken in appropriate cases to safeguard the right of the peoples concerned to use lands not exclusively occupied by them, but to which they have traditionally had access for their subsistence and traditional activities. Particular attention shall be paid to the situation of nomadic peoples and shifting cultivators in this respect." These provisions obviously establish nothing more but the right to use lands in case of non-exclusive occupation. The right of ownership and possession over land is thus only ensured in case of "traditionally occupied land". In this – second – provision of Art. 14 ILO Convention 169, the reference to "nomadic peoples and shifting cultivators" demonstrates a logic that has affected the legal assessment of colonized peoples – of having a rather "unsteady" relationship to their land – since the beginning of European expansion overseas. The renowned international law expert Emer de Vattel (18th century) for example emphasized that American "Indian tribes" could not claim more territory than the land they actually "occupied" and "cultivated". Even the founder of the modern liberal idea of constitutional law John Locke was particularly convinced that "uncultivated" land was not legally owned or possessed by anyone. Based on these approaches, the appropriation of land from non-farming peoples was not theft but original appropriation of *res nullius*.[6]

The *High Court of Botswana* could have assessed the relationship between the San and the *Central Kalahari Game Reserve* as intense enough to create an extensive title to land in the sense of aboriginal title. In contrast, at a central point the decision states that "the appellants were in possession of the land which they lawfully occupied *in their settlements* [in the *Central Kalahari Game Reserve*]" (emphasis R. Kuppe). From both an international and national perspective, the legal developments concerning indigenous land rights offer a certain range of opportunities but *Sesana* is doubtlessly located in the lower, rather moderate area. It is remarkable though that in the "land rights" part of its decision, the *High Court of Botswana* recognizes and at least implicitly addresses the evaluative parallels of the land titles of indigenous peoples in other, more progressive countries. At the same time, the court does not include a direct reference to groundbreaking decisions such as in *Mabo v. Queensland* (1992) of the *High Court of Australia* in its reasons, thus also suggesting a politically-motivated consideration not to somehow legally push the controversial indigeneity of the San applicants. The author of this book is absolutely right to point out that the time of this case's decision was far too much influenced by the national and regional political "mobilization" by African states against indigenous rights in the context of the negotiations on the *UN Declaration on the Rights of Indigenous Peoples*.

---

6   Barbara Arneil (1998): *John Locke. The Defence of English Colonialism*. Oxford: Clarendon Press.

In this case as well, the judges completely blocked out the normative relevance of specific indigenous rights claims for the other legal issues in question: the application of law for the necessary overcoming of marginalization and discrimination, the state's responsibility not to tolerate but to actively protect the needed conditions to practice cultural traditions. In the context of implemented international Human Rights instruments ratified by Botswana concerning indigenous rights, the judges could have additionally applied these considerations when they assessed the controversial welfare benefits or the denial of hunting licenses. Instead they treated these questions as technical problems and refused to take the opportunity of using law, as Zips-Mairitsch states, to contribute to "a process of reconciliation in terms of intercultural retributive justice".

Especially in a country where the negative assessment of nomadism in Western-European legal tradition overlapped and blended with autochthonous pre-colonial marginalization, this process of reconciliation would have been a very special order of the day.

In this book, the author masterfully succeeds in processing the detailed descriptions of the San's land rights dispute in such a way that its instructive relevance for fundamental questions of intercultural justice becomes obvious. This book is perfect to present the central questions to the issue of the rights of indigenous peoples. I wish this also stylistically exceptional publication that it will be widely distributed among experts as well as the interested public – an area where profound studies to this issue unfortunately are few and far between.

Introduction

"If we win the court case, government will be very very unhappy, because we will shoot some few gemsbok and we will party for two nights and we will dance and say thank you to our ancestors."
(Mathambo Ngakaeaja, interview on 8 March 2005)

It needed almost a small miracle for the hopes of Mathambo Ngakaeaja, a leading member of the NGO *Working Group of Indigenous Minorities in Southern Africa* (WIMSA) and Naro San, to really come true. In Botswana nobody would have expected the High Court to rule in favour of the San. The decision of 13 December 2006 unanimously confirmed the land rights of the G|wi and ||Gana San as well as Bakgalagadi in the *Central Kalahari Game Reserve* (CKGR). Although it was not recorded whether those who were relocated from the *Central Kalahari Game Reserve* and got involved in the legal struggle and their sympathizers really hunted for gemsbok and danced for two nights, their joy and content was obvious.

The crucial decision which stands at the centre of this book's contextual considerations was preceded by ten years of local political and physical conflicts deciding about the fate of the inhabitants of the CKGR. The Botswana government's numerous threats of forced relocation from the Game Reserve were realized in 1997 and 2002 and caught the attention of the international community. After all, the San of the Central Kalahari were groups of people who for many decades were regarded as the "archetypal hunters and gatherers" of southern Africa and who, therefore, had become subjects of countless documentaries, newspaper articles and (popular) scientific works. The many following years of struggle for their (indigenous) rights created a solidarity wave of almost global dimensions. International NGOs, such as *Survival International*, knew how to surf on this wave and how to successfully use it to gather more donations and international funding. The marketing of their campaigns for the "last hunters and gatherers of the Central Kalahari" who were about to suffer from land dispossession because of diamond mining operations worked as well as pictures of giant pandas by conservationist organizations. Romanticizing movies such as "The

Gods Must Be Crazy" and idealizing presentations in books (cf. Laurens van der Post 1958, 1961) provided the San with some form of cult status, which made them one of the most described peoples or cultures in anthropology.

With good reason, the majority population of Botswana refuses to accept such presentations as exoticizing forms of differentiation ("othering") which were each time ultimately used to construct the own "civilization" as particularly advanced. This legitimate refusal of, ultimately, racist concepts of evolutionist differentiations, however, was then used in a mirror-inverted way by consecutive governments to regard cultural expressions as well as social, political and legal ways of organization of the San as true causes for such external presentations and imagery of Africa. In this respect, similar views of "savagery" have in a rather complex way caused refusals of true contemporaneity and today shimmer through a great number of national development ideas. The judicial decision in favour of the indigenous land rights of the San was even more surprising as, at the very same time, Botswana became the driving force of a global, political "campaign" against the *United Nations Declaration on the Rights of Indigenous Peoples*. Botswana and its neighbouring country Namibia were able to convince enough state representatives (mainly of the African continent) to obtain an adjournment of the UN General Assembly's resolution in order to (once again) revise the draft version of this historic human rights document.[1] Their massive reservations against the text were mainly based on their concerns that the declaration would contradict the territorial integrity and political unity of the postcolonial state and would cause ethnic and tribal conflicts especially on the African continent.

Both of these legal processes – the development of a global, legal standard on the one hand and the Botswana High Court's evaluation of state policies on the other hand – are in multiple ways connected and form the opposing poles of the present work. This book, therefore, addresses both the way how Botswana locally treats the (indigenous peoples of the) San in the context of developments in southern Africa as well as the development of universal Human Rights towards indigenous rights and their (possible) consequences for national forms of development policies and governance. While indigenous peoples and rights in Canada, Australia, New Zealand and the United States have been extensively presented and dealt with, an impressive amount of works of various disciplines (law, anthropology, historical research, political science, and others) has also discussed indigenous peoples of Latin America, whose rights have gained constitutional character in most national contexts (Aguilar et al. 2009: 44 ff.). In regional-specific literature, India should be mentioned as well, although it may be narrowed down to "internal Indian" debates – national development and the "promotion" of so called "tribal societies".

---

1 *Amnesty International, Public Statement* 11/30/2006; Republic of Botswana, *Tautona Times no 32* of 2007; IWGIA *update*, June 2007.

In relation to these particular regional or national contexts, the term "indigeneity" did not just remain rather pale on the African continent but it even faced grave opposition in the context of postcolonial nation building. In general more than a few governments are quite indifferent concerning human rights and particularly refuse to accept the term "indigenous peoples" in Africa. Mere pretense or not, they suspect a new version of the "divide and rule principle" of former colonial and neocolonial powers by means of ethnic differentiations. Some African governments use the concept that "all Africans are indigenous" to struggle against this term and its related developments in international law. While this subject matter has just recently provoked a wide debate in social anthropology, I will refrain from a comprehensive and conclusive discussion because the debate just remotely (if at all) addresses legal questions or related existing literature. My following considerations about the clearly not unproblematic terms of "indigeneity" and "peoples" will to some extent deal with social-anthropological literature. However, I will focus on legal works which of course pay less attention to the problematic etymological, socio-cultural perspective or the history of science than to the pragmatic need of protection of communities who doubtlessly suffer in multiple ways. In any case, the legal use of these terms should not claim any ontological essence of "indigenous peoples" or take any essentialist contents as the basis of this compound term. Although several problems with the terms "indigenous" and "peoples" have been mentioned and a lack of semiotic clarity is obvious, both elements are used in this work because, from a legal point of view, they appear as the best way to address legal maladies (of discrimination, patronization, cultural hegemony, and occasionally even ethnocide) in lack of better or more adequate proposals.

Some governments, including Botswana, have not accepted "their" indigenous peoples or (indigenous) land rights yet. This is why it seemed necessary for the reader's overall understanding to discuss at first prevailing international (part 1) and then regional African legal norms (part 2) of their protection (and possibly compensation for past and continuing injustice suffered). Furthermore, I have placed all relationships in a context of legal pluralism, as such a perspective appeared essential to assess the relevant (development) policies of consecutive governments as well as the decision of the High Court. This approach would have been relevant in the same way, if the *High Court of Botswana* had not confirmed the land rights of the San in the *Central Kalahari Game Reserve*. Only after having exhausted all local remedies, there would have been a chance to take up international and/or regional legal instruments. In this context, I will present the development of "universal" indigenous rights which makes it more and more difficult for states to ignore such standards. An example of a positive development offers the neighbouring country of South Africa which I will use to compare current legal developments and governance measures with a special reference to judicial decisions on indigenous rights.

The "true actors" of the present work (apart from state authorities) are the descendants of Botswana's first "hunters and gatherers", amounting to about 50,000 out of southern Africa's total of 80,000 to 100,000 members. As this book's terminological part suggests, these indigenous peoples have never formed homogenous groups. Their different but comparable experiences of land dispossession due to both waves of immigration and the taking over of (colonial and postcolonial) power in southern Africa had far-reaching consequences for "the" San (of course keeping "their" huge internal differences in mind): they lost their cultures, identities, forms of self-determination, territories and natural resources to a great extent or even completely. In many cases they were also forced into institutionalized political and legal systems without any choice or form of influence. At different points of the past, they experienced various forms of oppression, domination, disenfranchisement and discrimination. There was only little or no space at all left for their own ways of life, legal conceptions and cultural practices.

In a further step to draw attention to the marginalized position of San societies in today's Botswana, it also seemed necessary to describe the country's (socio-)political past as well as the legal development up to current applicable law (part 4). The relationships between different ethnic, social and indigenous groups root back to the development of the early "Tswana proto-states". At this time the San communities held the lowest ranks of power. This structure of hierarchy was then continued in colonial times through the transformation to administrative "Tswana" units and/or "reserves" by the British protectorate. Thus a social structure developed which even continued in the independent state under "Tswana" rule from 1966. The Republic of Botswana basically claims to be a country of good governance, rule of law and democracy. Concerning their coexistence with the San and other (indigenous) minorities, however, the state developed an approach regarded by many as derogatory, paternalistic and assimilative. The majority population of Botswana judges San, generally called "Basarwa", as backward, child-like "people from the Stone Age" whose values, cultural practices and ways of life qualify as underdeveloped. Today this approach also legitimizes the country's claim for a protective and caring task to balance developmental disadvantages by means of targeted development measures (part 5). The idea constructed in former times of "hunters and gatherers" is confronted with the model of a progressive "free citizen" working in agriculture or the cattle industry. In the state representatives' discussions about development policies, each culturally "different(iated)" community is not only viewed as a contradiction to progress but, moreover, a threat and danger to the process of postcolonial nation building.

After having dealt with the relevant discourses mentioned above, I will finally address the central focus of my work in part 6: the problems all around the resettlement from the *Central Kalahari Game Reserve* (CKGR) and the lawsuit concerned with the lands the San thought were lost. This internal resettlement gained a level of international attention that the government of Botswana obviously had underestimated. The reasons for the (forced) relocation of about 2,300 G|wi und ||Gana San from the *Central Kalahari Game Reserve* officially included the already-mentioned social imperatives of state development, economic costs for social services in the reserve and the protection of nature and biodiversity. In order to resettle on their lands as soon as possible, 243 former inhabitants of the CKGR filed an urgent application on notice of motion before the *High Court of Botswana*. The lawsuit became the longest and most expensive case in Botswana history. In the end, a panel of three judges granted twelve out of a total of 18 motions for judgement. The most important claim for the San clearly was the establishment of their land rights which the panel unanimously ruled in favour for. Therefore, their (indigenous) land rights as well as the related right to resettle on the "territory of their ancestors" were acknowledged. In the legal struggle for the "lost lands" of the Kalahari, this at least was an important partial victory.

There are further closely connected and groundbreaking developments in the protection of indigenous rights on the African continent. After conclusion of the lawsuit, the latest developments in Botswana do not give rise to any exaggerated or optimistic expectations whatsoever though: for the most part, the orders included in the court decision have not been observed. The San had to file another claim to regain access to water sources in the *Central Kalahari Game Reserve*. This shows that a change of state policies towards a participatory type of relationship which is connected to (and even inherent in) the legalistic notion of indigeneity clearly lags behind legal developments. As it has been the case with the United Nations for several decades, a rudimentarily recognizable form of cooperative "governance of indigeneity" could build on a reassessment of cultural diversity.

Part 1: Indigenous Peoples in International Law

"The indigenous peoples hold a significant place in the planetary cultural landscape and are representative of cultural diversity. They personify a global vision of the world and of humankind that continues to be intimately linked to nature and the earth to which we all belong."

(UNESCO: Culture. Action in favour of Indigenous Peoples)[1]

---

1   www.unesco.org/culture as of 09/18/2007.

I. Historical Overview

The protection of cultural diversity has by far not reached the same status the conservation of biological diversity has achieved in the last few decades. In recent times, however, several groundbreaking instruments of international legal development have at least shown signs of possible progress in this matter. Two specific instruments should be pointed out: first, the UNESCO "Convention on the Protection and Promotion of the Diversity of Cultural Expressions" (2005); and second, the "United Nations Declaration on the Rights of Indigenous Peoples" (2007).[2] Both take into account that about 90 percent of our world's cultural diversity can be found in (an estimated) 370 million people – or about 5 percent of the planet's population – who are members of still existing groups of indigenous peoples (cf. Alcántara 1999: 105).[3] There are more than 5,000 languages spoken on the planet, 96 percent of which are spoken by only 4 percent of the world's population. Most of these 4 percent are indigenous groups.[4] This is why UNESCO primarily focuses on the need for protection of indigenous peoples whose cultural expressions as well as indispensable claims of land ownership are threatened:

"The fact that the cultures of indigenous peoples are in danger of dying out cannot fail to be a matter of concern to UNESCO. These populations number some 350 million individuals in more than 70 countries in the world and represent more than 5,000 languages and cultures. Today many of them live on the fringes of society and are deprived of basic Human Rights, particularly cultural rights."[5]

Keeping in mind the linguistic pluralism of indigenous peoples, it becomes obvious how much they contribute to this planet's rich cultural heritage. Nevertheless, many governments as well as private sectors involved in the exploitation of resources in nation states regard indigenous groups as "disturbing factors" and "inconvenient" obstacles to development.[6] This process concerns three areas of state inter-

---

2   Cf. UNESCO, "Convention on the Protection and Promotion of the Diversity of Cultural Expressions", CLT-2005/Convention Diversite-Cult Rev, Paris, 20 October 2005; and United Nations General Assembly, "United Nations Declaration on the Rights of Indigenous Peoples", 13 September 2007 (A/61/L.67).

3   Durand Alcántara (1999: 105) talks of 300 million. Based on the latest estimates, this number was revised upwards due to demographic growth.

4   UNESCO and Indigenous Peoples: Partnership to Promote Cultural Diversity (2006): p 34.

5   www.unesco.org/culture as of 09/18/2007.

6   Saugestad 2001: *The Inconvenient Indigenous*. For a detailed discussion see chapter 5, section II, this volume. In this context, see also the problem of internally displaced persons, e.g., Deng (1998); UNHCR (2010).

est: first, homogenization in the context of both postcolonial nation building and uniform cultural, social, and educational policies; second, undisputed sovereignty; and third, control over resources. Conflicts are continuously shifted to the symbolic (terminological) level, perhaps to distract from legal questions (central to this book). In the cause of progress and development, nature conservation, or public (state) interest, indigenous rights are diminished or often even negated as a whole:

Indigenous peoples live in the domain of (and often in conflict with) states that generally specify their economic goals in terms of 'growth' through commercial exploitation of so-called national resources, their political goals often in terms of 'nation-building', and their cultural programme predominantly in terms of a monolingual and homogenous state. Specific legal grounds are instrumentalized to achieve these goals – such as the declaration of sovereignty or the perception as a 'nation state' – in order to form the foundation for state claims: for this purpose, relevant concepts borrowed from the European context are adopted and often anachronistically exaggerated without hesitation (Kuppe 1990: 15).[7]

Our world's about 5,000 distinct groups of indigenous cultures (United Nations 2009: 84) have had to experience similar forms of historical, social and political discrimination. In consequence, they have lost large parts of their former territories and have been turned into "voiceless peoples". As late as 1967, for example, the passage denying Aborigines their humanity was removed from the Australian code of law (*Der Standard*, 08/19/2008). Numerous studies (primarily commissioned by the UN) confirm that indigenous peoples generally live under deplorable living conditions, which are closely connected to discrimination and other violations of human rights against individuals or whole groups. Their poor standard of living as well as various social constraints and legal obstacles, such as limited rights of participation and representation, make it even harder for them to improve their conditions in the long run.[8] Many still live on the margins of society, are poorer, less educated, die younger, commit suicide more often, and generally suffer from poor health care compared to the planet's population average (IWGIA 2006: 10).

In the 1960s, indigenous peoples in Australia, Canada, and the United States started to organize on a global level. With Central and South America following 10–15 years later, they sought to face these objective inequalities and subjective injustices in a more successful way and to use international law to reinforce their claims.[9] A committed and courageous approach was needed to use international law, the "law of peoples", against its historical grain because the roots of international law are found in the interests of powerful nations that called for

---

7   Original citation in German.
8   Cf. also Stavenhagen (2002).
9   For a detailed description of the development of the indigenous movement see e.g., Thornberry (2002: 21ff.).

I. Historical Overview

the submission and control of large parts of the inhabited world. Their "discoveries" of regions which were occupied by others had to be legally legitimized. In this respect, the "international law of peoples" originally focused on expropriating indigenous peoples and was, therefore, related to the "nature", character, and justification of rights, others (mostly European nations) claimed over indigenous peoples. In the second half of the 20th century, the scope of international law slowly shifted to include the protection of indigenous peoples and to develop indigenous rights. Not only this process but also the complex development of universal human rights as well as the under-the-gun process of decolonisation demanded international law to undergo a thorough reflective revision:

"The subject of indigenous peoples is not new to this genre of law but has figured with varying degrees of prominence in the legal discourse and practice related to international law's evolution over centuries" (Anaya 1996: 9).

Current international law has its deepest roots in the law of nature, in which the first approaches to a basic equality of peoples and sympathy for those "discovered" can be detected.[10] In the late 16th century, however, colonial rulers were supported by the Catholic Church to justify expropriating indigenous peoples: as nonbelievers and heathen, indigenous peoples were not on the same level as Christians and thus did not enjoy the same rights to land and resources (Keal 2003: 69f.). The Peace of Westphalia of 1648 and the development of the modern state caused the all-encompassing principle of sovereignty to cast a damp over the mindset of natural law.

As we can even see in current discourses concerned with national matters of law (including the litigation over the "lost lands" in Botswana's Kalahari as presented in this book), this legal-historical development is a lot more than only historically interesting. After a long diplomatic tug-of-war, the United Nations' General Assembly adopted the *Declaration on the Rights of Indigenous Peoples* by majority vote on 13 September 2007: even this instrument was ultimately about the principle of non-intervention in domestic affairs and exclusive national sovereignty. Rooted in the discriminating expressions of European modernism combined with the attributed natural state of non-European peoples, it is this sovereignty from which the "rightlessness" of indigenous peoples is implicitly derived:

"In the broader discourse of international law, while processes of secularisation continued, movements towards the aggrandisement of sovereignty, the further and narrower 'Europeanisation' of international law, and the diminishing of polities not modelled on European patterns, continues apace. (...) Clearly the

---

10 The clerics Bartolomé de las Casas (1474–1566) and Francisco de Vitoria (1486–1547) were among the first not only to question the justification and moral claims over the "New World" as well as the often brutal settlement policies of later times but who protected indigenous peoples too (Anaya 1996: 10). Nevertheless, they should always be read keeping their temporal context in mind.

turn given to natural law by Hobbes (1588–1679) which views it as an instrument of self-preservation, together with his bifurcation of law into 'real' law under the sovereign within the State, and the law of nations (*ius gentium*) still in a state of nature without, is a major influence. (…) The related aspect of Hobbes's thinking – the brutish state of nature from which sovereignty was an escape – continues even now to furnish unattractive metaphors for those who wish to caricature indigenous societies" (Thornberry 2002: 70–71).[11]

The concept of a nation state was based on the following three criteria: sovereignty, exclusive territorial power, and central hierarchical power. From the elevated point of view of the European conquerors, however, indigenous peoples were organized by kinship, did not have any laws whatsoever, usually showed decentralized political structures, and lived on shared or overlapping territories. These characteristics did not qualify them as "states" and were the reason why indigenous peoples were *de facto* deprived of their rights of self-determination (Anaya 1996: 13–15). The continuous secularization of international law helped the status of indigenous groups to increasingly become part of legally comparative considerations about the status and hierarchy of entire "civilizations". The ideas of different hierarchical stages of development were mainly supported by explanations of evolutionist anthropologists and promoted the development of "scientific racism" (Thornberry 2002: 72f.). 18th and 19th century European jurists regarded some indigenous groups as the embodied "most primitive, wild" stage of human evolution. Their indigenous forms of social organization, legal land concepts and the related rights to both land ownership and use were seen as incomprehensible and incompatible with the "advanced" models Europeans ascribed to themselves. This was the basis of the dogmatic principle that the territory of indigenous peoples was land belonging to no one and that intruding powers had the right to occupy this land. The doctrine of "terra nullius" saw indigenous land as "uninhabited by law" that could thus be "legally" occupied (Anaya 1996: 22).[12]

Based on the (legal) negation of indigenous existence, colonial power combined this jurisprudence with the doctrine of "trust or guardianship". This principle obliged those "advanced" to civilize the "less developed, backward races". Hence, it implicitly included the obligation of paternalistic custody which pursued the goal of "improving" the evolutionist stage of development of indigenous peoples.[13] At the conference of European imperialists to partition Africa, the

---

11 Thornberry (ibid.) proves his point by citing the Chief Judge of the famous Canadian "Delgamuukw decision", who at that time had cited Hobbes to characterize the indigenous groups concerned and their lives as "nasty, brutish and short".

12 For a more detailed explanation of this doctrine see chapter 2, excursus "Aboriginal Title".

13 The concept of paternal state welfare for "underdeveloped" parts of the population (analyzed by various authorities) is still effective today and has its roots, *inter alia*, in this development.

I. Historical Overview

doctrine of "trust or guardianship" manifested itself in Art. VI of the *General Act of the Berlin African Conference* 1884–85: "All the Powers (…) bind themselves to watch over the preservation of the native tribes, and to care for the improvement of the conditions of their moral and material well-being."[14]

These short historical considerations should demonstrate that the international so-called "law of peoples" was extremely one-sided and definitely not the law of all people(s) until the second half of the 20th century. The dogmatic discourse was dominated by legal theories that deprived indigenous peoples of their rights. Influenced by such doctrines, international law predominantly followed the purpose of justifying intrusions into indigenous territories and refusing to recognize their cultural identity. It is, therefore, quite a reversion that international law has further developed towards the legal protection of indigenous peoples. This process does not emerge unanimously or frictionless and is partially undermined or at least weakened because of various forms of opposition often obliged to national but also global economic self-interest. In a time of extensive juridification which J.L. Comaroff and J. Comaroff attempt to comprehend adequately as "(global) lawfare" and "fetishism of law" (2006: 22ff.), this process is a strong parameter for state and private relationships to indigenous peoples. Whether it is "soft law" or not, international law is more and more turning from a former instrument of colonialism to an "advocate" of indigenous peoples (Anaya 1996: 4).[15] Today's legal determinations concerning indigenous peoples are mostly the result of their own instigation. When it comes to their legal status, indigenous peoples have stopped to be nothing but objects of others' discussions at a transnational level. On the contrary, they have become indispensable participants of an extensive multilateral dialog. Although indigenous rights have found their way into many both "hard law" and "soft law" instruments, concerned parties are still divided over the term "indigenous peoples". This lack of a precise definition causes a controversial, terminological classification which I will shortly discuss in the next part.

---

14 Cited in Thornberry (2002: 76). More than 30 years later, Art. 11 of the *Treaty of Saint-Germain-en-Laye* of 1919 extended the validity of the *Berlin General Act* to include all African territories (ibid.: 77).
15 See chapter 1, section III, 1.2. this volume for the concept of "soft law" and its relation to "hard law".

II. "Indigenous Peoples": Term, Concepts, and Definitions

The concept of "indigenous peoples" does not only involve terminological problems but also related, complex questions of inclusion and exclusion. Let us have a look at an example from 1995: at the annual session of the *United Nations Working Group on Indigenous Populations*, a group of South African Boers claimed their right to be recognized under the umbrella of indigenous peoples.[16] These descendants of Dutch and German settlers, migrated to South Africa in 1652, invoked the characteristics which at that time were ascribed to indigeneity: identity-establishing "cultural otherness" and "non-dominant status in society". Countless participants at the session felt snubbed by the downright ironizing way the members of a former ruling group, infamous for their discriminating exercise of power, used this terminology. In direct response to this claim, the Working Group and their *chairperson-rapporteur* considered the spontaneous development of a definition for indigenous peoples. After long discussions, however, the Working Group refrained from determining a definition appropriate for the occasion and decided that the already-existing open criteria still provided the best protection against misuse. According to their decision, a preconception of the term indigenous peoples was sufficiently ensured. Nevertheless, each single case had to be individually specified due to its relational character (Daes 1995a: para. 6).

If we try to keep in mind the multitude of indigenous peoples as mentioned above, it is hardly surprising that there is no universally accepted definition of indigenous peoples getting to grips with and doing justice to this diversity. In the last 40 years, the terminological definition has changed on the various levels of global, regional, national, and local contexts. Concerning the chronological legal development for the protection of indigenous interests, *UN Special Rapporteur* José R. Martínez Cobo was the first (1972) to create a working definition for his *"Study of the Problems of Discrimination Against Indigenous Peoples"* which was launched by the *UN Sub-Commission on Prevention of Discrimination and Protection of Minorities*. In 1986/87, his defining explanation of indigenous peoples was used in a UN document and became widely known and accepted. Even so, we cannot formally conclude the discussion about adequate terminology and its content. In contrast to the current understanding, the former definition vigorously differentiated between indigenous peoples and (ethnic) minorities:

---

16 See also the "Kennewick debate" over the discovery of the oldest human skeleton ever found in North America, predating the American Indians, the ensuing question of who got to America first, and, therefore, should be accredited the right of "first come" due to prior inhabitation (e.g., Thornberry 2002: 35–40). The *Working Group on Indigenous Populations* was abolished in 2007 and replaced with the *Expert Mechanism on the Rights of Indigenous Peoples*.

II. "Indigenous Peoples": Term, Concepts, and Definitions

"Indigenous communities, peoples and nations are those which, having a historical continuity with pre-invasion and pre-colonial societies that developed on their territories, consider themselves distinct from other sectors of the societies now prevailing in those territories, or part of them. They form at present non-dominant sectors of society and are determined to preserve, develop and transmit to future generations their ancestral territories, and their ethnic identity, as the basis of their continued existence as peoples, in accordance with their own cultural patterns, social institutions and legal systems" (Cobo 1986: para. 379).

Since the first working definition in 1972, its central statements have shown a development towards the protection of indigenous cultural societies as autonomous peoples. Thus, in a period of roughly 15 years, we can detect a paradigm shift from a former assimilative basis to a bilateral, "sovereign" relationship to the states. The working definition certainly was inspired by ILO Convention No. 107 (1957) which was using the term 'populations'. In the document of 1986/87, this relatively undefined demographic expression evolved to the stable sociopolitical units of 'communities, peoples and nations'. Furthermore, the former practice of "linking indigenousness with the task of tracing ancestry" was replaced by a contextual perspective, including not only kinship but predominantly historical continuity in terms of land (rights), culture, language, economic systems, and ways of living. Keeping all that in mind, the 1972 working definition covered merely the "blue water colonisation", while the official report of 1986/87 referred to a continuity of life worlds before indigenous territories were conquered and colonized.[17] The concept of "blue/salt water colonisation" is only concerned with oppression and physical expropriation by settlers from overseas. Therefore, this definition does not apply to Africa or Asia. According to *Chairperson Rapporteur* Daes, such a restrictive classification would unjustifiably differentiate between aggressions originating geographically further away and those from shorter away. She continues by stating that it would be undoubtedly impossible to differentiate between intrusions into the laws of concerned communities based on objective criteria (Daes 1996: para. 63). In contrast, the concept of historical continuity also includes invasions or colonisations within a certain territory.[18]

One of the most contested criteria on the terminological level of Cobo's report is the highly stressed element of self-definition which was used for the first time. When it comes to self-identification, Cobo emphasizes that this "power to define (oneself)" clearly discontinues formerly established ascriptions: "On an individual basis, an indigenous person is one who belongs to these indigenous populations through self-identification as indigenous (group consciousness) and

---

17   UN Doc. I/CN.4/Sub.2/L.566, para.34 and UN Doc. E/CN.4/Sub.2/1986/7/Add 4 para. 379.
18   Cf., inter alia, Kuppe (2004: 44), Thornberry (2002: 48).

is recognised and accepted by these populations as one of its members (acceptance by the group)" (para. 381).

As history and ethnicity are of such complex nature, this self-identification is of utmost importance for representatives of indigenous peoples. They agree that it is the defining criterion for belonging to and being recognized as a certain indigenous community. Numerous members of the *Working Group on Indigenous Populations* (WGIP) have argued that a final and universal definition was not necessary and hardly desirable because it would reproduce existing relations of power and, thus, contribute to exclusion. Instead of developing a universal and abstract definition, they stressed the importance of self-definition as a crucial element of belonging (Keal 2003: 12). If we kept the requested clarity of legal categories and applications as well as the state institutions' interest of control in mind, all this might seem quite problematic. From the perspective of those concerned, however, it may become more understandable, if we thought of their century-long experiences with ascriptions by others and legally relevant classifications.

Although the request of a definition "providing legal certainty" was perhaps justified, the reasons mentioned above caused the 1982 WGIP to regard the request as less relevant: "The Working Group on Indigenous Populations considered a working definition of the term 'indigenous' (…), but subsequently concluded that justice would best be served by allowing the scope of this concept to evolve flexible over time, through practice."[19] While the 1993 *Draft Declaration on the Rights of Indigenous Peoples* considered the right of self-identification as indigenous in Art. 8, the *Declaration on the Rights of Indigenous Peoples*, adopted by the *UN General Assembly* on 13 September 2007, did not even define concerned legal persons. In addition, Art. 9 establishes the (collective and individual) right of belonging to an indigenous community or nation, thus satisfying the demand of flexibility and respectful recognition of the "power to define (oneself)".

It goes without saying that this development also expresses the presumably unsolvable defining problem: a definition too narrow would arbitrarily exclude certain groups, while a definition too broad would water down its application to the point that all human beings could be included, making the scope of legal protection in turn highly questionable. In contrast, the continuation of already-existing terminological preconceptions, as developed with strong participation of indigenous communities and their representatives, has the advantage of embracing the dynamic development of the discourse, thus refraining from allegedly "essential" elements or cumulative lists. It would also remain unclear whether regional or local differences could be too big for a supposedly precise, universal definition to comprehend concrete needs of protection at all. If this was the case, it would contribute to the abuse of definatory power ultimately rested in the states.[20]

---

19 Daes (1995b: para. 18).
20 Confirmed also by Capotorti's study (1991: paras. 561f.).

II. "Indigenous Peoples": Term, Concepts, and Definitions

The criteria and factors mentioned above are not even supposed to form an inclusive definition covering all possible particularities due to exactly these reasons. Concerning the scope and performance of their task, however, the WGIP used the elements as suggested by Cobo as a "vague gatekeeper" (Thornberry 2002: 33). His central statements still serve as instruments of orientation and understanding, a fact that contributed to their wide distribution through the media. As they are easily comprehensible, they have been recognized in legal discourses, especially concerning self-definition. As *Special Rapporteur* Rodolfo Stavenhagen stresses in connection with the Cobo Study: "(I)t has become increasingly accepted that the right to decide who is or is not an indigenous person belongs to the indigenous people alone. (…) States must respect the right of self-definition and self-identification of indigenous people" (2002: para. 100).

In the same way, representatives of indigenous peoples stress the inappropriateness of definitions by others, especially when originating in the sphere of states. In its alternative proposal to the *Draft American Declaration on the Rights of Indigenous Peoples*, the *National Congress of American Indians* called upon: "[I]t would not be appropriate for states to define the concept of 'indigenous populations', this being the sole province of the communities involved. Self-identification, as an essential criterion for the recognition of an indigenous people, is not subject to any obligation. No term could encompass the multiplicity and variety of such communities existing in the Hemisphere." The *National Congress of American Indians* emphasized that they were neither "ethnic minorities", nor "racial minorities", nor "populations" but defined themselves as a collective: "[P]eoples, or collective, autonomous entities, with age-old languages, whose organizations, shaped by lands, waters, forests, and other natural resources, afforded them a special cosmovision and a unique social structure ensuring their continuity".[21]

As it is quite unlikely that each of these factors sufficiently applies to all "indigenous" environments, a certain flexibility of terminological attribution is at hand. Although indicators of various analyses are chosen differently and concrete descriptions better apply to the situation of a certain region, the level of shown similarities is nevertheless significant. So it was not by accidence that international law avoided all too-inflexible definitions of the collective group rights of peoples, minorities, and collectives. Although by some rejected as *fuzzy logics*, the scope of discretion in international law is seen as a quality which prevents all terminological components to be canonically defined for a long time (Thornberry 2002: 57). As stressed by numerous authors, the preconception developed by those indigenous peoples concerned seems to be the crucial criterion for both the choice of terminology as well as the definition of its content: "Therefore, when

---

21 Section 1, Working Document comparing the original proposed American Declaration on the Rights of Indigenous Peoples and Proposals by Indigenous Representatives. GT/DADIN/doc.50/01 of 6 December 2001.

we ask who indigenous peoples are, we may not have a formal definition but we do have a concept. (...) We do not need a formal definition in order to articulate the interests that should be protected (...) it is in our interest (...) to avoid the pitfalls of creating a label. Otherwise, in our attempt at being all encompassing, we may hurt those whom we most aim to protect" (Dias 1999: 3).

When it comes to discussions concerning law and jurisprudence, we can, therefore, detect both a pragmatic approach – resulting in the focus on a really existing need of protection – as well as a historically aware interest in rights violated in the past. On its long way towards the adoption of the *Declaration on the Rights of Indigenous Peoples* (2007), the international development of law has refrained from determining stringent and clear characteristics of a definition with good reason. Therefore, it has not only impeded the danger of essentialist interpretations but also prevented the pressure related to such an understanding of law to stabilize a certain way of living as well as its corresponding cosmovision. An abstract and generalizing definition of indigenous characteristics could easily oblige indigenous peoples to continue their lives as static and culturally determined groups "without change", because they would have to watch out not to endanger or ultimately lose their once-established rights as indigenous groups. In this case, the extremely problematic obligation of developing and adapting to universalized perceptions of "the" modernity would have changed to an at least as questionable obligation of stagnation (cf. Thornberry 2002: 59).

The anthropologist Adam Kuper used these concerns that rather have to do with the practical implications of the term "indigenous" and the discourse of certain NGOs for his polemic against the movement for indigenous rights which he defamed as a *Return of the Native*, a kind of "return to the more or less noble savage" (2003). He is right to criticize several romanticizing motives of the political commitment for indigenous peoples as idealizing versions of the "primitive indigenous". This construction once developed by anthropologists lacked crucial characteristics of modern life in the areas of political organization, law, culture, technology, and religion: "But whatever the political inspiration, the conventional lines of argument currently used to justify 'indigenous' land claims rely on obsolete anthropological notions and on a romantic and false ethnographic vision. Fostering essentialist ideologies of culture and identity, they may have dangerous political consequences" (Kuper 2003: 395).

However, Kuper obviously confused the essentialist perceptions of a world in close touch with nature and opposed to Western modernism with the elaborate legal discourses about "indigeneity" generated in indigenous fora. These discourses avoid definitions of "primitive societies" widely spread in anthropological literature exactly because of de-essentialist reasons. They are further based on decades of legal debates and related political negotiations with those concerned in leading roles. As Zips (2006: 28f.) clarifies with regard to the extensive discussion started by Kuper:

II. "Indigenous Peoples": Term, Concepts, and Definitions

"The redefinition of indigenous peoples in international law bears little or no resemblance to the layman's connotations of self-acclaimed saviours of 'the pure, authentic, and primitive indigenous' in NGO circles that Kuper rightly criticises, but wrongly mistakes for being the outcome of a long and differentiated process of deliberations and negotiations that has involved, and been substantially driven by indigenous peoples themselves. (…) Human rights discourses on the recognition of indigenous rights as a remedy for (past and present) injustice appear much more advanced in this respect. *Urkultur* and related concepts of primitivity are of no relevance whatsoever for the legal issues at stake in ongoing debates of the UN Draft Declaration on Indigenous Rights."[22]

Furthermore, the reproaches of questionable "authenticity" hardly apply to the only binding agreement of international law: ILO Convention 169. In its definition of indigenous peoples, this legal instrument of 1989 even includes the relevance of self-identification as well as historic continuity and the recognition of specific social, economic and cultural rights: "Self-identification as indigenous or tribal shall be regarded as a fundamental criterion for determining the groups to which the provisions of this Convention apply" (Art. 1 para. 2). Although it is not the only one, it is still one of the most fundamental criteria of "indigeneity" and runs like a golden thread through conventions (ILO Convention 169), directives (World Bank OP 4.10, UNDG Guidelines on Indigenous Peoples' Issues 2008) and studies (Cobo 1986, Daes 1996, Stavenhagen 2002) of international development. As historic and ethnic complexity (as mentioned above) make it impossible for a restrictive definition to apply to all existing situations, it is especially indigenous peoples themselves who see self-identification as an essential element. In contrast to defining a kind of "checklist of indigenousness" with specific characteristics, as it was done by the World Bank (1991), the legally flexible connection to self-positioning in time and space definitely offers the advantage of identification that is not determined from outside.[23] As Kuppe (2004: 46) emphasizes, the probably unique potential of self-determination in international law also accounts for the extraordinary achievements of the communities concerned in communicating beyond national and linguistic barriers: At least in its predominant connotation, the term [indigenous peoples] is one of the direct consequences of the mobilization of a globally-acting liberation move-

---

22 As this debate takes legal conditions and literature only vaguely into account and seems to be of relatively low legal relevance, these short considerations should suffice; for further aspects see Asch/Samson et al. (2004) and Barnard (2006) as well as comments following this work.

23 Cf., for example, Li (1999: 151): "(A) group's self-identification as tribal or indigenous people is not natural or inevitable, but neither is it simply invented, adopted or imposed. It is, rather, a positioning which draws upon historically sedimented practices, landscapes and repertoires of meaning and emerges through particular patterns of engagement and struggle."

ment (…) under the sole leadership of 'indigenous peoples'. (…) It was the commitment to a common struggle for similar rights that inspired various peoples to find a common language and eventually a unifying bond."[24]

Differentiation from the Term "Minority"

As the early terminological development of "indigeneity" (as mentioned above) focused on elements that mostly applied to so-called "blue-water colonisation" societies, many governments in Africa and Asia regarded this terminology as inadequate for their social relationships. This is why they proposed to use the new term "national minority".[25] First, however, we should keep in mind that even the most severe critical voices of the concept of indigeneity concede that the legal protection of minorities is extremely assimilative and even repressive in most Asian and African countries (with only a few notable exceptions) (Kuper 2003: 392). In this respect, the established definition of minorities (as in the following quote) was obviously not enough to satisfy the demands of indigenous peoples for compensation for past injustice as well as for present and future legal protection:

"The term minority, may be taken to refer to as: A group numberically inferior to the rest of the population of a State, in a non-dominant position, whose members – being nationals of the State – possess ethnic, religious or linguistic characteristics differing from those of the rest of the population and show, if only implicitly, a sense of solidarity, directed towards preserving their culture, traditions, religion or language" (Capotorti 1991: para. 568).

In his United Nations "Study on the Rights of Persons Belonging to Ethnic, Religious, and Linguistic Minorities", the proposed definition by *Special Rapporteur* Capotorti (Capotorti 1991: para. 567f.) seems to sufficiently apply, if at all, to indigenous peoples only at first sight.[26] For indigenous peoples can hardly be reduced to small groups in a non-dominant position, whose members possess certain characteristics differing from those of the rest of the population and show a sense of solidarity directed towards preservation. Of course there is the complex problem of indigenous societies (as in Guatemala or Bolivia) forming majority populations and thus making the criterion of numerical inferiority inapplicable. It is, however, the key characteristic of non-dominance that causes complex problems

---

24 Original citation in German.
25 In the second chapter concerned with the use of the term in Africa, I will offer a more detailed view of this discussion which encouraged the UN study by Miguel Alfonso Martinez.
26 As Thornberry (2002: 52) explains with the crucial emphasis on the missing self-definition as "peoples": "While it does violence to their self-perception as peoples, the stress on cultural difference, non-dominance and the desire to transmit culture, etc., to their successors rings true for the indigenous also."

because its application would result in a paradox: a group would stop being a minority or indigenous group as soon as their human rights were established and their non-dominant status lost (Eide/Daes 2000: para. 30).

As there are no generally recognized definitions for minorities or indigenous peoples, the obviously overlapping categories sufficed for the term 'minority' to be continuously and misleadingly equated with 'indigenous peoples'. In this respect, it should be stressed that the values involved in the protection of minorities and indigenous peoples are not the same. The protection of the latter also includes territorial relations and the political rights of self-determination and self-government. Terminological differentiations are therefore almost bound to be of ideal-typical nature; as Eide and Daes (2000: para. 48) comprehensively argue, they cannot and also should not have such dividing precision that it would be opposed to their common needs of protection: "Bearing the conceptual problem in mind, I should like to suggest that the ideal type of an 'indigenous people' is a group that is aboriginal (autochthonous) to the territory where it resides today and chooses to perpetuate a distinct cultural identity and distinct collective social and political organization within the territory. The ideal type of a 'minority' is a group that has experienced exclusion or discrimination by the State or its citizens because of its ethnic, national, racial, religious or linguistic characteristics or ancestry."

Moreover, minority rights are defined as individual rights, while indigenous rights are a perfect example of collective rights. Special minority rights, however, are concerned with non-discrimination and cultural integrity. It is their goal to balance current cultural disadvantages within a sovereign state or the "cultural 'imbalance' of a state" (Kuppe 2004: 54). Of course this principle also applies to indigenous peoples, although with a clear emphasis on past injustices ranging to expropriations and ethnocide. If the approaches developed to establish rights for conventional cultural minorities are then applied to indigenous peoples, the different dimensions of legitimized indigenous rights would be blinded out. This would threaten, amongst other things, the crucial aspect of driving back the sovereign omnipotence of states as declared in colonial times by (*a posteriori*) recognizing indigenous rights as genuine rights. When it comes to the differentiation of indigenous and minority rights, we should not only focus on content but also on historic categories and how they influenced the legal bases of both kinds of rights (Kuppe 2004: 54).

The sense of community of indigenous peoples created from within and, thus, the process of self-understanding is based on different but basically comparable historical, political and social experiences: colonialism, discrimination, and the postcolonial assumption of the monopoly on the legitimate use of force, so characteristic of modern states. Keeping all this in mind, normative provisions covering all aspects of protecting and preserving indigenous groups and their independent (political) cultures become necessary. In the following chapter, I will present relevant legal provisions which on the one hand are subject to international treaties, and on the other hand specifically apply to indigenous peoples.

III. Special Indigenous Rights or Special Circumstances? Indigenous Protection Standards, Rights of Freedom, and Self-Determination

1. Sources of Law

At the outset we have to ask the question whether special indigenous rights make sense at all or not. Critical voices argue that there is no justification for a specific legislation because existing international law and the principles of human rights are sufficient for all peoples and societies.[27] From a legal point of view, however, we have to ask which material protection these "general" rights could provide for indigenous peoples and whether they are able to compensate for historically sustained disparities and injustices. For a long time, many member states of the United Nations have considered the UN Charter and existing human rights conventions (CCPR, CERD, Convention against Genocide, etc.) as sufficient for the protection of indigenous peoples. This position is inextricably linked to the question of the scope of legal protection though. In some cases, existing general instruments of law provided adequate protection against massive expulsions and genocide, although a sad history of cases of indigenous peoples who *de facto* suffered these fates leaves many grave doubts unanswered. Anyhow, existing instruments have been unable to sufficiently protect the cultural, economic and social way of life as well as the intangible rights, occasionally rather vaguely summarized as "cultural identity", of indigenous peoples. These shortcomings are exactly what James Anaya refers to and why the *UN Declaration on the Rights of Indigenous Peoples* was considered a legal desideratum.

In line with that, this Declaration does not grant indigenous peoples any material human rights different from those that others are already enjoying. On the contrary, it only guarantees those rights that indigenous peoples should have always enjoyed to remedy historical, current and systemic rights violations: "The Declaration, in essence, contextualizes human rights with attention to the patterns of indigenous group identity and association that constitute them as peoples. It is precisely because the human rights of indigenous groups have been denied, with disregard for their character as peoples, that there is a need for the Declaration in the first place. In other words the Declaration exists because in-

---

27 Brownlie (1992: 62), for example, claims that: "There can be little doubt that the normal application of human rights standards should take care of most of the claims of indigenous peoples."

digenous peoples have been denied self-determination and related human rights. It does not create for them new substantive human rights that others do not enjoy. Rather, it recognizes for them rights that they should have enjoyed all along as part of the human family, contextualizes those rights in light of their particular characteristics and circumstances, and promotes measures to remedy the rights' historical and systemic violation" Anaya (2010: 193f.). The following UN legal norms on human rights seek to address these shortcomings.

1.1 Binding Norms

1.1.1 *ILO Convention 169*

The International Labour Organization (ILO) was founded in 1919 and is not only the oldest special agency of the United Nations but also regarded as the most important human rights organization in the field of economic and social rights (Nowak 2002: 156). Many of their conventions created additional minimum standards of international law, ranging from protection against discrimination at work to the rights of indigenous peoples. The ILO Convention 169 (*Convention Concerning Indigenous and Tribal Peoples in Independent Countries*) provided a legal instrument at international level that has standardized most elements of a culturally adequate protection of indigenous rights on a legally binding basis for its member states since 1991. In the 1980s, the obvious limitations of the preceding ILO Convention 107 (of 1957) were already tackled by the indigenous movement(s). The *Meeting of Experts* assessing ILO Convention 107 criticized early terminological deficits that apparently tended towards a concept of assimilation and were not conceived as adequate provisions to prevent potential ethnocide in certain cases:

"The Meeting of Experts was unanimous in concluding that the integrationist language of Convention 107 is outdated, and (…) the application of this principle is destructive in the modern world. In 1956 and 1957 (…) it was felt that integration into the dominant national society offered the best chance for these groups to be a part of the development process of the countries in which they live (…) In practice it had become a concept which meant the extinction of ways of life which are different from that of the dominant society (…)."[28]

As I have mentioned, Art. 1 of ILO Convention 107 still spoke of "populations" in the sense of "temporary" demographic phenomena whose integration had to be supported due to their backward development.[29] In the course of such integration, the only interests that had to be protected were the rights of land and resources which were supposed to be recognized as social rights.[30] In con-

---

28 Partial Revision, Report VI (1) (1988), p. 107; cited in Thornberry (2002: 338).
29 Art. 4 and 5 ILO Convention 107.
30 Art. 11–14 ILO Convention 107.

trast, ILO Convention 169 establishes permanent relationships between (indigenous) "peoples" (Art. 1) as permanent sociopolitical units and "their" states. In consequence, it is supposed to enable a legal perspective that takes the priorities and ideas of independent development of indigenous peoples into account. The current convention promotes the rights to land (Art. 13–19) as a decisive condition to ensure identity.[31]

Although ILO Convention 169 is a progressive treaty for indigenous peoples, it still shows several problems on various levels. From a procedural point of view, the convention was not participatory at all. On the contrary, it was at least partially closed to the "parties" of those directly concerned, while it was based on internal considerations and processes of decision-making of the ILO in cooperation with the UN special agencies FAO, UNESCO, WHO and the *Inter-American Indian Institute of the Organizations of American States*. As the agreement for indigenous peoples was designed without participation of indigenous representatives, the organizations were criticized for establishing a convention that was ultimately paternalistic and again handed the basic authority of shaping internal relationships as an exclusive property of states (Howard 2003: 122–124). From a material point of view, a clear lack of rights of self-determination is obvious. When the convention was adopted, many states were extremely concerned with the term "self-determination" as related to indigenous peoples. This is why not even a restricted right, such as a form of regional autonomy, could be included, thus interpreting the term "peoples" rather restrictively (Thornberry 2002: 342ff.). Furthermore, ILO Convention 169 formally shows a clear flaw due to its selective number of ratifications (22 states as of March 2013) which are predominantly located in one region of the world, namely Latin America.[32]

In spite of all these deficits, increasing political discourses and demands are ultimately turning the convention into a symbolically relevant parameter for the actions of both states and indigenous organizations. It also provides the legal basis for further drafts, such as the development of the *UN Declaration on the Rights of Indigenous Peoples, Agenda 21, Chapter 26* (26:2), or the revision of the World Bank's internal operational policies (OP 4.10).[33] Just as well, the *Report of the African Commission's Working Group of Experts on Indigenous Populations/Communities* mentions ILO 169 as many as five times. In their 1994 "Resolution on Action required in-

---

31 For a detailed historical and material discussion see Thornberry (2002: 320–367).

32 Only two Commonwealth countries (Fiji and Dominica) have ratified ILO Convention 169. Most ratifications took place in the 1990s. After Argentina acceded in 2000 and Brazil, Dominica and Venezuela in 2002, the ratification process stagnated until 2007 when Spain, Nepal and Chile in 2008 and Nicaragua as well as the Central African Republic (as the first African member state) in 2010 ratified the convention. Since then, the number of signatory states has been higher than the number of ILO Convention 107. www.ilo.org/ilolex/cgi-lex/ratifce.pl?C169 as of 06/26/2012.

33 World Bank Legal Department, 8 April 2005.

ternationally to provide effective protection for indigenous peoples", the European Parliament used para. 1 of the ILO definition of indigenous peoples and considers the convention a "model text" in terms of its indigenous rights.[34] In 2002, the Parliament explicitly confirmed to support indigenous peoples and encouraged its member states to follow the example of Denmark, Norway and the Netherlands, the only European countries that had ratified ILO Convention 169.[35] Furthermore, complaints procedures of ILO bodies are increasingly filed and also give audience to those concerned with matters of indigenous human rights.[36] As mentioned above, this is related to the increased relevance of legal processes, which cause both political actions and negotiations to shift to legal actions.

1.1.2 UN Convention on Biological Diversity
Another international instrument, namely the Convention on Biological Diversity (CBD) has consequences for the protection of indigenous peoples. While it sets the global stage for a connection between biological and cultural diversity for the first time, it abstains from glorifying the societies concerned as "environmental saints" that live "in tune with nature", or even in perfect harmony of culture and the environment.[37] The central objectives of the Convention on Biological Diversity include the sustainable use and conservation of biological diversity as well as the fair and equitable sharing of natural resources (Art. 1).[38] In addition, it comprises the (minimum) requirements for shaping the relationships with indigenous peoples by encouraging each contracting party to respect, preserve and maintain indigenous traditional knowledge, rights to intellectual property, and the customary use of biological resources (Art. 10.c). Art. 8 (j) accordingly states:

"Each Contracting Party shall, as far as possible and as appropriate: Subject to its national legislation, respect, preserve and maintain knowledge, innovations and practices of indigenous and local communities embodying traditional lifestyles relevant for the conservation and sustainable use of biological diversity and promote their wider application with the approval and involvement of the holders of such knowledge, innovations and practices and encourage the equitable sharing of benefits arising from the utilization of such knowledge, innovation and practices."

---

34 Eur.Parl.Doc. PV 58 (II).
35 European Parliament Resolution on the situation concerning Basic Rights in the European Union: Eur. Parl.Doc.2001/2014(INI))-A5-0451/2002, Brussels at para. 87.
36 For a detailed discussion of the ILO protection system and a presentation of the case of the "Huicholes" see Binder (2004: 68–77).
37 Some critics use such ideas of everyday life to disavow the indigenous rights movement (cf. Kuper 2003: 390).
38 The Convention was drafted for the 1992 *United Nations Conference on Environment and Development* (UNCED) in Rio de Janeiro, Brazil and entered into force on 29 December 1993.

The promotion of indigenous peoples is, therefore, seen as a measure for possible *in-situ* conservation. As can be seen right at the beginning of the article, however, the declared subsidiarity to national legislation as well as numerous formulations, obviously opening up a wide scope of discretion, such as "subject to its national legislation", "as far as possible", and "as appropriate", are opposed to clear state obligation (Schweighofer 1999: 180). This is probably the price (which has to be also paid in other areas of international law) for its extensive consent. Based on its ratification status (193 parties in 2013[39]), we can basically regard it as universally applicable for collectively respecting and protecting indigenous environmental knowledge and usages. The signatory states are obliged to report on the progress of the convention's actual implementation, thus discursively realizing convention standards. In consequence, political and legal discourses as well as opinion-forming processes for the protection of indigenous peoples are created. Aside from such opinion-forming legal progress, however, many indigenous representatives regard the recognition of the states' sovereign right to exploit all their own biological resources (Art. 3) as a problematic statist provision. Nevertheless, other human rights instruments as well as international environmental law limit the execution of state sovereignty. For this very reason, the relationship between the states' exclusive sovereignty and state obligations to recognize indigenous rights is rather tense. Based on the legal context, the obligations can neither be ignored nor abolished (Griffiths 2003: 26).

1.2 "Soft law" Instruments

So-called "soft law" as "additional sources" of international law are legal instruments whose binding character and force is weaker (compared to the "primary sources" international treaty law, customary international law, and the general principles of law). Soft law mainly includes international declarations, principles, standards, and "codes of conduct". According to Wolfram Karl (1997: 105), the latter should be, strictly speaking, regarded as political or ethical, moral and social norms, which may be more specifically considered legal sources *in statu nascendi*. From the perspective of legal pluralism which, first and foremost, also takes the guiding and sanctioning functions of law and thus social reality into account, this assessment would be aprioristic and irrelevant for the social meaning of legal relevance (cf. Woodman 1998).[40] Its main significance is found in the (legal) political arena of transnational or global governance which is by all means gaining substantial importance in development and nature conservation law.

---

39   www.cbd.int/convention/parties/list/ as of 15/03/2013.
40   See the discussions about legal pluralism as well, e.g., Benda-Beckmann, F. (1997, 2002); Benda-Beckmann, F. and K. (2007); Woodman (1998).

1.2.1 Agenda 21, Chapter 26 (1992)

Such normative "soft law" standards for the protection of indigenous peoples are also included in Agenda 21 which was adopted at the *United Nations Conference on Environment and Development* (UNCED) held in Rio de Janeiro in 1992.[41] Agenda 21 presented a comprehensive and detailed action plan to promote sustainable development and nature conservation. As many as ten chapters contain basic standards and bilateral obligations, all of which are directly or indirectly relevant to indigenous peoples. Furthermore, chapter 26 is completely committed to their legitimate interests and comprises further international standards related to indigenous peoples and their independent development. Its emphasis on the historical relationship between indigenous peoples and their lands as well as the demanded consultation process regarding relevant development plans is particularly worth mentioning. Moreover, it shows the basis for the desire to have indigenous peoples actively involved in development projects and programmes adapted to their own needs, priorities, and values. As it is the case with other "soft law" instruments and their lack of binding force, this detailed nature conservation programme is rather "encouraging", "warning", or at best "informing". Terminologies such as "urge", "call for", and "encourage" used in the programme prove this point. Furthermore, the programme exclusively turns to governments that are asked to take care of "their" indigenous peoples' well-being, thus suggesting a certain paternalistic tendency (Griffiths 2003: 26).

Similar to other forms of cooperative governance which regularly uses "open methods of participatory coordination" to realize goals of action, also this programme cannot do more but imposing the "soft sanctions" of "naming, blaming and shaming" (cf. Borrás/Jacobsson 2004). Nevertheless, the programme's clear suggestions as well as the encouraged active participation of indigenous peoples in developing relevant policies and laws is of utmost symbolic importance. In some respect, these points present a clear breakthrough because Agenda 21's recommendations do not only incorporate indigenous forms of participation but also, for the first time, indigenous rights of protection in global nature conservation (Anaya 1996: 54). Moreover, the programme also stands up for national and international efforts to promote, strengthen and especially legally ensure the role of indigenous peoples in sustainable development (chapter 26.1).

1.2.2 UN Declaration on the Rights of Indigenous Peoples

The *UN Declaration on the Rights of Indigenous Peoples* (UNDRIP) is the first document of its kind having representatives of indigenous peoples from all over the world participating in its development. *Inter alia*, the *Special Rapporteurs* Stavenhagen (2002: para. 15; Charters/Stavenhagen 2009: 10) and Daes (2009: 73f.)

---

41 UN Doc. A/CONF.151/26 (vol.3), at 16, Annex 2 (1992) of the *United Nations Conference on Environment and Development* (UNCED).

even consider it to be the most important human rights document for indigenous peoples. When it comes to indigenous self-determination, rights to land and resources, and rights to autonomy, the declaration is far more extensive than ILO Convention 169 which rather focuses on consultation and participation. In contrast, the UN declaration deals with past injustices and existing discrimination such as the lack of recognition of indigenous rights to language, education, autonomy, cultural expression and the collective use of lands and resources (IWGIA 2006: 548). After 22 years of development, the United Nations General Assembly adopted the draft version on 13 September 2007. As it is the case with ILO Convention 169, also this declaration is used as a reference document in various instruments of protection of international law. In this regard, I would like to especially highlight the many different UNESCO declarations.[42]

As soon as 29 June 2006, 30 out of the 47 elected member states of the *UN Human Rights Council* – or 64 percent – voted in favour of the *UN Declaration on the Rights of Indigenous Peoples*. With Cameroon, Mauritius, South Africa, and Zambia, four countries of the African Group voted in favour, while six further members of the group abstained from voting.[43] After two decades of drafting texts and consultations, this broad consent was a breakthrough for the "pro indigenous concept" – a result that proves the persuading impact of the indigenous peoples' and organizations' decades of work. Considering this result, we should keep in mind how concerned states used various tactics of watering down and delaying the process by portraying the draft declaration as being too extensive and unrealistic in the run-up to the vote. Nevertheless, Botswana as the driving force together with its neighbouring country Namibia were able to launch a last-minute "anti-declaration campaign" and convinced enough states (mainly of the African continent) to defer the declaration's adoption at the UN General Assembly (Res. 61/178 of 20 December 2006) in order to amend the draft once more.[44] According to many stakeholders, the strong reservations against the text expressed by the *African Group* were mainly based on their insufficient information status, simply because relevant state representatives had hardly shown interest in active involvement during the painstaking

---

42 *Progress Report on the Proposed World Heritage Indigenous Peoples Council of Experts*: WHC-2001/CONF.208/13, p. 19.

43 For the sake of completeness, I should mention that three countries of the African Group were absent: Djibouti, Gabon and Mali; a total of 12 countries abstained from voting: Algeria, Argentina, Bahrain, Bangladesh, Ghana, Jordan, Morocco, Nigeria, the Philippines, Senegal, Tunisia and Ukraine; only Canada and the Russian Federation voted against the Declaration (*Human Rights Council Res. 2006/2* of 29 June 2006).

44 On 28 November 2006 in the Third Committee of the UN General Assembly, Namibia put forward a motion to defer action concerning the draft declaration. With 82 votes in favour, 67 against and 25 abstentions, the UN General Assembly did not vote on the adoption of the draft; see IWGIA (2007: 558ff.).

III. Special Indigenous Rights or Special Circumstances?

legislative debate.[45] The press releases of Botswana's presidential office (Republic of Botswana 2006: 15) described the draft as disrespectful to the constitutions of individual member states: "The Draft Declaration makes proposals which have very serious economic, political and constitutional implications which, in the case of our continent, can only contribute to ethnic and tribal conflicts."[46]

Furthermore, the release pointed to fundamental differences of so-called "settlement colonies" (North and Latin America, Australia, and New Zealand) and emphasized the African "origin" of all Africans: "Our contention as Botswana is that all black Africans are of African origin. It has to be appreciated that the situation of Africa is different from that of the Americas and Australia. Unlike in both North and Latin America and countries such as Australia and New Zealand, we did not emigrate from elsewhere to Africa, we have always belonged here" (ibid.). At a later meeting of African ambassadors in New Delhi, Botswana's then president referred to the sensitive aspects of postcolonial African independence presumably threatened by interference in internal affairs: "However, there are some Non-Governmental Organisations and maybe even some Governments who would like to tell Africa that some Africans are less indigenous than others and that, therefore, they deserve some special dispensation" (ibid.).

The following months were shaped by (information) talks at various levels concerning the Declaration.[47] In May 2007, the *African Commission on Human and Peoples Rights* reiterated its positive stance towards the Declaration which in their opinion was in complete accordance with the *African Charter on Human and People's Rights* and the stance and jurisprudence of the *African Commission*. It therefore asked all member states of the *African Union* for a quick adoption.[48] In the end, an overwhelming majority (of 143 states) of the General Assembly vot-

---

45 As the *International Work Group for Indigenous Affairs* criticized, "At this late stage it emerged that some African States had serious difficulties with the text of the Declaration and were not prepared to accept the recommendation made by the *Human Rights Council* to adopt the Declaration. It should be noted that most African States had previously barely participated in the more than 20 years long process of developing the text of the Declaration" (www.iwgia.org/sw21505.asp as of 09/15/2007); see also Barume (2009: 171ff.).

46 Republic of Botswana (18/12/06): *Tautona Times* no 43 of 2006. The Weekly Electronic Press Circular of the Office of the President.

47 Amongst other talks, IWGIA helped to organize a meeting of six experts on Africa and 19 members of African embassies to discuss the Declaration in April 2007. The *UN Permanent Forum* arranged a roundtable at which African and other Permanent Missions participated. A group of esteemed African human rights experts composed a written response to the concerns of the *African Group*. Even the African umbrella organization of indigenous peoples (*Indigenous Peoples of Africa Coordinating Committee*) made reference to this response. www.iwgia.org/sw21505asp as of 09/15/2007.

48 See Advisory Opinion of the *African Commission on Human and Peoples' Rights* on the *United Nations Declaration on the Rights of Indigenous Peoples* (adopted May 2007).

ed in favour of the (amended) *UN Declaration on the Rights of Indigenous Peoples* on 13 September 2007. While a total of eleven member states abstained from voting, only Australia, Canada, New Zealand, and the United States voted against it.[49]

After tough negotiations, growing scepticism, and true resignation, indigenous peoples all around the world were relieved and celebrated the day. Although some stakeholders were disappointed and did not only criticize several of the most powerful nations with indigenous populations for rejecting the Declaration but also the last weakening alterations under pressure of some African states, most representatives and UN bodies called it a historic victory in their first press release: "After 22 years of long and cumbersome negotiations, leaders of the world's 370 million indigenous peoples have won a powerful symbolic victory in their fight for recognition of the right to self-determination and control over their land and resources. (…) 'It's a triumph for indigenous peoples around the world,' said U.N. Secretary-General Ban Ki-Moon after the Assembly vote. 'This marks a historic moment when member states and indigenous peoples reconciled with their painful histories.' (…) While pleased with the General Assembly's decision, indigenous leaders told IPS they had hoped the Declaration would be adopted by consensus, but since certain countries remained unwilling to recognise their rights until the end, a majority vote was the only possible option left."[50]

In their official statements, Botswana's political leaders were extremely pleased with the fact that the African Group was able to achieve amendments to the Declaration, which in their opinion would otherwise have caused division and conflicts on the African continent while undermining state sovereignty. In his welcome address on the occasion of an official visit of his presidential colleague from Benin, then President Festus G. Mogae particularly highlighted the inclusion of a paragraph which calls for an interpretation of the Declaration that does neither conflict with territorial integrity nor political unity: "Among other improvements, the now adopted Declaration includes an amended preamble paragraph, which confirms that nothing in the Declaration may be construed as

---

49   The states that abstained from voting were Azerbaijan, Bangladesh, Bhutan, Burundi, Colombia, Georgia, Kenya, Nigeria, Russia, Samoa and Ukraine. Since then, all four countries that voted against the adoption, have announced their official support for the Declaration (Australia in 2009 and Canada, New Zealand and the United States in 2010).

50   IPS Inter Press Service (http://ipsnews.net/print.asp?idnews=39258); printed on 09/15/2007. Also UNESCO Director-General Koichiro Matsuura praised the declaration as a milestone for indigenous peoples and rights: "[T]he Declaration acknowledges the significant place that indigenous cultures occupy in the world's cultural landscape and their vital contribution to our rich cultural diversity, which constitutes, as the text's preamble reminds us, 'the common heritage of humankind'. (…) The UNESCO is pleased to note that this Declaration sets promising international standards for the protection and promotion of the rights of indigenous peoples within the larger human rights framework and, more specifically, highlights their rights related to culture, identity, language and education" (Office of the Spokeswoman, UNESCO Flash Info N° 125–2007).

authorising or encouraging any action that would dismember or impair the territorial integrity or political unity of sovereign and independent states."⁵¹

The amended version adopted by the General Assembly shows the wish to preserve on the one hand state supremacy and sovereignty and on the other hand certain national interests, thus hierarchical forms of "governance". This can be seen in the fact that a paragraph was repealed which established the right of indigenous peoples to determine their relationship to states themselves.⁵² In addition, a guarantee of integrity as mentioned above was added to Art. 46.⁵³ From the perspective of the states involved in the amendments, this result proves the success of their unquestioned rights of control and to alter legal relationships.⁵⁴ From the vantage point of indigenous peoples but also in view of new cooperative forms of "governance", however, the loss of more sustainable, integrative and legitimate policy forms come to the fore. Keeping all that in mind, we cannot be sure whether the repeal simplifies or rather complicates policies (in the sense of "governance") for all parties involved.

A further new paragraph of the preamble recognizes the diverse situations of indigenous peoples: "Recognizing also that the situation of indigenous peoples varies from region to region and from country to country and that the significance of national and regional particularities and various historical and cultural backgrounds should be taken into consideration" (para. 23). At first sight, the paragraph presents a norm that basically stresses the cultural diversity of indigenous peoples in (almost) global multicultural contexts. It is my opinion, however, that it also opens a back door to question its universal binding force and gives reason to expect objections of non-applicability due to diverging historic conditions. It should, nevertheless, be emphasized *cum grano salis* that, after 22 years of negotiations, the adoption of the *UN Declaration on the Rights of Indigenous Peoples* finally established an instrument that confers a wide range of indigenous rights and will definitely be fundamental for future developments.⁵⁵

---

51 Republic of Botswana (14/09/07): *Tautona Times* no. 32 of 2007. The Weekly Electronic Press Circular of the Office of the President. The paragraph mentioned here, however, is not part of the preamble but of Art. 46 (1).

52 Former paragraph 13 Draft Declaration (of Council Res. 2006/2): "Recognizing also that indigenous peoples have the right freely to determine their relationships with States in a spirit of coexistence, mutual benefit and full respect".

53 "Nothing in this Declaration may be interpreted as implying for any State, people, group or person any right to engage in any activity or to perform any act contrary to the Charter of the United Nations or construed as authorizing or encouraging any action which would dismember or impair, totally or in part, the territorial integrity or political unity of sovereign and independent States" (Art. 46).

54 In this respect, some African authors ask whether it is not an African "phobia" thinking that the recognition of indigenous groups would directly lead to political confrontations and predicaments (cf. Chebanne 2002: 49).

55 Another declaration is the *American Declaration on the Rights of Indigenous Peoples* of the *Organization of American States*. Existing only as a draft yet, its content is so simi-

1.2.3 Declarations and Policies of various International Bodies

A further document of reference to indigenous peoples is the *Universal Declaration on Cultural Diversity* of the United Nations specialized agency UNESCO. With its specific mandate to ensure "the preservation and promotion of the fruitful diversity of cultures", the Declaration was adopted unanimously by the (185) member states in 2001. It clearly states that the defense of cultural diversity is an ethical imperative indissociable from respect for human dignity.[56] It also implies a legal commitment to preserve and protect the human rights and fundamental freedoms of indigenous peoples (Art. 4). This document was then turned into an international treaty and clearly shows the spirit of consent on an international level that took so long to achieve: adopted in 2005 and entered into force in March 2007, the preamble of the *UNESCO Convention on the Protection and Promotion of the Diversity of Cultural Expressions* indicates the universal importance of preserving culture(s), particularly of indigenous peoples.

The convention explicitly underlines the significance of their traditional knowledge and their positive contribution to sustainable development. In Art. 7, national states are requested to create an environment for the special circumstances and needs of indigenous peoples, which allows them to have access to their own cultural expressions and realize their full potential. Furthermore, one of the eight guiding principles of cultural diversity is based on respect for all cultures and explicitly mentions indigenous peoples (Art. 2 para.3).

The relatively high number of the convention's ratifications in short time shows the development of increasing consent regarding indigenous rights: in only two years, 67 member states ratified the convention, fifteen of which were African countries and the European Community (2013: 126 member states). In accordance with its content, UNESCO developed a programme of action as an internal guideline and elaborated five key objectives, defined by the UN General Assembly when proclaiming the *Second International Decade of the World's Indigenous People* (2005–2014).[57] In this respect, UNESCO stresses how extremely relevant it regards promoting full and effective participation of indigenous peoples in all decisions which directly or indirectly affect their lifestyles, the adequate use of their traditional territories, their cultural integrity and their collective rights. A further important key objective of the programme of action questions redefined development policies and whether they, similar to environmental impact assessments (as some kind of "cultural impact assessment") respect indigenous culture.

---

lar to that of the UN declaration that it is not discussed separately here. For an overview, cf. MacKay (2002: 100–148), Thornberry (2002: 397–404).

56 UNESCO today, Magazine of the German Commission for UNESCO, Edition 1–2, 2002: 1. For a detailed discussion of the Declaration, see Charters/Stavenhagen (2009).

57 UNESCO and Indigenous Peoples: Partnership to Promote Cultural Diversity (2006: 20).

III. Special Indigenous Rights or Special Circumstances?

We can detect a new and maybe even surprising openness for the further development of indigenous rights and the protection of their legitimate interests not only in the cultural sphere but also in the development sector of international financial institutions, such as the *World Bank, Inter-American Development Bank,* or *Asian Development Bank.* Obviously their campaigns for wider recognition by civil society and against their widely attributed lack of legitimacy may have influenced this perhaps surprising process. When it comes to implementing their projects and development processes, numerous internal policies by now require their official representatives and employees to respect the dignity, cultural uniqueness and human rights of indigenous peoples. In accordance with international developments, the World Bank released their new *Operational Policy* (OP 4.10) in cooperation with indigenous peoples in 2005. This policy mentions the special relationship between these specific "stakeholders" and "their territories" several times. According to this standard of protection, all projects applying for World Bank funding need to be subject to screenings to determine whether indigenous peoples are present in, or have collective attachment to, the project area. The World Bank conducts such screenings independently. In addition, the organization requests a further assessment by qualified social scientists concerning the positive or negative consequences of projects and possible alternative proposals. In this respect, the whole process should also be subject to free, previous and informed consultation with the indigenous peoples concerned.

Furthermore, a concrete development project proposed for Bank funding needs to develop an "Indigenous Peoples Plan" which ensures adequate social and economic benefits as well as measures to avoid or eliminate adverse effects (para. 6–15). If a specific project was realized without carrying out this process, the operational policy provides indigenous peoples with the opportunity to file complaints with the World Bank's *Office of Compliance Advisor/Ombudsman* as an independent recourse mechanism.[58] When such disputes occur, this monitoring institution assesses all facts independently and takes steps to solve the issues raised in the complaints. One of their further tasks includes checking whether clients of the World Bank Group have adequately consulted the indigenous peoples concerned and comply with World Bank guidelines. The office reports directly to the president of the World Bank Group.[59] Although such internal op-

---

58   The Office is an independent post of the *International Finance Corporation*, subsidiary of the International Monetary Fund and the World Bank.

59   When the *Office of Compliance Advisor/Ombudsman* received a complaint by the San, namely the NGO *First People of the Kalahari*, on 4 November 2004, the Office was unable to establish a causal connection between the diamond-prospecting project of the company and the dislocation of the San from the *Central Kalahari Game Reserve*. Nevertheless, it could not ignore the fact that there is a strongly held perception that the diamond industry and the relocation of the San are related. The Office recommends to better cooperate with the Government of Botswana to clarify the obligations as stip-

erational guidelines do not allow any expectations about their implementation, their mere existence indicates a new "awareness" developed under the pressure of civil forms of mediatisation and networking.

If this development of transnational instruments of governance is also translated into external guidelines, it will be almost impossible to overestimate its importance because the conditions of the World Bank and other international financial institutions generally are "tougher" than conditions of human rights instruments which (usually) are rather moral institutions of "soft law" character.[60] In this matter, we also should not forget the procedural standards of the European Union (and other regional and national donor organizations) concerning indigenous peoples and their independent development. Based on the signatory states' bilateral development assistance, these standards find their way into national laws, guidelines, and programmes of recipient countries.[61] In discourses of legal pluralism, guidelines of various donor organizations are usually discussed as a form of (informal) project law and have a similar pioneering influence.[62] Although these procedural guidelines are at best *informal law*, they are relevant for numerous legally-binding bilateral and multilateral development projects, turning them into guidelines crucial for project activities. Here the usual processes of

---

ulated in World Bank guidelines, especially Op 4.20 concerning indigenous peoples (now OP 4.10). In addition, it recommends the Government to continue talks with the San (*Assessment Report: Complaint Regarding IFC's Investment in Kalahari Diamonds Ltd, Botswana. Office of the Compliance Advisor/Ombudsman, June 2005*).

60   In contrast to other bilateral donor organizations, the World Bank's *Articles of Agreement* prohibit the involvement in internal matters. It can, however, use its principles of "Good Governance and Accountability" to sidestep this rule. These principles include a range of preconditions such as the already-mentioned procedural standards for indigenous peoples which prescribe financial aid for developing countries as conditions to obtain financing.

61   See, e.g., the bilateral development cooperation for the *Remote Area Development Programme* between the *Norwegian Agency for Development Cooperation* (NORAD) and the Government of Botswana: "[N]ORAD support reflects a concern for the plight of indigenous peoples which is a priority of Norwegian foreign policy in general and which was among the main justifications for becoming involved in the first place" (Saugestad 2001: 30).

62   ILO Convention 169, thus, is explicitly mentioned in the *EU Working Document of the Commission on support for Indigenous Peoples in the development co-operation of the Community and Member States* (1998); cf. Griffith (2003) for a detailed comparison of international donor and development assistance organizations with regard to their guidelines for indigenous peoples; see Weilenmann (2004) for the term of project law; cf. Tomasevsky (1989) for EU development policies and the human rights approach in general; for a comparison to ACP states, cf. Windmeißer (2002); in this respect, see also the human rights clauses in treaties (under commercial law) for external relations of the European Community, e.g., Hoffmeister (1998), Brandtner/Rosas (1999), Riedel (1999).

responsibility as well as project evaluations make these guidelines both assessable and politically enforceable.[63]

These considerations of the increasing inclusion of indigenous (minimal) rights in the cultural sphere but also the development and financial sector only exemplify the wide range of legal instruments and governance policies. Further examples would be: in the field of health care, the *World Health Organization* (WHO) adopting the *Geneva Declaration on the Health and Survival of Indigenous Peoples* in 1999; in the field of development cooperation, the UN development programme establishing a *Policy of Engagement* in 2001; in the field of intellectual property, the *World Intellectual Property Organization* which continuously carries out (bilateral) seminars, fact-finding missions, and studies. In the context of nature conservation, the Working Group for Art. 8(j) of the Convention on Biological Diversity developed a Code of Ethics for the protection of indigenous cultural heritage: *Code of Ethics to ensure Respect for the Cultural and Intellectual Heritage of Indigenous and Local Communities relevant for the Conservation of Biological Diversity* (Tkarihwaié:ri Code); Guidelines for the conduct of cultural, environmental and social impact assessment (Akwé:Kon guidelines) and accomplished the adoption of the *Nagoya Protocol on Access to Genetic Resources and the Fair and Equitable Sharing of Benefits Arising from the Utilization of Genetic Resources*. Furthermore, the international treaty for the protection of wetlands (*Ramsar Convention*) established guidelines for the inclusion of communities concerned in the management of resources: the *Guidelines for Establishing and Strengthening Local Communities and Indigenous Peoples Participation in the Management of Wetlands*; the *Convention to Combat Desertification* also standardizes two articles dedicated to the protection of indigenous knowledge. Keeping the relevant environments in mind on which indigenous peoples depend on for forging their living, both instruments addressing the important ecological zones desert and wetland are of utmost significance.

Given all these international legal developments, the world appears convincingly and explicitly dealing with indigenous peoples and their rights, be it in the sphere of nature conservation, development law, health care, education, science or culture. There are various forms of such documents that are based on "hard law" texts or guidelines or documents of reference. Obviously the scope and binding force of such documents differs significantly: some principles are based on normative instruments that directly focus on indigenous peoples, while others are not specifically committed to indigenous matters, but "delegate" such issues as crucial aspects of practical consideration to operational guidelines (governance or policy implementation).

---

63 Cf. the anthology *Global Law without a State* (Teubner 1997), particularly Wilder's article on the necessary re-evaluation of the concept of "indigeneity" in global legal discourses.

1.3 Indigenous Rights as Part of Customary International Law

In the context of prevailing multilateral processes of opinion and decision-making, we can now detect a common understanding as well as a tendency to create laws for the further development towards the protection of indigenous rights. Thus, the international sphere is increasingly agreeing on the effective preservation of indigenous minimal rights. As Anaya (1996: 50) assesses from a legal point of view, this development of a legal conviction points to the formation of customary law:

"The extended multilateral discussion promoted through the international system has involved states, nongovernmental organizations, independent experts, and indigenous peoples themselves. It is now evident that states and other relevant actors have reached a certain new common ground about minimum standards that should govern behaviour towards indigenous peoples, and it is also evident that the standards are in fact guiding behaviour. Under modern theory, such a controlling consensus, following as it does from widely shared values of human dignity, constitutes customary international law."

The rules of international customary law develop when states use them on a general and continuous basis. International legal theory differentiates between two central elements of this condition: state practice has to coexist with *opinio juris*, meaning the conviction must prevail that the relevant use or legal practice is legally binding. If, therefore, this use is generally regarded as law and, thus, supported by legal awareness (the subjective or psychological element) and is then connected to the objective (material) element of state practice, international customary law will be formed (Simma 1997: 39f.). Legislation, court rulings and scientific works provide ample evidence for these two elements.

For the present work, this means that all documents concerning indigenous peoples or indigenous rights contain central principles which can now be considered (at least emerging) customary law. States in turn are subject to norms under customary law for a mandatory relationship to indigenous peoples, if those norms are part of international law. As one of the sources of international law, the norms of customary law are thus binding for the various parts of the global community, notwithstanding a relevant formal act of recognition of these norms (Anaya 1996: 127).

All considerations presented in this chapter offer an overview of the specific norms which are part in a narrow sense of binding "hard law" and in a broader sense of "soft law" which is not always legally enforceable but sometimes as effective due to guidelines and conditionalities. In the following two chapters, I will address the content of protection. Adequate protection is ensured especially when the central role of territories for the lives, cultures and religions of indigenous peoples is both recognized and canonized. Therefore, the standards of those instruments specifically referring to indigenous peoples of ILO Convention 169 and the *UN Declaration on the Rights of Indigenous Peoples* are the starting point

III. Special Indigenous Rights or Special Circumstances? 57

as well as main point of reference. Afterwards, I will discuss which provisions of universal human rights treaties may be used for the protection of indigenous territories. After all, also the legal branches of UN treaty monitoring bodies, with the *Human Rights Committee* and the *Committee on the Elimination of Racial Discrimination* leading the way, increasingly protect indigenous territories. The last chapter then portrays indigenous participation and self-control necessary for a self-determined development process.

2. "Sources of Life": Lands and Natural Resources

2.1 Material Standards of Protection

The legal sources mentioned above (with strategic focuses as examples) clearly show the predominant opinion that the relationship between indigenous peoples and their territories has to be regarded as a crucial factor of their cultural identity. Since the *Working Group on Indigenous Populations* (WGIP) was established, indigenous peoples have been able to send their representatives to argue for and symbolically emphasize the unique nature of their relationship to their lands and territories.[64] Understanding this deep connection is of course necessarily based on the recognition of the varied spheres of experiences, cultural diversity and pluralistic value systems in relation to other segments of the population in their various countries of origin. At this point I would like to emphasize that these distinctions should not be hypostatized as "invariable" and essential differences. They should rather be seen as basically equal interpretations of the world in the context of alternative conceptions of the world. The special connection to their lands, territories as well as local fauna and flora is a central element of indigenous societies and can be empirically perceived. It shows spiritual, social, cultural, economic and political dimensions, which indigenous peoples unanimously regard as conditions for their collective survival:

"It must be noted that, as indigenous peoples have explained, it is difficult to separate the concept of indigenous peoples' relationship with their lands, territories and resources from that of their cultural differences and values. The re-

---

64 The *Working Group on Indigenous Populations* was established by the UN Economic and Social Council as the result of the Cobo Study in 1982 (Res. 1982/34, 7 May 1982). In December 2007, the WGIP was replaced by the *Expert Mechanism on the Rights of Indigenous Peoples* (EMRIP) (Res. 6/36) as a subsidiary body of the *Human Rights Council*. In the UN system, the EMRIP (like the WGIP before) is regarded as the real hot spot for promoting indigenous rights. The Mechanisms' sessions are open to all indigenous representatives, communities and organizations, making it one of the UN's largest human rights meetings (cf., e.g., Anaya 1996: 91f.; Keal 2003: 117ff.; IWGIA 2006: 544ff.; IWGIA 2012: 517ff.).

lationship with the land and all living things is at the core of indigenous societies" (Daes 2001: 7).

Land is inherited from previous generations and is then passed on to future generations; it is part of the social heritage and self-conception of indigenous culture. Conceptions of the world and cosmovisions regularly attach high religious and spiritual significance to the "lands of the ancestors". First and foremost, however, indigenous peoples regard their own territory as a "bridge of continuity" between the past, present and future and, therefore, more often than not a *conditio sine qua non* of a self-determined legal-political existence (Binder 2004: 6–8).

2.1.1 *Cause of Action*

Historical bodies of law are of central value for the substantial recognition of indigenous land rights. In this respect, questions concerning colonial rule are often essential as well.[65] In many cases, indigenous peoples base their cause of action in their former pre-colonial relationships to lands and resources, which was severed when colonial governments or their legal successors as well as other governmental and non-governmental stakeholders took over their territories:

Today almost every legal sphere considers the recognition of legitimate rights of ownership and possession as a crucial criterion for the assignment and appropriation of rights and goods; keeping that in mind, it is a basic principle of applicable law to also recognize and ensure those rights of ownership and possession, which precede state law or which, in other words, are not derived from state law but are rather based on original titles of ownership (Kuppe 2004: 47).[66]

International court rulings, e.g., of the *Inter-American Court of Human Rights* in the *Awas Tingni*[67] case, and national courts, such as the *Supreme Court of Canada* in the *Delgamuukw*[68] case or the *High Court of Australia* in the at least as "famous" *Mabo*[69] case subsequently corrected the historical expropriation of indigenous peoples and recognized their original titles of ownership. The various High Courts based their fundamental decisions on the understanding that indigenous (land) rights depended on titles of ownership according to neither British com-

---

65 Here territories are regarded as the "total environment of the areas which the peoples concerned occupy or otherwise use" (in the sense of Art. 13 ILO Convention 169 and Art. 25, 26 UNDRIP). Compared to the term "area", territories are wider in content and linguistic use and are the best concept for the special connection between indigenous peoples and their lands. It also fits to most important economic connotations because it encompasses the future basis of existence as well as the spiritual and historical dimension. Indigenous discourses clearly prefer the term "territory".

66 Original citation in German.

67 *Inter-American Court of Human Rights, The Mayagna (Sumo) Awas Tingni Community v. The Republic of Nicaragua*, judgement of 31 August 2001.

68 *Delgamuukw v. British Columbia* (1997): 3 S.C.R. 1010 or (1998) 1 C.N.L.R. 14.

69 *Mabo v. Queensland* (1992): 175 CLR1 F.C.92/014.

mon law, nor Anglo-American jurisdictions, nor any other larger legal tradition, such as Roman law, but to specific systems of customary law of indigenous peoples (*sui generis* rights to land and resources). This confirmation does not promote the goals of only decolonisation but also equal opportunities and the recognition of cultural identity (Kuppe 2004: 50–51):

"In contemporary international law (…) modern notions of cultural integrity and self-determination join property precepts in the affirmation of sui generis indigenous land and resource rights (…)" (Anaya 1996: 105).

Furthermore, this can be seen in the system of ILO Convention 169 which specifically recognizes the genuine rights of ownership and possession of indigenous peoples concerned over "the lands which they traditionally occupy" (in Art. 14 para. 1). Subsequently the UN Declaration establishes the rights of indigenous peoples to "lands, territories and resources which they have traditionally owned, occupied or otherwise used or acquired" in Art. 26 para. 2. The historical settlement already provides *per se* the basis for a cause of action, regardless of a formal recognition by a state or any other official legal title. Therefore, governments only need to demarcate indigenous areas of settlement and officially attest the already-existing rights.[70] In consequence, state recognition only testifies but does not constitute these rights.

2.1.2 The Relationship between Indigenous Peoples and their Territories

Opinions on legal protection generally agree that each case of specific protection for indigenous peoples begins with protection guarantees concerning their relationship to their lands. In this respect, it does not suffice to continue tolerating indigenous peoples on a small share of the territory in a quasi "act of grace". The findings and recommendations of *Special Rapporteur* José Martínez Cobo on the special relationship to their territories reflect the considerations of indigenous peoples as mentioned above:

"It is essential to know and understand the deeply spiritual special relationship between indigenous peoples and their land as basic to their existence as such and to all their beliefs, customs, traditions and culture. For such peoples, the land is not merely a possession and a means of production. The entire relationship between the spiritual life of indigenous peoples and Mother Earth, and their land, has a great many deep-seated implications. Their land is not a commodity which can be acquired, but a material element to be enjoyed freely" (1983: paras. 196–197).

In both *ILO Convention 169* and the *UN Declaration on the Rights of Indigenous Peoples*, the term "territory" includes this special and comprehensive kind of relationship with a historical, cultural, spiritual and collective dimension. Art. 13 of ILO Convention 169 explicitly ensures the extraordinary holistic relationship

---

70   Art. 14 para. 2 of ILO Convention 169 and Art. 26 para. 3 of *UN Declaration on the Rights of Indigenous Peoples*.

between indigenous peoples and their territories. Para. 1 of Art. 13 recognizes the "special importance for the cultures and spiritual values of the peoples concerned of their relationship with the lands or territories (…) which they occupy (…)". Art. 25 of the *UN Declaration on the Rights of Indigenous Peoples* specifically refers to the protection of this special relationship:

"Indigenous peoples have the right to maintain and strengthen their distinctive spiritual relationship with their traditionally owned or otherwise occupied and used lands, territories, waters and coastal seas and other resources and to uphold their responsibilities to future generations in this regard."

In my opinion, these provisions are of utmost importance because they counteract those Western approaches which mostly reduce land and territory to a commodity value and economic production factor based on the aspects of reification and monetization. Applicable international law regards adequate compensation as sufficient for the legal condemnation of land for the public benefit; at least as long as a country's (claimed and documented) public benefit requires the expropriation and anti-discrimination laws are observed.[71] In most of the cases, such monetary compensation will not suffice at all for indigenous peoples due to the deep rootedness with their territories. It could also involve further damaging their internal relationships as well as their connections to past and future generations. Several sections of Art. 16 of ILO Convention 169 take these considerations into account:

"(1) Subject to the following paragraphs of this Article, the peoples concerned shall not be removed from the lands which they occupy.
(2) Where the relocation of these peoples is considered necessary as an exceptional measure, such relocation shall take place only with their free and informed consent. Where their consent cannot be obtained, such relocation shall take place only following appropriate procedures established by national laws and regulations, including public inquiries where appropriate, which provide the opportunity for effective representation of the peoples concerned.
(3) Whenever possible, these peoples shall have the right to return to their traditional lands, as soon as the grounds for relocation cease to exist.
(4) When such return is not possible, as determined by agreement or, in the absence of such agreement, through appropriate procedures, these peoples shall be provided in all possible cases with lands of quality and legal status at least equal to that of the lands previously occupied by them, suitable to provide for their present needs and future development. Where the peoples concerned express a preference for compensation in money or in kind, they shall be so compensated under appropriate guarantees.
(5) Persons thus relocated shall be fully compensated for any resulting loss or injury."

---

71   Cf. Fischer/Köck (2004: 261ff.).

III. Special Indigenous Rights or Special Circumstances?

Comparing the protection standards of ILO Convention 169 and the UN Declaration, the latter come short in my opinion: they admittedly mention the protection against forced relocation which should not take place without the free, prior and informed consent of the indigenous peoples concerned; Art. 10 of the UN Declaration settles for nothing more than "just and fair" – as opposed to "adequate" in the sense of "equal" – compensation. Returning to their lands is only optional, while a new scope of discretion is revealed here.[72] Although demanded by the *UN Working Group on Indigenous Populations* in Geneva in late 2005, the clear protection against "arbitrary displacement" did not make it to the draft Declaration as adopted by the *UN Human Rights Council*.[73] Also the rights to redress of Art. 28 include restitution only as a provision that "can" be applicable and offer the alternatives of compensation in form of lands or money (para. 2):

"Unless otherwise freely agreed upon by the peoples concerned, compensation shall take the form of lands, territories and resources equal in quality, size and legal status or of monetary compensation or other appropriate redress."[74]

While ILO Convention 169 firstly establishes an indigenous community's right to physically return, secondly provides the right to *in rem restitution* and sees monetary compensation only as a last resort, the UN Declaration is not as restrictive. It grants states a wide scope of discretion between the alternatives mentioned above and even grants the general qualification for an unspecified "other appropriate redress". This is how Art. 28 limits the extraordinary protection guarantees mentioned above (of Art. 25) for the spiritual relationship to the lands and the (also spiritual) obligation towards future generations. In some sort of "emergency" (of whatever kind of forced loss of lands, territories and resources), these guarantees are limited to possible monetary compensation which is again subject to state assessment. In some respects, the Declaration reduces the intangible and ultimately irreplaceable significance of the lands to indigenous peoples to a quantifiable, material and, thus, legally replaceable asset.

2.1.3 Collective Land Rights

As we can see in the chosen terminology ("peoples"), indigenous rights to lands and resources are of collective character. In this matter, the collective aspect of the relationship between indigenous peoples and their territories is key. Both ILO Convention 169 and the UN Declaration explicitly and repeatedly establish this collective claim. Art. 13 of the ILO Convention specifically emphasizes

---

72   See Seidl-Hohenveldern (1997: 240) for the various standards of compensations.
73   Report of the 11th Session Dec. 5–16, 2005, *Working Group on the Draft Declaration*, p. 26.
74   The wording of Art. 27 (now Art. 28) of the "old" draft version was limited to the right to *in rem restitution* and "[w]hen this is not possible, they have the right to just and fair compensation. (…) [C]ompensation shall take the form of lands, territories and resources equal in quality, size and legal status".

the collective aspect of this relationship: "[G]overnments shall respect the special importance for the cultures and spiritual values of the peoples concerned of their relationship with the lands or territories, or both as applicable, which they occupy or otherwise use, and in particular the collective aspects of this relationship." The term "peoples" usually implies a positive recognition of collective identity and relevant relationships of indigenous peoples to lands and resources (Anaya 1996: 48), similar to the relationships of societies – as it is for instance the case with the Maroons of Jamaica – that do not see themselves as indigenous peoples:

An individual owns land only due to the status as a member of the community. As individuals, they only enjoy the right of disposal. (…) The individual right to use the collectively owned land can be compared to the institution of *ususfructus* as an inheritable, rentable, sellable or in any other way transferable right. (…) Capitalistic imperatives concerning the cultivation of the land contradict a concept of history in which the past is projected into the future by reproducing the present (Zips 2003b: 49f.).[75]

Communities concerned, therefore, do not uphold collective ownership of lands only because their lands is their primary source of food supply and income but also because it is the source of their identity and political status as well as a source of fundamental significance for their culture (Paul 1990: 218f.).[76] Even the World Bank attributes the "collective attachment" of indigenous peoples to the ancestors of their territory to the objectives of its development policies, defining it as follows:

"'Collective attachment' means that for generations there has been a physical presence in and economic ties to lands and territories traditionally owned, or customarily used or occupied, by the group concerned, including areas that hold special significance for it, such as sacred sites. 'Collective attachment' also refers to the attachment of transhumant/nomadic groups to the territory they use on a seasonal or cyclical basis."[77]

The World Bank has recently begun to consider these relationships extremely important: "A group that has lost 'collective attachment to geographically distinct habitats or ancestral territories in the project area' (paragraph 4 (b)) because of forced severance remains eligible for coverage under this policy." Operational Policy (OP 4.10) exclusively refers to development projects supported by the World Bank. In para. 2 it downright apodictically states, "the identities and cul-

---

75 Original citation in German; cf. Kuppe (1990: 1f.) for the problematic instrumentalization of Western state jurisdiction (especially in the context of individual ownership) for the alleged benefit of indigenous peoples. According to the author, such a transfer may lead to developments endangering identity due to a structural change of internal, indigenous legal relationships.
76 Cf. also Art. 25–27 *UN Declaration on the Rights of Indigenous Peoples*.
77 Fn. 7 to Art. 4 (b), Operational Policies 4.10, January 2005, The World Bank Operational Policies.

tures of indigenous peoples are inextricably linked to the lands on which they live and the natural resources on which they depend." Para. 4 then means by implication that indigenous peoples who lose the attachment to their territory also lose their identity and culture(s).

The astounding document OP 4.10 with its internal directives binding for the World Bank stipulates an impact assessment process which should in advance involve social scientists for all projects proposed for Bank financing. Quite typical for the World Bank's technocratic style, a technical assessment by experts (para. 8) is required: "Early in project preparation, the Bank undertakes a screening to determine whether Indigenous Peoples (see paragraph 4) are present in, or have collective attachment to, the project area. In conducting this screening, the Bank seeks the technical judgement of qualified social scientists with expertise on the social and cultural group in the project area. The Bank also consults the Indigenous Peoples concerned and the borrower. The Bank may follow the borrower's framework for identification of Indigenous Peoples during project screening, when that framework is consistent with his policy." Only empirical studies could determine whether the last sentence could be a loophole for investor-friendly decisions and whether the whole document could plainly be used to pay lip service. A discussion of these studies, however, would certainly go beyond the scope of this book.[78]

2.1.4 Scope of Indigenous Territories

In this context, we have to keep in mind that the term "lands" or "traditional settlement areas" as stated above should be regarded as a comprehensive concept. Therefore, it should not only and exclusively comprise areas that are "permanently occupied" in the sense of a strict (Western) understanding but "the total environment of the areas which the peoples concerned occupy or otherwise use" (Art. 13 para. 2 ILO Convention 169). Such a broad interpretation of the term is meant to ensure that indigenous peoples do not only have access to their religious and cultural sites (spiritual dimension), as established in Art. 12(1) of the UN Declaration, but are also able to practice their productive activities. This is especially but not exclusively relevant for so-called "communities of hunters and gatherers". As they use their hunting and gathering areas in many cases without regularity, they would otherwise lose these areas as well as their cultural and religious expressions related to their lands.

---

78   For an excellent study about the relationship between the World Bank, indigenous and local communities and a state (India) as related to development projects with legal consequences, cf. Randeria (2002).

2.1.5 Restriction of Alienation and Disposal

The collective ownership of lands can basically be interpreted as emanating from an "intergenerational contract". Based on these commons, the alienation of lands was seen as a danger to the foundations of society. It was, thus, perceived as a breach of norms under ancestral protection to alienate land until entrepreneurial, capitalistic and individualistic ideas increased and lead to continuous monetization (cf. Zips 2003b: 55). In case indigenous peoples inconsiderately alienated their land, Art. 17 of ILO Convention 169 provides a system of consultation and participation of the whole community as well as a special state obligation of protection (Art. 17 para. 3).[79] In this respect, third parties are to be prevented from taking advantage of indigenous peoples' customs or of a lack of legal understanding. The *UN Declaration on the Rights of Indigenous Peoples* (UNDRIP) does not contain a specific restriction of disposal for the protection of indigenous lands by states. This is the case because the UN Declaration regards the communities concerned as "mature" and accordingly establishes the absolute and unlimited freedom of decision over their territories in Art. 26 (1) and (2) (cf. Binder 2004: 59).

The significance of the relationship between indigenous peoples and their territories for their culture and spiritual values becomes obvious just by the number of references in the two most important legal instruments for indigenous peoples: the term "lands" is used 20 times in ILO Convention 169 and 19 times in UNDRIP. So far, I have explained the normative standards of protection which are specifically concerned with indigenous peoples. Apart from that, relevant legal protection is also subject to general (human rights) treaties of international law, which can be applied for the protection of indigenous land rights: including the right to property, to cultural identity, to physical integrity, and to both private and family life.

2.2 Universal Human Rights Treaties

The *Universal Declaration of Human Rights* was adopted as a resolution by the UN General Assembly in 1948. While it first served as a programmatic Declaration of intent without binding force under international law, a new dimension of international human rights was born.[80] In the beginning, the resolution focused on the protection of individual human rights but in the course of time, this protection was increasingly extended to group and collective rights as well as non-governmental entities. Although without binding force, this development also strengthened indigenous rights as well. Such provisions then found their way into the

---

79   Binder (2004: 59) is right to attest that this obligation of protection can be a problem because state interests could cause states not to observe their obligations.

80   According to prevailing theories, several rights contained in the UN Resolution are of internationa customary law status (cf., e.g., Fischer/Köck 2004: 248, Hummer 1997: 250).

human rights Covenants of 1966 (*UN Covenant on Civil and Political Rights*, in short CCPR and *UN Covenant on Economic, Social and Cultural Rights*, in short CESCR). In addition, the UN established international monitoring bodies, such as the *Human Rights Committee* (HRC) for the CCPR or the *Committee on the Elimination of Racial Discrimination* (CERD Committee). In their general comments, recommendations and quasi-judicial decisions, they specifically refer to the status of indigenous rights. In the following part, I will discuss selected international treaties relevant for the protection of indigenous land rights.

2.2.1 Right of Ownership
Neither of the 1966 human rights covenants explicitly contains the right to ownership. Nevertheless, we can discern an analogous protection by using the general prohibition of discrimination in Art. 26 of the *UN Covenant on Civil and Political Rights* (CCPR). As this article stands on its own terms in the Covenant, it does not only refer to the rights established in the CCPR and can accordingly be applied to "other" forms of discriminations – also including any infringement in rights of ownership. This broad interpretation of legal provisions (based on the basic principle of equality) offers, in consequence, an opportunity to protect the territories of indigenous peoples (Binder 2004: 81f.).[81]

The 1965 *UN Convention on the Elimination of All Forms of Racial Discrimination* (CERD) provides further opportunities for the protection of indigenous territories. Its Art. 1 (1) understands racial discrimination to be based, amongst other reasons, on "ethnic origin". Combined with Art. 5 (d) and (v) CERD, States Parties are not only required to prohibit discriminating interventions concerning the right of ownership but they should establish positive measures of protection as well. The *Committee on the Elimination of Racial Discrimination* followed the same direction in their *General Recommendation XXIII (51) on the Rights of Indigenous Peoples* (1997): First and foremost, it affirms that CERD could be applied to indigenous peoples. It then calls upon its member states to recognize and protect indigenous land rights and obliges them to restitution in case of arbitrary displacement from indigenous territories.[82] As soon as a pattern of discrimination based on past injustices is detected, states are obliged to immediately eliminate such discrimination. The CERD Committee also recognizes the strong connection between indigenous peoples and their territories because it specifically allows material compensation only when restitution is for factual reasons not possible. It also decrees that such compensation should (as far as possible) take the form of lands and territories.[83]

---

81   The basic principle of equality has been internationally accepted and does not only focus on formally equal treatment and equality under the law but also on equality of results.
82   Art. 2 *General Recommendation XXIII* (51): indigenous peoples (1997).
83   Art. 5 *General Recommendation XXIII* (51): indigenous peoples (1997).

2.2.2 Right to Culture

Only in connection to other legal provisions, the protection of indigenous territories can be derived from the right to cultural identity, as contained in Art. 27 CCPR: "In those States in which ethnic, religious or linguistic minorities exist, persons belonging to such minorities shall not be denied the right, in community with the other members of their group, to enjoy their own culture, to profess and practice their own religion, or to use their own language."

As we can see in the *General Comment of the Human Rights Committee on the Rights of Minorities, No. 23 on Art. 27 (1994)*, the protection of minorities can also be applied to indigenous peoples: In this context, indigenous cultures primarily manifest themselves in a particular way of life associated with a specific use of resources, such as fishing or hunting. Thus, the HRC does not explicitly establish the right to own property in indigenous territories. It does, however, regard it as necessary for their particular way of life and acknowledges a similar scope of protection (General Comment 23, para. 7). In consequence, Art. 27 CCPR ensures the protection of indigenous land rights by obliging states to undertake positive measures to prevent violations by the state or third parties.[84]

2.2.3 Right to Private and Family Life

The *Human Rights Committee* ascribed a similar scope of protection to Art. 17 and 23 CCPR as to Art. 27 CCPR for the protection of indigenous land rights. In the case *Hopu and Bessert v. France*,[85] the HRC subsumed the protection of traditional burial grounds of an indigenous society in Tahiti that took a stand against the construction of a hotel, under the right to private and family life.[86] In this way, the Committee assessed that the land rights were indispensable for the "private and family life" as well as the spirituality of the society that had a deep connection to its burial grounds. What is interesting about this case is the fact that the HRC did not base their assessment on the complex situation of ownership – the territory concerned was dispossessed before France ratified the CCPR – but highlighted the essential importance of the burial grounds for indigenous religion and spirituality. In this respect, we can determine that any such disruption presents a violation of Art. 17 and 23 CCPR (Binder 2004: 97f.).

On a universal level, a multitude of legal provisions can be used for the protection of indigenous land rights. The legally non-binding decisions of the quasi-judicial *Human Rights Committee* (Nowak 2002: 95) predominantly focus on

---

84 Cf., amongst others, Anaya (1996: 100f.), Binder (2004: 84f.), Thornberry (2002: 151–172), Windmeißer (2002: 328f.).

85 HRC, *Hopu and Bessert v. France*, Communication No 549/1993, UN-Doc CCPR/C/60/D/549/1993, views adopted in July 1997.

86 The originally more adequate provision for the right to cultural identity could not be applied due to the French reservations against Art. 27 CCPR (cf. Binder 2004: 97f.).

III. Special Indigenous Rights or Special Circumstances?

the right to cultural identity. It thus confirms indigenous land rights and to some extent "compensates" for the right of ownership missing in the *UN Covenant on Civil and Political Rights*.

2.3 Jurisdiction of International Monitoring Bodies

A committee of independent experts, chosen by the signatory states, monitors the compliance with each human rights treaty. The tasks of these committees may range from monitoring (obligatory) periodic reports by the states to implementing the rights recognized in the treaties and from developing "General Recommendations" to assessing (optional) individual complaints. In international human rights protection, the opportunity to voice individual complaints is a crucial prerequisite for the implementation of human rights. With the *Human Rights Committee* and the *Committee on the Elimination of Racial Discrimination* leading the way, the evolving jurisdiction of UN treaty-monitoring bodies includes many (also) specific recommendations concerning indigenous peoples.

2.3.1 Human Rights Committee

The monitoring body for the *UN Covenant on Civil and Political Rights* (CCPR) is relevant to indigenous peoples because it examines state reports and, in addition, can be called upon through an individual complaints procedure, if the state concerned has ratified the treaty's optional protocol.[87] We have to keep in mind, though, that the exclusively-written individual complaints procedure does not end with a binding conviction but "only" with the Committee assessing the violation of the treaty and requesting the violating state to cease all damaging actions and provide compensation. What we have here, then, is a combination of legal and political components giving convincing authority to quasi-judicial decisions. As Nowak (2002: 115) explains:

In practice, the individual complaints procedure before the *Human Rights Committee* of the *UN Covenant on Civil and Political Rights* is by far their most significant task. Although former socialist member states were opposed to this process in the beginning, this committee was painstakingly able to develop this procedure into a quasi-judicial one, following the example of the *European Convention on Human Rights* (ECHR). Although the committee's decisions are not of binding character, they are structured and reasoned like court decisions and include specific recommendations to signatory states.[88]

Art. 1 for the individual complaints procedure, however, only allows individuals to bring communications of complaint before the Committee. This especially

---

87   The obligatory periodic report system is established in Art. 40 CCPR. For a more detailed discussion, see, e.g., Hüfner (2002: 36–44).
88   Original citation in German.

contradicts the collective aspect of relationship between indigenous peoples and their territories. Nevertheless, the *Human Rights Committee*'s flexible stance has contributed to the effective protection of indigenous interests. In *Lubicon Lake Band v. Canada*, for example, it accepted the author of the communication Chief Ominayak as the representative of the *Lubicon Lake Band* on the understanding that all members were similarly affected by the measure or otherwise public act.

Its "jurisdiction" bears proof of a broad interpretation of the concept of culture, which includes the protection of indigenous territories as well. This protection comprises such an extensive dimension in the sense of Art. 14 ILO Convention 169 (as mentioned above) that is necessary to enable indigenous peoples to carry out their traditional activities. In this context, one of the most significant cases was the already-mentioned *Lubicon Lake Band* case, in which the HRC decided that Canada had violated Art. 27 CCPR because the Canadian Government had allowed the Provincial Government of Alberta to expropriate the territory of the *Lubicon Lake Band* for the benefit of oil and gas exploration.

In the *Lansman* cases in Finland, the HRC assessed stone extraction of a private company and logging operations on state-owned land in the *Saami Homelands*. In all these cases, the HRC evaluated the adverse effect to "sustainable" Saami land use by examining a disturbance prohibition (focused on "sustainability") and a "consultation" requirement. The first specific *Lansman* case dealt with the following question: are the Saami people able to practice their traditional activities, such as hunting or reindeer herding, in such a way that the protection of Saami society is ensured and were the Saami people consulted beforehand? The Saami people argued in a qualitative way by pointing out that the area concerned was of essential significance to their reindeer herding. The HRC, however, based their decision on the quantitative element of the actual size impact. It specifically held that Finland had not violated Art. 27 CCPR because the size and extent of quarrying was not substantial enough. Anyway, the Committee's more recent "jurisdiction" shows a development towards increasingly assessing a situation from an indigenous perspective. Any interference with land that is of fundamental significance to indigenous spirituality is, therefore, considered a violation.[89]

2.3.2 Committee on the Elimination of Racial Discrimination

Since its establishment in 1970, the *Committee on the Elimination of Racial Discrimination* with its 18 experts has been the first human rights treaty monitoring body of the United Nations. It has had a crucial pioneering role especially due to its development of a procedure to examine the periodic state reports (Nowak 2002: 98). In accordance with Art. 9 (1) of the *UN Convention on the Elimination of All Forms of Racial Discrimination* (CERD), all signatory states are obliged to

---

[89] For a more detailed discussion on the jurisdiction of international monitoring bodies see Binder (2004: 90–102).

III. Special Indigenous Rights or Special Circumstances?

submit a report on the legislative or "governance" measures which they have adopted and which give effect to the provisions of this Convention every two years. The Committee is entitled to examine these reports and has criticized government policies in several cases. In March 1999, it rated Australian legislation regarding the 1998 *Native Title Amendment Act* which particularly revoked concessions made in the 1993[90] *Native Title Act* as possibly discriminating: "[To] wind back the protections of indigenous title offered in the Mabo decision and the Native Title Act 1993 (…) might not comply with Articles 2 and 5 for the Racial Discrimination Convention."[91] Furthermore, it considered the lack of participation of indigenous peoples in developing the "amendments" as a violation of Art. 1(4) and 2(2).[92]

In another matter referring to policies of the Swedish Government directed to its Saami population, Sweden became the target of critique. The Committee expressed serious concerns regarding the privatization of Saami territory and the negative impact on Saami hunting and fishing rights. Sweden was even recommended to ratify ILO Convention 169 (Thornberry 2002: 214ff.).[93]

In accordance with Art. 14 CERD, the individual complaints procedure (provided that states have declared that they recognize the competence of the Committee, as stipulated in para. 1) makes both individual and collective complaints possible. No indigenous petition has been brought before the Committee yet though (MacKay 2010: 159). Indigenous peoples could use this basis and refer to Art. 2 (2) CERD which has established "discrimination in fact". In such a case, indigenous peoples could request "their" states to restitute arbitrarily displaced territories. As we can see here, the protective potential of the *UN Convention on the Elimination of All Forms of Racial Discrimination* for indigenous peoples is far from being exploited.

Not less than 167 states had ratified the *UN Covenant on Civil and Political Rights* by March 2013. Of these 167 states, 114 (38 African countries thereof) also ratified the optional protocol of the individual complaints procedure. The *UN Convention on the Elimination of All Forms of Racial Discrimination* has 175 member states.[94] When it comes to the quasi legal procedure of the *Human Rights Committee* and the activities of the *Committee on the Elimination of Ra-*

---

90 This Act was essentially based on negotiations with indigenous representatives after the decision of the High Court in *Mabo v. Queensland* in 1992. The CERD Committee considered this an extremely significant development and was pleased to note that the *terra nullius* doctrine was rejected.
91 CERD-Committee, UN-Doc. CERD/C/54/Misc.40/Rev.2, at 7 March 1999.
92 For a more detailed discussion see Thornberry (2002: 218–223).
93 The Committee similarly expressed its regrets that Finland had not ratified ILO Convention 169: A/55/18, para. 214.
94 See www2.ohchr.org/english/law/cerd as of 15/03/2013.

cial Discrimination, the number of ratifications allows us to regard their binding force concerning the protection of indigenous territories as almost universal. Considering the "soft law" consequences of these decisions – in the sense of the already-mentioned "naming, blaming, shaming" – it becomes obvious that more and more states are willing to recognize indigenous land rights both nationally and internationally. As we can see on the African continent, this international practice of states of course raises awareness in this matter. Thus, it seems possible to argue that at least certain minimum standards regarding indigenous land rights, which are based on other conceptions of ownership, cultural integrity and self-determination, have not only found their way into statutory law but into international customary law as well.

3. Sources of Freedom and Equality: Self-Determination

As my considerations above have shown, there is in general a relatively broad agreement on the significance of lands or territories for the "survival" of indigenous cultures. The representatives of numerous indigenous peoples have expressly underlined that they assume collective responsibility for lands and consider the deep spiritual and emotional connection to earth and its resources an essential element of their cosmovision. After what has been said, it goes without saying that such statements must bear close empirical examination to reasonably claim an indispensable connection between territoriality and existential social being. Portraying indigenous peoples as "environmental saints" does more harm than good to their often legitimate claims of self-determination.

If, however, cultural-ecological data in a historical dimension point to a connectivity between indigenous "ownership" of lands and sustainable use, claims of an extended idea of self-determination stand their ground quite well under international law. In the end, the freedoms applied in the dimension of indigenous self-determination are used to pass on these values, their cultural identities and ways of life to future generations. This is why indigenous peoples need the freedom, amongst others, to dispose of their natural resources, practice an uninterrupted relationship to their territories, carry out their traditional activities, and determine their development themselves.

The right to self-determination of indigenous peoples is, *inter alia*, established in both UN human rights Covenants of 1966. Their identical Art. 1 also includes an economic component: the right to freely dispose of their natural wealth (para. 2).[95] Since both Covenants went into effect in 1976, it has been

---

95   The universal right to self-determination of all peoples is found in Art. 1/2 and Art. 55 of the UN Charter as well as in numerous resolutions of the UN General Assembly. In this respect, the *Declaration on the Granting of Independence to Colonial Countries and*

III. Special Indigenous Rights or Special Circumstances?

impossible to convincingly deny the right to self-determination of indigenous peoples (as mentioned in the above constructively extended sense). In the meantime, it has become binding under customary law or as a universal legal standard. As its nature is mainly *ius cogens*, it can be regarded as a compelling norm under international law. The concept on which the term "self-determination" is based shows the common (fundamental and indispensable) values of the community of states, which derive from the international context of human rights. First and foremost, they include the fundamental values of freedom and equality:

"[S]elf-determination is identified as a universe of Human Rights precepts concerned broadly with peoples, including indigenous peoples, and grounded in the idea that all are equally entitled to control their own destinies. Self-determination gives rise to remedies that tear at the legacies of empire, discrimination, suppression of democratic participation, and cultural suffocation" (Anaya 1996: 75).

At the international level, the broader terminology of the concept of self-determination for indigenous peoples is still controversial. This controversy is primarily based on the equation of whatever kind of right to self-determination with the term "peoples". Then again, numerous interpretations force this term into the narrow application frame of the entire population of a (state) territory.[96] The conception that the right to self-determination should generally also include "external" self-determination, meaning the formation of an own state (secession), has long been prevailing in the discourse of international law. It is particularly this idea that governments see as threats to their territorial integrity: "Self-determination carries the baggage of state building and decolonisation" (Keal 2003: 152). International law increasingly opposes this restrictive interpretation because it arbitrarily and one-dimensionally hypostatizes secession as the primary meaning of self-determination. As it is the case, this political aspect could only, if at all, be applied to a very short historical fragment of decolonisation (Kuppe 1994: 118).

In contrast, some states concerned argue that the right of self-determination that is free of state contexts to such an extent could, from the point of view of legal policy, mean a threat to democracy, stability, peace and the political and territorial unity of the state. This is why they interpret Article 1 of both UN Covenants quite restrictively and invest only states or peoples in the mentioned process of decolonisation with the right of self-determination. In this historical context of usually contractually stipulated successor states of former colonies, relevant proto-national stakeholders were entitled to the right of self-determination. Therefore, it can be said that the historical connotations of self-determination derive from the anti-

---

Peoples 1960 (Res. 1514 [XV]) certainly was a milestone; a further document would be the *Friendly-Relation-Declaration* 1970. Cf. Malanczuk (2003: 326f.).

96 For the consequences of the term "peoples" and the three prevailing (shortened) interpretations in the context of self-determination, see Anaya (1996: 77–80).

thesis to foreign rule. In the constitutive discourses and constitutional narratives of most "postcolonial" states, this right was based on the universal values of freedom, equality, and peace (Anaya 1995: 325). As self-determination is reduced to the single exemplary case of independent statehood, the term is *de facto* equated with decolonisation. Anaya (1996: 80) convincingly argues as follows:

"Decolonization prescriptions do not themselves embody the substance of the principle of self-determination; rather, they correspond with measures to remedy a sui generis deviation from the principle existing in the prior condition of colonialism in its classical form. (…) The substance of the norm – the precepts that define the standard – must be distinguished from the remedial prescriptions that may follow a violation of the norm, such as those developed to undo colonization. In the decolonization context, procedures that resulted in independent statehood were means of discarding alien rule that had been contrary to the enjoyment of self-determination. Remedial prescriptions in other contexts will vary according to the relevant circumstances and not inevitably result in the formations of new states."

In the sense of the mentioned variations of legal solutions to obvious injustices, the core values of self-determination are derived from the principles of freedom and equality. These values apply in a very particular way to indigenous peoples concerned with relevant violations of their freedoms. While self-determination in its widest interpretation applies all segments of humanity, its rather narrow sense refers to the corrective aspects of a political justice that is oriented towards freedom and equality.[97] In the context of the right of self-determination, the international community has developed "remedial prescriptions". Their specific, last-mentioned objectives prove advantageous to those groups whose essential self-determination rights have been curtailed. Indigenous communities are in many ways "perfect" examples of such groups:

"(W)hile the substantive elements of self-determination apply broadly to benefit all segments of humanity, self-determination applies more narrowly in its remedial aspect. Remedial prescriptions and mechanisms developed by the international community necessarily only benefit groups that have suffered violations of substantive self-determination. Indigenous peoples characteristically are within the more narrow category of self-determination beneficiaries, which includes groups entitled to remedial measures; but the remedial regime developing in the context of indigenous peoples is not one that favors the formation of new states" (Anaya 1996: 80f.).

As indigenous peoples are within the narrower category of self-determination beneficiaries, the legal scope focuses primarily on the indicated remedial prescriptions. Based on the constructively extended rights of self-determination,

---

97 For the concept of political justice and its global dimension see Höffe (1987; and 1999: 412f.).

III. Special Indigenous Rights or Special Circumstances?

some states fear a legal development harming or even destroying the integrity of the state towards a further-evolving remedial regime for indigenous peoples. As my considerations above show, such fears can be invalidated from a legal point of view. This legal aspect that the self-determination of indigenous peoples does in no way advocate the formation of new states (Anaya 1996: 81) has continuously and consistently been confirmed by those concerned. Indigenous peoples all around the world almost unanimously underline that they do not have any secessionist aspirations whatsoever: "Indigenous peoples often emphasize that their understanding of the right of self-determination is that it gives them the right to be in control of their lives and their own destiny. This enables them to remain who they are and to live the way they want to live" (Henriksen 2001: 14).

Much to the indigenous peoples' regret, this understanding remained mostly unresolved in ILO Convention 169.[98] In this respect, Art. 1 (3) limits indigenous rights under international law, as "[T]he use of the term peoples in this convention shall not be construed as having any implications as regards the rights which may attach to the term under international law." From the perspective of the ILO, political separatism should in no account be concluded from using the term 'peoples'. This subjunctive wording leads to the obvious interpretation that the ILO seeks to stay out of the self-determination controversy and generally wants the United Nations to decide which "peoples" should be entitled to this right. Nonetheless, the mere use of the term – perhaps unintentionally – caused a paradigm shift:

"On the other hand, the adoption of 'peoples' by the ILO advanced the case for indigenous employment of the vocabulary of peoples' rights, and, ultimately perhaps the discourses of self-determination" (Thornberry 2002: 344).

Instead of separating self-determination into its "internal" and "external" aspects, Anaya (1996: 81f.) suggests two normative lines comprising the essence of self-determination. The first so-called "constitutive aspect" requires that the existing institutional order emanates from the will of the governed people or peoples. When it comes to processes of forming or changing state institutions, the constitutive aspect calls for participation and consultation, thus making it possible to regard the final result of political order as the collective will of the people or peoples concerned. These minimal standards are established in Art. 3 of the *UN Declaration on the Rights of Indigenous Peoples* as well as in the identical Art. 1/1 of both UN human rights Covenants: "All peoples have the right of self-determination. By virtue of that right they freely determine their political status (…)." The second normative line Anaya (ibid.) suggests, the "ongoing aspect" re-

---

98 For debates prior to ILO 169, see Thornberry (2002: 342–344). Such conception could not find its way into the *UN Declaration on the Rights of Indigenous Peoples* either: Art. 46 stipulates an interpretation of the Declaration that does not contradict territorial integrity and political unity.

quires that the people or peoples are able to live and freely develop under the existing institutional order. In provisions of self-determination found in the international human rights Covenants and other instruments, this minimal standard establishes that all peoples have the right, "to freely pursue their economic, social and cultural development" (Art. 1/1).

These central contents answer to the economic, cultural, political, and social dimension of the right of self-determination as a constructive further development of the terminology exclusively applied to "peoples of a state" (cf. Kuppe 1994: 118f.). As long as "self-determination" is interpreted in such manner, we can also identify certain aspects, such as rights of participation and (subsidiary) self-governance (Art. 6 and 7 ILO Convention 169). This constructively extended right of self-determination was first realized in the *UN Declaration on the Rights of Indigenous Peoples*. Established in Art. 3 to 5, it now serves as the Declaration's central subject matter. Art. 3 follows Art. 1 of both human rights Covenants by just replacing "all peoples" with "indigenous peoples", "(…) an emphasis stating that indigenous peoples are included in the term 'all peoples'" (Henriksen 2001: 14).[99] In conformity with this right of self-determination, indigenous peoples are entitled to autonomy and (likewise subsidiary) self-governance "in matters relating to their internal and local affairs" (pursuant to Art. 4). Art. 4 of their (former draft) 1993 version still included a list to explain these internal and local affairs, e.g. culture, religion, education, employment or the management of lands and resources.[100] The final version leaves it to indigenous peoples to define their own matters of self-determination.

Furthermore, Art. 5 of the latest and definitive UN Declaration emphasizes much more the recognition of legal pluralism because it is based on the independent right of indigenous peoples "(…) to maintain and strengthen their distinct political, economic, social and cultural characteristics, **as well as their legal systems** (…)".[101] This explicit emphasis of their legal systems limits the state's monopoly on the legitimate use of force for the benefit of the normative and legal competence of indigenous legal systems. It *expressis verbis* recognizes indigenous "customary laws" which was reason enough for France to argue against the right of self-determination as a whole because it allegedly "seemed to create a State within a State".[102] All this shows how difficult it was to find a reason-

---

99 In international law, the right of self-determination is predominantly interpreted as a right of "all peoples". From a jurisprudential point of view, indigenous peoples are not to be excluded in this interpretation. "Indigenous peoples strongly believe that it would be a discriminatory application of this fundamental principle of international law if it were to be applicable to all peoples other than indigenous peoples" (Henriksen 2001: 14).

100 UN Doc. E/CNA/1995/2, E/CNA/Sub.2/1994/56, at 105 (1994).

101 Emphasis added.

102 E/CN.4/1997/102, para. 329, cited in Thornberry (2002: 384).

ably substantive and common basis for the interests (of power) of various nation states. Among the numerous controversial subjects delaying the adoption by the *Human Rights Council* by thirteen years obviously were these appeals to a pluralistic system.

Under an "umbrella" of human rights, the concept of self-determination allows for considerably finer interpretations and applications. This is especially true in an increasingly interdependent world in which formerly uncontested attributes of sovereignty – such as claiming the right to non-interference in internal affairs even in case of extremely severe human rights violations and genocides – become less and less significant (Anaya 1995: 325). In the future, the right of self-determination could be regarded as a collective right of freedom. Although such a freedom on the basis of international law could possibly cause tensions in national contexts, it also potentially opens up an entire sphere for new, cooperative forms of governance. With that said, nothing would stand in the way of applying the protection of the existence and (independent) development of indigenous peoples according to their own conceptions anymore. This is why self-determination is a fundamental prerequisite for the preservation of indigenous peoples with regard to their long-denied freedoms. It is not at all about keeping these groups "frozen" in time and space but about the universal freedoms' basic principle of determining their future themselves as well as about preserving, developing, and transmitting to future generations a collective identity shaped by former generations (Cobo 1986b: para. 20). At this point it can only be implied that a radical sense of democratic standard is included, which is based on the collective participation of all stakeholders. The alleged freedom from domination brings upon itself the right to determine the conditions of one's own existence, or in other words, of "self-determination" – within or without the legal confines of a national state.

This conciliatory or integrative framework intrinsically connotes the further objectives of retributive and restorative justice as a new foundation of social peace as well as mutual recognition and respect: "It is perhaps best to understand the Declaration and the right of self-determination it affirms as instruments of reconciliation. Properly understood, self-determination is an animating force for efforts toward reconciliation – or, perhaps more accurately, conciliation – with peoples that have suffered oppression at the hands of others. Self-determination requires confronting and reversing the legacies of empire, discrimination, and cultural suffocation. It does not do so to condone vengefulness or spite for past evils, or to foster divisiveness but rather to build a social and political order based on relations of mutual understanding and respect. That is what the right of self-determination of indigenous peoples, and all other peoples, is about" (Anaya 2010: 196).

Part 2: "Being Indigenous in Africa": Legal Developments of Indigenous Peoples Law in Africa

I. Historical Overview

As I have sketched in the first part of this book, national indigenous organizations on the American and Australian continent were formed in the 1960/70s. While in these regions a process of developing and mobilizing indigenous rights took place, for most parts of Africa colonial rule ended and they became independent.[1] After the colonial era, the young African nations were of course mainly concerned with political emancipation. This is explicitly emphasized in the preamble of the foundation *Charter of the Organization of African Unity* (OAU[2]):

"Conscious of their [the African States members of the OAU] duty to achieve the total liberation of Africa, the peoples of which are still struggling for their dignity and genuine independence, and undertaking to eliminate colonialism, neocolonialism, apartheid, Zionism and to dismantle aggressive foreign military bases and all forms of discrimination, particularly those based on race, ethnic group, color, sex, language, religion or political opinions" (para. 8).

Apart from promoting unity and solidarity of the African states, their ultimate objective is defending sovereignty, territorial integrity, and non-interference in internal affairs.[3] It was their basic understanding that the respect for human rights was an internal matter, which, therefore, was only marginally mentioned in the OAU Charter.[4] The conception obviously prevailed that individual human rights were automatically ensured after colonialism (Nowak 2002: 224). As it continued to stay silent even in cases of severe human rights violations on the African continent, this African regional body increasingly discredited itself. From the perspective of human rights organizations, the OAU was hardly convincing because it repeatedly referred to its "principle of non-interference in internal affairs". In 1979 at the 16th Ordinary Session held in Monrovia, Liberia, the *Organization of African Unity* addressed human rights for the first time by deciding to prepare a preliminary draft on an *African Charter on Human and Peoples' Rights*.[5] After about five years, the OAU adopted the human rights document, also known as the *Banjul Charter*, which came into effect on 21 October 1986.[6]

---

1   Cf. for example Ki-Zerbo (1981: 538–652) and Oliver/Atmore (1981: 222–290).
2   Art. 2 of the *Constitutive Act of the African Union* (AU) replaces the OAU. The AU has existed since its Constitutive Act came into force on 26 May 2001.
3   Art. 2 OAU Charter.
4   For a historical overview of the OAU's foundation as well as the *African Charter on Human and Peoples' Rights*, see, e.g., Bortfeld (2005: 21–31) and Ouguergouz (2003: 1–48).
5   The starting point of this process was *Amnesty International* proving that Emperor Bokassa I (Central African Empire) was involved in the assassination of more than 100 schoolchildren (Bortfeld 2005: 29).
6   The "African Charter on Human and Peoples' Rights" is in short called "Banjul Charter" because it was adopted and transmitted to the OAU Council of Ministers at a

While indigenous rights developed in Australia and the Americas, Africa focused on nation-building, the elimination of racial discrimination and apartheid, extensive decolonisation, the establishment of economic justice, and ending the rule of the white minority population in southern Africa. None of these objectives, however, included policies in favour of indigenous peoples. In this sense indigenous rights got lost in the postcolonial imperatives of development and the fight against poverty (Thornberry 2002: 246).

In the last ten to twenty years, the indigenous movement in Australia and the Americas helped to continue the process which is sometimes called "indigenization", meaning that more and more social groups and indigenous communities started claiming their primary rights as indigenous peoples. This is hardly surprising because experiences of discrimination, domination, and marginalization are alike all around the world. As a group of experts of the African Commission stated, Africa is no exception: "'Indigenous peoples' is today a term and a global movement fighting for rights and justice for those particular groups who have been left on the margins of development, who are perceived negatively by dominant mainstream development paradigms and whose cultures and lives are subject to discrimination and contempt" (ACHPR/IWGIA 2006: 11).

According to the *Report of the African Commission's Working Group of Experts on Indigenous Populations/Communities* (in short *African Report*), more than half a million "hunters and gatherers" are living under precarious circumstances on the African continent alone (ACHPR/IWGIA 2005: 16f.). A significantly higher number of crop and livestock farming indigenous peoples can be added to this figure. The *International Work Group for Indigenous Affairs* (IWGIA 1994: 4f.) estimates some 14 million nomads to be affected as well.[7] At the 1999 Arusha Conference, representatives of indigenous peoples emphasized these alarming conditions: numerous indigenous communities suffered from severe discrimination and marginalization, land dispossession and forced relocation as a result of agricultural programmes, mining, dam building, the creation of national parks and game reserves, low-quality social benefits, the lack of education and development opportunities, comparable severe human rights violations, collective punishment, and genocide. Contrary to some states' anxiety of the written letters of indigenous rights provisions, it is rather in the realm of these actions that situations of dissatisfaction, organized protest, civil unrest, and, in some cases, even armed warfare invariably arise.

---

    meeting of the ministers of justice in Banjul, The Gambia, in January 1981. Pursuant to Art. 63 III, it came into effect after the required majority (26 out of the 50 OAU member states of that time) was reached.

7   The lack of precise numbers shows how little we know about some indigenous groups: exact population numbers of the Tuareg as part of the indigenous Amazigh peoples (generally known as "Berbers") range from 300,000 to 3 million (ACHPR/IWGIA 2005: 18).

I. Historical Overview 81

The appendix of the resolution adopted at the conference shows a table with examples of indigenous peoples who had experienced relocation from national parks and nature reserves in Botswana,[8] Kenya,[9] Namibia,[10] Rwanda,[11] South Africa,[12] Tanzania,[13] and Uganda.[14] This list impressively shows how the very legitimate conservation of nature in Africa is played off against the protection of human rights.[15] This is why I would like to introduce and discuss this aspect before presenting African initiatives on indigenous rights protection.

1. Nature Conservation v. Human Rights Protection

Almost unnoticed by the international community, the creation of virtually all African nature reserves has had drastic consequences for local (often indigenous) communities. This process was committed to imperatives of nature conservation, such as "Serengeti shall not die!". In contrast to the obvious understanding that it was their sustainable way of life that enabled the conservation of environments worth protecting, indigenous communities had to move to more remote areas. Some authors tried to find logical explanations for this form of *conservation governance* and pointed to the European idea of nature conservation while examining relevant discourses with regard to Africa (cf. Anderson/Grove 1987, Adams 2003). In this respect, we can find a clear connection between the discourse elements of "untouched wilderness" and the "disturbing, threatening existence" of indigenous peoples. Around these opposing poles, various conservation policies, which were considerably based on myths, developed. Postcolonial dependencies of economic and ideological character influenced these genuinely European connections of ecological preservation and pristine nature. In the form of exclusion, they ultimately found their way into postcolonial African legislation and policies, which strikingly corresponded in how they complied with the principle of "nature conservation under the exclusion of human influences":

"[T]he colonial relationship (…) allowed Europeans to impose their image of Africa upon the reality of the African landscape. Much of the emotional as dis-

---

8   G|wi and ||Gana San from *Central Kalahari Game Reserve* as well as !Kung from *Gemsbok National Park*. For the first group see chapter 6 of this book.
9   Ogiek from *Parc Volcan Makurarle* and *Mau Forest*.
10 Hai//om San from *Etosha National Park*.
11 Batwa from *Parc National des Volcans* and *Forêt Naturelle Gishwati*.
12 ǂKhomani San from *Gemsbok National Park*.
13 Maasai from *Serengeti National Park*.
14 Batwa (Abayanda) from *Gorilla Park*, *Echuuya Forest Reserve* and *Semliki National Park*.
15 For a detailed list of relocations from nature reserves in southern Africa see Hitchcock (2001: 140).

tinct from the economic investment which Europe made in Africa has manifested itself in a wish to protect the natural environment as a special kind of 'Eden', for the purposes of the European psyche, rather than as a complex and changing environment in which people have actually had to live" (Anderson/Grove 1987: 4).

In (pre-colonial and colonial) Europe, expeditions to allegedly undiscovered regions, most of them already inhabited for centuries, could only be funded by offering descriptions with audience appeal. They usually went hand in hand with corresponding adventure stories of explorers and missionaries, e.g. Mungo Park, David Livingstone, or Henry Morton, which produced and reproduced the image of a "wild Africa". Such "ethics of natural wilderness" (Kuppe 1998a: 102)[16] have to some extent been continued until today and regard the conservation of nature as protecting an allegedly authentic original state. Separating nature from culture, this concept does not see humans as a part of nature but as intruders (Adams 2003: 9). This idea may also be regarded as the (original) essence of the Western concept of nature conservation. When *Yellowstone National Park* was founded in 1872, the conception of a fauna and flora that needed to be protected was incorporated in African legislation and programmes that were supported by international organizations and NGOs.[17] East Africa played a leading role in the conservation of animals and plants in certain uninhabited areas (except for those groups regarded as "wild humans" at that time, e.g. the Maasai in Kenya and Tanzania).

It seems ironic that this protection is mainly limited to areas (often sustainably) used by indigenous communities, whereas extensive regions subject to private and state interests are exploited without any protection. In this regard, the approach "nature v. human (rights) protection" presented above privileges the exploitation of natural resources in all those regions not protected by law because they fit the description of economic interests (Kuppe 1998a: 102). If we try to analyze the origins of the national park idea, it will become clear that there is a direct connection to the practice and ideology of colonialism. The idea of colonial masters as the exclusive holders of the right of disposal over nature directly caused the resettlement of indigenous communities; especially from areas with high biodiversity, which were interesting to nature conservation (ibid.: 104) and the prevailing hunting that preceded the conservationist agenda. Dislocations were often defended rather cynically by claiming that indigenous peoples were "backward" and "primitive" because their subsistence was based on natural resources. As the explanation was so easy to see through, they argued that indige-

---

16 "La 'Ética de la Vida Silvestre' considera al ser humano como invasor de la naturaleza, y no como parte integrante de la misma" (Kuppe 1998a: 102).
17 Cf. Chatty and Colchester (2002: 3), McCabe (2002: 65f.) and Kuppe (1998a: 101f.) for the origins of the idea of national parks.

I. Historical Overview

nous peoples needed "help" to further develop and that resettlements and dispossessions were in their own interests.

From time to time, however, indigenous ways of life also attracted tourists: in these rare cases, for which San peoples may be taken as an example, colonial rulers established a reserve for certain indigenous communities to conserve a piece of "primitive Africa" as some kind of "open-air museum".[18] Nonetheless, the end of colonial rule did not bring an end to human rights violations and discrimination against indigenous peoples: "The failure to distinguish between different peoples contained within the boundaries of new states established by formal decolonisation meant that for many indigenous peoples one set of oppressors had been replaced by another. It is then hardly surprising that many indigenous peoples (…) do not accept that colonialism has ended" (Keal 2003: 8).

As far as I can tell from the extensive literature of the various African countries, legal initiatives of indigenous groups in Africa remained nothing but fragmented until the 1990s. Only when the work of NGOs had at least to some extent success on other continents (mainly Australia and the Americas) and global networking was born, national and regional organizations formed in Africa and Asia and increasingly participated in international developments. In case of Africa, there were on the one hand bottom-up initiatives of groups that were in general highly marginalized and isolated from each other as well as on the other hand top-down tendencies. Among the first was the foundation of new NGOs, such as (in southern Africa) *First People of the Kalahari* 1993, *Working Group of Indigenous Minorities in Southern Africa*, or *South African San Institute*, both 1996; among the second various corresponding discourses and forums of the *African Union*, in which NGOs participated to address the issues of indigenous peoples. Supported by new developments in communication technology, these groups were not isolated anymore and focused on the recognition of their special, legal status as indigenous peoples instead of social minorities.

2. African Initiatives for the Protection of Indigenous Rights

The reactions to a UN study by *Special Rapporteur* Miguel Alfonso Martinez of the *Sub-Commission on Prevention of Discrimination and Protection of Minorities* were the first signs of a significantly strengthened pan-indigenous discourse. Indigenous from all around the world joined to take a stand against the *Special Rapporteur*'s conclusions. In the 1999 final report to his 10-year study, Miguel Alfonso Martinez recommended the *UN Working Group on Minorities* as the adequate forum for all social groups regarding themselves as "indigenous peoples in African and Asia":

---

18   Cf. Chatty and Colchester (2002: 5).

"[It is an] obvious fact that in post-colonial Africa and Asia autochthonous groups/minorities/ethnic groups/peoples who seek to exercise rights presumed to be or actually infringed by the existing autochthonous authorities in the States in which they live cannot, in the view of the *Special Rapporteur*, claim for themselves, unilaterally and exclusively, the 'indigenous' status in the United Nations context" (Martinez 1999: para. 88).

This recommendation would have made irrelevant all privileges indigenous peoples in Africa and Asia had begun enjoying. This is why indigenous representatives were outraged and dismissed this point of view. In Martinez' opinion the concept of "indigenous peoples" did not apply in Africa and Asia because it was supposed to be limited to the colonial migration of European powers. He was convinced that Africa and Asia only experienced a "territorial expansion by Indigenous nations into adjacent areas", calling them therefore "state-oppressed groups/peoples" and "minorities" (ibid.: paras. 73, 83).

Nevertheless, he made a few exceptions, such as the Ainu, Maasai, San, and indigenous peoples in Siberia. At the 17th meeting of the *UN Working Group on Indigenous Populations* in Geneva, present African and Asian representatives of indigenous peoples heavily criticized Martinez' view because his methodical approach only included former colonies in North America and the Pacific Ocean. In their opinion, he thus failed to produce universal results. The indigenous peoples' argumentations were supported by numerous legal instruments and judicial considerations because the term "indigenous" was applied to African and Asian peoples in legally relevant provisions and studies, including the World Bank, the European Commission, the UN studies by Martínez Cobo (1986) and Erica-Irene Daes (2000), and of course the *African Commission on Human and People's Rights* (ACHPR/IWGIA 2006: 11):

"The linking up to a global movement – by applying the term 'indigenous peoples' – is a way for these [indigenous] groups [in Africa] to try to address their situation, analyze the specific forms of inequalities and repression they suffer from, and overcome the human rights violations by also invoking the protection of international law. It is the modern analytical understanding of the term 'indigenous peoples', with its focus on (…) criteria of marginalisation, discrimination, cultural difference and self-identification, that has been adopted by the ACHPR."

In addition the terminology is firmly established in the overwhelming political opinion of indigenous peoples, "indigenous peoples of Asia and Africa are unequivocally regarded as indigenous peoples by themselves and by others" (Roy 2003: 7f.).

Keeping in mind the fundamental principles of equality, it would of course also be possible to argue against the rejection of the indigenous status for African and Asian indigenous peoples. This is why Roy (2003: 8) calls this differentiation simply unethical and clearly discriminating. According to the *Working Group on Indigenous Populations*, indigenous peoples, indigenous rights, and indigenous issues cannot be defined in a specific historical and geographical context.

I. Historical Overview 85

The 17th WGIP meeting was then followed by seminars with various focuses: in Arusha, Tanzania (2000) on the indigenous situation in Africa[19], in Kidal, Mali (2001) on Amazigh peoples,[20] in Gaborone, Botswana (2002) on multiculturalism[21] and a consultation and training workshop for the Pygmies in Yaoundé (Cameroon 2002).[22] In mid-September 2006 the African Commission organized a regional seminar to raise awareness for the right of indigenous peoples in Africa.[23] It was not only the United Nations that experienced an increasing focus on indigenous peoples and rights in Africa.[24]

Since the year 2000, the African Union, too, has increasingly addressed these problems. In 2001 at the 29th Ordinary Session in Tripoli, the African Commission appointed a *Working Group of Experts on Indigenous Populations/Communities* (in short *ACHPR Working Group*).[25] The Expert Group comprises three members of the African Commission, three experts of African indigenous communities, and an independent expert. Their mandate calls for the Working Group to: examine the concept of indigenous people and communities in Africa, study the

---

19 E/CN.4/Sub.2/AC.5/2000/WP.3, 13–15 May 2000. The indigenous African participants of this seminar referred to Martinez' differentiation as well and stated in their conclusions, "In differentiating between indigenous peoples and minorities it was suggested that indigenous peoples had an attachment to a particular land or territory and/or a way of life (e.g., pastoralists, hunter-gatherers, nomadic or others) which was threatened by current State policy and affected by the shrinking of their traditional resource base" (para. 29).

20 E/CN.4/Sub.2/AC.5/2001/3, 8–13 January 2001.

21 E/CN.4/Sub.2/AC.4/2002/4, 18–22 February 2002. This workshop adopted a remarkable resolution and encouraged African governments to ratify ILO Convention 169, consider it in national legislation and support the *UN Draft Declaration* (see points 38 and 39 of the document, the *Gaborone Declaration* (United Nations 2002); Mogwe 2002).

22 E/CN.4/Sub.2/AC.4/2003/11, 11–15 November 2002. Information on achievements of the Working Group, E/CN.4/Sub.2/AC.4/2006/CRP.1.

23 The seminar took place in Yaounde, Cameroon 13–16 September 2006. See: www.achpr.org/english/news/Seminar.htm.

24 African indigenous peoples appoint their own representative at the *Permanent Forum on Indigenous Issues*; in his 2001 report, the *UN Special Rapporteur for Indigenous Peoples* made various remarks on the situation of indigenous peoples in Africa; indigenous African organizations used the *UN Draft Declaration on the Rights of Indigenous Peoples* over the years. The *UN Voluntary Fund for Indigenous Peoples* (GA Res. 40/131 of 1985) has an African Board Member (Maasai); in 2001 in Tanzania, the ILO opened an indigenous (regional) office to promote indigenous peoples in Africa; also the World Bank organized a series of consultation conferences with indigenous peoples in various African regions. As we can see, however, this process mainly springs from the United Nations themselves or from African indigenous peoples. Most African Governments have not been really interested in recognizing indigenous rights withing the UN context as human rights instruments (ACHPR/IWGIA 2005: 59).

25 Pursuant to the *Resolution on the Rights of Indigenous Populations/Communities in Africa*, 28th Ordinary Session in Cotonou, Benin from 23rd October to 6th November 2000.

implications of the Banjul Charter on indigenous communities, consider appropriate recommendations for the monitoring and protection of the rights of indigenous communities, and to present a report to the *African Commission on Human and Peoples' Rights* (in short ACHPR or *African Commission*). The Working Group presented its 120-page report in May 2003, which was adopted at the 34th Ordinary Session in The Gambia in November 2003.[26] It addresses the human rights situation of African indigenous peoples in general, specifically the *Banjul Charter* as well as possible criteria of and (dynamic) "characteristics" for identifying indigenous peoples.[27] The *African Report* was summarized in a 29-page brochure and now serves as guideline of the *African Commission* on indigenous peoples' issues (ACHPR/IWGIA 2006: 9).

On the basis of this mandate, the Working Group has developed a comprehensive programme including regular bi-annual meetings, country visits,[28] sensitization seminars,[29] information activities,[30] and research.[31] The report of the *ACHPR Working Group* talks about commonalities among indigenous peoples and how they share experiences of problematic human rights warrants. Negative experiences of human rights violations are particularly stressed:

"The indigenous peoples of Africa display remarkable commonalities. Unlike other indigenous peoples outside Africa, where the aboriginal type of indigene-

---

26   The resolution adopted the report as well as its recommendations and included publishing the report, ensuring its wide distribution, maintaining on the agenda of its ordinary sessions the item on the situation of "indigenous populations" in Africa and establishing a Working Group of Experts for an initial term of two years. The mandate of the Working Group has already been renewed.

27   The "Report of the African Commission's Working Group of Experts on Indigenous Populations/Communities" was published in book form in 2005.

28   The Working Group has visited 13 countries so far; for the Botswana *fact-finding mission* in 2005, see chapter 5, section V.2. this volume.

29   Such a seminar on the region of central Africa took place in Cameroon in September 2006. Their goal was to learn from the *African Commission* about tasks and guidelines concerning indigenous peoples. Aiming the central issues discussed were indigenous land rights, poverty in indigenous communities and their access to health care and education. Not least because of that a successful dialog between the *African Commission*, its member states, NGOs, indigenous communities and organizations developed. The *ACHPR Working Group* organized two more sensitization seminars: in Addis Abeba, Ethiopia in 2008 and in Brazzaville, Congo in 2011; cf. www.achpr.org/mechanisms/indigenous-populations/about/.

30   The *ACHPR Working Group* finalized a promotional video film on indigenous peoples in Africa entitled "A Question of Justice: The Rights of Indigenous Peoples in Africa", which is being widely distributed to various stakeholders in and outside of Africa.

31   The *Centre for Human Rights at the University of Pretoria* conducted a comparative legal study on legislation in 24 African countries with regard to the protection of indigenous rights. This three-year project was commissioned by the *ACHPR Working Group* in cooperation with the ILO (ILO/ACHPR 2009).

ity is the characteristic feature, Africa's indigenous peoples have their own specific feature of the African state and its role. (...) However, a common feature of indigenous peoples and communities is the type of human rights violations they experience. Indigenous peoples and communities experience a range of human rights violations that ultimately boil down to a threat towards their right to existence and to the social, economic and cultural development of their own choice" (ACHPR/IWGIA 2005: 106f.).

In their struggle to counteract discrimination, domination, and marginalization as well as for the recognition of their fundamental human rights, indigenous peoples from Africa have joined the worldwide indigenous rights movement. In the meantime, we can talk about "one" or even "the" international indigenous movement.

There are still significant obstacles to overcome before an effective implementation of indigenous law appears within reach in most of Africa. The rest of the book will discuss these obstacles in further detail based on the example of the San. First and foremost in this context, I should highlight how governments feel their country's sovereignty threatened and do neither implement the relational denotations nor meanings of the used terminology. Since indigenous rights were recognized, some African Governments have seemed to see themselves as forced into colonizing roles. This is at least what the recurring rhetorical questions, whether or not all Africans are indigenous peoples, suggests. On the occasion of adopting the *UN Declaration on the Rights of Indigenous Peoples*, Botswana's ambassador to the United Nations Samuel Outlule raised this objection in no uncertain terms:

"As Africans and citizens of Botswana who are (...) **all indigenous to the country** and the African Continent, we are concerned that the Declaration [*on the Rights of Indigenous Peoples*] suggests that sections of the population have the right to claim to be the sole indigenous peoples of specific regions of a sovereign Republic."[32] (emphasis added)

As these concerns are voiced quite often and cannot be denied inconsiderately, I will discuss the etymological and historical understanding of the term "indigenous" as well as its use in international law and consider whether it is adequate for and can be applied to the African context.

---

32 Statement by Samuel Outlule, Ambassador and Permanent Representative of the Republic of Botswana to the United Nations to 3rd Committee of UN-GA on Agenda Item 68 (Indigenous Rights), 19 November 2006. Republic of Botswana (11/19/06): *Tautona Times* no 41 of 2006. The Weekly Electronic Press Circular of the Office of the President.

II. "Indigenous Peoples in Africa": Applying the Concept

Does the quote from above by Ambassador Outlule convincingly argue that the term "indigenous peoples" cannot be applied to relevant population groups in Africa? In 1990 Kuppe asked this question and started with analyzing its denotation to which various connotations can be attributed: Although the immediate meaning of the word [indigenous as 'native' or 'aboriginal'] comprises everything 'born in a country' and can thus be applied to everything connected to a region or country, a new dimension of meaning was added to the term in the context of the European overseas expansion[33] (Kuppe 1990: 9). In colonized countries, everybody who was not a European settler and showed divergent ways of life was called "indigenous". In this context, the term suggests a tension, or a contradiction first perceived from a European perspective, between on the one hand the European colonial system and its valuations and on the other hand the – often rather obstructive – real ways of life of the population which was seen as 'aboriginal'. This environment of tension is partly responsible for the term's very negative original connotation (ibid.).[34]

The 1960/70s indigenous movement (of the Australian and American continents) mentioned above again altered the connotation of the term. This process was started by indigenous peoples themselves and now manifested itself institutionally as well. Continuous and actual experiences of injustice relating to "their" nation states were added to the term's character, thus pointing to postcolonial tensions as well. 'Indigenous' is – within this approach – a dynamic concept which stands out in the context of a conflict constellation between two poles. (…) By applying (…) the term to characteristic population groups in certain conflict situations, it makes sense for us to talk of an 'indigenous Africa'[35] (Kuppe 1990: 10f.). Specific societies with cultural particularities and a deep connection to their environment find themselves in tension with modern statehood equipped with exclusive and sovereign claims to power and obligatory legislative competence.

When the *ACHPR Working Group* speaks of the term "indigenous" and how it is used in the African context, it basically also means these specific conflict situations: "When some particular marginalized groups use the term indigenous to describe their situation, they use the modern analytical form of the concept (which does not merely focus on aboriginality) in an attempt to draw attention to and alleviate the particular form of discrimination they suffer from" (ACH-

---

33 Original citation in German.
34 Original citation in German. International law was full of "primitive" and "backward" terminology until the 20th century; a good example is ILO Convention 107 which categorized humans according to their stage of development and worked with today-anachronistic terms, such as "semi-tribal".
35 Original citation in German.

PR/IWGIA 2005: 88). Today's prevailing connotations and denotations of the concept of "indigeneity" are considerably wider than the exclusive question of primordialism. Now it is both a term and a global movement championing the rights of those groups, whose predominating development paradigms are perceived negatively. Modern states categorize the cultures and ways of life of these groups *inter alia* as backward and sometimes even see them as a "national disgrace". If nothing else, this causes indigenous groups to often experience discrimination, thus threatening their existence as it is (ACHPR/IWGIA 2005: 87):

"[I]t is indeed a fact that Africa is characterized by multiculturalism. Almost all African states host a rich variety of different ethnic groups (…). All of these groups are indigenous to Africa. However, some are in a structurally subordinate position to the dominating groups and the State, leading to marginalisation and discrimination. It is this situation that the indigenous concept, in its modern analytical form, and the international legal framework attached to it, addresses. It addresses the root causes of the subordination and it emphasizes the human rights dimension for addressing the issues" (ACHPR/IWGIA 2005: 113f.).

From a discourse analysis point of view, the close reading of the quote and the use of the notion "indigenous" points to a legal policy on the part of this Working Group. This unit obviously tried to call on the nation states to observe their obligations of protecting the weakest parts of their population. Keeping in mind the highly sceptical stance of many African states towards the term and its related legal problems of indigeneity, this cautious way of formulating reports meant for benevolent consent is more than understandable.[36] Everything ultimately revolves around having as many states as possible agreeing on the legitimate need of protection of indigenous peoples in Africa as well.

This approach stands in stark contrast to the often-voiced concerns that the situation of the African continent could not be compared to the historical conditions in North and South America, where states were similarly founded or ruled by European settlers after the *conquista* and colonial migration as it was the case on the Australian continent.[37] Such a differentiation between indigenous and

---

36 The majority of African states impressively exemplified this approach with regard to the *Declaration on the Rights of Indigenous Peoples*. At the Third Committee, the Namibian delegation brought forward a motion to defer action concerning a reassessment of the Declaration, thus proposing not to put it to vote at the General Assembly. 82 member states voted in favour including New Zealand, Canada, Australia, the United States and basically the whole African continent; 67 delegates voted against and 25 states abstained from voting (www.iwgia.org, Public statement 30 Nov. 2006). In contrast it should be mentioned that in 1999, indigenous representatives noted a lack of African Governments (except Libya, Morocco and Sudan) present at the meeting of the *Drafting Group for the Declaration on Indigenous Rights* and pointed to their obvious lack of interest (E/CN.4/2000/84, para. 41).

37 "[T]here had been this move historically to focus on uniting peoples against colonialism. So we are a bit of a hotchpotch, we have different bits of history which con-

settler societies could thus not be applied to Africa.[38] In my view this narrow understanding of the term ultimately leads to a wrong contradiction which interferes with constructive solutions in the mutual (negotiated) interest of all parties involved. Several African Governments simply postulate that "all Africans are indigenous" and thus refuse to accept the development of international law associated with the term. The rather cautious terms of *inter alia* "marginalized", "vulnerable groups", "certain forms of inequalities", or "sufferings" refer to this politically sensitive context.

From the general perspective of a wider legal discourse of indigeneity, however, we have to ask on the one hand whether legitimate claims to indigenous rights are not set aside right from the beginning because such soft and morally-motivated appeals to state benevolence towards "marginalized, vulnerable, oppressed, and suffering population groups" present some sort of preemptive obedience. On the other hand we should also ask whether in the medium run a de-essentializing definition of indigeneity would not work as well. Such a definition would interpret indigeneity as a relationship between various social groups, states, and local communities with regard to a defined piece of land ("territory") instead of being based on essential, biological-genetic or cultural characteristics.[39] In this relational sense, indigeneity describes the interrelation between social groups, including particularly the relationship between the entire population of a state and a local community which holds the older rights to a certain territory.[40] This could not only take away the threatening character of indigeneity but also make essentialist denotations which seem to be so problematic less relevant:

"It is suggested that the usefulness of a concept such as 'indigenous' cannot be found in a strict definition, but in the appropriateness of a number of characteristics that appear in various combinations. Indigenous, like ethnic, is a relational

---

tribute towards us being farely sensitive or hesitant of how to deal with difference" (Interview Alice Mogwe on 22 February 2005).

38   In times before decolonialization, all non-settlers and non-European inhabitants of European colonies were considered indigenous population groups. This process caused the definition of indigenous peoples to be closely connected to colonialism, with European settlement or, as it was the case in China, "saltwater settler colonialism" being used as the exclusive basis (Keal 2003: 8). Cf. also Stavenhagen, *Mission to South Africa* 2005: "This meaning ["indigenous" in contrast to minority European settler populations] is the norm in southern Africa where both Botswana and Zimbabwe regularly use the term indigenous to distinguish the black majority from the European and Asian settler minorities" (Stavenhagen 2006: para. 24).

39   It would also avoid the misunderstanding that the concept of "indigenous peoples" leads to tribalism and ethnic conflicts. Cf. ACHPR/IWGIA (2005: 88).

40   The term "indigenous" basically refers to a claim of validity to a certain territory on the part of indigenous peoples or nations. In contrast to those definitions which are based on genetic heritage, this understanding is connected to the original relationship to the land (Interview Roger Chennells 20 October 2005).

II. "Indigenous Peoples in Africa": Applying the Concept

term. A group is only indigenous in relation to another, encompassing group, and thus the meaning depends on the context" (Saugestad 2001: 228).

Such denotations would certainly allow for African states to regard all their populations as being indigenous. It would be conceivable in such a relative or better relational approach, however, to recognize former rights of certain indigenous communities in relation to other social groups and their society. Such a practice would not produce hierarchical categories of "more or less" indigenous communities but rather lead to a differentiation within a democratically negotiated relationship, which consciously recognizes historical conditions especially related to land rights. But this definition is without doubt neither understood nor accepted by all parties involved. Numerous discussions in various forums, however, are in favour of such a definition, e.g. the *Working Paper of Chairperson-Rapporteur Erica-Irene Daes* (1996: para. 64):

"Underlying the arguments made by many observer Government delegations is a conceptual critique of the use of the term 'indigenous' to distinguish between groups that have been neighbours for millennia. To the extent that the English and Spanish terms which are currently in official use in the UN system imply a distinction between persons originating in a country, as opposed to immigrants or settlers, the unease of many African and Asian Governments is understandable. Plainly, most of the persons who have control of the contemporary State are not less native to the soil of the country as a whole than groups that are identified as 'indigenous' or 'tribal'. It should be pointed out, however, that this conceptual difficulty disappears if we think of 'indigenous' peoples as groups which are native to their own specific ancestral territories within the borders of the existing State, rather than persons that are native generally to the region in which the State is located."

This relational definition could certainly counteract the understandable concerns that the development of indigenous rights would in many cases delegitimize the often fragile postcolonial African states. Such altered meaning could perhaps lead to more stable and rather comprehensive results concerning interests of indigenous protection than a discussion – see the quote from above of the *ACHPR Working Group* (in their report 2005) – that changes from a legal discourse to the moral discourse of state care and the particular custody over "marginalized and vulnerable groups".

Furthermore, this relational idea of indigeneity could perhaps help to further foster the key concept of indigenous peoples, which refers to "characteristic and severe conflict situations relevant for human rights" (Kuppe 1990: 11). Protective provisions can only be effective, if their contents are accepted and exceed the possible agreement to international declarations and future conventions. While it may be interpreted as progress when instruments protecting human rights exist on paper, several African examples have demonstrated that those who should enjoy the protection have not experienced too many positive changes. It would therefore be desirable to convince African Governments that a de-essentialist understanding of indigeneity does not equal the end to state sovereignty some seem to fear inordinate. In this sense we could talk of an indigenous Africa that is shaped by a complex set of relationships. Realizing this interdependence could help to solve and prevent conflicts. Such a refined concept of indigeneity could then be hopefully defined outside two rather problematic constrictions:

On the one hand concerning a definition that sees 'indigenous' only in the sense of 'aboriginal' as related to the ancestral population in European emigration states, and on the other hand concerning a recourse that seems almost cynical to the original meaning of the word which sees all populations born in a country as indigenous[41] (Kuppe 1990: 11).

---

41   Original citation in German.

III. Indigenous Rights in the African Context

There can be no doubt that the term "indigenous peoples" raises questions of state policy that are difficult to solve in the African context. While leading to various interpretations and controversial discussions, it is clear that some of its related, essential elements, static understandings of tradition, and evolutionist tendencies should be criticized and rejected. Nevertheless, this provocative thematization of former paternalistic relationships and forced ideas of development, which together see the (post)colonial state as the sole sovereign decisive power, stimulates a discourse of ("good") governance that is relevant to democratic and legal policies. In the end, those thought-provoking discussions make it possible to critically reflect on and get rid of the term's pejorative connotations of insinuating meanings of "primitive, backward, underdeveloped" etc. This is why the international community in general as well as (self-identified) indigenous peoples in particular increasingly understand this term as a "common road map" to recognize, analyze, and fight against certain forms of injustice and oppression.

This process, therefore, does not focus on establishing special rights for certain ethnic groups. Keeping in mind the historical experiences of colonialism, slavery and apartheid (also including white "positive discrimination"), such an objective would be highly questionable.[42] It rather revolves around universal rights against particular forms of injustice that are relevant for special cases and, thus, only to certain groups. This form of retributive justice is becoming more and more important in international law. As we cannot put an end to past injustices and they still influence our present and future, these sectors of law need a differentiation which makes it possible to combine compensation and protection:

"[T]he issue is that certain marginalized groups are discriminated in particular ways because of their particular culture, mode of production and marginalized position within the state. This is a form of discrimination which other groups within the state do not suffer from. It is legitimate for these marginalized groups to call for protection of their rights in order to alleviate this particular form of discrimination" (ACHPR/IWGIA 2006: 12).

In this respect, the claims of indigenous peoples do not present calls for "betterment", privileges, or "positive discrimination" but rather for protection based on but not sufficiently ensured by the general protection of human rights. Indig-

---

42   Cf. for example Suzman who assesses the applicability of ILO Convention 169 on the African continent: "It is wholly inappropriate to the peculiarities of the post-colonial African situation where memories of apartheid ensure that there is staunch opposition to the granting of special rights to any group solely or even primarily on the basis of their ethnicity or ancestry (…) Indigenous per se claim no greater legitimacy as a basis for special rights than blue-blood, white skin or red hair (…)" (Suzman 2002: 6).

enous rights should therefore not be regarded as special rights based on essential characteristics but as legitimate claims to eliminate all forms of discrimination.[43] In the following part I will analyze the opportunities existing institutions and legal provisions of Africa's regional organization present as a fundus for indigenous rights.

1. Regional Indigenous Rights

1.1 The African Charter on Human and Peoples' Rights

The Governments of the OAU member states are bound by the *African Charter on Human and Peoples' Rights (Banjul Charter)*[44] as a human rights instrument that reflects their culture(s) and social system(s). In contrast to its representation in European media, the African continent is home to a significant diversity of values and cosmovisions, which of course also manifests itself in the legal sphere. Not least because of the huge differences in Africa, this African human rights instrument is a unique and complex amalgamation of philosophical and legal dimensions, based on generations of human rights drafts.[45] It connects a wide range of "discursive spheres" which "acclimatize" fundamental principles to

---

43 Cf. also the substantial principle of equality in chapter 1, section III, 2.2.1. this volume.

44 The OAU adopted the *Banjul Charter* in 1981 which then entered into force on 21 October 1986; in the meantime all member states have lodged their ratifications with the Secretariat General. For the historical background, cf. Bortfeld (2005) or Ouguergouz (2003: 26–48). Ölz (2002) emphasizes the *Banjul Charter's* "difficult birth in the truest sense of the word" which would not have been possible without the contribution of NGOs, the UN and other stakeholders.

45 Many western states stress the fact that only the so called "first generation", thus civil and political rights, as liberal defense rights and democratic rights of participation are "real" human rights in the sense of subjective, individual rights that can be enforced against the state. The socialist conception of the "second generation", meaning economic, social and cultural obligation rights on part of the state, is also included in the "real" human rights. As the "third generation", collective rights of the peoples (of the south) shall add another dimension to human rights based on the philosophy of universalism. The most important rights of the "third generation" are the right of self-determination of peoples as well as the right to self-determined development. The "generation" terminology has its roots in the language used in the cold war; nowadays, the emphasis lies on the principles of universality, indivisibility and interdependence of all human rights (cf. Nowak (2003: 23f.). The rights of the "first generation" were established in the CCPR (1966), of the second in the CESCR (1966) and of the third basically as collective rights in Art. 27 CCPR, ILO Convention 107 and 169, in the 1992 *UN Declaration on Minorities* and the *UN Declaration on the Rights of Indigenous Peoples*. The *African Charter*, however, protects all rights in one single document without hierarchical preferences.

III. Indigenous Rights in the African Context

the African context (Thornberry 2002: 247). The Charter contains a preamble and a total of 68 articles divided into three main parts: the first 29 articles are dedicated to the material part and proclaim rights and duties; the second part is titled "measures of safeguard" and provides organizational as well as procedural provisions to establish the "African Commission on Human and Peoples' Rights" (*African Commission*), its competences and its rules of procedure; the last part named "General Provisions" stipulates norms for the Charter's ratification, entry into force and conditions for amendments.

The Preamble shows two significant definitions: first, that peoples' rights have necessarily to guarantee human rights,[46] and second, that rights and freedoms also imply the performance of duties on the part of everyone.[47] Both may be interpreted in a community-spirit way by emphasizing the strong collective way of thinking in the African context as well as in local communities. They are, however, ambiguous when they are contextualized, depending on the fact whether the term "peoples" is applied to the community or state level. "The notion of individual responsibility to the community is firmly engrained in the African tradition. (…) It is an open question, however, as to whether 'community' equals 'State'" (Thornberry 2002: 248).

Many African states, especially those with socialist systems, have not distinguished between the rights of peoples and the rights of states for a long time. Various forms of planned economy or centrally controlled economic systems turned the state into the sole owner of land, thus making the terms 'peoples' and 'state' exchangeable (Nanjira 2003: 223). So what does the term really mean in the *African Charter*? Articles 19–24 explicitly refer to "all peoples" but as it is the case with both 1966 UN Covenants, the *African Charter* does not define the term.[48] The *African Commission's Working Group of Experts on Indigenous Populations/Communities* interprets this silence in such a way that the former preconception is continued, which relies on determining the sense from existing legal instruments and norms (ACHPR/IWGIA 2005: 72f.).

---

46   Para. 6 of the Preamble: "(…) the reality and respect of peoples rights should necessarily guarantee human rights".

47   Para. 7 of the Preamble: "(…) the enjoyment of rights and freedoms also implies the performance of duties on the part of everyone (…)". Some authors see the stipulation of duties in a human rights instrument as dangerous because the duties could be used as as condition for enjoying the rights. A list of individual duties to the state is not an African phenomenon though. Para. 3 of the Preamble of the *American Convention on Human Rights* refers to the *American Declaration on the Rights and Duties of Man*, which provides such an extensive list of duties. Bortfeld (2005: 56) is right when he explains that such an imposition of duties is hardly relevant because they cannot be enforced through international trials but would have to be defined and enforced on a national state level.

48   See Nanjira (2003: 221–223) for a detailed discussion of the various definitions of "peoples".

At this point we can draw two conclusions: firstly, the *African Charter* seeks to arrange for group or collective rights. These rights can evidently be only enjoyed collectively, e.g. the right of self-determination, independence, or sovereignty. Secondly, keeping in mind the political environment of the time, the *African Charter* justifies the anti-colonial aspirations of the continent. Based on the principle of *uti possidetis*,[49] the OAU legally recognized the sacredness of the (arbitrary) colonial borders. Therefore, it is hardly possible to deduce any other definition of "peoples" from this provision than (a narrow) one based on the nation state (ACHPR/IWGIA 2005: 73).

Ouguergouz (2003: 204ff.) interprets the Charter's silence concerning the term "peoples" quite differently and comes to the conclusion that its authors deliberately refrained from explaining it. Behind this abstention may lurk the two related reasons to remain indecisive to a far-reaching definition on the one hand and open to future interpretations. Keeping everything said in mind, this controversial term may refer to any of four legal entities, each of which suggests a related facticity: the national population (or all citizens of a state), the population of a state (or all inhabitants of a state), peoples under colonial or racial domination, or the ethnic group (or human community integrated into one or more states). In his opinion, indigenous peoples are part of these latter societies and may be entitled to the legal status of "peoples" in the context of the *African Charter*:

"In our view, only these communities, to which 'indigenous' peoples and communities could be added, are eligible for the status of people in the context of the African Charter; and the alternative nature of this eligibility must be emphasized. The word 'people' is in fact a 'chameleon-like term' here, whose content is dependent on the function of the right concerned; it is the context in which the term is used that gives it its contours. In the African Charter, the people are therefore a social entity which varies in nature according to the right which is to be implemented" (Ouguergouz 2003: 211).

The *ACHPR Working Group's* interpretation of the term "peoples" in the *African Charter* was at first based on the historical context of the anti-colonial movement and state sovereignty, thus suggesting the denotation of "national population" or nation. This understanding seems to go hand in hand with the European idea of a nation state. Nonetheless, the *ACHPR Working Group* comes to the conclusion that the fundamental applicability and extensive interpretation of

---

49 This principle was originally developed in South America in the context of independence from Spanish and Portuguese rule to protect the territorial integrity within former administrative borders. It helped to avoid border conflicts by keeping the borders exactly as they had been under colonial rule. As these borders had often been drawn with the ruler, they cut right through ethnic communities or economic units (Cf., *inter alia*, Malanczuk 2003: 162 or Seidl-Hohenveldern 1997: 142). For the Latin American context of this doctrine, cf. Kuppe (2004: 48).

III. Indigenous Rights in the African Context

the *African Charter* could possibly also include indigenous peoples.[50] The *ACHPR Working Group's* interpretation has certainly changed from the national-state term "people" to the cultural diversity indicating term "peoples".

This change may suggest that the Working Group has tried to read the originally vague wording against the grain to replace it with a new and perhaps even contradicting denotation. At this point, the *ACHPR Working Group's* conclusion could indicate a paradigmatic shift from the original understanding of "peoples" as closely associated with the necessary, national liberation from foreign, colonial domination. In contrast to the OAU Charter which explicitly stipulated to "eradicate all forms of colonialism" in Art. II (d), the Constitutive Act of the *African Union* does not include such a provision. From the perspective of the *ACHPR Working Group*, this missing definition allows for new opportunities of interpreting the extended term of "peoples". When interpreting the *African Charter*, the present realities seem to demand for human rights protection of "vulnerable" groups and peoples within nation states, according to the *ACHPR Working Group*, and this fact should always be kept in mind (ACHPR/IWGIA 2005: 79)[51]: "No international human rights regime should be static and neither is the African Charter" (ACHPR/IWGIA 2005: 11).[52]

This allows us to conclude that the *ACHPR Working Group* assumes cultural diversity within the unit of a nation state and regards it as worth protecting. Keeping in mind the collective rights of indigenous peoples, the Working Group recommends the *African Commission* to continue and further develop the concept of "peoples" (ibid.: 115). Also the *African Commission* now encourages this "continuation" (discussed in the next chapter) due to recent, terminological discourses.

Although the Charter was evaluated in a mostly positive way, there are also critical voices which point to inherent tensions between, on the one hand the attempt to continue pre-colonial and anti-colonial essential ideas and "values", and on the other hand the clear definition of the *status quo* of existing postcolonial sovereignties.[53] They mainly address the contradiction between African historical

---

50 "The overall conclusion is (...) that the African Charter is an important instrument for the promotion and protection of the rights of indigenous peoples and communities (...)" (ACHPR/IWGIA 2005: 106).

51 Cf. in this matter, "The Working Group also takes the view that, as the African Charter recognises collective rights, formulated as rights of 'peoples', these rights should be available to sections of populations within nation states, including indigenous people (sic) and communities" (ACHPR/IWGIA 2005: 79).

52 This interpretation is rather teleological, thus referring to the objective and purpose of the international treaty pursuant to Art. 31 para. 1 of the *Vienna Convention on the Law of Treaties*. It therefore stands in stark contrast to originalism which combines the interpretation of the original meaning with an objective version of a historical interpretation.

53 Cf. Kuppe (1990: 8–16).

traditions and values, and the legal conception of a "type of state foreign to African tradition".⁵⁴ These values on which criticism is based are explicitly mentioned in Para. 5 of the Preamble: "Taking into consideration the virtues of their historical tradition and the values of African civilization which should inspire and characterize their reflection on the concept of human and peoples' rights".

It is definitely true that the Charter as well as a whole range of national constitutions reflect the unsolved problems and contradictions of both the political and legal decolonisation. Of course we have to ascribe to these processes the good will of eliminating the tremendous "sins of their colonial past" by adapting adequate postcolonial constitutions to African experiences. Some of the Charter's normative rights could also be used to protect indigenous peoples: in this respect, Art. 2 of the *African Charter* prohibits accessory discrimination "without distinction of any kind such as race, ethnic group, color, sex, language, religion, political or any other opinion, national and social origin, fortune, birth or other status." All signatory states are therefore obliged to ensure all rights established in the relevant conventions to all people without discrimination of any kind as well as to counteract particularly proscribed forms of distinction (Nowak 2002: 76).

This Article 2 of the *African Charter* corresponds to Art. 1 of the *American Convention on Human Rights* and Art. 14 of the *European Convention on Human Rights* (ECHR), with the only exception that the latter also explicitly mentions the term "minorities". The included list is obviously not exhaustive (hence the words "such as") but rather exemplary. It can therefore be argued that courts are able to employ further interpretations. Although the fundamental principles of non-discrimination and equality are limited to the rights included in the Charter, this restriction does not seem to be very restrictive because of the rather exemplary character of the list in Art. 2. As Bortfeld (2005: 41) argues, Art. 2 *African Charter* is worded in such an open manner that it could be used for restrictions to rights ensured by the signatory states, which are established in the Charter and thus legitimate, as long as these restrictions are not sufficient themselves for the principle of equality. It is interesting in this context that the *ACHPR Working Group* deduces the prohibition of discrimination from the fundamental principle of respect for human dignity (Art. 5 *African Charter*) and the right of equality (Art. 19 *African Charter*).⁵⁵

---

54 Kuppe (1990: 16): [The Charter] explains (...) the philosophy and legal conception of Africa but at the same time establishes rights – with completely different origins – of a type of state foreign to African traditions. The Charter then stipulates 'collective duties' towards some form of state which is becoming overly powerful exactly because of such rights. Original citation in German.

55 The latter goes as follows, "All people shall be equal; they shall enjoy the same respect and shall have the same rights. Nothing shall justify the domination of a people by another" (Art. 19 ACHPR). See also on this matter ACHPR/IWGIA (2005: 34–38).

III. Indigenous Rights in the African Context 99

The civil and political rights following the prohibition of discrimination are kept to a minimum. Art. 8, Art. 9 para. 2 and Art. 10 para. 1 guarantee the freedoms of conscience, religion, information, opinion, and free association under national statutory provisions. This means that the freedoms can be limited on grounds of public safety and order. Public order in particular is an opportunity of restriction that opens up a wide range of hardly-limitable justifications to intervene in the protected legal position. As similar provisions do not include such non-limitations to state authority, we have to ask whether or not the Charter falls behind international and national human rights instruments and even undermines them on the African continent. An interpretation of the whole text, however, leads us to the formal conclusion that the scope of limitations should be considerably put into perspective due to the introductory remark that the Charter adheres (*inter alia*) to the UN human rights standards and the provisions of Art. 60 and 61 (Thornberry 2002: 251).[56] Thus, the list of civil and political rights comprises several fundamental individual rights in the same manner as they are also included in universal and regional human rights documents. The guaranteed rights, however, are restricted by an impressive amount of clauses, which enable national legislation to intervene in these norms.

Art. 14–17 of the *African Charter* address economic, social and cultural rights, such as ownership, work, health, and education. The *African Commission* has established several guidelines for member states to report on measures they have undertaken to promote the understanding, tolerance, and friendship among all ethnic and religious groups as well as on special precautions for "children belonging to linguistic, racial, religious or other minorities, and children belonging to indigenous sectors of the population".[57] When it comes to these rights and especially their enforcement, the *African Commission* is definitely entering *terra incognita*. No other international treaty phrases these rights as clearly, not to mention as completely enforceable.[58] As the *African Commission* requires state reports, it

---

56 In Art. 60 ACHPR, "The Commission shall draw inspiration from international law on human and peoples' rights, particularly from the provisions of (...) the Charter of the United Nations, the Charter of the Organization of African Unity, the Universal Declaration of Human Rights (...)". In Art. 61 ACHPR, "The Commission shall also take into consideration, as subsidiary measures to determine the principles of law (...) African practices consistent with international norms on human and peoples' rights (...)." The Article, too, mentions customary law, general principles of law (recognized by African states) as well as legal precedents and doctrine.

57 The *African Commission* established these guidelines to extend the *African Charter*'s human rights and fundamental freedoms (Amnesty International 2006: 4). See the *Guidelines for National Periodic Reports II.47* and *II.48*, in the *Second Activity Report of the African Commission on Human and Peoples' Rights* (adopted June 1989), annex XII; cited in Thornberry (2002: 252).

58 Many European states have recognized only civil and political rights constitutionally as national, fundamental rights and still regard economic, social and cultural rights

seems to ensure the enforcement of the rights mentioned above. In consequence, there can be no doubt that the potential judicial implementation to enforce these rights can be affirmed (Bortfeld 2005: 49).

There are two things, however, that are uncertain in this context: first, the rights are phrased rather vaguely and appellatively;[59] second, their implementation depends on available resources but the question how much money should be spent for what is decided by judicial and executive authorities. Answering this question in court to some extent breaks with the principle of division of powers (ibid.: 49). If the *African Court on Human and Peoples' Rights* decides to address economic, social and cultural rights in the future, it will basically have to face a lot of new challenges. It is quite difficult to predict whether the Court will at least be able to define the central areas. It seems even more problematic, however, for the court to establish enforcement and to control as well as enforce, if necessary, that states observe binding court rulings (ibid.: 51).

Art. 19–24 of the *Banjul Charter* comprise the rights of peoples: Art. 20 para. 1 stipulates the "right of all peoples" to self-determination; Art. 21 the free disposal of their natural resources. In the context of the legal protection of indigenous peoples, Art. 21 para. 2 is especially relevant because it provides the binding principle of compensation for dispossessed people, "[I]n case of spoliation the dispossessed people shall have the right to the lawful recovery of its property as well as to an adequate compensation." Art. 22 governs the peoples' right to their own development; para. 1 contains the provision that, "[A]ll peoples shall have the right to their economic, social and cultural development with due regard to their freedom and identity (…)."

This is the first time that positive rights of development are connected to the idea of freedom and self-determination of indigenous peoples.[60] It also expresses a versatile concept of development that is not exclusively reduced to economic aspects anymore. In addition, these provisions oblige states to ensure the exercise of the rights mentioned above. And finally, Art. 24 proclaims the right of peoples to a satisfactory environment. All these collective rights have been and still are mostly denied to indigenous peoples. Therefore, their recognition is not only a le-

---

as "not actionable" at the international level. The *European Social Charter*, often called the "little sister" of the *European Convention on Human Rights*, does not establish these rights as strigently and bindingly. When ratifying the Charter, signatory states can choose "*à la carte*" which rights they regard as binding. Apart from that, only two thirds of all *Council of Europe* states have already ratified the *Social Charter*, whereas countries are required to ratify the ECHR to become members of the *Council of Europe* (Nowak 2002: 189).

59 How fair and satisfying must be working conditions, for example, under Art. 15 ACHPR?

60 See also the *ACHPR Working Group's* report (2005: 20f.).

III. Indigenous Rights in the African Context

gal breakthrough but also an actual precondition for their chances to survive in the future. As the *ACHPR Working Group* explicitly emphasizes:

"Such fundamental collective rights are to a large extent denied to indigenous peoples. (...) The different types of human rights violations experienced by indigenous peoples all boil down to this fundamental issue: many marginalized indigenous peoples in Africa are denied the right to exist as peoples and to determine their own development" (ACHPR/IWGIA 2005: 57).

In the following part, I will first present the *African Commission on Human and Peoples' Rights* and then discuss how the *African Commission* deals with these young categories of rights.

1.2 The African Commission on Human and Peoples' Rights

Based on Art. 30,[61] the *African Charter* established the *African Commission* as its sole genuine body of protection. While its official inauguration took place in 1987, its permanent secretariat was established in Banjul, The Gambia two years later. As only two ordinary sessions are held every year, the secretariat is of crucial importance. The Commission consists of eleven members, "chosen from amongst African personalities of the highest reputation, known for their high morality, integrity, impartiality and competence in matters of human and peoples' rights" (Art. 31 para. 1 *African Charter*).[62]

Chapter II *African Charter* stipulates the mandate of the Commission: to promote human and peoples' rights (Art. 45/1)[63], to ensure their protection (Art. 45/2) and to interpret all the provisions upon request (Art. 45/3). The *African Commission* has three monitoring procedures at its disposal but each of them is significantly less efficient than their counterparts in comparable universal and regional conventions (Nowak 2002: 228). While one of its tasks is to examine state

---

61   Part II of the *Banjul Charter* includes provisions concerning the *African Commission*: Art. 30–40 administrative provisions, Art. 45 its mandate, Art. 46–59 its procedures and Art. 60 63 the Commission's applicable principles.

62   The members are elected by secret ballot by the *Assembly of Heads of State and Government* for a six-year renewable term. The AU Assembly is the supreme decision body of the *African Union*, decides on amendments and extensions of the *Banjul Charter*, considers the Commissioners' activity reports and can add additional tasks to its mandate. But principally it decides on the Commission's cases of severe human rights violations (cf. Bortfeld 2005: 60). Only men could become members of the Commission until 1993. After NGOs demanded to include women, the Commission has begun to have female members as well. Today more than half of all Commission members are women (in 2013 seven).

63   In 1998, the Commission specified what this promotion of human rights should look like: its "Mauritius Plan of Action" initiated promotion measures, such as the "African Day of Human Rights" on 21 October, the anniversary of the day the ACHPR entered into force.

reports, it is one of the least intervening mechanisms of control into state sovereignty.⁶⁴ This procedure also reveals serious shortcomings: almost half of the members have not even submitted their initial reports, others have not submitted their periodic reports or have only presented them orally before the Commission (Bortfeld 2005: 74).⁶⁵

As the *African Commission* protects human and peoples' rights, it assumes quasi-judicial functions. All African States, with the exception of Morocco, are parties to the *African Charter*. On becoming a party, States automatically accept the complaints procedures (ILO/ACHPR 2009: 13). The *Banjul Charter* provides two kinds of parties entitled to bring forward complaints before the *African Commission*: member states by means of communications (Art. 47–54) and individuals by means of so-called "other communications" (Art. 55–59). While the first has only happened once,⁶⁶ the latter leads to a much more feasible individual complaints procedure, which not only victims but also NGOs as well as other groups⁶⁷ and individual may use to assert "the existence of a series of serious or massive violations of human and peoples' rights" (Art. 58 *African Charter*).⁶⁸ Victims, however, are not subjectively entitled to a procedure because the Commission considers their complaints only by majority vote. Even then, the matter is only pursued, if it is possibly related to massive and systematic human rights violations.

So far, the *African Commission* has been highly flexible and interpreted the *African Charter* quite liberally (Ouguergouz 2003: 560). It understood the phrase "a series of violations" as either a violation affecting a series of individuals or repeated violations affecting one individual. A procedure may be initiated because

---

64 Pursuant to Art. 62 ACHPR, "[E]ach state party shall undertake to submit every two years (…) a report on the legislative or other measures taken with a view to giving effect to the rights and freedoms recognized and guaranteed by the present Charter."

65 Botswana, for example, has not submitted any report at all yet (ACHPR/IWGIA 2008a: 90). Nevertheless, the issue of indigenous peoples shows slow progress: when states presented their reports at the 29th Ordinary Session, it was the first time that the *African Commission* asked the member states about their measures to protect the human rights of indigenous peoples (ACHPR/IWGIA 2005: 78).

66 Cf. Communication 227/98, *Democratic Republic of Congo v. Burundi, Rwanda and Uganda*. Nonetheless, it works similar to the Inter-American Human Rights System where no state has filed a complaint yet; only under the *European Convention on Human Rights* sixteen state complaints had been lodged until 2012.

67 This means that this is a real *actio popularis*.

68 In accordance with Art. 56 ACHPR, formal prerequisites for communications to be considered are: knowledge of their authors (name, address, profession and age), exhaustion of local remedies unless it is obvious that this procedure is unduly prolonged and the existence of the principle of *ne bis in idem* (meaning that a procedure was not and is not pending at the universal level, e.g., before the *UN Human Rights Committee* or the *CERD Committee*). It is neither required for the victim and the author to be the same party, nor for the complainant to be citizen of a state (cf. Ouguergouz 2003: 559).

of one "massive" violation, but a violation may also be of that character due to special circumstances (Bortfeld 2005: 79f.). If a communicated violation has been recognized as a relevant case to initiate a complaints procedure, the *African Commission* informs the state concerned and asks for a statement.[69] If the Commission does not receive an adequate reaction, it will be entitled to conclude its considerations and submit recommendations based on existing evidence. Their consideration, however, only follows the tradition of "naming, blaming, shaming" regardless whether they try to solve a present conflict or just want to confirm the violation of rights.[70]

Anyhow, the Commission submits the results of their considerations to both the state concerned as well as to the *Assembly of Heads of State and Government*. Similarly the Assembly can only recommend appointing a commissioner as *special rapporteur* to further examine the case (Art. 58 *African Charter*). This has – probably not by accident – never happened though. In its first 15 years since its foundation in 1987, the *African Commission* has received 289 individual complaints (Bortfeld 2005: 78).[71] Although the big picture allows us to detect a symbolic commitment to human rights, its actual implementation faces the priority of the member states' sovereignty as an obstacle it can hardly overcome in the regional context (this basic thrust is also highly relevant for indigenous rights to be recognized).

In times of increasing mediatisation (in African countries as well), we should of course not underestimate this symbolic significance which is also playing a major role for the conditionalities related to the allocation of development funds. Although states that are not cooperating will not face any legal sanctions, public opinion can put states under pressure to "behave". The *African Commission* may also put states under pressure by appointing *special rapporteurs* for specific purposes, such as monitoring whether states observe the rights of women as well as indigenous peoples' needs of protection. NGOs cooperate quite well with the

---

69 Art. 57 ACHPR.
70 Cf. Viljoen/Odinkalu (2006. 28). "[T]he Commission is a quasi-judicial body. Its decisions do not carry the binding force of decisions from a court of law, but have a persuasive authority akin to the opinions of the UN Human Rights Committee."
71 In 2001, for example, the *African Commission* found a clear violation of the rights of the indigenous Ogoni community in Nigeria, including their rights to freely dispose of their natural resources (Art. 21 Banjul Charter). Cf. *The Social and Economic Rights Action Center and the Center for Economic and Social Rights v. Nigeria* (ACHPR 2002; Com. No. 155/96). In 2009, the *African Commission* found violations resulting from the displacement of the Endorois community, an indigenous community in Kenya, from their ancestral lands, failing to adequately compensate them for the loss of their property, disruption of the community's pastoral enterprise and violations of the right to practice their religion and culture, as well as the overall process of development of the Endorois people (ACHPR 2009; Com. No. 276/03). Cf. www.caselaw.ihrda.org

Commission which (not least because it is always short of staff) depends on their professional knowledge.[72] In addition, NGOs have been the driving and supporting force behind a legal body to be established within the African system.

At this point it should be emphasized, though, that the *African Commission* does not even hold the power of final decision in its "own" procedures because of the Commission's close organizational and procedural connections to the *Assembly of Heads of State and Government*. A procedure assumes regional and geopolitical character as soon as the Assembly decides to intervene. In this case, the Commission does not only lose a lot of its power but also its significance. Although it receives external funding, it is extremely limited in terms of finances and, thus, in effectively exercising its tasks. This is why it is hardly surprising that, at least in the beginning, it phrased its goals rather vaguely and lacked clear words for human rights violations in some sort of preemptive obedience.[73]

1.3 The African Court on Human and Peoples' Rights

As the Commission does not have the power it would need as mentioned above, the demands for a court of justice voiced by organizations of groups concerned as well as other forces of civil society become increasingly important. In this respect, the role of international comparable examples such as the *European Union* should not be underestimated, especially because "Africa" (in the context of the OAU and its successor organization AU) does not want to lag behind the developments in other regions of the world. Entered into force on 1 November 1998, Protocol No. 11 to the *European Convention for the Protection of Human Rights and Fundamental Freedoms* (ECHR) significantly upgraded the Strasbourg system of legal protection. In this process, the *European Court of Human Rights* (ECtHR) became a full-time court with permanent judges (Nowak 2002: 179). Around the same time, to be exact on 10 June 1998, the OAU *Assembly of Heads of State and Government* adopted an additional protocol to the *Banjul Charter* to

---

72 NGOs may be granted observer status which offers them a lot more opportunities than any status with other human rights institutions. They are entitled to participate in public sessions as well as to add additional items to the agenda. As it is not limited to African NGOs, 447 (March 2013) NGOs have been granted observer status. The Commission has no choice but to depend on the work of NGOs due to its difficult organizational situation suffering from a lack of funding, a shortage of staff and the occasional wrong person for a task (Bortfeld 2005: 64ff.).

73 For a detailed assessment of the Commission, see Bortfeld (2005: 56–74). In his conclusion of the year 2003, he stated that when it comes to realizing their tasks, the Commission's work could and also needs to be improved. *Amnesty International* shares this sentiment in their annual report 2007: "The African Commission on Human and Peoples' Rights (…) continued to be denied the much needed human, material and financial resources to fully respond to the many human rights problems in the region."

establish an *African Court on Human Rights*, the only regional court existing in Africa today.[74] It came into effect on 25 January 2004 but – in contrast to the *European Court of Human Rights* – states are not obliged to become members; 26 states had ratified the protocol by March 2013.[75]

The preamble of the protocol emphasizes that "freedom, equality, justice, peace and dignity are essential objectives for the achievement of the legitimate aspirations of the African peoples". It also points out that the *Banjul Charter* is only one of several legal sources among other human rights instruments. The Preamble (para. VII) explicitly mentions that the establishment of an *African Court on Human and Peoples' Rights* is required to complement and reinforce the functions of the *African Commission on Human and Peoples' Rights*. This may also be interpreted as indicating that the OAU admitted the Commission's lack of range. Anyhow, the court now serves as the second protective institution next to the commission,[76] thus suggesting equal power of both bodies in terms of protective tasks.[77]

The second judicial institution is the *African Court of Justice*, which was established under the 2003 *Protocol establishing an African Court of Justice*. Its role would have been to adjudicate matters related to economic integration and of political nature, such as border disputes. Although this Protocol has in fact been

---

74 In 1991 at the first NGO workshop, the demand for a judicial body was voiced for the first time. In June 1994, the *Assembly of Heads of State and Government* passed a resolution for the OAU Secretary to commission a draft. Afterwards, the development process did not go that smoothly: three expert conferences and four councils of ministers took place; as the member states did not show much interest (although asked repeatedly, they neither submitted statements nor showed up at the conferences), a conference of ministers of justice was created. In the end, diplomatic representatives had to be summoned to force member states to discuss the protocol (Bortfeld 2005: 93ff.).

75 A minimum of 15 states had to ratify the additional protocol. Although the protocol had been ready to be ratified since June 1998, the required quorum was only achieved in December 2003. As we can see here, states continued not to be interested in the ratification as well. In the meantime, all but two states (Cape Verde, Eritrea) have signaled their agreement by signing the protocol. Cf. www.african-court.org/en/index.php/documents-legal-instruments/basic-documents as of 06/26/2012.

76 For a detailed discussion of the African court concerning its historical and political background, its jurisdiction and procedures as well as comparisons to the *Inter-American Court of Human Rights* and the ECtHR, see Ouguergouz (2003: 688–756) and Bortfeld (2005: 96–147). The latter detects significant structural deficiencies in the additional protocol, manifesting itself in a combination of institutional, administrative and jurisdiction-wise determinations and procedural provisions (ib. 95f.).

77 Bortfeld (2005: 97, 222–225) is right to emphasize that tasks that are not sufficiently distributed do not only lead to double the work but also to overlapping responsibilities. As it is for example the case with the *Inter-American Commission* and the *Inter-American Court of Human Rights*, the commission could also insist on its responsibilities without adequately including the court. The *African Commission*, however, vehemently advocated the direct access without optional declaration for complainants.

ratified by the required 15 AU member states, this Court has not become operational – and will in all likelihood not emerge in the near future. The *African Court of Justice* may therefore rightly be described as 'still-born', despite the fact that the Protocol establishing this Court entered into force on 11 February 2009 (Viljoen 2012). The explanation why the AU is not bringing this Court to life lies in the political agreement to merge the two courts into a single institution. At the 11th AU Summit (in July 2008), the *Assembly of Heads of State and Government* finished the merging process by adopting the *Protocol on the Statute of the African Court of Justice and Human Rights*. One of the reasons for merging two separate courts was the lack of resources.[78] Fifteen state parties need to ratify this Protocol to secure its entry into force. By 2013, only five states, namely Benin, Burkina Faso, Congo, Libya and Mali, have become a party to this Protocol, indicating that the political will to set up this Court is weak.

The court consists of sixteen instead of the former eleven independent judges[79], all of which except the President of the Court are elected for a period of six years on a part-time basis.[80] The new *Statute of the African Court of Justice and Human Rights* stipulates that each geographical region of the continent should, where possible, be represented by three judges except western Africa with four judges (Art. 3/3). In terms of egalitarian principles the provisions of Art. 7 (5) are quite unique because they establish an equitable gender representation. If the states do not keep this in mind when electing their judges, the *Assembly of Heads of State and Government* will intervene.[81] The seat of the "new" court will be the same as the seat of the ("old") *African Court on Human and Peoples' Rights* (Art. 25/1 new Statute), which the AU General Assembly established in Arusha, Tanzania.

As the new name of the "African Court of Justice and Human Rights" suggests, it covers two fields of jurisdiction. This becomes quite obvious in its internal organization with functions assigned to two different sections. The "General

---

78   Cf. www.africancourtcoalition.org as of 09/11/2008.

79   See Art. 3 as well as Art. 12 for the clause of independence of the *African Court of Justice and Human Rights*. The judges must be nationals of AU member states (not necessarily signatory states!), qualified jurists, or at least have recognized competence and experience in the fields of international law or human rights law (Art. 6 Abs. 1).

80   A part-time court brings with it the disadvantage of significantly elongated proceedings, thus of course staying the effect of legal protection. It goes without saying that this lack of efficiency also goes hand in hand with their constantly worsening reputation. In addition we have to question whether the court will be able to find top jurists for such a part-time employment, especially if the position is not prestigious enough.

81   In contrast to these provisions of equality, there has been quite a difference in theory and practice at the *African Court on Human and Peoples' Rights*: nine male but only two female judges (Viljoen/Chidi 2006: 31). Comparing these numbers to the other two regional systems of protection, only nine female judges (out of 44 positions) are employed at the ECtHR and the *Inter-American Court* has had only one female judge (1989–1994) who prematurely resigned from the post (Bortfeld 2005: 99).

Affairs Section" has jurisdiction over all cases pursuant to Art. 28 of the new Statute, except all cases relating to an alleged violation of a human or peoples' right. Such cases as well as all disputes that are subject to relevant human rights instruments fall within the competence of the "Human Rights Section" (new Statute Art. 17/2).[82] One of the peculiarities of this assignment of competences is the opportunity to claim human rights established by various legal instruments. Other regional courts only have jurisdiction over cases related to their own human rights Conventions.[83] While Art. 7 of the *African Court on Human and Peoples' Rights* still limited the sources of law to "provisions of the Charter and any other relevant human rights instruments ratified by the States concerned", Art. 31 of the "Merged Court" Protocol extends applicable law to international custom, general principles of law and any other legal sources relevant to the determination of a case.

While the vast majority of AU member states is still struggling to ratify the "Merged Court", the *African Court on Human and Peoples' Rights* has begun its work and delivered its first judgement in 2009. In accordance with Art. 5 (3) of the *Protocol of the Establishment of the African Court on Human and Peoples' Rights*, the following entities are entitled to submit cases to the court: states, the Commission, African intergovernmental organizations, and national human rights institutions. When it comes to complaints by individuals and NGOs, Art. 5 (3) refers to Art. 34 (6) of the Protocol which is a clause to accept the court's competence. The court has optional jurisdiction over individual and popular actions. When ratifying the Protocol or at any time thereafter, however, member states may make a special declaration accepting the competence of the court. Only five states, Burkina Faso, Ghana, Malawi, Mali, Rwanda and Tanzania had submitted such a declaration to the *Human Rights Court* by 2013.

Individuals and NGOs can still sue states but they first have to involve the *African Commission* to immediately transfer the case to the court by submitting an individual communication pursuant to Art. 55 *African Charter*.[84] Court judge-

---

82 Relevant human rights instruments are both regional African treaties (*African Charter on the Rights and Welfare of the Child, OAU Convention on Refugees, Protocol to the African Charter on Human and Peoples' Rights, Protocol on the Rights of Women in Africa*) and universal treaties (e.g., the two human rights Covenants, *Convention on the Elimination of All Forms of Discrimination against Women, Convention against Torture, Convention on the Rights of the Child*), see Art. 3 of the Additional Protocol ACHPR.

83 This extended jurisdiction involves the danger of colliding decisions by different international bodies though. As international law shows a lack of enforcement, this could negatively affect the unity of the international law system and thus jeopardize legal certainty.

84 Although this provision may be disappointing, an optional clause protects state sovereignty and makes it easier for states to ratify the Protocol (Bortfeld 2005: 142).

ments obtain both formal and material legal effect.[85] According to Art. 28 of the Protocol, "[T]he judgment of the Court shall be final and not subject to appeal." The formal legal effect of judgements does not mean that they cannot be revised: Art. 28 (3) provides the opportunity of revising a judgement, if new facts have been discovered. Art. 30 lays down the material legal effect of a judgement: parties must comply with the judgement in any case to which they are parties and guarantee its execution within the time stipulated. States are basically free in how to execute the judgement. In addition, compensation in material legal effect is included by obliging states to act. The *Assembly of Heads of State and Government* in form of the "Executive Council of Ministers of the Union" is entitled to monitor the execution of judgements.[86] The court also has a further monitoring mechanism at its disposal because it has to submit to the General Assembly a report on its work and include the cases in which a state has not complied with the judgement (Art. 31 *Protocol of the African Court on Human and Peoples' Rights*).

As the *African Court on Human and Peoples' Rights* has only existed for a short time (the Court delivered its first judgement in 2009; it has received 24 applications and finalized 11 cases and rendered decisions thereon by June 2012) and the newly merged *African Court of Justice and Human Rights* is still in ratification process, it is hardly possible to say anything about the consequences for indigenous peoples. Compared to its counterparts around the world, the court offers some potential: its crucial competence of considering complaints brought forward by individuals (*ratione personae*), for example, is completely left out at the *Inter-American Court of Human Rights*.[87] The previous version of the *European Court of Human Rights* did originally not have the competence to consider individual complaints either. In accordance with the new *European Convention on Human Rights*, any person, non-governmental organization or group of individuals may bring a complaint before the court but only if they can claim to be the victim of a violation themselves (Art. 34 amended ECHR). NGOs can therefore not submit such an "application" to report a violation of rights against others.

As NGOs are often legally trained, they are crucial in the African context because the concept of indigenous rights is relatively new and indigenous peoples are not as experienced in taking legal steps. In addition, NGOs are also equipped to

---

85 In accordance with Art. 28 (1), judgements are to be rendered within ninety days of having completed the deliberations. Pursuant to Art. 28 (2), they have to be decided by a majority of the judges present and the reasons on which they are based must be stated as well (Art. 28 (6)).

86 This is the successor body to the OAU *Council of Ministers* and, pursuant to Art. 10 *Constitutive Act*, consists of the ministers of foreign affairs or other ministers of the member states (Bortfeld 2005: 205f.). Following the European example, the General Assembly commissioned the Executive Council to monitor judgement execution (Ölz 2002: 381).

87 Art. 61 *American Convention on Human Rights*.

both reach people in remote areas and exchange experiences rather quickly because of two developments: first, they have established networks of national, regional, and global cooperation; and second, the vast distribution of virtual communication technology. In line with Art. 55 *African Charter*, a communication of violation to the *African Commission* is sufficient for an NGO initiative. After considering the communication, it may be forwarded to court. If the state concerned has declared its acceptance of the court's competence, there is also the opportunity of direct intervention by bringing a claim directly before the human rights Court. The protocol to the *African Human Rights Court* has refrained from establishing nationality (to a signatory state or an AU member state) as a legitimate precondition for the court to consider communications by NGOs. This is why also international NGOs such as *Amnesty International* can contest violations of rights on behalf of indigenous peoples. Experience has shown that this alone increases the chances of success because more financial resources are involved. The structure and independence of these relatively powerful organizations is crucial as well.

At this point in time, we can only notice the basic potential of the consequences the *African Court on Human and Peoples' Rights* has for the promotion and protection of the rights of indigenous peoples. Only time will tell whether the court will be able to pursue the direction the Commission has set and address this matter so delicate in many African states. In spite of all the political opposition, the related lack of funding and staff, and the public critique of the last couple of years, the *African Commission* has achieved quite a bit in (symbolically) advocating the rights of indigenous peoples. Although it depends on the good will of its member states, the Commission is not as cautious as in the beginning anymore and has appointed a *Working Group of Experts* to learn about the situation of indigenous peoples and the adequacy of the concept in the African context. The *ACHPR Working Group* does not only ask relevant institutions of member states about the measures undertaken for indigenous peoples, it also encourages those concerned to obtain observer status at the *African Commission*. Furthermore, it understands the term "peoples" in such a way that it is possible for indigenous peoples to claim legal protection as provided by Art. 19–24 of the *African Charter*. Finally, the *ACHPR Working Group* internationally championed the right of indigenous peoples and took a stand for adopting the *UN Declaration on the Rights of Indigenous Peoples*.[88]

---

88 In his letter of 20 November 2006 to the *Permanent Mission of the Republic of Namibia to the UN, acting for the African Group at the UN*, the *Chairperson of the African Commission's Working Group on Indigenous Populations/Communities* called on the UN General Assembly to support the UN Declaration: "We firmly believe that the UN Declaration (…) as adopted by the Human Rights Council is essential for the survival, dignity and well being of Indigenous Peoples."

2. National Indigenous Rights

In the last couple of years, it has become more and more evident that some African nation states are about to revaluate their position regarding the full recognition of "their" indigenous peoples. There is a growing number of African States which have taken steps that signify an emerging sensitivity towards indigenous peoples (rights). These steps are, for instance and primarily, the ratification of ILO Convention 169 by the Central African Republic (in 2010); but also the promulgation of "Law No. 5-2011 of 25 February 2011 on the promotion and protection of the rights of indigenous populations of the Republic of Congo"; the adoption by the Cameroonian Government of an *Indigenous Peoples Development Plan* and the elaboration of similar plans in Gabon and the Democratic Republic of Congo; the inclusion of a Batwa representative in a national land commission by the Burundian Government; the new Kenyan National Land Policy that addresses indigenous peoples' land rights; and the land restitutions (to the ≠Khomani San and the Richtersveld Community) in South Africa (cf. Barume 2010: 225f.). In the following part, I will compare and discuss some examples of national developments in the realm of state law towards the possible protection of indigenous peoples in Africa.

2.1 Selected Constitutional Guarantees

First and foremost it should be mentioned that basically all African constitutions guarantee the fundamental freedoms, contain human rights clauses, and refer to the 1948 *Declaration of Human Rights* (Nanjira 2003: 216). But, unlike the constitutionalization of indigenous rights in the three Commonwealth countries Australia, Canada and New Zealand[89] as well as Latin America in the 1980/90s,[90] the African continent has hardly followed this legal advancement in the field of collective human rights. As the *ACHPR Working Group of Experts* emphasized some years ago, "very few African countries recognise the existence of indigenous peoples in their countries. Even fewer do so in their national constitutions or legislation" (ACHPR/IWGIA 2005: 47).[91]

---

89 Cf. for example Bartlett (1999) for Australia; Asch (1999) for Canada; and McHugh (1999) for New Zealand.

90 Most Latin American constitutions, e.g., in Bolivia, Colombia, Peru, Venezuela, Ecuador and Mexico, even recognize the right to an own indigenous jurisdiction with own bodies. For a detailed state overview concerning the rights of indigenous peoples to cultural identity as well as the undisturbed relationship to their territories, see Daes (2001: para 105).

91 For *UN Special Rapporteur* Stavenhagen the legal development of indigenous rights are long overdue to counteract persistent abuses against indigenous peoples: "Despite a changing legal environment, however, human rights violations of indigenous peoples continue to be reported" (2002: para. 33).

III. Indigenous Rights in the African Context

Only one state explicitly protects indigenous rights in its Constitution: the Republic of Cameroon. The preamble of its 1972 Constitution (amended in 1996 and in 2008) contains fundamental and human rights, which are recognized as integral elements of the Constitution and therefore are of direct and normative character.[92] It affirms the belief in the fundamental freedoms enshrined in the *Universal Declaration of Human Rights*, the *Charter of the United Nations* and the *African Charter on Human and Peoples' Rights*, and all duly ratified international Conventions relating *inter alia* to the protection of indigenous rights: "[T]he State shall ensure the protection of minorities and shall preserve the rights of indigenous populations in accordance with the law" (para. 5.2).

Of course this rather general wording makes us wonder whether this constitutional guarantee should be interpreted restrictively or extensively.[93] We can assume, however, that Cameroon consciously wanted the Constitutional amendment (No. 96-06 of 18 January 1996) to be a statement for the protection of indigenous rights. However, we should keep in mind the international context of the *UN Decade of Indigenous Peoples* declared in 1994 and its symbolic importance in international development cooperation circles. Similar to Botswana (with its large San population), Cameroon enjoys much more attention concerning its indigenous-related policies and legislation due to the country's "Pygmy" societies, the Bedzan, Bakola-Bagyeli and Baka. In this respect, the constitutional statement of respect ensures the increase not only in symbolic capital in terms of international recognition for the state but also in terms of development funding. As mentioned above, it is increasingly connected to the human rights conditions of respect for, participation of, and protection of indigenous peoples. As the first paragraph of the preamble suggests, the amendment associates the preservation of cultural diversity with the idea of national unity:

"We, the People of Cameroon, Proud of our linguistic and cultural diversity, an enriching feature of our national identity, but profoundly aware of the imperative need to further consolidate our unity, solemnly declare that we constitute one and the same Nation (...)."

---

92   Art. 65 *Constitution of Cameroon* 1996: "The preamble shall be part and parcel of this Constitution". This article certainly is significant because preambles are generally not regarded as directly legally relevant. It usually rather consists of a mission and vision, while stating and explaining the objectives of the treaty or act (Creifelds et al. 1997).

93   The Report by the ILO in cooperation with the *African Commission's Working Group on Indigenous Communities/Populations* and the *Centre for Human Rights*, University of Pretoria, regarding the constitutional, legislative and administrative protection of the rights of indigenous peoples in 24 selected African countries, sees this constitutional guarantee rather restrictively: "Doubt may be expressed as to whether the use of the term 'indigenous' in this case refers to what is understood under UNDRIP" (ILO/ACHPR 2009: 19).

Still the question remains whether the extensive interpretation has also been able to legally take into account further developments of indigenous legal protection since the Constitution's amendment in 1996. The *European Court of Human Rights* has made it clear for the European context that it is the court's task to use court rulings to adapt the fundamental rights established by the *European Convention on Human Rights* (ECHR) to the changed social reality (Öhlinger 1999: 284). Unfortunately we can only speculate whether such an "evolutionary understanding" would be imaginable for indigenous legal aspects in Cameroon. In this sense, "all duly ratified international conventions" indirectly addressed by Cameroon's Constitution would be subject to constitutional law. This would also include Conventions protecting indigenous peoples with respect to substantive law, such as ILO Convention 169, both UN Covenants (1966), and other legal instruments. As Cameroon has not enacted any laws specifically for indigenous rights, such a reference to the constitutional character of indigenous legal protection could become quite relevant in case of conflicts. Keeping in mind the contextual interpretation of the Constitution, the state would also have to fulfill its explicit duty of protecting "traditional values" (as long as they conform to democratic principles, human rights and the law).[94]

Cameroon, too, faces the problems of its legislative and administrative duties of protection in its enforcement: "The failure of States to implement or enforce existing laws for the protection of indigenous lands and resources is (…) a widespread problem" (Stavenhagen 2002: para. 42). Specifying such protective duties is exactly one of the primary competences of legislators. If institutions do not fulfill these duties, the sometimes rather pathetic constitutional narratives will remain nothing but "dead paper". And if legislation fails in such a way, there is basically almost nothing anybody could do to counteract this failure. Now, if a so-called "action of warranty" existed against legislative institutions, the beneficiary protected by constitutional law could bring a claim of implementation against the legislator.

As Öhlinger (1999: 284) suggests when discussing a possible future development of law, fundamental rights are not only regarded as (negative) constraints of legislation anymore but they are also values ("principles") obliging legislators to positively implement them. Positive actions by a state, such as identifying, demarcating, and declaring indigenous territories, is a basic prerequisite to implement the harmonious constitutional narratives in legislation; non-constitutional laws realize therefore a *conditio sine qua non* of any adequate and effective protection. In Cameroon, only Art. 8 (1) of the 1994 *Law on Forest and Fauna* recognizes the "resident communities" rights of use but neither does it establish the right of ownership nor monitoring right for indigenous peoples. In consequence,

---

94   Art. 1 (2) "The Republic of Cameroon shall be a decentralized unitary State. (…) It shall recognize and protect traditional values that conform to democratic principles, human rights and the law (…)."

III. Indigenous Rights in the African Context

both the legal situation for the "Pygmies" and the protection of Cameroonian forest eco-sites are precarious (Barume 2002: 3).[95]

In comparison to Cameroon's Constitution, the following Constitutions establish nothing more but a general prohibition of discrimination: Angola 1992, Kenya 1998, Lesotho 1993, Malawi 1994 (as amended 2001), Mozambique 2004, Tanzania 1977 (as amended 1997), Zambia 1991 (as amended 1996) and Zimbabwe 1979 (as amended 2005).[96] The 1995 *Constitution of Uganda* (amended in 2005) at least provides the right of participation and the right to be legally heard in state (development) programmes and plans for undefined "minorities".[97] It also includes the extensively interpreted freedom of collective practices (including the freedom of religion).[98] Nonetheless, this protection of minorities can only be used to protect indigenous rights, if it conforms to international human rights instruments and institutions, especially the *United Nations Human Rights Council*. As mentioned in the first part of this book, the Council's interpretation of Art. 27 of the *UN Covenant on Civil and Political Rights* (1966) suggests a universal legal opinion. This opinion derives the adequate protection of indigenous territories from the right to cultural identity (as confirmed by Uganda's Constitution) because the indigenous way of life is connected to a certain way of using resources, which then in turn points to the necessary protection of land rights.[99] Hence, the protection of cultural identity does not bring any explicit positive rights of ownership with it but the interpretation provides similar substantive protection.

When it comes to Uganda, we should always keep in mind (not least because of its postcolonial past of genocide, ethnocide, and civil wars) that "positive discrimination", as stipulated by Art. 32 of the 1995 Constitution, for marginalized groups can also be abused as well.[100] As some authors have stressed for other contexts, it would be as well possible to argue in favour of assimilative in-

---

95 For the consequences to and the revision of the *Forest Act* in 2011 as well as the general situation of indigenous peoples in Cameroon, see the *International Work Group for Indigenous Affairs* (2007: 525–529; 2012: 475–480).

96 In the Ethiopian Constitution (1994), the definition for nation, nationality and people (Art. 39 para. 5) may be implicitly used for "indigenous peoples" as well, although the term "people" is used synonymously with the terms "nation" and "nationality".

97 Art. 36 of the 1995 Constitution of Uganda: "Minorities have a right to participate in decision-making processes and their views and interests shall be taken into account in the making of national plans and programmes."

98 Art. 37 of the 1995 Constitution of Uganda: "Every person has a right as applicable to belong to, enjoy, practise, profess, maintain and promote any culture, cultural institution, language, tradition, creed or religion in community with others."

99 See in this matter the above-mentioned *General Comment of the HRC on the rights of minorities*, No. 23 on Art 27 CCPR: para 7 (1994).

100 Art. 32 of the 1995 Constitution of Uganda: "Affirmative action in favour of marginalised groups. (1) Notwithstanding anything in this Constitution, the State shall take affirmative action in favour of groups marginalised on the basis of gender, age, dis-

terventions under the label of "state promotion and adaption to other population groups" instead of eliminating present forms of discrimination: It appears *prima facie* the main objective of such promotive measures to elevate the members of (a) discriminated group(s) through all reasonable efforts to the standards of the privileged group(s). In this context, however, the background of these standards, namely the criteria and values of mainstream culture, remain unquestioned. Affirmative action under such auspices ultimately serves the purpose of taking on the semblance of a pretended ideal of equality (Kuppe 2004: 49).

According to these warnings, the (legitimate) claim of indigenous peoples should not end with the compensation of historical injustice and the elimination of present discrimination. Indigenous legal protection may rather stretch further to comprise the preservation of their independent cultural expressions as well as achievements in communication.

In relation to these considerations the 1990 Constitution of Namibia proclaims a list of fundamental and human rights and establishes the right of every citizen to practice their culture (Art. 19). It certainly stands out as a unique document because it applies to principles of general transformation to international agreements.[101] As Namibia ratified the *UN Covenant on Civil and Political Rights* (in 1994), the *UN Covenant on Economic, Social and Cultural Rights* (in 1994), and the *UN Convention on the Elimination of All Forms of Racial Discrimination* (in 1982), these documents became elements of Namibian law and thus legally binding. All three international treaties offer indirect ways of protecting indigenous rights and can be used by indigenous peoples to achieve similar protective standards as provided by their special rights.[102]

As the Constitution of Botswana is discussed in a separate part (4) of this book, I will only address the Constitution of South Africa (1996) at this point. It explicitly provides the term "indigenous" in the context of language rights and mentions the languages of the San, Khoe and Nama by name.[103] Furthermore, it protects self-determined communities in the preservation of their cultural identity against

---

ability or any other reason created by history, tradition or custom, for the purpose of redressing imbalances which exist against them."

101 Art. 144 of the 1990 Constitution of Namibia: "(...) unless otherwise provided by this Constitution or Act of Parliament, the general rules of public international law and international agreements binding upon Namibia (...) shall form part of the law of Namibia". In Botswana, however, international agreements become effective only when relevant laws are enacted ("special transformation"; cf. Boko 2002: 104f.).

102 Cf. Part 1 "Universal Human Rights Treaties". There have been no signs of their application yet; but anyhow, the legal position of indigenous peoples in Namibia is stronger than in other countries due to this constitutional provision (Harring 2004: 70). In this context we have to always ask whether or not international treaties are specific enough to be applied by nation states.

103 See Section 6 (5) of the *Constitution of the Republic of South Africa Act 108* of 1996. Cf. also the *Report of the African Commission's Working Group of Experts on Indigenous*

III. Indigenous Rights in the African Context

violent assimilation and discrimination.[104] The Constitution of South Africa additionally provides for the establishment of the *Commission for the Protection of Rights of Cultural, Religious and Linguistic Communities* (Art. 185). This Commission follows the mandate of monitoring, examining, training, educating, lobbying, consulting, and reporting on matters related to the rights of cultural, religious and linguistic communities. After the formal end of apartheid, these constitutional provisions are associated with the prevailing idea of national reconciliation.

Within this historical context, it becomes obvious why constitutional prescriptions for nation-building in South Africa preferred the terminology of "communities" over the usual terms "minorities" or "indigenous peoples". It goes without saying that this process, based on the enormous distortion of a political and social community (namely apartheid), is highly sensitive and requires particular caution. South Africa is facing the immensely complex situation of eliminating extreme inequalities, compensating, if possible, for past injustices, and still creating a common state of a multitude of partially politically organized, ethnic groups. The main focus is oriented on the one hand towards protecting or even promoting minority rights, while on the other hand questioning the (exclusive) awareness of minorities for the benefit of a common national identity. Like other states, South Africa tries to strengthen the loyalty of minorities to an emerging nation and to turn former enemies into fellow citizens. Kymlicka (2004: 70f.) regards this process as a joint African project as well as an ultimately global phenomenon:

"I believe that most African countries are nation-building in this sense. As we have seen, this nation-building takes different forms in different African countries, some of which have little in common with Western forms of nation-building. But each form of nation-building puts its own pressures on minorities, and it is only reasonable to expect that they will respond by seeking to modify these nation-building policies, to ensure that they are not disadvantaged by them. In my view, justice in multi-ethnic countries will always require some balancing of nation-building and minority rights."

Although – as Kymlicka stresses above – the situation on the African continent is different for each country, many postcolonial African states show clear tendencies of centralizing the control over land and resources for the benefit of national unity.[105] At the dawn of independence, numerous indigenous peoples in

---

Populations/Communities (205: 48f.); and Tong (2003: 3). See chapter 3 this volume for the definitions of the terms San, Khoe and Nama.

104 See Section 31 of the *Constitution of the Republic of South Africa Act 108* of 1996: "Persons belonging to a cultural, religious or linguistic community may not be denied the right, with other members of their community, to (a) enjoy their culture, practice their religion and use their language; and (b) form, join and maintain cultural, religious and linguistic associations and other organs of civil society."

105 For a legal comparison of Angola, Zambia and Zimbabwe, see Akpan/Mberengwa/Hitchcock/Koperski (2004).

many African countries who had preserved at least some of their self-determination under colonial rule became inconvenient obstacles to nation-building due to the often (if at all) democratically weak and politically hardly communicated measures of nationalization. More often than not, development projects and state dispossessions turned them into illegal occupiers of now state territory. For this matter the legal or constitutional recognition of indigenous land rights is a crucial precondition for their further legal protection. It offers indigenous peoples a politically reliable instrument to take a stance against unilateral state development plans and other threatening scenarios, which originate from states institutions, multinational corporations, and other groups that are usually competing for resources. Only a rights-based approach gives them a chance to effectively counteract the various interests which as a rule are opposed to their self-determined development. If such a legal recognition does not or not sufficiently exist, indigenous peoples have no choice except launching media campaigns and contacting international institutions and/or taking legal actions to protect their right of ownership. As not a lot of African cases of indigenous land rights have already been through all stages of the appeals process, I would like to use the well-documented South African legislation as an example.[106]

2.2 Jurisdiction using the example of South Africa

However dynamically and flexibly the term "indigenous peoples" is interpreted and applied in various African contexts and environments, they all share the essential significance of (land) rights. Legal disputes are fed by emancipatory interests in accordance with present relations of power. They are certainly not based on a "blood and soil ideology" (as argued by Adam Kuper 2003) which has hardly any empirically verifiable importance whatsoever in the cosmovision of indigenous peoples. With all due caution against making exaggerated generalizations, this cosmovision is generally based on a complex community of all living beings and even "living nature", thus opposing the motive of the utilitarian and ethnocentric appropriation of land (Kuppe 1998a: 106f.).

The economies of indigenous peoples in southern Africa do not only include (subsistence) agriculture and the keeping of cattle but also – in the case of the

---

106 Also cf. for the Ogiek of Kenya: Stavenhagen (2002 Add.1). The collective claim of "immemorial occupation" of the Barabaig (Tanzania) was dismissed because only individual claims are considered. In 1999 the *Court of Appeal* ruled that the Maasai were not entitled to any rights based on "immemorial occupation". See Barume (2010: 86–105) for an overview of indigenous peoples' land claims in Kenya and Tanzania (Barume 2010: 123–138). In Namibia the Khoe filed an "aboriginal title" claim which was never processed because politics had interfered (Barume 2002). See also ILO/ACHPR (2009) "Overview Report on the constitutional and legislative protection of the rights of indigenous peoples in 24 African countries".

San – (to an increasingly limited extent) hunting and gathering. In consequence, their territories are crucial to their physical survival but also to the spiritual conception of an often integral cosmovision of holistic interconnectedness.[107] Particularly in the various religious contexts, many indigenous peoples emphasize the obligation to their ancestors to preserve the land. As Mathambo Ngakaeaja (interview 24 February 2003), one of Botswana's most important San representatives, impressively describes, the communication with these ancestors is extremely important in both religion and the spiritual geography of their ancestral lands:

"This is also the case for the Bushmen, because when we go hunting, and we come across a site where our forefathers had been buried, we do respect them, and we do talk to them and we go: 'Oh, my grandfather, I am here, help me, we are going to go hunting, please bless my hunting.' So we do communicate with them in a way that is still showing that we have a lot of links with those ancestors. So our burial sides are still of great value and significance to us."

In past legal disputes, indigenous representatives used similar arguments and thereby caught the attention of the media. They stressed that the undisturbed relationship to their territories – next to practicing their language and culture – is a crucial element in preserving their self-determined but fundamentally alterable cultural identity – in contrast to some indelible perceptions of their static primordial existence. As these litigations of land were primarily related to historical events and the assertion of past injustices, legal discourses focused on the unilateral dispossession of land in colonial times and during apartheid in southern Africa. Since the beginning of European settlements, both the ruthless dispossession of land by European intruders and the measures to protect the economic and hegemonic interests of "settlers" under colonial law have conflicted with local populations.[108]

2.2.1 The Case of the ǂKhomani San

When the (South African) "Southern Kalahari San" lodged a land claim in 1999, it was the first time that a state's official recognition of indigenous self-organization and a specific form of *empowerment* became evaluated. In the early colonial phase, the San as well as other groups were either expelled from newly dedicated farming regions or integrated as a cheap workforce in commercial farming. In the second phase of territorial reorganization, the colonial government established reservations and homelands, which forced the San to live in smaller territories and suffer from unfavourable environmental conditions (Hohmann 2003: 21). Then in the 20th century, national parks were founded in the context

---

107 See, e.g., B. Söfterstad (1998: 12).
108 "[T]he expansion of international society cannot be separated from dispossession, genocide and the destruction of cultural identity" (Keal 2003: 35).

of state environmental protection (as discussed above) and caused further relocations and dispossessions of San communities.[109]

So the ‡Khomani San shared a similar "destiny" with many indigenous peoples in southern Africa: the forced eviction from the *Kalahari Gemsbok Park* just after its formation in 1931.[110] At the end of the 20th century – the time of renewal after the formal end of apartheid – they were supported by South African human rights attorney Roger Chennells and the *South African San Institute* (SASI). Together they referred to legislation which particularly focused on the restitution of lands and was supposed to remedy as far as possible injustices based on former discriminating laws and practices.[111] They claimed land use rights within the national park as well as six farms totally comprising 36,900 hectares of land south of the park. The parties involved[112] needed two phases of negotiations to settle their disputes out of court.

Of course we have to keep in mind the aforementioned atmosphere of renewal and a lot of good will to "eliminate" the past injustices that affected the negotiations.[113] In the first phase of negotiations, the farms which the San claimed as former community land were returned. When the second phase ended in August 2002, the San were able to successfully claim further 25,000 hectares of land within the *Kgalagadi Transfrontier Park* and enjoy significant cultural, symbolic, and commercial rights in an additional area that comprised about half of the former *Kalahari Gemsbok Park*.[114] In this context, religious and cultural rights were central to the negotiations:

"The San were awarded cultural and heritage rights over the entire area of their original land claim. (…) In this area they were to be entitled to visit, and to carry out various medicinal, gathering, cultural, educational and related activities" (Chennells 2006: 4).

---

109 See section I.1. of this chapter.
110 In 1999, this park merged with Botswana's "Gemsbok National Park" and formed the renamed "Kgalagadi Transfrontier Park", the first international and transboundary "Peace Park" in Africa; cf. Pabst (2002: 14–17).
111 *Restitution of Land Rights Act 22* of 1994, the claim was formally lodged before the *Northern Cape Land Regional Claims Commissioner* in 1995.
112 The parties involved were the *Department of Land Affairs* representing the government, the ‡Khomani San, *South African National Parks* (with the ironic acronym SANParks) and a group of Mier farmers.
113 Also in South Africa the idea prevails that extra-judicial settlements in form of mutual agreements have much more sustainable effects than unilateral court rulings.
114 For further details concerning the second phase of the land claim as well as the "!Ae!Hai Kalahari Heritage Park Agreement", see Chennells (2002: 51–53 and 2006: 2–4). Cf. also an assessment from a different source: "This agreement, seen in contrast to the client-relationship persisting in other Southern African states' interaction with 'their' indigenous peoples or 'remote area dwellers', stands out as a remarkable breakthrough towards a rights-based approach and legal readjustment of historically strained relations" (Zips/Zips-Mairitsch 2007: 45).

III. Indigenous Rights in the African Context

Although the ǂKhomani San with their leading elder Dawid Kruiper were granted indigenous land rights while recognizing the spiritual relationship to their territories, their situation today remains ambivalent. Even the most benevolent and sophisticated form of restitution is not able to turn back time as such. When it comes to a collective group that had to "reinvent" itself after decades of complete fragmentation, legal agreements have only limited effect (Roger Chennells, interview 9 February 2007). As these "indigenous communities" are considered homogenous social units, they rather are constructs of NGOs and legal specialists involved than actually existing collectives with related structures of organizing and decision-making. This should not mean that they could not reclaim certain of their former organizational principles and competences; yet, after the legal and political decisions in their favour, they find it difficult to live up to some perhaps unrealistic expectations of a new bright future, nurtured among themselves as well as in NGO circles. How to use the partially regained resources for their economic upliftment still remains as thorny a social landscape as the bush veld they love so much.

During several travels and interviews with ǂKhomani San involved, I learned that a lack of concepts following a legally successful land claim could cause much frustration and even more internal social conflicts. Before continuing this discussion, I should mention that "the" ǂKhomani San, if ever at all, have not formed a social unity of whatsoever kind in the last couple of decades.[115] The following two factors contributed to disputing opinions and even conflicting ideologies between two "camps" which could quite imprecisely be distinguished into "traditionalists" and "modernists": First, their social composition is far from being homogenous; and second, individuals and small groups who had been completely dependent on external labour for a long time were not easily able to develop the expected "management plans" for the cultivation of restituted farm land. This process went hand in hand with two leading figures dividing the community in such a "(party) political" dimension that was previously unheard of.[116]

As Roger Chennells (interview 20 October 2005) implicitly suggests, the following observable signs are but a few factors for the disappointing aftermath of the original "groundbreaking success story": the six restituted farms went rack

---

115 While the current number of members of the ǂKhomani San community has surpassed 700 individuals, the original group that lodged the claim consisted of 350 adults (Chennells 2006: 4). This number could rise even more due to the growing awareness of development and income opportunities from the land rights agreement. It is still unclear which rules of inclusion and exclusion are applied to define membership rights and grant access to ǂKhomani San resources (Robins 2001: 246).

116 "The ǂKhomani San did not have any prior tradition of hierarchical decision making, or of representative structures. As the claim progressed, so the institution that represented this essentially broken and then re-formed community went through different stages" (Chennells 2006: 5).

and ruin, the (by far too small) region outside the national park was overhunted, hopes of development remained unanswered, tourists stayed away, conflicts within the community developed, and people suffered from further serious social problems, such as poverty, alcohol abuse, or domestic violence:[117]

"The Kalahari Transfrontier case was a reconstruction of a community that had lost everything, and I think, it has been very positive, because the Government has generally put a framework in place, that allowed the legal settlement to happen. Now the crisis that is happening on the ground, the development crisis, began as the San peoples tried to start becoming managers of the land, as opposed to peoples who belong to a landscape. That is a transforming process that is taking place now. People now have their land; it is their traditional land, but circumstances have changed and they are busy finding their feet."

2.2.2 Richtersveld Case
The Richtersveld community mainly consists of Nama including some individual San who married in.[118] Their ancestors were semi-nomadic herding people in the province of Northern Cape and shared the same culture, including language, religion, social and political structures, and certain forms of land use, which were relevant to the decision of the *South African Supreme Court* in the so-called "Richtersveld case":

"One of the components of the culture of the Richtersveld people was the customary rules relating to their entitlement to and use and occupation of this land. The primary rule was that the land belonged to the Richtersveld community as a whole and that all its people were entitled to the reasonable occupation and use of all land held in common by them and its resources" (*Supreme Court of Appeal of South Africa* 2003, para. 18).

In 1847 the British Crown annexed the Richtersveld territory but local communities suffered from forced dispossession only after large diamond deposits were discovered in 1925. The Government (of the South African Union) immediately claimed the whole territory as inalienable Crown Land on which only the Government was entitled to mine diamonds. Step by step, the community lost access to its traditional areas of settlement. Under apartheid as well, the community was banned from entering their territories. In 1994 after the formal end of apartheid and the first free democratic elections, the property rights of Richters-

---

117 See also Robins (2001 and 2003a: 375–380). *UN Special Rapporteur* Stavenhagen discusses the same problems in his "Addendum Mission to South Africa" (E/CN.4/2006/78/Add.2, para. 40).

118 The Nama are a subgroup of the Khoe; the Dutch gave them the derogatory name "Hottentotten" which even found its way into German literature. "Khoe means 'a person' in many languages and is also the name of the largest of the three families of languages. (…) However, as an ethnic (not linguistic) label it has been used to refer to people who come from a mainly herding tradition" (Saugestad 2004: 23).

III. Indigenous Rights in the African Context

veld were transferred to the state-owned diamond company Alexkor. This was the time when the power of a court to change the situation and restore the former legal status was revived (Chan 2004: 116).

As a result, the descendants of the former indigenous community of Richtersveld actually lodged the first direct land claim in December 1998. The claim contained two separate claims to be exact: one to land restitution under the *Restitution of Land Rights Act*[119] before the *Land Claims Court of South Africa*; one to restore the land rights based on the claim of an *aboriginal title* before the *Cape High Court of South Africa*. The community then decided to wait with the second claim until the first one was decided based on the *Restitution Act*.[120] The reasons for that were quite simple: on the one hand a rather pragmatic position that it was easier to prove the claim under the *Restitution of Land Rights Act* which was explicitly established to deconstruct the system of racist-motivated injustices; on the other hand the realistic expectation that the *Land Claims Court of South Africa* could refer in its decision to "indigenous law ownership" or "aboriginal title" as part of the lodged claim.

After the Anglo-Boer wars, the newly founded 1909 Union of South Africa enacted numerous repression laws and thus radically limited all civil and human rights for non-white South Africans. The *Restitution of Land Rights Act*, however, mainly addressed dispossessions as result of the *1913 Native Lands Act*.[121] This law was enacted to control the land ownership of the "native" population and forbade the predominant majority to purchase, rent or cultivate land outside of territories designated for Blacks. These territories comprised only 7.5 percent of the whole country. It therefore paved the way for the later homelands and racial segregation legislation which deprived Black South Africans even of their most fundamental civil rights and institutionalized the ideology of separate ("apart") development (Zips 2008). Keeping in mind these specific historical conditions, the discussion on the existence of a right to lands that vests in an indigenous community may be regarded as equivalent to the "aboriginal title" in South Africa.

---

119 Since the year 1994, the South African Government has sought to reverse the dispossessions of the apartheid regime. "During apartheid, over 85% of South Africans did not have the vote and could not legally own land" (Chan 2004: 114). South African parliament established the *Restitution of Land Rights Act* as well as the *Land Claims Court* to ensure an effective and fair land reform.

120 The crucial article for a land claim is *Art. 2(1) Restitution of Land Rights Act, No.22* (1994) stipulating as follows:
"A person shall be entitled to restitution of a right in land if –
d) it is a community or part of a community dispossessed of a right in land after 19 June 1913 as a result of past racially discriminatory laws or practices and
e) the claim for such restitution is lodged not later than 31 December 1998."

121 At this time, the legal foundations of the later apartheid regime were laid, the main architect being Hendrik Verwoerd.

Excursus: "Aboriginal Title"

For the purpose of better understanding this subject matter, I consider it as crucial to offer a short comparison to the term "aboriginal title". While it is characterized in comparable jurisdictions as *native title, indigenous title* or *Indian title*, Australia and Canada call the doctrine of original land ownership (or traditionally maintained vested rights) of originally resident populations "aboriginal title". In Anglo-American case law, the related legal opinions were formed by courts recognizing (in so-called precedents) that certain indigenous land rights had survived colonial rule. This is why relevant decisions were usually named after the individual claimants.

In the 1990s, the concept of the aboriginal title became really famous because of the "Mabo case",[122] which in direct consequence of positive law was integrated into the Australian code.[123] Also in other regions of the world, indigenous peoples began claiming their rights over certain territories they (had once) owned. As a result, the colonisation of settled or occupied territories first developed from a historical and social-scientific discourse to a legal one and its manifold consequences kept the Supreme Courts of so-called "settler colonies" busy. South Africa may historically be seen as a very special case with the uniquely monstrous development of legal apartheid. International law recognized three effective ways to acquire sovereignty: occupation of *terra nullius* meaning uninhabited territory; conquest; and cession (Mabo 1992: para. 33).[124] As most of the territories Europeans "discovered" were inhabited though, various theories to justify their acquisition of sovereignty found their way into colonial policies. On the occasion of a 1919 court decision, Lord Sumner explained:

"The estimation of the rights of aboriginal tribes is always inherently difficult. Some tribes are so low in the scale of social organization that their usages and conceptions of rights and duties are not to be reconciled with the institutions or

---

122 *Mabo and others v. Queensland* (No.2) (1992) 175 CLR 1 F.C. 92/014. In 1981, the Meriam community lodged a land claim. They were agricultural indigenous peoples from the Torres Strait Murray Islands who lived in permanent settlements. In 1992, the *High Court of Australia* recognized a form of native title which granted them the right to their traditional territory in accordance with their rights and customs.

123 The doctrine of the aboriginal title is nothing new and was developed by Spanish jurists in the 15th and 16th century (Bartlett 2000: 73). It was mainly Francisco de Victoria who concluded that, "the aborigines in question were true owners, before the Spaniards came among them, both from the public and the private point of view" (Lindley 1926: 128, cited in MacKay 2004: 87). His theories of an "indigenous title to ownership" were incorporated into Spanish, Dutch and British laws and thus applied to their colonial territories. As early as 1823, the *Supreme Court of the United States* mentioned them in their recognition and affirmation of an aboriginal title (Johnson v. McIntosh [1823] 8 Wheat 543 USSC).

124 Cf. for the classification of territories as well as for methods of acquiring sovereignty: McNeil (1989: 110–133).

the legal ideas of civilized society. Such a gulf cannot be bridged. It would be idle to impute to such people some shadow of the rights known to our law and then to transmute it into the substance of transferable rights of property as we know them."[125]

The grounds to this decision seem to be outrageous today but at that time they conformed to the prevailing evolutionist assumptions of anthropology. According to the various versions of these "theories of savages", the territories were regarded as "no man's land" (*terra nullius*) and thus ready to be appropriated. When the Europeans "discovered" new territories and expelled the local population, they justified their actions by officially establishing the indigenous peoples' "lack of interest in property" and regarding them as "uncivilized". It was therefore ultimately a question of power relations and its related *raison d'état* to qualify which political unity was "civilized" enough to be entitled to (ownership) rights. As basically no colonial power was consistent in its decisions, they decided rather pragmatically and arbitrarily on the recognition of land rights:

"Some African polities, including Swaziland, Morocco, Algeria and Tunisia, were accepted as states, with the implication that they were civilised. Others might not be treated as states, but might still have recognised legal systems" (Bennett/ Powell 1999: 459).

In the course of the 20th century, the idea of connecting *terra nullius* to a "lack of civilization" lost its grounds not least because of the advisory opinion in the *Western Sahara Case*.[126] It did not matter how colonial property was acquired: if (indigenous) peoples concerned showed some sort of social organization, they were entitled to bear rights from that time on. These rights included property rights which derived from their indigenous legal systems. According to objections to these legal interpretations, it may have been possible for pre-colonial (indigenous) rights to have survived colonisation but only if the new colonial governments had recognized them by means of an executive or legislative act of positive law. This is how the two opposing doctrines of recognition and continuation of indigenous rights developed.[127] The latter is based on the legal assumption that private property rights continue even after a change of sovereign-

---

125 *In re Southern Rhodesia* [1919] (60) AC 211 PC, pp 233–234. In this case, an African ruler claimed the right of ownership on behalf of his people against the *British South African Company* of Cecil Rhodes which was commissioned to "conquer lands on behalf of the Crown".

126 *Western Sahara Case 1975* ICJ Reports 12. Morocco and Mauretania annexed the former Spanish colony since 1884 of Western Sahara without their inhabitants' agreement. In accordance with the advisory opinion of the *International Court of Justice*, the annexing states had to recognize the inhabitants' right of self-determination (Akehurst 2003: 331f.). In addition, it declared the concept of *terra nullius* to be obsolete. See also Mabo [1992], Judge Brennan, para 40f.

127 For a detailed discussion of both doctrines, see: McNeil (1989: 165–179).

ty. The majority of colonial decisions was made because of this assumption which then again became (legally) pragmatic with the momentum of legal certainty.[128] Therefore, all legal titles would have been uncertain for an indefinite period until they were explicitly recognized. In the meantime, however, all inhabitants would have been unauthorized trespassers on their own land. Today the doctrine of continuation is unquestioned in Anglo-American legislation.[129] And in addition, parties claiming the termination of pre-existing rights have to take on the burden of proof (McNeil 1989: 177f.).

Courts recognize this principle of indigenous customary rights which – under certain conditions – continue even after the (post)colonial acquisition of sovereignty as *common law* or as a *sui generis* legal norm. As already mentioned, legal titles to land ("aboriginal title") are recognized because of the specific indigenous system of customary law. National or international courts have then declared this system to be directly legally valid. These "aboriginal titles" are considered either a "burden" to the genuine law of the Crown (as in Australia) or a "unique" characteristic (*sui generis*), "[which] must be understood by reference to both common law and aboriginal perspectives" (*Supreme Court of Canada*).[130]

Notwithstanding the legal source mentioned here, "aboriginal title" can also be applied based on international customary law: as I have explained in the first part of this book (indigenous rights as part of international customary law), many legislations, court rulings, treaties, resolutions, international conferences, conventions, and scientific papers provide ample evidence for the existence of both elements of customary law: a state practice (*usus*) which occurs out of the belief of obligation that the relevant practice is legally binding *(opinio iuris)*. This means for the "aboriginal title" that the doctrine becomes enforceable in national courts as international customary law: "Because international law is deemed to be part of our law, it follows that, to the extent that aboriginal title is internationally recognised, the doctrine becomes enforceable in our courts" (Bennett/Powell 1999: 451).

If you want to claim "aboriginal title", you will have to fulfill certain principles. Although these principles are different in all national legislations, a few general

---

128 As Lord Sumner argues, the cases of *In re Southern Rhodesia* [1919] AC 211 (PC), *Amodu Tijani v. Secretary*, Southern Nigeria [1921] AC 399 (PC) and *Bakare Ajakaiye v. Lieutenant-Governor*, Southern Provinces [1929] AC 679 (PC) support, amongst others, the doctrine of continued pre-existing property rights: "[U]pon a conquest it is to be presumed in the absence of express confiscation or of subsequent expropriatory legislation, that the conqueror has respected (private property rights) and forborne to diminish or modify them" (*In Re Southern Rhodesia*, p 233).

129 Cf. Mabo [1992], Justice Toheey, para 27f., Calder [1973], para 195ff.

130 Delgamuukw [1997] at 1081. See also Borrows/Rotman (1997: 25) in respect of the existence of Aboriginal rights in Canada: "A *sui generis* approach will place 'equal weight' on each perspective and thus achieve a true reconciliation beween the [European and Aboriginal] cultures".

trends may be observed.[131] The essence of *aboriginal title* is the factual proof that the claiming party or its ancestors had occupied the relevant land at the time of colonisation: "[O]ccupation is a matter of fact involving exclusive physical control of land, coupled with an intention (usually implied) to hold or use it for one's own purposes" (McNeil 1989: 201).[132]

In a legally relevant sense, occupation by indigenous peoples is based on three components: first, land use which requires a relationship to their customs and ways of life; second, the exclusion of other groups from their territory; and third, a temporal factor. These components are based on the concept of interest in indigenous (customary) law, which includes the relevant community's undoubted claim to occupation or use of the land. This claim to property or use must then be so evident and stringent that a special relationship between the community and its territory was (historically) established and is thus recognized by third parties.[133]

Experience shows that these requirements are only unproblematic for agricultural economies because cultivation is based on a permanent relationship to land. Providing legally relevant evidence of occupation becomes a lot more difficult in case of non-permanent ephemeral activities (such as hunting and gathering in a certain area). Here a territorial relationship focusing on occupation was *a priori* not undoubtedly established and is therefore extremely difficult to prove. This is, however, not the case in as many so-called hunting and gathering communities as state discourses in colonial (but occasionally also in postcolonial) times sometimes claimed:

"Whatever the perceptions of early British colonists, however, modern anthropological research has revealed that few hunting and gathering groups are indiscriminate wanderers. On the contrary, they tend to be attached to definite areas, where they often have spiritual ties, are familiar with the resources available, and are able to keep conflict with potentially rival groups to a minimum. Boundaries may or may not be clearly defined, and there may be peripheral strips of shared or no man's land, but generally a group's territorial range will be known both to its members and to neighbouring groups" (McNeil 1989: 202f.).

When courts now evaluate cases of former occupation, they usually base their decisions on an indigenous (legal) perspective and ask whether their connection to the lands ecologically conforms to the lands' condition and meets the econom-

---

131 See, e.g., Mabo [1992], Judge Toohey, para 29–39, concerning British, Australian and North American requirements.
132 Cf. *Delgamuukw v. British Columbia* [1997] 153 DLR, para 145, in which the court only required evidence of exclusive occupation. If present ownership was used as evidence for pre-colonial occupation, continuity between both was required.
133 Mabo case, Judges Dean and Gaudron, para 16. In this context, the Privy Council states in *Amodu Tijani v. Secretary, Southern Nigeria* [1921] 2 AC 399 (PC), p 197 that British concepts of ownership are not adequate for their assessment.

ic and cultural needs of the community.¹³⁴ Regardless of national contexts, nowadays courts seem to share the awareness that the character of occupation is not necessarily constant and that it inevitably changed because of the contact with "settlers". While a possibly still-existing and substantial relationship to the lands is increasingly used as a central feature, courts also pay attention to the indigenous recognition of normative foundations and customs in the dynamic context of their ancestors' traditions (Bennett/Powell 1999: 465).

At this point I should note that indigenous cultures and practiced traditions are in many cases hypostatized as far too homogenous and static. These legal opinions are in line with the stiff evolutionist assumptions this work discusses (and criticizes because of its mistaken essentialist categories and untenable consequences) at several points of the book. In terms of control over land, the exclusive character of occupation of lands, meaning the practice of excluding all others from the lands, is a crucial factor claimants have to prove:

"As to the extent of their occupation, it would include not just land in actual use by them at any given moment, but all land within their habitual range, for occupation, once acquired, is not necessarily lost by temporary absence (particular if seasonal), so long as the intention and capacity to retain exclusive control and return to the land continue, and no one else occupies it in the meantime" (McNeil 1989: 204).

As courts want to keep in mind the specific situation of each indigenous community, they are usually not too strict about this extent of occupation.¹³⁵ Therefore, the claimant's proof of occupation does not have to prejudice the fact that other groups frequented or temporarily lived in the territory. "Aboriginal title" also depends on a point of reference in time: the claimant's ancestors must have owned the lands at the time of colonisation. In this context, the length of occupation remains subject to the specific conditions of each case.

While in *Calder v. A-G of British Columbia*¹³⁶, the Canadian Court indicated the time frame "as their forefathers had done for centuries" and "for time immemorial", "[a] reasonable number of their ancestors were probably present in and near the villages of the territory for a long long time" in *Delgamuukw*. Concerning this really unspecified "long long time", the Supreme Court did not assume a "time immemorial"; according to the reasons of the decision, the claimant rather had to prove that indigenous peoples occupied the land at the time the British Crown asserted sovereignty.¹³⁷ While former decisions required the continuation from past to present occupancy, recent international precedents are

---

134 Cf. *Ward v. Western Australia* [1998] 159 ALR 483, p 501. Also *Delgamuukw v. British Columbia*, para 149 paid attention to indigenous economy, culture and religion.
135 Delgamuukw [1991] 79 DLR (4th) paras. 152–154; Mabo [1992] paras. 18ff., 42.
136 [1973] 34 DLR (3rd), paras. 170–173.
137 Delgamuukw [1991] 79 DLR (4th), paras. 142 und 144–145.

based on the material protection of the relationship between (indigenous) peoples and their territories.[138] If occupation at the time of colonisation can be proven, relevant courts will assume that it continued until the time the claim was lodged.[139]

As *aboriginal title* is a permanent and imminent right of (indigenous) peoples, the territory is collectively owned and passed on from generation to generation. The claimant (group) has to prove that they are a specific community which has existed from colonial times until today.[140] If a community, however, loses "its" (interpreted quite statically) "character" and its (interpreted quite homogenously) identity as a group, the (collective) holder of rights ceases to exist from a legal point of view and the rights are lost.[141]

In accordance with the present understanding of jurisdiction in indigenous land disputes, a legally valid act of state can terminate any right and thus also "indigenous title", including private property rights. In other words, the rights are not superior to the state because of their pre-state origins and their related character.[142] Nevertheless, such a legal action requires the legislative act to (have) proclaim(ed) a clear and unmistakable intention of termination. This principle was already expressed in *In Re Southern Rhodesia [1919]*, in which the Privy Council assessed that the continuation of ownership rights has to be assumed, "(…) in the absence of express confiscation".[143] This is why Anglo-American adjudication regularly considers the possibility of a law or formal dispossession terminating a legal title. An example of such a case would be a detailed investigation whether a newly formed reserve for a specific indigenous community would have terminated their "indigenous title" as a possible side effect of such an act.[144] All cases are based on the above-mentioned clear and unmistakable intention of the historical legislator. This, however, cannot be the only criterion: another criterion would be the act's effectiveness, meaning the question whether the legal provision really entered into effect or failed due to resistance of those concerned (Bennett/Powell 1999: 474ff.). As soon as the *aboriginal title* is terminated, it is assumed to be permanently lost. As it is the case with other procedures of expropriation, it should be assessed, nonetheless, whether or not the state has provided fair compensation.[145]

---

138 Cf. for example Delgamuukw [1991] 79 DLR (4th), para. 153.
139 Calder [1973] 34 DLR, para. 190 (Hall J).
140 Mabo [1992] para. 67f. (Brennan).
141 Mabo [1992] para. 83 Pkt. 7 (Brennan).
142 Cf. for example McNeil (1998: 8–13); Gilbert (2007: 602–610) for a critique of the termination of "indigenous title".
143 See also Mabo, para 61 (Brennan).
144 As Bennett/Powell (1999: 484) explain, such new reserves should be regarded as measures of protecting and preserving indigenous rights and titles, rather than measures of their termination.
145 As stated in Mabo, para 61 (Brennan).

The considerations about "aboriginal title" on which case decisions are based clearly suggest that indigenous peoples could have had land rights *sui generis* in many particular situations. As these rights would have originated in their own legal systems, they would not have had to alternatively require state recognition. I have offered this excursus for a better understanding of the Richtersveld case. This practical example is also crucial because for the first time in the South African context, the famous *aboriginal title* cases were used as models to argue before a court of third instance, namely the *Constitutional Court of South Africa*.

2.2.2.1 "Aboriginal Title" before the South African Constitutional Court

The Richtersveld Community first brought their claim before the *Land Claims Court of South Africa* (LCC).[146] It specifically asked for an assessment of *aboriginal title* and claimed their "right in land" under the *Restitution of Land Rights Act 22* (1994). This claim was based on three different demands: "a) ownership; b) a right based on aboriginal title allowing them the exclusive beneficial occupation and use of the subject land, or the right to use the subject land for certain specified purposes; or c) 'a right in land' over the subject land acquired through their beneficial occupation thereof for a period longer than 10 years prior to their eventual dispossession."

After the LLC had dismissed their claim in first instance, the Richtersveld Community appealed this decision before the *South African Supreme Court of Appeal* (SCA).[147] Many were surprised that the community was proved right before the Supreme Court of Appeal and granted the *title of collective ownership*. The diamond mining company Alexkor Ltd. then appealed this consenting decision before the

---

146 *Richtersveld Community v. Alexkor Ltd., 2001* (3) SA 1293 (LCC). In a nutshell, the court rejected the claim to property on the following grounds: the colonial government had regarded the territory as *terra nullius* because its inhabitants, the indigenous Richtersveld Community, were "too uncivilized" to occupy land. Therefore, indigenous land rights could not have survived the annexation by Great Britain (para. 37–41). The court also dismissed the claim of "aboriginal title" because its adoption into South African law is not subject to the LLC's jurisdiction but to courts with general jurisdiction (para. 48–53). Furthermore, the court declined the "right in land" based on occupation because the *Restitution Act* was only supposed to eliminate discrimination based on apartheid. In the court's opinion, however, the present case was not based on racial discrimination (para. 93). In consequence of these considerations, the Richtersveld Community was not entitled to restitution under the *Restitution Act*, which is why the LLC dismissed the claim (para. 120).

147 *Richtersveld Community v. Alexkor Ltd., 2003* (6) BCLR 583 (SCA). The Court of Appeal set aside the order of the LLC and granted the Richterveld Community restitution under the *Restiution Act*. The restitution focused on "the right to exclusive beneficial occupation and use of the subject land". What was extraordinary about this decision was the fact that it also included extensive rights to resources, including minerals and gemstones. As only the Supreme Court of Appeal explains (para. 111), this legal extent is similar to "common law ownership". So basically the court judgement may be seen as a partial victory because the Richtersveld Community obtained rights in land but not rights of ownership.

South African Constitutional Court.[148] The Constitutional Court ultimately confirmed the claim and upheld the decision to restitution of the right to ownership of the subject land (including non-renewable resources) and to the exclusive beneficial use and occupation (para. 103). In order to evaluate a claim to restitution of a "right in land", the court previously had to determine the nature and content of the right which the community of the subject land had before annexation.[149] According to the Constitutional Court, their evaluation was based on indigenous (customary) law because it was the applicable law for land rights at that time:

"[T]he nature of the indigenous law rights exercised by the Richtersveld Community (…) must be considered in their own terms and not through the prism of the common law. The dangers of looking at indigenous law through a common law prism are obvious. The two systems of law developed in different situations, under different cultures and in response to different conditions (paras. 55f.)"[150]

The court accordingly applied the international law standard measures of proof to the *aboriginal title* by analyzing evidence of the existence of indigenous rights as well as the relationship to the subject territory. The community had to provide evidence of their occupation of the land by proving that their ancestors owned the land: furthermore that they have been able to exclude others from the subject land, that they controlled and sanctioned their internal relationships of occupancy, ownership and use, and that they had ensured that other communities respected their rights of ownership. Based on these considerations, the Constitutional Court assessed that the land was collectively owned by the community (para. 62). Their rights included all natural resources because the ancestors of the Richtersveld Community had mined copper and iron and had granted mineral leases to outsiders long before the British annexation (paras. 61ff.). In the light of the evidence provided, the Constitutional Court concluded that the true nature of the title had been a right to collective occupancy under indigenous (customary) law (para. 62) and defined it as "indigenous law ownership".[151]

---

148 *Alexkor Ltd. v. Richtersveld Community, 2003* (12) BCLR 1301 (CC).
149 Art. 1 *Restitution Act* defines the "right in land" as "any right in land whether registered or unregistered and may include the interest of a labour tenant and sharecropper, a customary law interest, the interest of a beneficiary under a trust arrangement and beneficial occupation for a continuous period of not less than 10 years prior to dispossession in question."
150 In *Amodu Tijani v. The Secretary 1923*, a community in southern Nigeria, represented by their chief, lodged a collective claim to compensation. In this case, the Privy Council assessed that "The [native] title [to land] (…) may not be that of the individual, as in this country it nearly always is in some form, but may be that of a community. (…) To ascertain how far this latter development of right has progressed **involves the study of the history of the particular community and its usages** in each case. Abstract principles fashioned a priori are of but little assistance and are as often as not misleading" (2 AC [1921] 399 (PC) at 402–4) (emphasis added).
151 Paras. 70, 81, 86, 87, 92, 96, 99.

After having recognized this historical "right in land", the court addressed the question whether this right was terminated due to the British annexation[152] in 1847 or by means of a law or action.[153] Concerning the cases of indigenous land rights, the court upheld the paradigmatic opinion that the Richtersveld Community was entitled to these rights until the reference year of 1913 (the *Natives Land Act 27 of 1913*).[154] When the new democratic Government established this date, it limited the court's jurisdiction to the time when apartheid had unofficially begun due to the first prototypical racist laws. After this year, claimants must have lost their land in consequence of these racist laws and must have been dispossessed before 19 June 1913 (Art. 2(1) (d) *Restitution of Land Rights Act, No. 22)*:

"This date was chosen because of its association with the apartheid regime. 1913 was the year in which the first of the so-called 'pillars of apartheid' was passed, the Natives Land Act 27 of 1913, which laid the foundation for systematic racial segregation in South Africa" (Bennett/Powell 1999: 450).

The *South African Constitutional Court* decided in its judgement that the Richtersveld Community had actually lost its collective ownership rights due to government actions in the 1920s. As these actions could only be considered racially discriminating, the court decided to repeal them as unlawful actions.[155] In consequence, the Richtersveld Community was entitled to restitution under the

---

152 *Oyekan and others v. Adele [1957]* 2 ALL ER 785 at 788E-I. already assessed that a change of sovereignty alone does not affect the right to private property: "In inquiring, however, what rights are recognized, there is one guiding principle. It is this: The courts will assume that the British Crown intends that the rights of property of the inhabitants are to be fully respected. Whilst, therefore, the British Crown, as Sovereign, can make laws enabling it compulsorily to acquire land for public purposes, it will see that proper compensation is awarded to every one of the inhabitants who has by native law an interest in it; and the courts will declare the inhabitants entitled to compensation according to their interests, even though those interests are of a kind unknown to English law (…)" (cited in *Alexkor Ltd. v. Richtersveld Community, 2003* (12) BCLR 1301 (CC), para. 69).

153 Cf. in this matter also *Mabo and others v. Queensland* (No.2) (1992) at p 73–96.

154 Nevertheless, we have to ask whether an established date of reference should, in the interest of legal certainty, also prevent indigenous land claims from being extended indefinitely until the time of European intrusion. This aspect is emphasized by concerns of legal policy. As the *Land Claims Court* expresses in its grounds for dismissing the *aboriginal title*, "[I]n South Africa, of course, [the extension of the land claims process right back to the time of colonial settlement] would have proven disastrous. Not only would the entire land surface of the country have become subject to claims, but the very ethnic tensions which the land claims process hopes to resolve would simply have been exacerbated" (para. 94).

155 "In this case, the racial discrimination lay in the failure to recognise and accord protection to indigenous law ownership while, on the other hand, according protection to registered title. The inevitable impact of this differential treatment was racial discrimination against the Richtersveld Community which caused it to be dispossessed of its land rights" (para. 99).

Restitution Act. In legal history, this judgement was not only a victory for the Richtersveld Community but it was also significant for a legal development in the realm of indigenous rights because of its incorporation of a form of *aboriginal title* in South Africa. From the perspective of substantive law, "indigenous law ownership" may be equaled with *aboriginal title* as it was developed in comparable legal systems. The title of "indigenous law ownership" can therefore be regarded as the counterpart of aboriginal title in South African law (Chan 2004: 127).

As with almost all comparable cases, this decision can be criticized from a viewpoint of legal philosophy and anthropology: it is clearly based on a hierarchy of rights according to which the genuinely European legal systems and their ideas prevail over indigenous conceptions of law.[156] Furthermore, we can detect the colonial and postcolonial states' redundant expression of exclusive sovereignty. These states may grant, if at all, limited autonomy to indigenous peoples and otherwise insist on their monopoly of exclusive sovereignty. Although this judgement recognizes indigenous rights, the recognition is only second to a possible acceptance of equal rights. Keeping in mind the concept of equality though, this lack of acceptance causes more and more problems in many similar legal disputes and is ultimately considered untenable:

"[T]he asserted 'sovereign' subordination fails because the positivistic legal terms in which it is supposedly effected cannot be sustained in the face of the indigenous challenges to its historical and ontological basis" (Mostert/Fitzpatrick 2004: 2).[157] Anyway, both the *indigenous law ownership title* and the *aboriginal title* basically pursue the same purpose by granting indigenous rights from outside the paradigms of colonial and postcolonial jurisdiction and British common law. Both doctrines establish a right of indigenous peoples who owned the land before and at the time of annexation. It conforms to the universal principles of justice and equality and has survived both colonisation and other changes of regime unless – meaning the mentioned "relapse" into hegemonial thought – it was explicitly terminated by means of a legislative or executive act.

Both legal concepts refer to collective land ownership. The first and decisive evaluation of such collective titles always addresses the question whether a title already existed under indigenous (customary) law (at the time of annexation). This evaluation needs to analyze the community's history and understanding of law at the time in question. This is the same standard the *South African Constitutional Court* applied to "its" "indigenous law ownership". Chan (2004: 128) is right to note that the Constitutional Court did neither try to differentiate be-

---

156 Cf., e.g., Keon-Cohen (2000) for the Mabo case.
157 Mostert/Fitzpatrick (2004) suggest that the validity of indigenous rights, which is at best subsidiary, stems from an evolutionist understanding of law. In contrast to the idea of decolonisation, this understanding still places European rights over pre-European/indigenous rights.

tween the two doctrines nor did it invalidate the notion that "indigenous law ownership" was another form of *aboriginal title* in the sense of South African law:

"It is clear that the Constitutional Court meant to formulate 'indigenous law ownership' as a South African version of aboriginal title. Along with native title, indigenous title, Indian title and aboriginal title, the Constitutional Court has added 'indigenous law ownership' as the South African contribution to the pantheon of names representing this most important aboriginal right to land."

Before the Constitutional Court's judgement, scholars discussed the *aboriginal title* as an alternative remedial claim for those (indigenous peoples) who cannot meet the temporal requirements of the *Restitution Act* (cf. Bennett/Powell 1999: 450f.). Now it has been established in the guise of "indigenous law ownership" as a part of South African law and provides reliable legal protection for indigenous land rights. As this development has not affected intangible rights, I will present another famous case about the protection of indigenous knowledge: the case addressed the medicinal properties of the Hoodia plant which various San groups have used during long hunting trips to stave their hunger.

2.2.3 "Hoodia Gordonii" Case

Indigenous peoples do not only consider their rights to land and resources but also the protection of their traditional knowledge as pressing legal problems. NGOs that were acquainted with international law and its protective measures for intangible values were crucially responsible in raising awareness for relevant interests that had to be legally protected or otherwise become lost. For this purpose they developed a "rights-based approach" in addition to accompanying symbolic media campaigns. While discussing these rights with indigenous peoples, intangible property law is often referred to with the broader term of "intangible heritage", thus extending rights to all aspects of cultural heritage including ideas and culture (myths, songs, knowledge, images):

"The 'intangible cultural heritage' (…) is manifested *inter alia* in the following domains: (a) oral traditions and expressions, including language as a vehicle of the intangible cultural heritage; (b) performing arts; (c) social practices, rituals and festive events; (d) knowledge and practices concerning nature and the universe; (e) traditional craftsmanship" (Art. 2/2 *UNESCO Convention for the Safeguarding of the Intangible Cultural Heritage*).[158]

Traditional knowledge of resources presents a problem that is often overlooked: it is not protected by conventional intellectual property rights as soon as its use is of public interest (Chennells/du Toit 2004: 109). The present case

---

158 This UNESCO Convention entered into force on 20 April 2006. It already has 151 signatory states (as of 30 March 2013).

dealt with the traditional use of the desert fat plant.[159] In southern Africa, San communities have used *Hoodia Gordonii* or *!Khoba* to suppress hunger and thirst during their hunting trips for thousands of years. In 2001 they learned that the *Council for Scientific and Industrial Research (CSIR) of South Africa* had patented the desert plant as "P57" as early as 1995. Should the San have accepted to lose their rights in an invention? During the entire process of researching and patenting, nobody has consulted the original holders of the traditional knowledge (Duda 2005: 174).

The license for trials and a possible commercialization as an appetite suppressant was issued to the British company Phytopharm which then passed it on to Pfizer Inc. (U.S.). When San representatives negotiated with the *Council for Scientific and Industrial Research (CSIR) of South Africa*, they strategically demanded (by threatening with a legal dispute catching media attention) the explicit recognition of their traditional knowledge as well as a share of all royalties and other benefits. In March 2003, the involved San who were represented by two NGOs, namely the *South African San Institute* (SASI) and the *Working Group of Indigenous Minorities in Southern Africa* (WIMSA), were able to achieve a landmark success concerning collective intellectual property rights by agreeing to settle their dispute with CSIR out of court. The settlement recognized that the knowledge of the traditional use of the Hoodia plant could be traced back to the San. It was therefore a relevant inspiration for the "P57" patent:

"The San people are custodians of an ancient body of traditional knowledge and cultural values, related *inter alia* to human uses of the Hoodia plant, resulting from their interrelatedness with nature in all its forms, over the ages."[160]

In return, the San recognized CSIR's technological and financial effort for research and field studies (Stephenson 2003: 35). The San were supposed to receive 8% of all royalties Phytopharm paid CSIR and additionally 6% of all profit shares as soon as the medicinal product was available on the market (Duda 2005: 177).[161]

All three South African cases I have presented here are groundbreaking legal achievements of indigenous peoples in South Africa. In the first case, the ǂKhomani San (at least partially) reclaimed their land rights in an out-of court settlement. The

---

159 See for a detailed discussion Duda (2005); Stephenson (2003) as well as WIMSA (2004a: 54ff.) and (2004b). See also Wynberg/Schroeder/Chennells (2009) for the Hoodia bioprospecting case and use of San traditional knowledge, placing it in global context of indigenous peoples' rights, consent and benefit-sharing and for questions of justice in the *Convention on Biological Diversity*.

160 *Benefit Sharing Agreement between the CSIR and the San Council* (2003).

161 In July 2003, Pfizer dropped its license. As one of the world's biggest consumer goods companies, Unilever has been holding the license since December 2004. The company has been planning to launch a "hoodia bar" (for USD 5.- or EUR 2 to 3.-) which they advertised as "healthy and slimming" with nuts, chocolate and hunger-suppressing properties (Duda 2005: 204).

Richtersveld Community (in the second case) took legal action and was not only granted their demands but also established the "indigenous law ownership" title as a part of South African law and a basis of a cause of action for indigenous peoples. Keeping in mind the widely discussed and media-hyped problem of "biopiracy", the agreement in the last-mentioned "Hoodia case" is significant because for the first time in the South African context, patent law deviated from the Western concept of protecting individual inventors and the procedural principle of "first come" (patent application) for the benefit of protecting indigenous knowledge which was based on the San's collective (intellectual) property.

Two of the three cases also show that it is not always necessary to involve legal actions to obtain one's rights: other ways of solving conflicts and disputes, e.g. negotiations, may be rewarding as well. Indigenous peoples may benefit from this rather informal approach because they are not *a priori* disadvantaged or even hopelessly losing out due to a lack of finances in lengthy legal actions. Even well-financed and powerful corporations are at least willing to compromise under the pressure of public opinion and threats to take legal actions if no agreement is reached. In addition, such proceedings may have better chances of receiving financial support because the media have already been prepared to show interest in this subject matter. An out-of-court decision is based on mutual agreement and therefore shows the advantage of rather long-term conflict solutions. As a general rule, acceptable and even successful negotiations will also depend on the present legal background and possible legal options. In Commonwealth countries in which indigenous rights are not explicitly recognized by (constitutional) law, the concept of *aboriginal title* is crucial to the prospects of success in formal legal proceedings. Enforceable rights may be claimed if it first seems possible to prove the exclusive use and occupation of a territory since time immemorial. "Where aboriginal title is recognized, indigenous peoples have at least some legal right that can be asserted in the domestic legal system" (Daes 2001: para. 38).

All communities that call themselves indigenous peoples of Africa experienced – as in other parts of the world – specific forms of systematic discrimination, subordination and marginalization. In the past 20 to 25 years, they have used the term "indigenous peoples" which is highly controversial in Africa to find a common (global) voice which enabled them to collectively draw attention to any human rights violations and systematic discriminations at a national, regional, and international level. Although we should not underestimate the etymological and ideological problems of the term "indigenous" particularly in various African contexts, the multifaceted artificial collectivization presents the opportunity of defusing existing conflicts and making every effort to cope with historical injustices. Of course the term could be abused to politicize ethnic differences and fuel tribalism. As there is no empirical evidence for such abuses, they are only based on the preemptive concerns of a few governments.

According to the rules of symbolically exchanging respect, the following assumption would be true: if nation states recognized all their groups, respected their differences, and created a democratic environment offering equal opportunities of development, we could rather expect possible agreements and integrative solutions than ethnic or other conflicts over power that are based on essentialized categories. Especially pluralistic African societies share the difficult heritage of the European powers' colonial division of the continent. When the understanding of a unified nation was imported from Europe and combined with the other imports of party democracy and Western legal systems, it was almost inevitable for the above-mentioned African societies to face a multitude of ethnic conflicts and civil wars, which have been threatening Africa since the time of decolonisation.

What would happen if in these complex relationships postcolonial states recognized historically violated rights? In my opinion, this practice would be far more promising for ensuring peace, defusing conflicts, and promoting nation-building which has violently failed in numerous cases. According to the logics of symbolical exchange, it is not a new paradox at all that the recognition of the rights of self-determination could rather lead to state consolidation than conflictive tendencies of secession. A central statement of the *African Commission's Working Group* (2005: 88) underlines such an understanding: "Conflicts do not arise because people demand their rights but because their rights are violated." It seems to me that this statement especially applies to various San peoples. In the following part, I will outline their self-conception, historical conditions, legal understandings, and environments; this should help me to better determine the context for my exemplary discussion of the (legal situation of the) San in Botswana.

Part 3: Legal Perspectives of San Communities

"Nobody has ever asked us what our name is and how we should be called."

(Komtsha Komtsha, Chairman Kuru Development Trust, 1992)

I. Terminology: San, "Bushmen", Basarwa, Khoesan, N/oakwe or Kwe?

The assumed representatives of early stages of human development were defenseless victims particularly of anthropology's evolutionist thinking. In the myth of an ancient human society ("Urkultur"), "the San" had a special place in the historical development and evolution of the world's population (Barnard 2006): they represent(ed) a way of life that has survived since the dawn of mankind. This Western way of thinking applied its hierarchical ideas to various extremes from the "brutal savage" to the "harmless little people" but even romanticized and idealized versions were (and still are today) nothing more than intellectual colonialism. As Bargatzky conclusively argued in 1986 (21): In my opinion the practice of glorifying the other as 'primitive peoples' (*Naturvölker*) should be called 'intellectual colonialism' because it skews the image of members of foreign cultures, which in turn deprives them of their human character and thus colonizes them intellectually.[1]

The almost-obsessive fascination with the "last wild Bushmen" of scientific journalism and documentary film addresses the same self-interest of creating alternative worlds. The peoples subsumed under these and similar (judgemental) terms are among the most comprehensively described in the global historical context. The two commented bibliographies *The Khoe and San* (Willet et al. 2002; Willet 2003) alone with a total of 1,470 titles of contemporary literature virtually speak "volumes". If we keep in mind that these titles include only the English ones, the enormous quantity is even more impressive. Depending on location, time and perspective, the books talk about San, Bushpeople (Bushmen and Bushwomen), Basarwa, Khoesan, N/oakwe or Kwe (Khwe, Khoe) who do not and never have formed a homogenous political group, which is the basis of the (emic) diversity of ethnic self-designations. Time and again, (etic) generic terms for these communities were introduced due to scientific as well as state political reasons. The persistent tradition of outside labelling even dates back to pre-colonial contacts with Khoekhoe und later Bantu migrants from other regions of Africa. While such terms included characterizations, usually only one feature was used to define them. In this context, it is crucial to understand that the choice of this criterion was based on the intellectual history and experience of the defining group. In general, their definitions did not conform to the designations of those defined; they often even contradicted them. Intruding Europeans continued this

---

1 Original citation in German.

"etymological tradition" of a unilateral terminological development but their chosen criteria clearly reflected the racist attitudes of Europe at that time.[2]

The above-mentioned terms "San, Bushmen, Basarwa, Khoesan, N/oakwe or Kwe" refer to about 80,000 to 100,000 descendants of early "hunters and gatherers" in southern Africa.[3] All are problematic and heteronomous. When about 4,000 years ago the pastoral Khoekhoe or "Hottentots", as they were derogatively called by the Dutch, immigrated into southern Africa, they came into contact with "hunters and gatherers". They called them "San" referring to their purely economic activity of "gathering food" (Sanders 1989: 107). Nevertheless, there were times when derogatory connotations, such as "tramps", "vagabonds", "rascals", "robbers" or "bandits" were ascribed to this relatively neutral Nama term of the Khoekhoe (Barnard 1992: 8). "Unfortunately, a derogatory connotation is the fate of any appellation of a marginal group, even when in its original form the appellation was merely descriptive and meant no harm" (Sanders 1989: 107).

In the 1960s, however, the *Harvard Kalahari Research Group*[4] upgraded the term "San" to replace the term "Bushman" which was commonly used at that time and presents various problems at first sight until today (not only because of its reductionist identification of those concerned with their natural environment but also because of its androcentric omission of women). The term "Bushman" goes back to the first Dutch settlers at the Cape. The earliest historical accounts of 1685 show various variations, such as "Bosjesmans, Bosmanekens, Bosiesmans". Still in 1930, Schapera (1930: 31) did not find any reason why this term should not be used, especially because the term had found its way into ethnological literature. The trivial representations gave the term enough space for derogatory and even ridiculing "observations". The "Bushmen" were said to hide in the bush, just to jump out in front of unwary travellers (Lewis-Williams 2002: 1). The term implicitly also connotes a "primitive", "simple" and "uncivilized" life because it assumes a group of individuals who do not own anything and live in the bush – "natural" like animals. This was a perfect way to reproduce the opposed concepts of nature and culture: the "primitive, natural peoples" were seen as the antithesis to civilization. As all these reasons clearly explain, we can ascribe negative conno-

---

2   Even in the 21st century, some authors still regard it as necessary to note certain defining characteristics, as can be seen in the following examples: "The state of debate about 'San', 'Bushmen', or 'Basarwa' as possible appellations for the general group of small, click-speaking, yellow-skinned peoples in southern Africa can be illustrated (…)" (Hitchcock/Ikeya/Biesele/Lee 2006: 5); or "The Bushmen are the longest-term inhabitants of southern Africa. They are the last survivors of a Stone Age people who were once scattered all over eastern, central and southern Africa and have distinguishable traits" (Sanders 1993: 116).

3   Suzman (2001a) estimates the San population to: Angola 1,200, Botswana 47,675, Namibia 32,000, South Africa 4,350, Zambia 300 and Zimbabwe 2,500.

4   See the next section.

I. Terminology: San, "Bushmen", Basarwa, Khoesan, N/oakwe or Kwe?

tations to this term as well. "Any term which is applied to low-status individuals can acquire negative connotations. The English word 'Bushman' (from the Dutch Bosjesmans) has much the same history as 'San'" (Barnard 1992: 9).

Botswana officially uses "Basarwa" (singular: "Mosarwa") for the San and regards it as a "politically correct" Bantu word. The term was even attached at one point to the government's website which describes "The Relocation of *Basarwa* from the Central Kalahari Game Reserve".[5] Also the leaflet "Botswana" published by the country's Tourism Board states under the headline "the people of Botswana": "The *Basarwa*, commonly known as Bushmen (…)". The word originally derives from *bao ba-basa-ruing dikgome* which means something like "those who do not rear cattle" (Mogwe 2002: 3) or "people who have nothing" (Godwin 2001: 94).[6] The implication of this designation suggests that cattle-rearing people are the norm and that all those who do not rear cattle are defined by means of this negative criterion. The San usually know about these connotations which determine unilateral relationships. Taylor (2001: 164) cites a dialog in which a San describes the term "Mosarwa" as follows: "Mosarwa means *mo sa rua*; someone that does not own stock. That is our name because we are poor. (…) The opposite of Mosarwa is *morui*, a person that has livestock, a person that is rich."

These connotations indicate a lack of essential criteria of equality – "the notion of lack" as Laura Nader (2005: 201) describes it – and already point to an implicit objective of such a terminological development: to serve as a hierarchical structure to justify the legal dispossession of land, as Nader explains for the U.S. American context. Indigenous peoples lack the necessary modernity and development, capacity and knowledge to perfectly and economically exploit their natural environment. Accordingly we should not expect law, forms of organization, the ability to form alliances, e.g. using agreements and even culture in a specifically evaluated sense. Therefore, the related designations refer to an alleged state of absence, as if culture was not needed to survive in the natural eco-zones of southern Africa (Kalahari, Namib, Richtersveld, etc.).[7] Others, however, trace back the term "Basarwa" to a purely geographical connotation, meaning "people from the south" (Hitchcock/Biesele n.d.).

Some linguists proposed the term "Khoesan" as a scientific umbrella term for all groups who use "click consonants" and are therefore members of the Khoe-

---

5 www.gov.bw/basarwa/index.html from 2007.
6 In the court case *Sesana v. Government of Botswana* (chapter 6), Judge Unity Dow also pointed out the discriminating use of the term: "Until recently, perhaps it is still the case, 'Mosarwa', 'Lesarwa' (…) were common terms of insult, in the same way as 'Nigger' and 'Kaffir' were/are" (High Court 2006: 232).
7 These arguments are based on Thomas Bargatzky (1986) who criticized the term "primitive, natural peoples" (*Naturvölker*).

San language family in southern Africa (ibid.).⁸ But also this term leads to numerous problems of transferring a linguistically generic term for a certain language family to ethnic designations. These are then summed up under a category that can hardly be formed due to historical and social reasons. In the ethnic context, it was thus predominantly applied to peoples with pastoral traditions. Some authors consider these reasons as well as extensive further social differences as sufficient to conclude that it would be misleading in the socio-political context to subsume Khoe and San under one category (Saugestad 2004: 23).

In this complex etymological debate, the perspective of those concerned should be kept in mind as well. It goes without saying that this perspective is not completely homogenous and often even subject of controversial processes of self-understanding. Such a discussion forum amongst others was the NGO "First People of the Kalahari" (FPK). Founded in 1993 on the initiative of the San from the Central Kalahari, it proposed the collective term "N/oakwe" which in the Naro language means something like "red people" as opposed to the Bantu "black people" (Saugestad 2001: 29). This NGO also used the term "Kwe" meaning "person" which included all San groups of Botswana. Nonetheless, both terms are only common in Botswana and therefore lack a transnational, regional context. Umbrella organizations, such as the *Working Group for Indigenous Minorities of Southern Africa* (WIMSA), should be reason enough to seek such a context though.

The problem of terminology reflects the often-stressed fact that the indigenous peoples of southern Africa are not a homogenous group: "These former hunter-gatherers called themselves by the names of their individual groups, such as Ju|'hoansi, Khwe, ||Ani, G|wi, Naro, Hai||om, !Xōò, ǂKhomani, !Xun, ||Gana, Tshua, ||Xekgwi, !Ui, which, in most cases, mean 'real people', 'first people' or just 'people'" (Le Roux/White 2004: 2). The relevant language group comprises more than 35 Khoesan languages. We can see this diversity also in various cultural practices, divergent political economies, and different lifeworlds, which are not only geographically spread over almost all of southern Africa. Only in recent times, it has become necessary for the 80,000 to 100,000 individuals concerned to find an "umbrella term": first, they needed to show their unity in certain aspects of identity (Hohmann 2003: 3) and especially in the field of international legal development; second, they needed to find common features among themselves and in relation to other indigenous groups; and third, they needed them to become legally effective.

For the purpose of this book as well as the related common problems and (legal) solutions, I have been trying to find a general term for various groups, which preferably has no pejorative connotation at all. On my search for such a term,

---

8   Khoe also means "a person" in many San languages. As a language group, Khoe is one of the three biggest Khoe-San language families. See Saugestad (2004: 250–252) for an overview.

I. Terminology: San, "Bushmen", Basarwa, Khoesan, N/oakwe or Kwe?   159

on the one hand the etymological "burden" of virtually all etic umbrella terms, and on the other hand the dynamically changing connotations because of social change under various historical and political contexts become obvious. Unfortunately, a certain extent of negated contemporaneity remained unquestioned: "Primitive, savage, hunter-gatherer, forager, Bushman, Basarwa, San; the names have changed, their predicates and the premises from which these are drawn retain their negation of historically constructed objects" (Wilmsen 1989: 32).

An analysis of historical and scientific literature shows that it seems hardly possible to find a flawless, politically correct term. Also the scientific use of these terms is subject to the state of discussion as well as its underlying attitudes. While in the past, it may have been motives of exoticizing and alienating subsumed groups from "modern beings", today it is political correctness which dominates the choice and use of terms. As the following quote shows, those concerned share this opinion. When he was asked for the politically correct term, WIMSA staff and San Mathambo Ngakaeaja replied:

"You see, there is no political correct term for referring to us. Whatever term you find, be it Bushmen, be it San, be it Basarwa or whatever, is a foreign term and it lies in the repudiating connotation depending on the person who uses it at a particular time to refer to us. I refer to myself as a Naro, a Tsila person refers to himself as a Tsila, a Ju|'hoan refers to himself as a Ju|'hoan and so on. So there is no uniform term that refers to us, it has never existed."[9]

Of course not even this political activist can deny that reasons of unity and transregional cooperation of groups concerned make it necessary to find a relatively – concerning the present – politically correct or neutral term. In the last few years, it has become evident that the term "San" shows the least negative connotations and accompanying ideas. After long and intensive discussions at the 1997 Khoe and San conference in Cape Town, the decision was made to use the term "San".[10] This development is closely connected to the beginning of a pan-San-movement which tries to assert its common issues, legal interests and needs of protection in transregional contexts of southern Africa. Mathambo Ngakaeaja (WIMSA) puts the growing pan-San mobilization in a nutshell:

"You will find that the indigenous movement is actually growing throughout the southern African region. In South Africa they have established an institution called South African San Council, a purely political platform for the San to hear their views and interests. In Namibia such a board is under formation, here in

---

9 Interview 8 March 2005.
10 Conference "Khoesan Identities and Cultural Heritage", Cape Town, 12–16 July 1997. See Lee/Hitchcock (2001: 271f.) for an overview of the conference and the diverging wishes on the one hand of the Khoe who focused on their cultural heritage and identity and on the other hand of the San who stressed the importance of land, hunting and grazing rights as well as recent discrimination.

Botswana, we had a first meeting with a brainstorming session, and an organization such as WIMSA goes a long way indicating the pan-San-movement characteristic in terms of uniting in a regional organization such as WIMSA. There is a pan-San-movement that is growing."[11]

In 1998, the San organizations of southern Africa met in Shakawe (Botswana) and agreed on their shared commitment to a common movement. Their proclaimed principles ("Shakawe Principles") also include *inter alia* a call to support newly-formed regional San organizations and emphasize the necessity of solidarity in these wide transnational relationships.[12] Nowadays, it is not special in any way to use the term "San".

When using the term "San" in this book, I am fully aware that this general designation will not necessarily be valid or the politically most correct version for ever. It will of course be subject to changing contexts as well. At a certain point in time, the critical factor for such a decision should ultimately be the discursively established will of those concerned, especially if scientific analysis was not only based on descriptively explicative but also emancipatory interests. In this sense, I agree to the following clear positioning in terms of a self-defining designation (described with the formula "power to define"):

"As any term takes on a derogatory meaning if it is used to express negative attitudes about a group of people, it is the social context, and as far as possible the wish of the people being named, that should guide the use of the terms" (Saugestad 2004: 23).[13]

Art. 33 of the *UN Declaration on the Rights of Indigenous Peoples* too proclaims the same position with the right of indigenous peoples to determine their identity or membership in accordance with their customs and traditions. Anyhow, the most important San NGOs *Working Group for Indigenous Minorities of Southern Africa* (WIMSA), *South African San Institute* (SASI), *Kuru Family of Organisations* (KFO), *Indigenous Peoples of Africa Coordinating Committee* (IPACC) and *First People of the Kalahari* (FPK) use the term "San".[14]

---

11 Interview 8 March 2005. In the meantime, three San Councils have been founded and efforts are made to create a fourth: The *South African San Council* (established in 2001), the *Namibian San Council* (established in 2006) and the *Khwedom Council* (Botswana San Council established in 2008). At present, there is still no Angolan San Council. Cf. www.wimsanet.org.

12 "An increase in solidarity is needed as we find ourselves in a changing environment. Therefore we should: (…) support our own San organizations" (principle 5, Principles adopted by an Indigenous Peoples' Consultation on empowerment, culture and spirituality in community development 1998).

13 In 2001 Saugestad also noted that personally she would prefer the term Kwe (or Khwe) meaning "person".

14 www.san.org.za as of 06/06/2007.

II. Historical Overview until the End of Colonial Times

A chronology of the history of indigenous peoples in southern Africa may be outlined as follows: for thousands of years, the San lived in small groups of hunters and gatherers and were the only inhabitants of southern Africa. Clear archaeological finds outside of Cape Town date back to about 120,000 years (Lee/ Hitchcock/Biesele 2002: 9–12). All over southern Africa, we can still find rock paintings and engravings that are up to 20,000 and 25,000 years old and depict many of their cultural, economic and religious practices. After the cattle-rearing Khoekhoe immigrated about 8,000 years ago, they have shared the same environment.[15] In the first century AD, Bantu-speaking peoples from northern regions immigrated and formed the Zulu, Xhosa, Tswana and Sotho kingdoms (Stephenson 2003: 21).

Following the violent intrusion of Dutch invaders in 1652, a long and bloody chapter began which almost ended with the complete genocide of the San. At the symbolic level of violence, the history of the genocide was reflected in an entirely unilateral historiography. From this time on, it was characterized by the self-righteous narrations of settlers, colonial authorities, missionaries, adventurers, and anthropologists who directly influenced the fate of the San. In this respect, we can consider the entire view of history documented in written form as burdened with the Western (racist) sentiments of that time. Virtually all of these allegedly "factual reports" pursued interests that were not based on the perspectives of "their objects". They rather focused on the "explorers'" multifaceted claims to power over (to them) unknown territories and their hence "discovered" inhabitants of absolute "otherness": "Until the middle of the 20th century, emphasis was more often placed on their physique and their lifestyle than on the facts of their history. Historical accounts have usually revealed more about their authors than about the San themselves" (Le Roux/White 2004: 6f.).

Historical portrayals basically shared the opinion that although the San were the "first human beings" and had a place in evolutionary history, they more specifically belonged to the peoples without history: "[T]hese people, who are universally considered to be the longest-term living residents of the Kalahari, are permitted antiquity while denied history" (Wilmsen 1989: 10). In the last few decades, the extensive and self-critical history of relevant disciplines has clearly worked out that – keeping in mind the white interests of power – they were not allowed to have a history.[16] European colonial historiography thus deprived

---

15 See section I, this chapter.
16 Wilmsen (1989: 3) criticizes , e.g., the description by Professor Emeritus of Anthropology, Richard Lee, who presents the San as ahistorical people until ethnographic fieldwork introduced them to history: "In fact, Lee (1979: 6) goes so far as to believe

those subjected of their history in exactly the same way as colonial powers deprived them of their territories, resources, and living environments:

> The statement that human beings have always used their experiences to make their environment livable is undoubtedly a banal one. It appears also a basal insight, however, if we try to keep in mind how simplified and marginalized the historical practice of those colonized, missionized and dominated was described. Since 'otherness' had been discovered, they were damned in two ways: to serve and to stay quiet. The military, political and economic ruling power coincided with the power of representation (Zips 2003a: 21f.)[17].

From today's point of view, an adequate methodological approach of a historical study would also focus on the historical understanding of the San. As such studies hardly exist, though, we still have to rely mostly on the consciously and unconsciously distorted and fragmentary impressions and anecdotes. These are found in written documents that are the result of complex and alienating perceptions of European immigrants and colonial rulers. Therefore, the following historical outline should be read on the meta level of narrative strategies of historical representations: especially concerning omissions and marginalizations but also human beings glorified or diabolized as "savages" (cf. Zips 2003a: 28). As the comprehensive and yet redundant literature addresses extremely selective aspects of culture, the following considerations can be nothing more but a short overview.

It is assumed that between 250,000 and 300,000 San lived in southern Africa before European occupation. The relative autonomy of individual San groups did not implicate a lack of contact or trade relations though. In pre-colonial times, social relationships with Bantu peoples generally ranged from small-scale wars to coexistence and mixed marriages (Saugestad 2004: 24). Wilmsen (1989: 64–76) documents early trade and exchange networks, such as the exchange of skins, ostrich feathers and ivory for tobacco, weapons and other goods with Great Zimbabwe and the east coast.

With the Dutch intrusion in 1652, the San became victims of ruthless dispossessions of lands and targeted genocides which intensified the catastrophic consequences of epidemics, diseases and systematic slavery. Numerous sources confirm that targeted mass murder (which at that time was as "legal" as hunting wild animals) and taking prisoners happened every day: "In 1774, we are told, a commando in the Roggeveld killed 503 Bushmen and took 239 prisoners, while it is calculated that between the years 1785 and 1795 no fewer than 2,504 were killed and 669 made captive" (Schapera 1930: 39). Just by considering that in only 10 years 2,504 individuals were killed in the area of Roggeveld, the true extent of European atrocities becomes clear. The prevailing opinion of settlers as

---

that it is the very act of ethnographic fieldwork itself that "can begin to place this 'ahistorical' society into history."

17 Original citation in German.

well as officials that "the only good Bushman was a dead Bushman" caused campaigns of extermination on a regular basis.[18]

The period of symbolic violence in science began considerably later: in accordance with European interests of domination, science developed an evolutionary concept of hierarchy at the expense of the San (and other indigenous peoples) who had been wiped out in large numbers. It is the time when the theory of evolution spreads to anthropology and first peaks in Lewis Morgan's (1877) "Ancient Society" (Hildebrandt 1979: 1). Morgan develops the theory of four fundamental stages of development with different economies based on the first (and lowest) stage of hunting, followed successfully by pasturage, agriculture, and finally commerce based economies (Keal 2003: 74). His theory explained human "progress" from savagery and barbarism to civilization.

Other "armchair anthropologists" evaluated the various developmental stages completely contrarily. Their objectifications ranged from the (significantly rarer) positive "exotic, noble and peaceful savages" (à la Rousseau) who lived in harmony with their environment and nature to the much more often used "wild, primitive and animal-like creatures", thus offering an image of European customs as well (Keal 2003: 75). Reasons enough for ruthless "entrepreneurs" to see "individuals of the lowest stage" as objects they could make money with: "In the nineteenth century, living persons were taken from their homelands to be displayed in colonial capitals as representatives of their savage state" (Wilmsen 1989: 35). Among these victims, for example, was Sara Baartman, a Khoekhoe who was deported from the Cape of Good Hope in 1810. In London at the Piccadilly, she was shown to paying customers as "Hottentot Venus" at the age of 20 years.[19] She exemplifies all others who were victimized by the exploitative nature and racist, literally "wild psyche" of European thought reflected in the entertainment industry.[20]

From the second half of the 19th century on, evolutionary and racist paradigms profoundly shaped early "scientific" research on the San. As they were re-

---

18 The figures speak for themselves: in August 1774 in only 10 weeks, Dutch commando troops led the following campaigns: "The first section of the General Commando, under the command of Nicolaas van der Merwe (…) destroyed 167 kraals, killed 142 Bushmen and took 89 prisoners. (…) The second section, under Gerrit van Wyk, (…) its body count was slightly smaller, (…) 96 Bushmen killed and 21 captured, as against no commando members. The third section, under Opperman, (…) killing 265 Bushmen and capturing 129" (Gall 2002: 66f.).

19 When she died five years later, a plaster cast of her was made before she was dissected. Georges Cuvier then sent her skeleton, preserved brain and sexual organs to the *Musée de l'Homme* in Paris, where it was displayed until 1985 (Cf. Parsons 2002a: 3ff.). In 2002, Sarah Baartman's remains were returned and buried on 9th August 2002, South Africa's Women's Day, in the Eastern Cape Province.

20 See for the history of "El Negro" see, e.g., Parsons (2002b: 19–29) as well as Hitchcock's contributions "The Kalahari Earth Man" and "Klikko, the Wild Dancing Bushman" (1987: 289).

garded as living fossils, representatives of the animal-like stage of humankind and missing links in the theory of evolution, particularly their physiognomy caught the researchers' attention: they measured and compared each centimetre of their skin, calculated the layer of subcutaneous fat, and documented the curvature of their prominent buttocks, the thickness of eyelids, the angle of the (not) erect penis, the length of genital lips, etc. (Hudelson 1995: 3).[21] True "hordes" of anthropologists, parasitologists, linguists, dentists, physiognomists, ethnographic movie makers, and others got their teeth into the San's blood, urine, saliva, languages, dances, myths, stories, fire-making techniques and hunting skills with bow and arrow.[22] Starting in 1850, social Darwinism favoured the development of "scientific racism" (Keal 2003: 66).

Around 1880, the basic classification schemes and alleged defining characteristics of a "primitive, wild stage" of human existence formed for the most part the prevailing doctrine of anthropology and even beyond. Lubbock (1865) did not only introduce the term "prehistoric" for the time before European historiography, he also extended it to "modern savages" and used them as the decisive factors of comparison for the European development of civilization: "[I]f we wish clearly to understand the antiquities of Europe, we must compare them with the rude implements and weapons still, or until lately, used by the savage races in other parts of the world" (Lubbock cited in Wilmsen 1989: 13).

Also the "VIPs" of European intellectual history stayed with a self-righteous and simple-minded view of the world though: Engels (1884) for example speculated about evolutionary stages and how they could affect sexuality and marriage; Marx, Engels and Lubbock theorized about the transitions from the stage of savagery to civilization; and both Hegel and Schopenhauer were convinced that all Black people would remain on the most primitive stage and that Europeans would only use them to ascertain their own progress, just to name a few.[23] The "Vienna school of ethnology" became rather questionably famous as well due to Wilhelm Schmidt's concept of *Kulturkreis* (1939), roughly meaning "culture circle". He understood primitive hunters and gatherers as *Urkultur* ("ancient society") and was convinced that these prehistoric culture circles could be reconstructed by using the remaining modern "primitive hunters" forced to live in the periphery as role models (Schweitzer 2004: 72f.; cf. also Barnard 2006).

Evolutionist theories as well as the romanticized "noble savage" as their positive counterpart tenaciously held their ground in science until the 20th century.

---

21 For a detailed description of evolutionist and racist research, see Skotnes (1996).

22 Some Botswana administrators ironically desribed a "typical" San household as being made up of man, woman, two children and an anthropologist. Or you could describe it as follows, "[T]here were reputedly more anthropologists than Basarwa in the Kalahari" (Hitchcock 1987: 286).

23 For detailed criticism and an overview of the literature see Wilmsen (1989: 1–26).

Both conceptions, however, were not only reductionist in their crude cultural materialism and critique of civilization; they were both also based on "cultural purity". They suggest that at least individual groups have made it homogenously and without cultural relations or influences into the present. Based on an isolationist theory, this conception on the one hand is right to emphasize the rich cultural heritage of San cultures but on the other hand reduces their essence to an unalterable existence of hunters and gatherers. Wilmsen (1989: 8ff., 33–38) comprehensibly criticizes this essentialism which is one of the most common forms of simplified representations.

Before I will summarize the Kalahari debate, two contradictions should be pointed out which seem to make use of some anthropological concepts: the first contradiction refers to a part of anthropological research trying to find undisturbed communities of hunters and gatherers because they realized an epistemological prerequisite to reach their evolutionist goals. As representatives of an alleged *Urkultur*, these still existing, antique and static peoples were supposed to offer insights into cultural evolution as well as the reconstruction of characteristics of early societies and economies. Thus, Richard Lee openly and without compunction explains his chosen fieldwork region of the northern Kalahari as a question of desirable isolation: "[T]he research goals required a population as isolated and traditionally oriented as possible" (Lee 1965: 2).[24]

If researchers could not find this state of isolation in (prehistoric) time and space, it was ignored or simply disregarded: "[These] things we ignored, relatively speaking, because we didn't come all the way around the world to see them. (…) and although we remind each other once in a while not to be romantic, we consciously and unconsciously neglect and avoid the !Kung who don't conform to our expectations" (Howell [1986], cited in Wilmsen 1989: 35).[25] Of course also a fair number of research projects unconsciously work with untruthful assumptions of reality. This practice which Wilmsen (1989: 33–63) appropriately analyzes as "poverty of misappropriated theory" is closely connected to a scientific habitus of evolutionist, biologistic and objectivistic approaches.

The second contradiction refers to the (assumed) necessity of isolation to conserve culture, the way of living and the environment. On the one hand, our time (and especially postcolonial states) owes the existence of wide ecologically-intact regions of the Kalahari to various San groups but on the other hand, this obviously sustainable use of resources does not turn them into "environmental saints" or romanticized "Stone Age people in harmony with the natural environment". This is also why it is more than questionable whether the isolation or assumed lack of contact of San cultures is really crucial to the cultural and ecological pres-

---

24 For this case as well as other methodological criteria see Wilmsen (1989: 8).
25 In a legal sense, we could draw an analogy to the term of fiction: in this understanding, fiction would mean a consciously untruthful assumption of reality.

ervation of the Kalahari. We could ultimately argue as well that it was especially the interaction with other social groups and their economies that provided the basis for the survival of various San cultures as well as their occupied and cultivated biomes.

This isolated representation of the San in their wider social environment of the Kalahari fueled a debate that divided the factions of the "traditionalists" and the "revisionists". The vital spark originated in the scientific-methodic induction of the *Harvard Kalahari Research Group* under Lee and DeVore. For five years (1967–1972), more than a dozen scientists had more or less continuously undertaken research on the !Kung in north-western Ngamiland (Botswana) (Hitchcock 1987: 302f.). The harshest critique came from Edwin Wilmsen who accused them of representing the groups of hunters and gatherers as isolated ahistorical units. According to Wilmsen, Lee wants the human "original innocence" to be reflected in the !Kung and achieves this goal by virtually "freezing" these peoples in an arbitrarily chosen evolutionist moment and then projecting them into the present (Wilmsen 1989: 34f.). Wilmsen and other critics, referred to as "revisionists" or "historical particularists", see the range of interaction and historic relationships of present hunters and gatherers as much more complex. Since the beginning of the geographic contact situation, the San have interacted with immigrating Bantu as well as Europeans (Saugestad 2001: 92).

Based on archaeological data and historical sources, Wilmsen documents early trading routes into the heart of the Kalahari. Wilmsen's as well as other's findings prove the existence of ceramics-producing pastoralists in the Kalahari over a period of 2,000 years: glass pearls, iron and copper ornaments as well as kauri and freshwater shells from the Indian and Arab region provide evidence for the San trade with other peoples. The San probably also cultivated sorghum, corn and melons; archaeological findings of mongongo nuts and grewia berries suggest that gathering continued to be important though (Wilmsen 1989: 64–77). So-called "traditionalists", with Lee (2001, 2006) leading the way, on the other hand accuse "revisionists" of representing the subordination of the San to the economically stronger pre-colonial African centres of power as a universally valid fact. In their eyes, "revisionists" underestimated the clear diversity of the historical conditions of the pre-colonial period. In the 19th century, San groups lived very differently: "There were wretched San peoples in the 19th century living in abject poverty; there were also independent cattle-holding San peoples, and a number of very successful San groups who lived by the hunt and maintained a proud independence" (Lee/Hitchcock 2001: 267).

Although I cannot address the Kalahari debate in more detail, some of the contradictions seem to be based on individual local facts and it remains highly questionable whether or not they can be generalized. The essence of this scientific controversy is obviously formed by ideological contradictions which "compete" for the assessment of the recent history of "hunting and gathering" especially

II. Historical Overview until the End of Colonial Times

in southern Africa. While the "traditionalist and authenticistic" faction regarded San groups as representatives of an original and essentially isolated culture of hunting and gathering, their counterpart negated their ethnicity as "peoples" all together and reduced their collective existence in recent history to communities of fate controlled from outside, which they assessed as "mere class categories":

"The thrust of my argument has been that it is useless to speak about 'Bushmen'/Basarwa/San as a separate category unless we realize that these terms are class categorizations having nothing to do with ethnic entities or persons and only occasionally relating to particular, restricted ways of life. The first step to this realization leads away from a fascination with a fixed forager image, a fascination that sets the present of peoples so labelled out of focus and circumscribes any vision of their future" (Wilmsen 1989: 324f.).

At this point it must remain unresolved to what extent these positions owed their overgeneralizations to limited archaeological and empirical data and a lack of source criticism. When the Kalahari debate was at full speed, Lee (1996: 247) at least stated that he did not recognize any conception as absolutely superior or "truer" but saw them all as partial aspects of a whole. In a later article, however, he opposed the possibility of subsistence economy with limited cattle breeding for some San groups because he portrayed several in-depth interviews with two elder Ju|'hoan as representative for the oral tradition of about a dozen informants. They had confirmed a long history of independent hunting and gathering without farming and cattle breeding. At this point we have to keep in mind that oral traditions can only reach back so far into the past and claim to be valid but they should not be considered the "truth".[26] Lee's (2006: 463) further evidence as well as methodological shortcomings (e.g. he sees a close connection – without any source criticism – between the remarks of the German geographer Siegfried Passarge who gave his name to a valley in the *Central Kalahari Game Reserve* and his own interviews about 80 years later) turn oral traditions into some sort of meta discourse about the allegedly "unalterable characteristics" of hunters and gatherers.

This theoretical point of view shows the limitations of one-dimensional interpretations based on methodologically questionable "strategic interpretations" of various source types – oral traditions, archaeological evidence or other sources. "Strategic essentialism", however, as Lee (2006: 455) proposes for the concept of "indigeneity" remains limited in its scope. It does not resolve the problematic aspects of essentialist thinking and thus seems to be counterproductive in contrast

---

26 Cf. Gingrich/Zips (2003: 284): As 'oral history', narratives are just as little able to portray the past as any written text (Original citation in German). Because (e)ach narrative and each text is a presentation using symbolic means and contains a range of interpretations for which the narrator both searches for and finds a composition in the act of talking (Original citation in German), (Sieder 2001: 152).

to its proclaimed benevolent attitude towards the issues of indigenous peoples. As this book seeks to argue, legal claims of indigenous peoples cannot be derived from "essential authenticities" after evolutionist circular arguments but from violations of law within historical (particular but often overlapping) relationships as well as the protection needs within historically accumulated political economies. At the methodological level, elaborate source criticism is needed, which also has to question and resolve as far as possible any relationship between existing sources. Such a praxeological approach was not used in the Kalahari debate. Saugestad expresses this shortcoming most clearly:

"For one who stands outside the debate, the two approaches appear to complement more than to contradict each other. The Harvard project brought forward a series of rich and detailed studies that illuminate local life among the !Kung of the Dobe area, and uncover the systems logic of a foraging mode of production. (…) The weakness is that trade and relations with neighbours are not as closely investigated, and the hunter-gatherer subsistence system may easily appear as a somewhat timeless, functional entity. The picture presented by the other, more diffusely defined school is less clear cut, but perhaps that is part of the message. (…) The focus is more on inter-group relations than on the internal cultural traits. (…) It is the history of contact that is the focus of study, and the relationship between foraging groups and their neighbours that is being traced" (Saugestad 2001: 93).

If we read through the common European repertoire of suggestive, adventurous and romantically-glorifying narratives of the "savage, noble, primitive, shy and peaceful last survivors of human prehistoric times", we will probably also from a self-critical and reflective point of view have to ask to what extent such narratives mirror the secret desires and wishful thinking of Western idealists. This indeed benevolent conception reduces the historical experiences of the San in many ways, though. Furthermore, it especially simplifies their rational communication accomplishments of defending their interests (e.g., to land use) and ways of living by limiting the existence of those concerned to virtually passive instinctive beings who are adapted to nature and thus automatically in balance with their natural environment.

Such structures of interpretation are deeply embedded in Western cosmovisions and are further complemented by trends of regional historical (political) developments. Based on trade routes and types of settlement, these developments depended in turn on fertile ground, natural resources and climate conditions. The historical differences – and I basically confine myself to the states of southern Africa – are significant to figure out the present situation of the San.

1. Regional Historical Differences

Quantitative estimates about San populations in southern Africa have varied quite heavily. As censuses, if undertaken at all on a regular basis, hardly provide plausible data especially on the San (because of their social conditions in remote areas or informal ways of urban living), there are drastic variations in existing sources. In addition, the relatively high mobility, migration, wars, changes of identity as well as the ecologic pressure of their specific biomes cause demographic data to be unreliable: "Although the data is currently more complete than ever before, identity switching, movements and migrations in response to war, population pressure, ecological constraints and the inaccuracy of census data all hinder the accurate enumeration of southern Africa's San population" (Suzman 2001a: 4). According to an EU assessment of the human rights and socio-economic situation of the San in southern Africa, about 85,000 to 90,000 San live in six countries.[27] The largest San populations are in Botswana (47,675) and Namibia (32,000), while significantly smaller groups are found in South Africa (4,350), Zimbabwe (2,500), Angola (1,200) and Zambia (300) (Suzman 2001a: 4f.).

Historical records as well as rather recent research including archaeological findings produce the rather pessimistic picture that different San groups share similar experiences of conflicts, oppression and exploitation as well as in the worst case physical and cultural annihilation. When it comes to their political influence, legislative measures, and the economic exploitation of their workforce and natural resources, there are huge differences among the countries of southern Africa. In the following part, I will offer a short outline of these differences.[28]

1.1 Botswana

Botswana has remained an extremely sparsely populated country with just over two million inhabitants on 570,000 square kilometres due to its geological and climatic conditions. The largest part of the country (more than 85 percent) comprises the Kalahari. This semi-dry grass and bush savannah which is often mis-

---

27 This study was the result of development cooperation between the EU and the so-called ACP states (African, Caribbean, Pacific): *ACP-EU Resolution on the San People* 1736/96/fin. Adopted by the ACP-EU General Assembly in March 1996, this resolution recognizes "the special difficulties encountered in integrating hunting and gathering peoples in agricultural industrial states" and notices "the lack of accurate overall information on the present condition and prospects of San". In consequence, the European Commission was asked to conduct a comprehensive study about San societies. This series of studies was headed by anthropologist James Suzman (1999–2000) and five reports were eventually published.

28 For a presentation of the situation and legal conditions of the San in southern Africa, cf., e.g., Suzman (2001a), Hitchcock/Biesele/Lee (2003).

taken for a "desert" was uninhabitable for the first Sotho-Tswana and other Bantu-speaking, cattle-breeding groups who immigrated 1,800 years ago. There they encountered the local Khoekhoe and San and turned them into their subjects within their social forms of organization. This was also the starting point for some groups retreating to the extensive regions uninhabited by Bantu-speaking groups. Numerous further waves of Tswana immigrants established *merafe* or kingdoms and founded larger settlements predominantly in border regions where rivers and other water resources made it possible to permanently live and rear cattle. From a historiographical point of view, it is rather difficult to differentiate between settlement and origin myths on the one hand and conceivable historical sources on the other (Hopf 1991: 63). We can be certain, however, that there is no coherent historical picture due to high social mobility of migrations caused by wars, drought periods and fissions until roughly 1800 (cf. also Ramsay/Morton/Mgadla 1996: 11–17; as well as Obeng 2001: 3–7).

In the last two centuries, eight Tswana kingdoms shaped a political history in which the San played a highly marginalized role. Today the Tswana are the country's clear majority and share a common medium of communication (from the Sotho language group) with the (today official) language Setswana (Altheimer/Hubert 1991: 11). These Tswana groups or "nations" which the British called "tribes" were hierarchically organized with a king (the so-called chief or *kgosi*) and did not even change their political existence under the British Protectorate of Bechuanaland. At the beginning of the 20th century, the most powerful kingdoms which later found their way into the 1966 Constitution as the "eight main tribes" controlled most parts of Botswana. The only exceptions were the (today) districts Chobe, Ghanzi and Kgalagadi, which remained sparsely populated and became British crown land in 1910.[29] Only various San peoples lived in these remote and often arid regions due to the climatic and ecological conditions.

Great Britain proclaimed the protectorate in 1885 because of, amongst other things, general geo-strategic considerations.[30] Therefore, it is hardly surprising that the British influence was minimal in internal economic and political matters and allowed more or less space for self-determination in a relatively permissive system of indirect rule. The protectorate administration established *Native* or *Tribal Reserves* and generally assumed that each territory occupied by a "tribe" was, in fact, owned by this "tribe". This is why the administration granted exten-

---

29 *Bechuanaland Protectorate (Lands) Order-in-Council* 1910, announced on 10 January 1910. For further details see chapter 4, section I.2. this volume.

30 The British Government, for example, was afraid that the German colony (today Namibia) would merge with the Boer Transvaal which was sympathizing with Germany. In this context, Great Britain decided to establish Bechuanaland quasi-preemptively as a "buffer zone" (Hopf 1991: 67). The second consideration concerned a northern expansion searching for further diamond deposits and using Bechuanaland as some sort of "British Suez Canal" (Oliver/Atmore 1981: 112).

sive autonomy to these political units. Non-Tswana communities and thus also the San were, in consequence, subjects of the chiefs and basically the Tswana system of land rights. Land (if it was not crown land) was collectively owned by the entire "tribe" and administrated by the chief *(Kgosi)* on behalf of the "tribe" (Obeng 2001: 6). While the social status of all members of these societies depended on their kinship to the chief and the royal family, all "non-Tswana" individuals were incorporated into the general class system: citizens, foreigners and serfs. The Tswana, too, classified the San in the latter category and forced them to live under semi-feudal conditions without legal status or fundamental rights (Obeng 2001: 7ff.).[31]

Only in the late 20th century, the – until then completely indifferent – colonial government began to recognize the extremely discriminatory situation of the San – maybe also because of the pressure of scientific research on the San (especially by Isaac Schapera who bemoaned the "dying way of life" of the "Bushmen") – and was ultimately committed to become actively involved (Hitchcock 1987: 290). In 1931, the protectorate government commissioned the *Tagart Commission Report* which revealed the San's slave-like conditions: "The commission, which was inquiring into the conditions of the Basarwa reported that many were still treated as serfs. They [San] were unable to dispose freely of their labour, enjoyed limited property rights, had no control over land, and were liable to be transferred as property on the death of their master" (Datta/Murray 1989: 62).[32] Only two years later in 1933, the British abolished slavery in the protectorate.[33] Until the country's independence and even later, however, the Tswana's feeling of superiority over the San did not change much (Obeng 2001: 7). At this point I should add that the lands of the Kalahari were not particularly attractive due to its raw climate. Only "white hunters" but not any white large-scale farmers, colonial civil servants and traders could be found there. Thus, the real control mainly remained with Tswana societies. Botswana did not attract many white adventurous settlers except a few short-time trade expeditions.

---

31 San were not entitled to take legal steps against Tswana people. San men were not allowed to marry or have sexual relationships with Tswana women. Tswana men in turn could have sexual relationships with San women without consequences and without being held accountable in case of eventual pregnancies. When missionaries established schools in the protectorate, San children were not allowed to attend them (Obeng 2001: 7ff.).

32 In the same year, a cattle breeder was accused of having murdered "his" San serf. Before the High Court he stated, "I have never beaten dogs like I beat those Masarwa [San] and never would" (Datta/Murray 1989: 68).

33 As Charles Rey, plenipotentiary from 1930 to 1937, attested, the many years of inactivity were the result of the colonial government's ambivalent stance: in his opinion, "preserving a decadent and dying race [...] is perfectly useless from any point of view"; he still condemned the drastic discrimination against the San because they should have had the opportunity to be "civilized" (Bennett 2002: 9).

1.2 Namibia

The historical development of the Namibia we know today (the former German colony South-West Africa) is quite similar to that of South Africa when concerning the San. As it was the case with Botswana, though, white colonists were less economically interested in the less fertile regions. The first immigrants, the ancestors of today's Herero and large-scale cattle breeders, encountered the indigenous San peoples (Hai||om, Ju|'hoansi, !Xōō, !Xun and Khwe) as well as the cattle-breeding Khoekhoe (Le Roux/White 2004: 82f.). At the end of the 15th century, the first significant waves of Bantu groups immigrated and lead to similar consequences for local San communities as in Botswana. As Suzman (2001b: 5) summarizes, internal forced displacement and land dispossession were among these aftermaths:

"This large-scale in-migration of Bantu speakers saw a significant displacement of local peoples, such that by the late 19th century and the advent of white colonialism, only a proportion of San populations – spread mainly through the east of the country – remained functionally autonomous of the new arrivals. This process of land dispossession established a pattern that remains the leitmotif of relations between San and Bantu speakers today."

Nevertheless, individual San groups quite successfully put up resistance against the Bantu immigrants or lived more or less peacefully side by side. Only when white hunters, settlers, soldiers and administrators entered the territory with superior firearms prior to German colonisation, they had no choice but to completely retreat. After the colonial annexation by Germany in 1884, the process of marginalization continued (Ki-Zerbo 1981: 448).[34]

German South-West Africa may be regarded as synonymous for colonial cruelties in which the German "master race" were at least equal, if not even superior, to other European nations. Their racist hierarchies and phantasies of omnipotence corresponded to those of the Boers and could not have been any more excessively violent.[35] The life of a San was even less valuable than the life of other Africans. In contrast to Botswana where the San rather retreated to remote areas, however, some San in today's Namibia did not accept becoming passive victims but actively made a stand against the German oppressors. This is why in 1911, the German "Siedlerpresse" (settlers' press) wrote about a "Bushmen plague" and "Bushmen threat" (Gordon [1992] cited in Saugestad 2004: 28).[36] When

---

34 In response to the German annexation, Great Britain proclaimed the protectorate of Bechuanaland (Oliver/Atmore 1981: 65).

35 At this point it may be interesting to add that at the beginning of the 20th century, the Governor General of German South-West Africa was Rudolph Göring, father of Hitler's right hand Herman Göring (Le Roux/White 2004: 92).

36 For a more detailed presentation of the Khoekhoe and San resistance see Le Roux/White (2004: 96–100).

the administration of German South-West Africa was transferred to the Union of South Africa (1920), this development certainly changed the land rights situation of the San. Both colonial powers presumed that the extinction of the San – due to assimilation into their "civilized" society – was only a matter of time. Therefore, they did not have to pay attention to their land rights, as Suzman (2001b: 5) also explains for the power following the Germans:

"Although German colonists were often ruthless in their dealings with San, the fact that they had their hands full pacifying Otjiherero- and Nama-speaking groups meant that many San escaped the excesses of that particular regime. It was really only after the Union of South Africa took over administration of South West Africa (SWA; today Namibia) that San came to find themselves at the sharp end of the colonial enterprise. In particular, San were to suffer great losses as a result of the SWA Administration's land policies, so that by the mid-1970s fewer than 3% of them retained even limited de jure rights to land anywhere in the country."

From today's point of view, I would like to add that the so-called "pacification" of the Otjiherero and Khoekhoe is considered the "first German genocide" (cf. Ki-Zerbo 1981: 464). For about two decades, the Otjiherero with their representative Chief Kuaima Riruako have demanded reparation payments. Now they are ready to take legal steps. Similar to basically all cases of colonial cruelties, these demands too have to face a German policy of denial. In an article of the German magazine "Der Spiegel", Hielscher (2007: 59) comments this policy in his closing remarks in a way that could be applied to so many human rights violations, including those against the San:

The question why it is so difficult to reconcile the Herero with Germany was answered by the renowned Norwegian conflict researcher Johan Galtung as follows: 'The basis of any reconciliation is a dialog at eye level' – and such a dialog has not begun yet![37]

1.3 South Africa

From 300 AD until the 18th century, Bantu-speaking peoples slowly migrated into the southern regions of Africa. Also in the area of today's South Africa, the newcomers encountered land occupied by the San and Khoekhoe. Archaeological findings prove that they were able to coexist at least in some cases. The Khoekhoe might have been of great value to the immigrants because of their knowledge of the land and cattle breeding. When white settlers arrived at the Cape in 1652, the

---

[37] Original citation in German. For a detailed description of the historical facts for each region in Namibia, current Government policies and laws concerning land rights, resources and participation as well as the current conditions and legal situation of the San in Namibia, see, e.g., Suzman (2001b) or the *Report of the African Commission's Working Group on Indigenous Populations/Communities: Mission to the Republic of Namibia* (ACHPR/IWGIA 2008b).

San and Khoekhoe began to gradually lose their remaining land. Boer settlers were searching for farmland and pressed more and more forward, thus threatening the traditional pasture areas of the Khoekhoe as well as the territories of the San.

The San and Khoekhoe developed one form of resistance that also helped them to survivor: they began hunting for cattle and looting farm houses. These attacks were considered the first guerrilla wars in southern Africa. They provoked campaigns of revenge and destruction: until the middle of the 18th century, Dutch military commands murdered thousands of San, including many women and children. The number of enslaved San in 1795 is estimated to be about 17,000 (Le Roux/White 2004: 18–32).

The few descendants of Khoekhoe and San communities who had not been completely eradicated in the 18th and 19th century and who had not died of disease or extreme poverty because they had lost their economic base entered the 20th century suffering from the symbolic violence of apartheid classification: "They became doubly invisible, as the drama of South African politics was dominated by the overriding black-white dichotomy, with 'coloured' a residual category of diverse individuals lumped together for administrative purposes" (Saugestad 2004: 28). This "double annihilation" meant that the San did not only lose their traditional territories but also their identity and thus their cultural roots.[38]

1.4 The "Northern San"

There are far less sources addressing the history of the San in the three countries Angola, Zambia and Zimbabwe than for the rest of southern Africa. One of the reasons may be the less intense research interest for these relatively small groups but we should also keep in mind political factors, such as armed conflicts and long civil wars (e.g. in Angola). About 3,500 San, mainly !Xun and Khwe, live in southern Angola. For more than 40 years, war has shaped their living conditions. At the beginning of this bloodshed, the Portuguese used them to fight against the liberation movement in Angola. Later on, the South African military committed them against the national liberation movement SWAPO in Namibia. Most San moved to southern Namibia and a few even to Zambia in the east. The majority of the remaining 300 to 400 Khwe lived in the border region of Angola, Zambia and Namibia. When the conflicts in this region intensified, more border controls, land mines and violent exchanges fragmented and isolated them from each other. Now many are considered refugees and thus do not receive any state support (Saugestad 2004: 30).[39]

---

38   Cf. for a regional overview of the San's situation in South Africa, Angola, Zambia and Zimbabwe: Robins et al. (2001).
39   The *Working Group of Indigenous Minorities in Southern Africa* (WIMSA) and two other NGOs commissioned Richard Pakleppa to assess the situation of San communities

II. Historical Overview until the End of Colonial Times

Although Zambia was never involved in any war after its independence, it has a strategic location at the border to Angola and the hard-fought Caprivi Strip in Namibia. This location was the reason why time and again, armed conflicts terribly affected especially the many San communities in the border region. Fights, land mines and military border controls isolated these groups. As these communities are relatively small with 300 to 400 individuals – compared to hundreds of thousands of civil war victims – they have never entered the regional or international limelight and never received any support. In addition, also the Zambian Government saw them as refugees or immigrants of neighbouring countries, whereas they presumably are the earliest inhabitants of the western region of Zambia (Le Roux/White 2004: 212–218).

An estimated 2,500 San (Tyua) live in the western border region between Zimbabwe and Botswana and are ethnically related to the Tyua of Botswana. Similar to the other countries of southern Africa, they were dragged into the country's conflicts and liberation fights. In the 1920s and 1930s, the Government resettled them from the Hwange National Park and thus took away their basis of existence. Now they survive as pastoralists and on subsistence economy (Le Roux/White 2004: 206–212).

In a nutshell, the historical human migration from other parts of Africa, especially of Bantu-speaking peoples, caused more and more pressure on the land and natural resources of the San communities of southern Africa. The immigrants' agriculture and cattle breeding needed large extensions of land and caused a highly competitive situation over water and pasture land for wild animals, both of which the San needed for hunting and gathering. In consequence, the San were forced into border regions with less agricultural potential.

The geographical marginalization was not the end of the story though. The immigrating communities also brought a feeling of superiority with them, especially concerning socio-economic characteristics: these focused on the San's decisive "lack" of grazing animals and thus of wealth. As Nader analyzed for a different context (of European and later U.S. American imperialism), this regional version of her "theory of lack" sought to establish three things: the authority to dispose of the territory, the subordination of the encountered "indigenous peoples" and the dominance of the rights they brought with them. This (as mentioned above) historical and rhetorical strategy worked with the central "notion of lack" and today is reflected in multiple ways in the current social situations of the San and the legal attempts for "indigenous" rights:

---

in Angola. The report *Where the First are Last: San Communities Fighting for Survival in Southern Angola (2003)* concludes that the San communities experience social marginalization, discrimination and economic exploitation. They also live in alarming conditions of servitude and dependence. Cf. also WIMSA Report (2004a: 65–70).

"As an imperial instrument, law calls upon this key principle of control – the notion of lack – to legally justify the taking. Indigenous lack modernity and development; they lack capacity and knowledge that allows full utilization of their environment; they lack law, they lack treaties, although exceptions were noted" (Nader 2005: 201).

Also in these historical situations of land dispossession in southern Africa, the new sovereigns insisted that "indigenous peoples" were denied any leadership and thus any (efficient) organization as well as the right to live in settlements. In their eyes, therefore, "indigenous peoples" lived similar to "Stone Age peoples", if not even to animals. All this meant different but basically comparable forms of marginalization. When the Europeans began their so-called "blue water" colonisation, a history of almost complete and violent demise as well as all imaginable forms of oppression, domination, slavery and discrimination began. As a consequence of this new power situation, the San lost most of their culture, identities, and forms of self-governance, territories and natural resources. They were forced into an institutionalized political-legal system which provided hardly any or no space at all for their way of living, understandings of law and cultural practices. In the following section, I will describe the aspects of what was in many ways "blinded out" and "destroyed".

III. Reflections on Indigenous Legal Perspectives and World Views

To begin with, it is my opinion that the reciprocal translation of indigenous and Western legal systems, understandings and terms is problematic. The "indigenous world", as some may call it, is separated from the "Western world" by different "terminological worlds", first and foremost in their legal cosmovisions. In this sense, Roberts (1979) and later also Wilmsen (1989: 165) concurring in his opinion, warn that it would have adverse effects on indigenous claims and interests, if their understandings of law were embedded or even frozen in Western categories. They suggest that a research area narrowed down by Eurocentric criteria derived from our legal understandings should be replaced by questions that refer to their understandings of law, procedural traditions, historical experiences of maintaining order, processes of social control and the settlement of disputes. As we do not know a lot about the legal system(s) of the San, we should avoid classifications based on legal categories, such as constitutional, property or hereditary law.

Anthropologists mainly focused on the San's various forms of economy, technological and material forms of expression, kinship structures, sexual behaviour, biological aspects, and also recently questions of gender. Researchers, however, hardly addressed their religion, political and legal processes of both self-organization and decision-making, or the relevance of their ancestors in normative systems, especially concerning their indispensable relationship to their territory. The San regularly emphasize how important their territory is to them: "We understand in our culture, in the Sesarwa culture, that land is central to our lives because the graveyards of our ancestors are in our land. (…) Land is crucial to our culture" (Sesana 2000: 175). At the (according to their own accounts) first historic process of consultation of various southern African San organizations (in Shakawe, Botswana, 6–9 September 1998), a catalogue of principles and guidelines was developed as an indigenous resolution (interestingly, they were supported by experienced indigenous representatives from other continents)[40]. The resolution stresses both the spiritual and metaphysical significance of their traditional territories:

- "Respecting the significance of our traditional territories is vital for our survival as a people.

---

40   The published document of this consultation process justified this step of a political counter-globalization as follows: "Many of them (other indigenous peoples around the world) can look back at experience over a much longer period than we can in southern Africa. That way we have learned from each others' successes and failures" (Kuru Development Trust and WIMSA 1999: para. 1).

- Our land is part of our origins and thereby of our identity, as the land is the owner of its people.
- Our land is the link to our ancestors, and sacred places bear witness to this.
- Our land is alive and requires our protection; through its soil and vegetation we are connected to its animals and these are the resources necessary for our spiritual and physical life."[41]

Why then is the geographical environment so important for the San and for all indigenous peoples? Some social anthropologists have tried to generalize these spiritual aspects of legal arguments and to develop them to essential characteristics of indigenous peoples. Durand Alcántara (1999: 104–111), for example, addressed the question whether it would be possible to work out certain models of social organization and related philosophical forms of expression – notwithstanding the cultural diversity among indigenous peoples – that shared similar features and thus common characteristics of the essential relationship between indigenous peoples and their territories. The author calls these presumed archetypical structures the "four 'levels' of identity" between indigenous peoples and territories. According to Durand Alcántara, indigenous peoples understand "nature" and their cultural-ecological interactions as guided by a holistic principle of the harmonious and well-structured order of the universe. This understanding is also the basis for the first level of the cosmovision of any indigenous culture:

If these peoples talk about the earth, they refer to the most fundamental element which in their global cosmovision includes the universe as well. From this perspective, all processes of social life are connected to each other. In this total sense contained in indigenous peoples' cosmovisions, earth is of holistic meaning (Durand 1999: 107).[42]

Thus, the earth is sacred (to them); they are born on it, live from it, and will be part of it again. In contrast to Western understanding, earth is not reduced to its significance as a factor of production. It is rather (also) the foundation of the spiritual existence of indigenous peoples. The territorial space forms a community (the so-called "level of communalism") out of (any?) indigenous peoples but these communities must not be understood as independent and autonomous units. As Durand Alcántara continues, the community life of indigenous peoples manifests itself on levels of organization: the collective right of *usufruct* is ensured by a "legal oral tradition" which is passed on to the whole community. Based on the level of kinship, the right of *usufruct* determines the basis of domes-

---

41 Principle 8 adopted by an *Indigenous Peoples' Consultation* (Kuru Development Trust and WIMSA 1999). Also the *Gaborone Declaration on Indigenous Peoples and Minorities in Africa* explicitly mentions the spiritual relationship concerning their ancestors to their traditional trerritories and resources (United Nations 2002).

42 Original citation in German.

tic subsistence economy. Ultimately, all indigenous peoples exist in both "internal" and "external" relationships with a territory that is subject to the socio-political control of a hegemonic power. Exercising this hegemony has caused transformations ("hybridization" between the conventional and the new culture) and losses (mainly as a result of land grab) of the former as well as current meaning of the soil (Durand 1999: 108).

The third level is identity: the indigenous community derives its specific identity from the understanding that it is organized as a specific population on a historically qualified territory. This identity – that must not be considered as static – both determines and defines the relationship to their territories because it established a feeling of belonging to a certain geographical space and its socio-cultural environment. This feeling is then passed on from generation to generation and paves the way for their heritage claims as handed down from their ancestors (Durand 1999: 109f.).

The fourth and last level addresses the cosmological principle of the sacredness of earth. It is not only both a subjective and objective relationship to earth but it also regulates the balance between nature and humans. In the end, a territory provides the material basis of existence for indigenous peoples and comprises their entire environment as well as their sacred places. Indigenous conceptions of "mother earth" share a crucial characteristic: the respect for nature. Thus, "mother earth" is in a certain way the "social" relationship between nature and humans (Durand 1999: 110f.).

Similar discourse elements may be found in the statements of San and their representatives: "[The Kgalagadi Transfrontier] Park is our whole heritage, our life is there, the graves of our ancestors are in the Park. So what I can say actually is that it's our life, the park is our life, it's our history, our heritage."[43] The director of the NGO DITSHWANELO shares comparable experiences and observations about the central significance of land for the San: "If you would have raised the word 'land' to any Basarwa in Botswana, you would emotionally get the response 'the land is my mother, the land is my identity, the land is my culture' and as Roy Sesana once said, land is their human rights."[44]

Needless to say, these considerations essentialize the close connection between indigenous peoples and nature and thus assume a perspective of indigeneity that does not conform to the legal discourses. Also here, however, we have to ask whether such a homogenous perspective may be applied to an entire collective or whether it may rather be that other less spiritual statements are simply blinded out in a relatively heterogeneous spectrum. Therefore, it may happen that particularly those contents and arguments that conform to the prejudices from outside (e.g. from a European perspective) about alleged "characteristics" of

---

43 Interview with the ǂKhomani San Vetpiet Kleinmann, 12 February 2004.
44 Interview Alice Mogwe, DITSHWANELO, 12 September 2003.

indigenous peoples are privileged in the media and public discourses. Of course this does not mean that such emotional statements, e.g. about the motherhood of earth – as a metaphor for their land – are irrelevant or even impermissible. On the contrary, they demonstrate how indispensably crucial territorial ownership is for many indigenous communities. Furthermore, they also show both cognitive and discursive commonalities and points of contact, which have certainly provided the basis for global interactions about "indigenous" aspects in international law. In other words, spiritual and cosmological reference points should not be played off against proper rational "worldly" arguments of law. We can detect a false contradiction between an alleged cosmological view of the world and rationality in the following often-observed fact: whenever indigenous peoples had full control and unrestricted ownership of land, it has much more often lead to a sustainable use of resources than the economization of land and resources of Western industrial societies.

From a legal point of view as well as from empirical contact with the voices of those concerned, a certain theoretical restraint towards some metaphysical generalizations from the outside – as interesting and perhaps (at least partially) valid they may be in a limited empirical segment – appears at order. Statements from the viewpoint of those directly concerned have a different theoretical status than the "essential characteristics" sometimes elaborated from a social anthropological perspective. We can imagine how problematic such generalizations may be in legal practice (of promoting indigenous rights) by looking at the simple fact that states will quite probably not recognize and rather reject indigenous claims or even deny indigenous identity at all, if such generalizations are not deemed applicable in a particular case. Furthermore, it is evident in the various attempts of social anthropology to elaborate some kind of common metaphysic or cosmology of indigenous peoples that there is a significant lack of empirical work, especially concerning the rational processes of decision- and opinion-making.[45] In this particular aspect, however, numerous accounts of oral traditions allow us to assume that there really are empirical common features implying the significance of the communicative process of finding consensus in various San communities as well as, beyond that, indigenous societies. "The byword of Bushman politics in general and G/wi politics in particular is consensus" (Barnard 1992: 108). In contrast to certain conceptions of a so-called consensus democracy in party-political European contexts, this consensus certainly refers to a significant notion of actual discourse based on arguments and is not in any way connected to conceptions of intransparent trades.[46] The following interview shows what a San representative of the NGO WIMSA understands as a consensual process of decision-making:

---

45 For more details see Zips (2009).
46 For more details see Barnard (1992: 108ff.) as well as Silberbauer (1982: 31–34).

"Generally, our life is not built on principles of individualism, on building of wealth and power. Decision-making is by consensus by a group. Equity, trust and respect for all are some of the principles that our way of life was built and set upon. In most cases when you are looking for consensus, you have to get the elderly people, including men and women and consult with them. Consultation is important, views of other people are important. They must be taken on board and be respected."[47]

The interview cited above focuses on the current situation of the San in Botswana as it is related to their resettlement from the Kalahari and its subsequent legal dispute. This is why the quote above on the one hand includes strong historical references, suggesting regrets that parts of political and legal practices have already been lost. On the other hand, however, Mathambo Ngakaeaja refers to his current experience of NGO work that needs to integrate many different interests and viewpoints – also and especially concerning future developments. In addition, the WIMSA spokesperson held a leading position in the former KURU Trust. This umbrella organization of various project groups is the material and intellectual property of the San, amongst others of D'kar, and practices processes of decision-making according to the criteria mentioned above.[48]

At the level of empirical research, the current reconstruction of such processes is facing severe problems. Hardly any group lives in a social environment that would allow them to practice "democratic self-determination" according to their own criteria. Only to a certain extent, qualitative and narrative interviews are able to close this gap of former research. Many researchers have focused on the area of absolutized differences with European systems due to the explicit or implicit evolutionist preconceptions I have mentioned several times. Therefore, not only religious and spiritual aspects but primarily the economic foundation of the San, namely hunting and gathering, occupied the centre stage of interest. From a perspective of today's source criticism, we may again perceive various aspects of an ambivalent context. On the one hand, it is quite understandable in the context of the land rights dispute that the San invoke their (historical) identity as hunters and gatherers.[49] This is closely connected to hunting dances which try to tran

---

47 Interview Mathambo Ngakaeaja, 24 February 2003. For more details see Zips-Mairitsch (2011).
48 Since 2001, the *Kuru Family of Organisations* (KFO) has been a group of NGOs owned by the San. For this subject matter see especially chapter 5.
49 Mathambo Ngakaeaja answered the questions, "Are there still some groups that live the lifestyle that they are known for internationally?" as follows: "You mean the romanticised way of life of hunting and gathering? I personally haven't met any and I'm keen to meet some. But this does not mean to say that there are no groups that live more traditionally in comparison with others. I am quite aware that even here in D'Kar there are people who still use the healing dance to heal themselves, who go to the veld to gather fruits and eat them and use them for medicine. There is still a lot

scendentally pick up the scent of an animal before the hunt starts or comfort and reconcile the spirit of killed animals after the hunt.⁵⁰

On the other hand, stressing an identity as hunters and gatherers reduces their subsistence to a form that is in stark contrast to modern worlds. After all, the political and legal structures shown above become less important because the San's economic ways of life are overemphasized. However, the insistance of San activists (and the communities they represent) on sufficient living environment and land ownership as a prerequisite to their historically accumulated lifestyle is another matter. Vast areas of land stocked with wild animals are indispensably necessary to retain their special competences of hunting and gathering as well as their well-attested biological and ecological expertise which they have, for example, used extremely successfully in natural medicine.⁵¹ As Taylor (2001: 157) explains in Botswana's political economy of today, this "otherness" of "hunters and gatherers" is still symbolically significant:

"[H]unting and gathering is important in understanding Basarwa identities, not because Basarwa represent leftovers of a prehistoric way of life, but because contemporary contexts make 'hunting and gathering' an important label of self-designation by Basarwa in certain contexts. In other words, the salience of hunting and gathering today is more as a symbol that carries meaning to both Basarwa and their neighbours in the contemporary political economy of Botswana, especially considering experiences of dispossession and alienation from land and wildlife."

As indigenous peoples (or their representatives) increasingly began to communicate with each other by means of international conferences, common activities, transnational legal developments and of course also the new media, they "discovered" and intentionally developed common features. In light of this development, however, it would be of course wrong to disregard the diversity and all the differences. One of such cultural events is, for example, the Kuru Dance Festival near Ghanzi, which politically is an important medium of the already-mentioned pan-San policies. Its foundation in the spiritual world and the arts offers insights into their impressively diversified cultural capital as well. Nonetheless, there is a common communicative base going beyond the linguistic di-

---

of subsistence on a traditional way of life, although it is not the 100% pure hunter-gatherer who is putting on a loin cloth and is hunting with bow and arrow" (Interview 8 March 2005).

50   Interview Seloka !Xuntai 19 February 2003, leading elder of the Ju|'hoansi (!Kung) San in Tsodilo.

51   As a member of the ||Anikhwe stresses, "The way they lived with the animals did not scare the animals away and they stayed close to our people, almost as if they understood that they had to feed us and that we would look after them. Our people followed conservation ways and knew the land. Almost as if we were farming with game, like people nowadays are keeping cattle and goats!" (Interview Kotsi Mmaba, Sekandomboro, Botswana), cited in Roux/White (2004: 148).

versity and divergent symbolic systems. As we can see in the context of the festival, this common base makes it possible for San groups with different historical experiences from remote areas of southern Africa to come together and practice a healing dance.

If you once have experienced the common healing dances of different San communities from southern Africa moving around enormous bonfires in a cold Botswana winter night, it will be hard for you to depreciate the shared significance of the communication with ancestors, trance, and collective healing.[52] Although I cannot focus on these spiritual and transcendental aspects in a book about legal and political questions, I still want to point out how significant they are in the self-understanding of the various San communities. Such events become extremely important especially in a period of on the one hand high social stress due to pressure by the surrounding majority population and on the other hand the threat of continuously losing (the last remaining piece of) land and thus one's culture.[53] Even though we are talking about creative representations of former cultural practices and their meanings, they fulfill the crucial task of enabling the San to collectively remember well as cognitively passing it on to the younger and youngest generations. In the course of this two-day festival, hunting practices and their spiritual support is invoked:

"If they hunted for the whole day without seeing any animals, the elders used to talk to the spirits by taking a piece of wood and putting it on the ground. They spoke to it as if they were speaking to a person, asking questions about which way they should take to find the animals. Then if that piece of wood became hard to pull out they would know that the spirits were agreeing that they should take that way to find the animals. This is true because we did find animals. That is the way we lived in the past."[54]

---

52 Even if such events that are to some extent advertised as tourism attractions do not have much to do with the spirit of the "olden days", it is still possible to see the intense joy and content of continuing the cultural experiences of the past in the faces of participants from South Africa, Botswana and Namibia: "In the olden days we used to sit around the fireplace for story telling by our parents and grandparents, which was in the form of jokes and very funny. The stories were mostly about animals. These stories told us how to live our lives and when hunting in the bush to be clever and brave. The other lessons were about taking care of the land, culture and relationships with other tribes. We were also taught to respect our elders in the community and to take care of children and to be generous. Those were our lessons during the old days" (Interview Peter Goro, Tobere, Botswana [Bugakhwe]), cited in Le Roux/White (2004: 82).

53 So, for example, co-organizer and host Bau Dukuri of the Kuru Dance Festival: "My culture is very important to me, because when we were still staying out in the Kalahari we used to heal ourselves with our culture. We sing, we dance, healers would heal us and we predict what is happening tomorrow and we predict what has happened before which we haven't seen" (Interview 20 August 2005).

54 Interview Dinge Masele, Ngarange, Botswana [Bugakhwe], see Le Roux/White (2004: 177).

Culture is always dynamic. Therefore, it should not be frozen in time neither because of scientific interests of preservation nor touristic reasons of economization. The various activities of intentionally remembering and preserving the cultural traditions of the San rather follow the purpose of counteracting the loss of culture due to external influences and force. As countless statements of those concerned confirm, this loss leaves them with a desert-like emptiness that does not give reason to expect any further development in the field of aesthetic creativity, skilled craftsmanship or spiritual expressiveness.[55] Their history and culture is crucial both in terms of self-awareness as well as for future generations: at the end of this chapter, I would like to illustrate this point by "giving the floor" (in the sense of the book title "Voices of the San")[56] to three San from three different countries:

"This project ["Voices of the San"] has told me so much about the traditional life of our people. I am now much more proud of who I am, and will be even more when I can see my language being written in books. Learning about my history has hurt me a lot, but also given me the power to stand up against the other groups. I think now I want our government to empower us, to make space for the San people" (Interview Xhwaa Tsae, Yooshe, Botswana [Ju|'hoansi]).[57]

"I want people to be happy about the old stories, the *kulimatji*, of our people. If we just sit still and do nothing to keep the beauty of our culture, all will be lost. So much is already gone. One thing we can do is to write it down, as the time for our culture to be an oral one only is past" (Interview Mario Kapilolo Mahango, Schmidtsdrift, South Africa [!Xun]).[58]

"I would like my life story to be told, as a Hai||om daughter growing up. The reason for this is to keep the historical background for our children, so that in the future they can know in whose footsteps they would like to go" (Interview Victoria Geingos, Outjo, Namibia [Hai||om]).[59]

---

55 Roy Sesana, Chairman of the NGO *First People of the Kalahari*, explained the consequences of his peoples' relocation: "Relocating the Basarwa communities is just a way of killing them – a way of detaching them from their ancestral spirits and a way for impoverishing them. By nature the Basarwa are richer than Batswana and white people. Now they are poor because of repressive systems that come from other tribes like the Batswana" (Sesana 2000: 175).

56 In the course of various projects, leading figures were interviewed by their own people. They all then formed the unique illustrated book "Voices of the San" (Le Roux/White 2004).

57 Cited in Le Roux/White (2004: viii).

58 Cited in Le Roux/White (2004: vii).

59 Cited in Le Roux/White (2004: viii).

Part 4: Botswana: State and Society

I. Sociopolitical History

Before decolonisation, the Republic of Botswana was the economic and political "Cinderella" of Africa (Obeng 2001: iii). In the 1950s, it was described as a country without a future and in the 1960s, it became the economically dependent neighbouring country of South Africa. Since its independence, however, Botswana has been regarded as "everybody's darling" (Interview Mogwe 2003) and a role model for the rest of Africa. After huge diamond deposits were found, the country earned this reputation because it used its significantly grown state assets sustainably. In contrast to other African countries where the political elite became richer and richer, Botswana invested in education, health care and its infrastructure.

In 1966, Botswana gained political independence with a self-understanding as the "Nation of the Tswana". In short "Tswanadom" developed into the key signifier of the emerging national identity (cf. Datta and Murray 1989: 58). Thus, the various Tswana societies were clearly privileged in political institutions and consolidated their domination of other ethnic groups. Since independence, the country has admittedly been an exemplary democracy with one blemish: its ethnocentric treatment of minorities and indigenous peoples put under constant pressure to adapt to the official version of "Tswanadom". The following historical outline focuses on how Botswana's current social makeup came into being: this will allow us to probably better understand why the country steadfastly refuses to politically recognize indigenous peoples as a part of a multi-ethnic state. In the beginning, I will describe the pre-colonial phase, how the region was settled and how early society was formed. The second part of the chapter presents the time of colonialism and its consequences on the region and its peoples. Both the specific form of colonial rule as "indirect rule" and the beginning of nationalism significantly shaped Botswana's way to independence. The last part of the chapter then shows how the former British protectorate has impressed the world with good governance, rule of law and democracy since then, even though without the complete participation of its indigenous population.

1. Pre-colonial Phase

The ancestors of the Sotho-Tswana were among the earliest Bantu immigrants in southern Africa. They are supposed to have entered the area of today's Botswana about 1,800 years ago. All current traditional Tswana ruling houses may trace back their origins to ancestors who, in the 13th century, allegedly lived in today's South African Witwatersrand in the Transvaal. From this time and space on, they presumably immigrated to today's Botswana. Later, others also left the region due to the Zulu expansion wars (Hopf 1991: 62f.). Anyhow, they all encountered San communities of hunters and gatherers as well as the cattle-breeding Khoekhoe.[1] At this time, the Tswana kingdoms were diversified enough to regard them as independent communities.[2] In their new territories, the Batswana founded large settlements with complex district structures reflecting the political organization of the community. These were always concentrated around the central power of the *Kgosi*.[3] The organization of the kingdoms as well as tribute payments enabled them to easily welcome and integrate other groups into their settlements (as the lowest social class) (Hopf 1991: 62; Tlou/Campbell 1984: 57f.).

Both internal and external factors, such as fissions of minorities and new social lineage segments, crises and wars resulted in new foundations of *merafe* as well as emigrations into other regions, thus in turn pressuring relevant local populations. As a result of these formation processes, strong and dominant Tswana kingdoms developed right to the edge of the Kalahari. In fact, "Tswana" is a collective name for eight different groups: Bangwaketse, Bakwena, Bamalete, Bakgatla, Bangwato, Batawana, Batlokwa and Barolong.[4] Nevertheless, also several "non-Tswana" societies settled down in the area of today's Botswana, including the ethnic minorities of the Bakalanga, Bakgalagadi, Wayeyi, Basubija, Mbukushu, which were mostly assimilated by the Tswana (Hopf 1991: 62ff.).

The so-called *Difaqane* or *Mfecane* wars then caused the most extensive migration in the history of Botswana and southern Africa.[5] The conflicts started in South Africa's Zulu society but the exact reasons are quite controversial and most sources name several triggering factors: a) the growing competition over land, especially good pasture land, perhaps also due to the severe droughts between 1800 and 1810; b) the (economic) fight for trade routes to Mozambique's Portuguese ports; c) the increased demand for "commodities", not least due to the generally extended trade relations because of the slave trade (Ramsay/Morton/Mgadla 1996: 62f.). Apart from inner-African aspects, however, the emerging of colonial influence may have played a decisive role as well (Hopf 1991: 64). Never before had wars become that extensive, cost so many human lives and destroyed so many settlements and culti-

---

1   For the history of the San (and Khoekhoe) see above chapter 3, section II this volume.
2   These proto-states were called *merafe* (sg. *morafe*) in Setswana. Individual *merafe* consisted of smaller wards with a sub-chief; kings or paramount chiefs, however, enjoyed absolute sovereignty.
3   The members of a *morafe* have always recognized a *Kgosi* (pl. *Dikgosi*) as "king" or *chief* and the highest executive, judicial and legislative authority (now with limited powers within the nation state though; cf., for example, Hazdra 1998).
4   The prefix Ba- is attributed to the "tribal name" but it is also the plural form for Botswana's citizens: singular Motswana, plural Batswana. The term "Batswana" is used as an adjective for customs, traditions, characteristics, opinions and positions of Botswana's population as well.
5   These wars between 1820 and 1840 are called *Difaqane* in Sotho (Setswana) and *Mfecane* in Isixhosa (Zulu). The literal translation would be "crushing" or "scattering" ("time of crushing"); local Botswana oral traditions refer to them as "times of tumult" (Ramsay/Morton/Mgadla 1996: 61).

I. Sociopolitical History

vated land. The consequences of the *Difaqane* wars could even be felt in Namibia and Ngamiland. They broke up all social structures of that time and caused all Tswana *merafe* to be newly formed after 1840. As a result of this reconstruction, many kingdoms later could not stand up to the Boer incursion. Choosing between bad and worse, they asked the British colonial power for protection (Wilmsen 1989: 90).

2. Protectorate Bechuanaland

After the *Difaqane* wars, the phase of social restoration went hand in hand with new pressure from outside: the continuing process of colonisation and the European "scramble for Africa", the increasing influence of Christian missionaries and traders on African societies, and the related spreading of new technologies. At the political level, the extended British imperialism in southern Africa as well as the newly-established Boer Republic in South Africa increasingly threatened the Tswana kingdoms. At the same time, the *merafe* of the Bangwato in the north, the Bangwaketse in the south and Bakwena in central Botswana developed to become strong trading and military powers (Hopf 1991: 65).

After Great Britain had recognized the independent Boer Republic in 1852, a Boer command attacked southern Tswana territories, including the mission station of Livingstone. In consequence, the Tswana chiefs closed their ranks and formed an alliance that would later lead to the united Tswana kingdoms of Botswana (Hopf 1991: 66). Since the 1870s, British missionaries had both recommended and urged the *dikgosi* to seek British protection against the raids of Boer settlers. On 30 September 1885, the British Crown decreed "Proclamation No. 1 of 1885" and thus unilaterally declared the area of today's Botswana a British protectorate. The territory south of Molopo River was turned into a colony and later became part of South Africa under the name Northern Cape.[6]

It was not the pleas of the Tswana chiefs that influenced Great Britain to make that decision, though, but general economic, political and geo-strategic changes and interests in the region. Crucial events, such as the discovery of diamonds in South African Kimberley and gold in Witwatersrand (Transvaal) would change the economic and political map of southern Africa in the long run. Also the growing demand in workforce for mining and railroad construction influenced Great Britain's interest in Botswana. Particularly Cecil Rhodes' *British South African Company* (BSAC) that dominated gold mining in South Africa was supposed to gain more influence in the north (Ki-Zerbo 1981: 369f.).

---

6   At this point we should keep in mind, however, that the formation of the protectorate did not comprise all areas of today's Botswana. Some areas gained British protectorate status only later, e.g., Ngamiland and Chobe in 1890 (Ramsay/Morton/Mgadla 1996: 128, 163).

When the German Empire annexed South-West Africa in 1884, Great Britain had another reason to establish the protectorate. The British Crown was afraid the German colony could form a confederation with the sympathizing Boer Transvaal because this would have blocked their expansions northwards. In this context, Great Britain, so to speak, "preemptively" proclaimed the protectorate of Bechuanaland (Hopf 1991: 67).[7] Moreover, Great Britain wanted to "rescue" all remaining countries after Germany's annexation of East Africa. In the context of this "Scramble for Africa", European imperialists met at the Berlin Conference (1884–1885) to negotiate the infamous distribution of Africa. In 1879, Africans still governed more than 90 percent of Africa. At the turn of the century, however, European powers controlled the entire continent except the kingdom of Ethiopia and Liberia.[8]

At first in the protectorate of Bechuanaland, the British "protection" posed the threat of becoming part of the High Commission Territories of South Africa and losing the independence of the Tswana kingdoms. For the time being, however, the proclamation hardly affected the internal structures of power. The proclaimed protectorate meant for the chiefs *de facto* that they could keep their territorial sovereignty, whereas the colonial government had a more or less strong influence on foreign and defense policies. In practice, there was no formal government with effective control over the entire protectorate area. Great Britain was thus officially responsible for both internal and external affairs (Quansah 2001: 1). As Bechuanaland was only strategically relevant to the British Crown, which also tried to keep administrative costs as low as possible, the chiefs (deemed complacent enough) were preferably confirmed in power or were to a certain extent even strengthened in their position.[9]

Then in 1889, the British Crown was facing a severe legal problem: in Bechuanaland, some kings granted other (mining) companies than the *British South African Company* (BSAC) mining concessions on their land. On behalf of the British Crown and directly granted by Queen Victoria, however, the *British*

---

7 Great Britain negotiated the eastern border with the Boer Government of the Transvaal, while for the western and northern borders they had to bargain with the German colonial administration of South-West Africa. For the German rulers, the Caprivi Strip was a corridor into the central territories of German East Africa and Ruanda-Urundi (Obeng 2001: 17). This arbitrary drawing of borders, however, separated San communities, e.g., the !Xo, Naron, Ju|'hoansi and Kxoe in the Botswana/Namibia border area as well as the Tua in the Botswana/Zimbabwe border area from each other (see figure in: Suzman 2001a: 7).

8 Oliver/Atmore (1981: 103–113), for example, explains why all colonial powers recognized the "distribution of Africa" as well as its reasons; see also Ramsay/Morton/Mgadla (1996: 145–148).

9 In pre-colonial times, the subjects could overthrow an unpopular chief: "[A] chief who became too unpopular might be displaced by force, or people could secede from his rule." Under British rule, however, the displacement by force was prohibited. The colonial government had to approve any loss of power (Bennett 2002: 7f.).

I. Sociopolitical History

South African Company was entitled to any and all sovereign rights, and thus concession rights, in Botswana, Zambia and Zimbabwe.[10] In consequence, the concessions granted by the Tswana kings contradicted the royal document of 1889 (*Royal Charter*). This was of course not acceptable for the British Crown which now had to find a legal way to revoke the concessions. The chiefs insisted on their sovereignty over their land though: when in 1885, the protectorate was proclaimed and accepted by the chiefs – so they argued – they did not *per se* convey the authority of legislation and jurisdiction within their territories to the British Crown (Queen Victoria). British jurists then confirmed this legal position and the Crown realized that the Tswana kings would never voluntarily renunciate their sovereignty (Ramsay/Morton/Mgadla 1996: 159–164).

In February 1891, the British Assistant Under-Secretary of State for the Colonies John Bramston produced a document to overcome these problems of international law: this memorandum dealt with the jurisdiction and administration of European powers in protectorates.[11] Accordingly, Europeans were entitled to undertake anything "necessary" for the control and safety of their nationals and natives in "uncivilized territories" because native rulers were not qualified for that task (due to their "uncivilized" state). Bramston thus concluded that in "uncivilized territories" sovereignty could be exercised in the same way as if the whole country had been assigned to the Crown. If Great Britain was henceforth allowed to protect the subjects of its protectorates, it would also as a "civilized power" be entitled to appoint own courts and government officials with legislative powers in "uncivilized territories" (Ramsay/Morton/Mgadla 1996: 164f.). In the same way slavery was legitimated, racist "rationalizations" made it possible to cynically justify their ruling power.

In consequence, this was the end of previously limited interventions in the internal affairs of Tswana kingdoms. Based on the Bramston Memorandum, the colonial government issued the *Bechuanaland Protectorate General Administration Order-in-Council* 1891 which adopted the colonial law of the Cape.[12] It entitled the High Commissioner to enact laws, establish a court system, levy taxes and do everything necessary to ensure peace, order and responsible governance (Pain 1978: 163; Obeng 2001: 19f.). Nevertheless, the British colonial power limited itself – at least

---

10   Cf. for more details concerning development, exploitations and downfall of the *British South African Company* in southern Africa, e.g., Sauer (2003: 242f.).

11   "Memorandum as to the Jurisdiction and Administration of Powers of a European State Holding Protectorates in Africa" 1891.

12   In the previous year, a decree was issued that made the High Commissioner the representative of the Queen in southern Africa. He thus was granted absolute ruling power and could even revoke laws that had been enacted in the past (Ramsay/Morton/Mgadla 1996: 162f.). The general legal basis for applying British law to protectorates (the Crown had in principle no authority of legislation and jurisdiction in territories that were not part of the English dominion) may be found in the *Foreign Jurisdiction Acts* of 1843 and 1890.

partly – to have the High Commissioner respecting "(…) any native laws and customs by which the civil relations of any native chiefs, tribes or **populations** under Her Majesty's protection are now regulated, except so far as the same may be incompatible with the due exercise of her Majesty's power and jurisdiction" (section 4 of the *Bechuanaland Protectorate General Administration Order-in-Council 1891*).[13]

This section was crucial (for the context of indigenous rights presented in this book) because it did not only protect the laws and customs of Tswana societies but also those of "populations" not further defined. In my opinion, the relevant provision may reasonably be interpreted as covering the indigenous peoples' understandings of law in Bechuanaland as well, including *inter alia* those of the San. Otherwise the terms *chief* and *tribe* would have been sufficient to describe the Tswana kingdoms. The use of the term "populations" meaning "temporary demographic phenomena" suggests a certain understanding of indigenous communities of that time as well.[14] Needless to say, we should not overrate this provision. As we can see, it also includes a clause concerning the compatibility with all provisions decreed on behalf of the Crown ("the due exercise of her Majesty's power and jurisdiction"). Nonetheless, it at least shows circumstantial evidence for a certain recognition of the existence of the San and their rights.

In Proclamation 1891, two provisions of section 19 need to be further discussed: on the one hand the reception of the Cape Colony's law and on the other hand the undefined time of reception: "Subject to the foregoing provisions of this Proclamation, in all suits, actions, or proceedings, civil or criminal, the law to be administered shall, as nearly as the circumstances of the country will permit, be the same as the law for the time being in force in the Cape of Good Hope: Provided that no Act passed after this date by the Parliament of the Colony of the Cape of Good Hope shall be deemed to apply to the said territory." The reception of the Cape Colony's law differed from the normal practice of the British administration because "it was the usual practice for such reception of laws to be of English common law, the doctrines of equity and statutes of general application in England" (Quansah 2001: 3). Given the proximity of the countries, considerations of administrative convenience probably led to this decree of reception of the Cape Colony's law in Bechuanaland.

The proclamation's second provision did not show a specific date defining the beginning of the law's reception and thus caused legal uncertainty.[15] The colonial

---

13 Emphasis added. Cited in Sanders (1989: 116).

14 Since the 1980s, the term "peoples" meaning permanent socio-political units is clearly preferred. Cf. in this context the considerations to ILO Convention 107 of this book's first chapter.

15 This practice was not unusual though: the British colonial government usually chose between two formulas of reception concerning time. Some countries, e.g., Ghana, introduced the foreign law as it had been in its country of origin (England) at a certain point in time ("cut-off" day). It happened more often though – as in Bechuanaland

I. Sociopolitical History

administration resolved this lack of definition in *Proclamation No. 36 of 1909*. It thus derogated the proclamation of 1891 and imported the "entire" Roman-Dutch common law or, as it was named, Cape Colonial Law as a crucial element into the legal system of Botswana (Quansah 2001: 2f.; Fombad 2003: 87).[16] In addition, the British rulers established a system of superior courts responsible for disputes between Europeans as well as between Africans and Europeans. They also controlled all matters related to trade, the hunting by foreigners and concessions (Mgadla/ Campbell 1989: 49f.). Everything else was still subject to traditional Tswana legal provisions and institutions unless they contradicted colonial law, European values and occasionally the moods of the colonial administration too.[17]

In accordance with Her Majesty's decree, the administration of the protectorate was to be transferred to Cecil Rhodes and his *British South African Company* (BSAC). He did everything in his power to exercise *direct rule* in Bechuanaland because he wanted to integrate it into the Cape Colony. It was hardly surprising that the Tswana kings saw their positions and territories threatened and were determined to resist. Supported by the *London Missionary Society*, the *dikgosi* of three large kingdoms – Khama III of the Bangwato, Sechele I of the Bakwena and Bathoen I of the Bangwaketse – travelled to London in July 1895. They wanted to protest against the planned transfer of the colonial administration to the BSAC (and thus Cecil Rhodes) and asked for continued British protection (Obeng 2001: 14).

They had the idea of presenting themselves as "African gentlemen" and "exemplary Christians" and convinced the British population as well as the media

---

– that the foreign law was "timelessly" adopted. It was then used as applicable for the decision of an individual case (Pain 1978: 161ff.). In this case, the provision stated as follows: "The law for the time being in force in the Colony of the Cape of Good Hope". Cf. also Hazdra (1998: 53f.).

16 Pain (1978: 164ff.) argues that the proclamation of 1909 did not affect the "timeless" character of the 1891 proclamation. This basically means that the courts of today's Botswana would still be bound to South African precedents. As such a situation is hardly compatible with the sovereignty of a modern state, a dispute of doctrines developed concerning the question whether it was perhaps necessary to assume a "cut-off" day due to later events. Pain, however, advocates a defined separation of laws.

17 At this point it should be mentioned, though, that the British administration was inconsistent in many cases: *Kgosi* Sekgoma Letsholathebe of the Batawana, for example, could fight a divorce case under British law before a British court (Ramsay/Morton/Mgadla 1996: 247f.). The British, however, began to regard the same *Kgosi* as disreputable and arrested him allegedly to prevent a riot. He then appealed to his right to protection against arbitrary arrest. When his claim of *habeas corpus* was not granted in the Cape Colony, Sekgoma went before the Court of Appeal in London. The court then decided that British law also applied to the protectorate and that basically all subjects of British rule were entitled to *habeas corpus*. The peoples of Bechuanaland, however, were found to be "semi-savages" and thus excluded from any kind of legal protection (*The King v. The Earl of Crewe, ex parte Sekgome*, [1910] 2 K.B. 576 (C.A.). Kgosi Sekgoma stayed in prison without judicial inquiry for a total of six years (Ramsay/Morton/Mgadla 1996: 248).

with moral appeals that the Government could not decline their request. The campaign of the three chiefs was successful to some extent. Although the protectorate remained under British rule, the *Dikgosi* had to make some concessions and accept the following terms: to leave land to the BSAC to build a railroad to the north, not to exercise jurisdiction over Europeans, to grant appeals against their decisions before British courts, and to allow the demarcation of their territories in order to integrate all the remaining land into the protectorate (Obeng 2001: 15). In consequence and over a period of three decades, Great Britain added five more *native* or *tribal reserves* to the original three. These eight reserves represented the eight (dominant) Tswana-speaking communities, the chiefs of which were recognized by the British administration (Ng'ong'ola 2000: 163).[18] The rest of the country was proclaimed crown land (47%) or freehold land (5%):

> "Now therefore, His Majesty, by virtue of the powers by the Foreign Jurisdiction Act, 1890, or otherwise in His Majesty vested, is pleased by and with the advice of His Privy Council to Order, and it is hereby ordered as follows:
>
> 1. In addition to the Crown Lands defined by the Bechuanaland Protectorate (Lands) Order-in-Council, 1904, all other land situated within the limits of the Bechuanaland Protectorate elsewhere than in the Tati District shall, with the exception of
>   (1) Such land as is either
>   (a) included in any native reserve duly set apart by Proclamation; or
>   (b) the subject of any grant duly made by or on behalf of His Majesty; and
>   (2) the forty-one farms known as "the Baralong Farms" held by members of the Baralong tribe (…)
>
>   vest in His Majesty's High Commissioner for South Africa and be subject to all the provisions of the said Order-in-Council as Crown Lands.
>
> 2. His Majesty may at any time add to, alter, or amend this Order.
>
> 3. This Order may be cited for all purposes as the Bechuanaland Protectorate (Lands) Order-in-Council, 1910."

---

18 This was the first legislative act of recognition and proclamation reserving certain parts of the country for certain Tswana communities (Batawana in the north-west and Bakgatla in the southeast): *Proclamation No. 9 of 1899*, followed by the establishment of crown land and freehold land (or farms, blocks) in accordance with *Bechuanaland Protectorate (Lands) Order-in-Council 1904. Proclamation No. 28 of 1909* recognized the Bamalete community in the southeast, *Proclamation No. 44 of 1933* the Batlokwa of Gaborone. The last "reserve" – of the Barolong in the south – was granted in accordance with *Proclamation No. 77 of 1935*.

I. Sociopolitical History

The colonial administration's stance towards the *native reserves* which more or less represented the district structure after the country's independence granted the chiefs relative autonomy over their territory. As certain reserves were excluded from the decree cited above and established mainly for Tswana-speaking communities, the colonial rulers claimed legal titles for all territories not owned by Tswana communities. For the San, Bakgalagadi and ethnic minorities, this meant that henceforth they either lived in a reserve or on crown land.[19] In this sense, the 1910 decree may be regarded as the first legal instrument for the area of today's Botswana that legitimated the dispossession (without compensation) of indigenous peoples.[20]

Although colonial imperatives cut through all Tswana societies, the communities resisted quite successfully. Nonetheless, they could not permanently prevent or stop those severe structural and economic changes that increasingly both integrated in and subordinated Bechuanaland to the economic and political development of South Africa.[21] Colonial legislation was, for example, closely connected to the development of Botswana as a source of cheap workers, especially for South African mines and industries. Similar to other colonies, the collected so-called hut tax was a crucial instrument of economic submission (Obeng 2001: 21f.). This is how legislation demanded each and every "Bechuana household" to own money. As the country lacked larger businesses and industries, workers were hardly needed. The predominant mode of earning money thus became wage or migrant labour.[22]

There is still a debate going on from various social-theoretical and political viewpoints as to what these historical changes meant for the San of Bechuanaland. My considerations about the Kalahari debate presented above essentially showed that both perspectives had their deficits: one focusing on relations of production and class according to Wilmsen (1989) and one focusing on the evolutionist-biologistic idea of isolated communities of hunters and gatherers as used by the *Harvard Kalahari Research Group*. In fact, many of the still-unre-

---

19 Cf. in this context the doctrine of *terra nullius* in chapter 1, section I. as well as the excursus "aboriginal title".

20 Cf. also Saugestad (2001: 98): "To the extent that the colonial administration considered the rights of non-Tswana communities at all, they were conveniently assumed to be subject to the Tswana land-use regime. Those who inhabited Crown Lands became in legal terms tenants of the Crown and could be dispossessed of the land at a moment's notice, which became apparent whenever land was needed for settler occupation or other purposes."

21 For a more detailed account see Parson (1991: 117–121).

22 In the 1940s, migrant labourers earned almost half of the total income of the protectorate's African population (Hazdra 1998: 113). At the end of 1943, the record number of 21,200 migrant labourers – men between 18 and 50 years – from Bechuanaland resided outside of the country (Kiyaga-Mulindwa 1987: 106).

solved questions can hardly be answered due to a lack of sources. Therefore, both scientific "factions" draw quite extensive conclusions from particular data. This is also why none of the conclusions seems to be convincing: neither of the dependence theory (Wilmsen 1989) which regards practically all San as a lower class of Tswana society, nor of the Harvard "isolation" or "independence theory" (Lee 1965: 2) which regards today's San communities as "peoples" that have survived since times long past (just not to mention the proverbial "Stone Age").

Perhaps there are not enough sources for an illuminating, praxeological assessment of the diversity of various historical accumulations. Hence, the perspective of action remains rather vague. For the time being, a historical interpretation seems to be the most comprehensible solution: such an approach does not see "the" San as a homogenous "community of peoples" but considers them as heterogeneous groups with distinct but reciprocally comprehensible collective identities. These groups were the first inhabitants of the Kalahari and reacted in various dynamic ways to new social, external forces. Such an approach would also go beyond both diametric poles of the Kalahari debate and offer (at least) a third perspective that (based on existing sources and probably complemented with oral traditions) focuses on a multitude of creative and adaptive achievements of social organization as well as individual decisions. I also understand Saugestad in this sense, although I would love to see her "diversity of adaption" extended to include the perspective of (productive) creativity (seeking self-determined solutions).

When she refers to Wilmsen's (1989: 132–157) emphasis of the permanent "outside" relations[23] of the San who, as he claims, had never been completely isolated again since the immigration of the Sotho-Tswana, she is absolutely right to point out the significance of interactions which successively robbed the San of their autonomy and livelihood:

"This perspective has contributed important documentation of historical links between the San and the Bantu and invading Europeans. Many of the findings are provisional, many conclusions are debated, many details are contested. (...) For the last 1000 years or so there have been agro-pastoral peoples in eastern Botswana. There are traces of exchange networks extending to Great Zimbabwe and the East Coast, of regional differentiation of settlements, and of a stratified society. Some Bushmen groups were affected by historical events such as the 1820 population explosion in South Africa, Shaka Zulu's wars and the influx from the south. The period of 1850–1890 was a peak of European commerce, depleting large areas of commodifiable animals (skins, fur, ivory), and breaking

---

23   Cf. in this context, e.g., his conclusions: "The conclusion is inescapable: it is not possible to speak of the Kalahari's isolation, protected by its own vast distances. To those inside, the outside – whatever 'outside' there may have been at any moment – was always present. The appearance of isolation and its reality of dispossessed poverty are recent products that unfolded over two centuries and culminated in the last moments of the colonial era" (Wilmsen 1989: 157).

I. Sociopolitical History

down trade routes. This turbulent process must have had an impact on San people" (Saugestad 2001: 92).

Following this understanding, it becomes possible to believe in particular reconstructed aspects of the more or less dependent conditions of production in which the San were connected in and to Tswana societies as well as trade relations to the white population. This understanding becomes even more plausible, as it does not see all indigenous peoples of Botswana as a lower class in a double sense and, as a result, does not make them "disappear" (from a historical perspective). Some San obviously traded in animal products or hunted in subordinate positions to "their" Tswana masters. When trophy hunting decimated animal populations especially near larger settlements, we can assume that many of these dependent hunters were forced into even more subordinate positions in cattle breeding because – as Wilmsen (1989: 131) argues – they no longer owned the means of production as in hunting (as well as the symbolic capital of hunting technologies, as we should add here). Thus, cattle replaced ivory as the main source of income in the Kalahari.

As the cattle industry grew and hunting opportunities became rarer, a hardly quantifiable share of the San population *de facto* turned into pastoral peoples: "Those San-speakers who could capture a cattle post position obtained a measure of security in the system – at the bottom of the heap, but in it" (Wilmsen 1989: 132). Others became migrant labourers in the mines of South Africa. In my opinion it remains highly questionable whether Wilmsen (1989: 157) is right when he postulates that all other members of the San peoples were only forced into inaccessible and difficult ecological areas of the Kalahari because of these economic developments and that only then, they "fell" back (?) deeper and deeper into a "foraging way of life". Therefore, it seems that this part of historical reconstruction can neither be confirmed by empirical sources nor is it free of basic (ideological) assumptions that all social segments of Bechuanaland, including the vast majority of the San, were involved in the developing monetary economy and could, thus, be analyzed by means of a homogenous and preconceived social theory.

Anyhow, the introduction of the above-mentioned "hut tax" as well as the recruiting of labourers turned the colonial administration, the (mine) industry and the Tswana kingdoms/chiefs into a community of common interests. The chiefs became tax collectors and did not only receive British salaries but also ten percent of all tax revenue. In consequence, the British administration permanently changed the economic position of kings and royal families and, thus in turn, ensured their loyalty and cooperation (Obeng 2001: 21f.). In the course of time, they extended the territory in which English law was to be applied and gradually left administration to the chiefs. A system of indirect rule was born in which African customary law still played a significant role (Woodman 1993: 276ff.).[24]

---

24 There was the adopted Roman-Dutch law that regulated all trade relations and became the "personal" law of the educated urban population and the middle class. Tra-

From a political point of view, the British administrated the protectorate with a mixture of *laissez faire* and forced loyalty. Chiefs that did not oppose their rule and approved the European-Christian imperialism in their territories were rewarded with money, honour and protection. Chiefs who opposed them, however, were removed and replaced by (supposedly) more submissive successors. The two following proclamations of 1934 changed the character of the kingdoms as well as jurisdiction in the protectorate: *Native Administration Proclamation No. 74* and *Native Tribunal Proclamation No. 75*. The first proclamation did not only entitle colonial rulers not to recognize a person as chief but they could also indefinitely replace him with any person (that did not necessarily have to be a member of the royal family). And as if this was not enough, the second proclamation imposed a new court system upon the native reserves: it created two new court levels (Senior Tribal Tribunal and Junior Native Tribunal) to replace traditional jurisdiction, granted appeals against these new institutions before English courts and limited the chiefs' former jurisdiction in terms of criminal law and punishments.[25]

The colonial rulers probably wanted to be kept in the loop concerning the mood of the kings deprived of their power and "compensated" the chiefs with an advisory council, the so-called *African Council*.[26] As the name already implies, it was only a national forum of discussion without any legislative power. Nevertheless, the *African Council* was the first political body with Africans from the whole protectorate. Apart from its advisory role, it was also a crucial breeding ground for the first ideas of an independent Bechuanaland. Founded in 1921, the *European Advisory Council* only had European members and was dedicated to the issues of about 2,000 European settlers and traders. Still, its influence on colonial administration was much more direct than the *African Council's* impact ever was. In 1951, representatives of both councils formed the *Joint Advisory Council* (JAC). Established on principles of equal status, it was comprised of eight Africans, eight Europeans and four representatives of the colonial administration (Obeng 2001: 50f.).

(African) Council members referred to other British colonies and increasingly called for participation in the protectorate's legislation. As international political events worked in their favour, especially a wave of decolonisation through Africa

---

ditional African customary law was used for the lives of ordinary people in rural areas and standardized cattle transactions, marriages, legal succession, and inheritance. Criminal trial law before the Magistrates' Court or the High Court, however, was stipulated by English law (Obeng 2001: 40). Thus, a "legal dualism" or "legal pluralism" of adopted law and traditional African customary law was created.

25 For a more detailed picture see Obeng (2001: 22ff.).
26 In 1920, the first such forum was established as the *Native Advisory Council*. In 1940, it was renamed *African Advisory Council*. When 11 years later, the chiefs of the eight big Tswana communities were declared *ex officio* members, it was again renamed *African Council* (Obeng 2001: 50).

as well as first protests against the South African regime of racial segregation, the colonial administration answered their demands and replaced the advisory council with the *Legislative Council* (Mgadla/Campbell 1989: 52f.). Bechuanaland was home to 0.7% Europeans and 99% Africans but although both groups were equally (and not proportionately) represented in the council, its establishment was an important preparatory step towards political independence (Hopf 1991: 77).

In 1959, the council appointed a committee of eight members to draft a constitution.[27] The British administration accepted the proposal and, thus, the Constitution of the Bechuanaland Protectorate entered into force in 1961. Needless to say, this was not enough for the African population: they wanted to be independent. Step by step, all laws based on racial categories were repealed; the Constitution was amended towards self-governance and the *Bechuanaland Independence Conference* organized in London in 1966.[28] Prime Minister of Bechuanaland Seretse Khama (since the amended Constitution of 1965), his representative Quett Masire, *Kgosi* Bathoen II representing the *House of Chiefs* and the British colonial administration negotiated a whole week long.[29] The conference produced a document that was enacted as law by the British Government and entered into effect on 30 September 1966. This act has become the Constitution of the now independent Republic of Botswana.

3. Republic of Botswana

When the Constitution entered into force in 1966, it had taken exactly 81 years since the proclamation of the British Protectorate for Botswana to obtain peacefully – and without any resistance or violent struggle for liberation (as in most neighbouring countries) – its political independence. The colonial power's heritage may be summarized as sparing and shameful: at cut-off day, Botswana had about five kilometres of paved road (between the train station and the High Court in Lobatse). The total national budget amounted to less than 6 million Pula (a bit more than 600,000 Euros at the current exchange rate) and the annual per capita income was below 50 Pula (today about 5 Euros). More than 80 percent of the population lived in rural areas. When the country became independent, the cap-

---

27   The members of the constitutional committee were Tshekedi Khama, Seretse Khama, Chief Bathoen II and Dr. Molema of the African representatives and Russel England, J.G. Haskins, H.S. van Gass and G.W. Sim representing the Europeans (Obeng 2001: 51).

28   For a more detailed discussion of the 1963 and 1965 Constitution as well as the Independence Conference of 1966, see Obeng (2001: 52–57).

29   Philip Matante, leader of the opposition in Bechuanaland, boycotted the conference. In his opinion, the draft Constitution had not been sufficiently discussed neither with the chiefs nor the population.

ital of Gaborone had just about 4,000 inhabitants. City expansion only started with independence on the horizon around 1963. With 87% of state revenues, cattle breeding was the main source of income. The country did not have any industry except a slaughter house. Most of the population found no other employment but in the mines of South Africa or Southern Rhodesia (now Zimbabwe). Less than half of all children attended school and the country only had six institutions of higher education. In consequence, 80% of the population was illiterate and a total of 20 to 30 individuals could show a university degree. More than two thirds of the entire population depended on donated food rations.[30]

Keeping in mind this summary, the colonial period was basically characterized by gross default in the social, political and economic field. At the time of independence, this situation created a "technical and political vacuum" (Molutsi 1989: 104). Notwithstanding problems from the past, a government had to be formed for an independent Botswana. The first elections of 1965 were a tremendous success for the *Botswana Democratic Party* (BDP): in accordance with the plurality voting system, the party of Seretse Khama won 28 of the 31 seats in parliament. While the BPP (*Bechuanaland Peoples Party*) could win the remaining seats, the *Botswana Independence Party* came away empty-handed.[31]

After Botswana had become independent in 1966, the parliament elected Seretse Khama as first president and re-elected him twice until his death in 1980. He was then succeeded for an even longer period, 18 years, by his vice-president and former BDP Secretary General Quett Masire who, as his successor ensured stability in the "post-Khama era" by continuing *cum grano salis* his policies (Hopf 1991: 81). Vice-president then followed vice-president: Festus Mogae in November 1997 and Ian Khama in spring 2008.[32] The constitutional amendment of 1997 stipulated that a president cannot be elected to office any number of times

---

30   See United Nations (2001: 1), Obeng (2001: 59) and Grant/Ramsay (1987: 187ff.).

31   Founded in 1960, the BPP was the first party to gain political influence. It was partly inspired by the South African ANC and allegedly – probably because they demanded Botswana's independence – with militant tendencies. When internal differences caused the BPP to split up, the *Botswana Independence Party* (BIP) was born. In 1961, the BDP developed as a rather "moderate" answer to the BPP and was essentially lead by "modern" chiefs and wealthy farmers educated according to Western standards. For a more detailed overview of the three parties and the elections, see Murray/Nengwekhulu/Ramsay (1987: 172–186). Since independence, Botswana has been dominated by a single party, the ruling BDP. The opposition has remained weak and fragmented, often splitting the vote and lessening its chances of winning more parliamentary seats. Moreover, although elections are free and non-violent, the opposition and civil society have consistently complained about unfair polls. The political playing field is not balanced, since the BDP is the best resourced of all parties and enjoys the other benefits of incumbency. Additionally, factionalism is a challenge that all the political parties confront (Somolekae 2005: 18ff.; IDEA 2006: 5).

32   Good/Taylor (2006) criticized the early handing-over of the office without elections.

I. Sociopolitical History

but that presidential administrations are limited to two terms or a maximum of 10 years (Obeng 2001: 132).

Botswana is one of the few African states that have maintained the Westminster-derived parliamentary system of liberal democracy since independence. While free and democratic elections are held every five years, a functioning multi-party system at least formally exists. The opposition, however, is *de facto* split up into many smaller parties, in friction with each other and thus lacks power.

"[B]otswana has become a mono-party state, that is to say, a state with one strong party and many weak opposition parties" (Obeng 2001: 70). This can just as well be seen in the fact that the opposition is weakly represented in parliament.[33] This is why discussions in parliament are nothing more but a formal act. Needless to say, this situation is an obstacle to an effective parliamentary control. The BDP has continued to be so dominant because of the historically-accumulated structure of the ruling class: elements of traditional chieftaincy, former white settlers, and predominantly Western-style educated groups. The latter are not only the main source for politicians and leading government officials in the public sector but also for managers in the private sector.[34] In addition, the favourable economic development produced a "state alliance of classes" that determined the country's policies. In terms of political parties, this "alliance of cattle and diamonds" was mainly organized in the BDP (Hopf 1991: 81).

Botswana's economic upturn was caused by the "lucky fate" that huge diamond deposits were discovered only eight months after its declaration of independence. While the country still was among the world's ten poorest states in 1966, its annual gross domestic products (GDP) on average rose by 6 % annually in the 30 years to come – the highest continuing economic growth in the world for that period. In the category of "developing countries", Botswana was considered a 20th-century economic story of success among international financial institutions and donor associations (United Nations 2001: XI). In its *Index of Economic Freedom*, the conservative U.S. Heritage Foundation has ranked the country 30 in the world.[35] With the lowest rate of corruption in sub-Saharan Africa, a GDP per capita of USD 16,030 and an inflation rate of 8.5 %, Botswana (after Mauritius) also enjoys the reputation of being the economically most

---

[33] The BDP has always won the absolute majority in parliament since the country's independence. In 1969, the opposition parties gained 7 out of the 32 seats in parliament – the highest number of political representatives until the 1990s (Molutsi 1994: 29). In October 2004, they achieved 13 out of 57 seats and in October 2009 twelve seats, which means that percentage-wise nothing has changed. The Botswana parliament is now comprised of 63 members (being the State President, 57 directly elected members, four specially elected members, and the Attorney General); five are women.

[34] For a more detailed discussion see Molutsi (1989: 104–114).

[35] In comparison, Austria is ranked 25, France 62 and South Africa 74 (*Index of Economic Freedom* 2013). See online www.heritage.org/index.

connected country to liberalism. Therefore, Botswana is currently the third-richest African state.[36] The diamond industry produces more than 32% of the country's GDP, half of all foreign exchange revenue and 70–80% of export earnings.[37] Thus, Botswana's economy is extremely dependent on this one product. The other sectors of agriculture and tourism are hardly able to strengthen the success story's very narrow economic base.[38]

In spite of the otherwise positive economic development, one third of the population survives on more or less one USD per day. The huge difference in income suggests a strong urban-rural divide, whereas up to even 71% (in the north) or 90% (in the west) respectively earn the least in remote areas.[39] Difficult climatic conditions in huge parts of the country are responsible for this problem but that is not all there is: the heavy focus on a narrow economic base, a resulting high unemployment rate (2012: 7.5%) and other problems of distribution contribute to the social reasons as well.[40] In addition, HIV/AIDS has caused a "national crisis" in the health sector that weakens the productivity in all economic areas in the long run. As the *Weekly Electronic Press Circular of the Office of the President* indicates, life expectancy sank from 65 years in 1993 to 33.7 years in 2007. Probably one third of the entire populations are HIV positive.[41] Of course these hard facts can only scratch the surface of the resulting dramatic situation. If the chances of healing stay the same, a huge part of the young population will hardly reach working age. Out of the total numbers of people living with HIV/AIDS worldwide in 2009, 34% resided in 10 countries of southern Africa. In this list, Botswana ranks number two with nearly 25% of infected adults. According

---

36 *Index of Economic Freedom* 2013. In sub-Saharan Africa, the average GDP per capita is only USD 2.334,34 in 2011 while the average inflation rate is at 8,01% (without Zimbabwe).

37 Cf. CIA World Factbook 2012; www.indexmundi.com/botswana/economy_profile.html (accessed on 20 September 2012).

38 "[B]otswana can no longer look to the sustained expansion of mineral production to be the engine for further economic growth. (...) The structure of Botswana´s economy and the nature of its resource endowment make it highly vulnerable to external political and economic changes. (...) Synthetic diamonds pose a distinct threat in the longer term. The cattle industry also faces daunting problems. Botswana's favoured status under the Lomé Convention cannot prevail forever. (...) Slow global economic growth might even militate against tourism if rich people in the northern hemisphere become less willing to take expensive holidays in the southern hemisphere" (Hermans 1994: 129).

39 *Botswana Institute for Development Policy Analysis* (2001: 100).

40 For a more detailed discussion see United Nations (2001: 19ff. and 47f.).

41 Republic of Botswana (18/3/07): Tautona Times no 9 of 2007. *The Weekly Electronic Press Circular of the Office of the President*. According to "Fischer World Almanac 2007", this is the lowest life expectancy rate of the world (worldwide average 67 years).

to estimates, 93.000 children in Botswana are orphans due to AIDS (UNAIDS Report 2010: 181, 186).[42]

The Government tries to face these deficits with an ambitious development plan that pursues to following general objectives: sustainable economic growth, diversification, social justice, economic independence from South Africa, and continuing self-sustaining development. The policies to reach these goals are included in national development plans, currently *National Development Plan 10* (April 2009 to March 2015) as well as *Long Term Vision for Botswana 2016* (in short *Vision 2016*). The first have a planning period of five years, are revised every other year and, if necessary, adapted to social changes. Especially the first two development plans (prior to the HIV/AIDS epidemic) established Botswana's reputation of a both efficient and cautious planning authority. In consequence, the country received more international financial support (Hopf 1991: 82).

Vision 2016 and its democratic development strategies are the result of a comprehensive process of consultation that included various sectors of civil society and concerned social and economic aspirations of development. It is Botswana's long-term goal to realize the defined strategies as much as possible by means of continuously evaluated and implemented programmes by 2016, the 50th independence anniversary.[43] Both of the current national development plans obviously focus – quite understandably because of the poverty from times before independence – on the economic sector. The basic attitude of these objectives suggests that Botswana's cultural heritage is the source of the national political principles, meaning democracy, development, self-confidence and unity. These principles then formed the wider context for the country's development goals: sustainable development, fast economic growth, economic independence, and social justice (Vision 2016: 2).

Like Botswana's whole policy towards ethnic minorities and indigenous peoples, the country's emphasis on unity on the one hand and cultural diversity on the other hand remains contradictory and ultimately unresolved in the context of development paradigms. Needless to say, neither paradigm rules out the other one. If Botswana stresses its rich cultural and linguistic diversity, though, and at the same time finds it necessary to define the criteria of a true "Motswana" and thus citizen, a general tendency of contemporary (genuinely European) constitutionalism with a strong emphasis on the state's nation and uniform culture (the implicit "dominant culture") becomes obvious. Such constitutionalism is usually

---

42   However, five countries – Botswana, South Africa, Tanzania, Zambia and Zimbabwe – showed a significant decline in HIV prevalence among the younger generation in national surveys (UNAIDS Report 2010: 21).

43   The working group of 30 was appointed by the president and came from the following fields: political parties, the private sector, NGOs, trade unions and religious organizations. Long Term Vision for Botswana 2016 (1997: 80ff.).

based on three unquestioned social premises: society is exclusively comprised of equal citizens, the common good of society holds these citizens together, the citizens as a whole form a culturally rather uniform nation. Differing traditions are at best recognized in terms of minority rights that are determined by the state (Kuppe 2004: 55). Both communitarianism and nationalism are extremely underlined and reflected in *Vision 2016* which asks the national community to determine the "best elements of tradition":

"Botswana has not yet succeeded in enlisting the social and cultural diversity of the country in a shared Vision of the future. The people are the strongest asset of any nation, and Botswana is well endowed with a rich variety of cultures and languages. There must be an emphasis on the **characteristics that typify a Motswana** – the best elements of traditional behaviour must be strengthened and projected" (Vision 2016: 3; emphasis added).

Although several passages of the goals also stress the obligation to tolerate and respect both ethnic and cultural differences, I do not think that this is sufficiently established in the principles of nation-building. This is where national (Tswana?) unity and social harmony are concentrated. Quite understandably, tribalism is seen as a central problem but it is at least also implicitly used to justify the assimilatory stance against "less positive" cultural traditions. The whole context of public political discourses allows us to conclude, however, that these cultural traditions could be understood as the "backwards" indigenous communities "living in the past" (as the following chapter discusses in more detail):

"Botswana must deal with problems related to tribalism, and to **perceived** discrimination against minority ethnic and language groups. (…) Botswana must rediscover a collective identity based upon shared values and a respect for ethnic or cultural differences, or differing views or religious beliefs" (Vision 2016: 26 and 27, emphasis added).

Neither of the last two quoted passages can clarify what is meant on the one hand with the limited focus on "perceived" discrimination and on the other hand with the "rediscovered" collective identity. *Vision 2016* leaves open whether minority ethnic and language groups (as the document calls them) should be reintroduced into a historical relationship of integration/assimilation under a hegemonic majority culture of recognized (culturally different yet similar) Tswana ethnic groups. This again leaves room for interpretation of how the imperatives of uniform nation-building could be combined with the idea of protecting diversity.[44] In this sense, behind the targeted understanding of a homogenous nation state Botswana lurks the political dominance of the Tswana as it has historically existed for a long time already. As quoted above, *Vision 2016* appears to have

---

44   In this sense, Botswana's legal and social behaviour towards indigenous peoples and ethnic minorities is extremely similar to ILO Convention 107 and its integrationist and assimilatory character. See part 1.III. for a detailed discussion of the convention.

I. Sociopolitical History

a member of the eight Tswana communities or tribes in mind when drawing the picture of a "typical" Motswana:

"Like the process of establishing official nationalism elsewhere, 'Tswanafication' (...) has been an attempt to create and promote a unified nation while sustaining, if not strengthening existing suzerainty" (Solway 2004: 131). It seems probable that the plans for such suzerainty of a Tswana "dominant culture" had already started in the above-mentioned historical development since the early times of immigration. It was then both legally and politically established in the Constitution of independence: English became the official and Setswana the national language. All government matters, national media, legal institutions and education have thus been limited to these languages. Keeping such preconditions in mind, the government's often-confirmed good will of supporting pluralism (especially concerning languages) should neither be understood too extensively nor read without its connection to measures of social assimilation.

Botswana's policy of assimilation is also reflected in its legislation: establishing the position, recognition and function of the king, the *Chieftainship Act* defines "tribe" as the eight "classic" Tswana kingdoms of the Bangwato, Batawana, Bakgatla, Bakwena, Bangwaketse, Bamalete, Barolong and Batlokwa.[45] This means that the traditional authorities of the San, Kalanga, Kgalagadi, Herero, Wayeyi and Mbukushu were not recognized as chiefs. With the exception of state land, also the *Tribal Territories Act* attributes the districts of administration to these eight tribes.[46] Therefore, the eight Tswana groups represent a historical metamorphosis of pre-colonial *merafe* or proto-states in tribal reserves during colonialism to "districts" after independence (Solway 2004: 134f.). Two years after the country's independence, parliament proclaimed a law to end the chiefs' control and administration of tribal land by establishing "land boards".

Art. 3 of this act stipulated the formation of main authorities in the administration districts defined by Art. 2 *Chieftainship Act*, thus meaning in the Tswana territories.[47]

Moreover, the Constitution of Botswana has suppressed ethnic-cultural pluralism at the highest level of the newly-introduced *House of Chiefs* (a second advisory committee of the parliamentary system). Three articles – 77, 78 and 79 – exclusively granted the eight Tswana chiefs automatic membership in the *House of*

---

45 Art. 2 *Chieftainship Act* (Republic of Botswana, 1987, Cap. 41:01).
46 *Tribal Territories Act* (Republic of Botswana, 1933, Cap. 32:03).
47 *Tribal Land Act* (Republic of Botswana 1968, Cap 32:02). It also established subordinate authorities for each region within the tribal areas (Art. 3/1 und Art. 19/1). In 1976, the land was restructured: in the districts Chobe, Ghanzi and Kgalagadi, state land was reclassified as tribal territory in accordance with *Tribal Land (Amendment) Act no 21 of 1976*. State land was thus reduced from about 47% at the time of independence to about 24% in 1998; in consequence, the tribal territory grew from originally 48% to 75% (Ng'ong'ola 2000: 167; Adams et al. 2003: 56).

Chiefs.⁴⁸ Art. 79 entitled these "ex officio" members to elect four more members who would then also have a vote for the last three representatives. The *House of Chiefs* is subordinate to the Botswana parliament. Although it does not have too many constitutional competences (mainly in matters of chieftaincy), its advising influence on the central government should not be underestimated from a pragmatic point of view.⁴⁹

In the context of membership and representation in the *House of Chiefs*, the country's other ten ethnic communities were absolutely right to repeatedly indicate that they were discriminated (Obeng 2001: 72). In February of 1995, the parliament finally requested a constitutional amendment after long discussions.⁵⁰ In July 2000, then President Mogae appointed a commission of 21 members headed by former Member of Parliament and former Minister of Local Government Patrick Balopi (known as the *Balopi Commission* after the chairman). The commission was charged with the following tasks: to review the relevant articles and to assess the charges of (ethnic) discrimination against them, to amend the articles, if necessary, to make them more "neutral", and to propose a more effective method of selecting members of the *House of Chiefs*. Perhaps for the first time, these broad discussions put the question of ethnicity into the limelight of both public and media interest. The commission assumed a rather evading and diplomatic stance by stating that it would not serve any useful purpose to determine possible discrimination.⁵¹

"The Commission is of the view that it was empowered to pronounce on the question of whether or not the three Sections are discriminatory. But, we do not think that it is **either necessary or wise** to do so. We are satisfied that pronoun-

---

48 Art. 77 Constitution of Botswana: "(2) The House of Chiefs shall consist of (a) eight ex-officio Members; (b) four Elected Members and (3) three Specially Elected Members." Art. 78 Constitution of Botswana: "The ex-officio Members of the House of Chiefs shall be such persons as are for the time being performing the functions of the office of Chief in respect of the Bakgatla, Bakwena, Bamalete, Bamangwato, Bankgwaketse, Barolong, Batawana and Batlokwa Tribes respectively." Art. 79 Constitution of Botswana: "(1) The Elected Members of the House of Chiefs shall be (…) Sub-Chiefs in the Chobe, North East, Ghanzi and Kgalagadi districts, respectively."

49 The members of the *House of Chiefs* are the spokespeople and interpreters of their traditional culture(s). As traditional rulers, they have an alternative status of representation based on traditional (but in no way static) forms of organization. They do not contradict democracy but complement the democratic process. Cf., inter alia, Kotrba (2002) or Sharma (2003).

50 For more details see *Report of the Presidential Commission* (2000: 3–9). It already was the third motion though. The first two in 1969 and 1988 were rejected (Nyati-Ramahobo 2002b: 699).

51 Of course not all members of indigenous peoples and ethnic minorities as well as NGO stakeholders were satisfied with this view.

I. Sociopolitical History 207

cing on this question would serve **no useful purpose**. In this context, we make the following additional points that: a) Such a finding would do more harm than good. (...) b) It would entail an unnecessary and lengthy legal discourse (...) c) Such legal analysis would serve no real purpose (...)" (*Report of the Presidential Commission* 2000: 83f.; emphasis added).

Based on the *Balopi Commission*'s recommendations, the Government decided to amend the Constitution to end the dominance of the eight Tswana peoples, in Botswana called "tribes", in the *House of Chiefs* and to establish "tribal balance" in its composition. It amended Articles 77, 78 and 79 due to the explicit parliamentary motion "(...) to render them (articles 77, 78, 79) tribally neutral" (*Government White Paper No. 2* of 2002: 2). The Government thus responded to the charges that the Constitution of Botswana would privilege the eight dominant Tswana "tribes" and discriminate against all other segments of society. What is interesting about this broad discourse for a planned, decisive correction of the Constitution is the fact that even before parliament started to discuss such a process, the most important view seemed to believe that symbolic discrimination but not substantive interference was possible. Ultimately adopted by the Government (*Government White Paper No. 2* of 2002: 5), this opinion was first voiced by none other than Vice-President (and later President) Festus G. Mogae. In a parliamentary debate concerning the appointment of a commission to develop the constitutional amendment, he stated on 17 February 1995:

"But the point I am making is that, we agree that we should look at the constitution. I do not think that the Constitution is discriminatory. It guarantees the equality of individuals. Sections 3 and 15 as you have been quoting do that. But as I say, it is certain perceptions, certain words that are now considered unacceptable by most people or by some sections of the community and we have to pay heed to that. It is just to say that if they are mere perceptions, then let us get rid of them, not because the Constitution does not say that individuals are not equal. That is the spirit in which we support this motion" (Festus G. Mogae, cited in *Report of the Presidential Commission* 2000: 5).

It is, therefore, hardly surprising that the constitutional amendment focused on terminology and linguistic expressions: *tribesmen* was changed to "citizens of Botswana", *tribal territory* to "District", *Chief* to "*Kgosi*", and *House of Chiefs* to "*Ntlo ya Dikgosi*". The amendment paid special attention to changing the "tribal principle" to a principle of regional representation. It was not the membership to an ethnic group anymore but the regional origin from a certain district that henceforth became the official base of representation in the *House of Chiefs*.[52] More than a few critical voices regarded this amendment as nothing more but a cosmetic correction and "window dressing": "The intention was clearly not to bring about equality, but to seek a safer language to maintain tribalism" (Nyati-

---

52 *Government White Paper No. 2* of 2002: 7ff.

Ramahobo 2002b: 700). The new construction of the articles is still based on the foundation of the eight Tswana groups because they belong to those 12 members that are now automatically determined by their regional origin.

The amendment only changed the size of the *House of Chiefs* from 15 to 35 members but now in three categories: as already mentioned, eight of the twelve members of the first category come from the eight "major" tribes. In contrast to their new colleagues, they are still "Kgosi".[53] In the second category, a regional election committee elects twenty individuals from the districts but this committee is comprised of paid *Headmen of Record* or "Kgosi". In the last category, the president nominates five individuals at his discretion (and because of their particular qualifications) to "balance" the committee. This is why many forces of civil society evaluate this amendment primarily as a symbolic measure that corrected certain aspects that "some perceived as discriminatory" without dealing with latent policies of discrimination as established in certain parts of legislation.

"This Amendment Bill fails to recognise and build on the inherent strength which lies in the diversity of opinions, cultures, languages, traditions and peoples in Botswana. Instead, the 'window-dressing' exercise has largely effected superficial changes, which can be interpreted as dealing with discrimination through 'inclusion' of those ethnic groups which have hitherto been excluded from governance" (DITSHWANELO 2004).[54]

This debate in the realm of constitutional law focuses on the understanding of ethnicity as a relationship between various ethnic, social and indigenous groups in Botswana. As past discussions suggest, it is a dynamic conception of a multi-layered and constantly re-evaluated social structure that is confused and obscured by ambiguous terminology and as Bennett (2002: 10) so conclusively substanti-

---

53 In 2001, the first draft of the *Government White Paper* originally eliminated the *ex officio* membership of the eight Tswana tribes and stipulated regional parliamentary elections in all districts. The Tswana tribes opposed this step so vehemently that on 30 March 2002, then President Mogae proclaimed to re-establish the *ex officio* membership of the eigth Tswana-speaking tribes. In this context, "non-Tswana" regions would still elect their members of parliament (Nyati-Ramahobo 2002b: 700).

54 DITSHWANELO *Press Statement on Constitutional (Amendment) Bill 2004* of 18 April 2005. The representative of the NGO WIMSA shares this opinion: "I believe the Balopi Commission came up with a cosmetic solution to the problem. Instead of according everybody the same starters in terms of recognition for their leadership, major groups still remain and they have their leaders still granted some sort of special recognition, called 'Paramount Chief'. That is why I am saying: it is a fabricated or cosmetic solution to the whole problem, but the problem still exists. The commission failed to solve the issue" (Interview Mathambo Ngakaeaja 24 February 2003). The *UN Human Rights Committee* concluded as well: "The Committee is concerned that, despite recent amendments, the current rules regarding appointments to the Ntlo ya Dikgosi do not make provisions for fair representation of all tribes" (United Nations 2008: para. 24). Cf. also the "Concluding Observations" of the CERD Committee (United Nations 2006b: para. 10).

ates, particularly the term "tribe" imposed by colonial powers. Although he discusses the problem with the term "tribe" in the context of Botswana, his considerations could be generalized for several African and even other contexts. Aside from the importance of understanding constitutionally-established social justice, this is why I would like to quote him at some length:

"The word 'tribe' was adopted by European observers to describe patterns of social and political organization which seemed to have no close equivalents in their own societies. The word, which derives from classical Latin, had been used by the ancient Romans to describe 'barbarians' in western Europe. The term was not in itself racist, since it originally applied to the Europeans' own ancestors, but it did imply an idea of a 'lower stage' of cultural development. Unfortunately, it became reified in the twentieth century, especially as the concept of 'Indirect Rule' became the dominant model for the British administrators. Colonial government could operate through existing institutions, which were believed to be 'tribal'. This encouraged the fixing of previously fluid ethnic identities, and the conversion of other forms of group identity into ethnic ones, since it was 'tribes' which the British would recognize and deal with."

The author is convinced that this preconception is essential to understand the historical interpretation of the Constitution. The recognition of the eight chiefs as permanent *ex officio* members of the *House of Chiefs* would accordingly not have implied ethnically privileging the eight major Tswana "tribes" but only representing the power relations of that time. This composition was even supposed to prevent any tribalism or ethnic conflicts. In his opinion, it was based on the pre-colonial understanding of the political proto-national organization unit of a *morafe* that was then confused by introducing the term "tribe". In contrast to the political concept of a *morafe* under leadership of a chief, the term "tribe" was interpreted statically as well as characterizing a certain ethnic homogeneity. Needless to say, also Bennett sees how Tswana "tribes" were privileged but not primarily deriving from ethnicity but from the secondary consequence that some territorial and political units were not represented:

"It is frequently stated that the Constitution recognizes eight 'major tribes', at the expense of other ethnic groups, but in fact the Constitution does not, formally, recognize any ethnicities. What the Constitution provides, in section 78, is that the eight Chiefs who had the status of Paramount in the colonial era enjoy ex officio membership of the House of Chiefs. That is, the 'tribes' recognized are polities, not ethnic groups. (…) Obviously this does in fact, advantage Tswana at the expense of others since the eight major chiefs are all Tswana, but the Constitution recognizes them as heads of polities, not as ethnic representatives" (Bennett 2002: 11).

Although I can share this opinion from a legal perspective, it negates the special position of indigenous peoples as well as ethnic minorities. These were basically excluded from any form of political and democratic representation either because of the clear hierarchies within a *morafe* or because they did not belong to any recognized *morafe* at all. If, therefore, *tribal territories* were nothing more but territorial and political units and the chiefs did not represent any *specific* ethnic group, Botswana's public sphere would still be shaped by clear power structures: "Thus neutral public space is not, in fact, neutral. The so-called 'normal' or unmarked public cultural space is coterminous with the perceived majority (Tswana) and the perceived minority (non-Tswana) then becomes the marked or exceptional category in need of 'special' dispensation" (Solway 2004: 136).

In addition, sociological studies clearly show that ethnicity does play a subtle and possibly even hidden role: so the first question the "elders" ask a couple wanting to get married is, "*Ke mo kae?*" meaning, "to which ethnic group does he/she belong?" Mafisa (1990: 35) used elaborate questionnaires to find out that Batswana would hardly allow anyone but a member of their ethnic group to represent them politically.[55] If marginalized groups (want to) exercise their collective rights, it will usually be considered as ethnic agitation against the Constitution of Botswana with its fundamental principle of neutrality proclaimed as a firewall against (the threat of) "tribalism". If, however, Tswana groups advocate their own issues "in the spirit of the Constitution", it will be perceived as constitutional in the sense of an ethnically neutralized nation state (Nyati-Ramahobo 2002a: 21).[56]

The second crucial aspect related to the term "tribes" (aside from political representation in a nation-state democracy) is the control of access to land titles. In real life, it becomes clear that the claimed ethnic blindness leaves much to be desired. Also this is connected to the specific ambiguous retranslation of British tribe-terminology into (Tswana) understanding of a *morafe*. In this respect, the same political structures that are already inhibiting adequate representation of indigenous peoples and ethnic minorities (e.g. in the *House of Chiefs*) also prevent the access to land. As the Botswana representative of the *Working Group of Indigenous Minorities* (WIMSA) Mathambo Ngakaeaja (during an interview on 24 February 2003) clarified (in connection to the eviction from the CKGR or "Park"):

"That is the problem: it lies in non-recognition of the Basarwa as a tribe that is entitled to the same sort of rights as the other tribes in the country. This is historic, it comes from the Bantu-Basarwa relationship, whereby, for example, a myth such as 'Basarwa do not own land' already came to peoples' mind, and

---

55 Cf. Kotrba (2002: 102f.).

56 A further example for the importance of ethnic membership and the dominance of certain groups: the first president of Botswana was Seretse Khama. He stepped down from his position as *chief* of the Bangwato because it was legally incompatible with a political office. After his demise, President Masire who was a member of the Mongwaketsi affiliated to the opposition party had to appease the powerful Bangwato by appointing Seretse Khama's cousin Lenyeletsi Seretse as vice-president. In the same way in 1999, then President Mogae "appeased" the mighty tribe by appointing Seretse Khama's son Ian Khama as vice-president (Nyati-Ramahobo 2002a: 24).

that was carried on even into nation state building and they don't recognize the Basarwa way of living, of hunting and gathering, as a form of land use. That is why they are saying 'get out of the park' because essentially they don't recognize hunting and gathering as a land use. Our traditional leadership structures are not recognized, that's why we don't have a chief in the house of chiefs."

When Botswana became independent in 1966, the former crown land as one of three forms of land title was turned into state land: the other two forms continued to be "freehold land" and "tribal land".[57] According to this understanding, the vast majority of the San (or "Basarwa" in Botswana) lived on state land (especially in game reserves) because they hardly owned any tribal or private land. When Botswana launched a land reform, it exclusively focused on revising the allocation of land for the cattle industry. As the economy heavily depended on the cattle industry and more and more huge areas were overgrazed, the state wanted to assume control of land allocation. The Government of Botswana was convinced that the collective system under the chiefs' rule was responsible for mismanagement and the exploitation of resources, thus causing the degradation of soil. Cattle owners were regarded as the main culprits of this development. Some authors see the source of the land reform in elitist interests of "beef barons" who were tired of competing against smaller cattle owners. Therefore, they used their political and administrative positions to influence the normative opportunities of a law reform in their favour (White 2000: 7).

As early as 1968, the *Tribal Land Act* transferred the chiefs' former competence over land titles to state authorities. Since then, the newly-established land boards as state institutions have administrated the "tribal land" that is still owned collectively. At the substantive level, however, this institutional reform hardly changed the former understanding of "customary land law". The chiefs' competence of allocating "allodial titles" was effectively only transferred to the land boards. In addition, certificates of a transfer of land titles under customary law were developed to ensure legal certainty (White 2000: 4; Adams/Kalabamu/ White 2003: 59).

Since the *Tribal Amendment Act 1993*, also individuals who are not members of a certain tribe have been entitled to receive so-called tribal land either in accordance with customary grants or in form of a common law lease.[58] The first kind of title does not involve any fees; the relevant customary grants are limited to the use of wells, boreholes, farmland and land parcels. Transfers must be authorized by

---

57 State land currently amounts to 23% (mainly national parks and game reserves), freehold land to 5.7% and collective land to 71.3% of Botswana's whole territory (581,720 km²) (Hitchcock 2006: 239). For a more detailed outline of land ownership, land use and property in Botswana, see: Cassidy (2000: 8ff.).

58 In this respect see White (2000: 4): "Since 1993, Land Boards have been required to administer the tribal land in their area in the interest of all citizens of Botswana and are not allowed to discriminate against nontribesmen in allocations."

the land boards. If the land is not used adequately, land titles can be withdrawn as well. In this sense, any kind of non-disposal, such as not cultivating the soil, without credible justification may be sufficient to withdraw the land title.[59]

In case of land use that cannot be subject to customary grants, the land boards allocate (in return of payment) leasable land for possible businesses, gated ranches and other commercial undertakings.[60] The Government also issued the *Tribal Grazing Land Policy* (TGLP) 1975 to get the problem of increased overgrazing under control. It was supposed to alleviate the threat that individual beneficiaries could use the land in a non-sustainable way at the community's expense – in literature renowned as the alleged "tragedy of the commons" (Hardin 1968). The policy was based on the assumption that individuals or syndicates would pay much more attention to pasture land, if they were allowed to fence and control it. This is why legislators separated common land into two zones: a commercial and a collective one.

Originally a third zone was reserved for future land developments in poorer areas. When the needed size of areas was miscalculated, however, it had to be given up.[61] In the context of the separation into two zones, the large cattle owners were supposed to herd their cattle into commercially usable (fenced) areas. This should have helped to counteract overgrazing and decrease soil degradation. The implementation of the policy as well as subsequent developments did not bring the desired success, though, because the "beef barons" cattle did not leave collective areas but plied between collective and commercial land. In addition, the binding regulation of livestock was dropped. Individuals and farming syndicates received 6,400 hectares of land and full control of the land including hunting rights in return for a symbolic lease of 4 Thebe (~0.1 Cent) per hectare over a period of one hundred years. In consequence, the local populations of predominantly indigenous communities that lived in commercial areas had to make way for the new farms and fences (Saugestad 2001: 130).

Therefore, we have to conclude that the original purpose of the *Tribal Grazing Land Policy*, namely protecting the interests of those who did not own a lot of cattle or not any cattle at all, failed. The hopes of the poorer and poorest social classes to finally receive land for their own purposes as well were far from being realized. On the contrary: as the new owners were granted the exclusive rights of land and resources, hunting and gathering became *de facto* impossible in these areas. According to a World Bank report commissioned by the Ministry of Agriculture, the implementation of the *Tribal Grazing Land Policy* caused the displacement and more or less forced resettlement of between 28,000 and 31,000 individuals (Taylor 2004: 160).

---

59   Art. 13 and Art. 15 *Tribal Land Act Cap. 32:02* and *Tribal Land (Amendment) Act 1993.*
60   Art. 22ff. *Tribal Land und Amendment Act 1993.*
61   *Report of The Presidential Commission on Land Tenure* (1983: IX).

I. Sociopolitical History

Both policies thus still draw on the tradition of on the one hand ethnocentric forms of allocation based on the interests of cattle breeding and on the other hand of the related assimilation since the early beginnings of multi-ethnic coexistence in Botswana. It might be, therefore, that they mainly focus on the following three issues: more effective control, a tendency of privatization by granting relatively extensive individual rights in the context of collective customary land rights, and the process of administrative rationalization:

"Since about 1975 there has been a slow but accelerating reversal of policy towards centralisation of land administration, towards de-linking of communities from the land they occupy (and collectively own), and towards increasing privatisation of tenure arrangements. The main beneficiaries of this shift in policy are the elite, who are largely synonymous with the large cattle owners. (…) The main losers are the poorer households of lower social status in the rural areas, and in particular those from marginalised, sometimes ethnically distinct, sections of the community" (White 2000: 8).

In this sense, the land reform as a process of modernization/development follows a direction of allocation in which both assimilation and differentiation are simultaneously processed. Despite its policy of open access to resources free of tribal limitations, land titles are *de facto* even increasingly based on capital historically accumulated by Tswana groups. This structural relationship is enhanced by titles of land use being limited to housing, agriculture and cattle breeding. This excludes all those parts of the population that can neither raise the necessary means nor the resources. If we keep all this in mind, the fundamental principle of an amended system of land ownership based on "traditions" or customary law, in which everybody has as much land as needed – "[I]t is the right of every tribesman to have as much land as he needs to sustain him and his family" (*Government White Paper* No. 2 of 1975: 4) – sounds like pure irony.

Empirical observations confirm this pessimistic assessment. The *Tribal Grazing Land Policy* further disadvantaged indigenous lifeworlds that did not obey to dominant forms of economy: "In the peri-urban areas, households have lost arable fields to urbanisation while in the remoter areas numerous BaKgalagadi, BaLala and Basarwa have lost access to land and resources, they have used for generations. In the latter case, policy has failed to recognise these groups' need for substantial areas of land to pursue distinctive lifestyles as hunter-herders and hunter-gatherers" (White 2000: 8f.).

Limited land needs to enclosed properties, cultivation areas or fields and cattle farms are traditional Tswana systems and derive, as Parsons (1994: 3) notes, in their privileged meaning from a "cattle post mentality". Transfers of land are controlled by Tribal Land Boards open to influence from state authorities. Although every citizen may apply for land titles successfully (under customary or common law), there still remain two unresolved questions: how democratic is this process; and can these institutions be made accountable?[62] And in light of the illiteracy rate common in rural areas, we should not underrate the intricacies for local community members involved in the new bureaucratic process of land transfer.[63]

The principle of open access to resources is another consequence of the prevailing system of land rights: "A further implication is that under the current system, local communities have no rights to exclude other citizens of Botswana who are from outside their communities even when they consider that they have valid reasons to restrict access. Botswana's common land system has therefore become very close to being an open access system for all Batswana. An open access system promotes market failure, where prices do not provide proper signals to producers and consumers to promote locative efficiency. Environmental externalities (such as overgrazing and over-harvesting of firewood) will not assist the rural communities or rural poor to achieve a social optimum" (Botswana Institute for Development Policy Analysis 2001: 89f.). Indigenous representatives criticize that this open access causes a *de facto* exclusion of all those communities that also in the past have been regarded as inadequate for acceptable land use. In the same way, the historical denial of equality can be applied to Botswana's system of land rights. As Mathambo Ngakaeaja (WIMSA) reminds us:

"The issue of land rights is of great importance to our people, because basically we have lost all sorts of land rights. It was based on non-recognition of Basarwa culture. Our people do not have any land rights recognized by the legislation of this country and it all started even before colonialism. Again assumptions like hunting and gathering is not a way of life, therefore hunting and gathering is not a land use. And when the British came up with any piece of legislation together with the Batswana, they did not include our way of life and hence our land use system was ignored and we are outside the law. That marked the beginning of the loss of our land rights and even today, there are no land rights guaranteed for Basarwa in any legislation in this country".[64]

The legal situation portrayed in the medium of the fundamental right of equality focuses on the understanding of ethnicity as a relationship between various ethnic, social and indigenous groups in Botswana. The following developments did not *per se* cause inequalities between Botswana's communities: the formation

---

62 White (2000: 18f.) negates both the democratic process as well as the institutions' accountability and criticizes the transfer of authority from the chief to Tribal Land Boards. Today these are obliged to manage communal lands in the interest of all citizens subject to directions from central Government: "Most land reform programmes aim to promote equity in access to land and democratisation of the allocation process, usually by encouraging decentralisation and subsidiarity (the taking of decisions as close to their point of implementation as is practical). Land reform in Botswana thus runs counter to the norm."
63 The San's illiteracy rate amounts to 77% (Mazonde 2004: 140).
64 Interview 24 February 2003.

of the *House of Chiefs*, the establishment of district boundaries, the election of an official and national language, and legislation, especially concerning land rights – these inequalities also date back to an earlier point in time. The marginalization of "non-Tswana" communities had its beginnings in the socio-political structures of the early Tswana proto-states. It was then increased when British colonizers established administrative "Tswana"-units and reserves, when the Tswana participated in constitutional negotiations, and finally when the Tswana ruled in an independent Botswana. The laws, policies and practices discussed above, however, limited the elimination of inequalities between groups in Botswana – they may have even reproduced disparities.

Notwithstanding the above discussion of deeper – i.e. hidden – forms of ethnic disparities, the Republic of Botswana represents a positive example of democratization. These undeniable achievements seem even more outstanding, as the social, political and economic structures were shaped by general poverty at the time of independence in 1966. Still, the country and its government had the courage to choose a full-fledged version of democracy.[65] In comparison, many countries have decided for a rather "minimalist approach" that prioritizes the economy while limiting political liberties (Weimer 1989: 290). Botswana has taken a different path: the Democratic Republic still enjoys the reputation of a state under rule of law with a liberal Constitution, a catalogue of fundamental rights, independent jurisdiction and a free market economy. Furthermore and in particular, the "inherited" legal dualism of passed-on (customary) and adopted (Anglo-American) law still exists. In the next chapter, I will discuss these legal and constitutional structures.

---

65   One of the public sector's deficits we should not forget is the bombastic administrative organization that significantly lacks efficiency. Whoever once asked for a VAT refund in an overstaffed but basically inactive administrative machinery could tell you a (sarcastic) thing or two about it. After more than three years of empirical "field trials" with a customs officer who refused to even know that such a tax existed and a grotesque amount of submitted red tape, I still have not had success in this matter and know from personal experience about the problems in Botswana's bureaucracy.

II. Sources of Law and Legal Pluralism

The following overview of Botswana's fundamental legal structures establishes the context for questions relating to the rights of indigenous peoples (primarily San communities). It is, therefore, necessary to discuss the crucial aspects of constitutional law, the current (pluralistic) legal system, the application of international law, and finally fundamental and human rights.

1. Constitutional Law

Similar to other processes of gaining independence, the draft independence Constitution was agreed on at a conference, the Bechuanaland Independence Conference (1966) in London. It did not take more than a week for the following participants to come to terms on a draft independence Constitution: Prime Minister of Bechuanaland (since the constitutional amendment in 1965) and later President of the Republic Seretse Khama, his Deputy Prime Minister Quett Masire, the representative of the *House of Chiefs* Kgosi Bathoen II, and of course the British protectorate power. In accordance with constitutional paternalism, the British Government enacted the legal foundation of the state of Botswana as a law. On 30 September 1966, this law came into effect and has served as the Constitution of the Republic of Botswana ever since.[66]

Any Constitution is based on certain fundamental principles ("component laws"). This body of guiding principles forms the constitutional order which has its own – the highest – status in a state's legal system (Öhlinger 1999: 50). Although the Constitution of Botswana does not explicitly stipulate that it is of the highest status in the state's legislation, it is generally assumed: "The Constitution is the supreme law of the land and it is meant to serve not only this generation but also generations yet unborn."[67] This Constitution of Botswana only proclaims the republican principle with the president as the head of state, who is elected (indirectly) by the parliament.[68] The entire text of the Constitution established Botswana as a representative parliamentary democracy. This interpretation is essentially based on how the people elect their representatives (parliament)

---

66 For a detailed account of the conference with clearly too many colonial representatives, see Obeng (2001: 55).
67 *Attorney General v. Unity Dow* [1992] B.L.R. 119 (C.A.), p. 166.
68 "Botswana is a sovereign Republic" (Art. 1 Constitution of Botswana). The Constitution explicitly mentions sovereignty, meaning the highest political authority in a sovereign territory, in its first article probably also because of the country's colonial history.

and the specific dependence of all other state authorities from parliament (except the president). In this context, the constitutional committee – following the British example – was oriented towards a bicameral parliament and established a Lower House of elected representatives as well as the *House of Chiefs* with its traditional rulers as an (advisory) Upper House.

Although the principle of so-called "tribal" authorities survived, it remained highly controversial: as traditional rulers are legitimized by inheritance, opponents have criticized this institution because it negates democracy.[69] Moreover, they see "chieftaincy" as the centre of the country's "tribal" consciousness. In contrast, proponents regard it as a both legitimate and legitimized institution with integrative effects on various social sectors. The institution of the *House of Chiefs* could solve regional and tribal differences before they get out of hand and become the foundation of balanced development. According to this opinion, it would be inconsiderate to give up such an institution that draws on older forms of discourse democracy (Obeng 2001: 57). The process of royal opinion and decision making would add an "African" approach to democracy that in a certain way could balance the multiparty system of European origin in the sense of checks and balances. The *kgosi* or king made use of the traditional community council *kgotla* to consult with and vote on decisions.[70] Former President Festus G. Mogae considered this institution the real basis of how the country understands democracy and also how Botswana is different from its neighbours. Although these countries knew about chieftainship (*bogosi*), they did not develop comparable structures of "democratic" opinion and decision making in his view (interview 29 September 2005):

"The Kgotla system as distinct from bogosi, which we share with other communities in southern Africa is our indigenous democracy, the kgotla system that is. That is our distinguishing characteristic between either the kingdoms or the chieftainships in the region among the different tribes in South Africa, Zimbabwe, Namibia, Zambia. So that enables us to say that democracy in our country is indigenous, because in the kgotla system the chief or the king was required to consult with the people on any issue, even if in certain cases he will end up getting his way, but he was required to consult and people were free to express them-

---

69 Apart from that, this legal succession has always been reserved to male rulers: "The Chieftainship is hereditary in the male line, passing normally from father to son (…). [A]s a rule the Chief succeeds automatically to his office by right of birth. Kgosi ke kgosi ka a tetswe, say the Tswana: 'A Chief is a Chief because he is born to it'. Women never succeed (…). Nor can any son of a Chief's sister or daughter claim that Chieftainship through his mother's right of birth" (Schapera 1984: 53f.). Today also female succession is possible: on 30 August 2003, Mosadi Seboko a Mokgôsi was crowned as the first female *Paramount Chief* of the Bamalete in southern Botswana (Mmegi, 5–11 September 2003; see in more detail Zips 2011: 181–212).
70 For more detailed information see inter alia Ray/Reddy (2003), Rouveroy van Nieuwaal/Dijk (1999), Rouveroy van Nieuwaal/Zips (1998).

selves with stunning views and even opposing views. So that way the chief was constrained, but it also enabled those with constructive suggestions to come up with something to improve on what the chief or the king was proposing, or had in mind, or dissuading him from it. But like in any democracy there were ups and downs: some chiefs were more autocratic than others, just like in the democratic system sometimes, presidents or leaders are perceived to be stronger men than others. So that is the importance of the kgotla system, it is the source of our traditional democracy. So our adaptation of the kgotla system into formal democracy was easy. Let me say that the transition into modern political party democracy was easy, because of the tradition of the requirements to consult, on the part of our leaders."

The institution of chieftaincy has a certain federal element but it combines two levels of legitimation and thus hardly has anything to do with the European-style federalist system (e.g., in the Republic of Austria). The "architects" of the Constitution neither included self-government of regional bodies or other legal entities performing public duties, nor the autonomy of the nine districts. Therefore, Botswana has a relatively strong central state. This, however, does not affect the principle of the separation of power as based on the three "classic" state functions of legislation, jurisdiction and execution: according to the Constitution of Botswana, the president represents the executive power, while parliament assumes legislative and the courts judiciary powers.[71] In the sense of a "separation of state and society" as a crucial constitutional element, the state limits its own power of disposition. The details of this limit are established by the liberal principle of fundamental rights (cf. Öhlinger 1999: 56).[72]

The Constitution of Botswana has nine chapters with 127 sections. The formal part stipulates the highest organs of state and their appointment, the processes of lawmaking and the highest principles of state structure (separation of powers, centralism, republicanism, democratic structures and the principle of traditional authorities). Interestingly, the material part is exclusively comprised of fundamental rights. In contrast to, e.g., South Africa, the Constitution of Botswana does not provide values, goals and contents, thus meaning primarily state objectives such as environmental protection, equality between men and women and equal treatment between the disabled and non-disabled.[73] The most probable reasons for that are on the one hand the historical development of the Consti-

---

71 Chapter IV Constitution of Botswana ("The Executive"), Chapter. V, Part IV ("Legislative Power of Parliament"), Chapter VI ("The Judicature").

72 These are found in Chapter II Constitution of Botswana ("Protection of Fundamental Rights and Freedoms of the Individual"), ss 3–18.

73 The Constitution of South Africa (1996) is often considered one of the most progressive and liberal Constitutions of the world, especially with regard to its human rights catalogue; cf. Mubangizi (2012: 33).

tution under more or less British dictation and on the other hand its date of formation. Unlike Botswana, most African states have developed new Constitutions or amended their independence Constitutions in keeping pace with postcolonial modes of thinking. Botswana's Constitution is still regarded as a "modern" document in European understanding. In line with Western tradition, it stipulates individual rights of the abstract citizen without paying attention to African conceptions of the community taking precedence over the individual.[74] As African jurists suggest apart from the republican Constitution with its catalogue of fundamental rights, the independence Constitution hardly changed the basic structure of the former, colonially "inherited" legal order:

"The view has been expressed that the post-independence legal system is dominated by the common law regime, especially, in the fields of constitutional, administrative, criminal and labour laws. The customary regimes, it is said, apply mostly to the rural population in civil or private law matters" (Quansah 2001: 7).

2. Customary Law

When common law was introduced in 1891, it became superior to the once exclusive sovereignty of traditional authorities. Although this development did not cause the end of African customary law, it was forced to retreat into the sphere of civil law that was still subject of the *kgotla*. In general, it was only applicable if it did not contradict common law (repugnancy clause). The state's independence did not change that except for some cosmetic corrections concerning terminology: legislators changed terms like "native" to *tribesmen* and "native law and custom" to *customary law*. Still, people tend to see customary law as a single and universally recognized set of norms based on a community or group (Molokomme 1994: 347).

"Thus officially, customary law continued to be defined subject to its compatibility with the written law and to the repugnancy clause. The common law gained even more importance in the public sphere, in keeping with the Government's policy of rapid economic growth. Customary law continued to be left to the private sphere, with the majority of the population being primarily subject to it in civil matters, unless they opted out" (Molokomme 1994: 356).

In Botswana, traditional customary law is a rather vague concept that is usually applied to a body of law explaining principles, customs and expectations that have their roots in pre-colonial Tswana societies (Quansah 2001: 24). It is often forgotten, however, that it is not a static law but reproduces and necessarily changes its normative, traditional and cultural aspects by means of oral tradition

---

74 Art. 31 Constitution of South Africa 1996 includes, for example, the collective right to culture, language and religion.

passed on from generation to generation. "The" customary law realizes a homogenous system just as little. Quite on the contrary, Botswana is home to many communities ("tribes") with their own rights concerning marriage, trade, inheritance, taboos, succession in office, etc. (Obeng 2001: 40; Griffiths 1997). The *Common Law and Customary Law Act* defines Botswana's customary law as follows:

"Customary law, as comprised in the laws of Botswana, consists of rules of law which by custom are applicable to any particular tribe or tribal community in Botswana, not being rules which are inconsistent with the provisions of any enactment or contrary to morality, humanity or natural justice."[75]

In this sense, customary law continues to be applicable unless incompatible with statutory law and the fundamental principles of justice. We may understand the notion of "morality, humanity or natural justice" as a postcolonial version of the so-called "repugnancy clause" – as some sort of British rule of inconsistency. Colonial rulers used this clause to prevent the application of certain norms of traditional African law and referred to the principle of "Ordre Public Colonial", meaning the universal principle of "civilization" and the colonial rulers' understanding of justice.[76] With regard to customary law and its institutions, the political line of independent Botswana has generally been consistent with the colonial Government's policies. The law mentioned above and its 1987 amendment entitle legal subjects to choose between laws in civil matters.

Jurisdiction for an individual case under customary law depends on the customary court assessing that either both parties are "tribesmen", the defendant has issued his/her written consent, or the defendant is ordinarily resident in the jurisdiction of the court.[77] In addition, the cause of action under dispute must arise wholly in the jurisdiction of the court. There are also certain matters that are excluded from the jurisdiction of customary courts: e.g. divorce of civil marriage, cases of testamentary succession, and bankruptcy law. The exceptions go even further concerning criminal law: no customary court has jurisdiction in case of

---

75 Sect. 4 (1) *Common Law and Customary Law Act* (1969, Cap. 16:01). Cf. also the definition of Sect. 2 (1) *Customary Courts Act* (1961, Cap. 04:05).

76 This clause is not uncommon in southern Africa. While Swaziland defines it as "contrary to natural justice or morality", South Africa calls it "opposed to public policy or natural justice". For a more detailed discussion of the "repugnancy clause" see Hazdra (1998: 34, 73f.).

77 Stipulated in Sect. 11 (1) *Customary Courts Act* (1961, Cap 04:05). Furthermore, customary courts are subordinate to the "local government". The Minister of Local Government, Lands and Housing is entitled to establish such a court or recognize an existing one (Obeng 2001: 197). The *Customary Courts Act* establishes the following three kinds of courts, each being superior to the one before: Lower Customary Court, Higher Customary Court (usually as *chief's court*), and Customary Court of Appeal. Any person aggrieved by a decision of one of the country's two customary courts of appeal (in Gaborone and Francistown) may appeal to the High Court under certain provisions (except "petty offences") (Molokomme 1994: 358ff.).

e.g. treason, bigamy, corruption, malpractice, homicide, robbery, rape and other severe offenses (Molokomme 1994: 358f.). Despite of this limited jurisdiction, customary courts are surprisingly popular because – apart from its transparent decision process – it is easily accessible and its proceedings are rather short and free of charge (Sekgoma 1994: 414).

As the customary courts' jurisdiction in criminal matters is even more limited, the courts mainly use statutory instead of customary law and thus primarily the penal code. State law in general and the *Customary Court Procedure Rules* in particular also regulate all procedural principles: "It seems that the ultimate aim is to have the penal code regulate all criminal matters: customary courts are required to be guided by the provisions of the penal code in such cases. More specifically, they must follow the Customary Court Procedure Rules which lay down pleading and other procedures along the lines of the common law" (Molokomme 1994: 359).

In contrast, civil matters are rather tried under customary law. As in all postcolonial African states, these standards of customary law are not homogenous at all. It thus happens in the sense of legal pluralism that customary courts base their decisions on diverging criteria and traditions. This is also one of the reasons why legal channels show a certain unifying tendency. Often customary law as used by state courts in cases of appeal deviates from the regional legal understanding of customary courts (Molokomme 1994: 360f.). The legal system results in pluralism and becomes rather complex without having even paid attention to the factor of time in the dynamic further development of "customary law".

All these reasons lead to "the" customary law being often implicitly presented in an oversimplified and ultimately wrong way as a homogenous and static legal regime.[78] Although the situation is undoubtedly complex, legal certainty is sufficient in local contexts to ensure the customary courts' high popularity. Relevant figures clearly confirm this tendency. In Botswana, about 80 % of all criminal offenses and civil matters are tried by customary courts (Sharma 2003: 261). Some voices even indicate higher figures, e.g. Chairman of the *House of Chiefs* and king of the Bangwaketse *Kgosi* Seepapitso IV (interview 27 September 2005) who also confirms the reasons mentioned above for the popularity of customary courts:

"About 98 percent of cases, both civil and criminal are tried in the customary courts. This is so because you don't have to engage a lawyer – it is not expensive – and you are tried by your fellow men. So people find it convenient rather to go to the customary court than to go to the magistrate court. We understand what is going on. We speak our own language; there is no question of translation, so one is able to express oneself and to defend oneself, as much as he can. This is why it is very convenient and used every day."

---

78 This is also why the universal courts' and especially the High Court's use of Schapera's "Handbook of Tswana Law and Custom" of 1938 in customary law is criticized.

Nevertheless, Botswana's "legal pluralism" is not only based on the various forms of customary law as only subsidiarily used by customary courts but also on common law which found its way from England and the Netherlands to the neighbouring "Cape Colony" and finally to Botswana. The 1969 *Common Law and Customary Law Act* (Cap. 16:01) was established to regulate the complex relationship between legal developments of customary law rooted in a pre-colonial understanding of law and a hybridized version of common law ("An Act to consolidate the enactments relating to the common law and customary law"). Based on the definition of customary law cited above, this act defined Botswana's common law more or less negatively as "Any law, whether written or unwritten in force in Botswana other than customary law".[79]

3. Common and Statutory Law

Botswana inherited a form of common law from the British colonial administration that has always been quite difficult to execute: it extraordinarily blends Roman-Dutch and Anglo-Saxon law from South Africa. The first dates back to the Dutch independence from Habsburg rule in 1648, when Roman and Germanic law was combined in the province of Holland (Hazdra 1998: 44). Then in 1652, the *Dutch East Indian Company* commissioned Jan van Riebeeck to introduce this law in the Cape Colony: "Roman-Dutch law was introduced into the Cape Colony, and in fact, the whole of what eventually became the Union of South Africa by the Dutch East Indian Company in the mid-seventeenth century. It was a blend of Roman law, Canon law, the Law Merchant and Germanic civil law as found in Holland" (Fombad 2003: 87).

In a simplified way, English law has three legal sources and common law is the primary one.[80] In contrast to Continental European law, English common law sees the decisions of certain (higher) courts as binding "precedents" for decisions in similar future cases.[81] If judges do not want to apply the rules established in precedents, they have to "distinguish" between the cases' material particulars and state them in their reasons.

So-called "equity law" is a second legal source. As common law seemed to become too static, this more flexible system developed in the 15th century. In the context of precedents, this system is subject to the judges' "equity" and discretion.

---

79 See Obeng (2001: 41).
80 Cf., e.g., Hazdra (1998: 45ff.) for a more detailed discussion of the British system of "case law".
81 This practice is based on the axiom *stare decisis et non quieta movere*, meaning "to stand by decisions and not disturb the undisturbed". The principle of *stare decisis* (or case law) is the foundation of common law (Quansah 2001: 30).

II. Sources of Law and Legal Pluralism

Although the Anglo-American legal system formally defines "statutory law" to merely complement case law, it is becoming more and more important as a legal source (Fombad 2003: 88). Colonisation also introduced English law in the colonies. In the Cape Colony, it significantly influenced Roman-Dutch law. When in 1891 Bechuanaland adopted the Cape Colony's law, common law blended with Roman-Dutch law, thus going beyond the former strong influence.

In the course of time, (post)colonial statutory law replaced at least some parts of the "judges' law", e.g., the *Penal Code* in 1964 or the *Matrimonial Causes Act* in 1973 (Quansah 2001: 29). But even in statutory law, it is almost impossible to overlook the great significance of jurisdiction: thus, the principle of binding precedents also applies to the interpretation of laws (Quansah 2001: 68).[82] This means that decisions of the High Court are consulted for similar future cases and the interpretation of positive law. When in 1969 the parliament of Botswana enacted the *Common Law and Customary Law Act*, it syncretized Roman-Dutch law, English law and laws applicable under Botswana's common law. As mentioned, the latter is defined as "Any law, whether written or unwritten in force in Botswana other than customary law" (Sect. 2). The same act also establishes rules of collision for cases of conflict between differing legal sources caused by legal pluralism.[83]

4. International Law

The construction of laws is not only based on the aforementioned principle of binding precedents but state law must also be interpreted in accordance with international law. Botswana's Court of Appeal addressed this rule in the "Unity Dow case" (see below) and argued that the country was a member of the world's "civilized states" and could not execute laws and proceedings that contradicted the legal imperatives of the international community: "I am in agreement that Botswana is a member of the community of civilised States which have undertaken to abide by certain standards of conduct and unless it is impossible to do

---

82   An established hierarchy of courts is the fundamental prerequisite to efficiently apply precedents: at the very top, the Botswana Court of Appeal's decisions are binding to all other courts. The subordinate courts are the High Court followed by the Magistrates' Court which does not establish precedents. Then finally the three stages of customary courts are in ascending order: Lower Customary Courts, Higher Customary Courts and the Customary Court of Appeal. Appeals against decisions of the latter are tried before the High Court. For a detailed list of each court's jurisdiction and its duties, see, e.g., Obeng (2001: 185–199) or Quansah (2001: 31–68, 77–100).

83   Sect. 6 (1) *Rules of Application* 1–6 *Common Law and Customary Law Act*. Cf. also Quansah (2001: 69–76).

otherwise, it would be wrong for its courts to interpret its legislation in a manner which conflicts with the international obligations Botswana has undertaken."[84]

This principle of interpretation in consistence with international law is particularly relevant for fundamental rights because these are based on the idea of limiting state power to protect individual liberties. In this sense, the state's protection of fundamental rights is seen as embedded in universal human rights standards that emerge from human rights treaties and the jurisdiction of monitoring bodies (Öhlinger 1999: 283). From this perspective, international law increasingly determines the interpretation of the fundamental rights catalogue.

In turn, however, the international protection of human rights still lacks an effective enforcement mechanism and thus depends on a functioning national protection of fundamental rights. This is the case because international law leaves the manner in which international human rights standards are implemented mostly to state law (Nowak 2002: 48). When it comes to the relationship between international law and state law, there are two methods of how to implement obligations under international law: the monist approach automatically incorporates international legal instruments into national law (adoption method), whereas Botswana applies the dualistic theory, also known as transformation theory. According to this approach, international human rights treaties require a national law to explicitly translate them into state law: "Treaties and Conventions do not confer enforceable rights on individuals within the State until parliament has legislated their provisions into law."[85]

This means, for example, that although Botswana adopted the *International Convention on the Elimination of All Forms of Racial Discrimination* (CERD) on 22 September 1974, it was not automatically incorporated but had to be "translated" into national law.[86]

---

84 Judge Ammissah in *Attorney General v. Unity Dow* [1992] B.L.R. 119 (CA) at p. 154.
85 Judge President of the *Court of Appeal of Botswana*, cited in Boko (2002: 104).
86 Botswana has ratified the following international treaties: International Covenant on Civil and Political Rights (CCPR) on 09/08/2000; Convention on the Elimination of All Forms of Discrimination against Women (CEDAW) on 08/13/1996; Convention on the Rights of the Child (CRC) on 03/14/1995; Convention Against Torture (CAT) on 09/08/2000 but with reservation concerning the definition of torture; Convention Against Transnational Organized Crime on 08/10/2002; World Heritage Convention on 11/23/1998; Convention on Biological Diversity (CBD) on 06/08/1992; Cartagena Protocol (Agenda 21) on 06/11/2002; United Nations Convention to Combat Desertification (UNCCD) on 09/11/1996; Rome Statute of the International Criminal Court (ICC) in September 2000; African Charter on Human and Peoples' Rights (Banjul Charter) on 07/17/1986; African Charter on the Rights and Welfare of the Child on 07/10/2001; OAU Convention Governing the Specific Aspects of Refugee Problems in Africa (CGSARPA) on 05/04/1995; furthermore, 15 ILO Conventions between 1988 and 2000. Botswana incorporated the four Geneva Conventions on International Humanitarian Law (1949) in the *Geneva Act, Cap 39:03*; the Convention on the Legal Status of Refu-

II. Sources of Law and Legal Pluralism

In terms of conformance with international law, it is less relevant whether a human rights treaty is incorporated into national law word by word. It is the result that counts – all obligations under international law need to be implemented in state law (Nowak 2002: 49). If a state does not fulfill its obligation to translate international law, Judge Ammissah (*Unity Dow* case) ruled as follows: the treaties and conventions will still be used to help interpreting statutory provisions including the Constitution, even if they do not establish enforceable individual rights.[87]

5. Fundamental and Human Rights

The first two sections of the Constitution of Botswana declare that it is a sovereign republic with a public seal. At next, it guarantees the subjective fundamental rights and freedoms: thirteen sections establish that the classic sources of fundamental rights are applicable in the national context. Section 3 proclaims the fundamental rights and freedoms of the individual, whatever his/her race, place of origin, political opinions, colour, creed or sex – limited by a substantive reservation.[88] In accordance with Sect. 4 (2), for example, the individual's right to life may be limited for the defense of any person from violence or for the defense of property, in order to effect a lawful arrest, for the purpose of maintaining public order, or to prevent criminal activities. All such restrictions, however, are only valid as long as they are necessary in the public interest of democratic society: "The basis of all the exceptions or restrictions is the preservation of the society itself" (Obeng 2001: 321).

In this way, the scope of intervention is much more limited than it would be the case for a merely formal but basically unrestricted reservation. The latter is only limited insofar as it shall not violate the nature of a fundamental right. Such an intervention would then be tantamount to abolishing the fundamental right (Öhlinger 1999: 296). Thus, an intervention based on a legal reservation does not *per se* mean a violation of a fundamental right. We rather have to ask the question of constitutionality or unconstitutionality of such an act. In Botswana, it is the High Court's task to address such questions.[89] One of the most controversial

---

gees (1951) including the Additional Protocol (1967) in the *Refugees (Recognition and Control) Act of 1967*; and the Vienna Conventions on Diplomatic and on Consular relations (1969) in the *Diplomatic Immunities and Privileges Act No. 5 of 1968* (Cap. 39:01). Other than that, Botswana had not incorporated any international human rights instruments into national law. This was also criticized by the African Commission (ACHPR/IWGIA 2008a: 89).

87 Judge Amissah in *Attorney General v. Unity Dow* [1992] B.L.R. 119 (CA), p. 153.
88 This means that the legislator is entitled to intervene in the fundamental rights and freedoms under the listed conditions that need to be protected (Öhlinger 1999: 297).
89 Section 18 Constitution of Botswana.

substantive reservations concerns the state's right to intervene in the individual's right to life as guaranteed in Sect. 4 Constitution of Botswana. In pursuance of Sect. 4 (1), the state is entitled to violate this right in execution of the death sentence of a court. The *Botswana Penal Code* also stipulates that the state is entitled to intentional killing in execution of a sentence of a court in respect of murder, treason and war against the people of Botswana. In contrast to many other countries, Botswana actually executes death sentences.[90] A further fundamental right limited by reservation I would like to mention is the "freedom of movement". "Non-Bushmen" were restricted from entering certain areas until the Constitution was amended in 2004:

"[F]or the imposition of restrictions on the entry into or residence within defined areas of Botswana of persons who are not Bushmen to the extent that such restrictions are reasonably required for the protection or wellbeing of Bushmen" (Sect. 14 (3) (c)).

The Constitution of the independent Republic of Botswana thus recognized the presence of the San in the *Central Kalahari Game Reserve* (CKGR) and limited the freedom of movement for "non-San".[91] As Botswana intended the Constitution to be "more neutral" concerning the eight major groups (see the *Balopi Commission* above), the entire subsection including the privilege of the San was deleted. It remains questionable, however, why this subsection was really deleted: if the concerns were related to limiting the freedom of movement of "non-San" and thus acting contrary to the principle of equality, this measure remains disputable because equal treatment in unequal initial situations rather creates discrimination under the pretext of formal equality. Accordingly, the constitutional restriction of the freedom of movement for "non-San" basically observed the substantive principle of equality because it protected the San ("Bushmen") and resulted in a compensation for the historical discrimination concerning land rights.[92]

In its periodic report on Botswana, the CERD Committee shared this opinion in its concluding remarks and saw the already-deleted constitutional provision as fully compatible with the letter and spirit of the *Convention on the Elimi-*

---

90 Death by hanging is still practiced (e.g., Oteng Modisane Ping on 1 April 2006, Sepeni Thubisane Popo on 6 November 2007, Modise Mokwodi Flyor on 24 March 2010, Zibani Thomo on 31 January 2012) (Amnesty International Report 2007, DITSHWANELO Press Statement 3 February 2012). South Africa abolished the death penalty in 1997, Namibia when it became independent in 1990, and Angola in 1992. For a regional critique see cf. Kerchoff (2000: 79).

91 See also Judge Phumaphi in *Roy Sesana v. Government of Botswana 2006* at p. 349. See part 6 for a detailed discussion.

92 When in *Roy Sesana v. Government of Botswana* 2006 the government argued that it did not discriminate against the San because of their ethnicity, Judge Dow (2006: 247) noted as well: "[E]qual treatment of unequals can amount to discrimination."

nation of All Forms of Racial Discrimination which Botswana had ratified as early as 1974: "[T]he Committee draws the attention of the State party to the fact that special measures for the advancement of disadvantaged ethnic groups, such as section 14 (3) (c) of the Constitution, are fully compatible with the letter and spirit of the Convention" (United Nations 2006b: para. 13). If the legal-political considerations of deleting the provisions instead focused on the term "Bushmen", which as discussed has in fact a derogatory meaning, it would have been sufficient and much easier to consult those concerned to find an acceptable term for the relevant section.

The last fundamental right I would like to discuss is the protection from discrimination in Sect. 15 Constitution of Botswana. Neither legislation nor public authorities shall treat any person in an objectively unjustified discriminatory manner on the grounds of race, tribe, place of origin, political opinions, colour or creed (Sect. 15 (2)). In terms of unequal treatment, it strikes me that the Constitution neither explicitly mentions indirect discrimination nor the grounds of ethnicity and sex. In this context, one of the most interesting examples to compare Botswana to is the post-apartheid Constitution of the new democratic South Africa. Needless to say, it was developed in a completely different context of time. Anyhow, it includes the provision that the state may not discriminate directly or indirectly on grounds of (inter alia) ethnic or social origin, gender, sex and even sexual orientation (Sect. 9 (3)). Gender equality has become a priority and is implemented in numerous laws in the context of South Africa's "empowerment policy". In Sect. 3, Botswana settles for the general principle of equality:

"Whereas every person in Botswana is entitled to the fundamental rights and freedoms of the individual, that is to say, the right, whatever his race, place of origin, political opinions, colour, creed or sex, but subject to respect the rights of others and for the public interest to each and all of the following, namely – (a) life, liberty, security of the person and protection of the law (…)."

In the CKGR case, Judge Unity Dow interpreted this "protection of the law" as a general prohibition of discrimination and "equal protection" of the law (High Court 2006: 213). We could argue from the perspective of Botswana on the one hand that it stipulated basic equal treatment between men and women long before any of the region's other states did. In consequence, Botswana has a relatively high share of women employed in public service.[93] From a rather critical stance on the other hand, Botswana lacks several legislative developments in the constitutional context as well. All around the world, the women's movement and its emancipatory legal initiatives have caused and encouraged such de-

---

93 Under the current administration (2009–2014) only 5 out of 63 Members of Parliament are women – (7.9%) (www.ipu.org/wmn-e/classif.htm). Interestingly, former President Mogae sees the roots of this unequal situation in the "fact" that women obviously do not elect enough women (*Tautona Times* no 9 of 2007).

velopments (since the early 1960s).[94] In 1992 the Court of Appeal counteracted this deficit at least with regard to the *Citizenship Act 1982* (*Citizenship Act* [Cap. 01:01]). This law established that exclusively the citizenship of the father determined the citizenship of a child according to *ius sanguinis*. A Motswana woman could therefore not pass on her citizenship to her children, if she was married to a foreigner. High Court Judge Unity Dow claimed the relevant provision to be discriminatory on grounds of sex as pursuant to Sect. 3 Constitution of Botswana.[95] Judge Amissah interpreted Sect. 15 (3) as not complete in terms of explicitly listed group factors ("race, tribe, place of origin, political opinion, colour, or creed"). The judge argued that just because the Constitution failed to mention a certain factor, this lapse could not lead to the rule *expressio unius exclusio alterius* (the express mention of one thing excludes all others).[96] In consequence, the listed categories are only examples and may be applied to "sex" as well (Quansah 2001: 63). As the constitutional provision stipulates formal equality as a prohibition against unequal treatment of equal, it is not entirely clear whether it may be applied to measures of "positive discrimination" as pursuant to the principle of substantive equality.

In light of an analogous application, the discussed provision against discrimination could perhaps be applied to indigenous peoples/ethnic groups. This was also the opinion of Botswana jurist Duma Boko even before he became the legal representative in the San case: "[I]t would be possible to make a tenable case under the Constitution of Botswana for a more proactive approach to safeguarding the Basarwa. A more positive obligation to facilitate the enjoyment of the fundamental rights of the Basarwa as an indigenous people, and in conformity with the norms of international law, can be defended" (2002: 105). As I will go into more detail in chapters 5 and 6 (especially concerning the High Court's decision in the CKGR case), this is primarily significant because there are no explicit legal measures of protection for these communities (except the aforementioned former privileges of limited freedom of movement against non-San in the Central Kalahari).

---

94   Although domestic violence is a serious problem in Botswana, there is no law against neither such violence nor rape within marriage (1,173 rapes had been reported to police between January and September 2011; however, they rarely lead to convictions) nor sexual harassment. In social practice, discrimination against women continues especially in rural areas: e.g., a woman married under traditional law or in "common property" is held to be a legal minor (U.S. Department of State 2011). Until the High Court ruling on 12 October 2012, women were denied the right to inherit the family home under a customary law (*Mmusi and others v. Ramantele and others*, MAHLB-000836-10).

95   The claim was accepted and the *Citizenship Act 1982* declared unconstitutional. In November 1995, parliament adjusted the law retroactively and issued the new *Citizenship Act* in 1998.

96   Judge Amissah in *Attorney-General v. Unity Dow* [1992] B.L.R., pp. 143–146.

The way Botswana's contemporary political elite aims to define the national identity in legal terms suggests a mode of nation-building governed by the ideology of an emerging homogenous society (thus privileging the idea of uniform "Tswanadom"): "At Independence, the Government deliberately turned a blind eye on ethnic differences within Botswana in a bid to create a unified nation. The ethnic diversity of the nation was undercommunicated in the name of national unity (...)" (Mazonde 2002: 64). In this sense, the legally institutionalized and thus official self-conception of Botswana as a homogenous nation state points out the legal, political and social dominance of the Tswana that has already existed for a long time.[97]

In a certain way, Botswana's two supreme courts, the High Court and the Court of Appeal, balanced this legalistic trend of levelling the ethnic differences as established in statutory and constitutional law. A reconstruction of the relevant decisions of these legal institutions reveals their compensating role against the state's cultural "imbalance" (Kuppe 2004: 54). The courts' decision practice completely exhausted their scope of competence in interpreting the law; in some cases, they may even be seen in their legislative role as correcting one-sided state policies. In 2001, the High Court provided such an example by recognizing the cultural rights of minorities in general as well as the Wayeyi as an independent – not subordinate to the Batawana – ethnic community ("tribe") in particular.[98]

In this case, the claimant was the minority group of the Wayeyi. As the first Bantu-speaking emigrants, they arrived in the Okavango Delta in the 18th century and maybe even earlier (Nyati-Ramahobo 2002b: 686). Those who settled down in the North West District (Ngamiland) were soon dominated by the Batawana, one of the eight ("major") Tswana tribes.[99] In 1995 members of the Wayeyi community founded the *Kamanakao Association* to promote and preserve their language and culture. On 24 April 1999, the Wayeyi opposed the will of *Kgosi* Tawana Moremi II as well as the Minister of Local Government responsible for tribal affairs and crowned Shikati Calvin Diile Kamanakao I as their own *Kgosi*. In consequence, they claimed both political self-determination and the demarcation of their territory to execute their own jurisdiction before the *House of Chiefs*. As Government representatives referred to the country's legal order in force and rejected their claims, they lodged an official claim before the High Court. The three-judge panel ruled that ss. 77, 78 and 79 of the Constitution of Botswana (cf. above Balopi Commission) were discrimina-

---

97 See my detailed discussion in the previous section.
98 *Shikati Calvin Keene Kamanakao, Kamanakao Association and Motsamai Keyecwe Mpho v. The Attorney General of Botswana and Kgosi Tawana Moremi II* MISCA No 377/99.
99 According to the 1991 population census, 37,000 out of the 94,000 Wayeyi are subject to Batawana rule.

tory on grounds of ethnicity.[100] It also ruled that the *Chieftaincy Act* was discriminatory and thus unconstitutional because it did not adjudicate the same protection and equal treatment for the Wayeyi as for the eight Tswana-speaking tribes:

"We therefore order that Government should amend Section 2 of the Chieftainship Act in such a way as will remove the discrimination complained of and to give equal protection and treatment to all tribes under that Act."[101] The High Court explicitly recognized the Wayeyi as well as all other minorities as distinct ethnic communities ("tribes") with their own languages and cultures (and therefore different from the eight "major tribes").[102] In terms of consistency with international developments in both minority and indigenous rights, the court followed a similar new direction as in the San case (see part 6) that still needs to be discussed.

Aside from the High Court, Botswana's range of national organs to protect fundamental rights also includes the institution of the *Ombudsman*. This complaints institution was established by a 1995 Act of Parliament. It is characterized by its low-key procedural formality concerning accessibility, competence, proceedings and decisions. The Ombudsman's duty is to investigate abuses and claimed violations of fundamental rights of the state's administration. As this role is not of executive power, the Ombudsman makes recommendations based on the investigated matter. If these recommendations are not answered, a special report concerning the relevant case may be presented to parliament (cf. Ayeni/ Sharma 2000).[103]

As we can also observe all around the world, more and more non-governmental organizations and forces of civil society assume crucial control functions in Botswana. At this point I would like to mention these stakeholders, not least because they have been extremely important in legally advocating the interests of the San. Non-governmental organizations (NGOs) for the protection of human rights provide more publicity and a wider presence in the media to the expression of solidarity with victims. Moreover, they undertake adequate measures of redress and "compensation" for possible rights violations. Their tasks may range from documentation and public accusation of human rights violations as well as

---

100 The court ruling took place (on 23 November 2001) after the report of the *Balopi Commission* which could not find any discrimination and thus unconstitutionality in sections 77 to 79. The commission only recommended a more balanced representation in the *House of Chiefs*. In March 2002, the Government implemented these recommendations.

101 *Shikati Calvin Keene Kamanakao, Kamanakao Association and Motsamai Keyecwe Mpho v. The Attorney General of Botswana and Kgosi Tawana Moremi II*, MISCA No 377/99 at p. 61.

102 Cf. for a more detailed discussion of the case as well as reactions to the court ruling: Nyati-Ramahobo (2002b).

103 Cf. also Obeng (2001: 327–332) as well as Maine (2000).

raising awareness to the development of new legal standards. Many organizations are also specialized both in legal support for national court proceedings and in initiating international proceedings (Ölz 2002: 49–57).

Like with many state institutions, Botswana is not always all too happy about such activities. As the policy definition indicates, the Government/Ministry of Labour and Home Affairs interprets the task of NGOs as limited to the field of economic development: "The policy defines NGOs as legally formed autonomous organisations that possess non-profit status whose primary motivation is to improve the well-being of the people. They are service driven and serve in diverse and complex activities that relate to the development processes that promote social transformation and sustainable development."[104]

Aside from the San NGOs to be discussed in the next chapter, there are five other human rights organizations in Botswana: the probably most active one in the field of human rights is the *Botswana Centre for Human Rights* (DITSHWANELO), in the field of women's rights *Emang Basadi*, in the field of children the NGO *Childfare*, the *Botswana Network on Ethics, Law, and HIV/AIDS*, and finally *RETENG*, the Multicultural Coalition of Botswana (13 organizations and informal groups) devoted to the promotion and preservation of the linguistic and cultural diversity of Botswana's heritage. They all can basically act without government restrictions and are partly even subsidized.[105] For all that, they have not been able to push through some of the crucial aspects (such as the abolition of the death penalty or the guaranteed freedom of the press) yet.

In spite of the Tswana dominance over ethnic communities in the legal field, some NGOs and those concerned still criticize certain restrictions on the freedom of the press as well as the freedom of opinion. There is a Tswana proverb that propagates the general freedom of speech by focusing on both the emotional and political dimension of this fundamental right: *mualebe obua lega gagwe*, "Let any person speak his mind".[106] Although the Constitution establishes this right in Sect. 12, the Government sometimes censors reports or news sources. In consequence, journalists working in government-affiliated media often censor themselves.

The best example to characterize this situation may be former Minister of Presidential Affairs and Public Service Honourable Kedikilwe; on the occasion of the symposium "Democracy in Botswana" (1988), he was criticized for the restrictions on the freedom of press (cit. in Egner/Grant 1988: 264) and reacted quite significantly: "[I]n news writing like in football, someone must be referee and raise the yellow card, when need arises." The newspaper and Government's media organ *The Daily News* is still distributed free of charge all over the country.

---

104 *National Policy for Non-Governmental Organisations*. Ministry of Labour and Home Affairs (February 2001: 9).
105 *Country Report on Human Rights Practices 2011* (U.S. Department of State (2012)).
106 See Obeng (2001: 318).

All three private newspapers – *The Gazette*, *The Botswana Guardian* and *Mmegi* – were founded in the 1980s and together are only read by one out of six inhabitants of Botswana.[107]

The situation is not any different in the field of broadcasting: both Government radio stations cover the whole country. As the radio is still the most accessible medium of Botswana, this radio coverage is even more effective. Although only founded in the third millennium, the state-owned "Botswana Television" has become the most important source of information in the relatively small TV network with a practical monopoly. Also foreign correspondents are mostly controlled: in 2005 the Government deported at least two foreign journalists. In state eyes, their reporting was too critical and the deportation justified with national security concerns.[108]

All things considered, – and despite all criticized aspects and overt human rights deficits – the Republic of Botswana may be regarded as a country of good governance, rule of law and democracy. This is also why I cannot agree with those authors who have predicted the end of Botswana's "exceptionality". On the one hand, the development of a growing gap between rich and poor as well as many parts of the population (primarily the San) depending on state care is alarming. On the other hand, however, the Government is willing to counteract these problems at least in the fields of economic development, social security and education policies. While education has been free in elementary schools since 1980, free higher schools were established since the end of the decade. Health institutions and schools are opened all over the country. Since 1980, the state has offered financial support in drought periods and guaranteed old-age and orphans pensions (Solway 2004: 132).

In my opinion, one thing we should not forget is the high transparency in politics and legislation; another thing to keep in mind is the population's basic op-

---

107 While the Government newspaper has a daily circulation of 45,000, the three private newspapers together have a weekly (!) circulation of 33,000 (Grant/Egner 1989: 255).

108 *Country Report on Human Rights Practices 2006* (U.S. Department of State (2007)). In 2007 the Government demanded visa applications of 17 foreigners including seven journalists, although they usually would not need a visa (U.S. Department of State (2009)). Moreover, the Government does not only focus on journalists: on 18 February 2005, it issued a presidential decree and declared Australian Professor Kenneth Good of the University of Botswana a "prohibited immigrant". He was deported on 05/31/2005 (inter alia *Mmegi*, *The Botswana Gazette*, both as of 02/23/2005). Cf. also *Good v. Attorney General [2005] 1 BLR 462* (High Court) and *Good v. Attorney General [2005] 2 BLR 337 (CA)*. See also Communication 313/05 – *Kenneth Good v. Botswana*, in which the *African Commission's Working Group on Human and Peoples' Rights* found Botswana violating several articles of the *Banjul Charter* EX.CL/600 (XVII) Annex IV, 28th Activity Report of the ACHPR. Foreign Affairs Minister Phandu Skelemani, however, announced in the media that Botswana would not follow the recommendations of the ACHPR. In my opinion, this fact indicates Botswana's ambiguous attitude towards human rights; see also Cook/Sarkin (2010: 22f.).

portunity to express their opinions and critiques. Virtually all laws and administrative policies are available to the public; all laws, policies and drafts I have cited in this book are sold for a small amount of money in a special store for publications in Gaborone – the renowned *Government Printer*.[109] Botswana hosts symposiums, conferences and congresses on human rights, democracy and even indigenous rights almost every year. As mentioned above, I would like to note that the freedom of expression seems to be higher in the informal sector than in foreign NGOs and media. At least in those fields that are considered rather sensitive, the Government does not really see critique as a reflective offer: "We have been praised for so long time, that we don't quite know how to deal with criticism" (interview Director of DITSHWANELO Alice Mogwe, as of 12 September 2003).

In the last few years, Botswana and its public authorities were most under fire in the field of human rights for (ethnic) minorities and indigenous peoples. The state leadership often seems to be unable to cope with this criticism and feels provoked. Particularly concerning this sensitive issue, objections are often seen as interventions into internal affairs and thus quickly rejected. In light of the country's ethnic complexity, maybe we should not underestimate this delicate issue of governance of ethnicity. The territory is home to sixteen different San communities that together with other minorities form one fifth of the entire population.[110] We should also keep in mind that Botswana's good example for the rest of Africa especially concerning regional African as well as international developments would fade away, if it ignored, restricted or even assimilated these parts of the population – for the benefit of "the eight Tswana groups". Once progressive with its anti-racist policies and its liberal system, the state could lose its international reputation and fall behind the region's "new democracies" like South Africa and Namibia.

---

109 These texts, however, are in English which to a certain extent limits their accessibility.
110 *World Directory of Minorities*. www.minorityrights.org. As Appendix "D" of the *Report of the Presidential Commission of Inquiry into Sections 77, 78 and 79 of the Constitution of Botswana* (2000) indicates, there are several lists on the country's ethnic composition. Nyati-Ramahobo (2002a: 17) talks of 55 ethnic groups with 26 languages. See Saugestad (2004: 250–252) on Khoe-San languages.

Part 5: San in Botswana

I. San as Citizens: Basarwa and/or Batswana?

"Basarwa are Batswana and they should stop living in the 18th century when the rest of the nation is in the 21st. Sure, a couple of goats can't make them rich, but it can improve the quality of their lives. For one, they will have better diet and I say that is better than the practice of posing for 'Human Rights activists' who then go back to England and say to their brethren 'hey look at these African savages', only to sell pictures taken of Basarwa for thousands of pounds."[1]

This letter to the editor speaks volumes for one dominant view in Botswana's public opinion. It also points to the complexities involved in the divergent views from inside and outside. Since the time when the San were relocated from the *Central Kalahari Game Reserve*, the idea of an intact and former way of life as "hunters and gatherers" has dominated in reports. On the one hand, this representation can be traced back to the media interests of various NGOs and those concerned to portray the internal relocation as a forced disruption of their "traditional" way of living. On the other hand, it tries to connect to existing constructions of a presumed San identity generated by ethnological representations and pseudo-scientific documentaries for more than a century. The more the used stereotypes supported certain initiatives to raise public awareness (and donations) in the West, the more they negatively affected public views as well as published opinions in Botswana. In numerous interviews and informal conversations with Botswana nationals I have learned that there might be a connection between the Government's hardened position and unwelcome international interventions. In this sense, it seems that at least some campaigns – especially those of the London-based NGO *Survival International* that is committed to the protection of endangered (indigenous) societies – have been counterproductive in one way or another.

Needless to say, the following discussion of the internal relations between Botswana's San and other Batswana cannot be about which side is guilty of what but about a dialectic view to find new ways of assessing past measures of governance. Both sides (Government and critics) have oversimplified the real living conditions of San communities in today's Botswana (and generally in southern Africa). Only a very small part (about 3 percent) of all Botswana's San lived in the *Central Kalahari Game Reserve* (CKGR) until 1997. The vast majority carved out a rather modest existence as day labourers or unemployed inhabitants in the district capital of Ghanzi. If you drove through the sandy streets of Ghanzi, you would see completely different scenes along the roadsides and near the inevitable bottle shops than those portrayed in commercials of state and private tourism corporations. As the citation above (used as the preamble of this chapter) from a

---

1   Anonymous letter to the editor of *The Botswana Gazette* on 02/27/2002.

letter to the editor of a newspaper in Botswana criticizes, these commercials really reproduce a romanticized image of the "eternal Bushmen".

Particularly these hopeless social conditions in Ghanzi as well as the surrounding cattle farms at the edge of the Central Kalahari turned this ancient environment into a significant symbol not only as an area of retreat but also as a point of reference of a self-determined social existence. Primarily for those San who lived near the CKGR and maybe still had relatives living in there, the freedom inside the Central Kalahari was at least an imaginable alternative to their dependent living conditions. Other groups that settled down in villages outside the boundaries of the CKGR in a landscape that ecologically belonged to the Kalahari as a biome in western and eastern Botswana were less affected. Nevertheless, they were extremely marginalized as well – under the telling official label of *Remote Area Dwellers (*RADs*)* in development policy lingua – and had accordingly a special status in the state's development plans. It would be wrong to accuse state institutions of not wanting state development programmes to improve the subordinate social situation of the San and their low-income existence (see sections III and IV of this chapter). We have to question though, how and how much those concerned were "allowed" to participate in determining their own development.

The extensive cattle industry and the related increased need of space and water caused many of the formerly important San hunting and gathering territories to shrink. As the San needed to survive somehow, many had no chance but to start working for Afrikaner farmers and Tswana cattle owners. As early as the 1960s, the subsistence situation of many Kalahari residents drastically deteriorated: when fences were built and the beef industry commercialized, the San faced fewer opportunities of self-preservation and income. In consequence, more and more San were unemployed and their economic and social status weakened (Hitchcock 1987: 307).

As early as the mid-1950s, the British colonial administration was alarmed by the aforementioned scientific research and became concerned about the fate of the San. The only thing they did, however, was to commission a situation report ("Bushman Survey Report 1965"). In the end – and this is somewhat significant for the discussed CKGR legal dispute – the British administration founded the CKGR also and especially to protect the reserve's San who needed an intact environment to survive on hunting and gathering.[2] In terms of protecting San land rights against the majority population, the rulers of the British protectorate did not go any further though, probably also because of the approaching end of their colonial "mandate".

When Botswana became independent in 1966, there was only one institution focused on the interests of the San but their motives were quite obviously to missionize them. The D'Kar mission station of the Dutch Reformed Church was

---

2 See chapter 6.

I. San as Citizens: Basarwa and/or Batswana?

dedicated to "development aid" and schooling specifically for the San. Even today, a church oversized for the settlement conditions of the region forms the centre of the D'Kar artist village that is funded by the *Kuru D'Kar Trust (Kuru Development Trust* until 2002). In the first years of independence, Botswana's Government was of course committed to the following three tasks: the development of the economy, political stabilization, and forming a national identity distinct from the surrounding apartheid regimes of South Africa and its satellite South-West Africa. Thus, their form of nation-building intentionally focused on both blinding out and overcoming ethnic differences (Suzman 2002: 3).

Politicians hardly addressed the country's situation of the San and other marginalized communities in the beginning. In line with this stance, the Constitution established the San's full and equal citizenship and made no distinction in their enforceable fundamental rights and freedoms. The following example of a criminal case of 1978 impressively shows that the state took the principle of equality seriously: a San pastoralist of 23 years was accused of murdering a policeman when he used a knife and tried to avoid unreasonable arrest. His legal counsel attempted to explain the long cultural history and the ideas of customary law prevailing in this region (the Kalahari). In the context of these origins, the counsel wanted to show that his client had acted like a "reasonable person" in his cultural environment. Chief Justice Hayfron-Benjamin, however, referred to the standard of conduct of reasonable individuals/citizens as stipulated by law for the entire national context and thus rejected this form of "cultural defense" as irrelevant. He explicitly emphasized that "underdevelopment" was not to be assessed as a privilege: "Under-development is a misfortune, and no useful purpose would be served by treating it as a privilege. The standard of conduct required by law of all persons is that of a reasonable man."[3]

At first sight, one may conclude from his reasoning that the San were deemed equal in terms of obligations but not in their citizen rights compared to other Batswana. In the end, many were surprised when the judge assessed the facts and found a different reason to rule in favour of defense: according to his reasons, the policeman had illegally arrested the culprit and thus violated the principle that all citizens were entitled to equal prosecution. In consequence, the accused San was entitled to get out of this illegal situation by means of "reasonable violence". The judge then referred to the Constitution to assess the extent of reasonable violence: "The right to liberty is enshrined in the Constitution, and to subject its enjoyment to conditions of humiliation would be demanding and unreasonable. To fight to be free cannot be regarded as unreasonable conduct." Chief Justice Hayfron-Benjamin thus interpreted the right of freedom in such an egalitarian

---

3 Baoke Case, *High Court of Botswana, Criminal Trial 32 of 1978*, 23 November 1978, unreported.

way that in the present case using a knife was considered an adequate and reasonable act of self-defense (Sanders 1989: 117).

Considering the San's social status in Botswana, this court ruling was more than remarkable. It basically also clarified that the San could not expect any special – neither positive nor negative – status. This result and the judge's stance reflect in my view the general approach of nation-building that does not want to determine any special rights or duties "for San only" and sees privileges of whatever kind as a threat to the idea of a nation state. There is only one contradiction though: the prevailing idea about the San that qualifies their values, cultural expressions and ways of living as underdeveloped and comes up with hierarchical intellectual-cultural stages. Accordingly, targeted development measures are the only way to balance such underdevelopment: "To most Tswana officials San 'underdevelopment' and poverty was (and indeed still is) understood to be a contemporary manifestation of their 'hunting and gathering culture', which in turn was seen not only as an obstacle to development, but the subject to development" (Suzman 2002: 3).

From this viewpoint, economic development could be equated with cultural transformation. Development processes then primarily concentrate on taking "the" San from the 18th to the 21st century. This governance attitude fails to take self-perceptions of history into account though. The majority population thinks that the acculturation of the San and other minorities frees them from their alleged under-age and backward state. The role model of this process is the economically independent citizen working in agriculture or the cattle industry. Such ambitions do not allow the legal or symbolic recognition of other "traditional" skills because they are part of a specific cultural knowledge from the past that one should move on from. Therefore, numerous skills and artistic competences of the San are not only ignored but also denigrated. They are seen as elements of a "different identity" that stand in the way of the interests of homogenous nation-building and thus become part of the problem. These ideological principles form the foundation of the Government's "San policy" that seeks to level ethnic differences without changing material possessions and vested rights. This is why development ideas and related programmes focus on facilitating social integration, combatting poverty, providing infrastructure, and improving the access to state aid.

II. Dominant View of the San in Botswana

The letter to the editor of a newspaper in Botswana cited above (in the preamble of this chapter) was published one month after the social benefits in the *Central Kalahari Game Reserve* had been ceased and just before the San were relocated (in 2002). It highlights the characteristic public opinion in Botswana. Social scientists and those concerned agree that there is every indication of a prevailing *communis opinio* concerning the San in Botswana. In her key work *The Inconvenient Indigenous*, Saugestad (2001) cuts straight to the chase of the matter. It is embedded in a framework of attitudes and perceptions that could be best described with terms like contempt, condescension and ambivalence.

In the same way opinions also agree that it does not indicate any outspoken rejection or even hostility. The author uses the term "inconvenient" rather as a form of habitus description for the attitude of mainstream society: "The term is not a description of the group, it conveys an attitude to the group" (ibid.: 28). The positive side of this habitus uses the identification process towards a "Tswanadom" to refer to the postcolonial goals of "nation-building". We may at least see some irony in the past: why did the process of postcolonial nation-building have to stress of all things the old Western concepts of nationalism? In many African contexts – and also in Botswana – the state felt compelled to combat "ethnicity" as a preliminary stage of tribalism and thus an obstacle to state unity and homogenous national development. This must be taken into consideration with regard to the aforementioned ambivalent attitudes:

"Underlying this ambivalence are some internal challenges that Botswana, like most other African nations, has had to address in the process of nation-building. A main project has been to create a unified and unitary old western concept of nationalism to the context of new African states with mostly arbitrary boundaries. In this process, 'ethnicity' has been linked to 'tribalism' and has been seen as anathema to unified national development. Ethnicity and nationalism have been understood as different, and often conflicting, forms of social classification, representing a choice between unity or diversity" (Saugestad 2001: 28).

The mentioned strategies of cultural unification for the purpose of (homogenous) nation-building are basically equivalent to three interdependent and complementing fundamental structures of governance in Botswana: a) policies that seek the economic and ultimately also cultural homogenization of the entire population; b) development measures that contribute to the tendency of reducing cultural differences/diversity; and c) centralistic development plans that follow the principle of the welfare state with a distinct paternalistic attitude. Therefore, the slogan "Basarwa are Batswana" corresponds to the strategy of an ethnically homogenous state.⁴

As the state of Botswana does not have a mono-ethnic structure but on the contrary more than 52 (even 55 according to other sources) ethnic communities (*Report of the Presidential Commission 2000*: Appendix D), especially those groups that are perceived as "ethnically different" and thus perhaps as "inconvenient, annoying and disturbing" feel a lot of pressure to adapt. In 1989, the second president of Botswana Ketumile Masire had the honest intention of resolving any threat to the unified state, when he made his point perfectly clear and asked his compatriots: "(…) not to spoil the prevailing peace and unity in the country by fighting for ethnic language groupings to take precedence over Setswana, and that tribes insisting that their languages become media of instruction within their respective areas would break up the nation".⁵

The three mentioned fundamental structures of governance in Botswana are also reflected in conceptions of educational policies with an integrated model of modernity. Although I do not want to elaborate on school policies, I would like to point out the obvious parallel between the attitudes of mainstream society towards the allegedly (evolutionary) backwards "oldest cultures" of the country and the temporal dissociation of the "underdeveloped part of humanity" in school books.

In such (often indirectly) evolutionist and originally Eurocentric representations and conceptions of development, Africa as the origin of humankind is still excluded from the present ("the modernity") as a representative image of past eras.⁶ Following this, the San or Basarwa are people from an ancient past and, therefore, not really "genuine" contemporaries:

"In school textbooks they are generally dealt with in a chapter between Stone Age and the Iron Age, representing a past which the greater part of society has abandoned. In the common discourse on modernity and progress, the argument is that 'we have all come from where the Basarwa are' but now we have progressed, and we want them to develop like we have" (Saugestad 2001: 65).

The debate about modernity and progress can be verified as representing both public and published opinion. In this long line of similar related statements, a famous quote of the later president of Botswana stands out. The leading question Festus G. Mogae answered himself could not be any clearer in showing the fundamental elements of the three aforementioned governance positions (homogeneity, uniformity, paternalism):

---

4 See also the state's perspective of "nation-building" strategies in chapter 4, section I.3 this volume.
5 Cited in Nyati-Ramahobo (2002a: 19).
6 Cf. in this context also the doctrine of trusteeship and its mission to "civilize" (Anaya 1996: 24ff.).

"How can you have a Stone Age creature continue to exist in the time of computers? If the Bushmen want to survive, they must change or otherwise, like the dodo, they will perish."[7] It is a debatable point whether the former vice president was aware of the various implications of this comparison. The dodo was a flightless swan-sized dove endemic to Mauritius. While sailors hunted them for their delicious meat, imported pigs and monkeys disturbed their breeding places. In 1681, the bird was extinct.[8]

The disregard for certain lifeforms certainly is a child of its time. Let us just think of the dodo that was hunted into extinction so long ago. Of all animals, the dodo is the national symbol of Mauritius and thus also portrayed in the national coat of arms. In this sense, Botswana and its leadership would certainly not be the first case in which the symbolic value of uniqueness is not or too late recognized. The analogy between the San ("Basarwa") and the dodo may by implication be also interpreted as a concession that the cultural value of indigenous groups in Botswana has not been recognized (yet). When I interviewed human rights activist and Director of the NGO DITSHWANELO (on 12 September 2003), she regretfully states:

"I think it's incredibly important that we do not allow the essential aspects of the identity of the people within their cultures to be lost and we are also talking even beyond Botswana, because we know the Basarwa live in southern Africa, not only in Botswana, although many of them live in Botswana. I think it will be an incredibly sad chapter in our history, if many many years down the line we are forced to say: 'once upon a time, Basarwa lived in the region'."

There are many good reasons to criticize the aforementioned comparison and its inherent stance that the San's cultural past is not relevant in the present. We should not forget, though, that the paternalistic way of thinking (of saving lost cultures in contemporary modernity) also implies the usual benevolence, as some human rights activists (like Alice Mogwe, ibid.) concede: "The ultimate development paradigm is responsible for a particular linear way of thinking that you want to develop the Basarwa. In the development paradigm of the Government, they are doing their best and they are spending a lot of money on them. They are genuinely thinking they are doing the right things and they don't understand why the world is criticizing them as they are doing their best, as for any other Batswana, so why shouldn't they do it for the Basarwa."[9]

---

7   Festus G. Mogae, *The Star*, 19 June 1997; cited in Suzman (2001c: 286).
8   See Gooders, John (1975: 17): *Birds. An illustrated survey of the bird families of the world*. The Hamlyn Publishing Group Limited, London.
9   NGO DITSHWANELO Director Alice Mogwe does not have an easy public role as she stands up for the San of the CKGR. This has also to do with the prejudices already discussed (interview 12 September 2003).

Completely in line with this representation of Government opinions, many of the leading state representatives voice their indignation especially with regard to the lack of understanding of international media. They even consider this foreign criticism as malicious falsehood against Botswana that downright ignores their achieved progress. In his annual *State of the Nation Address 2004*, former President Festus G. Mogae was more than clear on "promoting" the San and other so-called "remote area dwellers" (see next chapter):

"Mr. Speaker, notwithstanding the ignorant and/or malicious comment of some external critics, we can take special pride in the progress of our Remote Areas Development Programme. By 2003, for example, education enrolment among Basarwa and other Remote Area Dwellers already stood at over 16.500 at Primary, 3.500 at Secondary and 300 at Tertiary level. This is strong evidence that these communities, too, are also now beginning to truly enjoy the benefits of our national development."[10]

A further contradiction concerning governance of San development becomes obvious in the tourism industry: it seems – at least in advertising – that there is only one way to effectively market the relevant communities – as "representatives of the Stone Age". When you come to Gaborone and have just passed the airport exit, you are greeted by an advertising poster saying "Welcome to Botswana". It is quite an eye-catching paradox, however, when the poster shows the portrait of a San boy drinking from an opened ostrich egg. It is also unconsciously ironic that tourists are the only ones buying such items, while probably most San have replaced this traditional and cooling water carrier by a plastic bottle. Anyhow, the picture completely contrasts Botswana's self-understanding as a modern, emerging regional economic power. It symbolizes that the other way around, prejudices against alleged "Stone Age cultures" correspond to what many tourists expect. Needless to say, the tourism industry is happy to use such symbols. Even the former Government's homepage that was designed for touristic purposes advertises Botswana's "earliest inhabitants" that still are Africa's second-largest group of indigenous hunters and gatherers after the pygmies of Equatorial Africa.[11] The announcement shows – probably because of market-based interests – how proud Botswana is that reportedly 3,000 Basarwa still subsist on hunting and gathering. In this context, the mentioned paradox shows a further aspect: the Government publicly voiced its indignation that first, the tourism industry has commodified the "Bushmen" particularly for Europe, the U.S. and Japan and second, foreigners

---

10 *State of the Nation Address 2004* by Festus Mogae (1st session of the ninth Parliament, 8 November 2004).

11 At www.gov.bw/tourism/culture-and-his/people.html (08/08/2004). Also the new homepage of *Botswana Tourism* shows in a slideshow a picture of traditional "Bushmen/Kgalagadi District" as a single ethnic community among Botswana's tourism attractions (www.botswanatourism.co.bw accessed on 20 September 2012).

have such a huge influence on human rights matters. The paradox also includes the aspect that on the one hand the marketing value of indigenous cultures is both recognized and used. On the other hand, however, the state is ashamed of this fact and wipes out the marketing value instead of questioning the underlying evaluation (Saugestad 2001: 104).

There is even another crucial aspect concerning the motives for deciding on the aforementioned prevailing governance structures in Botswana: according to the official visions of that state, as they are reflected e.g. in the national development plan "Vision 2016", Botswana clearly follows in the direction of the international community and thus the conceptions of progress of those nations that are economically most developed. According to these modernist parameters the so-called "hunting and gathering cultures" are to be viewed as development stages or obstacles on the way to full development that need to be overcome. In addition, they are perhaps secretly regarded as a "blemish" on the state's striving for modernity. It is thus quite understandable that the political elite proves proud of what it has achieved in terms of development: "If you look at where the Bushmen are coming from, and where they are now, I feel the government of Botswana has done a lot. It is clear that the international reactions still lack some understanding seeing what the government has done" (Member of Parliament Chris Grayling).[12]

For sedentary Tswana farmers and cattle breeders, the San represent a difficult past full of material shortage and social signs of deficiency they have turned their back on long ago. This leads to the false contradiction between primitiveness and progress because it misses that social goals may vary as much as individual ones do and that there is no such thing as a universally valid ideal way to development. Especially in leading positions, more than a few people are ashamed of the continued existence of individuals who (at least a small share of them) still live on hunting and gathering "like savages". This shame is reflected in many statements (see also the citation used for this chapter's preamble). Such social (psychological) considerations refer to the fact that the country's political governance of indigenous progress applies a top-down approach. As a rule, they provide the unquestioned context for the dispute that was transferred to the field of law and that became the point of reference for the court cases discussed in chapter 6.

---

12 Republic of Botswana (6/11/04): *Tautona Times* no 41 of 2004. *The Weekly Electronic Press Circular of the Office of the President.*

III. Development Policies

In the context of the governance positions of homogeneity, uniformity and paternalism as development guidelines, the Government of Botswana thought it was acting in the best interest of the San not to treat them as a "special case" so they could be brought nearer to mainstream society. It regarded any form of privileged special rights or rights of self-determination as a threat of social fission. In consequence, this was perceived as potentially causing negative or even racist reactions of other segments of society. Apart from that, conventional socio-economic criteria showed that the San were so disadvantaged that – again from the perspective of state institutions – any kind of measure combatting poverty and creating better employment opportunities did not need further legitimation in form of agreement by those concerned. In this context, the following two discussed governance programmes were and still are meant to, first and foremost, remedy economic marginalization.

1. Remote Area Development Programme

Botswana's San found themselves in a difficult and precarious situation because of two related processes: first of all, monetization and mechanization in some fields of agriculture and the service sector; secondly, regional development planning in favour of the cattle industry and especially the fragmentation of the Kalahari zones by putting up fences around huge areas. This rampant fragmentation of land by more and more fenced grazing grounds for farm animals on the one hand and national nature and game reserves on the other hand drastically limited the freedom of movement of numerous San groups. This caused their economic and social status to become weaker and weaker. Eight years after Great Britain had commissioned a situation report on the San, the Government of independent Botswana launched a development programme for their benefit – the *Bushmen Development Programme 1974*.[13] This programme granted direct state aid to indigenous "hunting and gathering communities" and raised Botswana to a special position among the region's many other countries which did not pay any such attention to this population group. Therefore and despite all shortfalls, Botswana has been Africa's (positive) exception (Lee/Hitchcock 2001: 265).

---

13 New Zealander Liz Wily of 22 years was appointed head of the programme. In her five years of work, she produced nine detailed documents and only granted research permits to scientists, if their research was combined with practical development approaches. For more details see Hermans (1995: 46ff.).

The programme's leading principles concentrated on integration into the national socio-economic system by promoting autonomy and local development (Hitchcock 1987: 311, Saugestad 2001: 117). Nevertheless, the *Bushmen Development Programme* in a certain way still contradicted the pursued objectives of nation-building. Two years later, the interests of homogenization were incorporated at least in the programme's title and the ethnic focus on the San (or "Bushmen") was replaced by a more neutral and geographical one. After the programme was then renamed several times, the Government proclaimed the still effective *Remote Area Development Programme* (RADP) in 1977.[14]

One of the programme's strengths was a certain flexibility that made it possible to react to special local conditions and the identification of negative socio-economic factors. As some parts of the population were particularly disadvantaged, specific forms of support were intended to mobilize adequate means to combat poverty. In this sense, relatively open policies enabled RADP to be operated as a special programme. It was approved by the Presidential Directive of 1987 (Cab. 28/87) and thus still has no legal basis today. Consequently, the RADP neither pursues concrete objectives and strategies nor does it establish systematic monitoring and evaluation systems, objective performance measures or deadlines. While the Ministry of Local Government administrates and coordinates the programme, it is decentrally implemented in seven administrative districts that are subordinate to the superior authority of the ministry and thus state control and influence.[15]

The state provides public funds to improve the infrastructure, e.g., public health departments, schools and water supply; further goals are the promotion of employment in agriculture and access to land rights (*Botswana Institute for Development Policy Analysis* 2003: V, *National Development Plan 8* (1997): 71). If a settlement wants to qualify for this programme, it needs at least 250 inhabitants who live at least 15 kilometres from any existing village.[16] According to the ministry responsible, the main objectives are the integration of marginalized population groups as well as the development of their living conditions:

"To facilitate the social integration of the marginalised sections of the population into the mainstream of the society and to develop rural settlement on

---

14   The progamme names were in 1975 *Basarwa Development Programme*, in 1976 *Extra-Rural Development Programme* and finally in 1977 *Remote Area Development Programme*. For three years, it was even called *Accelerated Remote Area Development Programme* to show the Government's serious implementation ambitions after ten years of rather few actions. See also Saugestad (2001: 113ff.).

15   For more details concerning the organizational structures as well as their evaluation, see "Review of RADP Draft Report" (Botswana Institute for Development Policy Analysis 2003: 111–124).

16   *National Settlement Policy* (1999: 69). There are 64 recognized RAD settlements (Raphaka 2003: 3).

to a level that is comparable with that of other rural villages in the country by providing adequate supply of potable water, education, health and other facilities necessary to improve the living conditions in those settlements" (Ministry of Local Government, Lands, and Housing 1992–93).[17]

Henceforth, the programme targets all "Remote Area Dwellers" or in short RADs. According to the *Botswana Institute for Development Policy Analysis* (2003: v), this should comprise all those groups that do not have any or only insufficient access to social benefits and other development institutions because they live in remote settlements or villages. In this context, the decisive factors are economic poverty, low education standards and insufficient ecological resources: "The programme is intended to target citizens of Botswana who live in settlements located far from centres of basic services and facilities, where there is severe poverty, low levels of education and literacy, and a deteriorating resource base" (ibid.). This should make clear that the centrally planned development focuses on material living conditions and (at least officially) not, as the former *Bushmen Development Programme* did, on ethnicity anymore.[18]

According to rough estimates, the RADP addresses about 51,000 individuals or about 4.2 % of the overall population. If we asked, however, about ethnicity in the purely economically defined group of reference, the change of label would become quite clear. Between 70 % and 80 % of all San are among the so-called RADs (Saugestad 2001: 127).[19] In this sense, a third underlying dimension can be added to the two proclaimed dimensions of – geographical and economic – "remoteness": "Stakeholders generally understood the objectives of the RADP to be linked to the economic 'upliftment' of people in remote areas. However, despite the stated geographical focus of the RADP, many people felt that the true focus of the programme was on one ethnic group – the Basarwa" (Botswana Institute for Development Policy Analysis 2003: vii).[20]

---

17 Cited in Saugestad (2001: 156). Cf. also *Botswana Institute for Development Policy Analysis* (2003: 2).

18 This makes the programme also different from ILO Convention 107, although they share the basic tendency of their integrationist and assimilative character: "Considering that there exist in various independent countries indigenous and other tribal and semi-tribal populations which are not yet integrated into the national community and whose social, economic or cultural situation hinders them from benefiting fully from the rights and advantages enjoyed by other elements of the population (…)" (Preamble, para. 6).

19 The number of *remote area dwellers* varies from source to source; Hitchcock et al. (2006: 6) assumes an estimated 60,000 to 100,000 RADs in Botswana, 47,675 and thus 47.6 % and 79 % of which are San. In contrast, the former Government homepage (www.gov.bw/basarwa/background.html) spoke of 37,771 RADs, whereas the *Review of RADP* (Botswana Institute for Development Policy Analysis 2003: 29) is based on the 2001 census with 28,487 RADS.

20 See also Wilmsen (1989: 274).

III. Development Policies   249

This critical analysis was commissioned by the Ministry of Local Government to possibly revise the programme in 2002. The *Botswana Institute for Development Policy Analysis* (BIDPA) even used international experiences with indigenous peoples (in Malaysia and Australia) for their comparison. Time and again in their review of the RADP, they called the San "indigenous populations". The institute concluded that despite of the changed focus on geographical remoteness, the majority of those involved still perceived a concentration on the San and that the word "Basarwa" was interchangeably used for the term "RAD".[21] The official Tswana equivalent to "remote area dweller" is "*Ba tengnyanateng*" and literally means "those who are deep inside deep" (Mogwe 1992: 3). We may at least have our doubts that this special distinction can be interpreted without cultural undertones. Related public discourses suggest such a tendency. According to the really interesting RADP review by the *Botswana Institute for Development Policy Analysis* (2003: 51), these discourses indicate the mainstream population's as well as parts of the political elite's contemptuous attitude towards San:

"Some officials and extension workers, even at senior levels, expressed extremely negative views about Basarwa, using expressions such as 'spoiled', 'spoon-fed' or 'troublesome', and also some racist comments, such as that Basarwa are 'liars' or that they 'have small faces'" (Botswana Institute for Development Policy Analysis 2003: 51).[22] Although the district of Ghanzi has a population of about 45% "remote area dwellers" (RADs), even the official *Ghanzi District Development Plan 6* (DDP) describes these individuals as follows: "The RADs do not appreciate education, do not seek permanent employment and are ignorant of leadership and land rights" (Ghanzi DDP 2003: 32).

When the Ghanzi DDP determined its target group, it reflected exactly the same attitudes: accordingly, the "RADs" (the semantic and phonetic aspects of this universally used acronym drastically reflect its pejorative connotations) are defined by negation, reminding us of the Laura Nader's aforementioned "discourse of lack". Wherever the Ghanzi DDP includes cultural characteristics, they are perceived and represented as parts of the (development) problem. It thus con-

---

21 Nevertheless, the commissioned institute recommended not changing the programme's focus back to ethnicity because of the principle of equality. Instead it proposed to introduce income and poverty criteria to reach the poorest members of remote communities (Botswana Institute for Development Policy Analysis 2003: 46, 52f.).

22 Keitseope Nthomang, lecturer at the University of Botswana, found the same attitudes during her eight months of fieldwork with the authorities implementing the RADP. The interview with the Government official responsible for the San settlement Kanaku exemplifies such perceptions of prevailing stereotypes: "Masarwa are not people but animals (...) they will never change (...) I think they should be left alone in the bush (...) government is just wasting resources trying to tame them because they will never understand what development is all about. All they want is to be told what to do (...) given food (...) and again they do not want to work (...) they are lazy and stupid" (Nthomang 2004: 426).

centrates on certain characteristics of the Tswana majority that the target group reportedly misses, e.g., the development of political structures and leadership (in form of the institution of a *kgosi*); further such alleged characteristics would be: they do not speak Setswana, only have insufficient access to resources, do not live in villages, do not own land, have no territoriality due to their nomadic life, and many more (Saugestad 2001: 65, 106; Saugestad 2006: 172).[23]

According to development policies, all targeted characteristics could only be "developed" in settlements, making them an indispensable prerequisite for the "integration" of those concerned. Some critics call this ideal of Tswana development measures "villagization" or the "bricks and mortar approach to development" (after the principle of settling down) (Hitchcock 1987: 333; Lee/Hitchcock 2001: 265).

In contrast to these basic attitudes, anthropological as well as development studies have clearly shown that artificial settlements are generally characterized by poverty, unemployment, social conflicts, alcoholism, apathy and discontent of its inhabitants (Hitchcock 1987: 333). Most authors agree that the purely material redefinition of the target group from "Bushmen" to "Remote Area Dwellers" missed the core of the problem and thus also possible solution approaches. As it "paternalistically" claimed to know the best way to develop the programme's target group, it did not pay any attention to the needs and improvement ideas of those concerned. Instead it established a welfare programme for the poor and marginalized among the San who had all suffered from discrimination particularly concerning land rights. The new definition was not developed to change existing structures from scratch but to only "facilitate" their living conditions (Saugestad 2001: 31).

This support, however, rather deals with the symptoms and not with the underlying reasons of poverty. As a study of the University of Botswana analyzed: "[The] continued failure in the implementation of the RADP is a function of negative perception of the Basarwa by dominant Tswana groups. Efforts to realise the objectives of the RADP are bound to fail, as long as negative perceptions that are responsible for the contempt with which they are held by the dominant Tswana groups remain" (Nthomang 2004: 428).

What does this approach of state "welfare" mean for the recipients who may not even want this support and doubtful benefits? This well-intended patronization tends to cause a state of subordination because it denies the recipients any ("proper") ability, culture and way of life and makes them dependent on social benefits. Thus many are turned into passive welfare recipients who in a certain way have handed over their competence of decision-making. This usually goes hand in hand with them losing their self-respect and dignity as well as the

---

23   Cf., for example, also the opinion of Sigmund Freud (1969 [1913]: 1–2) on Australian aborigines: he called them "the most backward and miserable of savages" that do not build houses, do not produce pottery, do not have chiefs, do not believe in or worship a higher existence, and only allow dogs as pets (cf. Barnard 2004: 1).

control over their own individual life and social destiny: "[T]he programme 'disempowers' the Basarwa by making them dependent on handouts for their entire lifetime without any end in sight or any other sustainable empowerment strategies. The Basarwa lose dignity, and lack control of their own destinies" (Botswana Institute for Development Policy Analysis 2003: 50).

It is hardly necessary to further explain that individuals who have been humiliated in such (unintended) way find their solace elsewhere, e.g. often in alcohol: "[T]hey drink to fill themselves" (Mogwe 1992: 35). The Government has created a patronizing yet well-intended dependency relationship which some authors call "welfare colonialism". They see its real function in the extension of state hegemony: "[T]he RADP, [is] dressed in the language of concern and benevolence, but function[s] to retain, even extend, political and economic control over San. (...) Dominant constructions of San as people who lack skills, material goods, civilisation – in short, 'development' – function to invite the 'normalisation' and standardisation of their reality, legitimating bureaucratic intervention and control over their lives" (Taylor 2003: 273f.).

As certain humans are represented as underdeveloped, backward and (ontogenetically) child-like, the state may treat them accordingly and justify such an intervention in form of "development". The very heart of the development concept reveals its origins in Eurocentric conceptions which Europe and its specific developments regarded as the measure of all things and prescribed to the "rest of the world" as some sort of universal remedy.

This false conclusion of an apodictically claimed universal development paradigm – "the fallacy of developmentalism" (Dussel 1995: 66f.) – is part of the protected colonial heritage of many postcolonial states.

The imposed development initiatives without consultation and participation of those concerned may be interpreted as an element of this fundamental structure and have been criticized by the commissioned *Botswana Institute for Development Policy Analysis* (BIDPA) as well. Accordingly, public authorities and ministries unilaterally define problems, control their analyses and develop further programmes that are then delegated to the "district councils" and implemented on "community level" (in villages and settlements). The San themselves see this paternalistic development approach as the main problem. They criticize that the projects are imposed "top-down" without consulting them and that, nonetheless, they are blamed for any possible failure. As Nthomang (2004: 428) summarizes her interviews with San: "We have told them the kind of income generating projects we need but they ignore us and provide what they think is good for us. Unfortunately, what they think is good for us continues to fail. We think there is a problem with the way projects are implemented. The problem is, we do not sit together and talk about what could be the problem and better ways of dealing with it. Because they think we are stupid and useless, they do not want to talk to us when projects collapse, instead they shout at us and blame us for failing the government."

The same strategies are applied in the whole country and for a multitude of different ecological, cultural and economic conditions as well as divergent social and political structures. Those concerned neither have an (informed) choice nor are they adequately consulted in the process of planning and implementing programmes (Botswana Institute for Development Policy Analysis 2003: 51).[24]

Human rights activist Alice Mogwe called this uniform kind of governance "one size fits all" or "copy and paste" model (in an interview on 12 September 2003). In this context it is hardly surprising that the evaluation of the RADP could present its only success as providing infrastructure. Measures of promoting income, establishing access to land rights and strengthening the local communities mostly failed though. These deficits were addressed in *National Development Plan 9* which focused on land rights, employment and income opportunities (NDP 9 [2003]: 41). Furthermore, the commissioned *Botswana Institute for Development Policy Analysis* (BIDPA 2003: 54) recommends to take into account and even incorporate the unique culture and tradition of historically disadvantaged communities living in remote areas. This step would lead to sustainable development. The aspect of participation for sustainable development is also crucial to NGO representative Mathambo Ngakaeaja:

"Sustainable Rural Development can only take place if there is what is now in the International Indigenous World commonly referred to as free, prior consent of the people involved – participation. It means people must be properly informed of what decisions there are and what are the consequences."[25]

The BIDPA agrees with Saugestad (2001: 192) that the ethnic discrimination and social marginalization of the San as "RADs" is a result of the underlying negative attitude of mainstream society and that this is the real reason for the problems.[26] A solution to the problems would require changing the social and political structures: "It would seem clear that there need to be programmes to address the marginalisation through affirmative action targeted at disadvantaged remote area people, as well as public education programmes to counter the prevalent social attitudes towards them" (Botswana Institute for Development Policy Analysis 2003: 53).

We can assess in a nutshell that the one-sided, contemptuous and paternalistic basic attitudes towards the San in the background of the RADP are the cardinal problem and obstacle to a self-determined and sustainable development. On the "active side" (Government, decision makers) these approaches are reflected in imposed development initiatives without prior consultation or participation and

---

24 Cf. also the considerations of Mogwe (1994: 55), Saugestad (2001: 164), Suzman (2001a: 25), Nthomang (2003: 7).
25 Interview Mathambo Ngakaeaja 24 February 2003.
26 Norwegian anthropologist Sidsel Saugestad has worked as an expert of the Norwegian Agency for Development Cooperation (NORAD) for the RADP for two years.

express an unquestioned and in a certain way self-righteous cosmovision that tends to be Eurocentric as well. The benevolent aspects of these approaches – to integrate/assimilate the "backward" parts of the population so they can also enjoy the "fruits of civilization" – only confirm the vertical ("top-down") structures.

On the "passive side" (San, RADs) this dominant way of thinking and acting leads to less self-respect, hopelessness and the feeling of uselessness. The cited literature, state evaluations but also my own empirical observations and interviews confirm that many San feel humiliated as supplicants. Such self-perceptions cause obvious consequences of social conflicts, domestic violence, alcoholism and apathy that are all openly manifested in concerned local communities. A Ju|'hoansi from north-western Botswana describes this hopelessness caused by a helpless situation that is not their fault and is combined with the constant feeling that they are inferior to the Tswana majority population (using the term "black"): "If we were blacks like them maybe that's when we could manage, but today's blacks are on top of us and look down at us like [we are] nothing just because we are red. The government can help us but we are always behind the black people" (|/!ae N||aqu cit. in Le Roux/White 2004: 17).

The implementation, however, has neither changed the marginal social situation of the San in particular nor the low-income situation of the *remote area dwellers* in general (Mazonde 2002: 60). As the San feel that their way of life is not in keeping with the times, some socio-psychological consequences suggest a development in the opposite direction of an even further marginalization of the San. Therefore, the *Remote Area Development Programme* has not really touched the San's real problems of subsistence in today's Botswana. It has not even established an effective mechanism to address them yet (Boko 2002: 107). As the *Botswana Institute for Development Policy Analysis* is an independent institution and not overly critical of the Government, the reasons they have found may have been sufficient for the responsible authorities to search for an alternative that could be put to the test apart from the RADP. They decided to try out the *Community Based Natural Resource Management* approach that is widely used around the world. This programme tries to establish access to the (sustainable) use of natural resources for residents of remote area.

2. Community Based Natural Resource Management

Studies and evaluations of the *Remote Area Development Programme* indicate (as discussed above) a growing dependency of the target group (RADs) on state welfare in form of food rations, "food for work" programmes and other state benefits (Suzman 2001a: 22f.; Botswana Institute for Development Policy Analysis 2003: XII). As the programme was not successful in economically strengthening the communities concerned, a significant part of the population lived and still lives on hunting and gathering to ensure their subsistence. Botswana is rich in wildlife as well as in veld products. This is why the *Community Based Natural Resource Management* (CBNRM) was launched as a reasonable alternative to the hardly successful RADP. It links rural economic and social development to nature conservation. The management of natural resources is based on (local) communities and focuses on reducing poverty by means of organizational development, "community empowerment" (to empower the communities to act autonomously and self-responsibly) and the sustainable management of natural resources (Child 2003: 11, Government of Botswana 2010: 1).

This suggests a clear paradigm shift that primarily manifests itself in two aspects: on the one hand, the state has come to realize that poverty should not only be interpreted in terms of low income or lack of education and health institutions but also concerning a lack of voice. The key elements of this relatively new approach are empowerment and good governance: "Poverty reduction, broadly defined, requires processes that help people improve their capabilities and functioning, that enable people to take charge of local affairs instead of being supplicants before higher authorities" (World Bank 2000: 4).[27]

In the last decades many states, on the other hand, had learned that nature conservation cannot be successful without or even against local communities. Considering the amount and huge size of protected areas in Botswana, conventional strategies of nature conservation (without people) often caused extensive conflicts between rural communities and nature conservation authorities because the economy of the first directly depended on the availability of resources.

In many regions of the world, the *status quo* of conservation policies has at best caused the communities' resentment and apathy against nature conservation. But also extremely destructive behaviour, such as the occupation of land, arbitrary destruction of natural resources, poaching and physical threats against conservationists and tourists has been observed all around the globe. It was interpreted as a form of resistance against "nature conservation without people" based on, as Barrow and Fabricius (2002: 71) explain, the "frustration of exclusion". Some of the one-sided measures resulted in reduced natural resources and thus realized exactly the opposite of what conservation authorities had intended. As only the first such steps had been taken in Botswana and the relevant institutions anticipated a similar negative scenario, they decided to change state (top-down) nature conservation to a cooperative management of selected rural communities (Thakadu 2001: 1).

The paradigm shift recognized that it was necessary to include and empower rural communities. Thus both poles of economic and social development were connected to the conservation and management of natural resources. The concept of *Community Based Natural Resource Management* (CBNRM) linked interests that

---

27 The economist Amartya Sen lists five dimensions of poverty: political space, economic space, social space, transparency and protective security (ibid.).

III. Development Policies

had been regarded as diametrically opposed ones. Proponents see several advantages in the integrative approach of resource management: first, in positive contrast to the former inability of most state authorities to manage protected areas, people living in a certain biome are cognitively familiar with its peculiarities; second, the economic potential of savings in administration due to cost-effective local management; third, the value of traditional knowledge of ecological processes; fourth, people are more motivated to protect natural resources when nature conservation is combined with direct economic advantages (Barrow/Fabricius 2002: 68).[28]

In 1989, Botswana launched the CBNRM project to be implemented by the American NGO USAID which brought in USD 25 million and a true "army of advisors" (Rozemeijer 2003: 2). In accordance with the ideas of participatory governance as further developed by the *United Nations Development Programme* (UNDP 1997), the CBNRM relies on decentral decision-making and control to promote economic endeavours and combat poverty. This is one of the huge differences to other policies. However, the rights of voice and decision-making do not apply to how natural resources are used – this decision is still subject to the Government – but to planning consented rural development projects (Cassidy 2000: 19). The 2007 CBNRM policy affirmed the legal basis for community management on the one hand, on the other hand it compels the communities to deposit 65% of their revenues generated from the sale of natural resource concessions and hunting quotas into a *National Environment Fund* for financing CBNRM projects throughout the country (Poteete/Ribot 2011: 441, Government of Botswana 2010: 22, Atlhopheng/Mulale 2009: 137).[29] That implies a decisive turning point from the ideas of participatory governance towards recentralization of wildlife management. Prior to that, all revenues generated in community-managed areas flowed directly to the *Community Based Organization* (CBO), which had considerable discretion over their allocation.

In Botswana such programme activities mainly take place in *Wildlife Management Areas* (WMA). They comprise 22% of the country and clearly serve as buffer zones to adjacent national parks and game reserves (with 17%) (Government of Botswana 2010: XII).[30] The *Department of Wildlife and National Parks* as part of the Ministry of Trade and Industry decides which buffer zones are adequate for the CBNRM. These are then declared *Controlled Hunting Areas* (CHA)

---

28 Botswana has also ratified the *UN Convention on Biological Diversity*. Art. 11 recognizes the adoption of economically and socially sound measures that act as incentives for the conservation and sustainable use of biological diversity. The CBNRM is interpreted as such an approach (Motladiile 2002: 167).

29 However, money from other CBNRM activities such as operation of campsites and lodges can be retained by the community (Government of Botswana 2010: 26).

30 *Wildlife Management Areas* were established by the *Wildlife Conservation Policy* (No. 1 of 1986). For a better overview of land rights, see chapter 4, section I.3; for a detailed discussion of land rights and categories of use, see Cassidy (2000: 10f.).

with annual hunting quotas (Barnes 1994: 325). From a legal perspective, each community is granted absolute land use titles for activities related to commercial tourism, hunting and the commercial use of veld products for 15 years. It is not an unconditional right of ownership, though, but rather a "lease"[31] that entitles the community to exclude others from using their area. In return, the community becomes a legally recognized *Community Based Organization* (CBO, e.g., an association, society or cooperative) and is required to draft and implement a management and land use plan that is subject to government approval.[32] There is one obligation especially significant for the San: as the communities are entitled to sign joint-venture agreements, e.g., with safari businesses, they are obliged to take into account members whose successful subsistence depends more or less on hunting and gathering and ensure their customary rights (Cassidy 2000: 29f.).

Since a pilot project was launched in the Chobe enclave in 1994, CBNRM has involved 91 community based organizations (CBOs) managing 150 villages and more than 135,000 individuals in all districts of Botswana. A fair share of these figures only exists on paper though; 35 CBOs at best actively implement the CBNRM's activities to promote income. Their income in 2006 was estimated to 16.3 million Pula (about EUR 2.3 million at the time). This would be the equivalent of an average annual income of only P 580 (about EUR 83) per household. This is why such earnings cannot be seen as anything more than an additional (and not exclusive) income (Schuster 2007: 43–49).[33] Furthermore, many authors warn that although the options of tourism may seem quite attractive, they rarely contribute any increase of income to the communities worth mentioning: "[W]hile tourism is an attractive option, it will not address the acute short-term financial needs of communities. Investments in tourism typically take 25 to 30 years to realize returns, and poor rural people are seldom prepared to wait that long for development to become reality" (Fabricius/de Wet 2002: 151).

One such example would be the *Okavango Community Trust* (OCT): the impressive environment and location in the northern Okavango Delta as well as the region's abundant fauna and flora convinced a private investor that the area would be perfect for a CBNRM project. The local safari company Michellet and Bates Safaris established a foundation for the five communities Gudigwa, Beetsha, Eretsha, Gunotsoga and Seronga. They funded the development of a foun-

---

31   Not known in every legal system (such as the Austrian Civil Code ABGB).

32   We should not forget, however, that these obligations only apply in case of commercial use of resources. All citizens of Botswana enjoy the fundamental right of ensuring their subsistence. A legal basis for CBNRM only exists since July 2007. Prior to that, the following laws were used as programme guidelines: *Draft CBNRM Policy* (2004), *Revised Rural Development Policy* (2002), *Wildlife Conservation Policy* (1986), *Tourism Policy* (1990), *National Policy on Agricultural Development* (1991), *Tribal Grazing Land Policy* (1975). For a more detailed account see Cassidy (2000: 14–18).

33   Cf. Rozemeijer (2003: 3f.) for 2002.

III. Development Policies

dation charter and entitled extensive competences to a (small) community council. In return, the OCT sold its entire hunting quota including twelve elephants to the company. If the ultimately failed investments in five stores as well as some smaller financial contributions to funerals are deducted, the trust did not have any income in six years. In 2001, 1.4 million Pula (then about EUR 200,000) were spent on administration (offices, transport, and training of council members) (Rozemeijer 2003: 5f.). Four years later, total incomes amounted to 1.8 million Pula, so a distribution of profits was still unrealistic (Schuster 2007: 72). The project comprises five villages with a total of 6,431 inhabitants.[34]

If a community does not sign agreements with third parties but decides to establish an own business like hunting or phototourism, they often face many more problems than only the missing start-up capital: they usually do not have any management knowledge or experience in the tourism industry (Bolaane 2001: 155f.). Considering the real short- and medium-term success of *Community Based Natural Resource Management*, the general expectations seem to have been too high. So are there any reasonable prospects suggesting that the expected increase of income could be achieved in the near future and that, thus, subsistence in difficult regions could be sustainably improved? Most authors basically deny that there is any short-term probability of improved income for the community as well as individual households. To be fair, I would like to emphasize that the programme has never claimed to become the single or even main source of income of community members. The concept of CBNRM rather had the purpose of creating new options for additional income (Suzman 2001a: 14).

All things considered, many local expectations of this questionable project approach have been rather unrealistic right from the beginning. Perhaps some initiatives to encourage local populations have also pitched the hopes of quick material success too high and thus resulted in understandable disappointment. If the connection of business and the conservation of natural resources leads to economic frustration, the aspect of conservation is of course also threatened. Once such a connection has been established, it becomes quite clear that the failure of community entrepreneurship also makes nature conservation less attractive (Rozemeijer 2003: 7).

---

34 See also Leppers/Goebel (2010: 730ff.). Cf. Poteete/Ribot (2011: 242f.) for the *Khwai Development Trust*. Cf. Bollig (2003: 310f.) and Rihoy/Maguranyanga (2011: 76ff.) for other CBNRM projects in Botswana. The same project is called LIFE in Namibia, cf. Sullivan (2002: 168ff.) and ADMADE in Zambia. Once regarded as an exemplary project, a study has shown that Zimbabwe's CAMPFIRE caused the exclusion and dislocation of local communities for the benefit of private safari businesses and local elites, while it hardly contributed to the communities' income and failed the standards of environmental sustainability (Igoe 2002: 78); see also Child (2003: 3ff.). The project of the Makuleke community in the South African *Kruger National Park* showed rather positive progress. Although they had first been relocated from the park, they took legal steps and got their territories back in 1998; cf. Robins (2003b: 272ff.).

A further unresolved question addresses programme efficiency: have all stakeholders been adequately represented and have they participated in the decision-making process as the theory prescribes? This is also closely related to the problem of a relevant forum: which decision structures are linked to the term community? In accordance with CBNRM policy (2007), a community is a group of individuals with diverse socio-economic interests and skills, who share their interest in nature conservation and live in a legally specific area.[35] We should always keep in mind that communities are complex, historically-grown, social structures, for which such thing as a "fair representation" is difficult to achieve. This requires experienced leadership competences and empowered membership. If the latter is missing, it will be difficult to avoid small village elites monopolizing decision-making (Rozemeijer 2003: 8).

For the marginalized parts of a presumptive local "community" and especially the often subordinated and disregarded San, this problem is of particularly drastic character. Masilo-Rakgoasi (2003: 10) conducted interviews in two project communities and describes the low participation of San in processes of shaping opinions and policy because they are discriminated against: "If you are poor like myself, the board thinks that even your intelligence is low." There is no mechanism guaranteeing fair participation to weaker community members. As many authors agree, the question of representative and participative decision-making has, because of these reasons, only remained something to be desired.

Several critical analyses have emphasized that CBNRM is dictated by the primacy of nature conservation. Accordingly, the proclaimed economic empowerment of communities would be less relevant. This observation would at least be consistent with Botswana's pioneering role in nature conservation. Long before other African states, many successive administrations of Botswana established huge areas as national parks and game reserves. Another indicator would be that CBNRM was initiated by the *Department of Wildlife and National Parks*. In the meantime, several public authorities have begun to implement the programme. They all either stem from nature conservation or directly/indirectly benefit from conservation measures: *Agricultural Resources Board, National Conservation Strategy Coordinating Agency, Department of Tourism, Rural Development Coordinating Division and the National Museum, Monuments and Art Gallery* (Botswana Institute for Development Policy Analysis 2003: 87).

Considering the real beneficiaries of the programme, it seems that CBNRM is primarily a label for the benefit of nature conservation that mainly plays into the hands of the government, the private sector and some NGOs: "As identified by re-

---

35   This policy was developed by the *Ministry of Commerce and Industry* (*Department of Wildlife and National Parks*) as well as the *Ministry of Agriculture*. To give the CBNRM policy a legal status, it still needs to be casted in a legislative mold (CBNRM Act). Cf. Government of Botswana (2010: 21).

III. Development Policies

cipients, however, this 'new' conservation can be also viewed as a continuation of past conservation policies: in terms of who is driving and implementing policy and in the ways in which local differences and aspirations are masked by the associated 'communalizing' rhetoric" (Sullivan 2002: 159). Even (former) programme employees informally admit that nature conservation was the real objective and that community development was only the way to this goal (Taylor 1999: 10).[36]

Needless to say, this direction is not criticized because it prioritizes nature conservation, which most regions of the world fail to do with dramatic consequences but because it suggests a referential context that is not sufficiently fulfilled. We should keep in mind from a global perspective of development that CBNRM originated from a worldwide initiative to improve conservation and did not primarily focus on economic development. "Clearly, it is preferable that local people benefit from the animal-wildlife with which they live instead of remaining alienated from these resources in a 'fortress conservation'" (Sullivan 2002: 179).

Nevertheless, this programme does not seem to offer the radically new and qualitatively exceptional approach to nature conservation it proclaims. This becomes quite clear by following the obvious idea that today's nature conservation is only possible in areas where local communities have treated their natural environment in a more or less sustainable way long before this term (sustainability) turned into the all-determining catchphrase of development and conservation discourses. In a nutshell, modern nature conservation in areas with long-standing human presence is based on the residents' original conservation measures and their cautious use of natural resources.[37] Only when "fortress conservation" was developed, many local (often indigenous) communities suddenly were denied this precautious ability of using natural resources: "[W]hen National Parks and Game Reserves were set up, hunting for subsistence became poaching and local people were alienated from managing the resources on which they had previously depended" (*Kuru Newsletter 2004*). Now if a community wants to make use of CBNRM, it will have to convincingly present itself as an "adequate" guardian of natural resources and begin to regard and use its territories as a source of generating economic capital.

---

36 See in more detail Sullivan (2002: 161). See also Poteete/Ribot (2010: 441) and Rihoy/Maguranyanga (2011: 63) as to the influence of President Ian Khama within the conservation sector: "Khama's allegiance to a protectionist conservation paradigm and the tendency that he has already demonstrated to personally dictate conservation policy in Botswana will lead to further shrinkage of policy space. His political dominance and influence throughout the country ensure that his conservation ideals permeate policy and have facilitated recent policy changes towards recentralization and 'nationalization' of wildlife revenues."

37 Overhunted or clearcut areas can, if at all, only be turned into conservation areas through expensive replenishing. In this context, one of the most impressive examples is the *Phinda Forest Reserve* in KwaZulu Natal, South Africa. It is based on the financial as well as immaterial effort of international investors and the cooperation between the private sector and the communities.

IV. Development – Nature Conservation: A Contradiction?

It was once assumed that wildlife and humans could not coexist. This basic assumption did not only lead to an unresolvable contradiction between (human) development and nature conservation, it also had serious consequences for the land rights of indigenous peoples. In line with this process, some states argued that on the one hand they could only ensure their obliged care for the further development of those concerned, if they were reasonably reachable for state institutions and outsourced authorities of health and general care as well as education (with necessary basic needs). On the other hand, nature conservation could only be guaranteed, if state interventions by relevant authorities were not "disturbed" by independently acting local groups.

In accordance with this understanding, those concerned should be seen as the beneficiaries of the relocation (discussed in the next chapter) and yet as human "disturbing factors" of an allegedly "pristine nature". The latter was both a dominant image and action-oriented motive up to the recent history of nature conservation. Such an attitude also reflects the result of the widely-spread image of a pre-modern and non-Westernized world. In their introduction of *Conservation and Mobile Indigenous Peoples*, Chatty/Colchester (2002: 7f.) explain how one-dimensional this conception was and how it was related to a certain positivistic as well as rationalistic paradigm of the separation of nature and culture: they convincingly question how this fragmented view of causalities could live up to the complexity of ecological and social relationships at a particular local level:

"This approach reduces the complex aspects of a problem into discrete parts that can be analysed, so that predictions can be made on these discrete parts. It is then assumed that knowledge can be summarized into universal laws or generalizations. Conservation science is firmly set within this paradigm, and so too are the inherently ethnocentric basic values and assumptions of its professionals. This has produced a body of work and industry based on a top-down transfer of technology model of conservation that has consistently ignored the complexity of ecological and social relationships at the local level."

Today this problem becomes even more severe because it matches the touristic expectations, originating from the same source, of a presumed, pristine nature. In this matter it should be sufficient to point out the relevant discourse elements of "discovery" that can be equally applied from Borneo over Brazil up to Botswana. This is why it is perhaps hardly surprising that the reproduced contradiction between development and nature conservation stems from a habitus that seems to be already adapted to the wishful thinking of Western modernity that a wild counterworld really exists. Until 2008, the *International Union for Conservation of Nature and Natural Resources* (IUCN) (until *2008 World Conservation Union*) represented this natural purity or the "ethics of natural wilderness" in its definition

IV. Development – Nature Conservation: A Contradiction?

of national parks. The Union was convinced that the only way to conserve certain ecosystems was to exclude human habitations.[38]

Both the reduction of development to a purely economic category and the equation of development and growth based on an increased production of material goods per capita are one-dimensional as well. Since "underdevelopment" was invented and introduced as a political emblem, development has described the economic system that followed the leitmotif of Western civilization and sought to extend the economy of goods to the rest of the world (Kaller-Dietrich 2002: 297).[39] In addition, development is only seen as increased complexity and in connection to technological progress, thus concentrating the aforementioned contradiction even further because Western lifestyles and technologies are incompatible with the idea of natural purity. If nature conservation did not only exist for its own sake but also for the economic development of the nation state, it would be quite logical to create nature reserves without humans that are adapted to the needs of touristic marketing.

This is particularly true for Botswana and its environmental conditions as the "Kalahari state"[40] because it regards tourism as one of its most important national-economic resources.[41] The argument that many tourists would love to visit indigenous societies that corresponded to their conception of "savages" is opposed to the state's legitimate opinion that such an image was of racist character. Although we can find these images of "Bushmen" everywhere in Botswana ranging from billboards and mural paintings in shopping malls even to objects of everyday life, official policies try to disassociate themselves from such an "eye-catching" use. Nevertheless, these understandable state conceptions are also the reason why the contradiction between development and nature conservation is still reflected at the level of land rights:

"We've come a hell of a long way since the 1960s, and that's why we hope [the San] will catch up with the rest of us. They belong in towns and cities like you

---

38 Cf. *inter alia* Kuppe (1998a: 101–105), McCabe (2002: 63f.).

39 Original citation in German; see also Kaller-Dietrich (2002: 294ff.) for a development concept in colonial style and as means of state control.

40 More than 85% of the state is part of this ecozone (Hupe 1999: 26). National Development Plan 8 assumes that the country has less than 5% arable land (NDP 8: 7).

41 In fact, Botswana is also signatory to almost all multilateral UN environmental agreements, including inter alia: UN *Framework Convention on Climate Change* (UN-FCCC), *Montreal Protocol on the Ozone Layer, Convention to Combat Desertification* (UNCCD), *Convention on Biological Diversity* (CBD), *Ramsar Convention* (Wetlands), *Convention on International Trade in Endangered Species* (CITES), *Basel Convention on Hazardous Wastes, Convention on the World Cultural and Natural Heritage* as well as the *African Convention on the Conservation of Nature and Natural Resources* (1968) and several regional SADC protocols. In addition, President Ian Khama is a member of the Board of Directors of the NGO *Conservation International*.

and me. They are not animals, they are not a tourist attraction" (Sidney Pilane, Attorney General).[42]

This statement of course expresses the often-mentioned unidirectional – meaning that it is included in the state's care obligations – conception of development. Although there are numerous examples of problematic self-dramatizations by members of indigenous societies conforming to preconceived categories and expectations of Western (and increasingly also eastern) visitors of the (wild) "other", these self-exploitations may only reflect current marketing strategies. But this pressure of economic adaptation to the imposed image of "the exotic other" is not engraved in stone. Take for example the Maasai in Tanzania: if structures were created that allowed them to be part of the value chain of the tourist industry in any other way than as photo subjects of warriors at the wayside of tourist paths, this form of self-commodification could become less relevant because of their alternatives. Therefore, Government statements of the often-claimed "rescue of the San" from their existence as "noble savages" seem quite clearly to be nothing but excuses. They may even serve as a straw man construed to deny any cultural assets (in expressive, visual, or fine arts, ecological knowledge and various historically accumulated competences, such as tracking, guiding, production of natural medicine and so forth) their validity. If such fictitious images were used, the motive could become an obstacle to more creative ideas of self-determined or at least participative development (e.g. in tourism) that would not necessarily have to contradict nature conservation. Apart from the legitimate rights of self-determination of those concerned in the context of belonging to a social entity, a complementary concept of reconciling development and nature conservation could also have the potential of deconstructing the mentioned expectations of tourism.

We have discussed the share of nation states in constructing this contradiction that is essentially based on preconceived ideas of development. However, international regulatory mechanisms of nature conservation by means of national parks are crucial factors as well. Of course states are interested in obtaining the status of an internationally recognized national park for the purpose of touristic development. In accordance with IUCN management category II, a protected area must be primarily administrated for the protection of the ecosystem as well as for recreation:

"[A National Park is a] Natural area of land and/or sea, designated to (a) protect the ecological integrity of one or more ecosystems for present and future generations, (b) exclude exploitation or occupation inimical to the purposes of designation of the area and (c) provide a foundation for spiritual, scientific,

---

42   In *The Guardian*: "Bushmen fight for ancestral land" of 10 July 2004. Sidney Pilane acted as Attorney General in the case *Roy Sesana & others v. Government of Botswana* that was concluded on 13 December 2006. See also chapter 6.

educational, recreational and visitor opportunities, all of which must be environmentally and culturally compatible."[43]

It would be quite difficult for any state including Botswana, though, to refer to the pressure of merely adapting to international conservation law or the soft law of various policies because the IUCN management goals unmistakably require the consideration of indigenous needs and the use of resources for subsistence purposes. In the year 2000 moreover, the IUCN issued a document concerning the compatibility of indigenous peoples and nature conservation and made it perfectly clear that unfortunately most protected areas were established without the explicit consent of those communities who had previously lived there. The "key stakeholders" were thus excluded. The document quite optimistically stated that this situation was about to be changed. This might be partly the result of the slowly spreading recognition of indigenous rights but also because of the wider-spread firm belief that the participation of indigenous population groups was essential to ensure long-term sustainability in protected areas, in which they have lived. The IUCN recommended developing new forms of co-management between government institutions and indigenous communities to eliminate the remaining deficits of adequate participation in planning and decision-making processes. International organizations could help to achieve these goals (IUCN 2000: VI).[44]

This also shows that there really are some international trends emanating from a basic and desirable complementary compatibility between state forms of planning nature conservation and indigenous knowledge. If state actors were willing to respect the capabilities of indigenous inputs particularly in terms of nature conservation, a new field of multi-level governance could be developed.[45] This would comprise the perspectives of bottom-up governance as well as the inclusion of various levels in developing and implementing political action programmes. As drafting perfect models of the integrated interests of development and nature conservation is quite problematic as it is, it seems more important to point out the significance of opening more relevant interaction channels. It is not

---

43 *IUCN Management Categories of Protected Areas* (1994). Under Botswana's law, its president may, by order published in the gazette, declare any area of state land to be a national park (Section 5 *Wildlife Conservation and National Parks Act*). According to Section 12, game reserves too are to be established by the president. See also IUCN (2004).

44 The IUCN also has a *Specialist Group on Indigenous Peoples and Environmental Law*.

45 These are relatively new concepts of cooperation between state players and civil society as well as the private sector and possibly indigenous communities. We can understand them as negotiated processes that may exceed legal definitions of competences, constitutionally stipulated jurisdictions and administrative agendas. From the viewpoint of political science, these concepts reflect the ambition to draft an adequate concept of the "real separation of power" for the complex forms of new networks (Peters/Pierre 2004: 80f.).

my intention to play off a certain approach like the CBNRM against another one such as pure self-regulation. Therefore, the options, chances and risks of co-operation in the field of national parks and game reserves should be assessed for each individual case.

As various stakeholders are involved, such an assessment is a difficult task and depends on decision-makers and socio-political goals and may result in the disadvantage of individual but primarily weaker parts of the population. This is why organizations were formed that are less interested in direct political power or profit and instead more committed to a wider public interest. In recent times, these global, national and regional "pressure groups" or "public interest organizations" have increasingly become more important than state organizations. The latter now outsource many current tasks to this kind of civil society organizations. In the following section, I will address the role of "non-governmental organizations" (NGOs) that lobby at various levels – and depending on their objectives – champion *inter alia* the San's rights, development and humanitarian aid in Botswana.

V. NGO Initiatives

Indigenous organizations as well as those committed to indigenous interests are formed to solve problems in a different way than that used by top-down models of governance. One of their main tasks is to arbitrate between nation states and indigenous peoples. In this context, their actions and ambitions are based on international experiences because they are convinced that certain problems have structural similarities. This fact has also been confirmed by empirical studies. Such processes of mutual learning promote the development of national organization forms that are very well regionally linked. Just 15 years ago, there were only a few and relatively weak indigenous organizations in southern Africa. As "San organizations" are a more or less new concept, we can detect three main areas of interest in regional contexts: economic development, activism in political relationships, and the advocacy as well as promotional activities predominantly in legal matters (Saugestad 2003: 8). National and regional NGOs offer support to each other in terms of the media.

1. National San NGOs

As it became increasingly clear that the San of various countries suffered from similar forms of economic and social marginalization, concentration shifted to the following issues: the deficits and failures of Government programmes, the growing internationalization of indigenous rights and matters, but also the active search of partnerships with (non indigenous and indigenous) NGOs. After the potential of such networking activities had been discovered, more and more organizations formed in Botswana as well. The following overview is of course not complete and mainly focuses on non-governmental organizations (NGOs) or community-based organizations (CBOs) respectively that are entirely or at least predominantly managed by San.[46]

Botswana's only NGO founded "by San for San" operates under the name of "First People of the Kalahari" (FPK) or *Kgeikani Kweni*. After the usual bureaucratic problems in the beginning, it was officially registered in October 1993. Supported by the *International Work Group for Indigenous Affairs* (IWGIA), its Ghanzi office opened in April 1994. The FPK was founded due to an initia-

---

46 Further NGOs are *Permaculture* and *Thusano Lefatseng*: both NGOs are specialized in small agricultural projects and not explicitly dedicated to indigenous issues. Also the CBO *Maiteko Tshwaragano Development Trust* is open to all members of the Zutshwa community, a RAD settlement in north-western Botswana (Bollig 2003: 285ff.). For a further overview of NGOs and CBOs committed to San issues: cf. Suzman (2001a: 30f.).

tive of a San group from the Central Kalahari that was inspired and supported by the "international indigenous movement" and was mainly concerned with activities related to the relocation of the San from the *Central Kalahari Game Reserve* (CKGR) as well as political emancipation (Bollig 2003: 285). Their board of trustees included Naro from the area of Ghanzi, Ju|'hoan (north Khoesan) as well as G|wi and ||Gana from the nature reserve. The central mission of the FPK reflected local yet still globally shared interests of indigenous peoples: the recognition of the N|oakwe as peoples and the legitimate representation of their rights in the public media as well as against the Government of Botswana; the formation of a national committee with elected representatives for the N|oakwe and the enforcement of their land rights; and the (re)vitalization of the individual identification with N|oakwe culture through related cultural education programmes (Saugestad 2001: 198).[47]

These objectives suggested that the NGO *First People of the Kalahari* (FPK) mainly saw itself as an organization of national pan-San interests. Accordingly, they concentrate on "lobbying" and raising awareness. Even the name they have chosen symbolically refers to international communication – a name and a related self-understanding they have probably borrowed from the Canadian "First Peoples". FPK is currently struggling because of a lack of manpower and funding.[48]

In 2005, their charismatic chairman Roy Sesana was awarded the Alternative Nobel Prize for his achievements in receiving land rights in the Central Kalahari as an indispensable prerequisite for the protection of cultural diversity (especially of the San). His opponents – predominantly Government members – accuse him of an unwelcome close connection to *Survival International* which was the very same international NGO whose campaign against the forced relocation of the San and the undisturbed exploitation of diamond deposits in the Central Kalahari discredited Botswana worldwide.[49]

This campaign also affected the national NGO and human rights organization *DITSHWANELO – The Botswana Centre for Human Rights* which is not specifically committed to San issues. Although the Government had previously commissioned DITSHWANELO to conduct a fact-finding mission, it terminated all consensual approaches to problems in 1996. The Government argued that the NGO was "hand in glove" with *Survival International* and wanted to harm Botswana. DITSHWANELO mainly advises and supports the San in legal matters: in 1995, for example, the NGO successfully intervened for a San community in Shaikarawe, North West District, when the authority responsible for land rights had requested them to leave their lands on behalf of a cattle own-

---

47 *N|oakwe* is a Naro word for "red people" (Saugestad 2001: 29, 176); cf. chapter 3, section I.
48 See: www.savethefpk.org (accessed 20 September 2012).
49 For a more detailed discussion see the next chapter.

er and the Minister of Local Government had dismissed their appeal (interview Alice Mogwe 12 September 2003). Their para-legal programme primarily focuses on the often difficult access to law but it also comprises the training of local activists in questions of human rights as well as providing general legal information to communities. DITSHWANELO publishes brochures and hosts focus seminars for these purposes.[50]

The increased formation of community organizations (CBOs, see above) probably is the latest organizational development in San communities. Although most of them only have a very limited budget and thus remain relatively small and institutionally weak, they receive media attention in local problem areas. Therefore, they answer the "widespread desire among San to take a more proactive and assertive role in their own development" (Suzman 2001a: 31).

The most prominent development and community organization was the *Kuru Development Trust* (KDT). In just 15 years, it had become a consortium of independent NGOs and CBOs as well as a regional support institution. As part of the *KURU Family of Organisations* (KFO), they all pursue the common goal of empowering the most vulnerable group of indigenous peoples in southern Africa to take control over their own destinies through a holistic approach to development (Kuru Family of Organisations Report 2004: 1).

Within the "Kuru Family", seven organizations are dedicated to specific development projects: e.g., the NGO *Bokamoso* provides training to elementary school teachers and native-language education, while many CBOs are represented by organizations that promote specific development agendas in local communities (Saugestad 2003: 8). Each of these NGOs has a board of trustees with a majority of San members, an almost equal representation of women and men, and several non-San advisors. They are horizontally structured, although the *Letloa Trust* with its office in Shakawe, north-western Botswana, is also the office of the *KURU Family of Organisations* (KFO) and thus takes on such tasks as fundraising, coordinating training programmes, public relations, and research related to development. In this context, the KFO (represented by the *Letloa Trust*)[51], also famous for its international art projects, arranged a meeting with

---

50 See, e.g., the brochure "Steps towards your Land Rights"; or the human rights educational programme "Tsa Bana!" which offers a guideline *inter alia* to San and human rights for secondary school teachers. In March 2002, DITSHWANELO also organized the seminar "Central Kalahari Game Reserve" which I will discuss in more detail in the next part. For current information and the latest news, see: www.ditshwanelo.org.bw.

51 The *Kuru Art Project* supports young San artists who have already attracted some attention at the international art market (through exhibitions in England, the Netherlands, Sweden, South Africa, Canada and Japan, just to name a few). Their contemporary paintings depict spiritual motives in the context of Kalahari cosmovisions as well as trance dances in which dancers contacted animals to be hunted; cf., e.g., "Bushman Art. Zeitgenössische Kunst aus dem südlichen Afrika" (2002), Arnoldsche

Chairman Nicky Oppenheimer of De Beers in 2004. Their goal was to negotiate a *Code of Conduct* for a joint-venture partnership with indigenous peoples (KFO Report 2004: 71f.).[52]

When in 2004 the *South African San Institute* (SASI) joined the *KURU Family of Organisations*, the NGO expanded its field of operation beyond Botswana.[53] Moreover, it intensively networks with the *Working Group of Indigenous Minorities in Southern Africa* (WIMSA) (see below) and provides financial and administrative support, even though WIMSA focuses on the human rights and political representation of the San in Botswana and thus differs from the rather apolitical agendas of the "Kuru Family" (KDT) (ibid.: 72).

2. Regional San NGOs

As the calls of those concerned for a regional San organization grew ever louder, various San NGOs began to discuss this issue both locally and regionally with San communities from five countries of southern Africa (since 1992). This consultation process mainly showed that various San organizations suffered from the same insufficient effective exchange of information and experience. In 1996, these findings and further extensive consultations resulted in the foundation of the regional *Working Group of Indigenous Minorities in Southern Africa* (WIMSA) in Windhoek, Namibia and shortly afterwards in D'Kar, Botswana. This San NGO formed a platform for San communities to express their problems, needs and concerns. WIMSA is required: "[t]o advocate and lobby for the San rights, to establish a network for information exchange among San communities and other concerned parties, and to provide training and advice to San communities on tourism, integrated development projects and land tenure".[54]

The regional NGO WIMSA works in the fields of political support, capacity building and networking for San communities in South Africa, Angola and Namibia. At the same time, WIMSA Botswana is responsible for similar affairs in

---

Verlagsanstalt, Stuttgart; or "Spuren des Regenbogens. Kunst und Leben im südlichen Afrika" (2001), Arnoldsche Verlagsanstalt, Stuttgart.

52 On its website, De Beers explains that it is crucial to consult with indigenous peoples as an element of their principles and community policy. As De Beers is the world's biggest diamond mining and trading company, this is a huge success for the global indigenous movement. As always in such cases, the actual implementation of such policies would have to be the subject of long-term empirical observations; see www.debeersgroup.com. See also *De Beers Report to Society 2011* – Supporting sustainable local communities.

53 When SASI was founded in 1996, it was the first and only South African NGO for indigenous affairs; see www.san.org.za (accessed 12.12.2012).

54 www.san.org.za (accessed 06.06.2007).

V. NGO Initiatives

Botswana, Zambia and Zimbabwe (WIMSA 2004a: 9). WIMSA's Board is comprised of San representatives from Botswana, Namibia and South Africa. The regional organization funds projects, connects and arbitrates between governments or NGOs and promotes both indigenous and human rights. Similar to the aforementioned NGO DITSHWANELO, WIMSA, too, is committed to providing information and thus publishes from time to time brochures specifically concerned with the San and their issues.[55] In the meantime, San representatives from the whole region have begun to meet regularly for the purpose of more effective networking. A total of 30 CBOs and NGOs have joined WIMSA as member organizations, more than half of which are in Botswana (WIMSA 2004a: 8).

In the last ten to fifteen years and inspired by the global indigenous movement, the organization process of San communities in southern Africa has continued. As they all share similar experiences of discrimination and marginalization, of the states' failure to secure the protection of indigenous interests and the growing dependency on states and welfare, this process is hardly surprising. The new and strengthened self-confidence is also based on a group of San who have completed their higher or university education and now contribute to the national and international networking of San communities to establish political awareness. This is also why it was possible for a further attempt of transnational integration of regional San NGOs to take shape.

In accordance with several "Shakawe Principles" (see chapter 3, section I), WIMSA, KDT, SASI and their member organizations agreed to form a joint Council. While such a Council will on the one hand represent San interests in many different national and international forums, it will on the other hand support small financially and organizationally weak San communities which lack the clout to represent their own interests effectively at the political level or within the media (cf. Suzman 2001a: 32).

The various NGOs in particular share the opinion that membership does not depend on belonging to a clearly demarcated and locatable ethnic group but that it is rather based on self-identification. National San councils have been elected in South Africa, Botswana and Namibia. These are representative bodies that advocate on behalf of San communities at different Government levels.

Although the value of a Regional San Council for the San of southern Africa should not be underestimated, each of the various states in the region has its own opinion of such a transnational network. While it is unlikely that South African authorities would voice reservations – there is, for example, a Griqua Council (Suzman 2001a: 33), the situation is rather different in Botswana. The structures of governance mentioned above have generated a centralistic atti-

---

55 WIMSA, for example, introduces the San of Namibia to the legal system (WIMSA 2001) or explains the problems of cultural heritage and intellectual property (WIMSA 2004b).

tude that could be extremely reluctant to appreciate and even possibly disapprove of such decentralization aspirations not recognized by the state. Such ambitions particularly include initiatives that are regarded as ethnic or "tribal" ones and focus on the development of more or less autonomous organizational structures. Basically all Botswana's postcolonial administrations have been extremely cautious, whenever the San called for independent decisions and self-determination. Needless to say, they were significantly less agitated, when recognized Tswana societies voiced similar demands. During a mission to Botswana from 15–23 June 2005, the *African Commission's Working Group on Indigenous Populations/Communities* made similar observations:

"During the mission, the delegation observed that there was a generally negative impression about the Basarwa in the country. This impression is not limited to members of the public but extended to high ranking Government officials. The delegation observed that the Basarwa were the least developed in all aspects of human development – education, health care, nutrition, etc. They were the least represented politically and most marginalised. Another troubling observation was Government's continuous insistence that there were no indigenous populations in the country despite volumes of literature to prove that the San/Basarwa were the original inhabitants of the region."[56]

As the hardly successful *Remote Area Development Programme* indicates, the Government's centralistic attitude also impedes development projects. Anyhow, the social situation of the San has not improved in any aspect worth mentioning. As Mogwe (1992: 43) explains, any aspirations of development are, therefore, significantly restricted: "development planned for them and around them, without reaching them". In contrast, *Community Based Natural Resource Management* seems to apply a more honest approach to decentralization. As this initiative is rather dictated by the primacy of nature conservation instead of human development, it hardly provides any operational opportunity to improve the San's living conditions in a sustainable and self-determined way. In consequence, many still define themselves by negation, as Aaron Johannes resonantly noted at the Gaborone Conference in 1993: "we are the people with no money".[57]

---

56 *Progress Report for the ACHPR Working Group on Indigenous Populations/Communities. Intersessional period between 37th and 38th ordinary sessions of the ACHPR.*
57 Cited in Taylor (2001: 163).

"In the olden days, we were free to hunt. But nowadays we are not allowed to" (Kgosi Molatwe Mokalake).

Figure 23: Today most of Botswana's over 50.000 San live in dependence of government handouts or poorly paid wage labour. Only a few support themselves as actors in a "living museum" that "preserves" their knowledge of hunting and gathering for interested tourists. The legal struggle for their land(s) may be read as a means to protect this important cultural heritage.

Part 6: "The Lost Lands": Relocation from the *Central Kalahari Game Reserve*

I. History of the *Central Kalahari Game Reserve*

The following outline of the history of the *Central Kalahari Game Reserve* (CKGR) and its significance for the local San shows the political context of the legal proceedings before the High Court for the land and resource rights of San communities relocated from their living environment. Only a historical perspective enables such a discussion to be adequately analyzed.

When the earliest Bantu-immigrants entered the area of Botswana, they encountered (as mentioned) the "hunting and gathering communities" of the San as well as cattle-breeding Khoekhoe.[58] In consequence, their living environment was increasingly reduced because – as the territories were extremely dry – the immigrants needed extensive grazing grounds for their cattle. The local peoples could hardly oppose the immigrants' striving for land occupation and control over the territories. When the politically dominant Tswana kingdoms expanded to the edges of the Kalahari, the San had no choice but to retreat to the dry areas unattractive for keeping cattle at the country's centre, if they wanted to lead a self-determined and more or less independent life.[59]

The so-called "Kalahari Desert" with its bush and grass savanna was mainly the home of G|wi (according to the Government, 47% of all San in the *Central Kalahari Game Reserve* were G|wi), ||Gana (15.3%) but also Tsira and Hai/nu San communities as well as the relatively sedentary Sotho-Tswana communities of the Bakgalagadi with 37.2%.[60] The average population living within the area of

---

58 For the history of the San, see chapter 3 section II and for the political history of Botswana chapter 4, section II.

59 These descriptions are rather simplified and should not create an overly homogenous picture. Over the course of time, the relationships to later immigrants were always dynamic. In certain situations, it may have been that individual San, whole families or even communities (temporarily) gave up hunting to ensure their survival on cattle farms (e.g., during droughts). It is difficult to estimate how many San permanently lived on these farms or in the growing cities (cf. Saugestad 2001: 83–97; Wilmsen 1989: 130ff., 153ff.); see particularly the considerations of the *Kalahari debate* in chapter 3, section II.

60 The former Government homepage – which in the meantime has been deleted – differentiated between these three groups according to the following official characterizations: until today, the G|wi (or G/wikwe as the Government calls them) have lived a "traditional" life as hunters and gatherers, who used bows and arrows to hunt wild animals. In contrast, the Bakgalagadi predominantly lived in villages, cultivated fields and kept goats, donkeys and horses. Their cattle were kept by relatives living outside of the reserve. Finally the ||Gana – still according to the Government – combined both mentioned lifestyles ("a unique cultural cross between the G/wikwe and the Bakgaladi"): they had egalitarian structures but still showed the abilities of hunters and gatherers, although they had adopted the social structures of villages and supplemented their subsistence as hunters and gatherers through cattle husbandry and

today's reserve varied from season to season: generally it amounted to about 4,000 individuals but the environment probably would not have been able to feed more anyway (Albertson 2002: 12). Contrary to certain conceptions, the San were not nomadic peoples in the narrow sense of the word. They rather applied complex strategies of survival that depended on the ecological and climatic conditions, seasonal rainfall, varying degrees of aridity, and the respective local access to resources. I guess you need to have experienced the different seasons of the Kalahari to really imagine in how many and difficult ways this biome challenges both the flexibility and mobility of its inhabitants:

"When the wild food and animals were not found near our camp, the old men gathered the community together to go to a new place to make a camp there. The day after the assembly meeting decided this, everyone left, but not for good, as they said that they would be back again in the old camp. They left all their clothes there, and this shows how the Khwe were a mobile people but not truly nomadic (…)" (interview Ôâna Djami, Ngarange, Botswana [Bugakhwe]).[61]

This description shows that the existing categories of nomadism and semi-nomadism do not exactly fit the concrete social arrangements of the San in the Central Kalahari. Although their communities were mobile, they did not leave their territories (*ngo's*). Individuals that did not belong to the local group had to obtain the community's approval, represented by the elders, to use the lands. In the Central Kalahari court case, this fact was also addressed to understand the San's relationship to their lands (High Court 2006: 157f.). This bleak and arid character helped the region of central Botswana to remain rather undisturbed until the beginning of the 20th century. Nevertheless, it would be completely wrong to regard the individual territories of San communities as isolated and self-contained units; instead archaeological findings have confirmed that the inhabitants also traded with outsiders and were subject to interventions from outside (Wilmsen 1989: 64–77).

As not unusual for that time, the British colonial Government unilaterally declared the area of today's Botswana as its protectorate in 1885. It thus incorporated – except for the eight Tswana kingdoms – the remaining "unoccupied" territories (*terra nullius*) into British Crown Lands.[62] In the 1920s/30s already, a

---

agriculture. About 75% of all CKGR residents left their usual environments during droughts and searched for other water resources. During such times, about half of them left the reserve.
Government homepage: *The Relocation of Basarwa from the CKGR – Background* at www.gov.bw/index.php?option=com_content&task=view&id=13&itemid=52 (accessed on 25 November 2008).

61 Cited in Le Roux/White (2004: 145).
62 Proclamation No. 1 of 1885 established the area of today's Botswana as a British protectorate; see chapter 4, section I.2. The *Bechuanaland Protectorate (Lands) Order-in-Council 1910* then proclaimed the (today's) districts of Chobe, Kgalagadi and Ghanzi

I. History of the Central Kalahari Game Reserve

debate – I have extensively addressed – that today would be regarded as terribly bizarre about the status of the "wild, primitive Bushmen" developed. At that time, Charles Darwin's doctrine of biological evolutionism was simplistically transferred to human societies as "Stone Age evolutionism". Based on these widely-spread evolutionist ideas, the representatives of the "ancient society" (*Urkultur*) had to be adequately protected as "agreeable to their nature". The former Government of the Union of South Africa commissioned two special advisers who (according to Hermans 1995: 41) determined the San as actually being part of the fauna. There would thus be "no problem" to have them stay in a planned game reserve.[63] This racist position obviously stabilized the fate of San communities in the Central Kalahari.

Twenty years after the so-called "Tagart Commission" had assessed the relations of dependency and forms of enslavement of the San working on Tswana and European cattle ranches, the concerns about the situation and treatment of San communities again grew louder.[64] An "ethnological study on the San's economy and forms of society" was meant to form the basis for the decision on future "Kalahari policies". It is one of the continued absurdities of arbitrary governance as related to the inhabitants of the Kalahari that this task was performed by an untrained administrative civil servant with the rank of a cadet. As this job was, to put it mildly, rather unattractive to colonial officers, the decisive criterion for this decision was this young man's thirst for adventure and his fascination for the African bush. District Commissioner George Silberbauer ultimately had the idea to establish a reserve as a "retreat for hunters and gatherers" as well as for wild life and other resources they needed in order to survive.[65] This had become clear in a *savingram* of the Resident High Commissioner in Mafikeng, the capital of Bechuanaland, to the High Commission in Cape Town:

"Briefly, the object of the Reserve is to protect the food supplies of the existing bushman population in the area, which has been estimated to number approximately four thousand, from the activities of the European farming community at Ghantsi and visitors to the territory who are entering this area in increasing-

---

as British Crown Land as well. The *Central Kalahari Game Reserve* is located in the latter district.

63 See Hitchcock (1987: 299) who based his considerations on an article in the South African newspaper *Cape Argus* from 25 August 1936.

64 See chapter 3, section II, 1.1. on the "Tagart Commission" which, at that time already, addressed the problematic situation of the San especially outside of the Kalahari and conducted the first study in this matter.

65 In this context, it is quite interesting to note that this person (now Australian professor of anthropology) was summoned to the High Court as a witness in the San legal case about half a century later. Also this fact indicates the unchanged historical continuity of unresolved legal questions.

ly numbers, either to poach game or to shoot predatory animals such as lions or leopards for their skins."[66]

In line with these objectives, the concerned territory was supposed to perform the mentioned dual function: to guarantee the protection of animals and resources as well as enough lands for the San (Mogwe 2011: 166, High Court 2006: 344, Botswana Institute for Development Policy Analysis 2003).[67] According to Silberbauer's "study", time was of the essence, if they still wanted to protect the San's cultural expressions and ways of life. Therefore as an immediate measure, the High Commissioner established the said territory as the *Central Kalahari Game Reserve* (CKGR) in 1961.[68]

As at that time, the control of protective measures and hunting bans was more than just fragmentary, the mere declaration was of course not sufficient. Many local farmers and cattle owners simply ignored the declaration and continued hunting in the Kalahari. These hunters were significantly more successful because they began to increasingly use the latest weapons and better vehicles. Thus, they threatened the basis of existence of the San communities who were still using their traditional weapons and hunted only with poisoned arrows and without any means of transportation. In consequence, Silberbauer sharpened the legal stipulations as well as their implementation and generally limited the entry to the reserve. This *Control of Entry Regulation* declared that it was illegal for "non-Bushmen" to enter the CKGR without a permit:

"No person other than a Bushman indigenous to the Central Kgalagadi Game Reserve shall enter the said Reserve without having first obtained a permit in writing from the District Commissioner, Ghanzi."[69]

---

66   *Savingram No-735* of 7th October 1960 (cited in Albertson 2002: 12).

67   On 15 December 1960, similar findings were wired to the Commonwealth Relations Office in London and were later cited by Judge Phumaphi in the Kalahari case (High Court 2006: 340): "Survey will take longer than originally expected to achieve satisfactory results. Proposal on interim report forwarded with my Savingram No-735 of 7th October 1960 is for declaration of game reserve, i.e., interim measure to satisfy most important need of primitive bushmen. Namely preservation of game on which they live (…)."

68   *High Commissioner's Notice No. 33 of 1961,* 14. February 1961: "It is hereby notified for general information that his Excellency the High Commissioner has been pleased to declare part of the Ghanzi District which lies to the east of meridian of longitude which passes through the highest point of the hills known as Great Tsau shall be a Game Reserve, to be known as The Central Kalahari Game Reserve." Pursuant to the provisions of Sect. 5(1) of the *Game Proclamation* (Chapter 114 of the Laws of the Bechuanaland Protectorate, 1948), the High Commissioner may, by Notice published in the Gazette, declare any territory to be a game reserve (High Court 2006: 104). This declaration competence for game reserves is now included in the *Wildlife Conservation and National Parks Act Chap. 38:01, second Schedule.*

69   *Sect. 2 (1) CKGR (Control of Entry) Regulation, Government Notice* No. 38 of 1963 of 3 May 1963.

I. History of the Central Kalahari Game Reserve

This Government regulation of 1963 was incorporated in the *Fauna Conservation Act* (Chapter 38:01) as one of fifteen annexed "Subsidiary Legislations". For decades later, it would play a key role in the legal dispute over the "lost lands of the Kalahari". The *Fauna Conservation Act* (of 1961) stayed in force also after the country's independence and was only amended in 1992 (No. 28) and later in 2000 (under the same-named Chapter 38:01) under the new *Wildlife Conservation and National Parks Act*.[70] The *Subsidiary Regulation/Order* (under Sect. 92) of the latter does not include the cited special regulation for the San of 1963 anymore. Instead it stipulates (under the *National Park and Game Reserve Regulation*) that generally no person is allowed to enter a national park or game reserve except under and in accordance with a valid entry permit (Sect. 4 (1)).

We have to ask ourselves, therefore, whether the new law had really changed anything because Sect. 94 (2) of the *Wildlife Conservation and National Parks Act* established that any subsidiary legislation shall be in force and effect notwithstanding the repeal of the *Fauna Conservation Act*. This is why perhaps a formal derogation of the repealed former regulation (of 1963) would have been necessary, which was only part of the *Fauna Conservation Act's* schedule.[71] As far as I know, this has not happened though. During the court case, also Judge Dibotelo (High Court 2006: 391f.) assessed the same regulation of 1963 with regard to the legal question of a necessary permission for the San to enter the CKGR. He emphasized that this regulation clearly established an exception for the San and had not been repealed ever since. In his opinion, it even found its way into Botswana's Constitution under Art. 14 (3) (c). This now repealed source of fundamental rights regulated the explicit restriction for any persons other than "Bushmen" to certain territories.[72]

If we wanted to apply a historical interpretation of the original law, we would find the clear intention of Silberbauer's survey, which also formed the basis of the decision, to *de facto* create an area for the exclusive and permanent use by the San (while not ruling out activities of tourism, recreation and research). This would have offered the San an opportunity to maintain their subsistence lifestyle of hunting and gathering.[73] Already at that time, some administrators criticized

---

70 Sect. 94 (1) "The Fauna Conservation Act and the National Parks Act are hereby repealed."
71 See Sect. 94 (2): "Any subsidiary legislation made under and in accordance with the provisions of the Fauna Conservation Act or the National Parks Act shall continue of force and effect as if made under the provisions of this Act (…) until revoked or amended by or under this Act."
72 Cf. also the considerations in chapter 4, section II.5, Fundamental and Human Rights.
73 Silberbauer summarizes the creation of the CKGR as follows: "The retention of Bushmen in the Reserve would appear to be a reversal of the policy of economic advancement advocated for the rest of the Bushmen of Bechuanaland. The resolution of this

Silberbauer for creating a "human zoo" in which anthropologists could study the so-called "primitive peoples".

This argument is also reflected in a few state argumentations of postcolonial Botswana and thus hinders the San's wish for self-determination and land rights. Instead it propagates the (unilateral) integration of the San whose autonomy derives from a European myth (of an "exotic race living in splendid isolation from other peoples, as subsistence hunter-gatherers").[74] Both cases – the colonial concerns against Silberauer's proposals and the current criticism against supporters of the San in the Kalahari – seem to be straw man arguments that pervert the real intentions of advocacy for the (indigenous) rights of the San. Silberbauer as well as other anthropologists championed the San and their rights to remain in the Central Kalahari primarily because, as Hitchcock (1987: 299) underlines: "Silberbauer (…) felt that the Basarwa should have the right to retain their dignity and to pursue their own options."

This opinion is also confirmed by Silberbauer's rarely mentioned additional recommendation to extend the education and development opportunities of those San who worked on Ghanzi farms and had long ago given up their traditional ways of life. This does not really agree with the accusation of dwelling on the image of the "noble savage", particularly since the San of the Kalahari would have been entitled to enjoy such opportunities (Hitchcock 1987: 299). In this context, I would like to mention that Silberbauer's fieldwork also affected the San's way of life and former mobility in the Central Kalahari: "When Silberbauer sank a borehole at Xade for his own use in 1961, he inadvertently set the ball of change rolling" (Suzman 2002: 1).

Access to water all year long was so attractive to many San that they moved from the regions they lived in during dry seasons to !Xade in the central-western CKGR. At this point it is crucial to know that contrary to many romanticized ideas, any form of living has always been precarious and without any existential security during dry season. Therefore, the building of a well radically changed seasonal mobility but also their subsistence strategies changed: as water now was always available, it was suddenly possible to keep livestock and cultivate the land at the same time. Some figures show a clear picture: as soon as 1962 (shortly after the well was built), the settlement of !Xade had 200 inhabitants. When their conditions were evaluated by the *Remote Area Development Programme* in 1976,

---

paradox is that it is not intended to preserve the Bushmen of the Reserve as museum curiosities and pristine primitives, but to allow them the right of choice of the life they wish to follow" (Hitchcock/Brandenburgh 1995: 8, cited in DITSHWANELO 1996: 27).

74 According to the already-deleted homepage of the Government of Botswana "The Relocation of Basarwa from the Central Kalahari Game Reserve" – Background. www.gov.bw/index.php?option=com_content&task=view&id=13&itemid=52 (accessed on 25 November 2008).

I. History of the Central Kalahari Game Reserve

the San had 1,500 goats, 100 donkeys, 21 horses, dogs and chickens (Hitchcock 1987: 309, 318).[75]

One possibly unintentional consequence of the original proclamation of the *Central Kalahari Game Reserve* (1961) was the henceforth *de jure* illegal character of hunting.[76] As hunting and gathering was central to the San's survival and the proclamation an official instrument to protect living conditions, the colonial administration ignored such violations, which was confirmed by Silberbauer when he was summoned as a witness for the CKGR legal case in 2004.[77] This situation of the state accepting violations of law only ended when Botswana became independent and the *Fauna Conservation (Amendment) Act* 1967 was amended. This law officially allowed members of communities that primarily lived on hunting and gathering to continue their forms of subsistence.[78]

After the *Remote Area Development Programme* was introduced in 1977, those population groups living in remote areas and dependent on hunting and gathering received so-called "special game licences" (SGL). As long as state authorities were convinced that their way of life fulfilled the further qualifications of the RADP, especially the aspects of extreme poverty and low education standards, such a license had been free since 1979. To obtain the license, though, they had to file an application with the *Department of Wildlife and National Parks* (DWNP) in written form. It is quite ironic that from now on, the region's first indigenous residents required legitimation by the state to exercise their subsistence practices on lands they had occupied since ancient times. These SGLs entitled them to hunt all year long. Animals that were particularly endangered or

---

[75] Before that time, the communities separated into family units during dry season. The average size of a community varied between 21 and 85 individuals. One individual per 14 km² lived in the CKGR (Barnard 1992: 102). For the *Remote Area Development Programme*, see chapter 5, section III.1.

[76] Section 5 (2) of the *Game Proclamation*.

[77] When Attorney General Pilane asked him, whether or not the colonial Government's law had to be observed, Silberbauer answered: "I do not think it could be fairly and truthfully said that law did not matter, however in many situations it was deemed expedient and wise to as it were to turn a blind eye (…) [a]t the continued of free hunting by the inhabitants of the CKGR" (High Court 2006: 347f.).

[78] Now hunting and gathering requires a written permission (Sect. 12 (3), Sect. 39 *Wildlife Conservation and National Parks Cap. 38:01*). In accordance with Sect. 30, all citizens of Botswana living primarily on hunting and gathering are entitled to such a permit. Other legal provisions establish such a right as well: Sec. 9 (3) *Wildlife Conservation Regulations* 2001: "The special game licence may only be issued to citizens who are principally dependent on hunting and gathering of veld products for their food (…)". This is also true for all CKGR residents as pursuant to Sect. 45 *National Parks and Game Reserves Regulations* 2000: "Persons resident in the CKGR at the time of the establishment of the CKGR, or persons who can rightly lay claim to hunting rights in the CKGR, may be permitted in writing by the Director to hunt specified animal species and collect veld products in the game reserve (…)."

protected, however, were generally excluded from this license and had a specific hunting quota that had to be observed. Hunting some of these animals, such as wildebeest and eland, however, had always assumed a special role in the cultural and religious expressions of the San (Hitchcock 2001: 144).

But what extent of economic dependency from hunting and gathering was necessary to qualify for special game licences (SGL)? As there was no legal provision establishing the exact criteria, we can find a wide range of determining factors – again according to (at that time) widely-spread evolutionist thinking: administrative practice classified individuals as hunters and gatherers in the proper sense, when they were *de facto* members of a "nomadic" and thus non-sedentary community. Public authorities also demanded the use of "traditional" hunting weapons, e.g. poisoned arrows, lances and traps all made from natural materials. The DWNP granted special licenses only to those applicants who did not use so-called "hunting aids", such as horses, donkeys, dogs or vehicles. This licensing practice sometimes seems quite grotesque and proves that the principle of "clothes make (bush)men" in a modified way also applied to Botswana. So it happened that some government officials only accepted applications of individuals wearing "traditional clothes" in form of a loincloth made of animal skins (Hitchcock 2001: 145). Therefore, people dependent on hunting and gathering for their subsistence had to look and live like "traditional Bushmen" from the picture book of exotistic psyche (non-sedentary, half-naked, wearing loincloth with bow and arrow) until such hunting licenses were abolished in 2001.[79]

As the provisions for granting special licenses to the poorest parts of the population allowed for a wide scope of interpretation, they created a situation of legal uncertainty and were severely criticized from various sides. The Parliament of Botswana was concerned that such free hunting licenses were equal to "special rights" for certain communities, especially *Remote Area Dwellers* (RADs).[80] In addition, some members of parliament considered "traditional" hunting techniques to be cruel and "inhuman". On the other side, those concerned, primarily San, criticized the restrictions both of numbers and certain animal species (Hitchcock 2001: 146). From an academic perspective, Alice Mogwe (1992) confirmed this critical stance in a report about the human rights situation of the San. She criticized that the special licenses on the one hand were supposed to ensure the survival of the poorest parts of the population, while on the other hand they established requirements that either questioned this survival when

---

79 Cf. the report by the animal researcher couple Owens (1986: 132) how they imagined to encounter the San in the Kalahari: "[W]e imagined that at any moment we would round a hedge and see little black men in animal skins, with bows and arrows slung over their backs, gathered around a small campfire, roasting a steenbok for their supper."

80 This concern again reflects the political fear that special rights for a part of the population could lead to social fission and threaten the unitary state.

I. History of the Central Kalahari Game Reserve

they were observed or had legal consequences ranging to imprisonment when they were ignored.

In practice many possible recipients probably failed to take advantage of this legal provision because their application had to be filed in written English. As most of the San (or "RADs") are illiterate and do not speak English, they would have needed others to help them – a help they would have only insufficiently received (Mogwe 1992: 7).[81] Moreover, the San actually hunt – in contrast to commercial and hobby hunters – "for their cooking pots" (in the words of Alice Mogwe). If they cannot trace one of the animals the license allows, they only have two options: they either starve or hunt an animal they are not licensed to and violate the law (Mogwe 1992: 13).

The license further stipulates that the San are only allowed to use "traditional" methods, such as hunting with bow and arrow. Younger generations are not that familiar with these weapons and techniques anymore and, therefore, face a problem they can hardly resolve (Mogwe 1992: 7). San-activist Mathambo Ngakaeaja (WIMSA) detects similar reasons and notes that the Government discriminates against the San by limiting their hunting rights. Even if the legal provisions apply to all citizens as legal subjects, Ngakaeaja argues, they will only *de facto* affect those who need hunting to survive:

"All these regulations and laws further impoverish, disadvantage and marginalize our people. In a way, I think all this is an institutionalized state-orchestrated racism, because it is dealt within a system. Of course, it is not written in black and white that 'you Basarwa need to do this', but if you say that everybody needs a hunting licence, of course you refer to Basarwa. The only people who suffer from the consequences of that law are Basarwa; so it is racism" (Mathambo Ngakaeaja, interview 24 February 2003).

If San did not have such special game licences (SGL) and still hunted for animals, they became "poachers" and faced severe consequences: they were arrested, imprisoned and punished with a fine. As the San participate in the monetary economy in a very limited way, they were often unable to pay such fines. In consequence, anything they possessed was seized, e.g., horses, donkeys, weapons or other material goods of their everyday life. Time and again, newspapers also reported cases of abuse – and even torture – during police or *Wildlife Department* custody. The formal reasons for official acts ranged from violation of their quota to expired licenses; numerous statements of San perceived the true motive of this extreme exercise of coercive power as harassment. In many such cases of complaints, the courts found

---

81 About 77% of so-called "illiterate" RADs are San (Mazonde 2004: 140). Also Mathambo Ngakaeaja (interview 24 February 2003) of the NGO WIMSA criticized the implications of the SGL: "How do you expect an old man here in D'kar, who doesn't have a telephone, who doesn't have a car to get a written permission from the Director, to fulfill the hunting regulation?"

them not to be guilty; this result could also be related to a certain sympathy towards the legal-politically questionable obligations of the "indigenous peoples of the Kalahari". In no case (that I know of), however, they were in any way compensated for asserted human rights violations or material losses.[82]

Nevertheless, the San who had to deal with completely unfamiliar bureaucratic procedures, were not the only ones to voice criticism. Also environmentalists, safari hunters and the *Department of Wildlife and National Parks* (DWNP) picked the concept of special game licenses for *Remote Area Dwellers* into pieces. They were convinced that too many licenses – more than 2,000 per year in the mid-1990s – would also lead to more hunting and ultimately to overhunted territories. In their eyes, this licensing practice was the main reason for Botswana's decreased game population (Hitchcock 2001: 146). From the perspective of protecting wild animals, this concern was of course understandable but it did not sufficiently differentiate between the San who had lived from hunting in the Kalahari for a long time and the new beneficiaries of the RADP.

In consequence, many such critical voices threw the San and all the other hunting companies in the same pot as "factors disturbing pristine nature". According to the principle of "nature conservation without human influence", all those who had received hunting licenses were seen as an undifferentiated group and declared a potential danger for "the" environment without adequately taking into account aspects of cultural ecology of a long-term historical relationship.[83] This position was also prominently supported, amongst others, by the renowned lion and hyena researchers of the Central Kalahari, Mark and Delia Owens. Although they had never encountered San during their research, they blamed three factors for the drastic decline of wildlife: severe droughts, fenced reserves and the San living in the Kalahari (Suzman 2002: 2).[84] Newly founded in 1984, the NGO *Kalahari Conservation Society* cleaved to the same mindset and proposed to relocate the San from the reserve because their presence would be incompatible with the reserve's protection status. This request provoked wild debates in the media and even parts of the NGO's own members vehemently opposed this position (White 2000: 19).

---

82   www.iwgia.org/sw9942.asp#516_10077 (11/09/2006).

83   Today only communities that are legally recognized as organizations are granted hunting rights and certain quotas by the CBNRM; cf. chapter 5, section III.2.

84   Mark & Delia Owens committed themselves to study the great predators before insufficient laws of nature conservation would presumably lead to the destruction of the African wilderness. Their results were published in "Cry of the Kalahari" (1984). Hundreds of kilometres of fences were built because of an agreement with the EU known as the "Beef Protocol" in 1972. The EU ensured Botswana the highest possible price on the market for beef exports within the EU as long as the meat was free of disease. This is why the nature reserves had to be fenced because Botswana wanted to make sure no wildlife could transmit any disease to their cattle. In consequence, hundreds of thousands of wild animals died (Gall 2002: 192).

I. History of the Central Kalahari Game Reserve 301

The Government of Botswana reacted by forming a commission of inquiry (*Fact Finding Mission* 1985).[85] The commission's task was to present adequate measures primarily to protect the fauna and flora. Nevertheless, they were also supposed to keep in mind compatible development opportunities for the "RADs" in the CKGR (Final Draft Management Plan 2001: 128).[86] Their study indicated that the communities living in the game reserve had mostly become sedentary and had begun to cultivate small pieces of land. Particularly 40 kilometres in any direction around !Xade, you could not find any wild animals or veld products anymore; also the settlements Molapo, Metsiamanong, Gope, Mothomelo and Kukama increasingly became permanent settlements where the inhabitants also kept cattle.[87]

The commission presented sixteen recommendations which included, amongst others, to separate the southern part of the reserve and turn it into a Wildlife Management Area, establish two communal cells in precisely defined areas of the reserve, to sink six wells, and to expand the DWNP's staff (Suzman 2001a: 71). It was also proposed to form a so-called *Biosphere Reserve* according to UNESCO standards (which basically did not only regulate nature conservation and the logistic functions of a game reserve but also promoted the social and economic development of the local population and protected the region's cultural values within the reserve).[88] The commission finally also mentioned that it would be possible to relocate the inhabitants of the *Central Kalahari Game Reserve*. It recommended the latter "solution", however, as the "least preferable" of all options.[89]

The Government's relocation homepage only selectively mentioned the results of the *Fact Finding Mission* (of 1985) and especially left out the negative recommendation against relocating the San.[90] After that, the justification homepage showed a short paragraph (about three quarts of a page) named "Findings

---

85   The study was commissioned by the *Ministry of Commerce and Industry*.
86   See also Mogwe (2011: 166ff.).
87   Depending on used sources, the settlements *Metsiamanong* may also be spelled "Metseamonong", "Metsiamenong", "Metsimanong" or *Kukuma* also "Kugamma", "Gukamma".
88   Today there are 610 Biosphere Reserves with a total area of over 5 million square kilometres in 117 countries around the world (March 2013). The African continent is home to 76 such reserves in 28 countries (not Botswana). Even the world's first reserve in a modern sense – Yellowstone National Park founded in 1872 – has partly been a Biosphere Reserve since 1976 (UNESCO heute 2007: 78). For Biosphere Reserves, go to: www.unesco.org/mab/wnbrs.shtml.
89   Interview Alice Mogwe (12 September 2003): "The report was produced for government in which one of the suggestions put forward was that the Basarwa should remain in the CKGR. Another was that the CKGR should be subdivided and what was called the least preferable option was that the Basarwa should be moved out."
90   www.gov.bw/index; "The Relocation of Basarwa from the CKGR" (11/25/2008). The homepage of the years 2002, 2004 and 2005 only listed the Government's reloca-

of independent researchers" which was only based on two authors. Thousands of pages about the San exist, which in my opinion clearly tend to indicate that the San way of life and the conservation of wildlife are in fact compatible. In contrast, the website only recalls selected notes of Japanese anthropologist Masazuka Osaki and his colleague James Suzman working for the European Commission. The Government used these studies and reports to quote Osaki (from 1982/83) that only one of 91 hunted hoofed animals was brought down using traditional bow and arrow.

The homepage also used the conclusion of Suzman's detailed report that, for example, almost all G|wi had cultivated gardens since 1985. Thus, they would not fear possible social change as long as they were adequately informed.[91] Despite the commission's recommendations (of 1985) and due to the aforementioned results that had been separated from the overall context, the Government obviously jumped to the premature conclusion that the inhabitants of the CKGR had given up traditional nomadism and thus their life as "traditional hunters and gatherers" in favour of a sedentary existence. The Government understood the latter as hunting by foot with bow and arrow and was convinced that this method had been replaced by hunting with horses, dogs and weapons. Its administrative actions were determined by the following conclusion: the development towards permanent settlements within the game reserve combined with new activities of hunting, cultivating and cattle keeping were incompatible with the protection of the fauna and flora. Therefore, the Government decided not to change the borders and status of the CKGR, freeze the social and economic development in !Xade and other reserve settlements due to their "inefficiency", find better places for their adequate social development outside of the reserve, and finally "encourage" the inhabitants to relocate.[92]

It seems quite ironic that the Government's official internet representation referred to a paragraph from the article "Kalahari conundrums: relocation, resistance and international support in the Central Kalahari Botswana" by James Suzman (2002). His article, however, actually "reads the riot act" to the Government:

"It appears that the Government of Botswana has not taken on board the implications of the ongoing crisis. Their treatment of Kalahari San populations remains paternalist, inappropriate and ultimately disempowering to the extent that it reinforces the very structures of inequality that the development process

---

tion decisions. However, this "background" of the relocation was removed from the homepage of the Government of Botswana in 2009.
91 The homepage www.gov.bw/index, *The Relocation of Basarwa from the CKGR – Background* quoted the study "The Social Influence of Change in Hunting Technique among Central Kalahari San" by Masakazu Osaki (1983) as well as a later article by James Suzman (2002).
92 Ministry of Commerce and Industry Circular No. 1 of 1986. www.gov.bw/basarwa/background.html (08/08/2005, 05/09/2006, 01/03/2007 and 11/25/2008).

I. History of the Central Kalahari Game Reserve

is intended to collapse. Botswana's attempts to integrate Bushmen into mainstream Tswana society through a rigidly unilinear development strategy and to treat them the same as any other Batswana has ironically had the opposite effect. Moreover they are guilty of denying the CKGR population the same respect that they are rightly demanding from Survival International" (ibid.: 7).

The Government's decision – although heavily criticized all around the world – was committed to (at least according to their official representations) a version of nature conservation that was based on the idea of so-called "ethics of natural wilderness". This approach regarded humans as intruders that were harmful to nature.[93]

The *Central Kalahari Game Reserve* is located in the district of Ghanzi and comprises about 11% of the country on an area of 52,313 km². Officially declared as state land, the CKGR and its southern neighbour *Khutse Game Reserve* form the third-largest game reserve of the world (Ghanzi DDP 6 [2003]: 1).[94] If we started from the assumption that the average San population amounts to 1,200 individuals, the game reserve would be home to one individual for every 44 square kilometres. Even having considered the specific environmental conditions of the Central Kalahari, this region should easily be able to cope with such a low population density.[95] The decision of relocation – not only because the Government chose the least favourable option – is hardly understandable and only partly rational. In the article cited above which also formed the basis of the Government's justification homepage, Suzman (2002: 7) clearly explained:

"I suspect that the Botswana Government has missed a great opportunity here. Had they resolved the CKGR situation they would not only have contributed greatly to rectifying their otherwise poor record in dealing with San, but they would also have made a far stronger case for rejecting the unwanted intrusion of foreigners in domestic affairs. Likewise they could have also shown how the needs of communities like the San could be reasonably addressed without cementing a concept as problematic as indigenous rights in international law."

---

93   Botswana chose IUCN Category IV (www.unep-wcmc.org) for the *Central Kalahari Game Reserve* and thus declared that the reserve was mainly managed for the purpose of nature conservation: "Area of Land (…) subject to active intervention for management purposes so as to ensure the maintenance of habitats and/or to meet the requirements of specific species" (*IUCN Management Categories of Protected Areas 1994*). It is quite interesting to know, though, that one of the management goals should create advantages for the human population of the concerned area.

94   The area of the reserve (alone) is larger than Bosnia and Herzegovina (51,129 km²) and far larger than Switzerland (41,285 km²) (Fischer Weltalmanach 2007).

95   If the natural environment cannot be compared to any other region in the world, a comparison to Austria with at least 97 individuals per square kilometre should put it into perspective. According to the census of 1991, the total population of the entire CKGR was 994; Albertson estimated less than 1,500 individuals for the year 1997 (Albertson 2002: 18); cf. also Barnard (1992: 102).

Suzman is not the only one who ultimately cannot understand why the Government of Botswana took the trouble of this "tragedy"; also because the consequences seem to be quite substantial: the international loss of image and the creation of a completely dependent and highly dissatisfied clientele. Particularly in times of considerably high awareness, in which the interests of indigenous peoples are generally considered to be legitimate, even the consequences of a legal dispute successful for the Government would have probably been traumatic. As Suzman condenses his argumentation, which was extremely simplified and erroneously twisted by the justification homepage, he concludes:

"The loss of the Kalahari is not a tragedy because it spells the end of a culture. Kalahari cultures have proved to be both dynamic and robust in the face of external pressure. It is a tragedy because the Central Kalahari was a marginalised people's single most important asset. Remaining in the reserve would have greatly facilitated their development and empowerment through letting them negotiate this transitional period at their own pace, under their own steam and without the additional trauma of dislocation" (ibid.).

II. The Relocation of the G|wi and ||Gana (San)

After the Government's decision (in 1986) to relocate the San from the *Central Kalahari Game Reserve*, the situation of San communities hardly changed at first. The authorities responsible for the communities continued to provide water and other social benefits. Only the presentation of the relocation plan by the Minister of Local Government in charge of the CKGR confirmed the Government's ambitions in 1989. As those concerned strongly refused to relocate, the Government flinched in the beginning from executing its plan. As a report by Alice Mogwe, Director of the human rights NGO DITSHWANELO, clearly states, the diverse understandings of law and terminology violently crashed time and again. The 1992 document about the problematic human rights situation of the San shows that the cosmovisions and ideas of development based on different historical and cultural experiences were diametrically opposed.[96]

In this empirical study, the San could for the first time voice recommendations or proposals concerning their situation themselves: from the allocation and designation of an own territory within the CKGR and the wish to investigate opportunities to regain their traditional territories to demands for adequate compensation for their loss of lands and resources (Mogwe 1992: 8f.). One month after the report was published, San representatives proposed similar options at the *Workshop on Sustainable Rural Development* in Gaborone. Their ideas attracted some attention of the press in Botswana as well as academic observers, e.g., the clear statements made by Komtsha Komtsha, a Naro from the district of Ghanzi and cited in Saugestad (2001: 176): "'God created the white man, the black man and the red man. Now they want us to change colour, like a chameleon. I am a Batswana as anybody else.' And he asked for the difference to be recognised: 'With all respect, let me live in my environment and enjoy the wealth around me.'" Certain state parties were obviously quite alarmed because they were not used to San speaking for themselves. When again one month later, a San delegation officially met with the Minister of Local Government, their meeting failed to be successful due to divergent (cultural) expectations. The Government reacted extremely sensitively and proclaimed in the media that "the" Basarwa (San) were seeking independence from Botswana:

---

96 Although the study on the human rights situation of the San was commissioned by the *Botswana Christian Council*, it was, for the first time, conducted by a Motswana: Alice Mogwe. Compared to former reports, "Who was (t)here first?" is rather short (51 pages) and relatively easy to understand. Therefore, it could not be inconsiderately rejected by politicians (Hermans 1995: 48f.).

"The [San] delegation, among other issues, requested that they be allowed to secede from Botswana and form their own state (...)";[97] "Basarwa people from the Central Kgalagadi District want their area to be declared independent from the rest of Botswana (...)";[98] "What they want is the establishment of Basarwaland and their own council".[99]

Whenever an official or individual statement of the San is reproduced in media in Botswana, their interpretations suggest not only simple misunderstandings owed to differing world views and life experiences but also diverging cultures of law from a legal perspective. This (national) version of legal pluralism ironically reflects the encounter between the San's view of "natural" land rights and justice, and legal thoughts of Botswana's political elite shaped by European conceptions of law. Based on the various options to influence the process of mediatisation, thus meaning the huge differences in power to control basically all instruments of public opinion-making, the perspectives of the San on (land) rights are usually misunderstood. As the media are to a certain extent controlled by the state, it was easy for the Government to use them for their purposes: in this case, they ignored the fundamental problem of insufficient recognition as well as the recommendations and proposals of the San, which they reframed as the most negative aspect of "tribalism" – the imminent risk of secession. In contrast, independent observers and involved human rights organizations rather considered the statements of various San representatives as an invitation for Government to begin a dialog.[100]

From this time on, however, the Government intensified its ambitions to (in the euphemistic words of the Government) "encourage" the inhabitants of the CKGR to relocate. At the same time, the San more often complained that the *Department for Wildlife and National Parks* (DWNP) as well as the *Botswana Defence Force* threatened to attack them, if they continued to oppose their relocation (DITSHWANELO 1996: 1ff.). In March 1996, San representatives brought these accusations of human rights violations and the first actual cases of forced relocation before the *UN Commission on Human Rights* in Geneva. At the United Nations as well as various other forums, Government representatives repeatedly ensured that it was not their intention to force individuals to leave the reserve or cease to provide social benefits. In this sense, the Government answered to an inquiry by the European Parliament and officially confirmed their position: "The Ambassadors of Sweden and the United States (...) were assured by the Govern-

---

97 *Daily News*, 02/21/1992.
98 *Mmegi*, 05/22/1992.
99 *Botswana Guardian*, 05/22/1992. Only one month later, a newspaper included a short paragraph in which the San delegation was allowed to state they had been misquoted.
100 Cf. also Saugestad (2001: 180f.) and Mogwe (1994: 52f.); for the general right of self-determination, see chapter 1, section V.

ment representatives that not only **no forcible resettlements** will be carried out but **social services** to people who wish to stay in the reserve **will not be discontinued** (...)."[101]

As the Government's statements and actions contradicted each other, the national NGO DITSHWANELO appointed a commission of inquiry to assess whether the concerned communities of the Kalahari were in fact really informed about the state's provisions of a planned relocation and understood all its consequences. The commission was also formed for the relocation's addressees to have a stronger voice and to listen to their concerns. The commission visited six (of the ten) settlements in the CKGR and conducted empirical studies. The report "When will this Moving Stop?" presents their results. Interviews with local stakeholders conducted by the commission contested the Government's reasoning for the relocation – that the San overhunted the regions and would reduce the wildlife population. Instead they understandably argued that they had lived with wild animals for generations and protected them, not least because they were the San's basis of existence. In their eyes, the single fact that the Central Kalahari as one of only a few regions of Botswana that was still home to a huge population of wild animals should be enough to prove their point. With regard to the basic assumption that wildlife and human settlements were incompatible in game reserves they objected that in no other case, such reserves had been established without the consultation and consent of the local population.

Moreover, many interviewees criticized that the communities profited from tourism, if at all, only indirectly and were still dependent on hunting. They also mentioned the crucial problem that applicable law denied them the right to adequately defend their livestock against wild animals because any act of killing predators was criminalized as poaching. Since the Government had relocated communities from Molapo, Mothomelo and other places to !Xade in the 1980s, they were afraid to be once more relocated and finally losing "their" lands for good. In a nutshell, they were concerned with the following question: "When will this moving – from place to place – stop?"[102]

The San had various reasons to oppose the planned relocation ranging from their deep cultural roots of coexisting with their natural environment "since time immemorial" and intensive relationship between fauna and flora as well as spiritual aspects. One of the latter we know from similar contexts is the special relationship to their ancestral lands which results in the identification of the lands with the burial grounds of their ancestors and their transcendentally-justified

---

101 Abstract of the written reply to the European Parliament, cited by Judge Phumaphi (High Court 2006: 305f.); emphasis added.
102 See DITSHWANELO (1996: 5–11). DITSHWANELO's commission of inquiry and their fundamental questions would later form the first discursive basis of the formulated legal case.

claim to territories. In addition, they were of course concerned that the new settlements would cause conflicts due to competing interests and increase food insecurity because they anticipated not to know the fauna and flora of the unfamiliar settlement area. Many also guessed that they would be even more dependent on the Government because they would have not been able to use their traditional subsistence practices they had learned in the intact ecosystem of the CKGR in case they did not receive water and food rations (DITSHWANELO 1996: 9f.).

Nevertheless, these communicative research processes also revealed that the communities did not homogenously oppose the planned relocation. Some were prepared to be relocated, even though only because they felt "constrained by the circumstances". Their positive motives ("pull factors") mainly comprised the Government's "relocation package" which they understood to be 5 cattle, 8 donkeys, 15 goats and ploughs for each and every household. Their statements saying that this would probably be their last relocation also suggest that they hoped to finally achieve "certainty of law and occupation". In contrast, they mentioned the negative motives ("push factors") that the Government threatened to cease supplying them with water and medicine and leave them in the hands of the military. In sum they were ready to leave the CKGR because they saw chances of development as well as the negative consequences of resistance. The commission thus concluded that not even those ready to relocate would leave of their own free will (DITSHWANELO 1996: 11–13).

In spite of the efforts from various sides and levels, all attempts of "appeasement" failed due to the lack of (mainly state) willingness to find an amicable agreement. The first relocations began in March 1997. Two months later, trucks came to pick up about 600 individuals from !Xade and took them and all their chattels to the new settlement of G'Kgoisakeni (administratively renamed New !Xade). Built virtually overnight, this village is located about 70 km from (old) !Xade outside of the reserve. Law enforcement officers as well as state officials relocated the inhabitants of Gope, Mothomelo and Kikao about 40 km to the new settlement of Kaudwane from the southern entrance to the reserve. In 1997, the Government resettled a total of 1,739 individuals. Neither of the communities of Metsiamanong or Kukama would move voluntarily, so 575 San remained in the CKGR.[103] The following table shows the census data for the inhabitants of seven settlements in the CKGR at two special points in time – five years prior to the first and one year prior to the second relocation and 2011:

---

103 180 inhabitants stayed in Molapo, 150 in Metsiamanong, 90 in Mothomelo, 12 in Kikao, 33 in Gukanba (Kukama) and 110 in Gope (Ikeya 2001: 188). It is striking how much the data used by Ikeya (2001) and the Government homepage diverge from each other: while the first assumes a total reserve population of 1,700, the Government relocated 1,739 inhabitants just in 1997. The Government does not mention how many individuals remained in the CKGR.

II. *The Relocation of the G|wi and ||Gana (San)* 309

Village/	1991 Population			2001 Population			2011*
Locality	Total	Male	Female	Total	Male	Female	Total
Old !Xade	528	254	274	5	3	2	-
Kikao	98	48	50	31	10	21	8
Mothomelo	149	60	89	245	118	127	2
Bape	41	27	14	-	-	-	-
Metsiamanong	71	30	41	141	83	58	98
Kaka	3	3	0	-	-	-	-
Gope	43	24	19	63	29	34	-
Totals	994	472	522	689	352	337	108
New Settlements outside the Game Reserve							
New !Xade	-	-	-	1049	522	527	1269
Kaudwane	-	-	-	551	267	284	1084
Totals	-	-	-	1645	789	811	2353

Source: *1991 and 2001 Population and Housing Census Report, CSO (http://www.gov.bw/basarwa/background.html, accessed 8 August 2004); 2011 Population and Housing Census.*
* *The population in Kukama amounts to estimated 30 San.*

These data indicate that significant parts of the relocated communities joined the hardly accessible San communities in Mothomelo, Metsiamanong and Molapo because their hopes for amenities in the new settlements had been deceived: "While, to be sure, some were in favour of resettlement, few remained positive about it once they had moved to the resettlement areas where an impoverished natural resources base and an almost complete absence of income generating opportunities immediately offset the benefits of improved state services" (Suzman 2002: 4). As soon as the beginning of the wet season in 1998, about 650 San and Bakgalagadi returned to the CKGR (Suzman 2002: 4). Instead of promised development, wealth and alleged "modernity", the resettled San became more and more pessimistic and increasingly expected the need to depend on the Government. This was also expressed in the words of one inhabitant:

"When the officer told me about the resettlement, I thought it was not too bad. Keeping cattle sounded nice and I like to earn money. When the new life actually started here [New !Xade], however, I soon realized I do not like this land. There are too many people here and we cannot find any wild food nearby. Now, I want to go back to my homeland."[104]

In the context of this resettlement, some sides speak of forced displacement. Nonetheless, we should keep in mind that there have hardly been any complaints of physical violence. Various sources rather suggest that they suffered from sym-

---

104 Cited in Maruyama (2003: 228).

bolic forms of coercion ranging from vague threats and the fact that they would not receive any more support in the future to possible military interventions:

"However, reports also confirm severe coercion: people have been approached individually, with promises of services in New Xade and threats of withdrawal of all services within the CKGR. A desperately poor population has been given a choice between two equally unattractive alternatives, and has left its ancient land with great sorrow" (Saugestad 2001: 224). Roy Sesana, a ||Gana from Molapo and chairman of the NGO *First People of the Kalahari*, too talks about a mixture of bribery and threats, a combination of money, lies and also threatened violence in case all the other forms of external pressure failed (Gall 2002: 11).[105]

Only detailed empirical studies could find out which reasons ultimately determined the (not really) "free" consent of the concerned San to be resettled. Currently, however, the Government hardly allows such studies. Without such communicatively collected data, we can only assume that a "combination" of various factors was reason enough: these were based on the one hand on threatened sanctions and on the other hand on hoped expectations of a "better life", meaning existential security (water, food, basic health care and medical treatment) as well as access to education and other state institutions.[106]

One crucial point in this mixture of "push and pull factors" certainly was the promised compensation in form of livestock and money. The Government guaranteed 10% of the overall compensation to those inhabitants who agreed to the relocation for adverse effects: between Pula 1,000 (USD 220) and Pula 100,000 (USD 22,000) per adult or family unit based on the estate they had to give up. In addition, each family received livestock in form of either five cattle or 15 goats (Government Homepage 2007: 4f.).[107]

In the new settlements, each house came with land for living and cultivation and was supposed to also include a certificate of their land title. As these lots are located on collective land, however, the beneficiaries cannot own them. In the worst case instead, they could lose their lands, if they did not cultivate the soil.[108]

The state of Botswana indicates to have made compensation payments of Pula 4.4 million (USD 900,000) to 730 households as well as 2,300 cattle and 2,018

---

105 The NGO DITSHWANELO reports the same: "It has spread fear amongst the people – it is fear which is making the people move" (1996: 18).

106 Cf. also the considerations by Hainzl (2005: 120–191) who critically discusses the various arguments of the Government, San communities and public opinion to propose solutions.

107 In contrast, Ikeya (2001: 192) indicates – after he had asked those concerned – a compensation between Pula 500 (USD 110) and Pula 17,000 (USD 3,740) depending on the size of their hut or house, fences for livestock and cultivated fields.

108 Sect. 13 and 15 *Tribal Land Act Cap. 32:02* and *Tribal Land (Amendment) Act 1993*. For as more detailed discussion see 4.I.3.

II. The Relocation of the G|wi and ||Gana (San)

goats to 602 beneficiaries between 1997 and 2002.[109] The Japanese anthropologist Ikeya (2001: 192) investigated how this monetary compensation was used and came to the hardly-surprising conclusion that it was spent on non-sustainable consumer goods (clothes, cassette recorders and simple status symbols) and alcohol. There were no investments whatsoever in effective means of production (Saugestad 2001: 223). These short-sighted compensations rekindled the aforementioned criticism against a prioritized assimilative development approach. In this sense, state institutions continued their paternalistic practice and determined what was adequate for the former inhabitants of the CKGR. They were neither interested in honest consultation with those concerned, nor in real participation or legal information. These more or less generous payments were thus clearly in line with the short-term concept of governance. As those concerned were not used to handling money and did not receive any advice, the payments achieved nothing but the exact opposite of sustainable measures of development.

At the end of 1997, those concerned found a possible alternative to the "one-way ticket of relocation" and appointed a team of negotiators to arbitrate between the parties and find a solution that was acceptable to all stakeholders. This "Negotiating Team" was comprised of two representatives from each of the seven settlements within the CKGR, named *CKGR Committee,* and the three San-specific NGOs *First People of the Kalahari* (FPK), *Working Group of Indigenous Minorities in Southern Africa* (WIMSA) and the *Kuru Family of Organisations* (KFO). In addition, the human rights NGO DITSHWANELO as well as *The Botswana Council of Churches* (BCC) also participated without a vote because they were non-San organizations. The team was entitled to negotiate with Government representatives and to take the matter to court, in case they failed to achieve a negotiated solution. Right from the beginning everybody agreed that there would be more than one possible way to resolve the dispute: a negotiated solution would be the best option and was considered their first choice (Mogwe 2011: 169). In March 1998, the *Negotiating Team* met with (at that time) President Quett Masire but he questioned their legitimacy and only made vague promises.

After several frustrating attempts to enter into constructive dialog with the Government, the team began to cooperate with the ministerial *Department of Wildlife and National Parks* (DWNP) which was responsible for the CKGR. In 2001, they finally drafted a management plan for the game reserve based on the consultation and participation of the communities. This "Third Draft Management Plan" recognized the San's traditional land use and aligned it with the strategic goals of conservation policies. The plan primarily focused on nature conservation, protection of the wilderness, sustainable economic use, development of tourism, recognition of traditional knowledge, and research.

---

109 Cf. www.gov.bw/index. "The relocation of Basarwa from the Central Kalahari Game Reserve – Background"; the homepage has in the meantime been deleted.

It identified three possible functional zones, each with its own form of management, that were supposed to divide the CKGR: a central zone exclusively for nature conservation and tourism, a tourism development zone, and finally a structure of five *Community Use Zones*. The latter should have been introduced to *Community Based Natural Resource Management* (CBNRM). They justified the formation of these three zones and especially the one reserved for communities with the fact that, in contrast to other game reserves, the CKGR was significantly bigger than the size necessary for conventional tourism. Moreover, the authors of the management plan wanted the Government to keep in mind that the CKGR was originally established for the use and advantage of local "Remote Area Dwellers" (CKGR Management Plan 2001: 35).[110]

Therefore, this third draft recognizes the local population as a part of the Kalahari's ecosystem that should not be excluded from the management of the reserve: "What was considered ideal in the Plan was what they dubbed a win-win situation whereby a compromise between conservation and communities will have been established. Under this situation there would be no need for relocation of communities from the CKGR" (Botswana Institute for Development Policy Analysis 2003: 69). Not least because the Wildlife Department had participated in this development, the Government tended to adopt this plan. In April 2000, it enacted a new game reserves regulation to implement it.[111] Thus, the Government clearly demonstrated that it was willing to follow and implement the plan.

Many neutral observers agree that this would have been a step in the right direction (Alice Mogwe, interview 12 September 2003). In stark contrast to former developments in Botswana that had been rather disadvantageous for the San, two positive characteristics stand out: firstly, the (basically first-time ever) application of a participatory process between state employees (of the DWNP) and the San to develop the management plan; secondly, the draft was based on the assumption that nature conservation and (indigenous) communities were not (necessarily) mutually exclusive.

The plan ultimately failed and Government authorities are not the only ones to blame the British NGO *Survival International* and their external intervention at the wrong moment.[112] When they launched an international campaign which connected the allegedly "forced relocation" of the San to diamond mining operations in the Kalahari, the Government of Botswana unilaterally ended all negotiations with the "Negotiating Team" and overturned the innovative draft of

---

110 From *Botswana Institute for Development Policy Analysis* (2003: 69); cf. Albertson (2002: 20) for further considerations on the *Community Use Zones*.

111 *National Parks and Game Reserves Regulations No. 28 of 2000*. The draft was also approved by the entire District Councils of Ghanzi on 30 March 2001 and Kweneng on 31 May 2001.

112 See, e.g., Mogwe (2011: 165) as well as Suzman (2002: 5).

II. The Relocation of the G|wi and ||Gana (San)   313

the management plan. The NGO *Survival International* was supported by some members of San communities and asserted that the relocation was actually a clever move by the Government against the San to obviate any future claims in case diamonds were found in the CKGR (CAO 2005: 9).[113]

The campaign "Bushmen aren't forever", twisting the diamond industry's slogan "Diamonds are forever" around, put Botswana in line with the category of states producing conflict and blood diamonds. It thus went for the country's economic jugular.[114] Although the "Negotiating Team" publicly distanced itself from the campaign, the targeted action by *Survival International* discredited all and even national advocates of the San. For many years to come, the Government would reject all voices in favour of alternative options to CKGR governance because it generally suspected them to belong to or at least be influenced by *Survival International*. Therefore, a campaign built on sand with highly undiplomatic means and very bad timing perhaps became a welcome excuse to reject any support for the San as a variation of *Survival International's* "neocolonial intervention".[115] The Government used this straw man argument to legitimize its top-down governance by means of the unilaterally enacted *Draft Final Management Plan* for both the CKGR and the adjacent *Khutse Game Reserve*.

Unfortunately, the new draft only ensures two out of the originally five *Community Use Zones*, both of which are located **outside** of the reserve. Thus, the new management plan did not allow any settlements within the CKGR (Botswana Institute for Development Policy Analysis 2003: 69). The Government soon implemented the plan's provisions and stopped the water supply. On 31 January 2002 for the last time, about 700 inhabitants of the CKGR had enough water and received fundamental state services.[116] Then the second relocation began. This time, however, the Government officials responsible did not settle for just

---

113 This source interestingly is a report by the *Compliance Advisor Ombudsman* to the World Bank.

114 In 2002, 80% of Botswana's entire export revenue came from diamonds. At this point I would like to mention that aside from the accusations by *Survival International*, there was no evidence to confirm this position. In the legal case discussed in the next section, the concerned court could not find any such indications either (High Court 2006: 194). It cannot be denied, however, that three legal cases concerned with indigenous rights to lands and intellectual property had already been taken to court and ruled in favour of indigenous peoples in the neighbouring country South Africa (cf. chapter 2, section III, 2.2 this volume). Perhaps Botswana preemptively wanted to rule out such a case.

115 For details to the campaign, see Suzman (2002: 4).

116 Assistant Minister of Local Government Kokorwe had issued press releases stating that all social benefits in the reserve would be ceased within half a year. When the parliament opened in October 2001, President Mogae confirmed this decision (High Court 2006: 68).

"encouraging" the remaining communities to resettle to a new environment. It was clear instead that they wanted to complete their task once and for all:

"The San were already on the margins of mainstream life and virtually excluded from the political process, but any possibility of their mounting united resistance to the removals was pre-empted by the way in which the Government implemented the programme. Households were often approached individually, offered a deal and told their neighbours had already agreed to the terms. The implication was that they would be left alone in the wild 'un-serviced' reaches of the Kalahari, while everyone else found new opportunities in the settlements" (Armstrong/Bennett 2002: 190).

Moreover, Government officials emptied all existing water tanks, sealed the well in Mothomelo, bulldozed away huts even without prior consent of those concerned, and separated families and households by relocating some to New !Xade and others to Kaudwane (High Court 2006: 185ff.). The Government did not only cease fundamental supply services but also all welfare benefits.[117] In addition, the DWNP also stopped granting special game licenses and thus made any act of hunting illegal. Only 17 individuals seemed to be determined and uncompromising enough to stay in the CKGR even under such conditions (Government Homepage 2004: 3).[118]

The Government generally presented three reasons to justify their decision of relocation from the CKGR: first, the costs of state supply services at the heart of the reserve; second, the decline in natural resources near settlements; and third, the improved development opportunities outside of the reserve. Since the *Remote Area Development Programme (*RADP) was introduced in (old) !Xade (in the CKGR) in 1976, the *Ghanzi District Council* had been responsible for providing fundamental supply and social services, such as water, mobile clinics, school education, pensions, financial benefits and food rations within the reserve. Whoever knows the region will have to concede that the sandy dirt lanes with deep ruts are extremely wearisome. This was one main reason for the Government to justify the end of all state services:

"In some areas, water was being bowsed in at great expense and inconvenience along very rough roads. The task of delivering entitlements, such as the destitute allowance, to mobile populations was becoming very time consuming and costly. (…) It is easy to conclude that services and social welfare can be delivered much more effectively and efficiently in accessible communities. It is therefore understandable that Government would take the position that these services will only be available at certain points outside the reserve, where they are within range of existing service points" (Botswana Institute for Development Policy Analysis 2003: 71).

---

117 *Mmegi* 15–21 February 2002, *The Botswana Gazette* 20 February 2002.
118 Henceforth, the Government (involuntarily) used these 17 individuals to prove that the relocation had never been a forced or violent one.

II. The Relocation of the G|wi and ||Gana (San)

These services cost the district of Ghanzi Pula 50,000 per month.[119] This would have been Pula 70 (~USD 15) per CKGR inhabitant and per month before they were relocated in 2002. Although these figures do not seem to be terribly high, the Government stated that: "Given the number of people remaining in the reserve, the continued provision of services to the CKGR proved unsustainable and unaffordable."[120] Instead, we have to question the Government's transparency of costs because the follow-up costs of resettlement, compensation as well as a permanent group of dependent individuals could be many times higher in the long run. It would also be worth discussing whether or not all citizens who do not enjoy the privilege of living in easily accessible urban centres are generally entitled to services and benefits under public law, especially in a state with extreme geographical and climatic conditions.

In the context of such a perspective on fair social distribution, this specific problem should not be easily disregarded. The government justified the relocation primarily with the costs of providing services in an area that had been occupied "since time immemorial". As this radical intervention was undertaken without commissioning related studies of cost and efficiency analyses, an assessment of the chosen "social policy" being oriented in the future must be rather critical. Furthermore, the government reasoned that the communities within the reserve grew quickly, especially concentrated in (old) !Xade, and thus caused the natural resources of their surroundings to decline. At this point I should mention, however, that it was the government itself that arranged the relocation from settlements like Metseamanong (also Metsiamanong) and Molapo to (old) !Xade:

"[T]he government had on a previous occasion told the Basarwa peoples that they should move to Xade because it was to be a permanent settlement. When they moved from Metseamanong, they were told that the move was to ensure protection of the wildlife at Metseamanong. At the time of the move, nothing was said about the need to protect the wildlife in Xade" (DITSHWANELO 1996: 24).

It seems probable that the new settlements reduce the natural resources even more. This is a logical consequence of human settlements in an area without infrastructure where the arriving population has no alternatives to earn their bread and butter.[121] The situation in New !Xade gets even more complex because more cattle, more settlements, more fences and longer droughts are obstacles even to the (sub-

---

119 Homepage Government of Botswana: Question and Answer (accessed 3 January 2007).
120 www.gov.bw/basarwa/background.html (accessed 8 August 2004).
121 The verification commission of the RADP (*Botswana Institute for Development Policy Analysis*) came to the same conclusion (2003: X): "Nevertheless, there are few livelihood options in the RADP settlements outside the CKGR, and resources around them are currently being depleted. (...) It would seem that this [community use zones within the reserve] could be made compatible with the conservation of resources within the CKGR as well as assisting with the goal of sustainable livelihood."

sidiary) subsistence of hunting wild animals and gathering wild crops. As there are still no other sources of income, many San are relatively dependent on successful hunting and gathering in their new settlements as well: "Despite drought relief labour, intensive employment, food handouts, handicrafts sales, casual labour, and small stock production, for a large portion of the population there are no other economic opportunities than hunting and gathering" (Ghanzi DDP 2003: 10).[122]

When the natural resources in the environment of the new settlements significantly decreased, the relocated communities were forced to change their livelihood from hunting and gathering to wage labour or agriculture and cattle keeping. The resettlement areas hardly offer any sufficient means to earn a living in the service sector (the nearest city in the case of New !Xade is Ghanzi about 120 km away). Moreover, hardscrabble soil conditions and a serious lack of water prevent any establishment of agriculture worth mentioning. This is of course also true for other remote areas:

"Employment opportunities are scarce in remote settlements (…) far from suppliers, and from markets (…) the market within the settlement is very small. (…) Livestock (…) has had mixed results, partly because herding is not a traditional activity for many of the people living in remote areas. There is also a general lack of grazing land, (…) problems with wild predators, or clashes over the use of land and water resources with the owner of cattle posts. (…) Arable agriculture is unlikely (…) because of the low rainfall and poor soils" (Botswana Institute for Development Policy Analysis 2003: XI).[123]

Most resettlement projects in variously similar ways failed to reestablish the more or less independent livelihood of those concerned. Lots of relocated inhabitants found themselves in even worse conditions because these projects primarily seek to balance the loss of living environment but neglect to compensate for means of production, such as land, grazing grounds and wild resources. Therefore, their former basis of social existence and individual income disappears without compensation (Hitchcock/Vinding 2004: 15). As a result, the former and already modest standard of living cannot be maintained. The development initiatives that were explicitly held out in prospect as "pull factors" of the relocation remained nothing but empty promises: "The intention of Government is to bring the standards of living of Basarwa up to the level obtaining in the rest of the country (…)".[124] In the end, the often-preached idea of development could not even begin to correspond to the projects that the government had rushed

---

122 This is true particularly in the district of Ghanzi with an unemployment rate of an estimated 58% (Ghanzi DDP 6: 8).
123 The commission generally refers to all RAD settlements, including New !Xade and Kaudwane.
124 www.gov.bw/basarwa/background.html (accessed 8 August 2004).

II. *The Relocation of the G|wi and ||Gana (San)* 317

through.¹²⁵ In this respect, a local inspection of the new villages provides perfect images for the bold statements of advocates for San rights, who are quoted in the articles of journalists from all over world: New !Xade was also called by its new and hardly flattering nickname "place of death" (Gall 2002: 10).

Although the relocation directly affected only a small share of Botswana's total San population – about 2,300 of an estimated 50,000 San – this matter gained dynamic media attention as well as symbolic value in international politics and far beyond the borders of the Kalahari. Local and international media made sure they had enough tragic headlines for many years to come: "The Hunters with Bow and Arrow Must Make Way for Tourists", the German newspaper *Süddeutsche Zeitung* wrote on 7 February 2002; others headlined: "Botswana: Where Cattle have more Value than People or Heritage" (*Day Independent* 31 August 1997); "The Struggle of the Last Hunters" (*Standard* 4 August 2004); or "Basarwa lose Kalahari" (*The Clarion* Sept./Oct. 2002), just to name but a few.

Many primarily international media, NGOs, government representatives and further organizations declared their solidarity with and explicit support for the San. BBC dedicated a special website to the incidents around the Kalahari. UN *Special Rapporteur* Rodolfo Stavenhagen (2006) repeatedly voiced his concerns about the relocation: "In the past three years, the *Special Rapporteur* has been monitoring the human rights problems facing the Bushmen of Botswana and has expressed his deep concern about the forcible relocation of hundreds of Bushmen far from their traditional homes and hunting grounds in the Central Kalahari."¹²⁶

Botswana and its relocation strategy comes off really badly especially compared to the positive developments of indigenous land rights in neighbouring South Africa and the international trends towards a complementary perspective of nature conservation and indigenous rights. This is even more unfortunate considering the country's otherwise good human rights reputation (except for the death penalty) and its downright exemplary nature conservation policy. Many benevolent observers could not really understand this self-inflicted "defamation". Some tried to psychologically explain this process as the result of injured pride due to *Survival International's* intervention and the state's aversion against such "(neo)colonial" interferences (Alice Mogwe, interview 12 September 2003).

After their relocation, many of the concerned San initially had access to drinking water – which is so crucial in the Kalahari – but also to education, health care, structures of administration, funding for small businesses, pensions, food rations and other social services. In addition, they received material compensation in form of a plot of living and farm land as well as livestock and monetary compensation. In 2004, the government homepage estimated the costs for the phys-

---

125 See especially chapter 5, sections II and IV but also chapter 3, section II as well as section I of this chapter.
126 E/CN.4/2006/78/Add.1, 18 January 2006 para. 18.

ical infrastructure of the new settlements New !Xade and Kaudwane with Pula 34,580,597 (USD 5,763,432).[127] The *Ghanzi District Council* indicates to have spent Pula 9,441,448.65 (~USD 2.1 million) just for buildings in New !Xade by 2002; here we should add the water supply from a well 40 km (!) away, the construction of an access road (of about 80 km), compensation, support programmes and monthly food rations for each family since 1997. Even if Botswana cannot provide precise data on the total expenses just for New !Xade in the first five years, Taylor (2004: 154) estimates the additional costs of the relocation to even exceed Pula 80 million (USD 17.8 million). An estimated census of 1,598 individuals for April 2002 showed that the state had spent about Pula 50,000 (USD 11,110) per inhabitant in New !Xade.[128]

The authorities distributed uniform plots of 25 × 40 metres of living space that were arranged in a grid like a village on a drawing board. They reminded Japanese geographer Junko Maruyama (2003: 227) of the new settlements of cramped Japan, which perhaps allows us to get an idea of how well these settlements were adapted to the vast Kalahari. Considering from where the San came, namely an area larger than Switzerland, it is easier to imagine how frustrated the San were. As the director of the human rights organization DITSHWANELO (Alice Mogwe, interview 22 February 2005) describes:

"When they moved to these settlements, they were given plots of land. If you have recently come from there, you see how small the plots are, as opposed to where people come from inside the Game Reserve, where the notion of land and space is so different, where the notion of territory, which is theirs per language group, is so vast and where they can move within their territory. Here you are talking about people being encouraged to make a settled community over night. All are living very close to each other. Even within the new settlements, they are living according to their former settlements within the Game Reserve but in a very huddled sort of way. And that is development? I am sure you saw the land degradation, erosion due to overgrazing, because people were given cattle once they settled, so you can see the contrast when you go inside the Game Reserve and these new settlements. And that is what development looks like, the face of modern development!"

In February 2005 near Kaudwane, I met a young American zoologist (N.N.) who had lived just off the settlement for several months and who expressed quite a similar opinion. At that time, the inhabitants of Kaudwane at the southern border of the CKGR had doubled. In the year 2000 and thus two years prior to

---

127 www.gov.bw/basarwa/background.html (accessed 8 August 2004). In November 2002, President Mogae explained the relocation for *Radio Botswana Studios* and spoke of Pula 30 million (USD 5 million).

128 At this time (of the year 2002), the conversion rate to USD 1 was about 4.5 Pula (Taylor 2004). Comparing the expenses per capita with the monthly costs before the relocation (Pula 70), we again have to question the purely economic sense of this process.

II. The Relocation of the G|wi and ||Gana (San)

the second relocation, however, the village only comprised 500 individuals. He was convinced that this rapid increase in population was related to state pension money which any relocated individual received. Thus, many people from nearby regions were drawn to Kaudwane because the only thing they had to do was claiming to be relocated San. He had observed that tourists who took the detour through Kaudwane were shocked and not only because the village without waste collection brimmed over with empty cans and other garbage.[129] As a result of this hopelessness and severe unemployment, the only vibrant place of the village was the local bottle shop, as liquor stores are called in Botswana. The American zoologist confirmed that there were no other businesses. Without any options of employment or leisure activities that could make sense, alcoholism was a widely-spread consequence of state payments.

Alice Mogwe too (interview 22 February 2005) analyzed this process of providing free services without transferring any personal responsibility as one of the main structural problems and hardly resolvable deficits of a dependency based on welfare: "In a settlement for example, if a tap breaks, I can assure you it will be like, 'oh, the government's tap is broken, water is being wasted, but it is not ours'. It is what is being given to us. So once we move more towards a true partnership in development, you also develop a sense of ownership, accountability."

Unlike anybody else, the zoologist anonymously cited above could observe the specific developments in Kaudwane during the period in question. He mentioned another version of how this role of living on charity was accepted: the downright eager conversion of livestock received as compensation to cash by means of local lions and leopards. According to his descriptions, the inhabitants were really happy to see their new goats and donkeys killed by predators. In such a case, they could expect a compensation (in cash) as provided by law.[130]

This also reflects the (legally relevant) value system that cannot be simply overcome by imposing attitude changes from outside. In line with this information, the San clearly seem to regard the monetary value of their newly-owned cattle as much higher than its symbolic value. This would be exactly the opposite in the value systems of many cattle-breeding societies. The zoologist continued by telling me how little the San cared about their cattle, how badly they treated the animals and how much they missed their coexistence with wildlife. These remarks may also help us to conceive how unsustainable these top-down imposed development measures are and how they dash against accustomed ways of living. Many of the San that have been relocated in the last few years still have a subsistence consciousness even though its basis was mostly lost due to the resettlement.

---

129 Kaudwane is not directly located along the road leading to the *Khutse Game Reserve* (as part of the CKGR). At this point I also want to add that Kaudwane made a far better impression on me than New !Xade.

130 This happened quite often because the game reserve is not fenced.

At the moment, this situation seems to be a dead end. There is every indication that the government has created life-long dependents.

In the language of the G|wi and ||Gana, "G'Kgoisakeni" (New !Xade) means "anticipating livelihood" or "expecting good life". In this settlement, I wanted to visit the chairman of the NGO *First People of the Kalahari* Roy Sesana in February 2003. After all, the government homepage invited anybody to review all presented facts with regard to the relocation in the entire country. It also ensured that you could speak to anybody willing to provide information on the social realities. These lines I had in mind, when I stopped to ask for directions at a bar in New !Xade. A mountain of beer cans higher than the building itself should have perhaps been enough to warn me.[131] A young man named Lobatse Beslag who introduced himself as the "chief" of New !Xade and the policeman Justice Makane finally asked why I "really" wanted to talk to Roy Sesana. They did not believe that I had told them the truth though.[132] Instead both men prohibited me to establish any contact to Roy Sesana without written permission from the office of the president. Even then, they insisted, it would not be possible to talk to Roy Sesana in private. When I asked for their names, our conversation became somewhat unfortunate to put it mildly. They suspected me to be a secret member of *Survival International* and informed me that the freedom of information guaranteed by the government homepage without doubt had to be a mistake. This happened to me before the situation for journalists and others observing the events in the context of the law case before the High Court got even worse and also before those areas of the southern Central Kalahari where the San had remained were generally closed to visitors.[133]

Any summary of the relocation process from the Central Kalahari apart from the hardly-encouraging situation of the new settlements should first mention the irretrievable loss of intangible goods. Those San who more or less voluntarily agreed to leave the lands of their ancestors did not only give up their dwellings but also (the objects of) their century-old knowledge and practices of subsistence, significant parts of their cultural inventory, their legal system, social structures, and ultimately also their territories. This is also why the government was criticized for having separated the bond between the San and their territories. As this relation-

---

131 New !Xade has 19 bars (Maruyama 2003: 230) for 1,598 inhabitants (estimated census April 2002).

132 According to Mathambo Ngakaeaja (interview 23 February 2003) and Alice Mogwe (interview 12 September 2003), Lobatse Beslag was elected as *kgosi* because he as well as the other candidates had in a certain way been appointed by the government. Otherwise it would be difficult to explain how a young man of 23 years could become chief of the San communities in New !Xade, who always set great value upon seniority.

133 Cf. also the informative report of the (on the first attempt) failed visit by the *African Commission's Working Group on Indigenous Populations/Communities* in New !Xade (ACHPR/IWGIA 2008a: 67f.).

ship was crucial to their cultural identity, the government had created rootless people according to neutral observers (Alice Mogwe, interview 12 September 2003).

Countless other regional and local contexts of the (in various ways threatened) living environments of indigenous communities underline the significance of land. Also Roger Chennells (interview 20 October 2005), the famous South African human rights attorney, refers to these spiritual, social, cultural, economic and political dimensions of land as the backbone of both their survival and social identity, when he speaks of the indispensable meaning of land for the San:

"You can't really translate these cultures away from the land. Their words all mean things related to the land, the plants mean something, the game – all related to their territory. And there, like most hunter-gatherers, they know their landscape backwards and forwards in all their myths and their stories and the knowledge goes around the land. So at some level, it's a personal loss and it's a collective personal loss as well, for the San people."

Let us now remember the government's three reasons why the relocation was necessary: "costs, development and nature conservation". The first two reasons can already be discarded *prima vista* as a possible basis for a positive summary. In the next few years, medium-term evaluations will assess the third reason too. In general, any positive consequences from the (forcible) relocation derive from two processes: first, the desirable expansion of protected areas in a world that is increasingly becoming a smaller place; and second, the reduced environmental destruction and land disturbance. When it comes to the entire Kalahari region, however, empirical studies could virtually find no evidence that the communities had posed any negative impact on nature conservation before they were relocated. In this respect, there is no clear and permanent damage from using the lands for hunting and gathering (Fabricius/de Wet 2002: 144).

In contrast, the negative consequences of the relocation are evident: the unsustainable use of resources outside of protected areas. One of the reasons for this process apart from population growth is the increasing pressure onto natural resources all around the new and permanently-growing settlements. "People's expulsion from biodiversity-rich areas led to their attitudes to conservation and conservationists becoming increasingly negative, with a measurable increase in poaching and unprecedented incidents of natural resources being vandalized, often accompanied by land invasion" (Fabricius/de Wet 2002: 145). Furthermore, relocation leads to the loss of traditional environmental knowledge. The name "Basarwa", which others attributed to those that had been relocated, increasingly assumes its etymological meaning. Now it also includes the "lost lands":

"Basarwa means 'people who don't own anything'. Yet, we had things. We had our land and they took it away from us and started calling us 'people who don't own anything'" (/'Augn!ao/'Un).[134]

---

134 Cited in Thornberry (2002: 13).

III. The Legal Dispute over the (temporarily?) "Lost Lands"

When Botswana's state institutions stopped to provide basic and essential services to the residents of the *Central Kalahari Game Reserve* (CKGR) on 31 January 2002, the by then quite promising negotiations found a sudden end. The former alternatives to leaving the settlements had dwindled away because the inhabitants of the CKGR had not expected the actual termination of the drinking-water supply that was so essential to their survival especially during dry season and had been delivered by tank trucks every week. Nevertheless, also the cessation of further public services, such as food rations, orphan care, school transports or mobile clinics contributed to this situation. Even the boreholes were not maintained anymore. Many of those concerned spoke of a *de facto* forced relocation. At this juncture, the *Negotiating Team* (comprised of San representatives and five NGOs) *nolens volens* chose their only remaining option and brought the matter before the High Court (Mogwe 2011: 173).

1. Roy Sesana v. Government of Botswana

On 19 February 2002, 243 former inhabitants of the CKGR filed an urgent application on notice of motion which basically corresponds to the legal content of a preliminary injunction. They claimed that the termination of state services was both unlawful and unconstitutional and called for restoration. As the emergency motion had failed to observe court rules, sitting Judge Dibotelo single-handedly dismissed the application but granted to re-institute their action on 19 April 2002. The applicants appealed against this decision. At the formal hearing before the Court of Appeal on 11 July 2002, the court took the view that the concerned issues were of fundamental relevance and far too important to be legally processed based on procedural defects. It recommended evaluating the relocation considering substantial legal facts and arguments. The court thus asked both parties to agree, which was a relatively difficult decision for the government to make. Therefore, it took another year until the proceedings finally returned to the Court of Appeal on 23 January 2003.[135]

On the same day, the Court of Appeal turned the motion into questions to be considered and referred the matter to the High Court with a corresponding or-

---

[135] At the hearing before the Court of Appeal, both legal representatives were recommended to agree on the court proposal that this matter should be referred back to the High Court for judgement on the substantial evidence of the appealed matter. As late as 23 January 2003, the parties agreed on the issues (High Court 2006: 127).

der. The court essentially ordered to evaluate the circumstances by hearing of oral evidence on the following legal issues:

> "(a) Whether the termination with effect from 31ˢᵗ January 2002 by the Government of the provision of basic and essential services to the Appellants in the Central Kalahari Game Reserve was unlawful and constitutional.
> (b) Whether the Government is obliged to restore the provision of such services to the Appellants in the Central Kalahari Game Reserve.
> (c) Whether subsequent to 31ˢᵗ January 2002 the Appellants were: (i) in possession of the land which they lawfully occupied in their settlements in the Central Kalahari Game Reserve; (ii) deprived of such possession by the Government forcibly or wrongly and without their consent.
> (d) Whether the Government's refusal to: (i) issue special game licences to the Appellants; and (ii) allow the Appellants to enter into the Central Kalahari Game Reserve unless they are issued with a permit is unlawful and constitutional" (High Court: 2006: 5f.).

Furthermore, the court ordered hearing of oral evidence by the applicants' witnesses to take place in Ghanzi and the respondent's witnesses at the High Court in Lobatse.[136] The legal proceedings were again significantly delayed. More than a year later, the former residents of the CKGR were eventually able to explain their legal perspective. While the termination of state services had been an "urgent matter" that was meant to be quickly resolved by restoring the *status quo* in February 2002, the proceedings dragged on for more than two years. Therefore, some legal representatives thought it would stand to reason to extend their application to land rights claims. This option was initially not taken into consideration to avoid the danger of imminent damage to the protection of both their way of life and cultural competences because of the anticipated lapse of time for such a substantive decision. Leading jurists appointed to the case assumed that a constant litigation lasting for several years with unknown ending would cause, in one way or another, the loss of capability to survive in the biome of the Kalahari.[137] When court proceedings started again on 28 May 2004, the appointed attorney filed a motion for adjournment to extend the relevant claims. As more than two years had already passed, however, the court dismissed the motion and continued with the original application.[138]

---

136 For the complete judgement by the Court of Appeal, see Court of Appeal, Civil Appeal No. 21 of 2002; and Dibotelo's judgement (High Court 2006: 5f.).
137 Personal conversation with Roger Chennells on 8 February 2007. His office in Stellenbosch/South Africa had represented the San until September 2004.
138 Their problem was that Attorney Du Plessis was only supposed to obtain adjournment because the case's real attorneys Williams and Whitehead had to be present at

At the beginning of July 2004, the court inspected the new villages of Kaudwane and New !Xade outside the game reserve as well as the settlements Kukama, Kikao, Mothomelo, Metsiamanong, Molapo and (old) !Xade inside the CKGR.[139] As the allegations continued that the real reason for the relocation was the undisturbed and especially exclusive mining of diamonds in the CKGR, the High Court conducted a further inspection *in loco* at the reserve's prospecting pit in Gope in 2005. On 12 July 2004, the trial commenced in New !Xade and went on for several weeks. The court heard three witness reports for the applicants' side: one by George Silberbauer, the administrative officer that had initiated the proclamation of the game reserve in 1961; and two others by former residents of the CKGR. Afterwards, the proceedings were postponed until November at the instance of the applicants due to insufficient funds. Commissioned and also supported by the British NGO *Survival International* that co-funded the case, Chairman of the *First People of the Kalahari* (FPK) Roy Sesana and Jumanda Gakelebone launched a (successful) promotion and fundraising campaign in England, Norway and the United States.[140]

Once they had returned from their campaign, they revoked the mandate for the former South African legal representatives and replaced them by the British litigator Gordon Bennett and the Tswana attorneys Boko, Motlhala, Rabashwa and Ketshabile.[141] At this point, only 215 of the original applicants were still alive, 189 of which transferred their mandate to the latter legal representatives, while the other 26 remained litigating parties without representation.[142] On 3 November 2004, the court continued to interview witnesses but some involved

---

another case in South Africa at the same time. As their appointed representative, Du Plessis was not able to argue the matter of application for amendment convincingly (High Court 2006: 128f.).

139 During the hearing of evidence, the court produced protocols, pictures and a video of the inspection (High Court 2006: 10).

140 Also newspapers in Botswana reported on the international lobbying of the San: "In the USA, the two Basarwa representatives visited the United Nations and Hollywood and met lawmakers and celebrities. They also addressed a press conference. In the UK they held a demonstration at the Botswana High Commission and the De Beers diamond shop" (*Mmegi* 15 October 2004). The campaign was funded by the so-called "CKGR Legal Rights Support Coalition", a loose coalition of international (human rights) NGOs, and *inter alia* also *the International Work Group for Indigenous Affairs* (IWGIA), and with DITSHWANELO, the *Botswana Centre of Human Rights*, as its secretariat (Saugestad 2005: 3).

141 Until the end of the process, the appointed Gordon Bennett was considered to entertain close connections to *Survival International*, also because his official assistant worked for this NGO (interview Alice Mogwe 22 February 2005).

142 Nevertheless, the information about the number of applicants is inconsistent; at one point, Boko represented 133 individuals, while 111 were not represented (High Court 2006: 196) and at another point, Bennett represented 182 with 29 remaining applicants (High Court 2006: 141).

III. The Legal Dispute over the (temporarily?) "Lost Lands"

and observing parties were under the impression that the proceedings were unnecessarily protracted. Some even considered Attorney General Pilane's taking of evidence to be tactics of delaying the proceedings and suspected him trying to exert pressure on the (tight) budget of the claiming San. One of the applicants' witnesses, for example was *de facto* cross-examined for more than twelve days, which of course seems to confirm their suspicions (interview Mathambo Ngakaeaja 8 March 2005).

From 12 September 2005 until 6 February 2006, the High Court again had to postpone the continuation of the case again at the instance of the San due to insufficient financial means. On the same day (12 September 2005), policemen and wildlife officers entered the CKGR to confiscate the livestock of the remaining San. Two weeks before, the Wildlife Department (DWNP) had closed the CKGR because the reserve's livestock had been diagnosed with an allegedly fatal and contagious disease. The San were convinced that this action was a further strategy to displace them once and for all (*Botswana Guardian* 16 September 2005).[143]

When on 24 September 2005, participants including women and children of an announced demonstration tried to enter the closed reserve to provide their families within the CKGR with food and water, policemen opened fire using rubber bullets and tear gas. All 28 involved individuals were arrested, according to them also tortured, and some released without charges days later. In an open letter published in *The Midweek Sun* (28 September 2005), the DWNP accused the NGO *First People of the Kalahari* of having organized and then used this demonstration as part of their fund-raising campaign. Afterwards, the situation continued to be rather tense; time and again, the media reported on threats, intimidation, arrests, torture and forced relocation until the judgement was proclaimed.[144]

After extremely time-consuming proceedings by Botswana's hitherto known standards, the judgement was delivered on 13 December 2006. In this final act, each of the panel's three judges read out his/her separate and full stand-alone judgement, thus also suggesting diverging conclusions. This is how the longest and most expensive case in Botswana's history ended. Although the original case was initiated as an urgent matter, it went on for more than four years, even though the proceedings actually took place on about 130 days spread over two years. The minutes amount to an estimated 18,900 pages. This spectacular case attracted an unprecedented attention of the media as well as a huge number of

---

143 Whether it was tactics or facts, this action was perfect for encouraging the San to relocate because hunting and gathering was prohibited and without livestock they did not have any chance of surviving in the reserve.

144 For an overview of all events between July 2004 and December 2006 from the perspective of *Survival International*, go to www.survival-international.org. See also the country report for Botswana by the *United States Department of State* (www.state.gov).

NGOs and individual stakeholders, which all together both narratively and argumentatively accompanied the developments of the case at the national as well as international stage (High Court 2006: 9, 134). Each of the panel members, one woman and two men (one of which is even member of a minority group), provided an own written judgement for the better understanding and critical recognition of their conclusions. In the following sections, I will discuss these conclusions in further detail based on the four legal questions (posed by the Court of Appeal) to be decided by the High Court.

1.1 Termination of Basic and Essential Services

The applicants claimed that the government's termination of providing basic and essential services was unlawful and unconstitutional because they had a "legitimate expectation to be consulted" before such a far-reaching act was executed.[145] Moreover, they alleged a violation of the *National Parks and Game Reserve Regulations* 2000. In the opinion of Judge Dibotelo, the legal question of legitimacy related to the termination of services was the central point of the whole case. These circumstances thus mobilized all other issues and causes of action (High Court 2006: 46).

Judge Dibotelo essentially assessed that he could not find any evidence that the applicants – who had the legal burden of proof – had not been consulted by the government. The judge also referred to statements of witnesses such as *inter alia* government representatives, as evidence in rebuttal, repeatedly suggesting the planned termination of services: "The admitted tape recordings of Assistant Minister Kokorwe's meetings at Mothomelo also show that at that settlement she repeated similar statements ["from January next year they will stop bringing water"] to the residents that **consultation** had been taking place since 1986" (High Court 2006: 63).[146] Needless to say, it remains questionable whether such statements could be regarded as "consultation". Considering the minimum standards of communication for an understandable consultation process, it seems that the needed requirements would have to be more comprehensive than just a single act of a subordinate ministry official pointing out the (future) termination of state services. Consultation requires both conversation and discussion, neither of which is indicated in any of the testimonies. Nevertheless, Judge Dibotelo still concluded that the alleged unlawfulness and unconstitutionality of the termination of services was not based on factual content and that, therefore, this issue was to be dismissed (ibid.: 70).

---

145 In this case, the universal principle of law may be applied stating that, except in urgent matters, those individually concerned by an encroachment of their rights shall be consulted first (*audiatur et altera pars*) (Raschauer 1998: 324).
146 Emphasis added.

III. The Legal Dispute over the (temporarily?) "Lost Lands"

Judge Unity Dow came to the view that the relocation was clearly forced, wrongful and without consent of those concerned. Furthermore, she concluded that the termination of basic and essential services was intended to force relocation (High Court 2006: 255). While the cost factor was certainly also a reason of termination, the government failed to take into consideration the fact that relocation always means a complete new way of life. In line of her arguments, such a far-reaching intervention into the living conditions of those concerned would have to be subject to a clearly noticeable assessment: "Was the financial saving worth the social and cultural loss? Did anyone do the maths? Was the potential loss to a people's identity worth the financial saving?" The unconstitutionality of the issue arose, so Dow (ibid.: 256), from the fact that the services, which included water and food to destitutes and orphans, were essential to the recipients' survival. In consequence, their termination endangered life and inevitably lead to relocation. She then argued that the right to life was a constitutional right and the termination of essential services had in essence been a breaching of that right (ibid.).

While interpreting the applicants' testimonies, Judge Phumaphi eventually came to the conclusion that the applicants would have been willing to continue living on their lands even without the provision of services: "[W]hen the Respondent intimated its intention to terminate the services, they told the Respondent to go ahead and do so. All they wanted was to be left undisturbed on their land" (High Court 2006: 289). In addition, he detected serious inconsistencies in the medium-term attitude of the defendant party ("Respondent") towards the residents of the CKGR. On the one hand, the government repeatedly threatened to terminate these services, while on the other hand its opposed factual actions of continuing to provide the relevant services questioned the serious character of their threat. As the government took the position that services were temporary while preserving the *status quo*, the applicants found themselves in unresolved contradiction to the 'policy of encouraging" the residents to voluntarily leave the Central Kalahari; a policy the government had applied in various ways since 1986. This contradiction was then even intensified by public statements of government members concerning the San as well as diplomatic representatives saying that they did not intend to unilaterally terminate their services (High Court 2006: 302, 305). These statements thus created the legitimate expectation of continued services.

The judge assessed, however, whether these assurances had really reached the applicants and found no such evidence (ibid.: 308). He also considered whether the participation of the applicants in developing the *Third Draft Management Plan* could have given rise to the legitimate expectation that the respondent would not make any decision inconsistent with this instrument. In his view, hope alone could not be legally elevated to legitimate expectation, especially as the concerned management plan was only a draft version. The further reasoning beautifully reflects all the complexities that make the judgement to seem hardly lucid to many parties involved. According to Judge Phumaphi, the applicants did not enjoy the doctrine of legitimate expectation to continue the provision of state services because the government had conducted sufficient consultations (ibid.: 313f.).

Pursuant to the *National Parks and Game Reserve Regulations* 2000 and in the absence of a management plan, the further development of the game reserve was to be guided by the draft version (*Third Draft Management Plan*) which stated that the San could coexist with the wildlife of the CKGR. Phumaphi also found that this third draft was not to be considered the final version and concluded that developments could deviate from the draft. As the judge could neither determine a violation of the concerned regulation nor insufficient consultation, he ruled that the allegedly legitimate expectation based on the respondents' promises or actions was essentially unfounded. Therefore, the termination of services was neither unlawful nor unconstitutional (ibid.: 318).

1.2 Restoration of Basic and Essential Services

In line with their answers to the previous issue, neither of the male judges found that the government was obliged to restore the state services. Dibotelo (High Court 2006: 73) referred to the applicants' own testimonies and argued quite pragmatically that they could also live in the game reserve without these services. Surprisingly, Phumaphi identified a possible court order to restore the services as potential assumption and transgression of the High Court's competences. In his opinion, such a decision would mean an order to re-prioritize the allocation of national resources. Considering the evidence that the provision of services in the reserve would prove to be unsustainable, the court was not be entitled to such an intervention in state matters except in cases of constitutional or other serious violations of law:

"It seems to me that, if this Court were to decide that the services should be restored, in the face of admitted evidence to the effect that provision of services in the reserve is unsustainable on account of costs, the import of the Court's decision would be to direct the Respondent to re-prioritise the allocation of national resources. In my view, the Court should be loathe to enter the arena of allocation of national resources unless, it can be shown that the Respondent has, in the course of its business transgressed against the Supreme Law of the land or some other law" (ibid.: 320f.).

Under these circumstances, the government was not obliged – as Phumaphi states – to restore their services in the CKGR. In her diverging reasoning of the judgement, Unity Dow argued that an alleged specific performance obliging the government to provide services was an extraordinary legal instrument. She also recognized that those applicants who had already built permanent houses and did not wish to return to the reserve were entitled to adequate damages. As related to those applicants, however, who wanted to stay in the CKGR – after all, the

III. *The Legal Dispute over the (temporarily?) "Lost Lands"* 329

inspection in July 2004 counted more than 90 individuals – the respondent was obliged to specific performance in form of restored state services because no other legal remedy would have been able to offer the protection required under the provisions of compensation: "Specific performance being an extra-ordinary remedy, it is only available where no other remedy will offer relief (…) For those Applicants who wish to remain in or if they relocated to return to the Reserve, an order for specific performance is indicated" (High Court 2006: 259f.).

1.3 Lawful Occupation

The third issue that had to be evaluated was the applicants' lawful occupation in the *Central Kalahari Game Reserve*: this question, too, was a rather difficult one. Right from the beginning, the simple occupation of the lands was uncontented because on the one hand, the respondent had conceded that the applicants had enjoyed such vested rights prior to the relocation, and on the other hand the applicants' legal claim was not to ownership but to a right to use and occupy the lands anyway. Nevertheless, the government disputed the applicants' **lawful** occupation because the settlements were located on state land and thus subject to government "ownership":

"The Respondent has argued that the occupation by the Applicants of the land in the settlements in the CKGR was unlawful because the CKGR is owned by the Government as it is state land. In the submission of the Respondent, this is so because the Applicants have not only claimed that they were unlawfully dispossessed of the land by the government but have also gone further to claim that their occupation of the land in question was lawful which the Respondent disputes" (High Court 2006: 84).

As the government had never lawfully terminated the applicants' occupation and continuously tolerated their presence or at least had implicitly permitted their presence before they were relocated, Justice Dibotelo (ibid.: 86) determined that ownership and occupation were not mutually exclusive and, therefore, found that the occupation of lands by the applicants in the CKGR was indeed lawful.

Unity Dow referred to several facts and concluded that the occupation was lawful. She began her reasoning by stating that the applicants were descendants of those people who had lawfully occupied the territories prior to the creation of the reserve in 1961. As the original reserve was specifically established for the benefit of its residents, their mobility in the entire Kgalagadi area was recognized: "At the time of the creation of the Reserve (…) it was the Bushmen who spent on average at least four months in a year in that area, who were expected to benefit from the creation of a Reserve that excluded all others, unless such others possessed entry permits to enter it" (High Court 2006: 209).

Furthermore, she doubtlessly attached great significance to the applicants being members of indigenous peoples: "[I] take the position that the fact the Applicants belong to a class of peoples that have now come to be recognized as 'indigenous peoples' is of relevance (…)" (ibid.: 201). Considering this definition and her subsequent considerations on the traditional occupation of "Bushmen" in the reserve, it is my opinion that a discussion of the "native title" doctrine would have actually been obvious.[147] It seems, however, that a discussion of pre-colonial indigenous rights – as opposed to her colleague Phumaphi – would have meant even for Dow going too far.

Nevertheless, Unity Dow finds that the (preferred) issuance of special game licenses as well as the permission to hunt in the CKGR implies the intention of simplifying the continued enjoyment of rights and, in consequence, the applicants' right of occupation. These special rights have even found their way into the Constitution of independent Botswana at Section 14 (1) and 14 (3) (c) (ibid.: 211). Dow continues by arguing that the constitutional character of these rights reflects the state's concern about their further development and future. As the Constitution could hardly protect what was unlawful, the applicants' occupation had to be considered as "lawful". Moreover, the provision of state services to the applicants in the reserve supports the legal interpretation of the clear lawfulness of their residence. A further indicator suggesting the recognition of lawful occupation is the policy of not seeking to regulate the entry and exit of the residents of the reserve (ibid.: 216).

With regard to the current policy that nature conservation and human settlements in the reserve are incompatible, Judge Dow remarked that the government had long recognized the dual use (game conservation and residence of the San) of the lands. As humans had lived in the reserve before the first policies of nature conservation (*ex post*) were developed, the policies were rather wishful thinking that was quite understandable from the perspective of nature conservation without humans. They could not be legally realized due to the recognized and lawful existence of human settlements in the reserve though. This is also why such policies could only be understood as the ideal version of perfect nature conservation that has its legal limitations always and everywhere:

"It has been said that human residence within the Reserve is inconsistent with the Respondent's policy of total preservation of wildlife. That may be so, and in that case, the Respondent has adopted a policy that cannot be realized. Alternatively, the Respondent policy must be read as an ideal with certain acknowledged limitations, one of them being the reality of human residence within the Reserve. After all, the policy came after the people" (ibid.: 218).

When Judge Phumaphi evaluated the legal question of lawful occupation, he went a significant step further than Judge Unity Dow. He realized that it was legally required to determine that certain land rights of the applicants could have survived both colonial rule and the creation of the reserve. As only one of three

---

147 See chapter 2 "Excursus" on Aboriginal (or native) title.

III. The Legal Dispute over the (temporarily?) "Lost Lands"

judges, Phumaphi also assumed a perspective of legal comparison and took into consideration other international land rights cases related to indigenous peoples. His evaluation thus also addressed the so-called "native title" of land rights and compared it to the famous "Mabo case" in Australia. Although the judge made clear that the Australian case assessing the "native title" and its decision was not binding on the *High Court of Botswana*, he still considered it to be quite similar to the relevant situation (ibid.: 330).

While his reasoning might be regarded as ground-breaking in the future, he developed the existence of a "native title" in Botswana based on the testimony of George Silberbauer. The witness had explained that, although the San had lived in the area of today's CKGR for thousands of years and practiced a mobile way of life, they still had established clearly-defined territories within the CKGR and Khutse:

"[T]he Bushmen are indigenous to the CKGR which means that they were in the CKGR prior to it becoming Crown Land, thereafter a game reserve and then State land upon Botswana attaining independence" (High Court 2006: 327).

Judge Phumaphi then discussed the question whether the declaration of the British Protectorate had extinguished the rights of the "Bushmen" ("native rights") in 1910. In his opinion, the *Bechuanaland Protectorate (Lands) Order-in-Council 1910* did not address the rights of those people living in the Crown Lands. This approach was based on the notion that "discovered" areas were uninhabited and thus *terra nullius* simply ignored the presence of indigenous peoples (ibid.: 332). The theory of *terra nullius* may today be obsolete but at that time it stated that all lands belonged to the Crown and did not distinguish between the process of obtaining sovereignty (e.g., by colonisation) and the acquisition of ownership of land within the colony itself. In accordance with current understandings of law, the land rights of indigenous peoples had not changed because they could only be extinguished by a specific act (e.g., alienation of land to a third party, or appropriation of the land by the Crown itself). If such an act (indispensable under applicable law) was not issued though, it would be justified to legally presume that the rights of private ownership continued to be valid even after a change of sovereignty. Phumaphi underlined his reasoning by extensively quoting Judge Brennan in the "Mabo case" (ibid.: 333–337), who had referred to the legal cases *Amodu Tijani* (1921) and *In re Southern Rhodesia* (1919). Phumaphi concluded from this legal comparison that the "native rights" of the San were not affected by the proclamation of the land they occupied to be Crown land. Also the fact that the British rulers had provided them with water so that they could remain in the CKGR was a clear indication that the Crown recognized their "native rights" with respect to the relevant territories (ibid.: 339).

Judge Phumaphi then finally asked whether the declaration of the game reserve may have extinguished the land rights of the San. Fortunately there was ample evidence (especially telegrams from colonial times) at hand to resolve this issue. It indicated that the British government had originally planned to turn the CKGR into a territory where resident San could hunt freely. The judge further explained that in 1961, however, the area had been declared a game reserve because the colonial government was constrained by circumstances and entangled in a complex "diplomatic web" just shortly before independence. Phumaphi confirmed these developments on several pages by providing comprehensive historical documentation (ibid.: 340ff.):

"There is copious documentary evidence indicating that, the British Government intended the CKGR to be a free hunting area for the resident Bushmen. However, it got itself entangled in a diplomatic web and ended up declaring a game reserve in which the Bushmen had no hunting rights, quite contrary to the ostensible reason for creating the reserve".

Judge Phumaphi again made recourse to Silberbauer's statements concerning the central problem that the proclamation of the game reserve had generally made hunting illegal and thus had officially prohibited the continued hunting activities of the San. Silberbauer had regretted that the original purpose of the reserve had created a downright diametrically opposed law. The colonial administration, however, dealt with this unwanted situation by permitting the continuation of hunting activities. In line with the reserve's originally designed purpose of protection, the administration had intentionally ignored the San's violations of law. Once again, Judge Phumaphi used Silberbauer's testimony to support his reasoning:

"Dr. Silberbauer who was the prime motivator for a dual purpose game reserve admitted that he had failed to prevail upon his superiors to declare a dual purpose game reserve. He regretted that his failure had resulted in rendering illegal, the hunting by the Bushmen, which had hitherto been legal. He, however, explained that the Colonial Government decided to turn 'Nelson's eye' at the continued hunting by the Bushmen, since one of the primary aims of declaration of the game reserve, was to provide them with a place where they could hunt" (ibid.: 345).

This legal situation persisted until the *Fauna Conservation (Amendment) Act 1967* was established. It explicitly allowed those communities that were primarily dependent on hunting to practice it in a regulated way. Subsequent legislation and even the Constitution had always recognised the presence of the San in the CKGR and adequately provided for their continued hunting (ibid.: 349f.). Considering all that, Phumaphi ultimately concluded that the applicants were in possession of the lands they had lawfully occupied in the CKGR.

1.4 Deprivation of Land Possession

In light of the unanimous confirmation of the San's lawful occupation in the CKGR by all three judges, the next issue that had to be addressed was the question whether the applicants had been deprived of possession by the government forcibly or wrongly and without their consent. In this sense, the applicants argued

III. The Legal Dispute over the (temporarily?) "Lost Lands" 333

that they had been relocated without their consent and referred to the structural violence caused by the termination of state services, the hunting ban, and further psychological threats in case they would have decided to stay on.

Judge Dibotelo's reasoning gave ample food for thought to many involved (and uninvolved) observers who doubted that state-oriented and genuinely Western postcolonial jurisdiction was in fact impartial and adequate for the interests of members of indigenous peoples.[148] Thus, the High Court's judge only used the testimonies of two selected applicants for his decision and to support his reasoning: both had agreed to the relocation either because of the desired access to clean water, schools for their children, and new income opportunities, or because of state-offered compensation (High Court 2006: 93ff.). It seems quite ironic that he even saw his selective evaluation confirmed by the fact that not everybody had left the reserve. He interpreted this situation as evidence that state authorities had not realized any (unlawful) coercion. Furthermore, Dibotelo's evaluation was also based on the mobility of many residents in the CKGR, who regularly left the reserve for certain periods without having the services being terminated. In his opinion, this verified the respondent's exonerating claim that the relocation had not been a direct consequence or result of the termination of services (ibid.: 100).

This reasoning does not only try to correspond to the state's arguments, it is also carried out in a strikingly different way: to a certain extent it turns the distress of those hoping for less poverty and a secured existence into a government virtue.[149] It would have been a great surprise, if not a single one out of an estimated 2,500 relocated residents had reacted to the promises of a "better" and particularly secured life as well as the chances of material compensation and ultimately had given in to the underlying pressure. In this sense, justice is far from being found in a "neutral" way because these temptations are used against the interests of preservation and self-determined development of their culture, history and identity. In addition, this type of reasoning seeks to assume a position of self-critical distance combined with inevitably ethnocentric perspectives. Perhaps true to his unquestioned modernist world-view of an "appropriate and future-oriented way of life", Dibotelo found that the allegedly forcible and unlawful deprivation of possession had no factual basis whatsoever.

It is remarkable how Judge Unity Dow applied a very different sensitivity to evaluate the circumstances according to the criteria of the legal system in Botswana. Her judgement took into account the specific history of oppression and discrimination of those concerned and also considered the San communities' alternative "culture of law" of consensual decision-making; a legal tradition with-

---

148 See below for this context.
149 It was hardly a surprise when Judge Dibotelo was appointed Chief Justice in February 2010.

out similar institutions of social and political organization in the majority culture of Tswana societies. Moreover, she assessed concrete relocation approaches of the government at the procedural level. Judge Dow concluded from the number of trucks employed, the amount of staff members and the diversity of the government departments involved that the government basically did its utmost to relocate most, if not all, residents of the CKGR (ibid.: 223).

With regard to the termination of state services without consultation of those concerned, Unity Dow investigated the requirements of the legal standards of legitimate expectation. She assessed a Court of Appeal reasoning, according to which legitimate expectation arose where policymakers had provoked reasonable expectation in those possibly affected by their decisions: "A legitimate expectation arises where a person responsible for taking a decision had induced in someone who may be affected by the decision a reasonable expectation that he will receive or retain a benefit or that he will be granted a hearing before the decision is taken (…) It is founded upon the basic principle of the rule of law, which required regularity, predictability, and certainty in government's dealings with the public" (ibid.: 224f.).[150]

In light of this legal understanding, Unity Dow then asked what an average resident of the CKGR could expect from the government prior to August 2001. According to her assessment of circumstances, some of those concerned might had at least expected that what had not changed for more than fifteen years and was supported by policy, law and practice: indispensable consultation before being relocated. Others perhaps had expected not be forced to relocate at all and yet others might had expected continued provision of services until a new policy with their input entered into force. Her consideration of evidence suggested that the government had operated under confusing and unclear principles. This point alone would have been sufficient to find that the applicants had been deprived of possession of the land they lawfully occupied wrongfully and unlawfully and without their consent (ibid.: 226f.).

Unity Dow also examined other factors that shed light on potential, involuntary and uninformed consent to be relocated: this included the state's ignorance regarding specific domestic and social relationships. The applicants were not people living "in an apartment building in New York", as the judge sarcastically remarked, but in families, informal compounds and small settlements that were linked together by kinship ties, marriage, mutual cooperations and general economic interdependence. Therefore, she concluded that the government's conceptions of individual ownership were inadequate and only shaped by the intention to force them into the process of relocation (ibid.: 227f.). There had been instances where husband and wife or children and their parents were

---

150 *Botswana Court of Appeal case of Labbeus Ditiro Peleowetse and Permanent Secretary to the President and Attorney General and Shaw Kgathi*, CA No 26/99, at 13–14.

played off against each other. Huts had simply been dismantled and existing water tanks emptied.

As all those who had wanted to stay on had to observe how they were not only deprived of their material possessions but also of their closest social relationships, they had had no choice but to give in to the relocation plans. In the eyes of Judge Dow, this was aggravated even more by the applicants' relative powerlessness based on the hegemonic relationships of ethnicity in Botswana, their literacy levels, and their marginalized political and economic situation:

"The Applicants belong to an ethnic group that has been historically looked down-upon, often considered to be no more than cheap, disposable labour, by almost all other numerically superior ethnic groups in Botswana. Until recently, perhaps it is still the case, 'Mosarwa', 'Lesarwa', 'Lekgalagadi' and 'Mokgalagadi' were common terms of insult, in the same way as 'Nigger' and 'Kaffir' were/are" (ibid.: 232).

In light of this legal understanding, the government had been obliged to put in place mechanisms that promoted and facilitated true decision-making and thus consensual agreement. Based on this provisional result, Dow then discussed what the applicants would actually gain by relocating. She explicitly asked what they could do with such a – for those concerned extremely abstract – piece of paper giving one rights to a plot of 25 × 40m when they had access to much larger territories. Although the fifteen goats or five cattle for material compensation corresponded to the cosmovisions of dominant Tswana society, they clearly were not enough to pull the beneficiaries out of the need to receive destitute rations (ibid.: 240f.). The state's allegations of the then possible access to water, health care and schools also had to run into nothing because the applicants had already enjoyed all that in the reserve as well.

In accordance with her interpretation, the government had only kept the economic development in sight but had failed to see the cultural and social problems (ibid.: 243). Unity Dow then used two examples to explain the insufficient inclusion of the applicants and how the government had also failed to take into consideration the knowledge, culture and ideologies of the applicants: the then Minister of Local Government Margaret Nasha wrote a letter to the NGO DITSHWANELO stating that it was simply unfair to allow certain parts of the population to remain "undeveloped": "[A]ll we want to do is treat Basarwa as humans, not Game, and enable them to partake of the development cake of their country" (ibid.: 244). Her second example was a court situation with Attorney General Pilane who had burst out laughing, when an applicant explained that she did not wish to relocate because of the graves of her ancestors.[151] The High

---

151 He explained his amusement by stating that he had not been aware that they actually buried their dead but had rather thought that they collapsed a hut over their dead and moved on (High Court 2006: 244).

Court judge then recommended the government to re-evaluate their at-any-cost "development" strategy which also included the possible disappearance of a people and their culture:

"I am not convinced, on the evidence, that the decision to terminate services and relocate the Applicants and what to offer them once they have been relocated, took into consideration such relevant considerations as the potential disruptions of their culture and the threat to their very survival as a people. I note the Respondent's position that it does not discriminate on ethnic lines, but equal treatment of un-equals can amount to discrimination" (ibid.: 246).

Judge Dow was also surprised at the practice of compensation payments: she particularly criticized that the government's decision process had only been one-sided and did not provide for any form of negotiations. The government had obviously assumed that the applicants would accept whatever had been offered. Thus, no attempt had been made to make any of the residents aware of how the amount would be calculated and what would be a fair compensation adequate to their loss. From this perspective, the whole compensation process had been hierarchical in its execution and just one more step to quickly achieve their tiresome goal. She then continued by explaining that also the manner of execution was unique: a normal compensation procedure would only require the people to leave after compensation was paid or an offer at least made (ibid.: 250).

In keeping with her reasoning, the unlawful hunting ban which had been based on the general rejection to issue special game licenses was to be read as part of the plan that the applicants were to be deprived of their existential livelihood by 31 January 2002. Without water and without food due to the hunting ban, they would have been virtually unable to survive in their old environment (ibid.: 253). There was no doubt in Dow's opinion that both actions and statements of the applicants had been consistent with their intention to remain in the CKGR. In line with this desire, they instructed the NGO *First People of the Kalahari* to negotiate with the government on their remaining within the CKGR. Similarly, the applicants instructed their attorneys to challenge the relocation, once the dialog had been unilaterally terminated. Judge Dow thus concluded that the applicants had never consented to the 2002 relocations and had, therefore, been unlawfully dispossessed of the land they had lawfully occupied (ibid.: 254f.).

The third involved Judge Phumaphi agreed with most parts of Dow's judgement and reasoning, although his considerations of evidence were not as detailed. In his conclusions, he remarked that the content of the testimonies of both the applicants' and the respondent's witnesses were fundamentally different (ibid.: 356). Similar to Unity Dow's reasoning, however, he referred to the practices of separating spouses and families, dismantling huts based on coercive power without the applicants' consent, threatening the residents of the CKGR, destroying veld products, emptying water tanks, and prohibiting hunting: "Once the provision of rations was terminated, hunting became a very important alter-

III. *The Legal Dispute over the (temporarily?) "Lost Lands"* 337

native for sourcing food. It is therefore unlikely that if the residents were not being pressured they would have been denied SGLs [Special Game Licences]. It appears the idea was to starve those remaining in the reserve so that the lure of the serviced settlements outside the reserve would loom large among their options for survival" (ibid.: 374).

Furthermore, he criticized that the applicants were not or only falsely informed in terms of relocation and compensation. At the end of these conclusions, he stated that the question remained unresolved, whether those who had voluntarily decided to relocate were also fully aware of all consequences including the compensation to be expected and the loss of rights to return to the CKGR. On this issue, the High Court judge clearly decided to the disadvantage of the government: "It is unlikely that, if the residents were relocating willingly, they would have been kept in dark about the purposes for which they were made to thumbprint documents, and the fact that once they had received compensation they would not be allowed back in the reserve" (ibid.: 374). Phumaphi thus explicitly concluded that the applicants' consent had been vitiated and, therefore, invalid due to insufficiently corresponding basic assumptions of the applicants and the government (ibid.: 375).

1.5 Special Game Licences

The fourth and last issue that was subject to the High Court's judgement may be divided into two aspects: the first one concerns the government's refusal to issue special game licenses and was unanimously – although based on diverging legal grounds – declared unlawful and thus decided in favour of the applicants by all three judges. They all found that the hunting ban as a result of the stopped issuing of licenses was one of those reasons that had virtually forced them to relocate from the CKGR. They initially referred to Sect. 12 (3) *Wildlife Conservation and National Parks Act* (1992) to legally confirm their considerations; this act generally prohibited hunting within the game reserve, unless individuals were issued with a permit under the provisions of Sect. 39.[152] Pursuant to Sect. 45 (1) *National Parks and Game Reserves Regulations* 2000, the director of the Department for Wildlife and National Parks (DWNP) had the authority to issue such licenses:

"Persons resident in the Central Kalahari Game Reserve at the time of the establishment of the Central Kalahari Game Reserve, or persons who can rightly lay claim to hunting rights in the Central Kalahari Game Reserve, may be permitted in writing by the Director to hunt specified animal species and collect veld products in the game reserve and subject to any terms and conditions and in such areas as the Director may determine."

---

152 Furthermore, Sect. 26 and 30 (1) *Wildlife Conservation and National Parks Act* established that special game licenses were to be issued to those citizens of Botswana who were principally dependent on hunting and gathering.

Judge Dibotelo remarked, however, that the use of the word "may" indicated that the provision was not to be understood as mandatory but had been subject to the discretion of the state and thus the director of the DWNP (High Court 2006: 110f.). In consequence, the cited section had not entitled the applicants to special game licenses. Judge Dibotelo found this view also confirmed in the original proclamation to establish the CKGR ("[H]is Excellency the High Commissioner has been pleased to declare part of the Ghanzi District (...) a Game Reserve, to be known as The Central Kalahari Game Reserve."). In accordance with his (narrow) interpretation of the relevant High Commissioner's Notice 1961, the wording had been clear and unambiguous because the CKGR had (only) been created for wild life and not for "Basarwa"; in his opinion (with an *argumentum e contrario*), the San (or "Bushmen") would have otherwise had to be explicitly mentioned. Therefore, the relevant proclamation was not to be interpreted extensively.

In contrast to Dow and Phumaphi, Judge Dibotelo did neither take into account the intentions of the historical legislator, nor the originally objective purpose of these provisions. In his opinion, the colonial administration had created the reserve for the exclusive protection of wildlife and, therefore, had (generally) prohibited hunting within the reserve (ibid.: 108). In consequence, neither the (historical) creation of the CKGR, nor the provisions of laws and regulations of the Republic of Botswana would have granted the applicants the subjective right to be issued a hunting license. He conceded, however, that the government's refusal to issue licenses had adversely affected the applicants or their interests. In accordance with applicable law, the parties affected by this decision would under certain circumstances have been entitled to a hearing. As the director of the DWNP had not given the applicants this opportunity before he had stopped the issuing of special game licences, his decision had been invalid and was, therefore, to be interpreted as unlawful (ibid.: 114).

Judge Unity Dow had already addressed the relevance of the stopped issuing of licenses, when she discussed the previous issue of whether the applicants had been deprived of possession of land they had lawfully occupied; meaning without valid consent to be relocated (ibid.: 251–253). In this context, she assessed the possible motives of the DNWP director's decision to stop the issuing of licenses and came to the conclusion that his underlying intentions had been to create impossible living conditions within the CKGR: "The plan, therefore, was that by the end of 31st January 2002, there would be no water, no food, and no hunting, within the Reserve. Life would simply be very hard, if not outright impossible" (ibid.: 253).

With regard to the present issue, Unity Dow found that the director of the DWNP had clearly acted outside the powers granted to him. His refusal to issue new licences as well as to render invalid those already issued had not been based on the alleged need to protect flora and fauna but rather on his legal understanding that a special game license would be a service in contradiction to the state's termination thereof by 31 January 2002. In contrast, Dow found that such a le-

III. The Legal Dispute over the (temporarily?) "Lost Lands"

gal understanding had been misguided and, therefore, not an adequate reason to stop the issuing of licenses. Neither the *Wildlife Conservation and National Parks Act* nor the relevant regulation of 2000 had given the director of the DWNP the power to such an extensive interpretation. In consequence, she concluded that his refusal of issuance had been unlawful and unconstitutional (ibid.: 264).

Judge Phumaphi again mostly agreed with Judge Dow and assessed that the director's decision had been *ultra vires* (outside of his powers) the empowering legislation because he had not exercised his general discretion at all, let alone exercising it reasonably in case of such an existentially crucial decision. In addition, the High Court judge also evaluated the issue of constitutionality in this matter: the state's simultaneous termination of providing food rations and issuing special game licenses had been tantamount to condemning the remaining residents of the CKGR to "death by starvation". Under these circumstances, the refusal to issue hunting licenses – so his judgement – had not only been unlawful but had also violated the right to life as pursuant to Sect. 4 (1) Constitution of Botswana (ibid.: 380).

1.6 Access to the *Central Kalahari Game Reserve* (CKGR)

In the end, the present legal case was all about the (denied) access of those concerned to the CKGR. In consequence of these circumstances, it was necessary for the High Court to evaluate the lawfulness and constitutionality of the denied access without explicit permission. In the context of this case, the government based its arguments on a presidential directive of 30 October 2002 that stipulated, *inter alia*, as follows:

> "(b) The National Parks regulations be strictly enforced within the CKGR. This should be reinforced by regular patrols within and along the CKGR boundaries by Department of Wildlife and National Parks;
> (d) The following strategies be employed to help retain people in the new settlements:
>   (i) Special Game Licences for domestic purposes be exclusively issued to 'resident' Kaudwane and New Xade members of the Community for hunting in the wildlife management areas;
>   (ii) All those people who have relocated and were compensated should not be allowed to resettle in the CKGR."[153]

As a result, this directive states that only those seventeen individuals who had not been relocated were allowed to remain in, and if they left, re-enter without special permits. Henceforth, all others who had been relocated and, therefore, had received compensation became subjects to the present directive and needed a

---

153 *Presidential Directive CAB 38 (a) 2002.*

permit to enter the reserve. According to Judge Dibotelo, the state (represented by the government) as the (undisputed) owner of the CKGR could exercise all rights of ownership in respect of the CKGR, including the right to determine who may come into the CKGR and under what terms and conditions (High Court 2006: 115f.).

Completely in line with his previous conclusions stating that the termination of state services had not been unlawful and that the applicants had not been deprived of their right of occupation, he simply determined without further explanations that the relocation had also coincided with the definitive relinquishment of possession. Therefore, Dibotelo did not doubt that the applicants had considered the plots they had received in the new settlements after relocation as compensation for the lands they had previously occupied in the CKGR. Although witness statements claimed the opposite – one witness (PW 5), for example, explained that she had not known what they were being compensated for on the ground that it had not been explained to her what the compensation was for – Judge Dibotelo was convinced of the applicants' causal understanding of law that they had understood the terms of compensation (ibid.: 117).

As he tended to follow a rather exclusive and objective terminological interpretation, he cited the definition of "compensation" from two English dictionaries. This may seem a bit awkward for a judge and jurist, given that the Botswana government had its own compensation guidelines for relocations (*Compensation Guidelines for Tribal Areas*). In addition, the protection from deprivation of property of Sect. 8 (1) Constitution of Botswana stipulates a reservation with regard to adequate compensation for expropriation. Although the amended *Tribal Land Act* 1993 (No. 14) does not *per se* define the term "compensation", the content of Sect. 33 (2) indicates what compensation should look like and is, therefore, a legal point of reference for evaluating adequate compensation.[154]

In my opinion, Judge Dibotelo intentionally excluded this assessment of evidence from the applicable legal sphere by simplifying it to correspond to the Oxford Dictionaries instead of addressing the guidelines of adequacy and procedural compensation requirements. From this legal understanding, he concluded that the receipt of compensation in the form of money as well as new plots had been in replacement of the rights of the applicants to occupy and possess land in the settlements inside the CKGR. As they had relinquished their rights in the reserve as soon as they had accepted the compensation, the government's refusal to

---

154 Sect. 33 (2): "Any person who is required to vacate land under the provisions of subsection (1) may be granted the right to use other land, if available, and shall be entitled to adequate compensation from the State for the following, if applicable – (a) the value of any standing crops taken over by the State; (b) the value of any improvements effected to such land (…); (c) the costs of resettlement; and (d) the loss of right of user of such land."

allow the applicants to enter the CKGR unless they had been issued with a permit was neither unlawful nor unconstitutional (ibid.: 119).

In contrast, Judge Dow found that the government's claim of an offered compensation connected *sine qua non* to the immediate termination of the applicants' right to return without previous permission was a problem that needed to be addressed. From her point of view, the applicants would have needed to explicitly agree to the terms of relocation to actually have their rights extinguished. Thus, it was necessary to assess whether these terms of relocation had been part of the legal act of compensation. Another question that needed to be addressed was the question of time: when had the respondent communicated those terms to the applicants? Had the applicants been adequately informed about the consequences of accepting compensation and had these new terms been applicable only to the 2002 relocations and not to earlier relocations?

Judge Dow also detected another problematic procedural aspect related to a further rather arbitrary process: as soon as one single member of a household had agreed to relocate, his/her hut was immediately taken down. Thus, the rest of the family had no choice but to relocate as well (ibid.: 268f.). In her opinion, this process had played off men, women and children against each other: "The second problem is that the reality on the ground was that many people vacated the Reserve not because they had made a personal decision to leave, but because a family member, who could point at a hut as his or hers, had 'registered' and the hut had been taken down. With a wife, husband, parent etc., leaving, such 'dependent' family members had no option but to get into the truck" (ibid.: 268f.).[155]

The High Court judge explicitly questioned this crucial lack of free will as related to the extinguished right to return to their former environment. Accordingly, for the rights of these individuals to return to the CKGR to be extinguished, it would have had to be assumed that the leaving with a family member constituted a "voluntary" agreement – in some form of "kin liability" – that all rights to return would be extinguished. If it was compensation that extinguished the right to return (without a permit), Dow found completely in line with her assessment of evidence that other members of a family could not have possibly been bound by the decision of an individual to extinguish his/her right to return. After all, relocation had been considered an individual decision and also compensation had been paid to the individuals who relocated. Having all this considered, she came to the conclusion that the applicants had been in lawful occupation of their settlements and that the entire relocation exercise had been wrongful, unlawful and without the necessary consent. In consequence, any rights that had been lost as a result thereof had also been lost wrongfully and unlawfully.

---

155 See also at another part of the judgement (High Court 2006: 186) where a witness felt that he was forced to join his wife who was ready to relocate.

She then continued by establishing that any attempt to regulate the enjoyment of those rights by permits was an unlawful curtailment of the right of movement of the applicants. Notwithstanding these findings, the government was always entitled, as part of its management of the CKGR through the DWNP, to monitor and regulate traffic, especially vehicular traffic, into the CKGR. Such monitoring and regulation could also have included keeping records of identities and numbers of the residents, the incidence of entry and exit from the CKGR, the nature and impact on the reserve of the transportation they had used for such entry and exit. But in her opinion, such conservation management could not have been used as a means of denying the applicants the right to reside in the CKGR. Therefore, she came to the conclusion that the respondent's refusal to allow the applicants to enter the CKGR unless they had been issued with a permit was unlawful and unconstitutional (ibid.: 273f.).

In his evaluation of evidence, Judge Phumaphi addressed the applicants' right of possession. In this context, he found that both the British and the government of Botswana could have been extinguished these "pre-existing (inherited) rights to live in the CKGR". As neither the protectorate's rulers nor postcolonial Botswana had done so and they obviously had not even had the chance to do so, it had to be assumed that the lawful and traditional vested rights still existed. In contrast, the colonial government had established the *CKGR (Control of Entry) Regulations* in 1963, which stipulated that no person other than a "Bushman indigenous to the Central Kalahari Game Reserve" was permitted to enter the reserve without having obtained a permit (ibid.: 381f.). Even from then onwards, the applicants had never been required to obtain entry permits into the CKGR, until after the *Presidential Directive* was issued in 2002.

Moreover – Phumaphi continued – Sect. 18 (2) and 45 (1) *National Parks and Game Reserve Regulations* (2000) established provisions for the communities within the reserve. This clearly implicated that their residence had not been considered to be unlawful: it explicitly mentioned "communities living in" and "persons resident in the Central Kalahari Game Reserve". The legal circumstances of the government pursuing a policy of "persuade but not force" combined with said provisions suggested that the government had recognized the applicants' right to occupation (ibid.: 383–388). Phumaphi even confirmed his legal opinion by quoting that the entire *CKGR (Control of Entry) Regulation* 1963 "Bushmen of the CKGR" had found its way into the Constitution of Botswana: Sect. 14 (3) (c) had provided the imposition of restrictions on the freedom of movement of persons who were not members of San communities "for the protection or well-being of Bushmen".[156] Thus, the applicants had been explicitly exempted from the obligation to obtain a permit.

---

156 As Botswana sought to develop a Constitution that is more neutral towards the dominant "Tswana" communities, the Constitutional (Amendment) Bill 2004 delet-

III. The Legal Dispute over the (temporarily?) "Lost Lands"

After Phumaphi had established the applicants' lawful right of occupation in the CKGR, he addressed the issue whether applicants had abandoned their rights to reside in the CKGR by virtue of an agreement they had entered into with the government upon relocation. The evidence clearly indicated that all those who had lost property at the time of the 2002 relocations had been compensated. It also suggested that such compensation had been based on the assessment made by state executive officers that were part of the relocation teams. These assessment teams had then compensated for property which had been either dismantled or abandoned. In addition to this monetary compensation, those who had been compensated had also been given the option to choose between being given five cattle or 15 goats, to assist them in starting a new livelihood (ibid.: 394f.).

In accordance with the judgement by Unity Dow (ibid.: 250), he found that this so-called "agreement" had been a unilateral one with serious deficits but without comparable legal consequences. Phumaphi held it sufficient to only assess that applicants had not been adequately informed of the terms of relocation. As the applicants had mostly been illiterate, he found that it was not clear how it could have been assumed that they had given their consent to the conditions of the alleged agreement. In consequence, this High Court judge decided that there had not been an agreement.

Phumaphi concluded that the refusal to allow the applicants entry into the CKGR without permits was both unlawful and unconstitutional for the reason that it violates the applicants' rights of freedom of movement (ibid.: 398).

1.7 Conclusions

There was one issue all three High Court judges agreed on: they complained about the lack of respect towards the court by public figures and institutions who gained the attention of the media by questioning the court's impartiality. On multiple occasions, both parties had defamed the legal proceedings and tried to damage the court's reputation. Also several applicants had repeatedly questioned its legal impartiality in the media. Furthermore, the judges were dissatisfied with the conduct of both parties who had announced to appeal the judgement even before it was pronounced with detailed reasoning. One of the applicants' attorneys, Duma Boko, was particularly criticized for his active agitation outside the courtroom. The judges especially resented Boko's media campaign stating that his clients could never see justice at a court whose rules they did not understand.

The judges also clearly expressed their discontent of first applicant Roy Sesana's behaviour who had gained international fame (at least among those in-

---

ed this subsection. For a more detailed discussion, see *Balopi Commission* in chapter 4, section I.3 as well as my critique to this amendment in chapter 4, section II.5.

terested) in the course of the proceedings. Notwithstanding the applicants' legal representative Gordon Bennett who claimed to the contrary, Roy Sesana had, from the viewpoint of the judges, continuously explained to the press that had become aware of the fate of the "first hunters and gatherers" that the real grounds for their forced relocation from the *Central Kalahari Game Reserve* was diamond mining. This was reason enough for Attorney General Pilane to request a court visit at the Gope diamond mine on reserve land. The judges did not only criticize Sesana's mediagenic appearances (with springbok-antler hat and other "Bushmen accessories") against the court's independence but also that he – as the person who had initiated the case – refused to give evidence in court and only provided written affidavits. Considering his rhetorical skills, this self-restraint was indeed surprising: in 2003 at the conference "Research for Khoe and San Development" held at the University of Botswana, I was able to experience his rhetorical mastery when his trenchant and ironic comments earned him a lot of attention (as well as significant approval at least among other San participants). Judge Dibotelo described this strategy of implicit (and sometimes also explicit) contempt of court as follows:

"Although the First Applicant as a party to these proceedings has decided not to go into the witness box to give evidence, it is unfortunate that during the trial when he made comments to the media, which were not disclaimed by him and which he was entitled to make, about the alleged forcible removal of the Applicants from the CKGR by the Government, he went out of his way to malign and cast aspersions on this Court to the extent that at one point his Counsel had to apologise on his behalf to the Court for what were undoubtedly disparaging comments by him in May 2005 about this Court in its conduct of this case" (High Court 2006: 27f.).

Dibotelo continued his remarks by stating that it may have been contended that Sesana should personally pay a portion of the costs of the defendant party. In his words, justice would be better served, however, if each party paid their own costs in this action. Both Judge Dibotelo and Judge Phumaphi warned the parties not to consider the social and political problem as solved due to a one-time court ruling. Instead, they rather explained that it was asking too much of a judgement to solve the original problem. Even though the court case was over, they thus asked both parties to seek – a negotiated – consent and to settle their differences through dialog and joint relationship building (High Court 2006: 120, 398).

In contrast, Judge Dow detected the core problem of the conflict rather in the government's attitude towards the applicants. In her opinion, the present case addressed the termination of water supplies and other services for a few hundred individuals as well as their access to and hunting rights on a certain piece of land in the Central Kalahari only at first sight. This dispute was embedded in a much wider historical context and could not be resolved as long as the government applied hegemonic or otherwise paternalistic approaches to see the applicants ex-

III. The Legal Dispute over the (temporarily?) "Lost Lands" 345

clusively as underdeveloped citizens. Her criticism even went so far as to draw an analogy between the government and their former colonial power as well as their arrogant attitudes towards those colonized. In this sense, Botswana alone would basically in a similar way determine the meaning of "development" while regarding itself as the measure of all things:

"This is a case that questions the meaning of 'development' and demands of the Respondent to take a closer look at its definition of that notion. One of colonialism's greatest failings was to assume that development was, in the case of Britain, anglicising the colonised. All the current talk about African renaissance is really a twisting and turning at the yokes of that ideology" (ibid.: 275). As one of the many impressive facets of this key case for Botswana and maybe even for southern Africa and beyond, the legal consideration exceeded the positive limits of applicable law and also included the legal history of unequal relationships. Judge Dow in particular extended the legal sphere to the central problem that a group of individuals – representative for a community and possibly even all indigenous peoples – claimed their dignity and demanded respect for their divergent way(s) of living at least in the future. Quite uncommon for High Court decisions (at least in Botswana), she repeatedly put herself in the applicants' position by recognizing their original wish of being able to determine their lives within society as a whole themselves: "It is a people saying in essence, 'our way of life may be different but it is worthy of respect. We may be changing and getting closer to your way of life, but give us a chance to decide what we want to carry with us into the future'" (ibid.: 275).

2. Consequences of the High Court's Decision: Summary

Notwithstanding several reservations discussed above, the judgement of the *High Court of Botswana* denoted a veritable and, above all, unexpected victory for local San communities. In the run-up to the decision, not only the applicants but also many NGOs and other international advocates for the San were quite sceptical of the High Court's undaunted political impartiality, unconditional (real) legal freedom of instructions and complete objectivity.[157] Considering this scepticism alone, the court's decision was a clear sign that the rule of law and independent jurisdic-

---

157 For instance South African human rights lawyer Roger Chennells expressed such a sentiment when interviewed on 9 February 2007: "The decision of the Botswana Court was very unexpected. I am really ashamed to say that I had so little faith in this African High Court of Botswana and as one of the lawyers that started the case I believed we would not get a fair trial. I had this belief that African High Courts are in the pockets of the presidents, but this Court has shown that it is completely independent and that rule of law is applied. And that is an amazing thing. And I am ashamed to say: quite to a surprise for us."

tion existed in Botswana. Moreover, the comprehensive and contextual judgement and its reasoning went far beyond the legal perspective that had realistically to be expected: on the one hand because the court recognized the San communities as indigenous peoples, while on the other hand their indigenous land rights that had strictly speaking not even been claimed were confirmed by the legal reasoning.

As the redundant politicians' statement "all Africans are indigenous" appeared to deny the notion and concept of "indigenous peoples rights", its specific legal function in public discourse, the judgement must be viewed as a legal breakthrough. The recognition of San as indigenous peoples will certainly prove significant in the African context in general and for Botswana in particular. For Judge Unity Dow, in contrast to the dominant political utterances, the applicants are clearly members of indigenous peoples and, therefore, protected by this relatively new concept of special (legal) attention: "[I] take the position that the fact the Applicants belong to a class of peoples that have now come to be recognized as 'indigenous peoples' is of relevance (…)" (High Court 2006: 201). Dow considered this defining characteristic – as one of three central points – to be so relevant that it gave direction to the answer of all other legal aspects in question.[158]

Furthermore, I would like to point out that Judge Dow made blatant use of the term "peoples" against a tacit political taboo in Botswana. This becomes more remarkable in the African context, as even the expert group appointed by the African Commission flinched from using this term and instead decided to call itself "Working Group of Experts on Indigenous **Populations/Communities**". Thus, by alternately working with the terms "people", "populations" or "communities", they more or less refused to answer the legally-relevant question of who the addressees are. The consequences of this consideration of facts (that the applicants are members of indigenous peoples with special rights) were quite momentous as well because Botswana ratified the *Convention on the Elimination of All Forms of Racial Discrimination* (CERD). As state party, the government is committed to have members of indigenous peoples effectively participate in public life and to ask for their informed consent in all matters that directly concern their rights and interests. Unity Dow explicitly reminded "her" government of this request, as provided by the *General Recommendation XXIII (51) on the Rights of Indigenous Peoples (1997), Art. 4 (d) CERD Committee* (ibid.: 201f.).

---

158 The second point addresses the judge's (quite dynamic) interpretation of the national Constitution in the light of international developments of human rights to enhance the protection of cultural integrity, self-determination and human dignity. Conceptions of values and norms were therefore reviewed not as stagnant, but rather as elements of an ever changing society in the context of international legal progress. Finally Dow also considered – as the third central point relevant for the final judgement – Sect. 24 (1) of the *Interpretation Act* as relevant, which provides the court with the opportunity to take into account any text books, commission reports, memorandums as well as international agreements or conventions (High Court 2006: 203–206).

Judge Dow ultimately also referred to the recognition of the special relationship between indigenous peoples and their lands – as "current wisdom" – for all forms of related governance. She then quoted the *Study of the Problem of Discrimination Against Indigenous Populations* by José Martínez Cobo of 1983 (paras. 196f.) as evidence: "It is essential to know and understand the deeply spiritual special relationship between indigenous peoples and their land as basic to their existence as such and to all their beliefs, customs, traditions and culture. For such peoples, the land is not merely a possession and a means of production. The entire relationship between the spiritual life of indigenous peoples and Mother Earth, and their land, has a great many deep-seated implications. Their land is not a commodity which can be acquired, but a material element to be enjoyed freely" (High Court 2006: 202f.).[159]

Therefore, Dow clearly and without any doubt lifted the lid on the standards she considered to assess this court case. She was obviously guided by the ongoing international as well as (in the context of the African Union) regional African development of law that increasingly guarantees legal protection of indigenous peoples. Apart from their recognition as special interest groups, legal guarantees for the peculiar relationship to their lands form a further key achievement in this regard. When it came to deciding on the legal question of the applicants' lawful occupation, Dow recurred to fundamental considerations of law regarding the land rights of indigenous peoples. Although she did not explicitly mention the doctrine of "native title" in international law, this concept that had been considered in various national contexts largely overlapped with her understanding of land rights. Accordingly, she expressed her opinion right at the beginning of this consideration of evidence: "Some of the Applicants are descendants of people who have been resident in the Kgalagadi area, more particularly the CKGR area, before the Reserve was established as such in 1961. They were, by operation of the customary law of the area, in lawful occupation of the land prior to the creation of the Bechuanaland Protectorate and they were in lawful occupation at the time of the creation of the Reserve" (High Court 2006: 207f.).

Moreover, the judge confirmed the exclusive character of their occupation by recognizing that they had excluded other communities from their territories and use of lands (through activities of hunting and gathering): "[T]hey have (…) lived as hunter-gatherers, carrying out subsistence activities within the confines of clearly defined territories called *ngo's* (…)" (ibid.: 157f.). Thereby, she addressed the three legally relevant components of the occupation of lands by indigenous peoples: the land uses, the exclusion of other communities from their territories, and the temporal factor meaning that the applicants' ancestors had already occupied the territory at the time of colonisation. Her adjudication then turned to the

---

159 Cf. also my considerations on the relationship between indigenous cultures and their territories in chapter 1 of this book.

postcolonial state's acts of law and administration as well as the Constitution of Botswana, all of which recognized and even protected the applicants' lawful occupation without ever clearly and unambiguously repealing them (ibid.: 211–217). This assessment made it possible for her to (basically) rule out that the "indigenous right to ownership" had been extinguished by formal acts of legislation.

Even if Judge Dow did not explicitly mention the doctrine of "native title" (or traditionally maintained vested rights) of originally resident populations, her assessment reveals that she was more or less guided by this doctrine. Nevertheless, she did not refer to legal developments in neighbouring South Africa with a comparable situation of San communities and a legal system similar to Botswana; considering her judgement, perhaps it would have stood to reason for her to use similar South African court rulings and especially the "Richtersveld case" as points of reference.

Although the Richtersveld community based their claim on the *Restitution of Land Rights Act* which does not address indigenous land rights, they pleaded for a "right in land" whose legal nature rested in the aboriginal title. In its judgement, the *Constitutional Court of South Africa* adjudicated "indigenous law ownership" to the community, a South African version of the native title. But even if the court considered statutory law, its decision implied a way for future applications of the native title in South African law.[160] Why Judge Unity Dow did neither pursue an analogous direction nor assessed the doctrine of native title as other Commonwealth countries had done must remain the subject of speculations though. There is every indication that such an interpretation would have clearly been too much for the government to tolerate; the court's decision would thus hardly have been accepted (without appeal).

It is even more interesting, however, that Judge Phumaphi, who was much more reserved in other legal questions than Judge Dow, went a significant step further in this aspect by "calling the spade a spade". Although he made it clear right from start that the Australian "Mabo case" did not have any binding effect on the *High Court of Botswana*, he still based his considerations on this precedence and its underlying principle of "native title". He justified this step by stating that the "situation was not very different".[161]

Phumaphi knew very well that he stuck to the evidential conditions of the "native title" doctrine and thus followed the example of the "Mabo case". In his considerations, he embraced several crucial questions, such as the factual evidence of the applicants' and their ancestors' occupation or the components of use, exclusion and time based on this occupation. In line with this approach, he also based his decision on Silberbauer's testimony, who had conducted research

---

160 For a more detailed discussion of the "Richtersveld" case, see part 2.
161 See chapter 2 "Excursus" for a general discussion of the "native/aborginal title" and the Australian "Mabo case".

III. The Legal Dispute over the (temporarily?) "Lost Lands"

on the "Bushmen" when the reserve was established. Silberbauer had confirmed their century-old and exclusive relationship to their territories: "It is known that Basarwa or San peoples have inhabited the region which is now Botswana for many thousands of years. Although they were mobile, their movements had limits, so it is reasonable to say that the area which includes CKGR and Khutse has been the domain of the Basarwa for many centuries" (High Court 2006: 326).

According to his testimony, moreover, also their "adaptation" to the environment, their knowledge of plants and their hunting techniques proved that they must have occupied the territory for several hundred years.[162] Even though Judge Phumaphi's court evaluation of their former collective and exclusive occupation at the time of colonisation as well as their legal systems and customs did not comprise the same material scope as the "Mabo case", he at least found evidence that the San were "indigenous" to their territory in the CKGR: "[T]he Bushmen are indigenous to the CKGR which means that they were in the CKGR prior to it becoming Crown Land, thereafter a game reserve and then State land upon Botswana attaining independence" (ibid.: 328).

In international law, maybe the most important precondition for a native title to (continue to) exist is to evaluate whether or not it may have been extinguished by a lawful act of state. Accordingly, Judge Phumaphi asked whether British colonisation itself or the reserve's proclamation had any effect on the legal title of the "Bushmen". The area of today's CKGR was proclaimed Crown Land by the colonial government's *Bechuanaland Protectorate (Lands) Order-in-Council 1910* (on 10 January 1910). This proclamation, however, did not address the issue of indigenous land rights (traditionally vested rights or "native title") of the area's residents.

Phumaphi used up seven whole pages (High Court 2006: 331–337) to compare the present case to the Australian "Mabo case". In this Australian counterpart, Judge Brennan differentiated between gaining sovereignty and ownership with regard to the "terra nullius" doctrine which was supposed to regulate the Crown's process of obtaining land rights. He also explained that colonial courts increasingly recognized indigenous occupation which they of course connected to common-law conceptions of lawful possession. As evidence, in the "Mabo case" Brennan referred to the 1921 court case *Amodu Tijani* in which the Privy Council not only spoke out in favour of usufruct but also of collective land rights. Such rights could be extinguished – according to Australian legal findings – by means of a specific act, such as the transfer of land rights to third parties or the explicit appropriation by the Crown itself.

Phumaphi stressed an obvious analogy to the following interpretation of law by his Australian colleagues as especially relevant: "The Court held that native

---

162 As I have mentioned several times, a strictly adaptionist interpretation is an approach far too simple, especially as it seems to be a proven fact that the San shaped their biome also actively and did not only passively adapt to their surroundings.

rights were not extinguished by the declaration of game reserves or Crown lands except where the use to which such land is put, is inconsistent with the continued existence of native rights" (High Court 2006: 336). The judge interpreted the transfer of lands to third parties for farming, living, etc., as such inconsistent use because the holders of "native rights" would not be able to enjoy their rights anymore. As Judge Brennan quoted from the court cases *In re Southern Rhodesia* of 1919 and *Odeyinka Oyekan* of 1957 though, the mere change of sovereignty did not extinguish the private rights of ownership and possession.

In this sense of legal comparison, Judge Phumaphi discussed the present legal question as analogous to the "Mabo case" and concluded from his systematic assessment that the rights of the "Bushmen" to their territories had not been affected by the British colonial government proclaiming their territories to be Crown Land: "The rights of the Bushmen in the CKGR were not affected by the proclamation of the land they occupied to be Crown land, as they continued to live on it, and exploit it without interference from the British Government. They continued to hunt and wander about the land, without let or hindrance (…). Not only is the British Government presumed (on the authority of *In re Southern Rhodesia* and *Amodu Tijani* supra), to have respected the 'native rights' of the Bushmen in the CKGR upon proclamation of the Crown land, but the fact that it considered providing them with water, so that they could remain in the CKGR, is a clear indication that it did not extinguish their 'native rights' with respect to the CKGR. The 'native rights' of the Bushmen in the CKGR were therefore not extinguished in 1910 when the Crown land was declared" (High Court 2006: 339).

In line with this approach in the Australian court case, Judge Phumaphi also evaluated whether the proclamation to become a game reserve may have extinguished the "native title". As I have described in the previous section, written evidence (primarily telegrams) indicated that the colonial government intended the game reserve to be of dual purpose: as a game reserve and as land the San can use for their economic activities. Since then, any further legislation has – after detailed evaluations – recognized the presence and thus the "native title" of the "Bushmen" to the CKGR: "I therefore find that creation of the CKGR did not extinguish the 'native title' of the Bushmen to the CKGR. It follows that since I have come to the conclusion that, neither the creation of the Ghanzi Crown land nor of CKGR extinguished the native rights of the Bushmen to CKGR, the Applicants who are part of the natives of the CKGR, were in possession of the land which they lawfully occupied in their settlements in the CKGR subsequent to the 31st January 2002" (High Court 2006: 350).

Although the *High Court of Botswana* ruled in favour of indigenous rights, this judgement should not be interpreted all too euphorically; it should be rather noted that the confirmation of the right to occupation of the San as applicants did not (explicitly) refer to the existence of indigenous land rights based on their traditionally vested rights (the "native title"). In this field of (indigenous) human rights, therefore, it falls behind the intentions of international legal developments that are based on the "honest reconciliation" for past experiences of injustice. In this regard, we should not forget either that the judgement was issued during a period of national and regional political "mobilization" against indigenous rights in the context of the *UN Declaration on the Rights of Indigenous Peoples.*

Only two weeks after Botswana had successfully put forward a motion before the *Third Committee* of the *UN General Assembly* to defer action concerning the draft declaration, the government referred to this unexpected legal defeat in various crucial points. So without any intention to overrate the judgement from the perspective of international development of indigenous rights, it still may be considered a groundbreaking success that the court's panel of three judges came to an unanimous decision, that is concerning the most important material questions of land and hunting rights. Moreover, at least one of the judges based the decision particularly and *expressis verbis* on the doctrine of "native title" as provided in the precedents of the *Privy Council* and the *High Court of Australia*, even if this reasoning did not address the actual subject of the judgement. Such a comparative perspective may, however, be interpreted as an indication that indigenous land rights based on traditionally vested systems of indigenous rights related to a certain territory are increasingly recognized on the African continent.

As with basically all comparable cases, this judgement too may be criticized from a perspective of legal philosophy and anthropology: it is based on a clear hierarchy of rights and genuinely regards European legal systems and their central ideas as hegemonically superior to indigenous understandings of law.[163]

Alice Mogwe used the present court case to question exactly this expression of the monopoly of sovereignty. The director of the human rights NGO DITSHWANELO was a member of the *Negotiating Team* which originally dealt with the problematic situation as a result of the displacement from the CKGR. She therefore had no choice but to back the decision of taking this matter to court. In her article "Human Rights Struggles Where Social Conflicts and Confrontations are Negotiated – The Case of the Displacement of Basarwa from the CKGR" (2011), she discusses those aspects opposed to a possible process of reconciliation in terms of intercultural retributive justice.

In her opinion, these disadvantages of court proceedings already begin with the official language in court: English. As generally speaking none of the San applicants knew this language, the court approved of a translation into Setswana. Therefore, one of the most important roles was given to the San college student Kuela Kiema who did not only translate for those not speaking Setswana but who also could help in case of (intercultural) misunderstandings because he

---

163 Cf. also my considerations concerning the "aboriginal title" before the South African Constitutional Court (chapter 2).

understood the deeper meaning behind the words.¹⁶⁴ In consequence, the applicants' legal representative had to trust this student's abilities when communicating with his clients. The Attorney General communicated with the San exclusively in his (own) language Setswana. All judges speak and understand Setswana. These considerations of communication theory on court proceedings alone made it clear for Mogwe (2011: 173) that the language of the dominant group in Botswana "dominated" the court case. Therefore, the omnipresent and historically-accumulated structures of dominance also continued at this level: "The language of the dominant group found its way into the court case, which itself is about the dominance of 'the other'".¹⁶⁵

In addition to this language problem, the author also reflected on other differences between the culture of the San and prevailing (western) jurisprudence. If we kept – in her words – just the nature of a court room with all its symbolism of alienation and social differentiation in mind, we would also realize the hierarchical structuring in the symbolic sphere. These structures then return in various aspects of real life: in form of individualizing witnesses or applicants, cross examinations sometimes conducted aggressively to convict a witness of lying or to shake his/her testimony, public humiliation as a consequence thereof, and generally the stark contrast to the consensual (hardly researched on) legal traditions as well as processes of dispute resolution of the San. Mogwe (2011: 174) quoted the anthropologist and witness in the proceedings Silberbauer as evidence: "[D]ecisions in a band are taken or made with consensus – it is not everyone saying that they agree or democracy, but it is a system where everyone consents to go along with the decision. The consent is made in the interest of group solidarity, even if necessarily at a cost to me or my interest."

A further problematic aspect in her analysis of interaction processes in court is the lack of understanding of western jurists for the connection between the San and their territories and the related relationship to their original birthplace. This caused quite some confusion during witness questioning, as the following example by Mogwe (2011: 175) clearly shows: the applicant Tshokodiso Botshilwane did not even leave the reserve when his hut was destroyed and the water tanks in

---

164 In 2010, the college student published the book *Tears for My Land: A Social History of the Kua of the CKGR*.
165 See also Kuela Kiema: "The court often used abstract legal and academic language, which when interpreted into the non-legal languages of Dxana or Tshila, quickly lost its meaning. Concepts such as 'wild Bushmen', 'peer review', 'social anthropology', 'colonial administration', 'master's thesis', 'research', 'government white paper', 'conservation laws' and many more simply do not exist in the Dxana languages. Although I tried very hard to 'professionalise' my interpretations of the proceedings and the use of the abstractions into Tshila/Dxana, the Kua found it hard to understand their own languages when used in this way." Cited in *The Sunday Standard* 9 May 2010.

Metsiamanong were emptied. The Attorney General put pressure on him by pointing out that his evidence of identity placed him in Kukama (around a hundred kilometres southwards). He thus tried to impeach the credibility of a witness who seemed not to even know his place of birth. As Tshokodiso Botshilwane tried to explain, the only thing that mattered to him was that he had been born on the traditional territory of his community – not the specific location: "[E]ven though they [Kukama and Metsiamanong] are different they are in the same location – they are the same to us. There are ponds which we use in both places as they are within our tribal territory and we regard them as one."

Furthermore, the San had to face numerous technical and semiological requirements due to the terminology and procedural law of the applied legal system. The *Daily News* from 4 December 2004 reported, for example, that the San Losolobe Mooketsi wanted to testify in court. All jurists involved tried to explain to him that he was not on the list of applicants and thus not a litigant. Losolobe Mooketsi, however, insisted that he could not be excluded from the proceedings because his relocation from Kikao would already characterize him as an applicant. The following example of a dialog in court (Mogwe 2011: 177) clearly illustrates the diverging understandings and concepts of law: when the Attorney General (SC) asked Amogelang Segootsane (AS) whether he was aware of the fact that the CKGR territory was state land, he answered:

> "AS: It is not mine?
> SC: In this country anybody who makes a claim to land must have a title deed to it. Are you able to show us a title deed in respect of the land which you say you own in the CKGR?
> AS: No, I have no paper – how do I get those papers?
> SC: Either answer 'yes' or 'no'!
> AS: Am I born having these papers?
> SC: Do you have any papers which show that you have the title to the land – the question is simply whether you were born with them or whether they were given to you!
> AS: As I stand here I do not have any papers.
> SC: Do they exist?
> AS: I just know that the land was given to us by God and he made us and made the land. I am not aware that God made papers so that we can go around showing papers.
> SC: When did God give you this land?
> AS: God gave it to my great great grandparents so that I would also use it as their descendant.
> SC: Where do you know this from?
> Judge: If it is a matter of law that it is State land – he would probably not know.

SC: He says ... he owns this land. When they make assertions of law they must be ready to prove them.
Judge: You expect them to know about the land tenure system?
SC: I expect them to know about the land tenure system in Botswana – they are Batswana.
Judge: He does not have any paper to show it. His view is that his land was given to his ancestors by God. I do not know if you can extract anything further."

This witness hearing does not only reveal a touching document of intercultural misunderstanding but also a redundant expression of conceptions of exclusive sovereignty in colonial and postcolonial states. In such states, the San were at best granted citizen rights whose scope and meaning they only knew selectively, if at all. So while the existing legal system is guided by the principle that "all are equal before the law", such discourse analyses show that various factors may influence any individual's chances to find "justice". Mogwe (2011: 178) proposes an innovative approach for appropriate processes solving intercultural disputes: "The appropriate processes should engage all parties in different ways, but ensure that they are rooted in mutual respect of difference and similarities, respect of cultures and concepts, ensure true consultation and participation in sustainable development, and construct coherent communities nurtured with a spirit of collective goals, mandate and mechanisms which enable accountable behaviour. For such progress to be achieved, the court route needs to be recognized as being merely a stage in the phases, which will ultimately lead to managed change for the benefit of the society."

Alice Mogwe quite rightly asks what happens after a legal dispute. For both her and the *CKGR Negotiating Team*, the only chance of a sustainable solution to the problem of relocation from the reserve was to resume negotiations supported by institutions for intercultural mediation. Considering the government's reactions after the legal dispute had ended, they may not be alone with this opinion.

On 14 December 2006, one day after the judgement in the case *Roy Sesana and others v. the Attorney General* was passed, Attorney General Athalia Molokomme issued a statement that explained how her office understood the panel's judgement. According to that, the government recognized that the applicants had lawfully occupied the CKGR before they were relocated in 2002. The reserve would continue to be state land and (unilateral) subject to its laws. Based on this legal understanding, the government intended – according to the official statement – to implement the court's judgement in the following way: all 189 applicants and their underage children may return and live in the CKGR without needing a permit; any livestock already in the CKGR may stay in the reserve but the applicants may not bring any new livestock; the applicants are considered to be entitled to take anything legal into the CKGR, this also includes building materials but only for non-permanent constructions; the applicants may arrange for water supply in the reserve which may be limited by the director of the *Depart-*

III. The Legal Dispute over the (temporarily?) "Lost Lands"

ment of Wildlife and National Parks (DWNP) as part of his management activities; any other individual (also all San not involved in the court case) still require a permit to enter the CKGR. As the government's refusal to issue special game licenses was found unlawful, the government interprets this unlawfulness as follows: the applicants are not automatically entitled to such licenses but need to file a normal application which is then individually assessed by the DWNP.

Five days after the panel of judges had come to a judgement, the government officially announced that it did not intend to file an appeal.[166] When Press Secretary Jeff Ramsay was interviewed by the newspaper *Mmegi*, he called the result of the court case a "lose-lose situation" and emphasized that the government was generally willing to enter into new talks to create a "win-win" situation (*Mmegi* 19 December 2006). Thus, the Government of Botswana showed its good will. In the beginning, it was also quite generous concerning thirty original applicants who had waived their claim in the course of proceedings. This group was granted to enter the CKGR without a permit as well. Furthermore, they were also allowed to carry an unlimited amount of water at their own expense.[167]

After the media presence of the case had slowed down, however, more and more reports came in that seemed to contradict the spirit of government's initial good will. In March 2007, for example, the government refused to issue entry permits in 17 cases, including staff of the NGO *Survival International*, BBC correspondent John Simpson and other journalists as well as human rights activists. It even denied *UN Special Rapporteur on Indigenous Issues* Rodolfo Stavenhagen to visit the country (*Anthropology Today*, June 2007). A total of 111 San had returned to the *Central Kalahari Game Reserve* by the end of March 2007. Between June and the beginning of July, police arrested 21 of them for alleged poaching. On 12 August 2007, police found five men with the carcass of an eland antelope and took them into custody. Press Secretary of the *Botswana Ministry of Foreign Affairs* Clifford Maribe commented on the arrest that hunting was prohibited in the game reserve: "The men were found in possession of an eland carcass. Hunting is not permitted inside all Game Reserves and National Parks in Botswana and the CKGR is no exception" (*Mmegi*, 5 September 2007).

Although the panel of judges of the *High Court of Botswana* unanimously found that the government's refusal to issue special game licenses was unlawful and unconstitutional, the responsible *Department of Wildlife and National Parks* (DWNP) had not issued a single such license by May 2012.[168] On the occasion of

---

166 Republic of Botswana (18 December 2006): *Tautona Times* no. 43 of 2006. *The Weekly Electronic Press Circular of the Office of the President*.
167 Republic of Botswana (18 March 2007): *Tautona Times* no. 9 of 2007. *The Weekly Electronic Press Circular of the Office of the President*.
168 Hitchcock/Daggett (2008: 510); www.survival-international.org/news/8318 as of 10 May 2012.

the consideration of Botswana's country report for the *UN Human Rights Committee*, former *Minister for Defence, Justice and Security* Phandu Skelemani justified this fact to present experts by stating that any applicant would have to apply for such a license according to the government's interpretation of the court judgement. He explained the actual rejection of several applications with the alleged poaching of the applicants. Concerning criticism against the government that the San were not allowed to use the well in Mothomelo (inside the CKGR), Minister Skelemani explained that, based on the High Court's judgement, they were not obliged to arrange for any supply or care and that the well was state property.[169]

In the meantime, several monitoring bodies of the United Nations, such as the *Human Rights Committee*, the *Working Group on the Universal Periodic Review* of the *Human Rights Council* or the *Special Rapporteur on the Rights of Indigenous Peoples*, conceded with some concern the Government of Botswana's narrow interpretation of the court's judgement.[170] According to this understanding, not all relocated individuals (a total of about 1,000) but only the 189 applicants would be subject to the High Court's ruling. In addition, the right to return to the CKGR would depend on an issued identity document. This is why, e.g., the *Human Rights Committee* recommended the Republic of Botswana to observe the court's decision and to ensure the effective protection of those concerned: "The State party should ensure that all persons who were relocated are granted the right to return to the CKGR, consistent with the reasoning of the High Court decision, and that all necessary measures are taken to facilitate the enjoyment of Covenant [on Civil and Political] rights by these persons upon their return" (United Nations 2008: para. 23).

Anyway, the Government of Botswana is still convinced that it has fully implemented the High Court's decision. Without offering any evidence of effective legal protection for the San, the only dry answer is: "The Government of Botswana has fully implemented the Court order."[171] They also recognize, however, that "real" disputes, such as the issue of the CKGR on which the court case was based, cannot be sustainably resolved in court and often need to be settled afterwards (cf. Benda-Beckmann, K. 2007: 107), as proclaimed in the *Joint Press Statement from the Government of Botswana, the CKGR Residents' Committee and the CKGR Non-Governmental Organisations' Coalition on the CKGR Consultation Process*: "Following the CKGR Court Case ruling on 13 December 2006, in which Judge Phumaphi stated that 'this judgement does not finally resolve the dispute between the parties but merely refers them back to the negotiating table'(…)".

---

169 See: www.un.org/News/Press/docs/2008/hrct696.doc.htm as of 14 April 2008. The expert meeting of the *UN Human Rights Committee* took place on 20 March 2008 (General Assembly HR/CT/696).

170 Cf. A/HRC/7/5/Add.1, para. 13f. and A/HRC/10/69: paras. 81, 91.17.

171 Republic of Botswana (6/12/08): *Tautona Times* no 40 of 2008. *The Weekly Electronic Press Circular of the Office of the President*.

III. The Legal Dispute over the (temporarily?) "Lost Lands"

On 12 June 2008, President Ian Khama sat down with five representatives of the CKGR and established an *Inter-Ministerial Committee* for further discussions to achieve such an effective result. On 26 November 2008, the first official meeting of both parties took place. They agreed that three representative bodies should be involved in the consultation process: the Government of Botswana represented by the aforementioned *Inter-Ministerial Committee* comprised of six ministries and the *Attorney General's Chamber*; the *CKGR Committee* comprised of representatives from the CKGR settlements Molapo, Mothomelo, Kikao, Gope, Kukama as well as the relocation settlements New !Xade, Kaudwane and Xere; and the *CKGR NGO Coalition* (that already operated before the 2002 relocations) comprised of six NGOs and the *University of Botswana Research Centre for San Studies* (established 2009). On 11 September 2009, the parties met again and established ground rules and an action plan for the consultation process. This plan included a schedule and programme of consultation visits of government officials in settlements inside and outside the CKGR, which actually took place in September, October and November of that year.

It took another six months for them to meet again and evaluate the *Government Official's Report on the Consultation Meetings*. In the meantime, there were more and more reports on confiscated livestock and arrests for poaching in the *Central Kalahari Game Reserve*.[172] Government officials still refused to issue special game licenses and justified their (non-) action with the never-ending litany that the *Wildlife Management and National Parks Act* (Cap. 38:01) prohibited hunting in game reserves and national parks – so for example *Minister for Defence, Justice and Security* Ramadeluka Seretse.[173] Notwithstanding the continuous rejection of special game licenses established by this act (Sect. 13 (3) and Sect. 26 or 30 (1) and Sect. 45 (1) *National Parks and Game Reserves Regulations 2000*), we still have to question whether such practice does not at least partly ignore the High Court's decision. Is Botswana really living up to the self-definition of a state under rule of law and the international image of a democratic state often described as an "African Miracle"?

After his country visit from 19 to 27 of March 2010, also *UN Special Rapporteur* James Anaya criticizes in his report *The Situation of Indigenous Peoples in Botswana* that the court order has not been implemented: "While the Government may or may not be following the order of the Court in the Sesana case in a technical sense, its position on who should be permitted to re-enter the reserve without obtaining entry permits, its restrictions on hunting and livestock possession and its denial of services to those currently living in the reserve do not appear to be in keeping with the spirit and underlying logic of the decision, nor with the relevant international human rights standards. The Sesana decision

---

172 IWGIA (2011: 476f.).
173 *The Botswana Gazette*, 7 August 2009.

would seem to suggest that all former residents of the game reserve who were relocated should be permitted to return without having to obtain entry permits and should be able to subsist and maintain a dignified life within the reserve".[174] Therefore, the question arises whether this may be considered a case of permanent, unlawful refusal of the government to implement the *High Court of Botswana*'s decision from 2006, which *inter alia* had found that not issuing special game licenses was unlawful and unconstitutional. This act of omission indicates a partial failure of the Government of Botswana to comply with fundamental principles of constitutionality and rule of law, while it backfires in providing ammunition to its adversaries to question the legitimacy of public administration in this respect.

---

174 A/HRC/15/37/Add. 2 as of 2 June 2010.

IV. The Legal Dispute over Access to Water

When the government terminated all basic and essential supply services in the *Central Kalahari Game Reserve* on 31 January 2002, its officials sealed the well in Mothomelo. Originally built for prospecting purposes, the diamond mining company De Beers had granted the *Ghanzi District Council* to use the well for supplying the settlements in the reserve with drinking water since 1986 (Maripe 2011: 55).[175] Based on the court ruling in favour of the San in 2006, (only) those San who (as the Attorney General's Chamber interpreted the decision) had been among the 189 applicants in *Roy Sesana v. Attorney General* could return to the lands of their ancestors. However, the government's failure to comply with the judgement deprived even these San of the very basis of their livelihood: they were confronted with a hunting ban and the refusal to issue special game licenses, thus facing the indirect pressure of turning from hunters to poachers. Although their livestock was (more or less) tolerated in the reserve, the situation became more than just precarious due to the lack of water.

In contrast to some romanticizing ideas about the life of hunters and gatherers, any form of living in the Kalahari has always – but especially during dry season – been extremely difficult without any existential security whatsoever. Of course the "Kalahari San" have always been able to draw on their rich ecological experience and survival skills by living on tsamma melons and other succulents in times of need. But if you have ever been to the Central Kalahari after the rainy season between June and September, you will know how inhospitable, barren, harsh and difficult this terrain really is, as the High Court judgement conceded: "The CKGR is a vast unique wilderness in an area in excess of 52,000 square kilometres. (…) It has a harsh climate, is prone to droughts and has limited and unreliable rainfalls" (High Court 2006: 145ff.).

If the residents of the CKGR wanted to have water – after Botswana's government had refused to reopen the well – there were only two ways: they could either hope that the collected water during the rainy season covered their needs over the entire period of the dry season and to afterwards live on the natural liquid from plants, or – depending on where they lived – they could take the weary journey of many kilometres on a donkey or car, if available. The nearest settlement for instance to Mothomelo is Kaudwane – over 100 km away; however, the way from Metsiamanong to the next water source is 175 km, from Molapo 223 km (200 km to New !Xade, "only" 60 km to Rakops in the north-west of the CKGR), and 70 km from Kukama or Gugamma (DITSHWANELO 2002: 23, *African Human Rights Law Report* 2006: 192ff). In the ongoing court case *Matsipane Mosetlhanyane & others v.*

---

175   See also *The Botswana Gazette*, 12 May 2010.

Attorney General, the applicants' founding affidavit (paras. 30, 31) describes the situation as follows: "Mothomelo is too far from Kaudwane to fetch water with donkeys. I can sometimes use a vehicle that I borrow from a relation in Gugamma, if I have enough money to pay for fuel and the vehicle is available and in working order. In 2008 I was able to make this journey only once. Moreover water is heavy, the track from Kaudwane to Mothomelo is very rough, and the vehicle is small. Although we are very careful with it, any water I bring from Kaudwane is normally exhausted within a couple of weeks or so" (High Court 2010: para. 26). Occasionally it was also reported that the wildlife officers only allowed each individual entering the reserve to bring 20 litres of water (Interview Mathambo Ngakaeaja 24 February 2003). It is not all too difficult to realize that these conditions make it almost impossible to live in the CKGR, or in the words of Judge Dow: "The plan, therefore, was that by the end of 31st January 2002, there would be no water, no food, and no hunting, within the Reserve. Life would simply be very hard, if not outright impossible" (High Court 2006: 253).

1. Matsipane Mosetlhanyane, Gakenyatsiwe Matsipane & further applicants v. Attorney General of Botswana (MAHLB-000393-09)

Considering the aforementioned conditions and the stagnant progress of negotiations with the government, it is hardly surprising that Matsipane Mosetlhanyane who had already been an applicant in the *Sesana case*, his wife and 18 other San filed a notice of motion with the *High Court of Botswana* on 16 July 2009 (High Court Civil Case No. MAHLB-000393-09). They sought the following orders:

"1. The refusal or failure of the Respondent to permit the Applicants to recommission at their own expense ("the Borehole") at Mothomelo (…) is unlawful and unconstitutional.
2. The refusal or failure of the Respondent to confirm that on the payment of the specified fees it will issue permits under Regulation 4 of the National Parks and Game Reserve Regulations 2000 to any reputable contractors (…) to enter the CKGR to recommission the Borehole for the aforesaid purposes is unlawful and unconstitutional.
3. The refusal or failure of the Respondent to confirm that the Applicants have the right at their own expense to sink one or more boreholes or other boreholes on land in the CKGR and to abstract and use water therefrom for domestic purposes in accordance with Section 6 of the Water Act is unlawful and unconstitutional.
4. The refusal or failure of the Respondent to confirm that on the payment of the specified fees it will issue permits under the said Regulation 4 to any reputable surveyors or contractors appointed by or on behalf of the Ap-

IV. The Legal Dispute over Access to Water   361

plicants to enter the CKGR to identify suitable sites for and to sink one or more wells or other boreholes for the aforesaid purposes is unlawful and unconstitutional" (High Court 2010: para. 1.1.–1.4.).

After the affidavits of all parties involved were filed and a consensual decision about the proceeding achieved, the court case took place before the single judge Lakhvinder Walia on 9 June 2010. The applicants, represented by Gordon Bennett (already involved in the *Sesana* case), claimed that they were in lawful occupation of their settlements in the CKGR based on the *Sesana* judgement (para. 22). Nevertheless, especially in the dry season they would suffer extremely from serious water shortages, with melons and other succulents not providing sufficient water substitutes (para. 25). This is why the applicants would be willing and able to recommission the borehole even without government resources. For this purpose, they would need the necessary permit which the government refused though (paras. 27, 31). In their affidavit, the applicants tried to illustrate the government's inhuman and humiliating attitude towards them: "(T)he government takes active steps to ensure that animals in the Reserve are given the water they require, at the same time as it refuses to allow the applicants to make their own arrangements to the same end. They are expected to grub for roots or beg from passing tourists while animals use watering holes. This is to lower in estimation or dishonour the applicants, both in their own eyes and in the eyes of others. Their need for water is regarded as less deserving of respect than that of wild animals. This constitutes degrading treatment because the applicants are thereby humiliated or debased. No respect is shown for their human dignity."[176]

The applicants based their claim on various international conventions (*Convention on the Rights of the Child*) and human rights instruments (e.g. *UN General Assembly Resolution 54/175, Report of UN High Commissioner for Human Rights on access to safe drinking water*) which had also been applied by the *High Court of South Africa* concerning the fundamental right of sufficient access to water[177] as well as Section 6 of the *Water Act* which basically regulates the right of a land's owner or occupant to sink or deepen any well or borehole.

On the whole, the defendant party represented by independent South African advocate Paul Belger basically provided statements concerning the explained water shortage and answered accusations of the government's callous and indifferent attitude towards the applicants. In their opinion, the applicants had chosen to settle in areas far from facilities provided by the government. Therefore, they did not really challenge the government's policy but had become victims of their own de-

---

176 Cited in Dinokopila (2011: 285). We may also detect the government's double standard in the fact that it granted tour operator *Wilderness Safaris* to build a tourist lodge with swimming pool in the northern part of the CKGR in December 2009.
177 *City of Johannesburg v. L. Mazibuko (489/08) [2009] ZASCA 20 (25 March 2009).*

cisions (para. 48). The respondent also stated that they would be aware of the fact that Mothomelo was almost 40 km of difficult roads from Kaudwane. Nevertheless, it had been their own choice to lead such a life and to live in areas without water: "I can therefore aver that whatever hardships the applicants are likely to face in the exercise of their choice such hardships are of the applicants own making" (para. 15 respondent's written submission in para. 34). Although the state had provided sufficient services for the "Basarwa", they would be reluctant to accept the state's decisions regarding the location of such services: "The Basarwa have been provided with reasonable access to water and other basic services outside the CKGR. In that way the Government has sought to maintain the dignity and humanity of its people by providing such services. That those resources are provided outside the CKGR enables the Government to meet both its obligation to respect the rights of its people, while still realizing its conservation objectives" (para. 53).

"Judge L.S. Walia came to the judgement on 21 July 2010: he rejected the San's claim to recommission the borehole in Mothomelo and to sink others in the CKGR. Right in the beginning, he pointed out the uncertainty on the number of applicants. The significance of the number, the judge continued, lied in the acknowledgement by the applicants' counsel that the only ones entitled to reside inside the CKGR were the 189 applicants in the *Sesana* case, while any other individual had to obtain an entry permit (paras. 4 and 7). He thus concluded that the eight persons who had not been applicants in the *Sesana* case were "not properly before me". This aspect, however, is not in any way supported by the aforementioned decision of the panel of three judges in the *Sesana* case. This ruling "only" states that the "applicants" had lawfully resided inside the CKGR before their relocations in 2002. The understanding that exclusively the applicants were entitled to live in the reserve (without permit) only arouse from the interpretation of the *Attorney General's Chambers*. As confirmed by the Court of Appeal (para. 23) and aside from not being subject of this matter, this aspect does also concern all San residing in the CKGR who are not among the applicants (2006, 2010 or for future cases) and thus violates their rights.

It is also rather surprising that Judge Walia suddenly referred to the applicants as "settlers" (paras. 25) who had "settled" in the CKGR between 2004 and 2007 (para. 24). Therefore, he does not only withhold the fact that the CKGR is the land of their ancestors from which they were relocated but also their status as indigenous peoples (in contrast to "settlers"). As the High Court noted in 2006: "[T]he Bushmen are indigenous to the CKGR which means that they were in the CKGR prior to it becoming Crown Land, thereafter a game reserve and then State land upon Botswana attaining independence" (High Court 2006: 327).

As a matter of fact, so Judge Walia continued, the present case was a sequel or consequence to the *Sesana* case and he deferred to the following majority decision: the termination by the government of basic and essential services within the CKGR was neither unlawful nor unconstitutional, the government was un-

IV. The Legal Dispute over Access to Water 363

der no obligation to restore the provision of such essential services and that the applicants were in possession of the land, they lawfully occupied (paras. 9 and 10). This basically meant that he adopted the government's attitude concerning the San's occupation and their application to recommission the borehole. The judge found that the applicants were entitled to reside in the CKGR but that this right was not confined to a specific area. Thus, they could opt to reside in an area closer to available water and other services. He laconically notes: "I therefore have some sympathy for the respondent's argument that having chosen to settle at an uncomfortably distant location, they have brought upon themselves any discomfort they may endure" (para. 74).

In essence, it should be remarked that Judge Walia seemed not to have spent too much time studying the High Court decision of 2006. Although he aligns himself with the majority decision concerning lawful possession, he does not recognize the special relationship between the San and their lands (as stated by Unity Dow in the respective decision) in any way: "For such people [indigenous peoples], the land is not merely a possession and a means of production. The entire relationship between the spiritual life of indigenous peoples and Mother Earth, and their land, has a great many deep-seated implications. Their land is not a commodity which can be acquired, but a material element to be enjoyed freely" (High Court 2006: 202).

If this fundamental understanding is missing, their free choice of settlement adapted to their special living conditions in the Kalahari does not enjoy the status it should have. Picking up on a sarcastic comparison by Judge Unity Dow between the Kalahari and New York (High Court 2006: 227), this would certainly not be the same as if applicants living in an apartment building in New York had to move from apt. 58 to apt. 18 because it would mean climbing fewer stairs and living closer to the entrance. Anyway, the judge concluded his considerations in this matter by stating that the applicants' argument would have been valid, if there had been an obligation on the government to provide water – which he deemed to be not the case (para. 77).

With regard to the issue of water law in Botswana under the *Water Act*, Judge Walia evaluated various regulations and came to the conclusion that Sect. 6 and 9 were mutually contradictory.[178] While Sect. 6 entitles the applicants according to their understanding to abstraction without approval, Sect. 9 prohibits abstraction without a water right granted under the act. If, therefore, Sect. 6 was to be interpreted as the applicants contended, Sect. 9 was superfluous (para. 92). The

---

178 "6 (1) Subject to the provisions of this Act and of any other written law, the owner or occupier of any land may, without a water right – sink or deepen any well or borehole thereon and abstract, and use water therefrom for domestic purposes (…)
9 (1) Subject to the foregoing provisions, no person shall divert, dam, store, abstract, use, or discharge any effluent into, public water or for any such purpose construct any works, except in accordance with a water right granted under this Act."

judge thus found that their interpretation was clearly inconsistent with the requirement of authorization provided in Sect. 9 (para. 102), which is why they were not entitled to abstract water in the CKGR, not even at their own expense. By applying the rules of interpretation, Judge Walia tried to resolve the inconsistency between both sections and came to the "obvious result that Section 9 prevails". In consequence, any person was only entitled to abstract water by authorization (para. 104). As, therefore, the respondent's refusal or failure to issue a permit was neither unlawful nor unconstitutional, the application was dismissed (paras. 108, 109).

Again the world was filled with headlines, such as "High Court Judgement Cuts the Ground (Water) From Under the Bushmen's Feet" (*Kurier* 23 July 2010) [179]. Of course the NGO *Survival International* too surfed on the wave of anger by trying once again to hit Botswana's economic nerve: "In the last ten years Botswana has become one of the harshest places in the world for indigenous peoples. If Bushmen are to be denied water on their lands when it is freely provided for tourists, animals, and diamond mines, then foreigners should be asked if they really want to support this regime with their visits and jewellery shopping."[180] There were also serious voices of concern regarding the situation of the San in the CKGR. The *African Commission on Human and Peoples' Rights* urged the Government of Botswana to act in the spirit of the decision from 2006 and to grant the San access to water (despite the dismissed application). The statement emphasized that the *Sesana* judgement was in full compliance with the *African Charter* and in particular with Art. 2, 4, 19 and 24, which Botswana had ratified on 27 July 1986: "Refusal to allow the Bushmen to use their existing borehole at Mothomelo can only be interpreted as a clear sign that the Government of Botswana is determined to continue what is perceived as a policy of keeping the Bushmen from returning home" (ACHPR Press Release 10, August 2010).

Exactly one week after the application was dismissed, on 28 July 2010, the *UN General Assembly* adopted the *Resolution on Human Rights and Access to Safe Drinking Water and Sanitation* with an overwhelming majority.[181] This resolution recognizes "the right to safe and clean drinking water as a human right that is essential for the full enjoyment of life and all human rights" (para. 1). On 30 September 2010, the *Human Rights Council* approved of the aforementioned resolution by adopting a resolution which affirmed that "the human right to safe drinking water and sanitation is derived from the right to an adequate standard of living and inextricably related to the right to the highest attainable standard

---

179 Original headline from the Austrian newspaper "*Kurier*": "Urteil der Höchstrichter gräbt Buschleuten das Wasser ab".
180 Director of *Survival International* Stephen Corry on 21 July 2010.
181 UNHRC Resolution (A/RES/64/292); 122 voted in favour of the resolution, while 41 states including Botswana abstained from voting.

of physical and mental health, as well as the right to life and human dignity" (A/HRC/15/L.14). All these resolutions as well as the dismissal of the application to recommission the borehole inside the CKGR took place in a period that the *UN General Assembly* had declared/proclaimed the *International Decade for Action*, "Water for Life", 2005–2015.[182] On 1 September 2010, the San appealed against the judgement of dismissal in order to claim their rights to water and thus their fundamental human rights.

2. Matsipane Mosetlhanyane & Gakenyatsiwe Matsipane v. Attorney General of Botswana, Court of Appeal (CALB-074-10)

The appeal against Judge Walia's judgement of dismissal was allowed and the hearing before the Court of Appeal's panel of five judges was scheduled for 17 January 2011. In their written judgement ten days later, the judges set aside the High Court's judgement and unanimously decided in favour of the applicants on all counts: the San were entitled to recommission the borehole in Mothomelo at their own expense, to sink further boreholes, and to abstract water for domestic purposes (para. 25). Furthermore, the conclusion stated that the government subjected the San to inhuman and degrading treatment by rejecting the applicants' request.

In contrast to High Court Judge Walia, the judges showed empathy dealing with the San's human suffering and despair: "I observe at once that it is a harrowing story of human suffering and despair caused by a shortage of water in the harsh climatic conditions of the Kalahari Desert where the appellants and their 'Basarwa' community live" (para. 4).[183] Four paragraphs later, they again emphasize the degree of suffering by quoting the applicants' conditions of living: "Very often the appellants and other members of the various communities in the reserve do not have enough water to meet their needs. They depend on melons which are either scarce or sometimes non-existent. As a result, life becomes 'extremely difficult'. They spend a great deal of their time in the bush 'looking for any root or other edible matter from which we can extract even a few drops of water'. The absence of water frequently makes them 'weak and vulnerable to sickness'. Some of them suffer from 'constipation, headaches or bouts of dizziness'. Often they do not sleep well. Young children 'cry a great deal'. Often they do not have water to cook or to clean themselves" (para. 8).

The panel of five judges did not consider it to be far-fetched that a dismantled and removed pump during the 2002 relocations could lead to the conclusion as a matter of overwhelming probability that this had been designed to induce

---

182 (A/RES/58/217)
183 Justice of Appeal M. M. Ramodibedi wrote the judgement on behalf of the court.

the residents to relocate by making it as difficult as possible for them to stay in the CKGR (para. 7). In their opinion, the reason for the relocations had exclusively been nature conservation: "The reasons for this decision [the relocation] were (1) that the CKGR should now be used solely for conservation of wildlife and (2) that human settlements were incompatible with conservation of wildlife" (para. 6). Therefore, the judges contradicted the government's repeated position that the entire relocation was only for the San's own benefit: "The intention of Government is to bring the standard of living of Basarwa up to the level obtaining in the rest of the country (...)".[184] Improved development opportunities outside of the reserve, as claimed by government, were not seen as sufficient reasons for a policy of "leave or die".

It also was the respondent's case that the bringing of water tanks or similar facilities into the CKGR would seriously and negatively compromise the reserve's purpose. Thus, there would be an undoubted probability that the CKGR would be turned from a game and conservation reserve into a human habitation, according to this view. This would then "endanger the life of wild animals and fauna generally". It so happened that the government had declared and "zoned" the CKGR a wildlife reserve and fauna conservation area, so whatever hardships the applicants were facing were of their own making (para. 10). The judges considered the reliance on this zoning policy to become a reserve as a "non-starter". On the one hand, the applicants' occupation of the CKGR had preceded the zoning policy. As the High Court unanimously found in the *Sesana* case: "Prior to 31 January 2002, the applicants were in possession of the land, which they lawfully occupied in their settlements in the CKGR." On the other hand, the decision upheld their right of continuing occupation because the court had established that the applicants had unlawfully been deprived of their possession and that the refusal of granting them access was unlawful and unconstitutional. The government did not appeal against this court order. This is why the argument of zoning was rejected and the only conclusion in those circumstances was to find the applicants lawful occupiers of their settlements in the CKGR (para. 12).

Afterwards, the panel of five judges addressed Judge Walia's assessment of the inconsistency between two sections of the *Water Act* as well as his conclusion that an owner or occupier of land intending to sink or deepen any borehole was only allowed to do so in accordance with a water right granted under the act. Considering the wording "subject to" in Sect. 9, the Court of Appeal concluded that Sect. 6 is the more dominant of both sections. The reason behind this norm is the fact that water is rare in Botswana, which is why lawful occupiers of land must be able to get underground water for domestic purposes. Otherwise their occupation of land would become meaningless. In line with these considerations, the

---

184 www.gov.bw/basarwa/background.html as of 8 August 2004.

applicants as lawful occupiers do not require a water right to use the borehole in Mothomelo (paras. 15–16).

The respondent then contended that the borehole at Mothomelo was in fact not a borehole but a "prospecting hole". It thus was not subject to the provisions and qualified as public water. In the judges' opinion, this argument ignored the uncontested evidence that the original prospecting hole had ceased to be such long before the time in question (para. 17). In a nutshell, the court had not heard any legal basis for the government's refusal to allow the applicants the use of the borehole at Mothomelo. Furthermore, they were not able to find that the government had been entitled to seal the borehole. The judges thus repeated for emphasis that the applicants did not need a water right to use the borehole at Mothomelo at their own expense for domestic purposes. They were exactly in the same position as the original applicants in the *Sesana* case (para. 18).

The last issue addressed by the panel was the violation of constitutional law which Judge Walia should have dealt with but rejected because it had not been pleaded. The Court of Appeal, however, considered this point sufficiently raised and referred to in the papers to have justified an appropriate amendment of the notice of motion (para. 19). Section 7 (1) of the Constitution established an absolute and unlimited torture ban without reservations: "No person shall be subjected to torture or to inhuman or degrading punishment or other treatment." The court's evaluation of a single case regarding this fundamental principle of prohibited torture or inhuman or degrading treatment involves a value judgement, which then entitles the court to consider international consensus: "It is appropriate to stress that in the exercise of a value judgement, the Court is entitled to have regard to international consensus on the importance of access to water" (para. 19). For this purpose, the panel of judges referred to two international legal documents establishing the right to water as a fundamental human right. Furthermore, specific forms of discrimination concerning indigenous peoples and other socially disadvantaged groups were taken into consideration:

"16. Whereas the right to water applies to everyone, State parties should give special attention to those individuals and groups who have traditionally faced difficulties in exercising this right, including woman, children, minority groups, indigenous peoples, (…) In particular, States parties should take steps to ensure that:
(d) Indigenous people's access to water resources on their ancestral lands is protected from encroachment and unlawful pollution. States should provide resources for indigenous peoples to design, deliver and control their access to water."[185]

---

185 *General Comment No. 15 (2002) of the UN Committee on Economic, Social and Cultural Rights: The Right to Water* (Art. 11 and 12 of CESCR) E/C.12/2002/11.

Applying a value judgement to the case, the court held: "Indeed, I accept that there is a constitutional requirement based on international consensus (…) for Government to refrain from inflicting degrading treatment" (para. 22).[186] The factors of the aforementioned account by the first applicant of the human suffering and difficult life without water in the CKGR (para. 8) eventually came down to degrading treatment. When the Government of Botswana had refused to grant the San access to water, it violated constitutional provisions. Therefore, the appeal was allowed and the order of the High Court had to be substituted. On 27 January 2011, the Court of Appeal unanimously made the following order (para. 25):

"1. It is declared that the applicants have the right at their own expense
1.1 To re-commission the borehole at Mothomelo in the Central Kalahari Game Reserve ("the Reserve") formally used to provide water to the residents of the Reserve, and to sink one or more further boreholes at such site inside the Reserve as the surveyor or borehole engineer they may employ may advise them is most likely to achieve the purpose referred to in paragraph 1.3.
1.2 To service, repair and maintain in good working order any borehole to which this declaration applies.
1.3 To use water abstracted from any such borehole for domestic purposes only, in accordance with section 6 of the Water Act.
1.4 By themselves or their agents to bring into the Reserve, and to the extent necessary to enable any borehole to which this declaration applies can be used for the purposes referred to in paragraph 1.3 to retain therein
1.4.1 any rig, machinery, plant or other equipment that they may reasonably require to carry out the works referred to in paragraph 1.1 and 1.2; and
1.4.2 any water tank that they may reasonably require to store water abstracted from any borehole to which this declaration applies, prior to its domestic use.
1.5 To obtain such advice or assistance from persons resident outside the Reserve as they may reasonably require to carry out the works referred to in paragraphs 1.1 or 1.2 and to transport the materials referred to in paragraph 4.
PROVIDED THAT
(1) Unless it has reasonable grounds to believe that a person for a purpose referred to in paragraph 1.5 is not competent or is of bad repute, on payment of the requisite fee the Department of Wildlife shall issue an entry permit to him on terms that enable him to complete his task within a reasonable period.

---

186 Thus, the court diverged from practicing the transformation theory, meaning not to adopt any international human rights treaty into state law without an explicit act of law; cf. also Maripe (2011: 57).

IV. The Legal Dispute over Access to Water   369

   (2) The Department of Wildlife may direct any such person to leave the
       Reserve if it has reasonable grounds to believe that he has failed to comply
       with the terms of his permit or that his continued presence therein is likely
       to be detrimental to the interests of the Reserve.
   (3) If and when the Department of Wildlife refuses to issue a permit under
       (1) or directs a person to leave the Reserve under (2) it shall inform
       the applicants orally and in writing and the applicants' authorised
       representatives in writing of the grounds on which it has done so.
   (4) Before the borehole at Mothomelo is deepened or any new borehole is
       sunk, the requisite notice shall be given to the Director of Geological
       Surveys of Botswana pursuant to section 4 of the Borehole Act and that
       Act shall apply to any work carried out in accordance with the notice.
 2. The respondent shall pay costs including the costs of two counsels."

From the perspective of legal anthropology, this decision is ground-breaking. Therefore, it seemed only fair in this context to discuss it in every detail. After all, the reviewed judgement of the Court of Appeal dealt with nothing less but the all-determining question of survival in the Central Kalahari: access to water. For this purpose, I considered also the legal technicalities to be essential. Their fundamental relevance could develop giving direction to future legal disputes in the complex relationship between the Government of Botswana and the country's indigenous communities.

3. Consequences of the Courts' Decisions: Summary

Both the judgement of the *Court of Appeal of the Republic of Botswana* 2011 and the High Court decision 2006 have meant a welcome development with regard to the indigenous (human) rights of the San in Botswana – and particularly after the judgement of dismissal of High Court Judge Walia in 2010. The latter ruling, however, can only be considered a misjudgement from a human rights point of view and may be owed to preemptive obedience to government. Since the principle of the indivisibility and interdependence of all human rights was realized, the understanding has gradually prevailed that all human rights go hand in hand with the states' obligations of recognition, enforcement and protection. The obligation to respect requires states to refrain from interfering with existing access. Obligations to fulfill or ensure call on states to adopt the necessary measures to enable and assist individuals to enjoy their human rights and to ensure direct provision as a last resort, when individuals are, for reasons beyond their control, unable to provide for themselves. Finally, obligations to protect require states to prevent third parties from interfering with the enjoyment of human rights by others (Nowak 2002: 62ff.).

As recognized in the appeal (2011: para. 19) and established by several UN resolutions by the *General Assembly* and the *Human Rights Council* as well as reports and human rights documents (ICESCR, ICCPR, CERD), the right to water is a fundamental human right, the implementation of which states are obliged as comprehensively as possible. The right to safe drinking water is explicitly mentioned *inter alia* in the international UN conventions CEDAW and CRC as well as in regional documents in the context of the African Union, the *African Charter on the Rights and Welfare of the Child* and the *Protocol to the African Charter on Human and Peoples' Rights on the Rights of Women in Africa*. Furthermore, there is a close connection between the access to safe water and several human rights, such as the right to life, the prohibition of torture, the right to health, and the right to adequate standards of living.[187]

These state obligations of respecting human rights also need to both *de iure* and *de facto* eradicate all forms of discrimination as well as to pay special attention to weaker parts of the population, as Catarina de Albuquerque, an independent expert on the issue of human rights obligations related to access to safe drinking water and sanitation, states: "They [states] are obliged to pay priority attention to groups and individuals particularly vulnerable to exclusion and discrimination. Depending on the circumstances, they may need to adopt positive measures to redress existing discrimination" (Albuquerque 2010: para. 20). Considering especially this huge amount of international as well as regional legal documents and decisions, it seems more than surprising that High Court Judge Walia emphasized the relevance of water while negating these state obligations based on the applicants' place of residence in the CKGR. Like the Court of Appeal's assessment (2011: para. 7) of the real reasons for sealing the borehole at Mothomelo, it is my opinion that the intentions of making the San's life in the reserve as difficult as possible and to "induce" them to relocate were reflected in his judgement.

As already mentioned, the Court of Appeal's decision is exceptionally important because it has (once again) proved that Botswana is a state under the rule of law with an independent judiciary. In a matter that appears as a conundrum of value judgements on the "pro indigenous" vs. the "pro development" divide, both in Botswana and internationally, the Court of Appeal in fact amazingly demonstrated the independence of courts and ultimately also moral courage. It stayed clear of the emotional debate and weighed the disputed rights on the scale of constitutional regulations and international developments in human rights law, as Dinokopila (2001: 293) remarks as well: "It is beyond doubt that the issue of the Basarwa living in the CKGR is heavily contested, pitting the government of Botswana against local NGOs, such as DITSHWANELO – The Centre for

---

187 The question why the Court of Appeal only considerd two non-binding resolutions by the *UN General Assembly* must remain subject to speculations though.

IV. The Legal Dispute over Access to Water 371

Human Rights, and international NGOs, such as *Survival International*. By its [Court of Appeal] decision it has shown that, indeed, the judiciary in Botswana is committed to the protection of human rights as enshrined in the Constitution."

A further astonishing point of the Court of Appeal was the enforcement of socio-economic rights by making a detour to civil and political rights. Spread over thirteen articles, the Constitution of Botswana from 1966 guarantees so-called classic but not socio-economic civil rights.[188] As the court sought to legally enforce the San's right to water, it applied the civil right provided by the relatively extensive prohibition of inhuman or degrading treatment in sect. 7 of the Constitution. Aside from the fact that the applicants being lawful occupiers enjoyed the right to water anyway, the panel of five judges also found that their constitutional rights had been violated (2011: para. 22). In the absence of socio-economic rights, it happens quite often in similar cases that civil rights, such as the right to life, non-discrimination or freedom from inhuman and degrading treatment, are legally enforced. Also Judge Unity Dow assumed such a legal position in her dissenting opinion in the *Sesana* case: "The right to life is a constitutional right and the termination of essential services was, in essence, a breaching of that right" (High Court 2006: 256).

Similar to other cases of recognized cultural rights of minorities,[189] also the Court of Appeal fully exploited its scope of interpretive competence. Time and again, the progressive approaches of both supreme courts to come to a decision by taking into account legal standards of international human rights as well as indigenous rights seem to counterbalance ethnic differences enshrined in both statutory and constitutional law as well as insufficiently provided socio-economic rights.

In any case, this court order should definitely be considered a success for the applicants because they finally found a remedy for the injustice they had been suffering from. In addition, this case included another amazing development, as the application was extended to *all* members of the applicants' community in the CKGR: "It remains to say that the appellants litigated on their own behalf and for the members of their community in the CKGR" (Court of Appeal 2011: para. 24). Nevertheless, the question whether the court intended to use this extension to stress the collective character of the San as indigenous peoples or just sought to ensure the (individual) human rights of the entire San community in the CKGR must remain subject of further speculations. In this context, it may be criticized that the written court order did not mention the indigenous sta-

---

188 In their *Concluding Observations and Recommendations on the Initial Periodic Report of the Republic of Botswana*, also the *African Commission on Human and Peoples' Rights* voiced its concerns that Botswana's Constitution did not recognize economic, social, cultural or environmental rights (ACHPR 2010: para. 33).

189 Cf. *Shikati Calvin Keene Kamanakao, Kamanakao Association and Motssamai Keyecwe Mpho v. The Attorney General of Botswana and Kgosi Tawana Moremmi II* MISCA No 377/99.

tus of the San (and thus the related both historical and current inequalities and discriminations) at all. Although Judge of Appeal Ramodibedi quoted the *General Comment No. 15 (2002) of the Committee on Economic, Social and Cultural Rights* with regard to the specific consideration of, *inter alia,* indigenous peoples in terms of water rights, he did not in any way comment on or further elaborate this quote for the concrete case of the San in Botswana.

It may be that we can detect the indirect recognition of the applicants as indigenous peoples between the lines (specifically in para. 16(d)). The legal dispute of water rights, however, did not include the explicit legal terminology of the development of indigenous rights, as it had been used by the High Court in the *Sesana* case. The panel of judges may have backed away from using this terminology because they had arguably put their heads above the parapet already and possibly did not want to overstep the decision mark. Once you have recognized the special relationship and connection between indigenous peoples and their territories (and the related water rights) – "current wisdom" as Judge Unity Dow called it (High Court 2007: para. 196) – it is of course inevitable to ensure (international and regionally African) legal protection for indigenous peoples.

In the end, the Court of Appeal's decision received quite some positive feedback both at the national (with a few exceptions) and the international level. While the court first and foremost confirmed the right to water, it also ensured the San's right of possession of their territories in the CKGR. When it comes to the Government of Botswana's attitude towards "its" indigenous population, however, the result is less positive. They did not only gain national and international attention due to negative headlines but when the government *de facto* fell short to implement the *Sesana* court order, their reputation of acting sincerely obliged to the rule of law was damaged. "It would seem the attitude of the Government was motivated by a desire for revenge following the 'success' of the *Basarwa* in the *Sesana* case" (Maripe 2011: 58). Time will tell whether the government will reassess its negative attitude towards the San and their related diverging understandings of law. The latest developments do not seem to be all too positive though. On 28 January 2011, just one day after the court's order was proclaimed, the Government of Botswana released a *Press Statement on the Decision of the Court of Appeal*:

"The Government of Botswana has noted the decision of the Court of Appeal in the case in which some residents of the Central Kalahari Game Reserve succeeded in their claim to use the Mothomelo borehole located in the Reserve at their own expense. While we do not agree with certain aspects of the basis on which the decision was reached, we recognise that this is a decision of Botswana's highest court from which there is no appeal. As such, the Government of Botswana will, in line with its established policy of respect for the decisions of the Courts and the rule of law, facilitate implementation of the decision of the Court as reflected in the order. (…) The Botswana Government is of the firm

IV. *The Legal Dispute over Access to Water* 373

view that the CKGR is a national resource to be used for the benefit of all citizens of Botswana, and that any issues regarding the reserve cannot be resolved by recourse to the Courts (...)."¹⁹⁰

The first thing we can notice here is that the government does not agree with certain aspects on which the decision was based. As they are not mentioned, we could only speculate on them. It is much more serious, however, that a government questions a decision of an independent court of justice. It only recognizes the fact that the decision was made by Botswana's highest court, meaning that they cannot appeal against such a judgement. Although the government then proclaims its policy of respect for court decisions and the rule of law, which is why it intends to implement the court's decision, a sour aftertaste of reluctant and halfhearted obedience remains. Nevertheless from a pragmatic point of view, we should not overestimate this dogmatic political statement and rather pay attention to the government's good will of following the court order: "The Government of Botswana's compliance with this ruling is important not simply because non-compliance is an indicator of the failures of justice in Botswana, but also because it is indicative of the willingness of the GOB [Government of Botswana] to finally confront its poor relationship with the San and to work towards ameliorating many of the socio-economic issues that marginalize this group and other minorities in Botswana" (Cook/Sarkin 2010: 40).

Finally, the statement also emphasizes the government's strong conviction that the CKGR is a national resource to be used for the benefit of all citizens of Botswana. As it has already recognized after the *Sesana* case, a sustainable solution requires further dialog. Considering all the legal disputes after the initial case in 2002, this conflict seems to have an underlying problem: the government's attitude towards the applicants and the recourse to a top-down version of governance. There can be no doubt that the present controversy is embedded in a much wider historical context. As long as the government applies a hegemonic or even paternalistic approach to see the concerned San communities exclusively as underdeveloped citizens, the aforementioned problems will not be resolved. As *Minister of Environment, Wildlife and Tourism* Kitso Mokaila tried to enlighten everybody in a BBC interview: "I don't believe you would want to see your own kind living in the dark ages in the middle of nowhere as a choice, when you know that the world has moved forward and has become so technological."¹⁹¹

On the occasion of the opening ceremony of the diamond mine Jwaneng's Cut 8 extension project on 10 December 2010, President Ian Khama played quite a similar tune and understandably condemned *Survival International*'s an-

---

190 Republic of Botswana – Office of the President: *Government Press Statement on the Decision of the Court of Appeal* (28/1/11).
191 BBC News Africa 3 November 2010.

ti-Botswana campaign, while almost legitimizing their actions by describing the San's life in the CKGR as backwards and primitive:

"(…) It is only our misguided detractor Survival International who would like to see all the socio-economic benefits from diamonds for all our citizens reversed, by embarking upon a campaign of lies and misinformation that seeks to achieve for **a section of our population a life of backwardness** that appeals to their racist mentality of having people in Africa **live a primitive life of deprivation co-existing alongside wild animals as was the case in the past**. All our people must benefit from our development. No Motswana should exist as a tourist object to satisfy the desires of a few misguided foreigners living relatively well off with all the benefits they enjoy in a developed economy while wanting to satisfy their fantasies by trying to influence some of our people to live a primeval life of a bygone era of hardship and indignity. We at least in this country consider all people to be equal, whichever continent they live on. Their campaign to encourage people to boycott our diamonds and tourism would negatively affect the welfare of all Batswana thus exposing the myth that they claim to care for people. The opposite is the truth, as demonstrated by their on-going actions. They really only care for themselves and use these campaigns to appeal to donors' emotions, so they may benefit from funding" (emphasis added).

President Khama is quite right to criticize a few romanticizing themes of the political commitment for the San as idealizing versions of the concept of the "primitive native" which particularly anthropology developed in former times. Emerging from an isolationist theory of evolution based on separation and difference, this understanding on the one hand correctly emphasizes the rich culture and precious cultural heritage of the San, while on the other hand reduces their essence to a pre-constructed and isolated existence of hunters and gatherers. This essentialism is the most widespread form of simplified representation. Interestingly, it is particularly politicians who apply these "eye-catching" pictures of "primitive life of deprivation co-existing alongside wild animals" to all those San who have decided for themselves to live in the CKGR. In this sense they commit the same mistake of primitivism they accuse others of, yet with inverse intentions. This prejudice of a "primitive life" whether abhorred or adored is based on a simple value-judgement of appropriate ways of life. It appears fairly ironic that the negative appraisal of "a primeval life of a bygone era" shares the same base with the denounced "desires of a few misguided foreigners living relatively well off with all the benefits they enjoy in a developed economy" of a premodern "Stone Age" way of life. Its simplified juxtaposition of preconceived notions of modernity with a presumably anachronistic lifestyle does not do any justice to the legitimate free choice of individuals to determine their preferences. In the end, you do not have to be an ethno-romanticist to compare the living conditions of, for example, the "Kalahari capital" Ghanzi – with all archetypal "achievements of modernity" such as unemployment, ethnic discrimination, social hopelessness

IV. The Legal Dispute over Access to Water

and the related side effects of alcoholism, domestic violence and dependence on charity – and those in the Kalahari and consider the first to be hardly promising.

After all, about 600 San lived in five communities within the CKGR at the end of 2011 (IWGIA 2012: 497). This figure is completely different from what the *Botswana Population and Housing Census 2011* indicated: only 268 San in five settlements (Kikao 8, Kugamma 30, an estimated 98 in Metsiamanong, an estimated 130 in Molapo and Mothomelo 2). The reason the population census provided such vague data on the settlements Metsiamanong and Molapo possibly was the fact that the San of the CKGR were not allowed to vote at the general elections of 2009. *Gantsi District Commissioner* Utlwang Kerekang justified the fact that voters of the five settlements had not been registered with the (well-known) government policy that services are not provided within the CKGR. In consequence, the San refused to cooperate with the census bureau. Roy Sesana, first applicant of the 2006 dispute, commented on their rejection of the census as follows: "They should count us among the dead. We do not get water, the food basket, health services, or old-age pension. They say the main objective of the census is to keep records for planning, but we do not exist anywhere in government records."[192]

Of course such statements, attitudes and events create doubts about the positive development of legal-political relations and peaceful coexistence. Definitely positive, however, was the implementation of the order to recommission the borehole at Mothomelo. It is unclear whether this more or less quick implementation had anything to do with the involvement or funding of *Gem Diamonds Limited*, an international diamond mining company that obtained mining rights for the Gope mine in the CKGR in January 2011.[193] On 10 August 2011, the company published a press statement that they would work with the international development-aid NGO *VOX United* to present the residents of Mothomelo, Met-

---

192 *Mmegi Online* Vol. 27 No. 10, 21 January 2010 and *The Monitor*, 25 July 2011.
193 *Gem Diamonds Limited*, founded by current CEO Clifford Elphick, former personal assistant of Harry Oppenheimer and member of the De Beers executive committee, holds a 25-years mining license after buying the mine at Gope from De Beers and Xstrata for USD 34 million in May 2007. Interestingly, they renamed the mine "Ghaghoo Diamond Mine" in July 2011: "The name change to Ghaghoo Diamond Mine resulted from numerous consultations with the residents of the CKGR and reflects the Company's ongoing commitment to encouraging community involvement and building strong community relations. 'Ghaghoo' refers to a species of camel thorn acacia tree which is abundant in the area, and is the name which residents of the CKGR have historically used to refer to the Gope area, prior to the arrival of the geological exploration teams over thirty years ago who re-named the area Gope, which literally translated, means 'nowhere'" *(Press Statement Gem Diamonds* on 25 July 2011). For more information on the company's commitment to principles and practices of sustainable development and Corporate Social Responsibility (CSR), cf. their website http://www.gemdiamonds.com/gem/en/sustainable-development/our-policies (accessed 20 September 2012)

siamanong, Molapo and Gope with four new boreholes at the end of August. On 20 March 2012, the World Water Day, drinking and bathing San in Mothomelo caught the attention of the media.[194]

Unfortunately, the sinking of boreholes in the CKGR was the only observable progress. In the meantime, an increasing number of arrests for poaching of individual San have been reported. In contrast, not a single hunting license has been issued yet (contrary to the court order of 2006). Since May 2012, media reports indicated that the Government of Botswana has begun sending soldiers as well as police and DWNP officers into the reserve to intimidate the San and establish a permanent camp near Metsiamanong.[195] After the two court decisions (in favour of the San), it does not seem to be the case that the Government of Botswana is willing to start conversations on an equal footing in order to find a sustainable solution or to change the political climate towards participatory forms of governance. As (almost) always in such cases, a consensual solution to the problem will depend on the stronger side's intentions. Once again, it remains to be seen whether the government is willing to seek consent as well as to observe the decisions of both the High Court and the Court of Appeal in its administrative policies. In the context of the complex relationship between the government and "its" indigenous peoples, such an approach would certainly confirm the (good) reputation of a state under rule of law. At any rate, the settlement of disputes in court enabled the San to formally return to their territories in the CKGR. Not only can they enjoy their right to water but the courts also recognized their indigenous rights to the lands of their ancestors they had already believed to be lost.

---

194 *Survival International:* http://www.survivalinternational.org/news/8187; http://www.survivalinternational.org/films (accessed 20 September 2012); http://voxunited.org/back-in-the-ckgr (accessed 27 December 2011).

195 *Survival International* on 10 May 2012. Online: http://www.survivalinternational.org/news/8318 (accessed on 20 September 2012).

Part 7: Conclusion

Since its independence in 1966, Botswana's government has stood out among many other African countries because of its "triumvirate of democracy, rule of law and economic stability" – a combination that is quite rare on the African continent. The successive governments have undoubtedly achieved a lot: economic prudence, reduction of poverty, and the promotion of a liberal democracy with reasonable freedom of opinion and of the press. All these cardinal virtues of politics are reflected in various factors. Amongst other aspects, these include the accountability of state institutions, a level of corruption that is even below rates of some European states, the willingness to invest in infrastructure measures, and a variety of social norms: they are perhaps among the rather visionary postcolonial institutions in the field of protecting nature, landscapes and animals. At a time when environmental awareness was still in its infancy even in international contexts, Botswana began placing wide areas of its country under protection. This even included extensive zones that seemed not to be economically exploitable by tourism. From this point of view, the conservationist measures to preserve biodiversity can hardly be praised enough.

In the context of cultural diversity, however, quite the opposite is true although numerous state documents mention this sector affirmatively. Further research is certainly needed to resolve the formation of this obvious cognitive dissonance. While especially applying a discourse-theoretical or cognitive approach, such works would have to dare entering the sphere of the praxeological development of cosmovisions. This means all those processes of learning that have formed the basis of the prevailing paradigms of development (ideology) in the elite that received its education primarily in Europe and partly in the United States. The present work of legal anthropology may only raise the question whether such an analysis could reveal possible explanations for Eurocentric imperatives that seem to govern this unequal relationship. From the legal perspective of this book, I could only make certain well-founded assumptions about evolutionist attitudes that have been created in western (and primarily British) educational institutions, which many of today's elite leaders attended in the second half of the last century.

Drawing on Darwin's teachings of biological evolution may lead to a conservationist attitude towards nature but the same teachings in a Social Darwinist twist possibly also create a contrary impulse of adaptation and "progress" imposed on backwards-constructed parts of the population. Numerous aforementioned statements of "Stone Age cultures" and the "necessary adaptation to modern times" indicate such an interpretation of policies which allow minorities and indigenous peoples hardly any scope of self-determination and only few or no rights at all. Further reasons seem to be manifold and date back to colonial experiences before independence. Nevertheless, they are also clearly connected to the postcolonial objectives of a unified state, nation building and the general equality of the nation state and "Tswanadom". In this sense, the real reasons for the problematic approach to indigenous interests are rather found in unreflected values than in rational thinking. This is why I have addressed Botswana's "Kalahari policies" that have become the centre of national discussions and enjoy great international attention particularly in the context of the relocation of San communities from the *Central Kalahari Game Reserve*. My discussion of these policies is structured on three different levels: legally, politically and communicatively.

In the legal sphere, Botswana is for the most part shaped by a distinct constitutionalism. Along the lines of western democracies and the constitutional rule of law, the country makes decisions in parliament, basically observes civil rights, and ensures the separation of powers. When it comes to the protection and development of indigenous rights, however, Botswana falls behind other countries like South Africa and Namibia. It has not only refused to establish or at least recognize such rights in the context of its legal system, the Constitution as well as statutory laws also discriminate against all other members of ethnic communities in relation to the eight "major tribes" of the Tswana.

This analysis of the government's stance is not established on the political agenda of a few NGOs following arguably their own interests (such as *Survival International*) but is rather based on the decisions of the country's highest courts (aside from numerous national and international human rights organizations and expert opinions). Elements of prevailing inter-"Batswana" discrimination are reflected in the establishment of the *House of Chiefs*, the formation of district boundaries, the choice of the official and national language, development projects only focused on care and poverty, and of course legislation particularly with regard to land rights. It may be that these inequalities were created in the past but the Republic of Botswana still does not really try to correct such human rights deficits.

On the political level, the postcolonial governments of Botswana similarly departed from the British colonial government and focused on nation-building. Accordingly, they considered the Tswana as some sort of dominant culture directed towards nation-state unity as well as the central authority in a two-fold way of their power monopoly in state politics. In this sense, the state's elite time and again stresses – in spite of or even because of their affirmative emphasis on cultural diversity – "communitarianism" and nationalism. These concepts are at least implicitly also used to legitimize assimilative attitudes towards "non-Tswana" as "inferior or less appropriate" cultural traditions. For the purpose of balancing ethnic diversity and common citizenship as well as for the benefit of nation-building, the postcolonial government may have also implemented a strategy of Jacobin republicanism, as Berman/Eyoh/Kymlicka generally call it in their edited volume "Ethnicity & Democracy in Africa" (2004: 17f.). This way of thinking borrowed from the French model of integrative citizenship basically means "de-ethnicizing". It starts on the premise that all citizens must assimilate to a certain national language (Setswana), culture (dominant Tswana culture) and identity ("typical" Motswana). This citizenship is supposed to be equally shared by all and forms the essential precondition of national unity. Minorities and indigenous peoples interpret the government's actions to support the development of a "national" or "universal" state language and culture as attempts of the dominant group to privilege its specific language and culture over their own. In consequence, they hardly, if at all, identify with the state and rather pursue the contrary direction of questioning the (moral) legitimacy of the government or state.

As already mentioned, this has also to do with problems of interaction connected to vertical hierarchy. In my opinion, the key problem on a communicative level is also legally relevant. This can be clearly seen in the discussed example of discourses in the court case *Roy Sesana v. Government of Botswana*. Similarly, communicative misunderstandings also turn into problems of integration and public conflict.[196] From such a perspective, it was the next logical step to consider internal conflicts also and even especially as communication problems. So far, the government has always unilaterally established development guidelines for the San without including or consulting them or at least allowing them to participate.

All things considered, we can detect the problem in the objectification of the San correlating with older forms of reification based on implicitly evolutionist perspectives. In consequence, the San become objects of state policies and lose their intersubjective rights of participation. From the viewpoint of the government, the share of participation in governance is reduced to the problem of administrating the "nature" of these entities. In terms of (legal) sociology, these failed legal and political measures (of integration) can be regarded as disruptions of communication.

As the opportunities of communicative competence are only insufficiently exploited, mutually amplifying interactions of failed efforts to reach an agreement develop. To some extent, this is also based on the fact that the parties involved have not even agreed on the meaning of used terminology. Therefore, a lack of semantic understanding on the most basic level is evident. In consequence, the meanings of used signs, symbols and especially legal terms are obviously misunderstood. New constructions of a false "San nature" as potential separatists or secessionists then lay a rather unstable foundation. In the end, opponents or even internal "enemies" of the modern state are created without any rational backing. Closely connected to this dilemma, disturbed communication provokes further conflicts to escalate. When external forces get involved as well (primarily a few international NGOs), the conflicts become even more complex.

---

196 As I have been in Botswana on numerous visits, each time for several months since 2000, I could directly experience the intensity in which this matter dominated both public discourse and published opinion-making in the press.

Anyway, I have offered my interpretations as a small contribution to resolve these seemingly irreconcilable and opposing perspectives as well as to hopefully overcome the misunderstandings and differences that are really not based on the "nature" of those involved. On the one hand, a crucial aspect of this intersubjective approach was to deconstruct the overly-static perceptions of the "character" of the concerned parties. On the other hand, I have tried to offer a context as extensive as possible by shifting the focus to the (historically accumulated) relationship between the stakeholders (cf. Watzlawick/Beavin/Jackson 2007: 22ff.). I am convinced that this was a significant step because in the end, communication (and not only the legal sphere) is the solution to this conflict. Even in the aftermath of the High Court's decision in 2006 and the Court of Appeal's decision in 2011, there are many ways for Botswana to deal with the judgements. These may range from the recognition of indigenous rights and the prompt social improvement of the San to some sort of "reluctant governance in consistence with the court order". The latter version would formally grant the 189 applicants a (more than precarious) existence in the Kalahari, while putting them under pressure by means of various policies and ultimately "letting them starve with their rights".

The message of national jurisdiction was as surprising as impressive and clearly showed that the recognition of the San's land (and water) rights is a matter of justice and thus not subject to the contingent power of central-state policies anymore. In general, the High Court's decision was supposed to make amends for past and current forms of discrimination. It expressed the realistic hope of a win-win solution for all sides and did not have in mind the artificial conservation of indigenous cultures in some sort of open-air museum but rather the right of any human community to live within a (state) polity according to its own cultural standards and visions.

Against this backdrop, the Government of Botswana might be reminded to bethink of its fifth national principle "Botho" aside from democracy, development, confidence and unity. "Botho" refers to the African concept of earning respect by showing it first and achieving legitimacy by strengthening others. If I decided in the spirit of the High Court's judgement to finally adopt a cultural-optimistic perspective, I would leave the question I have raised in this book's title ("Lost Lands?") unanswered for now and thus not affirm it without reservations. Keeping in mind more than four decades of "good governance", Botswana is fully capable of learning from past experiences and questioning rigid attitudes. If the San were ready for reconciliation, the court orders could at least attribute some momentum to the recognition, respectful treatment and participatory development in the ever-contested Central Kalahari – and thus make a positive contribution to the internationally established protection of indigenous rights as envisioned by the *UN Declaration on the Rights of Indigenous Peoples*. It is highly probable that Botswana's symbolic gains in international recognition and agreement could "balance" the country's recovery for the San.

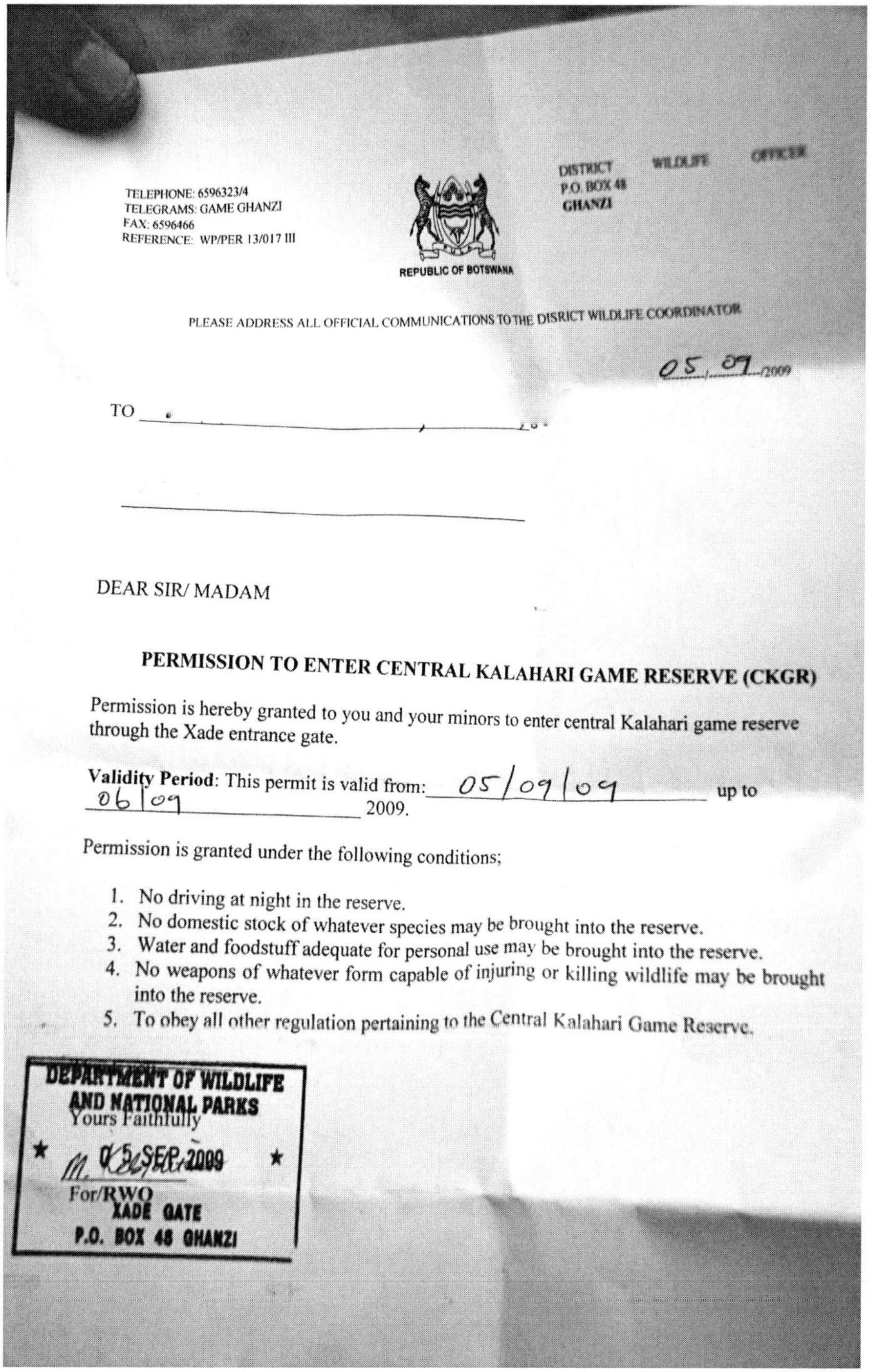

TELEPHONE: 6596323/4
TELEGRAMS: GAME GHANZI
FAX: 6596466
REFERENCE: WP/PER 13/017 III

DISTRICT WILDLIFE OFFICER
P.O. BOX 48
GHANZI

REPUBLIC OF BOTSWANA

PLEASE ADDRESS ALL OFFICIAL COMMUNICATIONS TO THE DISTRICT WILDLIFE COORDINATOR

05, 09, 2009

TO

DEAR SIR/ MADAM

PERMISSION TO ENTER CENTRAL KALAHARI GAME RESERVE (CKGR)

Permission is hereby granted to you and your minors to enter central Kalahari game reserve through the Xade entrance gate.

Validity Period: This permit is valid from: 05/09/09 up to 06/09 2009.

Permission is granted under the following conditions;

1. No driving at night in the reserve.
2. No domestic stock of whatever species may be brought into the reserve.
3. Water and foodstuff adequate for personal use may be brought into the reserve.
4. No weapons of whatever form capable of injuring or killing wildlife may be brought into the reserve.
5. To obey all other regulation pertaining to the Central Kalahari Game Reserve.

Yours Faithfully

DEPARTMENT OF WILDLIFE
AND NATIONAL PARKS
05 SEP 2009
For/RWO
XADE GATE
P.O. BOX 48 GHANZI

Figure 52: Entry permit to the CKGR for visiting San family member

The Return of the Outlaws: An Epilogue

by Werner Zips

"They do not use the term (indigenous) in order to deny all other Africans their legitimate claim to belong to Africa and identify as such. They use the present day wide understanding of the term because it is a term by which they can adequately analyse the particularities of their sufferings and by which they can seek protection in international Human Rights law and moral standards." (Report of the African Commission's Working Group of Experts on Indigenous Populations/Communities: ACHPR/IWGIA 2005: 88).

The present book approaches the extremely intense debate of various scientific disciplines and political arenas about "indigeneity" and its related or not yet related rights from a perspective essential to jurists: a pragmatic one. The first question we have to ask is whether it is a legal issue worth protecting and how such protection could be achieved. This prioritizing approach did not mean that the author dismissed all other possible perspectives but that the legal point of view was the first in line. In accordance with the Latin maxim *ubi ius, ibi remedium* (where there is a right, there must be a remedy), this book analyzes various forms of historical, legal discrimination of marginalized groups who could claim a relevant (legal) right and achieve its implementation.

Such an emphasis is clearly consistent with the essence of the aforementioned citation (of the *African Commission's Working Group*). Thus, striving for indigenous rights does not contradict the statement that all Africans in Africa are indigenous, which is one of the most striking redundancies in Botswana's political discourse. Neither are social groups using the label of indigenous peoples to claim special rights, nor should such claims lead to tribalism and ethnic conflicts. Such claims to indigenous rights rather focus on specific forms of discrimination and previous disenfranchisement, which quite ironically are often carried out by using the category of indigeneity. They usually demand the end of their discrimination as related to other groups within a state as well as possible compensation for the injustice they have experienced. In contrast to a common misunderstanding, this legal approach does not create but instead significantly helps to prevent or possibly resolve conflicts (ACHPR/IWGIA 2005: 88f.).

It is exactly the author's legal perspective on this issue that enables her to offer a crucial contribution to the debate on indigeneity in social and cultural anthropology. At least a few of my (own) colleagues show serious knowledge gaps in the field of law. In this context, Adam Kuper's (2003) unfortunate critique of the allegedly essentialist use of the term indigenous as the "return of the native" and the "ideological makeover of the old idea of primitive people" (2006: 21) is almost exemplary of all the common misunderstandings that the *African Commission's Working Group* (ib.) analyzes. Today's terminological meanings and their application in legal fields are neither based on the micro-discourses of social and cultural anthropology, nor the "unscientific intuitions" of NGOs and activists or the historical use of the term "indigenous" which in its original sense means belonging to an unoccupied territory from the perspective of the colonizer. In accordance with the doctrine of "terra nullius" the latter usage meant nothing less than an arrogate self-invitation to appropriate the land and "its occupiers". Instead the current understanding of indigeneity has emerged from a complex discourse universe that has developed around legal claims of self-determination. A minimum standard of self-determination can now be viewed as a fundamental principle of international customary law that Anaya (1996: 75) arguably regards as a peremptory norm (*ius cogens*).

While this right of self-determination was manifested in various legislative forums more than four decades ago, it has also become the foundation of the most important criteria of indigeneity – as a mode of relationships generally open for local variations. Therefore, the legal effects of indigeneity have nothing to do with those essentialisms of race, identity and culture that Kuper (2003: 395) considered to be open for racist criteria. If we embarked, as this piece of work has done, on the discourses of self-understanding on possible meanings and legal practices of indigeneity instead of simply ignoring them as being non-academic, it may happen that an interpretation leading right into the opposite direction reveals itself: as the political etymology of the term indigeneity allows for former connotations of being primitive, backward, aboriginal and underdeveloped to shimmer through, today's use of the term offers a starting point to connect to and (self-)critically review the historical roots of oppression and dispossession.

In this sense, the term is not a simple reproduction or a makeover of obsolete anthropological theories of "nativity" but an analytical tool for its deconstruction. This is why the present analysis of indigeneity as an emerging legal relationship in Botswana does not lead to the asserted, simple "return of the native" but rather to a legal evidence for a socio-political re-emergence that may be coined the "return of the outlaws". Moreover, the discourse on indigenous rights already adopts the reference to the origin of rightlessness in its terminology. In other words, the presented rights to self-determination of indigenous peoples refer on the one hand to a future of human rights yet to be further accomplished and on the other hand to the past of factual dispossession. So if the "native" was to return under the asserted guise of the indigenous, it would be at best a ghostly image reminding us of extreme injustice that may adequately be described in the categories of genocide, complete submission, total exploitation and disenfranchisement.

Botswana and the San communities of southern Africa may be a particularly good example to illustrate the historical dimension because it refers to consequences of decolonisation that have not been realized yet. Botswana has stood out due to its continuous democratic tradition since its independence in 1966 but these forms of participation are only unlimited for the governing ethnic groups or "major tribes" as established in the Constitution (cf. Nyati-Ramahobo 2009). In the last few years, those communities who under the term indigenous have sought to obtain equal rights of self-determination were only granted limited rights of participation. Nevertheless, the adequate participatory and consensual organization of internal self-determination rights in a state hierarchy can completely overcome structural, colonial inequality. In many respects, we can only expect a stabilization of social peace at a national level after the complete break with the colonial divide-and-rule policy. Anaya (1996: 75) then projects this stabilization onto the sphere of international law:

"Mention of self-determination within contemporary political discourse has at times raised the specter of destabilization and even violent turmoil. And indeed, as many have observed, self-determination rhetoric has been invoked in the world of late in association with extremist political posturing and ethnic chauvinism. Furthermore, a number of states have resisted express usage of the term self-determination in articulating indigenous peoples' rights. But notwithstanding rhetorical extremism or aversion to express invocation of the term self-determination, the concept underlying the term entails a certain nexus of widely shared values. These values and related processes of decision can be seen as stabilizing forces in the international system and as foundational to international law's contemporary treatment of indigenous peoples."

In Botswana the disputes over indigenous (land) rights coincided in a fully charged way with the international, legal development of the *UN Declaration on the Rights of Indigenous Peoples* (2007). Unlike hardly any other state, the Government of Botswana obviously feared that the establishment of protection norms (of a remedial regime) at the level of the United Nations could directly affect the tense situation during the legal dispute before the High Court over the land rights of the San in the Central Kalahari. Although not a single individual or group involved in the case ever even vaguely suggested separatist tendencies, the highest state bodies as well as parts of the media coverage conveyed the impression that the immediate dissolution of the nation was at stake. The state's "Kalahari governance" which is sometimes difficult to rationally understand and may be called a somewhat "chaotic policy", has been at the centre of public debates in Botswana since the 1990s.

In appreciation of the "remarkable political legacy" of President Festus Mogae, the Botswana journalist Keto Segwai (2008: 1) describes the obscure logics of "CKGR governance" and cuts straight to the chase:

"The real bone of contention (...) was the wholly embarrassing Central Kalahari Game Reserve (CKGR) saga. For Mogae and his coterie of advisors erroneously view what is basically a human rights issue, as some national security threat being fermented by foreign legions in the likes of their nemesis Survival International (SI). Up until its dying days, the Mogae administration dismally failed to give a convincing reason why the Basarwa of the CKGR were relocated from their home in the first place. Instead the administration's lies have effectively matched those of its archrival SI. (...) The Mogae administration's obsession with the CKGR blighted our otherwise impeccable foreign relations. Their recalcitrance on the issue has undoubtedly reached irrational proportions. This led some local political commentators to maintain that the Mogae administration's policy on Basarwa is premised on ethnic supremacy."

The deeper motives and reasons why the case of the Central Kalahari actually became so dramatic are subject of the author's alternative considerations and have repeatedly been the topic of many discussions during our joint travelling in Botswana. One of the most important achievements of this book is not to give way to monocausal interpretations, while having left the question of the "why" of in various ways adverse politics unresolved. When self-proclaimed saviours of the "last hunters and gatherers" internationally claimed that the relocation was only carried out for the sole purpose of making profits by facilitating diamond mining in the Kalahari without running risk of facing obligations to share with its original inhabitants, these accusations seemed to be quite too simple in our opinion. A thorough analysis of recurring key elements in the public discourse on the CKGR issue shows a much more complex relational structure revealing the real differences in the underlying world-views or "cosmovisions" of indigenous peoples and the Government. In her conclusion, the author interprets these as problems of communication. Only a long-term historical overview will probably be able to offer a somewhat reliable understanding of the real motives. In any case when we last travelled to Botswana in 2009, many of our former informants and interviewees who once had been convinced that diamond mining in the San's settlement area was of no significance were clearly hit by the latest developments and saw their previous beliefs refuted. According to reports of Botswana newspapers, economically viable mining rights were obviously assigned after the court's decision in favour of the San in 2006:

"Initially, government had argued on the conservation platform that human habitation is not compatible with the aegis of a game reserve. They denied allegations that the Basarwa were being relocated to make way for diamond mining. It has since turned out that a mining outfit by the name Gem Diamonds is about to start mining activities in the reserve" (Segwai 2008: 1f.).

As the Yearbook *The Indigenous World* (IWGIA 2012: 498) makes clear, we will have to continue paying close attention to how Botswana works or does not work to implement the court order. Well-informed observers argue on the quiet that the government factually refuses to observe the judgement and appears quite reluctant to consider a change of policies to more participatory forms of governance. They are concerned that the San may have won a battle while having lost the war. In contrast, the Government claims in its own media outlet, *Tautona Times* No. 40 (Republic of Botswana 2008: 20), to have fully implemented the order. In any case, the beneficiaries of the decision had yet to appeal again to the High Court and the Court of Appeal to restore their access to water in order to physically enable them to return to their former living environments. Botswana officially considers strict control of their ways of life (such as hunting and gathering) to be in compliance with the judgement. Some reports clearly show how hardened the fronts still are (IWGIA 2012: 495ff.). The present piece of work also followed the purpose of contributing its share in softening these conflict lines; it aims to comprehend the Government's Kalahari policies from a historical perspective and evaluates the benevolent aspects of the particular governance of indigeneity along with their discriminatory effects. The underlying scientific approach is based on the awareness that partial criticism and activism would be counterproductive particularly for the present case. The relevant commitment of *Survival International* has lucidly confirmed this fact.

The most promising approach to resolve the standoff of the current lose-lose situation appears to contribute relevant arguments to an internal process of reflection. Botswana's policies concerning the authoritarian relocation of the San from the Central Kalahari have seriously tarnished the generally-positive image of this African state for the first time. Any medium and long-term consequences for the crucial economic sectors of diamond mining and tourism will also depend on the conclusions that the Government will actually draw. Not only the state's reputation suffered internationally from insufficiently observing human rights, Botswana also had to bear the high follow-up costs of the relocation. As those concerned were basically deprived of any form of subsistence except for the unpopular keeping of cattle, a completely new class of dependents developed – a client society of indigenous peoples that are not recognized as such. Aside from symbolic costs of the grave image damage, further consequences became obvious: striking social costs of an uprooted San population suffering from alcoholism, domestic violence and mental deformation as well as considerable economic costs at the state's expense for sustaining a marginal group that will be significantly impaired for generations.

Finally we should not forget the political costs of destabilization that are already reflected to some extent in arbitrary arrests and the related increase in violent protests (IWGIA 2009: 567, IWGIA 2012: 498f.).

The carefully considered, legal political discussions in several chapters of this book may even contribute to familiarize those state institutions directly concerned with the "governance of indigeneity" with the insufficiently appreciated opportunities lying in an adequate recognition and promotion of indigenous rights of self-determination. The respect for and recognition of indigenous rights goes hand in hand with a paradox (as already mentioned in Anaya's quotation): they usually lead to the stabilization of state legitimacy and sovereignty and do not interfere with or even dissolve them. In many respects, recognition mobilizes those affirmative potentials that previously have been missing for a basically realizable version of internal stability. Botswana is not an exclusive example throughout the world, where such a political turnaround could provide a chance to prevent the dreaded destabilization all too often associated with cultural diversity. The probable consequences may then prove not to be in form of tribalism or secession but rather in the unexpected shape of an increased readiness for participation, approval and cooperation in overall governance.

There is a lot more than a simple increase in external and internal legitimacy speaking for a communicatively rational "governance of indigeneity" – meaning a participatory and basically respectful-egalitarian process of opinion and decision-making for an adequate future of those concerned in line with the international right of self-determination. Cultural diversity accommodates a cognitive, intellectual and creative pool of forms of capital that could be buried much deeper in states like Botswana than the diamond deposits of the Kalahari. Considering in addition the currently omnipresent imperatives of sustainability, the value of indigenous knowledge and competences seems much more stable and secure than the gemstone deposits that will almost certainly be exhausted in a not too distant future.

For all these reasons, I agree with the conclusions of the present book: also in Africa and against the backdrop of considerations based on pragmatism, law and politics, and the sociology of domination, the concept of indigeneity could assume a significantly higher status than it has done so far. The "return of the outlaws", in this sense, as a return of once marginalized and excluded peoples and communities to relevant fora of decision-making on various levels of local, national, regional and even global politics poses no threat for state sovereignty or risk factor for national integrity. From the perspective of complementary integration and sustainable peacekeeping, the recognition of indigenous rights would rather promise conflict resolution as well as symbolic, material and political winnings on both sides. Needless to say, this is not only true for small nation states like Botswana but also for major political players that place themselves as world or "super" powers but still fear indigenous communities that sometimes account to only a few thousand members. As the *African Commission's Working Group* (2005: 88) quoted above states: "Conflicts do not arise because people demand their rights but because their rights are violated." In this sense, the book title "Lost Lands?" does not only express hope honeycombed with considerations of political and social justice but also suggests the potential of alternative solutions to adamantly prevailing conflicts over land. All is not lost in the arena of indigenous rights, where David tends to get some assets at hand against Goliath.

March 2013   Werner Zips

Appendix

Examples of Indigenous Peoples in Africa (not exhaustive!)

Country	Group	Main economic activity
Algeria	Amazigh	Farmers
	Tuareg	Pastoralists
Angola	San	Hunter-gatherers
Botswana	San	Hunter-gatherers
Burkina Faso	Tuareg	Pastoralists
	Fulani	Pastoralists
Burundi	Batwa	Hunter-gatherers
Cameroon	Bakola/Bagyeli	Hunter-gatherers
	Baka	Hunter-gatherers
	Medzan	Hunter-gatherers
	Mbororo	Pastoralists
Central African Republic (CAR)	Baaka (Bayaka, Biaka) Mbororo	Hunter-gatherers Pastoralists
Congo, Republic of	Yaka	Hunter-gatherers
Democratic Republic of Congo	Batwa, Bacwa, Bambuti	Hunter-gatherers
Egypt	Amazigh	Pastoralists
Ethiopia	Somalis	Pastoralists
	Afars	Pastoralists
	Borana	Pastoralists
	Kereyu (Oromo) Nuer	Pastoralists Pastoralists
Gabon	Baka	Hunter-gatherers
Kenya	Ogiek	Hunter-gatherers
	Watta	Hunter-gatherers
	Sengwer	Hunter-gatherers
	Yaaku	Hunter-gatherers
	Maasai	Pastoralists
	Samburu	Pastoralists
	Elmolo	Pastoralists
	Turkana	Pastoralists
	Rendille	Pastoralists
	Borana	Pastoralists
	Somali	Pastoralists
	Gabra	Pastoralists
	Pokot	Pastoralists
	Endorois	Pastoralists

Examples of Indigenous Peoples in Africa

Libya	*Tuareg*	*Pastoralists*
	Amazigh	*Pastoralists*
Mali	*Tuareg*	*Pastoralists*
	Amazigh	*Pastoralists*
Morocco	*Amazigh*	*Farmers/Pastoralists*
Namibia	*San*	*Hunter-gatherers*
	Himba	*Pastoralists*
Niger	*Tuareg*	*Pastoralists*
	Fulani	*Pastoralists*
	Toubou	*Pastoralists*
Nigeria	*Ogoni*	*Small-scale farmers*
Rwanda	*Batwa*	*Hunter-gatherers*
South Africa	*San*	*Hunter-gatherers*
Tunisia	*Amazigh*	*Farmers*
Uganda	*Batwa*	*Hunter-gatherers*
	Benet	*Hunter-gatherers*
	Karamojong	*Pastoralists*
Tanzania	*Hadzabe*	*Semi-nomadic hunter-gatherer/small-scale agriculture*
	Akie	*Hunter-gatherers*
	Maasai	*Pastoralists*
	Barabaig	*Pastoralists*
Zambia	*San*	*Hunter-gatherers*
Zimbabwe	*San*	*Hunter-gatherers*

Source: ACHPR/IWGIA (2006: 15f.)

Abbreviations

ACHPR	African Commission on Human and Peoples' Rights
African Charter	African Charter on Human and Peoples' Rights (Banjul Charter)
AU	African Union (formerly OAU)
BDP	Botswana Democratic Party
CBD	Convention on Biological Diversity
CBNRM	Community Based Natural Resource Management
CBO	Community Based Organization
CCPR	Covenant on Civil and Political Rights
CERD	Convention on the Elimination of all Forms of Racial Discrimination
CESCR	Covenant on Economic, Social and Cultural Rights
CKGR	Central Kalahari Game Reserve
DWNP	Department of Wildlife and National Parks
ECHR	European Convention on Human Rights
ECOSOC	(UN) Economic and Social Council
ECtHR	European Court of Human Rights
FAO	Food and Agriculture Organization
KFO	Kuru Family of Organisations
FPK	First People of the Kalahari
HRC	Human Rights Committee
ILO	International Labour Organisation
IUCN	International Union for Conservation of Nature
IWGIA	International Work Group for Indigenous Affairs
KDT	Kuru Development Trust
NDP	National Development Plan
NGO	Non-Governmental Organization
OAU	Organization of African Union (cf. AU)
RAD	Remote Area Dwellers
RADP	Remote Area Development Programme
SASI	South African San Institute
SGL	Special Game Licences
TGLP	Tribal Grazing Land Policy
UNDG	United Nations Development Group
UNESCO	UN Education, Scientific and Cultural Organization
UNHCHR	UN High Commissioner for Human Rights
UNO	United Nations Organization
WGIP	UN Working Group on Indigenous Populations
WHO	World Health Organization
WIMSA	Working Group of Indigenous Minorities in Southern Africa
WMA	Wildlife Management Area

Bibliography

A

Albuquerque, Catarina de (2010): Report of the independent expert on the issue of human rights obligations related to access to safe drinking water and sanitation. (A/HRC/15/31).

ACHPR (2010): *Concluding Observations and Recommendations on the Initial Periodic Report of the Republic of Botswana*. African Commission on Human and Peoples' Rights: Forty-Seventh Ordinary Session, 12–16 May 2010, in Banjul, The Gambia.

ACHPR/IWGIA (2006): *Indigenous Peoples in Africa: The Forgotten Peoples? The African Commission's work on indigenous peoples in Africa*. Copenhagen: African Commission on Human and Peoples' Rights and International Work Group for Indigenous Affairs.

ACHPR/IWGIA (2008a): *Report of the African Commission's Working Group on Indigenous Populations/Communities. Mission to the Republic of Botswana*; 15–23 June 2005. Copenhagen: African Commission on Human and Peoples' Rights and International Work Group for Indigenous Affairs.

ACHPR/IWGIA (2008b): *Report of the African Commission's Working Group on Indigenous Populations/Communities. Mission to the Republic of Namibia*; 26 July–5 August 2005. Copenhagen: African Commission on Human and Peoples' Rights and International Work Group for Indigenous Affairs.

Adams, Martin/Kalabamu, Faustin/White, Richard (2003): "Land tenure policy and practice in Botswana – Governance lessons for southern Africa". In: *Journal für Entwicklungspolitik* XIX/1. Wien: Mandelbaum Verlag, 55–74.

Adams, William (2003): "Nature and the Colonial Mind". In: Adams, William/Mulligan, Martin (eds.): *Decolonizing Nature: Strategies for Conservation in a Post-Colonial Era*. London: Earthscan Publications, 16–50.

Aguilar, Gonzalo/LaFosse, Sandra/Rojas, Hugo/Steward, Rebecca (2009): "South/North Exchange of 2009 – The Constitutional Recognition of Indigenous Peoples in Latin America". In: *International Law Review Online Companion*. Vol.2, No. 2, 44–96. Online at: *digitalcommons.pace.edu/cgi/viewcontent.cgi?article=1017*.

Akpan, Joseph/Mberengwa, Ignatius/Hitchcock, Robert and Koperski, Thomas (2004): "Human Rights and Participation among Southern African Indigenous Peoples". In: Hitchcock, Robert/Vinding, Diana (eds.): *Indigenous Peoples' Rights in Southern Africa*. Copenhagen: International Work Group for Indigenous Affairs, 63–81.

Albertson, Arthur (2002): "Sustainable use of the Central Kalahari Game Reserve". In: DITSHWANELO. Central Kalahari Game Reserve. Focus Seminar Series. Gaborone: Pyramid Publishing, 12–24.

Altheimer, Gabriele/Hubert, Werner (1991): "Land und Leute. Ein einführender Überblick." In: Altheimer/Hopf/Weimer (Hg.): *Botswana. Vom Land der Betschuanen zum Frontstaat. Wirtschaft, Gesellschaft, Kultur.* Münster, Hamburg: LIT Verlag, 5–13.

Amnesty International (2006): A Guide to the African Charter on Human and Peoples Rights. London: Amnesty International.

Amnesty International (2007): Report 2007. Online at: http://thereport.amnesty.org/eng (accessed on 19 July 2007).

Anaya, James (1995): "The Capacity of International Law to Advance Ethnic or Nationality Rights Claims". In: Kymlicka, Will (ed.): *The Rights of Minority Cultures.* Oxford: Oxford University Press. 321–330.

Anaya, James (1996): *Indigenous Peoples in International Law.* Oxford: Oxford University Press.

Anaya, James (2010): Report of the Special Rapporteur on the situation of human rights and fundamental freedoms of indigenous people. (A/HRC/15/37).

Anderson, David/Grove, Richard (1987): "Introduction: The Scramble for Eden: Past, Present and Future in African Conservation". In: Anderson, David/Grove, Richard (eds.): *Conservation in Africa. People, Policies and Practice.* New York, Cambridge: Cambridge University Press, 1–12.

Armstrong, Sue/Bennett, Olivia (2002): "Representing the Resettled. The Ethical Issues raised by Research and Representation of the San". In: Chatty, Dawn and Colchester, Marcus (eds.): *Conservation and Mobile Indigenous Peoples. Displacement, Forced Settlement, and Sustainable Development.* New York, Oxford: Berghahn Books, 188–201.

Asch, Michael (1999): "From Calder to Van der Peet. Aboriginal Rights and Canadian Law, 1973–96". In: Havemann, Paul (ed.): *Indigenous Peoples' Rights in Australia, Canada and New Zealand.* Oxford: Oxford University Press, 428–446.

Asch, Michael/Samson, Colin et al. (2004): "Discussion: On the Return of the Native". In: *Current Anthropology*, Vol. 45 (2), 261–268.

Atlhopheng, Julius/Mulale, Kutlwano (2009): "Natural Resource-based Tourism and Wildlife Policies in Botswana". In: Saarinen, Jarkko/Becker, Fritz/Manwa, Haretsebe and Deon Wilson (eds.): *Sustainable Tourism in Southern Africa. Local Communities and Natural Resources in Transition.* Bristol, Buffalo, Toronto: Chennel View Publications, 134–149.

Ayeni, Victor/Sharma, Keshav C. (eds.) (2000): *Ombudsman in Botswana. Selected Papers, Cases and Materials.* London: Commonwealth Secretariat.

B

Bargatzky, Thomas (1986): *Einführung in die Kultur-Ökologie. Umwelt, Kultur und Gesellschaft.* Berlin: Dietrich Reimer Verlag.

Barnard, Alan (1992): *Hunters and Herders of Southern Africa. A Comparative Ethnography of the Khoisan Peoples.* New York, Cambridge: Cambridge University Press.

Barnard, Alan (2004): "Hunter-Gatherers in History, Archeology and Anthropology. Introductory Essay." In: Barnard, Alan (ed.): *Hunter-Gatherers in History, Archeology and Anthropology*. Oxford, New York: Berg Publishers, 1–13.

Barnard, Alan (2006): "Kalahari revisionism, Vienna and the 'indigenous peoples' Debate." In: *Social Anthropology*, No. 14, 1–16.

Barnes, Jonathan (1994): "Alternative Use for Natural Resources in Botswana: Wildlife Utilisation." In: Brothers, Sue/Hermans, Janet/Nteta, Doreen (eds.): *Botswana in the 21ˢᵗ Century*. Gaborone: The Botswana Society, 323–336.

Barrow, Edmund/Fabricius, Christo (2002): "Do Rural People Really Benefit from Protected Areas – Rhetoric or Reality?" In: Brown, Jessica/Kothari, Ashish/Menon, Manju (eds.): Parks: Local Communities and Protected Areas. *The International Journal for Protected Area Managers*, Vol. 12 No. 2. Gland, Switzerland: IUCN, 67–79.

Bartlett, Richard H. (1999): "Native Title in Australia. Denial, Recognition, and Dispossession." 1973–96." In: Havemann, Paul (ed.): *Indigenous Peoples' Rights in Australia, Canada and New Zealand*. Oxford: Oxford University Press, 408–427.

Bartlett, Richard H. (2000): *Native Title in Australia*. Sydney: Butterworths.

Barume, Albert K. (2002): "Constitutional Protection and Aboriginal Title in Commonwealth African Countries." Paper submitted at Indigenous Rights in the Commonwealth Project. Africa Regional Expert Meeting, Cape Town 16–18 October 2002. Online at: www.cpsu.org.uk (accessed on 7 August 2006).

Barume, Albert K. (2009): "Responding to the Concerns of the African States." In: Charters, Claire/Stavenhagen, Rodolfo (eds.): *Making the Declaration Work. The United Nations Declaration on the Rights of Indigenous Peoples*. Copenhagen: IWGIA, 170–182.

Barume, Albert K. (2010): *Land Rights of Indigenous Peoples in Africa*. Copenhagen: IWGIA.

Beck Verlag, (1989): *Menschenrechte*. München: Beck-Texte im dtv.

Benda-Beckmann, Franz von (1997): "Citizens, Strangers and Indigenous Peoples: Conceptual Politics and Legal Pluralism." In: *Law and Anthropology*, Vol. 9, 1–42.

Benda-Beckmann, Franz von (2002): "Who is afraid of legal pluralism?" In: *Journal of Legal Pluralism*, Vol. 47, 37–82.

Benda-Beckmann, Keebet von (2007): "Implementieren – Was heißt das? Die Implementierung von Gerichtsurteilen aus der Sicht der Rechtsethnologie." In: Franz und Keebet von Benda-Beckmann: *Gesellschaftliche Wirkung von Recht. Rechtsethnologische Perspektiven*. Berlin: Dietrich Reimer Verlag GmbH, 103–126.

Benda-Beckmann, Franz von/Benda-Beckmann, Keebet von (2007): "Transnationalization of Law, Globalization and Legal Pluralism: A Legal Anthropological Perspective." In: Antons, C./Gessner, V. (eds.): *Globalisation and Resistance: Law reform in Asia since the Crisis*. Oxford-Portland: Hart Publishing, 53–80.

Bennett, Bruce S. (2002): "Some Historical Background on Minorities in Botswana." In: Mazonde, Isaac N. (ed.): *Minorities in the Millennium: Perspectives from Botswana*. Gaborone: Lightbooks, 5–15.

Bennett, TW/Powell Ch. (1999): "Aboriginal Title in South Africa Revisited." In: *South African Journal on Human Rights*, Vol. 15, Part 4, 449–485.

Berman, Bruce/Eyoh, Dickson/Kymlicka, Will (2004): "Introduction. Ethnicity & the Politics of Democratic Nation-Building in Africa." In: Berman, Bruce/Eyoh, Dickson/Kymlicka, Will (eds.): *Ethnicity & Democracy in Africa*. Oxford: James Currey Ltd., 1–21.

Binder, Christina (2004): *Die Landrechte indigener Völker unter besonderer Bezugnahme auf Mexiko und Nicaragua*. Frankfurt a.M.: Peer Lang GmbH, Europäischer Verlag der Wissenschaften, Reihe II Rechtswissenschaft Bd/Vol. 3858.

Boko, Duma Gideon (2002): "Integrating the Basarwa under Botswana's Remote Area Development Programme: Empowerment or Marginalization?" In: Mazonde, Isaac N. (ed.): *Minorities in the Millennium: Perspectives from Botswana*. Gaborone: Lightbooks, 97–110.

Bolaane, Maitseo (2001): "Fear of the Marginalized Minorities: The Khwai Community Determining their Boundary in the Okavango, Botswana through a Deed of Trust." In: Barnard, Alan/Kenrick, Justin (eds.): *Africa's Indigenous Peoples: 'First Peoples' or 'Marginalized Minorities'?* University of Edinburgh: Centre of African Studies, 145–171.

Bollig, Michael (2003): "Between Welfare and Bureaucratic Domination: The San of Ghanzi and Kgalagadi Districts." In: Hohmann, Thekla (ed.): *San and the State. Contesting Land, Development, Identity and Representation*. Köln: Rüdiger Köppe Verlag, 281–324.

Borrás, Susana/Jacobsson, Kerstin (2004): "The Open Method of Co-ordination and New Governance Patterns in the EU." In: *Journal of European Public Policy*, 11 (2), 185–208.

Borrows, John/Rotman, Leonard I. (1997): "The Sui Generis Nature of Aboriginal Rights: Does it make a Difference?" In: *Alberta Law Review*, 36, 9–45.

Bortfeld, Matthias (2005): *Der Afrikanische Gerichtshof für Menschenrechte. Eine Untersuchung des Zusatzprotokolls zur Afrikanischen Charter für die Menschenrechte und die Rechte der Völker*. Baden-Baden: Nomos Verlagsgesellschaft.

Botswana Institute for Development Policy Analysis (2001): Report on the Review of the Rural Development Policy, Vol. 2. Analysis and Recommendations for the Ministry of Finance and Development Planning.

Botswana Institute for Development Policy Analysis (2003): Review of the Remote Area Development Programme. Draft Report. Republic of Botswana, Ministry of Local Government.

Brandtner, Barbara/Rosas, Allan (1999): "Trade Preferences and Human Rights." In: Alston, Philip (ed.): *The EU and Human Rights*. Oxford: Oxford University Press, 699–722.

Brownlie, Ian (1992): *Treaties and Indigenous Peoples*. The Robb Lectures. Brookfield, F.M. (ed.). Oxford: Claredon Press.

C

CAO (2005): Compliance Advisor Ombudsman. Assessment Report. Complaint regarding IFC's investment in Kalahari Diamonds Ltd, Botswana. International Finance Corporation/Multilateral Investment Guarantee Agency.

Capotorti, Francesco (1991): Study on the Rights of Persons belonging to Ethnic, Religious and Linguistic Minorities. (E/CN.4/Sub.2/384/Rev.1).

Cassidy, Lin (2000): Community Based Natural Resource Management and Legal Rights to Resources in Botswana. IUCN/SNV CNBRM Support Programme. Gland: IUCN.

Chan, Tung (2004): "The Richtersveld Challenge: South Africa Finally Adopts Aboriginal Title". In: Hitchcock, Robert/Vinding, Diana (eds.): *Indigenous Peoples' Rights in Southern Africa*. Copenhagen: International Work Group for Indigenous Affairs, 114–133.

Charters, Claire/Stavenhagen, Rodolfo (eds.) (2009): "The UN Declaration on the Rights of Indigenous Peoples: How it Came to be and What it Heralds." In: Charters, Claire/Stavenhagen, Rodolfo (eds.): *Making the Declaration Work. The United Nations Declaration on the Rights of Indigenous Peoples*. Copenhagen: International Work Group for Indigenous Affairs, 10–14.

Chatty, Dawn/Colchester, Marcus (2002): "Introduction." In: Chatty, Dawn and Marcus Colchester (eds.): *Conservation and Mobile Indigenous Peoples. Displacement, forced settlement, and sustainable Development*. New York, Oxford: Berghahn Books, 1–20.

Chennells, Roger (2002): "The ‡Khomani San Land Claim." In: *Cultural Survival Quarterly*, 26 (1), 51–53.

Chennells, Roger (2006): Report on the Land Rights of the ‡Khomani San Community for the Commission on Restitution of Land Rights. Unpublished.

Chennells, Roger/du Toit, Aymone (2004): "The Rights of Indigenous Peoples in South Africa." In: Hitchcock, Robert/Vinding, Diana (eds.): *Indigenous Peoples' Rights in Southern Africa*. Copenhagen: International Work Group for Indigenous Affairs, 98–113.

Child, Brian (2003): Origins and Efficacy of Modern Community Based Natural Resource Management (CBNRM). Practices in the Southern African Region. Online at: www.iucn.org/themes/ceesp/Publi cations/TILCEPA/CCA-BChild.doc (accessed on 10 August 2007).

Cobo, José R. Martínez (1983): Study of the Problem of Discrimination against Indigenous Populations. Final Report (last part). (E/CN.4/Sub.2/1983/21/Add.8).

Cobo, José R. Martínez (1986a): Study of the Problem of Discrimination against Indigenous Populations. Vols. 1–4. (E/CN.4/Sub.2/1986/7/Add.1) [Martínez Cobo Study].

Cobo, José R. Martínez (1986b): Study of the Problem of Discrimination against Indigenous Populations: Conclusions, Proposals, and Recommendations. Vol. 5. (E/CN.4/Sub.2/1986/7/Add.4).

Comaroff, John/Comaroff, Jean (2006): "Law and Disorder in the Postcolony: An Introduction." In: Comaroff, Jean/Comaroff, John (eds.): *Law and Disorder in the Postcolony*. Chicago, London: The University of Chicago Press, 1–56.

Comaroff, John/Comaroff, Jean (2009): *Ethnicity, Inc.* Chicago, London: The University of Chicago Press.

Cook, Amelia/Sarkin, Jeremy (2010): "Is Botswana the Miracle of Africa? Democracy, the Rule of Law, and Human Rights versus Economic Development." In: *Current Law Journal*, 19 (2), 453–489.

Creifelds, Carl et al. (1997): *Rechtswörterbuch*. 14. Auflage. München: C.H. Beck'sche Verlagsbuchhandlung.

D

Daes, Erica-Irene A. (1995a): Standard-setting Activities: Evolution of Standards concerning the Rights of Indigenous People – New Developments and General Discussion of Future Action. Note on Criteria which might be applied when considering the Concept of 'Indigenous Peoples'. (E/CN.4/Sub.2/AC.4/1995/3).

Daes, Erica-Irene A. (1995b): Final Report of the Special Rapporteur on the Protection of the Heritage of Indigenous People. (E/CN.4/Sub. 2/1995/26).

Daes, Erica-Irene A. (1996): Standard-setting activities: Evolution of Standards concerning the Rights of Indigenous People. Working Paper on the Concept of 'Indigenous People'. (E/CN.4/Sub.2/AC.4/1996/2).

Daes, Erica-Irene A. (2001): Prevention of Discrimination and Protection of Indigenous Peoples and Minorities. Indigenous Peoples and their Relationship to Land. Final Working Paper by the Special Rapporteur. (E/CN.4/Sub.2/2001/21).

Daes, Erica-Irene A. (2009): "The Contribution of the Working Group on Indigenous Populations to the Genesis and Evolution of the UN Declaration on the Rights of Indigenous Peoples". In: Charters, Claire/Stavenhagen, Rodolfo (eds.): *Making the Declaration Work. The United Nations Declaration on the Rights of Indigenous Peoples*. Copenhagen: IWGIA, 48–76.

Datta, Kusum/Murray, Andrew (1989): "The Rights of Minorities and Subject Peoples in Botswana: A Historical Evaluation." In: Holm, John/Molutsi, Patrick (eds.): *Democracy in Botswana*. Gaborone: Macmillan Botswana Publishing Company, 58–74.

Deng, Francis M. (1998): Internally Displaced Persons. Compilation and Analysis of Legal Norms. Geneva: Office of the UNHCR.

Dias, Ayesha K. (1999): International Standard-Setting on the Rights of Indigenous Peoples: Implications for Mineral Development in Africa. Online at: http://www.dundee.ac.uk/cepmlp/journal/html/vol7/article7-3.html (accessed on 16 December 2008).

Dinokopila, Bonolo Ramadi (2011): "The Right to Water in Botswana: A review of the Matsipane Mosetlhanyane Case." In: *African Human Rights Law Journal*, Vol. 11 No. 1. 282–295.

DITSHWANELO (1996): When will this Moving Stop? Report on a Fact-finding Mission of the Central Kalahari Game Reserve. Gaborone.

DITSHWANELO (1997): Tswa Bana! Human Rights Modules for Secondary School Teachers. DITSHWANELO – The Botswana Centre for Human Rights.

DITSHWANELO (2002): Central Kalahari Game Reserve Seminar. Focus Seminar Series. Gaborone: Pyramid Publishing.

DITSHWANELO (2005): Press Statement on Constitutional (Amendment) Bill 2004 of 18 April 2005.

DITSHWANELO **The Botswana Centre for Human Rights** (o. J.): Know your Law: Steps towards your Land Rights. A Booklet about the Land Allocation Process in Botswana.

Duda, Viktória Gy. (2005): Suppressed Hunger, Suppressed Rights – on the Protection of Indigenous Knowledge and the Rights of the South African San regarding their traditional use of the Hoodia Gordonii Plant. Unpublished Dissertation at the Faculty of Social Sciences, University of Vienna.

Durand Alcántara, Carlos H. (1999): "Die Erde und das Heilige – eine epistemologische Annäherung an die Territorialbeziehungen indigener Völker." In: *Journal für Entwicklungspolitik* XV/2, 1999. Frankfurt a.M.: Brandes & Apsel Verlag GmbH, 101–114.

Dussel, Enrique (1995): "Eurocentrism and Modernity. Introduction to the Frankfurt Lectures." In: Beverley, John/Aronna, Michael/Oviedo, José (eds.): *Folk Law. Essays in the Theory and Practice of Lex Non Scripta*, Vol. 1. Madison, Wisconsin: Duke University Press, 319–330.

E

Eide, Asbjørn/Daes, Erica-Irene (2000): The Relationship and Distinction between the Rights of Persons belonging to Minorities and those of Indigenous Peoples. Working Paper. (E/CN.4/Sub.2/2000/10).

F

Fabricius, Christo/de Wet, Chris (2002): "The Influence of Forced Removal and Land Restitution on Conservation in South Africa." In: Chatty, Dawn and Colchester, Marcus (eds.): *Conservation and Mobile Indigenous Peoples. Displacement, forced settlement, and sustainable development*. New York, Oxford: Berghahn Books, 142–157.

Fischer, Peter/Köck, Heribert Franz (2004): *Völkerrecht. Das Recht der universellen Staatengemeinschaft*. 6. Auflage, Vienna: Linde Verlag.

Fombad, Charles Manga (2003): "Protecting Constitutional Values in Africa: A Comparison of Botswana and Cameroon." In: *Comparative and International Law Journal of Southern Africa*, Vol. XXXVI. Pretoria: University of South Africa, 83–105.

G

Gall, Sandy (2002): *The Bushmen of Southern Africa. Slaughter of the Innocent.* London: Pimlico.

Gesellschaft für Bedrohte Völker (2005): Botswana: Alternativer Nobelpreis für inhaftierten Führer der San. Nr. 4/Dez. 2005.

Gingrich, Andre/Zips, Werner (2003): "Ethnohistorie und Historische Anthropologie." In: Fischer, Hans/Beer, Bettina (Hg.): *Ethnologie. Einführung und Überblick*. Berlin: Dietrich Reimer Verlag, 273–294.

Godwin, Peter (2001): "Bushmen. Last Stand for Southern Africa's First People." In: *National Geographic*, February 2001, 90–117.

Good, Kenneth/Taylor, Ian (2006): "Unpacking the 'Model': Presidential Succession in Botswana." In: Southall, R./Melber, H. (eds.): *Legacies of Power. Leadership Change and Former Presidents in African Politics*. Cape Town: HSRC Press, 51–72.

Grant, Sandy/Ramsay, Jeff (1987): "'One Botswana, One Nation': The Arrival of Independence." In: Morton, Fred/Ramsay, Jeff (eds.): *The Birth of Botswana. A History of the Bechuanaland Protectorate from 1910 to 1966*. Gaborone: Longman Botswana Ltd, 187–194.

Grant, Sandy/Egner, Brian (1989): "The Private Press and Democracy." In: Holm, John/Molutsi, Patrick (eds.): *Democracy in Botswana*. Gaborone: Macmillan Botswana Publishing Company, 247–265.

Griffiths, Anne (1989): "The legal heritage of colonialism: Family law in a former British Protectorate." In: *Law and Anthropology* 4, VWGÖ-Verlag, 75–105.

Griffiths, Anne (1997): "In the Shadow of Marriage. Gender and Justice in an African Community." Chicago, London: The University of Chicago Press.

Griffiths, Tom (2003): A Failure of Accountability. Indigenous Peoples, Human Rights and Development Agency Standards: a reference tool and comparative review. Forest Peoples Programme Briefing Paper, UK.

H

Hainzl, Gerald (2005): Ntwa Kgolo ke Ya Molomo (Die höchste Form der Auseinandersetzung ist der Dialog). Ökonomische und politische Aspekte der Umsiedlung der San aus dem CKGR. Unpublished PhD Thesis at the Faculty of Social Sciences, University of Vienna.

Hardin, Garrett (1968): "The Tragedy of the Commons". In: *Science*, Vol. 162, 1243–1248.

Harring, Sidney L. (2004): "Indigenous Land Rights and Land Reform in Namibia". In: Hitchcock/Vinding (eds.): *Indigenous Peoples' Rights in Southern Africa*. Copenhagen: International Work Group for Indigenous Affairs, 63–81.

Hazdra, Peter (1998): Zum Spannungsverhältnis von afrikanischem Gewohnheitsrecht und "modernem" staatlichen Recht (unter Berücksichtigung der aktuellen Situation im südlichen Afrika). MA Thesis at the Faculty of Social Sciences, University of Vienna.

Henriksen, John B. (2001): "Implementation of the Right of Self-determination of Indigenous Peoples." *Indigenous Affairs* 3/01, 7–21.

Hermans, Janet (1995): "Awareness through the Written Word: The Effect of Basarwa Literature on Policy Decisions in Botswana." In: Sanders, AJGM (ed.): *Speaking for the Bushmen*. A collection of papers read at the 13th International Congress of Anthropological and Ethnological Sciences, Mexico City, July 29–August 5, 1993. Gaborone: The Botswana Society, 40–53.

Hermans, Quill (1994): "Botswana in the 21st Century: Impact of External Political and Economic Changes on Botswana." In: Brothers, Sue/Hermans, Janet/Nteta, Doreen (eds.): *Botswana in the 21st Century*. Gaborone: The Botswana Society, 117–134.

Hielscher, Almut (2007): "Der erste deutsche Völkermord. Ein Kuhhandel." In: *Spiegel Special Geschichte* Nr. 2, 57–59. "

High Court (2006): *see under Law Cases*: Roy Sesana, Keiwa Setlhobogwa and Others v. The Attorney General.

Hildebrandt, Hans-Jürgen (1979): "Einführung." In: Morgan, Lewis H.: *Die Urgesellschaft. "Ancient Society". Untersuchungen über den Fortschritt der Menschheit aus der Wildheit durch die Barbarei zur Zivilisation*. Lollar/Lahn: Verlag Andreas Achenbach, 1–31.

Hitchcock, Robert (1987): "Anthropological Research and Remote Area Development among Botswana Basarwa." In: Hitchcock, Robert/Parsons, Neil/Taylor, John (eds.): *Research for Development in Botswana*. Gaborone: The Botswana Society, 285–351.

Hitchcock, Robert (2001): "'Hunting is our Heritage': The Struggle for Hunting and Gathering Rights among the San of Southern Africa." In: Anderson, David/Ikeya, Kazunobu (eds.): *Parks, Property, and Power: Managing Hunting Practice and Identity within State Policy Regimes*. Senri Ethnological Studies No. 59. Osaka: National Museum of Ethnology, 139–156.

Hitchcock, Robert (2006): "'We are the Owners of the Land': The San Struggle for the Kalahari and Its Resources." In: Hitchcock/Ikeya/Biesele/Lee (eds.): *Updating the San: Image and Reality of an African People in the 21st Century*. Osaka: National Museum of Ethnology, 229–256.

Hitchcock, Robert/Biesele, Megan (n.d.): San, Khwe, Basarwa or Bushmen?: Terminology, Identity and Empowerment in Southern Africa. Online at: www.kalaharipeoples.org/documents/San-term.htm (accessed on 24 August 2004).

Hitchcock, Robert/Biesele, Megan/Lee, Richard (2003): The San of Southern Africa: A Status Report, 2003. American Anthropological Association. Online at: www.aaanet.org/committees/cfhr/san.htm (accessed on 29 June 2007).

Hitchcock, Robert/Vinding, Diana (2004): "Indigenous Peoples' Rights in Southern Africa: An Introduction." In: Hitchcock, Robert/Vinding, Diana (eds.): *Indigenous Peoples' Rights in Southern Africa*. Copenhagen: IWGIA, 8–21.

Hitchcock, Robert/Ikeya, Kazunobu/Biesele, Megan/Lee, Richard (2006): "Introduction: Updating the San, Image and Reality of an African People in the Twenty First Century." In: Hitchcock/Ikeya/Biesele/Lee (eds.): *Updating the San: Image and Reality of an African People in the 21st Century*. Osaka: National Museum of Ethnology, 1–42.

Hitchcock, Robert/Daggett/Adrianne (2008): "Botswana." In: *The Indigenous World 2008*. Copenhagen: IWGIA.

Höffe, Otfried (1987): *Politische Gerechtigkeit. Grundlegung einer kritischen Philosophie von Recht und Staat*. Frankfurt am Main: Suhrkamp Verlag.

Höffe, Otfried (1999): *Demokratie im Zeitalter der Globalisierung*. Verlag C.H. Beck, München.

Hoffmeister, Frank (1998): *Menschenrechts- und Demokratieklauseln in den vertraglichen Außenbeziehungen der EG*. Berlin-Heidelberg-New York: Springer Verlag.

Hopf, Veit Dietrich (1991): "Von der Kolonialzeit bis zur Gegenwart. Ein historischer Überblick." In: Altheimer/Hopf/Weimer (Hg.): *Botswana. Vom Land der Betschuanen zum Frontstaat. Wirtschaft, Gesellschaft, Kultur*. Münster, Hamburg: LIT Verlag, 60–89.

Howard, Bradley Reed (2003): *Indigenous Peoples and the State. The Struggle for Native Rights*. DeKalb: Northern Illinoise University Press.

Hudelson, John (1995): "One Hundred Years among the San: A Social History of San Research." In: Sanders, AJGM (ed.): *Speaking for the Bushmen*. Gaborone: The Botswana Society, 3–39.

Hummer, Waldemar (1997): "Der internationale Menschenrechtsschutz." In: Neuhold/Hummer/Schreuer (Hrsg.): *Österreichisches Handbuch des Völkerrechts*, Teil 1. Wien: Manz Verlag, 243–290.

Hupe, Ilona (1999): *Reisen in Botswana*. München: Ilona Hupe Verlag.

I

IDEA (2006): "Botswana. Country Report based on Research and Dialogue with Political Parties." Stockholm: International Institute for Democracy and Electoral Assistance.

Igoe, Jim (2002): "National Parks and Human Ecosystems. The Challenge to Community Conservation. A Case Study from Simanjiro, Tanzania." In: Chatty, Dawn/Colchester, Marcus (eds.): *Conservation and Mobile Indigenous Peoples. Displacement, forced settlement, and sustainable development*. New York, Oxford: Berghahn Books, 77–96.

Ikeya, Kazunobu (2001): "Some Changes among the San under the Influence of Relocation Plan in Botswana." In: Anderson, David G./Ikeya, Kazunobu (eds.): *Parks, Property, and Power: Managing Hunting Practice and Identity within State Policy Regimes.* Senri Ethnological Studies no. 59. Osaka: National Museum of Ethnology, 183–198.

ILO/ACHPR (2009): Overview Report of the Research Project by the International Labour Organization and the African Commission on Human and Peoples' Rights on the constitutional and legislative protection of the rights of indigenous peoples in 24 African Countries. Geneva: International Labour Office.

IUCN (1994): Protected Areas and World Heritage Programme: Management Categories of Protected Areas. Online at: www.unep-wcmc.org/protected_areas/categories/index.html (accessed on 25 November 2008).

IUCN (2000): Indigenous and Traditional Peoples and Protected Areas: Principles, Guidelines and Case Studies. World Commission on Protected Areas. Best Practice Protected Area Guidelines Series, Final Draft.

IWGIA (1994): *The Indigenous World 1993–94.* Copenhagen: International Work Group for Indigenous Affairs.

IWGIA (2006): *The Indigenous World 2006.* Copenhagen: International Work Group for Indigenous Affairs.

IWGIA (2007): *The Indigenous World 2007.* Copenhagen: International Work Group for Indigenous Affairs.

IWGIA (2008): *The Indigenous World 2008.* Copenhagen: International Work Group for Indigenous Affairs.

IWGIA (2009): *The Indigenous World 2009.* Copenhagen: International Work Group for Indigenous Affairs.

IWGIA (2011): *The Indigenous World 2011.* Copenhagen: International Work Group for Indigenous Affairs.

IWGIA (2012): *The Indigenous World 2012.* Copenhagen: International Work Group for Indigenous Affairs.

K

Kaller-Dietrich, Martina (2002): "Zur Dritten Dimension der Menschenrechte. Das Recht auf Entwicklung." In: Grandner, Margarete/Schmale, Wolfgang/Weinzierl, Michael (Hg.): *Grund- und Menschenrechte. Historische Perspektiven – Aktuelle Problematiken.* Wien: Verlag für Geschichte und Politik, 292–315.

Karl, Wolfram (1997): "Sonstige Quellen des Völkerrechts". In: Neuhold/Hummer/Schreuer (Hrsg.): *Österreichisches Handbuch des Völkerrechts*, Teil 1. Wien: Manz Verlag, 104–112.

Keal, Paul (2003): *European Conquest and the Rights of Indigenous Peoples.* Cambridge: Cambridge University Press.

Keon-Cohen, B A (2000): The Mabo Litigation: A Personal and Procedural Account, Melbourne University Law Review. Online at: www.austlii.edu.au//cgi-bin/disp.pl/au/journals/MULR/2000 (accessed on 2 August 2006).

Kerchoff, Peter (2000): "Regional Perspectives of Democracy and Human Rights – The Death Penalty." In: DITSHWANELO (ed.): *Conference on Human Rights and Democracy*. Gaborone: Bay Publishing (Pty) Ltd., 79–84.

Keto Segwai (2008): CKGR saga soils Mogae's remarkable legacy (Mogae Legacy). In: *Mmegi Online*. Online at: www.mmegi.bw (accessed on 6 June 2009).

Ki-Zerbo, Joseph (1981): *Die Geschichte Schwarz-Afrikas*. Frankfurt a.M.: Fischer Taschenbuch Verlag.

Kiema, Kuela (2010): *Tears for my Land: A social history of the Kua of the CKGR, Tc'amnqoo*. Gaborone: Mmegi Publishing House.

Kiyaga-Mulindwa, David (1987): "The Protectorate and World War II." In: Morton, Fred/Ramsay, Jeff (eds.): *The Birth of Botswana. A History of the Bechuanaland Protectorate from 1910 to 1966*. Gaborone: Longman Botswana Ltd, 102–109.

Kotrba, Stefanie (2002): Das House of Chiefs in Botswana. Eine ethnohistorische Rekonstruktion der Tswana-Dominanz. MA Thesis at the Faculty of Social Sciences, University of Vienna.

Kuper, Adam (2003): "The Return of the Native." In: *Current Anthropology*, Vol. 44, 389–395.

Kuper, Adam (2006): "Comment. Discussion: The concept of indigeneity." In: *Social Anthropology*, Vol. 14, 21–22.

Kuppe, René (1990): "Indigene Rechte und die Diskussion um ‚Rechte für Gruppen'." In: *Law & Anthropology* Vol. 5, 1–23.

Kuppe, René (1994): "Zum Selbstbestimmungsrecht indigener Völker. Die Ausführungen in der Working Group on Indigenous Populations im Lichte des Völkerrechts." In: Muth, H./Seitel, F. (eds.): *Indigene Völker zwischen Vernichtung und Romantisierung*. Mönchengladbach: Infoe-Verlag, 101–122.

Kuppe, René (1998a): "Derechos Indígenas y Protección del Ambiente – ¿Dos Estrategias en Contradicción?" In: *Law and Anthropology* Vol. 10, 100–120.

Kuppe, René (1998b): "Indianerrechte: Vom Minderheitenschutz zum rechtliche Pluralismus." In: Kaller-Dietrich, Martina (Hrsg.): *Recht auf Entwicklung? Atención – Jahrbuch des Österreichischen Lateinamerika-Instituts*, Band 1. Frankfurt a.M.: Brandes & Apsel/Südwind, 121–136.

Kuppe, René (1999): "Rechte indigener Völker im Neoliberalismus: Der Zugriff der Bergbau- und Erdölmultis auf Mutter Erde." In: *Journal für Entwicklungspolitik* XV/2. Frankfurt a.M.: Brandes & Apsel Verlag GmbH, 187–206.

Kuppe, René (2004): "Diskurse zur Begründung multikultureller Autonomie in Lateinamerika." In: *Journal für Entwicklungspolitik* XX/4, 2004. Wien: Mandelbaum Verlag, 43–61.

Kuru Development Trust and WIMSA (1999): Principles adopted by an Indigenous Peoples' Consultation. Windhoek and Ghanzi: WIMSA and Kuru Development Trust.

Kuru Family of Organisations (KFO). Annual Report 2004.

Kuru Family of Organizations. Newsletter October 2004.

Kymlicka, Will (2004): "Nation-Building & Minority Rights: Comparing Africa & the West." In: Berman/Eyoh/Kymlicka (eds.): *Ethnicity & Democracy in Africa*. Oxford: James Currey Ltd, 54–71.

L

Le Roux, Willemien/White, Alison (2004): *Voices of the San living in Southern Africa Today*. Cape Town: Kwela Books.

Lee, Richard (1965): Subsistence ecology of !Kung Bushmen. Ph.D. thesis. Berkeley: University of California,

Lee, Richard (1996): "Laurens van der Post and the Kalahari Debate." In: Skotnes et al. (eds.): *Miscast: Negotiating the Presence of Bushmen*. Cape Town: University of Cape Town Press, 239–249.

Lee, Richard (2006): "Twenty-first Century Indigenism." *Anthropological Theory* 2006, Vol. 6 (4), 455–479. Online at: http://ant.sagepub.com/cgi/content/abstract/6/4/455.

Lee, Richard/Hitchcock, Robert (2001): "African Hunter-Gatherers: Survival, History, and the Politics of Identity." *African Study Monographs*, Suppl. 26. Center for African Area Studies, Kyoto: Kyoto University, 257–280.

Lee, Richard/Hitchcock, Robert/Biesele, Megan (2002): "From Foragers to First Peoples: The Kalahari San Today." In: *Cultural Survival Quarterly*, 26 (1), 8–12.

Lepper, Caitlin Mary/Goebel, Jessica Schroenn (2010): "Community-based natural resource management, poverty alleviation and livelihood diversification: A case study from northern Botswana." In: *Development Southern Africa*, 27 (5), 725–739.

Lewis-Williams, J.D. (2002): "Introduction." In: *Stories that Float from Afar. Ancestral Folklore of the San of Southern Africa*. Cape Town: David Philip Publishers, 1–41.

Li, Tania Murray (1999): "Articulating Indigenous Identity in Indonesia: Resource Politics of the Tribal Slot." In: *Comparative Studies in Society and History*, 42 (1), 149–179.

M

MacKay, Fergus (2002): *A Guide to Indigenous Peoples' Rights in the Inter-American Human Rights System*. Copenhagen: IWGIA.

MacKay, Fergus (2004): "Indigenous Peoples' Rights to Land, Territories and Resources: Selected International and Domestic Legal Considerations." In: *Land Reform, Land Settlement and Cooperatives*. Food and Agriculture Organization No. 1, 81–94.

MacKay, Fergus (2010): "Indigenous Peoples' Rights and the UN Committee on the Elimination of Racial Discrimination." In: Dersso, Solomon (ed.): *Perspectives on the Rights of Minorities and Indigenous Peoples in Africa*. Pretoria: Pretoria University Press, 155–205.

Mafisa, K.R. (1990): Ethnicity and Elections: The Case of 1989 National Elections in Botswana. MA Thesis at the University of Botswana.

Maine, Lethebe A. (2000): "Democracy and Human Rights in Botswana – an Ombudsman's Perspective." In: DITSHWANELO (ed.): *Conference on Human Rights and Democracy*. Gaborone: Bay Publishing (Pty) Ltd., 64–66.

Malanczuk, Peter (2003): *Akehurst's Modern Introduction to International Law (1997)*. London, New York: Routledge.

Markowitz, Arthur (1956): *With Uplifted Tongue: Stories, Myths and Fables of the South African Bushmen Told in their Manner*. Parow: Central News Agency.

Maripe, Bugalo (2011): "Development and the balancing of interests in environmental law: The case of Botswana." In: Fraue, Michael/du Plessis Willemien (eds.): *The Balancing of Interests in Environmental Law in Africa*. Pretoria: Pretoria University Law Press, 49–73.

Martinez, Miguel Alfonso (1999): Study on Treaties, Agreements and other Constructive Arrangements between States and Indigenous Populations. (E/CN.4/Sub.2/1999/20).

Maruyama, Junko (2003): "The Impacts of Resettlement on Livelihood and Social Relationships among the Central Kalahari San." In: *African Study Monographs*, 24(4), 223–245.

Masilo-Rakgoasi, Rosinah (2003): Where are the San in People-Centred Development? A Case of CBNRM in Botswana. Unpubl. Paper at the Conference "Research for Khoe and San Development". 10–12 September 2003. Gaborone: University of Botswana, Centre for Continuing Education.

Mazonde, Isaac (2002): "The San in Botswana and the Issue of Subjectivities – National Desintegration or Cultural Diversity?" In: Mazonde, Isaac (ed.): *Minorities in the Millennium. Perspectives from Botswana*. Gaborone: Lightbooks, 57–71.

Mazonde, Isaac (2004): "Equality and Ethnicity: How Equal are San in Botswana?" In: Hitchcock, Robert/Vinding, Diana (eds.): *Indigenous Peoples' Rights in Southern Africa*. Copenhagen: International Work Group for Indigenous Affairs, 134–151.

McCabe, Terrence J. (2002): "Giving Conservation a Human Face? Lessons from Forty years of Combining Conservation and Development in the Ngorongoro Conservation Area, Tanzania." In: Chatty, Dawn and Marcus Colchester (eds.): *Conservation and Mobile Indigenous Peoples. Displacement, forced settlement, and sustainable development*. New York, Oxford: Berghahn Books, 61–76.

McHugh, Paul G. (1999): "From Sovereignty Talk to Settlement Time. The Constitutional Setting of Maori Claims in the 1990s." In: Havemann, Paul (ed.): *Indigenous Peoples' Rights in Australia, Canada and New Zealand (1999)*. Oxford: Oxford University Press, 447–467.

McNeil, Kent (1989): *Common Law Aboriginal Title*. Oxford: Clarendon Press.

McNeil, Kent (1998): *Defining Aboriginal Title in the 90's: Has the Supreme Court finally got it right?* Toronto: Robarts Centre for Canadian Studies, York University. Online at: www.osgoode.yorku.ca/osgmedia.nsf/research/mcneil_kent.

Mgadla, P.T./Campbell, Alec C. (1989): "Dikgotla, Dikgosi and the Protectorate Administration." In: Holm, John/Molutsi, Patrick (eds.): *Democracy in Botswana*. Gaborone: Macmillan Botswana Publishing Company, 48–57.

Mogwe, Alice (1992): Who was (t)here first? An Assessment of the Human Rights Situation of Basarwa in selected Communities in the Gantsi District, Botswana. Study commissioned by the Botswana Christian Council, Occasional Paper No. 10.

Mogwe, Alice (1994): "Will Basic Human Rights and Individual Freedoms Continue to be Protected, Promoted and Respected?" In: Brothers, Sue/Hermans, Janet/Nteta, Doreen (eds.): *Botswana in the 21st Century*. Gaborone: The Botswana Society, 49–64.

Mogwe, Alice (2002): Report of the Chairperson-Rapporteur on the Third Workshop on Multiculturalism in Africa: Peaceful and Constructive Group Accommodation in Situations involving Minorities and Indigenous Peoples. Gaborone, 18–22 February 2002.

Mogwe, Alice (2011): "Human Rights Struggles. Where Social Conflicts and Confrontations are Negotiated – The Case of the Displacement of 'Basarwa' from the Central Kalahari Game Reserve." In: Zips, Werner/Weilenmann, Markus (eds.): *The Governance of Legal Pluralism*. Münster, Hamburg: LIT Verlag, 163–179.

Molokomme, Athaliah (1994): "Customary Law in Botswana: Past, Present and Future." In: Brothers, Sue/Hermans, Janet/Nteta, Doreen (eds.): *Botswana in the 21st Century*. Gaborone: The Botswana Society, 347–369.

Molutsi, Patrick (1989): "The Ruling Class and Democracy in Botswana." In: Holm, John/Molutsi, Patrick (eds.): *Democracy in Botswana*. Gaborone: Macmillan Botswana Publishing Company, 103–115.

Molutsi, Patrick (1994): "Botswana's Democratic Institutions: Their Strength and Prospects." In: Brothers, Sue/Hermans, Janet/Nteta, Doreen (eds.): *Botswana in the 21st Century*. Gaborone: The Botswana Society, 21–37.

Mostert, Hanri/Fitzpatrick, Peter (2004): "Law against Law: Indigenous Rights and the Richtersveld Cases. Law." In: *Social Justice & Global Development Journal (LGD)*. Online at: www.go.warwick.ac.uk/elj/lgd/2004_2/mostertfitzpatrick (accessed on 17 August 2006).

Motladiile, Mercy G. (2002): "The Role of NGOs & CBOs in Implementing the Convention on Biological Diversity through CBNRM Initiatives." In: John, Geryk/Tobedza, Geofrey/McColaugh, Doreen (eds.): *Proceedings of the Environmental Education Association of Southern Africa Annual Conference*. Gaborone: The Kalahari Conservation Society, 165–167.

Mubangizi, John Cantius (2012): "A South African Perspective on the Clash between Culture and Human Rights, with Particular Reference to Gender-related Cultural Practices and Traditions." In: *Journal of International Woman's Studies* Vol. 13#3 August 2012, 33–48.

Murray, Andrew/Nengwekhulu, Harry/Ramsay, Jeff (1987): "The Formation of Political Parties." In: Morton, Fred/Ramsay, Jeff (eds.): *The Birth of Botswana. A History of the Bechuanaland Protectorate from 1910 to 1966*. Gaborone: Longman Botswana, 172–186.

N

Nader, Laura (2005): "The Americanization of International Law." In: Benda-Beckmann, Franz/Benda-Beckmann, Keebet/Griffith, Anne (eds*.): Mobile People, Mobile Law. Expanding Legal Relations in a Contracting World*. Aldershot, Burlington: Ashgate Publishing, 199–213.

Nanjira, Daniel D.C. Don (2003): "The Protection of Human Rights in Africa: The African Charter on Human and Peoples' Rights." In: Symonides, Janusz (ed.): *Human Rights: International Protection, Monitoring, Enforcement*. Paris: UNESCO Publishing; Aldershot, Burlington: Ashgate Publishing, 213–237.

Ng'ong'ola, Clement (2000): "Legal and Practical Problems in the Administration of Tribal Land in Botswana." In: *Conference on Human Rights and Democracy 1998*. DITSHWANELO – The Botswana Centre for Human Rights. Gaborone: Bay Publishing (Pty) Ltd, 163–174.

Nowak, Manfred (2002): *Einführung in das internationale Menschenrechtssystem*. Wien: Neuer Wissenschaftlicher Verlag.

Nowak, Manfred (2003): *Introduction to the International Human Rights Regime*. Leiden, Boston: Martinus Nijhoff Publishers.

Nthomang, Keitseope (2003): "Development Practice and the Khoe and San Peoples: How Appropriate?" Paper at the conference "Research for Khoe and San Development". 10–12 September 2003. Gaborone: University of Botswana, Centre for Continuing Education.

Nthomang, Keitseope (2004): "Relentless Colonialism: The Case of the Remote Area Development Programme (RADP) and the Basarwa in Botswana." In: *Journal of Modern African Studies*, 42 (3). Cambridge: Cambridge University Press, 415–435.

Nyati-Ramahobo, Lydia (2002a): "Ethnic Identity and Nationhood in Botswana." In: Mazonde, Isaac (ed.): *Minorities in the Millennium. Perspectives from Botswana*. Gaborone: Lightbooks, 17–27.

Nyati-Ramahobo, Lydia (2002b): "From a Phone Call to the High Court: Wayeyi Visibility and the Kamanakao Association's Campaign for Linguistic and Cultural Rights in Botswana." In: *Journal of Southern African Studies*, Vol. 28 (4), Special Issue: Minorities and Citizenship in Botswana, 685–709.

Nyati-Ramahobo, Lydia (2009): Minority Tribes in Botswana: the Politics of Recognition. Online at: www.unhcr.org/refworld/docid/496dc0c82.html (accessed on 6 June 2009).

O

Obeng, Kenneth E. (2001): *Botswana. Institutions of Democracy and Government of Botswana*. Gaborone: Associated Printers.

Öhlinger, Theo (1999): *Verfassungsrecht*. Wien: WUV.

Oldham, Paul/Frank, Miriam Anne (2008): "'We the peoples ...' The United Nations Declaration on the Rights of Indigenous Peoples." In: *Anthropology Today*, Vol. 24 (2), 5–9.

Oliver, Roland/Atmore, Anthony (1981): *Africa since 1800*. Cambridge, London, Sydney: Cambridge University Press.

Ölz, Martin (2002): *Die NGO's im Recht des internationalen Menschenrechtsschutzes*. Wien: Verlag Österreich.

Ouguergouz, Fatsah (2003): *The African Charter on Human and Peoples' Rights. A Comprehensive Agenda for Human Dignity and Sustainable Democracy in Africa*. The Hague, London, New York: Martinus Nijhoff Publishers.

Owens, Mark and Delia (1984): *Cry of the Kalahari*. Glasgow: Fontana/Collins Publisher.

P

Pabst, Martin (2002): *Grenzüberschreitende Peace Parks im südlichen Afrika*. München: Südliches Afrika Initiative der Deutschen Wirtschaft (SAFRI).

Pain, J.H. (1978): "The Reception of English and Roman-Dutch Law in Africa with Reference to Botswana, Lesotho and Swaziland." In: *Comparative and International Law Journal of Southern Africa*, Vol. XI. Pretoria: University of South Africa, 137–167.

Pakleppa, Richard/Kwononoka, Americo (2003): *Where the First are the Last: San Communities Fighting for Survival in Southern Angola*. Windhoek: WIMSA, Trocaire Angola and OCADEC.

Parson, Jack (1991): "Botswana im Einflußbereich Südafrikas: Grenzen für die kapitalistische Umgestaltung im Arbeitskräftereservat." In: Altheimer/Hopf/Weimer (Hg.): *Botswana. Vom Land der Betschuanen zum Frontstaat. Wirtschaft, Gesellschaft, Kultur*. Münster, Hamburg: LIT Verlag, 117–129.

Parsons, Neil (1994): "Introduction. Botwana in the 21st Century – Tigers and Zebras." In: Brothers, Sue/Hermans, Janet/Nteta, Doreen (eds.): *Botswana in the 21st Century*. Gaborone: The Botswana Society, 1–8.

Parsons, Neil (2002a): "Introduction: El Negro and the Hottentot Venus." In: *Pula: Botswana Journal of African Studies*. Volume 16. Gaborone: University of Botswana, 2–7.

Parson, Neil (2002b): "One body playing many parts – le Betjouana, el Negro, and il Bosquimano." In: *Pula: Botswana Journal of African Studies*. Volume 16. Gaborone: University of Botswana, 19–29.

Paul, James S.N. (1990): "Participatory Approaches to Human Rights in Sub-Saharan Africa." In: An-Na'im, Abdullahai Ahmed/Deng, Francis M. (eds.): *Human Rights in Africa. Cross-Cultural Perspectives*. Washington: The Brookings Institution, 213–239.

Peters, Guy/Pierre, Jon (2004): "Multi-level Governance and Democracy: A Faustian Bargain?" In: Bache, Ian/Flinders, Matthew (eds.): *Multi-level Governance*. Oxford, New York: Oxford University Press, 75–89.

Poteete, Amy R./Ribot, Jesse C. (2011): "Repertoires of Domination: Decentralization as Process in Botswana and Senegal." In: *World Development* Vol. 39, No. 3, 439–449.

Q

Quansah, EK (2001): *Introduction to the Botswana Legal System*. Gaborone: Pula Press.

R

Ramsay, Jeff/Morton, Barry/Mgadla, Part Themba (1996): *Building a Nation. A History of Botswana from 1800 to 1910*. Gaborone: Longman Botswana.

Randeria, Shalini (2002): "Glocalization of Law: Environmental Justice, World Bank, NGOs and the Cunning State in India." In: *Current Sociology*, Vol. 51 (3–4), 305–328.

Raphaka, Thato Yaone (2003): Development Policy Dialogue: The Case of Implementing the Remote Area Development Programme: A General Brief. Paper at the conference "Research for Khoe and San Development". 10–12 September 2003. Gaborone: University of Botswana, Ministry of Local Government.

Raschauer, Bernhard (1998): *Allgemeines Verwaltungsrecht*. Wien: Springer-Verlag.

Ray, Donald I./Reddy, P.S. (eds.), (2003): *Grassroots Governance? Chiefs in Africa and the Afro-Caribbean*. Calgery: University of Calgery Press.

Riedel, Eige/Will, Martin (1999): "Human Rights Clauses in External Agreements of the EC." In: Alston, Philip (ed.): *The EU and Human Rights*. Oxford: Oxford University Press, 723–734.

Rihoy, Liz/Maguranyanga, Brian (2011): "The Politics of Community-Based Natural Resource Management in Botswana." In: Nelson, Fred (ed.): *Community Rights, Conservation & Contested Land. The Politics of Natural Resource Governance in Africa*. London, New York: Earthscan, 55–78.

Roberts, Simon (1979): *Order and Dispute. An Introduction to Legal Anthropology*. Harmondsworth: Penguin Books.

Robins, Steven (2001): "Whose 'culture', whose 'survival'? The ǂKhomani San Land Claim and the Cultural Politics of 'Community' and 'Development' in the Kalahari." In: Barnard, Alan/Kenrick, Justin (eds.): *Africa's Indigenous Peoples: 'First Peoples' or 'Marginalized Minorities'?* Edinburgh: Centre of African Studies, University of Edinburgh, 229–253.

Robins, Steven (2003a): "NGOs, 'Bushmen' and Double Vision: The ‡Khomani San Land Claim and the Cultural Politics of 'Community' and 'Development' in the Kalahari." In: Hohmann, Thekla (ed.): *San and the State. Contesting Land, Development, Identity and Representation.* Köln: Rüdiger Köppe Verlag, 365–400.

Robins, Steven (2003b): "Whose Modernity? Indigenous Modernities and Land Claims after Apartheid." In: *Development and Change* 34 (2), 265–285.

Robins, Steven/Madzudzo, Elias/Brenzinger, Matthias (2001): *An Assessment of the Status of the San in South Africa, Angola, Zambia and Zimbabwe.* Windhoek: Legal Assistance Centre.

Rouveroy van Nieuwaal van, Adrian/Dijk van, Rijk (eds.), (1999): *African Chieftaincy in a New Socio-Political Landscape.* Münster, Hamburg: LIT Verlag.

Rouveroy van Nieuwaal van, Adrian/Zips, Werner (eds.), (1998): *Sovereignty, Legitimacy, and Power in West African Societies. Perspectives from Legal Anthropology.* Münster, Hamburg: LIT Verlag.

Roy, Devasish (2003): The International Character of Treaties with Indigenous Peoples and Implementation Challenges for Intra-State Peace and Autonomy Agreements between Indigenous Peoples and States: The Case of the Chittagong Hill Tracts, Bangladesh. Background paper for the Expert Seminar on Treaties, Agreements and other Constructive Arrangements between States and Indigenous Peoples, 15–17 December 2003, HR/GENEVA/TSIP/SEM/2003/BP.8.

Rozemeijer, Nico (2003): Community Based Natural Resource Management in Botswana. Revisiting the Assumptions after 10 years of implementation. Online at: www.cbnrm.bw (accessed on 7 August 2004).

S

Sanders, A.J.G.M. (1989): "The Bushmen of Botswana – From desert dwellers to world citizens." In: *Law and Anthropology* 4, Vienna: VWGÖ-Verlag, 107–122.

Sanders, Douglas E. (1999): "Indigenous Peoples: Issues of Definition." In: *International Journal of Cultural Property*, Vol. 8 (1), 4–13.

SASI (2002): South African San Institute Annual Report Jan-Dec 2002. South African San Institute, South Africa.

Sauer, Walter (2003): "Südliches Afrika: Politik, Wirtschaft, Gesellschaft im 20. Jahrhundert." In: Grau/Mährdel/Schicho (Hg.): *Afrika. Geschichte und Gesellschaft im 19. und 20. Jahrhundert.* Wien: Promedia, 241–265.

Saugestad, Sidsel (2001): *The Inconvinient Indigenous. Remote Area Development in Botswana, Donor Assistance, and the First People of the Kalahari.* Uppsala: The Nordic Africa Institute.

Saugestad, Sidsel (2003): What has Changed? 1993–2003. Paper at the conference "Research for Khoe and San Development". 10–12 September 2003. Gaborone: Centre for Continuing Education, University of Botswana.

Saugestad, Sidsel (2004): "The Indigenous Peoples of Southern Africa: An Overview." In: Hitchcock, Robert/Vinding, Diana (eds.): *Indigenous Peoples' Rights in Southern Africa*. Copenhagen: IWGIA, 22–41.

Saugestad, Sidsel (2006): "San Development and Challenges in Development Cooperation." In: Hitchcock/Ikeya/Biesele/Lee (eds.): *Updating the San: Image and Reality of an African People in the 21st Century*. Osaka: National Museum of Ethnology, 171–180.

Schapera, Isaac (1930): *The Khoisan Peoples of South Africa. Bushmen and Hottentots*. London: George Routledge & Sons, Ltd.

Schapera, Isaac [1930](1984): *A Handbook of Tswana Law and Custom*. Münster, Hamburg: LIT Verlag and Gaborone: The Botswana Society.

Schuster, Brigitte (2007): *IUCN – The World Conservation Union. Towards Vision 2016: CBNRM's Potential to Contribute and CBNRM Status Report 2006*. Gaborone: IUCN CBNRM Support Programme.

Schweighofer, Erich (1999): "Schutz indigener Umweltbewirtschaftungspraktiken und -kenntnisse." In: *Journal für Entwicklungspolitik* XV/2, 1999, Frankfurt a.M.: Brandes & Apsel Verlag GmbH, 171–185.

Schweitzer, Peter (2004): "No Escape from being Theoretically Important: Hunter-Gatherers in German-Language Debates of the Late Nineteenth and Early Twentieth Centuries." In: Barnard, Alan (ed.): *Hunter-Gatherers in History, Archaeology and Anthropology*. Oxford, New York: Berg Publishers, 69–76.

Seidl-Hohenveldern, Ignaz (1997): "Die Staaten." In: Neuhold/Hummer/Schreuer (Hrsg.): *Österreichisches Handbuch des Völkerrechts*, Teil 1. Wien: Manz Verlag, 134–164.

Segwai, Keto (2008): CKGR saga soils Mogae's remarkable legacy (Mogae Legacy). In: *Mmegi Online*. Online at: www.mmegi.bw accest on 06 June 2009

Sekgoma, Gilbert (1994): "Does Chieftainship have a Future in the Next Century?" In: Brothers, Sue/Hermans, Janet/Nteta, Doreen (eds.): *Botswana in the 21st Century*. Gaborone: The Botswana Society, 403–418.

Sesana, Roy (2000): "Land Problem with specific focus on the Central Kalahari Game Reserve." In: DITSHWANELO (ed.): *Conference on Human Rights and Democracy*. Gaborone: Bay Publishing (Pty) Ltd., 175–176.

Sharma, Keshav C. (2003): "Traditional Leadership and Rural Local Government in Botswana." In: Ray, Donald/Reddy, P.S. (eds.): *Grassroots Governance? Chiefs in Africa and the Afro-Caribbean*. Calgary: University of Calgary Press, 249–262.

Silberbauer, Georg B. (1982): "Political Process in G/wi Bands." In: Leacock, E./Lee, R. (eds.): *Politics and History in Band Societies*. Cambridge: Cambridge University Press, 23–35.

Skotnes, Pippa (ed.), (1996): *Miscast: Negotiating the Presence of Bushmen*. Cape Town: University of Cape Town Press.

Söfterstad, L. (1988): "Indigenous Peoples and Land Rights: An Overview." In: *Geographica Helvetica*, No 4.

Solway, Jacqueline S. (2004): "Reaching the Limits of Universal Citizenship: 'Minority' Struggles in Botswana." In: Berman/Eyoh/Kymlicka (eds.): *Ethnicity and Democratization in Africa*. Oxford: James Currey, 129–147.

Somolekae, Gloria (2005): "Political Parties in Botswana." *EISA Research Report* No. 27. Johannesburg: EISA.

Stavenhagen, Rodolfo (2002): Human Rights and Indigenous Issues. Report of the Special Rapporteur on the Situation of Human Rights and Fundamental Freedoms of Indigenous People. (E/CN.4/2002/97 and Addendum E/CN.4/2002/97/Add.1).

Stavenhagen, Rodolfo (2006): Human Rights and Indigenous Issues. Analysis of country situations and other activities of the Special Rapporteur on the Situation of Human Rights and Fundamental Freedoms of Indigenous People. Addendum. (E/CN.4/2006/78/Add.1 and Add.2).

Stephenson, David J. (2003): The Patenting of P 57 and the Intellectual Property Rights of the San Peoples of Southern Africa. Unpublished case study, in Cooperation with and the Special Assistance of the South African San Council, as representatives of the Working Group of Indigenous Minorities in Southern Africa, and First Peoples Worldwide.

Sullivan, Sian (2002): "How Sustainable is the Communalizing Discourse of 'New' Conservation? The Masking of Difference, Inequality and Aspiration in the Fledgling 'Conservancies' of Namibia." In: Chatty, Dawn/Colchester, Marcus (eds.): *Conservation and Mobile Indigenous Peoples. Displacement, Forced Settlement, and Sustainable Development*. New York, Oxford: Berghahn Books, 158–187.

Suzman, James (2001a): *An Introduction to the Regional Assessment of the Status of the San in Southern Africa*. Windhoek: Legal Assistance Centre.

Suzman, James (2001b): *An Assessment of the Status of the San in Namibia*. Windhoek: Legal Assistance Centre.

Suzman, James (2001c): "Indigenous Wrongs and Human Rights: National Policy, International Resolutions and the Status of the San of Southern Africa." In: Barnard, Alan/Kenrick, Justin (eds.): *Africa's Indigenous Peoples: 'First Peoples' or 'Marginalized Minorities'?* Edinburgh: Centre of African Studies, University of Edinburgh, 273–297.

Suzman, James (2002): "Kalahari Conundrums: Relocation, Resistance and International Support in the Central Kalahari Botswana." In: *Before Farming*. Online at: http://www.waspjournals.com 2002/3_4(12)

T

Taylor, Michael (2001): "Narratives of Identity and Assertion of Legitimacy: Basarwa in Northern Botswana." In: Anderson, David/Ikeya, Kazunobu (eds.): *Parks, Property, and Power: Managing Hunting Practice and Identity within State Policy Regimes*. Osaka: National Museum of Ethnology, 157–182.

Taylor, Michael (2003): "'Wilderness', 'Development', and San Ethnicity in Contemporary Botswana." In: Hohmann, Thekla (ed): *San and the State. Contesting Land, Development, Identity and Representation.* Köln: Rüdiger Köppe Verlag, 255–279.

Taylor, Michael (2004): "The Past and Future of San Land Rights in Botswana." In: Hitchcock, Robert/Vinding, Diana (eds.): *Indigenous Peoples' Rights in Southern Africa.* Copenhagen: IWGIA, 152–165.

Teubner, Günther (ed.), (1997): *Global Law without a State.* Dartmouth: Aldershot.

Thakadu, O. T. (2001): The Concept of Community Ownership and Mobilization: Experiences from Community Based Natural Resource Management. Workshop on Community based Management of Animal Genetic Resources: A Tool for Rural Development and Food Security. Unpublished paper.

Thornberry, Patrick (2002): *Indigenous Peoples and Human Rights.* Manchester: Manchester University Press.

Tlou, Thomas/Campbell, Alec (1984): *History of Botswana.* Gaborone: Macmillan.

Tomasevski, Katarina (1989): *Development Aid and Human Rights.* New York: St. Martin's Press.

Tomasevski, Katarina (2003): "Sanctions and Human Rights." In: Symonides, Janusz (ed.): *Human Rights: International Protection, Monitoring, Enforcement.* Paris: UNESCO Publishing; Aldershot, Burlington: Ashgate Publishing, 303–323.

Tong, Maureen (2003): Indigenous Peoples' legal systems – examples, experiences and governmental, administrative and legal measures to accomodate customary law in national systems of justice. Background paper presented at the Expert Seminar on Indigenous Peoples and the Administration of Justice (OHCHR: HR/MADRID/IP/SEM/2003/BP.2).

U

UNDG (2008): Guidelines on Indigenous Peoples Issues. United Nations Development Group. New York, Geneva: United Nations. (HR/P/PT/16).

UNDP (1997): Governance for Sustainable Human Development: Report of International Conference, United Nations, New York, 28–30 July 1997

UNESCO heute (2007): UNESCO Biosphärenreservate: Modellregionen von Weltrang. *Zeitschrift der Deutschen UNESCO-Kommission* Nr. 2.

UNHCR (2010): Handbook for the Protection of Internally Displaced Persons. Online at: *www.unhcr.org/refworld/docid/4790cbc02.html*

United Nations (2009): State of the World's Indigenous Peoples. ST/ESA/328. New York. Online at: www.galdu.org/govat/doc/sowip.pdf (accessed on 25 October 2012).

U.S. Department of State. Country Reports on Human Rights practices – 2006, 2007, 2008, 2012: Botswana. Released by the Bureau of Democracy, Human Rights, and Labor. Online at: www.state.gov/g/drl/rls/hrrpt/2006/78720.htm (accessed on 7 July 2007, 21 November 2008, 28 June 2009, 15 October 2012).

V

Van der Post, Laurens (1958): *The Lost World of the Kalahari* (2002). London: Vintage.

Van der Post, Laurens (1961): *The Heart of the Hunter* (2002). London: Vintage.

Viljoen, Frans/Odinkalu, Chidi (2006): *The Prohibition of Torture and Ill-Treatment in the African Human Rights System: A Handbook for Victims and their Advocates*. Geneva: The World Organization against Torture.

Viljoen, Frans (2012): "AU Assembly should consider human rights implications before adopting the Amending Merged African Court Protocol." In: *AfricLaw*. Online at: www.africlaw.com/2012/05/23/au-assembly-should-consider-human-rights-implications-before-adopting-the-amending-merged-african-court-protocol/(accessed on 16 October 2012).

Vision 2016: see under *National Laws, Regulations, Policies*: 1997 Long-Term Vision for Botswana 2016: Towards Prosperity for All.

Vogler, Helmut (2002): "Der Menschenrechtsschutz indigener Völker." In: Jasse/Müller/Schneider (Hrsg.): *Menschenrechte, Bilanz und Perspektiven*. Baden Baden: Nomas Verlagsgesellschaft DSF, Band 137, 360–380.

W

Watzlawick, Paul/Beavin, Janet/Jackson, Don (2007): *Menschliche Kommunikation. Formen, Störungen, Paradoxien*. Bern: Verlag Hans Huber.

Weilenmann, Markus (2004): "Projektrecht" – normative Ordnungen der bilateralen Entwick lungs zusammenarbeit und sozialer Wandel. Zum Beispiel die Deutsche Gesellschaft für Technische Zusammenarbeit. Working Paper Nr. 66. Halle: Max-Planck-Instutute for Social Anthropology.

Weimer, Berhard (1989): "Democracy in Botswana: an outsider's view." In: Holm, John/Molutsi, Patrick (eds.): *Democracy in Botswana*. Gaborone: Macmillan Botswana Publishing Company, 289–294.

White, Richard (2000): Study on NGOs' Involvement in Land Issues. Online at: www.iucnbot.bw/pages_sub_dir/NGOLandstudy.html (accessed on 7 May 2003).

Wilder, Lisa (1997): "Local Futures? From Denunciation to Revalorization of the Indigenous Other." In: Teubner, Günther (ed.): *Global Law without a State*. Dartmouth: Aldershot, 215–256.

Willet, Shelagh/Monageng, Stella/Saugestad, Sidsel/Hermans, Janet (2002): *The Khoe and San: An Annotated Bibliography*: Volume One. Gaborone: Lightbooks.

Willet, Shelagh (2003): *The Khoe and San: An Annotated Bibliography:* Volume Two. Gaborone: Lightbooks.

Wilmsen, Edwin N. (1989): *Land filled with flies. A political economy of the Kalahari.* Chicago, London: The University of Chicago Press.

WIMSA (2001): *Traditional Authorities Handbook.* Windhoek: First Peoples Worldwide and Working Group of Indigenous Minorities in Southern Africa.

WIMSA (2004a): Working Group of Indigenous Minorities in Southern Africa. Report on Activities April 2003 to March 2004, Windhoek: Working Group of Indigenous Minorities in Southern Africa.

WIMSA (2004b): *Biopirates in the Kalahari? How Indigenous People are standing up for their Rights – the Experience of the San in Southern Africa.* Windhoek: Working Group of Indigenous Minorities in Southern Africa.

Windmeißer, Anette (2002): *Der Menschenrechtsansatz in der Entwicklungszusammenarbeit. Menschenrechte, Demokratie, Rechtsstaatlichkeit und "good governance" in der Entwicklungszusammenarbeit. Das Beispiel der AKP-EU-Beziehung.* Wien: Verlag Österreich.

Woodman, Gordon (1989): "The Peculiar Policy of Recognition of Indigenous Laws in British Colonial Africa. A Preliminary discussion." In: *Verfassung und Recht in Übersee* 22, 273–284.

Woodman, Gordon (1998): "Ideological Combat and Social Observation: Recent Debate about Legal Pluralism." In: *Journal of Legal Pluralism*, Vol. 42, 21–59.

WWF (2004): Statement of Principles on Indigenous Peoples and Conservation. Online at: www.panda.org/about_wwf/what_we_do/policy/indigenous_people/rights.cfm (accessed on 10 October 2004).

Wynberg, Rachel/Schroeder, Doris/Chennells, Roger (2009): *Indigenous Peoples, Consent and Benefit Sharing. Lessons from the San-Hoodia Case.* Dordrecht, Heidelberg, London, New York: Springer.

Z

Zips, Werner (2003a): *Das Stachelschwein erinnert sich. Ethnohistorie als praxeologische Strukturgeschichte.* Wien: WUV Universitätsverlag.

Zips, Werner (2003b): *Gerechtigkeit unter dem Mangobaum. Rechtsanthropologische Forschung zu einer Insel des Rechts.* Wien: WUV Universitätsverlag.

Zips, Werner (2006): "Comment. Discussion: The concept of indigeneity." In: *Social Anthropology*, Vol. 14, 27–29.

Zips, Werner (2009): "Justice ain't no System". Some reflections on "Justice" as an Empirical Category for Legal Pluralist Research. Unpublished Paper.

Zips, Werner (2011): "Fashion under a Leopard's Skin. Emerging Forms of Complementary Governance in Botswana." In: Zips, Werner/Weilenmann, Markus (eds.): *The Governance of Legal Pluralism. Empirical Studies from Africa and Beyond.* Münster, Wien: LIT Verlag, 181–212.

Zips, Werner/Zips-Mairitsch, Manuela (2007): "Lost in Transition? The Politics of Conservation, Indigenous Land Rights and Community-based Natural Resource Management in Southern Africa." In: *Journal of Legal Pluralism*, No. 55, 37–71.

Zips, Werner/Zips-Mairitsch, Manuela (2008): Kalahari San Tunes. The Kuru Dance Festival in Botswana. DVD and Booklet.

Zips-Mairitsch, Manuela (2011): "Kalahari Struggles. Indigeneity, Internal Displacement and Nature Conservation in Botswana – Interviews with Mathambo Ngakaeaja." In: Zips, Werner/Weilenmann, Markus (eds.): *The Governance of Legal Pluralism. Empirical Studies from Africa and Beyond*. Münster, Wien: LIT Verlag, 137–162

(Selected) Legal Texts

1. International Instruments

a) Universal Instruments

United Nations

1948   Universal Declaration on Human Rights, United Nations General Assembly. Resolution 217A(III), UN Doc. A/810 at 71

1965   International Convention on the Elimination of all forms of Racial Discrimination, GA-Res. 2106 A(XX) of 21 December 1965, entered into force on 4 January 1969.

1966   International Covenant on Civil and Political Rights, GA-Res. 2200 A (XXI) of 16 December 1966, entered into force on 23 March 1976.

1989   ILO Convention (No. 169) concerning Indigenous and Tribal Populations in Independent Countries, adopted by the ILO General Conference on 27 June 1989, entered into force on 5 September 1991.

1992   Agenda 21, UN Conference on Environment and Development, Rio de Janeiro, 13 June 1992, UN Doc. A/CONF.151/26 (vol. 1, 2&3) Annex 2 (1992).

1992   Rio Declaration on Environment and Development, UN Conference on Environment and Development, Rio de Janeiro, 13 June 1992, UN Doc. A/CONF.151/26 (vol. 1, Annex 1 (1992).

1992   Convention on Biological Diversity, Rio de Janeiro, 5 June 1992, entered into force on 28 December 1993.

2001   United Nations System in Botswana: Botswana: Towards National Prosperity. Common Country Assessment 2001. Gaborone, Botswana.

2002   Gaborone Declaration on Indigenous Peoples and Minorities in Africa. E/CN.4/Sub.2/AC.4/2002/4

2006a	Draft United Nations Declaration on the Rights of Indigenous Peoples, adopted by the Human Rights Council Resolution 2006/2 on 29 June 2006.
2006b	Committee on the Elimination of Racial Discrimination: Consideration of Reports submitted by State Parties under Article 9 of the CERD. Concluding Observations of the Committee on the Elimination of Racial Discrimination: Botswana. CERD/C/BWA/CO/16, 4 April 2006.
2007	Declaration on the Rights of Indigenous Peoples. A/61/L.67, 13 September 2007.
2008	Human Rights Committee: Consideration of Reports submitted by State Parties under Article 40 of the CCPR. Concluding Observations of the Human Rights Committee: Botswana. CCPR/C/BWA/CO/1, 24 April 2008.

UNESCO Universal Declaration on Cultural Diversity, adopted 2 November 2001.

UNESCO Progress Report on the Proposed World Heritage Indigenous Peoples Council of Experts. WHC-2001/CONF.208/13, 22 November 2001.

UNESCO Convention for the safeguarding of the Intangible Cultural Heritage. HISC/203/CLT/CH/14, 17 October 2003.

UNESCO Convention on the Protection and Promotion of the Diversity of Cultural Expressions. CLT-2005/CONVENTION DIVERSITE-CULT, 20 October 2005.

2010	United Nations AIDS Report on the Global AIDS Epidemic. Joint United Nations Programme on HIV/AIDS (UNAIDS).

World Bank

1991	Operational Directive 4.20 on Indigenous Peoples. Washington D.C.
2000	The Community driven Development Approach in the African Region: A Vision of Poverty Reduction through Empowerment. The World Bank, Washington D.C.
2005	Operational Policies and Bank Procedures 4.10 on Indigenous Peoples. Washington D.C.

b) Regional Instruments

African [Banjul] Charter on Human and Peoples' Rights, 27 June 1981, OAU Doc CAB/LEG/67/3/Rev 5, entered into force on 21 October 1986.

European Convention on Human Rights, Convention for the Protection of Human Rights and Fundamental Freedoms, Rome, 4 November 1950, entered into force on 3 September 1953.

2. National Laws, Regulations and Policies

Government of Botswana

1933	Tribal Territories Act, now Cap. 32:03. Government Printer, Gaborone
1955	Acquisition of Property Act, Government Printer, Gaborone
1961	Customary Courts Act, Cap. 04:05. Government Printer, Gaborone
1961	Fauna Conservation Act, Cap. 38:01. Government Printer, Gaborone
1962	Fencing, Cap. 33:03. Government Printer, Gaborone
1963	Central Kalahari Game Reserve (Control of Entry) Regulations, Government Printer
1966	Constitution of Botswana, Government Printer, Gaborone
1966	State Land Act, Cap. 32:01. Government Printer, Gaborone
1967	Mineral Rights in Tribal Territories, Government Printer, Gaborone
1968	Tribal Land Act, No. 54, now Cap 32:02. Government Printer, Gaborone
1969	Common Law and Customary Law Act, Cap. 16:01. Government Printer, Gaborone
1975	Government White Paper No. 2 of 1975. National Policy on Tribal Grazing Land. Government Printer, Gaborone
1975	Land Control Act, Cap. 32:11. Government Printer, Gaborone
1976	High Court Act, Cap. 04:02. High Court (Amendment) Act, 1999, No. 13, Government Printer, Gaborone
1976	Tribal Land (Amendment) Act No. 21. Government Printer, Gaborone
1987	Chieftainship Act, now Cap 41:01. Government Printer, Gaborone
1987	Common Law and Customary Law (Amendment) Act. Government Printer, Gaborone
1990	Tourism Policy, Government Paper No. 2 of 1990, Government Printer, Gaborone
1992	Wildlife Conservation and National Parks, Cap. 38:01. Government Printer, Gaborone
1993	Tribal Land (Amendment) Act No. 14. Government Printer, Gaborone
1993	Draft Policy on the Remote Area Development Programme, Ministry of Local Government, Lands and Housing
1997	National Development Plan 8. 1997/98–2002/03. Ministry of Finance and Development Planning Government Printer, Gaborone
1997	Long-Term Vision for Botswana 2016: Towards Prosperity for All, Presidential Task Group for a Long Term Vision for Botswana, Government Printer, Gaborone
1997	National Population Policy, National Council on Population and Development, Ministry of Local Government, Lands and Housing

1997	Population Projections 1991–2021, Central Statistics Office, Ministry of Finance and Development Planning
1998	Botswana National Settlement Policy, Government Paper No. 2 of 1998
1999	National Settlement Policy, Department of Town and Regional Planning, Ministry of Local Government, Lands and Housing
2000	National Parks and Game Reserves Regulations 2000, Government Printer, Gaborone
2000	Draft National Policy for Non-Governmental Organisations, Ministry of Labour and Home Affairs, 9th November 2000.
2002	Revised National Policy for Rural Development, Government Paper No. 3, Government Printer, Gaborone
2002	Government White Paper No. 2 of 2002. Presidential Commission of Inquiry into Sections 77, 78 and 79 of the Constitution of Botswana, Ministry of Finance and Development Planning. Republic of Botswana.
2002	Revised National Policy for Rural Development, Government Paper No. 3 of 2002 Ministry of Finance and Development Planning
2002	Game Ranching Policy for Botswana, Government paper No. 5 of 2002, Ministry of Trade, Industry, Wildlife and Tourism
2003	National Development Plan 9. 2003/04–2008/09. Ministry of Finance and Development Planning, Government Printer, Gaborone
2003	Ghanzi DDP 6: Ghanzi District Development Plan 6: 2003–2009, Ministry of Local Government, Ghanzi District Council, Republic of Botswana.
2004	Constitutional (Amendment) Bill, Government Printer, Gaborone
2009	National Development Plan 10. 2009/04–2016/03. Ministry of Finance and Development Planning, Government Printer, Gaborone
2010	Community based Natural Resource Management in Botswana Practitioners Manual, Ministry of Environment, Wildlife and Tourism, Department of Wildlife and National Parks, Gaborone.
2011	Population and Housing Census, Census Office, Gaborone

Republic of South Africa

1913	Native Land Act, Act No. 27 of 1913
1994	Restitution of Land Rights Act, Act No. 22 of 1994
1996	Constitution of the Republic of South Africa, No. 108 of 1996

2.1 Reports and Political Documents

Report of the Presidential Commission on Land Tenure (1983), Republic of Botswana

Report of the Second Presidential Commission on the Local Government Structure in Botswana (2001), Republic of Botswana

Report of the Presidential Commission (2000): Inquiry into Sections 77, 78 and 79 of the Constitution, November 2000, Republic of Botswana (*Balopi Commission*).

About the Autors

Manuela Zips-Mairitsch is a lecturer at the Department of Social and Cultural Anthropology at the University of Vienna, Austria. Aside from her extensive experience in the field of indigenous rights and legal developments in different nation states, she has conducted fieldwork in southern Africa for more than twelve years and holds a PhD in Law from the University of Vienna. Manuela Zips-Mairitsch has published several articles on legal anthropology, human rights, governance of indigeneity, court cases on indigenous land rights, borderland studies and community-based development. The keen filmmaker has directed numerous documentary films on  western and southern Africa, the Caribbean and Asia with international success in the broadcasting world.

René Kuppe is a Professor of Law at the University of Vienna, Austria. His research and teaching concentrates on the rights of indigenous peoples, especially land and resource rights and indigenous jurisdiction. He coordinated a European Commission project to support the participation of indigenous peoples in the demarcation and legalization of their traditional territories in Venezuela. More recently, René Kuppe joined an international research project on the "Recognition of Indigenous Property Systems within Arctic States" coordinated by the University of Lapland, Rovaniemi, Finland.

Werner Zips is a Professor of Social and Cultural Anthropology at the University of Vienna, Austria. The trained lawyer, anthropologist and former president of the Society for Caribbean Research is a member of the Steering Committee for the European Science Foundation's *African Borderlands Research Network* (ABORNE). Werner Zips focuses his research on legal anthropology, political and historical anthropology, Caribbean studies as well as governance in Africa. He is the author of numerous articles and books on Jamaican Maroons, Rastafari and Black Nationalism, and has edited volumes on Legal Pluralism, the African Diaspora and Black Economic Empowerment in South Africa.

3. Court Cases

Amodu Tijani v. The Secretary, Southern Nigeria [1921] 2 AC 399, 407 (PC)

Alexkor Ltd. v. Richtersveld Community, 2003 (12) BCLR 1301 (CC). South Africa.

Attorney General v. Unity Dow (1992) B.L.R. 119 (C.A.). Botswana.

Awas Tingni Community v. The Republic of Nicaragua, Justicement of 31 August 2001, Case text at www.indianlaw.org

Bakare Ajakaiye v. Lieutenant-Governor, Southern Provinces [1929] AC 679

Calder v. Attorney General of British Columbia [1973] S.C.R. 313. Canada.

Delgamuukw v. British Columbia (1997): 3 S.C.R. 1010 or (1998) 1 C.N.L.R. 14. Canada. Online at http://www.lexum.umontreal.ca/csc-scc/en/pub/1997/vol3/html/1997scr3_1010.html

Good v. Attorney General [2005] 1 BLR 462 (High Court). Botswana.

Good v. Attorney General [2005] 2 BLR 337 (Court of Appeal). Botswana.

Good, Kenneth v. Botswana Communication 313/05 (decision adopted in May 2010). African Commission's Working Group on Human and Peoples' Rights

Hopu and Bessert v. France, CCPR/C/60/D/549/1993 (views adopted in July 1997). Human Rights Council.

In re Southern Rhodesia [1919] AC 211 (PC)

Johnson v. McIntosh (1823) 8 Wheat 543 (USSC)

Länsman et al. v. Finland, CCPR/C/52/D/511/1992 (views adopted in July 1994). Human Rights Council.

J.E. Länsmann v. Finland, CCPR/C/58/D/671/1995 (views adopted in July 1996). Human Rights Council.

Lubicon Lake Band v. Canada, CCPR/C/38/D167/1984 (views adopted in March 1990). Human Rights Council.

Mabo v. Queensland (1992): 175 CLR1 F.C.92/014. Online at: http://www.austlii.edu.au/cgi-bin/disp.pl/au/cases/cth/high-ct/175clr1.html (accessed on 10 August 2004).

Matsipane Mosetlhanyane, Gakenyatsiwe Matsipane & further applicants v. Attorney General of Botswana [2010], High Court. (MAHLB-000393-09). Botswana.

Matsipane Mosetlhanyane & Gakenyatsiwe Matsipane v. Attorney General of Botswana [2011], Court of Appeal, CALB-074-10. Botswana.

Mmusi & others v. Ramantele &Attorney General of Botswana [2012], High Court. (MAHLB-000836-10). Botswana.

Oyekan v. Adele [1957] 2 All ER 785, 788 (PC) (Lord Denning).

Richtersveld Community v. Alexkor Ldt., 2001 (3) SA 1293 (LCC). South Africa.

Richtersveld Community v. Alexkor Ldt., 2003 (6) BCLR 583 (SCA). South Africa.

Roy Sesana, Keiwa Setlhobogwa and Others v. The Attorney General. MISCA No. 52 of 2002 (High Court). Botswana.

Shikati Calvin Keene Kamanakao, Kamanakao Association and Motsamai Keyecwe Mpho v. The Attorney General of Botswana and Kgosi Tawana Moremi II, MISCA No. 377 of 1999 (High Court). Botswana.

The King v. The Earl of Crewe, ex parte Sekgome, [1910] 2 K.B. 576 (C.A.).

The Social and Economic Rights Action Center and the Center for Economic and Social Rights v. Nigeria, (2001). ACHPR 2002; Com. No. 155/96. Online at: hppt://www.cesr.org/fi lestore2/download/579 (accessed on 9 November 2008).

Ward v. Western Australia [1998] 159 ALR 483

Western Sahara Case [1975]. International Court of Justice. Advisory Opinion. International Court of Justice 12.

4. Interviews

Chennells, Roger on 20 October 2005 in Stellenbosch, South Africa

Chennells, Roger on 9 February 2007 in Stellenbosch, South Africa

Dukuri, Bau on 20 August 2005 in Ghanzi, Botswana

Festus, Elias on 27 February 2005 in Twee Rivieren, South Africa

Kleinmann, Vetpiet on 12 February 2004 in Transfrontier Park, South Africa

Kruiper, Dawid on 26 February 2005 in Welkom, South Africa

Mogae, Festus on 29 September 2005 in Gaborone, Botswana

Mogwe, Alice on 12 September 2003 in Gaborone, Botswana

Mogwe, Alice on 22 February 2005 in Gaborone, Botswana

Ngakaeaja, Mathambo on 24 February 2003 in D'Kar, Botswana

Ngakaeaja, Mathambo on 6 March 2004 in D'Kar, Botswana

Ngakaeaja, Mathambo on 8 March 2005 in D'Kar, Botswana

Seepapitso IV, on 27 September 2005 in Kanye, Botswana

!Xuntai, Seloka on 19 February 2003 in Tsodilo Hills, Botswana

Index of Figures

Figure 1: Ju|'hoansi San Boo !Kunta hunting 137

Figure 2: The Ju|'hoansi San live in the Nyae Nyae Conservancy in north-eastern Namibia "Nature conservation with humans" 138

Figure 3: Kaqece Kxoara, Boo !Kunta and !ui Xao hunting for porcupines................ 138

Figure 4: !ui Xao on the land of his ancestors; the Ju|'hoansi have been collectively entitled to use it since 1998 139

Figure 5: G|wi, !Xóó and Ju|'hoansi (San) at the end of a so-called "Bushmen Walk" near Ghanzi in Botswana 140

Figure 6: Xlalka drinking rainwater 140

Figure 7: QGokwa (G|wi) looks over the "lost lands" of the Kalahari 141

Figure 8: Tzana and Tsawana hollowing out a Tsamma melon................................ 142

Figure 9: Bootsho, a Ju|'hoansi, explains the medicinal use of a root 143

Figure 10: Twyfelfontein, Namibia: "open-air museum" of San stone engravings 143

Figure 11: In Botswana all San are called Basarwa – "the people who own nothing" .. 144

Figure 12: Kayate gathering wild fruits...145

Figure 13: Traditional craftsmanship at the edge of the Kalahari 146

Figure 14: Today's living conditions of the San outside of the environments they had once lived in...146

Figure 15: Hunting performance: in South Africa most ǂKhomani San live from tourism...147

Figure 16: Relocated from "their" Tsodilo Hills: Ju|'hoansi (!Kung) in Botswana.........147

Figure 17: A group of Ju|'hoansi San in northeastern Namibia.................................. 148

Figure 18: Presenting traditional dances for tourists 149

Figure 19: Dancers connect to wild animals in trance dances 149

Figure 20: N≠aisa Kayece claps and sings to support the healing dance 150

Figure 21: Boo !Kunta, a traditional healer, at a healing session 151

Figure 22: Xlalka (G|wi) making fire... 152

Figure 23: Only a few of Botswana's San support themselves as actors in a "living museum" that "preserves" their knowledge of hunting and gathering 271

Figure 24: Molapo inhabitants depend on Tsamma melons during the dry season.......273

Figure 25: Kukama in the southern Central Kalahari Game Reserve (CKGR)........... 274

Figure 26: The last hut of Mothomelo where 245 San had lived before they were relocated in 2001 274
Figure 27: Fences protect the settlement against wild animals 275
Figure 28: Lenkagetse and Neo were among the last twelve San in Kukama 275
Figure 29: A sealed well is the only thing left of Mothomelo in the CKGR 276
Figure 30: Hunting is strictly prohibited in the CKGR 276
Figure 31: To the "starting stones": the way to the diamond mine Gope in the CKGR 277
Figure 32: Some San communities in Namibia still enjoy hunting rights 277
Figure 33: Tsodilo Hills, the "Louvre of the desert" in north-western Botswana 278
Figure 34: Old rock engravings as inspiration for contemporary San artists 278
Figure 35: Entertainment paradise Sun City: replica of San rock paintings 279
Figure 36: Thamae Kaashe in D'kar near Ghanzi: Botswana's contemporary art centre 279
Figure 37: Seloka !Xuntai, leading Ju|'hoansi (!Kung) elder with his great grandson ... 280
Figure 38: Tzana performing her traditional culture for tourists 281
Figure 39: Duu or eland dance, Kuru Dance Festival in Botswana 282
Figure 40: "My culture is very important to me." (Bau Dukuri, Naro healer in D'kar) 282
Figure 41: Choreographed hunting dance, Kuru Dance Festival 283
Figure 42: Healing performance: the festival is meant to help counteracting the loss of culture 283
Figure 43: Bosele Youth Group, Ghanzi 284
Figure 44: Hunting dance by the Naro Giraffe Dance Group, D'Kar in Botswana 284
Figure 45: Hamberere dance of the !Xun, Platfontein in South Africa 285
Figure 46: "Our culture, our pride, our dignity" – is the festival's slogan 285
Figure 47: San communities join for a healing dance at the Kuru Dance Festival 286
Figure 48: More than folklore: the collective experience forms a pan-San identity 286
Figure 49: Many cultures, many languages – one history of discrimination 287
Figure 50: The final chapter? "Relocating the Basarwa communities is a way of killing them" (Roy Sesana, First People of the Kalahari) 287
Figure 51: Xoallan !Kunta: Praying for a better future … 288
Figure 52: Entry permit to the CKGR for visiting San family member 383

Index

A

Aboriginal Title s. Native Title
African Union (AU) 49, 79, 83, 85, 97, 120, 347, 370
- African Charter on Human and Peoples' Rights (Banjul Charter) .. 79, 86, 94, 100, 102, 104f.
- African Commission on Human and Peoples' Rights (ACHPR) .. 80, 84–89, 91, 93, 95–98, 101f., 109f., 364, 383, 385, 393ff.
- African Court on Human and Peoples' Rights 106–109
- Working Group on Indigenous Populations (WGIP) ... 36f., 57, 85,
Agenda 21.............................. 44, 47, 224
Angola 113, 115, 156, 169, 174f., 226
Australia .. 13f., 19, 22, 30, 49f., 58, 80, 83, 89, 110, 122, 124, 126, 249, 331, 351
- Mabo case .... 122, 331, 348ff.

B

(Ba)Tswana.... 14ff., 24, 187–197, 204–210, 237–243, 354
Balopi Commission 206ff., 226, 230, 343
Basarwa 155–159, 182, 210f., 237–243, 248f., 299, 305f., 321
Bechuanaland Protectorate . 170, 189–199, 216, 223, 293ff.
Botswana
- Common Law............ 18, 220, 222f.
- Constitution.............. 111–115, 199, 205–207, 209f., 216, 218f., 225–229, 233, 239, 295, 339f., 342, 348, 371
- Customary Law .... 219f., 222f.
- Human Rights 225
- Independence... 70, 199f., 216, 229
Botswana Democratic Party (BDP) .. 200
Bushmen .... 14ff., 117, 155–159, 162f., 167, 171f., 196, 226f., 238, 243–250, 261f., 293ff., 329–332, 349f.
Bushmen Development Programme.. 246ff.

C

Cameroon....................... 48, 85, 86, 111ff.
Central Kalahari Game Reserve (CKGR) 24f., 237f., 226, 291, 325, 331f., 387
- Access to 14, 55, 296, 339, 359, 364
CERD (International Convention on the Elimination of all Forms of Racial Discrimination)
- CERD Committee 42 65, 68ff., 226f., 346
Chieftaincy.......... 201, 206, 217, 218, 230
- Chieftainship Act 205, 230
- House of Chiefs 199, 205–210, 215ff., 221, 229f., 338–342, 349f., 353–356, 359f., 366, 372f., 375, 387
Cobo Study 34–37, 84, 347
Colonialism 13ff., 33, 41, 72, 79, 82f., 93, 97, 155, 172, 187, 205, 214, 251
Community Based Natural Resource Management (CBNRM)....... 254, 312
Convention on Biological Diversity (CBD) 45, 224, 261

Covenant on Civil and Political Rights
(CCPR) 65, 67
Crown Land 120, 194f., 292f.,
331, 349f., 362
Customary International Law 46, 56f.,
70f., 124, 385

D

D'kar 181, 238f., 268, 279, 282, 284
Democracy 14, 24, 71, 135,
180, 187, 201, 203, 210, 215–218, 231ff.,
352, 379f., 382
Department of Wildlife and National
Parks (DWNP) 297, 300, 311, 355
Diamonds 54, 120, 189, 201, 313, 324,
374f., 388
Discrimination ... 34, 57, 65, 67ff., 83, 107,
114, 224, 227, 346f.
DITSHWANELO, The Botswana
Centre for Human Rights 11, 179,
208, 231, 233, 243, 266f., 269, 305–308,
311, 315, 318, 335, 351, 359, 370
Diversity, Cultural ...16, 25, 27, 29, 45, 51f.,
57, 97, 111, 178, 203f., 231, 266, 379f.
Dow, Unity 223, 225, 227f.,
327–330, 333–339, 341, 343–348, 360,
363, 371f.,
Draft Declaration on the Rights
of Indigenous Peoples 36, 85

E

European Convention on Human Rights
(ECHR) 67, 98, 112

F

First People of the Kalahari (FPK).... 158,
160, 265f., 311, 324

G

||Gana 21, 25, 158, 266, 291, 310, 320

G|wi ... 21, 25, 81, 158, 266, 291, 302, 305,
320
Ghanzi 170, 182, 205f., 237f., 249,
265, 292, 294, 296, 303, 305, 312, 314ff.,
318, 323, 338, 350, 359, 374

H

Harvard Kalahari Research Group 156,
166, 195
Hoodia Gordonii Case 6, 132f., 401
Human Rights Committee (HRC) .... 67f.
Human Rights Council 48f., 57, 61, 75,
109, 113, 356, 364, 370
Hunting and Gathering 63, 117, 125,
166f., 175, 181f., 211f., 214, 238, 240,
244ff., 253, 256, 291, 295, 297f., 316,
321, 347, 388

I

ILO Convention 107 ...... 43f., 88, 94, 192,
204, 248
ILO Convention 169 .... 19, 39, 43ff., 48,
54, 56, 58–61, 63f., 68f., 73f., 85, 93, 110,
112
Indigenous Peoples
– Terminology 34–39, 155
Indigenous Rights
– Collective Land Rights 61–63
– Land and Resource Rights 57–61, 65
– Restriction of Alienation
and Disposal 64
Individual Complaints Procedure 67, 69,
102f., 107f.
International Convention on the Elimination of all Forms of Racial Discrimination s. CERD
International Covenant on Civil
and Political Rights 224
International Law 30–33, 37,
42f., 46, 56, 59f., 70f., 84, 93, 122ff., 191,
223ff., 349, 386f.

K

≠Khomani San 117–120
Kalahari Debate .... 165–168, 195f.
Khama, Seretse 199
Khoesan 155–159, 266
Kuru Development Trust .. 153, 177f., 239, 267

L

Land Boards 16, 205, 211–213
Legal pluralism ...23, 46, 54, 74, 221ff., 306, 397

M

Minorities .... 34, 37, 40f., 66, 83ff., 98f., 111–113, 115, 187f., 209f., 229f., 379f.
Mogwe, Alice 11, 233, 243, 252, 267, 298f., 305, 312, 317ff., 321, 351–354

N

Namibia 48, 81, 114, 159f., 169–175, 268f.,
National Development Plan 203, 247, 252, 261
National Parks 80f., 117 118, 255, 258f., 261–264, 294f., 297, 306, 312, 326, 328, 337, 339, 342, 355, 357, 360
 – International Union for Conservation of Nature (IUCN) .. 260, 262f.
  Native Title 69 122–132, 330f., 347–351,
Nature Conservation 30, 46f., 55, 81ff., 138, 254f., 257–264, 270, 300ff., 311f., 317, 321, 330, 366
New !Xade 308f., 314–320, 324, 357, 359
NGOs .. 21, 83f., 102f., 107ff., 132f., 160, 180ff., 230f., 300, 311ff., 324ff., 345ff., 357, 370f.

O

Organization of African Union (OAU) 79 f., 96f., 104f.

P

Paternalism 216, 242, 246
Peoples
 – Terminology 71–75, 95ff., 155
Poverty ... 16, 80, 120, 165f., 174, 203, 215, 240, 246ff., 250, 254f., 297, 333, 379f.

R

Relocation .... 9f., 60f., 80f., 157, 266, 301–329, 333– 344, 353f., 365f., 380, 388f.
 – Compensation 340
Remote Area Development Programme (RADP) .... 247f., 297, 314f.
Remote Area Dwellers (RADs) . 238, 298
Richtersveld Case 120f., 128–132, 348

S

San
 – Terminology 155
Secession 71, 73, 135, 306, 381, 389
Self-determination, Right of ...32, 39ff., 44, 70–75, 100, 229, 296, 385ff.
Sesana, Roy... 179, 266, 287, 310, 320, 322, 324, 343f., 354, 359, 375, 381
 – v. Government of Botswana 157, 226, 262, 322–358
Silberbauer, Georg 15, 293–297, 324, 331f., 348f., 352
Soft Law 33, 46f., 54, 56, 70, 263
South Africa 48, 114–121, 128–134, 159f., 169, 172ff., 189f., 187–203, 218ff., 268f., 348
South African San Institute (SASI) .. 118, 133, 160, 268
Special Game Licence .... 297ff., 323, 337ff.

Survival International........... 21, 237, 266, 303, 312f., 317, 320, 324f., 355, 364, 371, 373f., 376, 380, 387, 389

T

Terra nullius 32, 122f., 292, 331, 349, 385
Territory......... 18f., 32, 35, 41, 58–63, 68f., 90, 120–129, 177ff., 207, 318, 321, 349–453
Tribal Grazing Land Policy (TGLP).. 212f.
Tswana s. (Ba)Tswana

U

Uganda................................ 81, 102, 113
UN Declaration on the Rights of Indigenous Peoples..... 19, 42ff., 47–51, 59–64, 73f., 87, 109, 160, 351, 382, 387
UNESCO 27, 29, 44, 48, 50, 52, 132, 301
- Convention on the Protection and Promotion of the Diversity of Cultural Expressions........... 29, 52
- Convention for the Safeguarding of the Intagible Cultural Heritage... 132
- Universal Declaration on Cultural Diversity 52

V

Vision 2016 .... 203f., 245

W

Wayeyi............................. 188, 205, 229f.
Wildlife Management Areas...... 255, 301, 339
Working Group of Experts s. African Union
Working Group on Indigenous Minorities in Southern Africa (WIMSA) 11, 14, 21, 133, 158ff., 180f., 210, 214, 268f., 299, 311
- World Bank 39, 44, 53f., 62f., 84f., 212,
- Operational Policy (OP 4.10)... 39, 44, 53f., 62f.
World Conservation Union (IUCN), s. National Parks: International Union for Conservation of Nature

X

!Xade 296, 301f., 307ff., 314–318

Z

Zambia......................... 48, 113, 156, 169, 174f., 191, 257, 269
Zimbabwe 113, 169, 174f., 190f., 257, 269